The Corporate Reconstruction
of American Capitalism, 1890–1916

The Corporate Reconstruction
of American Capitalism, 1890–1916

The Market, the Law, and Politics

MARTIN J. SKLAR

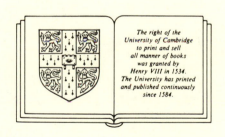

The right of the
University of Cambridge
to print and sell
all manner of books
was granted by
Henry VIII in 1534.
The University has printed
and published continuously
since 1584.

CAMBRIDGE UNIVERSITY PRESS

Cambridge

New York   New Rochelle   Melbourne   Sydney

Published by the Press Syndicate of the University of Cambridge
The Pitt Building, Trumpington Street, Cambridge CB2 1RP
32 East 57th Street, New York, NY 10022, USA
10 Stamford Road, Oakleigh, Melbourne 3166, Australia

First published 1988

Printed in the United States of America

Library of Congress Cataloging-in-Publication Data
Sklar, Martin J., 1935–
The corporate reconstruction of American capitalism,
1890–1916.
Bibliography: p.
Includes index.
1. Capital – United States – History. 2. Progressivism
(United States politics) 3. Antitrust law – United
States – History. 4. Business and politics – United
States – History. I. Title.
HC110.C3S58 1988   338.8'0973   87–9408

British Library Cataloguing in Publication Data
Sklar, Martin J.
The corporate reconstruction of American
capitalism, 1890–1916: the market, the
law, and politics.
1. Capitalism – United States – History
2. United States – Economic conditions
– 1865–1918
I. Title
330.12'2'0973   HC106

ISBN 0 521 30921 2 hard covers
ISBN 0 521 31382 1 paperback

Parts of Chapter 2 appeared in the same or similar wording as part of my contribution to Carl P. Parrini and Martin J. Sklar, "New Thinking about the Market, 1896–1904: Some American Economists on Investment and the Theory of Surplus Capital," *Journal of Economic History* 43:3 (September 1983), pp. 559–578. I wish to thank Carl P. Parrini and the *Journal of Economic History* for permission to include the material here.

TO NAO HAUSER

Contents

Preface

I have thought it useful over the years to examine in some close detail the antitrust debates of the Progressive Era, in their judicial, legislative, and political phases, in conjunction with a study of changes in property and market relations and in economic thought at the time. I have done so on the assumption that such inquiry might yield some altered perspectives on twentieth-century United States political history. I have long believed that, given the critical role of law and judicial process in a liberal-capitalist society, and at any rate in the United States, a close attention to the law is as necessary for interpreting twentieth-century United States political history as it has been found to be in relatively recent interpretations of earlier United States history.

A conclusion I have drawn from my efforts is that a closer attention to the law, in its judicial and legislative phases and as it relates to changing property-production relations, affords an understanding less ideologically predisposed and more receptive to retrieving past political discourses both on their own terms and in a larger historical context. In any event, as my study of these matters proceeded, my understanding of events, leaders, thought, and politics of the Progressive Era and subsequent times underwent changes, including those that carried me past some of my own earlier understandings, interpretations, and predispositions, as well as those of other writers in the field.

Since I introduced the term "corporate liberalism" in the late 1950s (first published in 1960 in my essay on Wilson, noted in the Bibliography), I have found it valid to retain the term and a good part of the meaning with which I then used it, but with continuing research, study, and reflection, my conception of corporate liberalism, with respect to both its meaning and its origins, has undergone further development and some corresponding change, along with my understanding of the politics of such leaders as Theodore Roosevelt, William Howard Taft, and Woodrow Wilson, and my understanding of twentieth-century American liberalism. Continuing research and study will undoubtedly bring still more change in understanding. The present volume is better to be regarded as *studies in* the corporate reconstruction of American capitalism, as it represents research and thinking in progress, addressed to parts of a story, the whole of which remains further or freshly to be researched and written about. Even in the parts treated here, I make no claim to be definitive, exhaustive, or error-free, only to present materials I have found and my understanding of them, so far, as best I can.

The broad theme of the corporate reconstruction of American capitalism and its relation to twentieth-century American political history has been a continuing interest of mine over the past three decades. The present studies have their immediate substantive origins in four different periods of work: in research and writing done in the latter 1950s, some of it published, the bulk of it remaining in unpublished manuscript form (including my initial inquiries into Sherman Act jurisprudence and its implications for corporate liberalism); in research done in the early 1960s; in research and writing done in the past several years since 1979; and, sandwiched between the latter two, in research, writing, and teaching at Northern Illinois University in the 1970s and, in particular, in the graduate seminar I gave there on The Corporate Reconstruction of United States Society, 1896–1929. For that seminar, I assembled for collegial reading, discussion, and analysis, contemporary sources, intermixed with historical and theoretical works, regarding the rise of corporate capitalism in its relation to such specific subjects as the reorganization of property ownership and investment practices, the banking and currency system, class formation and class relations, economic thought and public policy, law and government, international relations and foreign policy, the professions and higher education, as well as the significance of all this for the historiographical questions of periodization and interpretation. The present book represents findings in a small portion of those areas of study. I am pleased to have this opportunity, at last, to thank the remarkably talented people who attended the seminar, many of whom have since become working, and some published, historians, namely: Carl Beyer, Jeff Brunner, William Burr, Kim Butterfield, Helen Callahan, Stephen Cichy, Virginia Differding, Keith Haynes, James Livingston, Arlene Neher, John R. Nelson, Jr., William Nicklas, John Peer, Jon Robertson, Alana Ronne, Richard Schneirov, Robert Shaw, Keith Strinmoen, Thomas Suhrbur, and Paul Wolman.

At different stages of the writing, this work has benefited from readings in whole or in very large part, and from valuable critical comments, by Milton Berman, Robert M. Collins, Stanley Engerman, Eugene D. Genovese, Nao Hauser, Morton J. Horwitz, Michael C. Jensen, Walter LaFeber, Carl P. Parrini, Richard L. Sklar, Stephen Skowronek, and Alfred F. Young, and also from readings in certain parts, and critical comments, by Robert D. Cuff, William Duker, Louis Galambos, Charles H. George, Margaret George, Fred Harvey Harrington, Ellis Hawley, J. Willard Hurst, Stephen Kern, Arnold Lieber, Albro Martin, Arthur S. Miller, Stephen Presser, Warren J. Samuels, and members of the Workshop in Legal History, which met in Chicago in May 1986.

Discourses with Loren Baritz, John Bracey, William Burr, Lloyd Gardner, Eugene D. Genovese, Herbert Gutman, Nao Hauser, Ralph J. Kaufmann, Stephen Kern, Arnold Lieber, Carl P. Parrini, Richard Schneirov, Trent Schroyer, Richard L. Sklar, James G. Snyder, Warren I. Susman, James Weinstein, Hayden White, William A. Williams and Eli Zaretsky have given me knowledge and insights of particular relevance to the making of this book.

I particularly wish to note with gratitude the encouragement, critical engagement, and intensive interest, at crucial stages in the work on this book, of Eugene D. Genovese, from the very beginning, and of Fred Harvey Harrington, Nao Hauser, Carl P. Parrini, and Richard L. Sklar. I am solely responsible for the work, and particularly for its defects and shortcomings.

The collegial scholarly environment afforded by my colleagues in the History Department of Bucknell University and, also at Bucknell, by former vice-president of academic affairs Frances D. Fergusson (now president of Vassar College) and former president Dennis O'Brien (now president of the University of Rochester) greatly facilitated the writing of this book in its last stages. The research fund attached to the John D. and Catherine T. MacArthur Chair in American History, which I now hold, made possible the completion and enrichment of research for the book. Discussions with my colleague at Bucknell professor of modern languages Mills F. Edgerton, Jr., and with Christopher M. Sterba, a student at Bucknell, have been particularly stimulative and nourishing.

I wish to thank the staffs of the Bucknell University Library, the Rare Book and Manuscript Library of Columbia University, the Northern Illinois University Library, the Northwestern University Library, the Northwestern University Law Library, and, although it was some time ago that I labored among them, the staffs of the manuscript section of the New York Public Library, the Wisconsin State Historical Society Library, and the University of Wisconsin Library, for their attentive and patient assistance. As is my custom, I typed the manuscript myself, but for aid in preparing the manuscript for delivery to the publisher I wish to thank Ruth Snyder, secretary of the History and Classics departments of Bucknell, and for aid in preparation of the bibliography, Valerie Pullara Kamrath.

I am especially grateful to Frank Smith, editor at Cambridge University Press, for his diligent, critical, and always incisive work with me in the realization of the book. I also wish to thank Nancy Landau, my copy editor at the Press, for her intelligent and proficient care and mending of the manuscript.

Harrisburg, Pennsylvania
January 1987

Abbreviations used in the footnotes

AER	*American Economic Review*
AHR	*American Historical Review*
BC	Bureau of Corporations, Record Group 122, National Archives, Washington, D.C. (G.F. = General File)
BHR	*Business History Review*
Cong. Rec.	*Congressional Record*
EHR	*Economic History Review*
FAD	U.S. Attorney General, *Federal Anti-Trust Decisions*
FAV	Frank A. Vanderlip Papers, Rare Book and Manuscript Library, Columbia University
Fed.	*Federal Reporter*
GWP	George W. Perkins Papers, Rare Book and Manuscript Library, Columbia University
JAH	*Journal of American History*
JEH	*Journal of Economic History*
JPE	*Journal of Political Economy*
JRG	James R. Garfield Papers, Library of Congress (F. = File No.)
Link, *Papers*	Arthur S. Link, ed., *The Papers of Woodrow Wilson*
Link, *Wilson*, 1	Arthur S. Link, *Wilson: The Road to the White House*
Link, *Wilson*, 2	Arthur S. Link, *Wilson: The New Freedom*
MVHR	*Mississippi Valley Historical Review*
NA RG	National Archives, Record Group
N. Am. Rev.	*North American Review*
NCF	National Civic Federation Papers, New York Public Library
PPWW	Woodrow Wilson, *The Public Papers of Woodrow Wilson*, eds., Ray S. Baker and William E. Dodd

PSQ	*Political Science Quarterly*
QJE	*Quarterly Journal of Economics*
SL	Seth Low Papers, Rare Book and Manuscript Library, Columbia University
TR	Theodore Roosevelt Papers, Library of Congress
U.S.	*United States Reports*

1

Introduction: Corporate capitalism and corporate liberalism

Introduction

The period 1890–1916 in United States history, encompassing what is commonly called the Progressive Era, was both an age of reform and the age of the corporate reconstruction of American capitalism. Other ages of reform have punctuated the nation's history. It was, however, the intersecting of broad and lasting reform with the rise of corporate capitalism that made the years covered by this book historically distinctive and, more particularly, that made them the directly formative birth-time of basic institutions, social relations, and political divisions of United States society as it evolved toward and beyond the mid-twentieth century. In one and the same period were laid down and intermeshed the foundations of the corporate-capitalist economy, of the regulatory state, of internationalist foreign policy, and of modern political liberalism, as they would develop in mutually reinforcing and conflicting ways over the next several decades in the United States.

In marking the period as distinctive, the interrelation of reform and the ascendancy of corporate capitalism has also made the Progressive Era an intriguing object of historical inquiry, above and beyond its being, like any other time in the nation's history, a contested interpretive terrain. If the period was both an age of reform and the age of the ascendancy of corporate capitalism, how is the interrelation of the two best to be understood? The leading interpretations of the Progressive Era have largely turned on how they explain the interrelation, whether drawn in terms of reform as a modernizing or organizational concomitant of the rise of large-scale enterprise; reform as a response of smaller or traditional bourgeoisie and professionals to a changing status order brought on by large corporate enterprise; reform as a series of eclectic results of conflicts and compromises among myriad large corporate and other organized business and special-interest groups; reform as the instrument of limiting corporate power on behalf of the people or the general welfare; reform as a means of legitimizing and consolidating corporate power; or reform as a middle path between inordinate corporate power and radical or revolutionary impulses. As this implies, given the currency of such perspectives on more recent times, the several interpretations of the Progressive Era bear a close kinship to the prevalent ideas about the course of American political history well past mid-twentieth century. That kinship, in turn, indicates the large extent to which the events of the Progressive Era were directly formative of the subsequent course of the nation's sociopolitical development.

The interrelation of reform and the emergence of corporate capitalism manifested itself directly in what became, after the disposal of the monetary battle in the election of 1896, the preeminent set of issues in national politics in the years between the great depression of the 1890s and United States entry into World War I – the set of issues centered on the rise of large corporate enterprise and known as the Trust Question. Leaders of the time in political, economic, and intellectual spheres, who were most prominent in the debate on the trust question, defined it as in essence the corporation question and, accordingly, as one that addressed an economic transformation with its implications for the law, the role of government in economic affairs, and the state-society relation in general.

The present study takes as its point of departure the changing nature of capitalism, conceived not simply as economic change, but as change in social relations touching social history in the broad sense, and encompassing the political, legal, intellectual, and cultural, as well as the economic, spheres. As the trust question and the antitrust debates were in essence about the passage of American capitalism from the competitive to the corporate stage of its development, the study places its focus there.

Taking a social-history approach to capitalism and the capitalist class means seeing them not as static categories but as social formations changing in time. Specifically, with respect to capitalists, it means that they should be studied not simply, and certainly not in essence, as "interests," but like, say, workers and farmers, as a social movement or social movements. No less than other classes, the capitalist class consists of associated people with goals, values, ideas, and principles, as well as interests. They are people with a way of life to develop, defend, and extend, based on a definite type of property ownership and labor exploitation, the characteristics of which undergo historical change.

The study does not assume that small-producer, competitive capitalism was "natural" or the "true type" of capitalism, and that corporate capitalism was "unnatural," an artificial construct, or a "political" usurpation, a view corresponding with the populist outlook. Nor does it assume that corporate capitalism was the natural outcome of "objective" techno-economic evolution, a view corresponding with the pro-corporate outlook. In holding, rather, that capitalism and its class relations have a history, like all else in human affairs, the study assumes that the passage of capitalism from its proprietary-competitive stage to its corporate-administered stage, which transpired during the period 1890–1916, was a part of capitalism's historical development in the United States. It also assumes that neither stage was more "natural" or less "political" than the other, but that in whatever stage, historical development proceeded through human agency in such forms as social movements, political and ideological conflict, struggles over the shape and role of the law and government, and so on, and in such ways as usually to have yielded wide disparities between intentions and consequences. The trust question and the antitrust debates stood at the heart of those movements, conflicts, and struggles, transacting the passage of American capitalism from one historical stage to another. Understood in this way, rather than as sterile arguments over competition versus combination, they repay renewed inquiry both in some detail and in the larger principles they involved.

The study inquires into certain critical discourses of the period – economic, legal, and political – with a view to identifying the major contending positions on the trust question among those affirming the emergence of corporate capitalism, as well as with a view to pursuing some of their larger historical implications. Accordingly, it examines economic and legal thinking about property and market relations, policy-making thought engaged in legislative drafting work, and the pertinent thinking of the three major Progressive Era presidents: Theodore Roosevelt, William Howard Taft, and Woodrow Wilson. Because all three were persons of disciplined intellect – Roosevelt as an author, Taft as a jurist, and Wilson as a trained scholar in the field of political science – their thinking represented, more than is usual with presidents, serious and influential trends of thought in the larger society.

In a society such as that of the United States in the late nineteenth and early twentieth centuries, where capitalist property and market relations were the principal means of allocating resources, labor, and income, and where in general they constituted society's paramount social relations, economic discourse overlapped and intersected with legal and political discourse on every hand; each provided context for the others, and where they intersected, each assumed its most sophisticated expression, just as each is best comprehended, in the context of the others. The following inquiry begins with the metamorphosis in property, and in thinking about property and the market, corresponding with the passage of American capitalism from its proprietary-competitive stage to its corporate-administered stage, in the years around the turn of the century. From there it moves to a more complex level of discourse, that of legislation and jurisprudence as they related to the range of market activity encompassing competition and restraint of trade, and hence as they related to the emergence of corporate capitalism. The inquiry then proceeds to political discourse of a still more comprehensive kind, addressed to economic and juristic thought, to legislative and executive policy, and to the broad questions of property rights, economic and social efficiency, the government-market and state-society relation, and their bearing upon the larger questions of capitalism, socialism, and democracy.

Mode of production and social movements

The corporate reorganization of industry that crystallized in the merger movement of 1898–1904 and developed thereafter to World War I marked the passage of a relatively mature American industrial capitalism from its proprietary-competitive stage to an early phase of its corporate-administered stage. It marked, that is, the emergence of the corporate reconstruction of American capitalism.[1] The word "recon-

---

1. The term "proprietary-competitive" in this study refers to capitalist property and market relations in which the dominant type of enterprise was headed by an owner-manager (or owner-managers), or a direct agent thereof, and in which such enterprise was a price-taker, rather than a price-maker, price being determined by conditions of supply and demand beyond the control of the enterprise short of anticompetitive inter-firm collusion. The term "corporate reorganization of industry," or "corporate reconstruction of capitalism," in this study, means not simply the *de jure* incorporation of a property otherwise managed *de facto* along proprietary lines, but the capitalization of the property in the form of negotiable securities relatively widely dispersed in ownership, a corresponding separation of ownership title and management function, and management of the enterprise by bureaucratic-administrative methods involving a division, or a specialization, of managerial function, and an integration, or at least a centralization, of financial control. The term is also meant to designate a process occurring not merely in a few notable firms, or in a sector of the economy (e.g., railroads or public utilities), but pervasively, and hence involving the change in the broader economy from price-competitive

struction" is meant to connote, as with the earlier era of the Civil War and its aftermath, far-reaching and interrelated changes transpiring in the political, governmental, cultural, and intellectual spheres, as well as in the economy. The corporate reorganization of capitalist property and market relations substantially affected, or integrally related to, changes in intra-class and inter-class relations, in law and public policy, in party politics, in international relations, in prevalent modes of social thought, in education and philanthropy, in civic association, in the structure and role of government, and in the government-society relation in general. As Woodrow Wilson put it at the end of the new century's first decade, "the world of business" had changed "and therefore the world of society and the world of politics." With the change in "our economic conditions from top to bottom," he noted, had also come the change in "the organization of our life," so that the great "economic questions" of the day were also "questions of the very structure and operation of society itself." Or, as historian Richard Hofstadter noted almost a half century later, in the corporation question – the trust question – "nothing less was at stake than the entire organization of American business and American politics, the very question of who was to control the country."[2] In speaking of a corporate reconstruction of American capitalism, then, as distinctively periodizing, or defining, the years 1890–1916, and the Progressive Era in particular, we may also speak of a corporate reconstruction of American society.

Leaders in policy-forming politics of the time, including presidents Roosevelt, Taft, and Wilson, as we shall see in the ensuing examination of economic, legal, and political discourses, argued that the nation's laws, institutions, thinking, and habits must be reformed to facilitate and regulate the emerging corporate-capitalist order; that is, to adapt to natural economic evolution and thereby to assure the nation's development as a progressive society. In their view, capitalism as an economic system, or as a mode of production, evolved according to indefeasible economic law, from small-scale competitive to large-scale corporate enterprise, and society in its sociopolitical, intellectual, and cultural

---

to administered, or "oligopolistic," markets. The terms (a) "corporate" or "corporate capitalism" and (b) "pro-corporate," as used throughout this study unless otherwise indicated, refer, respectively, (a) to the rise of large corporations and administered markets to dominance in the United States political economy, and (b) to the outlook of those who affirmed it, whether as desirable or as inevitable or unavoidable. The terms do not connote or imply some special "organicist" or "corporative" organization, outlook, or ideology. See Chapter 6, below, in general, and, in particular, note 32, Chapter 6, also Chapter 7, below.

2. For Wilson, see Chapter 6, notes 26, 22, 25, and related text, below; Hofstadter, *The Age of Reform* (New York: Random House, Vintage Books, 1955), p. 252.

dimensions must adjust to that evolution in an appropriate way or suffer retrogression.

If, accordingly, in seeking to understand the politics of the Progressive Era, we begin with the idea of the passage of capitalism from one stage to another, we will have placed our thinking close to that of pro-corporate policy-forming leaders of the time. In order not merely to replicate their thinking, however, and to comprehend it, instead, in some critical historical perspective, it will be helpful to conceive of capitalism not simply as economics, not simply as an "economic aspect" of society, but as a system of social relations expressed in characteristic class structures, modes of consciousness, patterns of authority, and relations of power. Hence, although not necessarily identical with society as a whole, capitalism may be viewed as a complex of social relations that constitutes – where dominant over, or not subdued by, other social relations – the critical component of a distinct type of society, one that can be called, without undue violence to the empirical record and if left open to appropriate qualification, a capitalist society, as distinguished from, say, tribal hunting-gathering, slave, feudal, or state-socialist societies.

Even considered strictly as a mode of production, capitalism in the United States around the turn of the twentieth century encompassed not simply economics but property and class relations, values, ideas, law – in short, intersecting modes of consciousness – as well as such "material" phenomena as technique, equipment, labor power, and resources. The latter themselves, moreover, cannot be considered to be simply "material," as they are permeated by, and are the expression and product of, thought and feeling. If economics are a matter of input-output functions, the calculation of efficiencies in the allocation of resources and in the production and distribution of goods and services, and the like, no mode of production is simply a matter of economics. As a system of property and class relations, with their corresponding institutions and modes of consciousness, capitalism is the sociopolitical organization of economics, the larger social framework and relations of power within which input-output and allocative functions proceed at a certain stage of a society's history. "Political economy," which was still the prevalent term given to the study of economic matters in the United States at the turn of the century, denoted the study of the two subjects – sociopolitical and economic affairs – as inseparably interrelated. Accordingly, the term "property-production system," in denoting the sociopolitical determination of economics at a given historical period, may be used, as it is here, interchangeably with "mode of production." Viewing capitalism as a property-production system in this sense facilitates a social or sociopolitical interpretation of an "economic" order, or, in the particular case of the United States in 1890–1916, a social interpretation of an apparently "economic," or market, society where market relations are taken to permeate the society and to constitute its major extrafamilial institution of social integration.[3]

Property in its capitalist form, as in its other forms, is not simply a thing, nor simply an economic category, but is a complex social relation – of an intra- and inter-class character – that involves a system of authority inextricably interwoven with the legal and political order as well as with the broader system of legitimacy, the prevailing norms of emulative morality and behavior, and the hierarchy of power.[4] Even in its narrowest sense, capitalist business activity is not simply economic activity abstracted from the social and political spheres or from ideas and ideals. As modernization theory reminds us,[5] it is activity that

3. Cf., e.g., Charles E. Lindblom, *Politics and Markets: The World's Political-Economic Systems* (New York: Basic, 1977), pp. 8, 26, 34–35, 116; and J. Willard Hurst, *The Legitimacy of the Business Corporation in the Law of the United States, 1780–1970* (Charlottesville: University Press of Virginia, 1970), pp. 58–60, 62, 65, 66, 153. In noting that in the United States market activity serves as the main arena for the pursuit of utility and the accrual of legitimacy, Hurst (p. 153) points to "our long-term reliance on the market as an institution of social control."
4. "Slavery is an economic regime and a scheme of human relations. ... it is also a system of power." Hofstadter, *America at 1750: A Social Portrait* (New York: Random House, Vintage Books, 1973), p. 119. Substitute "capitalism" for "slavery" and is not the statement equally unobjectionable?
5. E.g., David E. Apter, *The Politics of Modernization* (Chicago: University of Chicago Press, 1965); Cyril E. Black, *The Dynamics of Modernization: A Study in Comparative History* (New York: Harper & Row, 1966); Bert F. Hoselitz, "Tradition and Economic Growth," Wilbert E. Moore, "The Social Framework of Economic Development," and Joseph J. Spengler, "Theory, Ideology, Non-Economic Values, and Political-Economic Development," all in Ralph Braibanti and Joseph J. Spengler, eds., *Tradition, Values, and Socio-Economic Development* (Cambridge University Press, 1961), pp. 83–113, 57–82, and 3–56, respectively; Dean C. Tipps, "Modernization Theory and the Comparative Study of Societies: A Critical Perspective," *Comparative Studies in Society and History* 16 (1973), pp. 199–226; E. A. Wrigley, "The Process of Modernization and the Industrial Revolution in England," *Journal of Interdisciplinary History* 3:2 (Autumn 1972), pp. 225–259; and with respect to United States history, Richard D. Brown, *Modernization: The Transformation of American Life, 1600–1865* (New York: Hill & Wang, 1976); Richard L. Bushman, *From Puritan to Yankee: Character and Social Order in Connecticut, 1690–1765* (Cambridge, Mass.: Harvard University Press, 1967); Ralph Lerner, "Commerce and Character: The Anglo-American as New-Model Man," *William & Mary Quarterly*, 3d ser., 36:1 (Jan. 1979), pp. 3–26; Kenneth A. Lockridge, "Social Change and the Meaning of the American Revolution," *Journal of Social History* 6:4 (Summer 1973), pp. 403–439; Eric Foner, "The Causes of the American Civil War: Recent Interpretations and New Directions," *Civil War History* 20:3 (Sept. 1974), pp. 197–214; Raimondo Luraghi, "The Civil War and the Modernization of American Society: Social Structure and Industrial Revolution in the Old South Before and During the War," *Civil War History* 18:3 (Sept. 1972), pp. 230–250.

presupposes, and is permeated by, a complex mode of consciousness, that is, by ideas and ideals about deliberate calculation of ends and means with respect to other persons; about the shape of society, its approved goals and moral standards; and about the law and jurisprudence, party politics, and the range and limits of government authority. Business activity presupposes, and is permeated by, expectations about one's own and other persons' character structure, values, and normal behavior, particularly as they relate to broader social relations in which some persons are taken to be superiors, some equals, and some subordinates – as they relate, that is, to social hierarchy. Singly and together, these expectations, ideas, and values are integral to activity pursued for pecuniary gain – for making profit and accumulating capital through private discretionary investment – and, in more general terms, pursued with a view to growth and development of firm and nation.

Business activity as such – buying, selling, allocating resources, employing and disemploying labor, making contracts, establishing and directing partnerships or corporations – corresponds with what Talcott Parsons, for example, designated as "power in a political sense" of the broader sort in a society: "the capacity to mobilize the resources of the society for the attainment of goals for which a general 'public' commitment has been made, or may be made ... mobilization, above all, of the actions of persons and groups, which is binding on them by virtue of their position in society."[6] In other words, what is often regarded as an "economic aspect" of society (the market and property relations) is rather the paramount web of social relations and modes of consciousness of that society, appearing as "economics."

It is empirically evident that the position of the business executive or capitalist in society is not purely "economic" but involves associations with others – social relations – on many intertwining fronts beyond the immediate marketplace: with business associates and their families, with employees, with government officials, with the media, to mention no others. "Business" involves a certain "standard of living," appropriate place of residence, sociability and standing with the "right" people and circles, engagement in clubs and philanthropies, the proper rearing of children. Business includes participation in trade and civic associations, and party politics. From one perspective, business is economic activity as the dominant mode of social relations in a capitalist society, permeated by ideas, ideals, and morality. From another perspective, it is

6. Parsons, "The Distribution of Power in American Society," *World Politics* 10:1 (Oct. 1957), pp. 123–143, at p. 140.

social and political activity as economic activity. Business, or capitalism, then, is not simply "economics," although it subsumes economics. It is property relations; it is class relations; it is a sociopolitical mode of control over economics and over a broad field of social behavior besides; it is a system of law and governance; it is ideology.[7]

From this perspective, we should not take at face value the claims of pro-corporate leaders in the Progressive Era that they were doing no more than adapting law and policy, and seeking the adaptation of the

---

7. Cf. Thorstein Veblen, "The Preconceptions of Economic Science. II," *QJE* 13 (July 1899), pp. 420–421, 426, and passim, pp. 396–426. Veblen observed that prevalent economic theory, like the prevalent everyday business mind, in taking capitalism as identical with economics as such, or as natural, could be regarded not as objective economic theory but as the prevailing interpretation of human nature drawn in terms of unverified a priori premises attributing pecuniary calculation, investment for gain, private ownership of income-yielding assets, as inherent to human nature. His observation found substantiation in the propensity of leading marginal-utility theorists of his day to declare, not unlike Adam Smith, that their theory was based upon, and gave adequate expression to, human nature.

It might also be remarked here that this general concept of "business," of capitalism and, more broadly, production-exchange relations, suggests the inappropriateness of Marx's structure-superstructure (or base-superstructure) metaphor. Karl Marx, *A Contribution to the Critique of Political Economy*, trans. N. I. Stone (Chicago: Charles H. Kerr, 1904), Preface (1859), pp. 9–15, esp. p. 11. The intent of that metaphor is to distinguish the sphere of production relations (structure, base) from the sphere of ideas, consciousness, law, religion, government, etc. (superstructure), and to designate the former as the cause and source of the latter. But because the sphere of production relations (the mode of production or property-production system) is existentially possible only as a definite form of social relations permeated by, and inseparable from, consciousness, values, the law, politics, etc., no such distinction is theoretically valid beyond a provisional level of abstraction for limited analytical purposes. A metaphor is often useful in this latter respect in clearing the ground for theory, but it becomes an obstruction when itself elevated to a principle of theory. Having no other significant meaning than the distinction between production and modes of consciousness, the metaphor is all but useless as theory. It is plainly inconsistent with Marx's repeated insistence through the body of his work that a mode of production always exists as a definite system of social relations, that is, as relations among people bearing historically specific states of consciousness, appearing under capitalism as a relation among things. The inconsistency is registered in Engels's and subsequent professedly Marxian thinkers' attempts at reformulating the structure-superstructure relationship as reciprocally causative except "ultimately," or "in the long run," thereby placing the concept on the same general basis as some theistic explanations of human events, in terms of which, however, the concept collapses as a regulative principle of nondevotional inquiry (that is, as a theoretical principle), and reverts to what it always was, a provisional metaphor. The inconsistency flows from conceiving mode of production as economics and economics as utilitarian manipulation of inanimate things, standing apart from the social, political, and cultural spheres, a view Marx repeatedly took pains to criticize. The inconsistency, it might be added, indicates that, like most other mortals living in western capitalist societies, neither Marx nor Engels, let alone their legatees, were able to extricate their thought entirely from the power of "bourgeois ideological hegemony."

people's thinking, habits, and expectations, to natural evolution dictated by indefeasible laws of economics. It was their way of explaining and justifying, to themselves and to the general public, the rise of corporate capitalism, in a society whose political culture placed great value on small-unit enterprise and the dispersal of economic power, and at the same time on improvement, development, and progress in accordance with "natural" laws. This was not a matter of premeditation or deliberate rationalization but rather of a way of thinking, strongly embedded in the late-nineteenth-century American mind, cutting across class and ideological lines, and receiving sanction from at least four venerable sources: (1) the older Protestant idea of predestination or its more modern, impersonal version of providential design manifested in the laws of nature; (2) principles of classical political economy that posited economic laws operating without reference to human will or preference and identifiable with the laws of nature and hence with providential design (if no longer the Invisible Hand of the old competitive market, then at least the Finger of God, as it were); (3) the idea that in the same way that the just government was a government of laws, not of persons, so the just market was one that operated and evolved in accordance with laws, not the design of persons; and (4) the more recent, prestigious principles of evolution by natural selection, applying to human history laws of cumulative and progressive development similar to those presumably governing the natural world of biology. From these premises, or some mixture of them, the demise of the older competitive captialism at the hands of a rising corporate capitalism could be understood, with convincing cogency, as the necessary result of a progressive evolution governed by natural economic laws, not the work of willful human design, and therefore as justified and ineluctable. As Wilson would put it, the large corporations were not hobgoblins, nor the work of the rascally rich; they were, rather, natural, and anything that was natural could not be called immoral.[8]

As American capitalism entered its transition from the competitive stage to the corporate stage, opinion among leaders in business, political, and intellectual spheres began shifting from the old classical economic laws of free competition and supply-demand equilibrium, to thinking centered on new economic laws of business cycles, crises, and disequilibrium, and on cooperation and administered markets as the progressively evolved alternative to "the wastes of competition." The elements of cooperation and administered markets in the new thinking

---

8. Wilson, "The Lawyer and the Community" (1910), *PPWW*, 2, pp. 254, 258; see Chapter 6, under "A world-wide economic tendency."

would pose an inconsistency with the principle of natural evolution proceeding apart from human design, an inconsistency lying at the heart of pro-corporate thought and placing it in dialogue with – or at jeopardy to – both populist and socialist thought. In any case, among pro-corporate partisans, as among others, there is to be found by the opening years of the twentieth century increasingly enfeebled appeals to dog-eat-dog social Darwinism: It was cooperation that now made firms, economies, and nations fit to survive; or, as Wilson phrased it in 1897, the American people were poised to realize "the triumphs of cooperation, the self–possession and calm choices of maturity."[9]

Something else, then, or at least something more, than supra-human laws of economics, was at work in the rise of corporate capitalism: namely, movements of thought and social action. We have little trouble comprehending that the rise of capitalism in early modern Western history involved to some decisive degree a rising bourgeoisie, a rising social class, and corresponding trends of social thought and sociopolitical movements. If that was the case with early capitalism and a rising bourgeoisie, so it was with a developing, maturing capitalism and a risen or regnant bourgeoisie. Capitalism as a mode of production and a set of social relations has a history, and so does the capitalist class, as do the other classes and the class relations, the property and market relations, associated with capitalism. If the establishment of the "natural" competitive marketplace took for its attainment powerful political movements and modes of thought suited to creating the necessary governmental, legal, intellectual, and cultural conditions, no less so did the subsequent evolution of capitalist market relations, including their passage to the corporate-administered stage.

The history of capitalism, in its very property and market relations, involves not simply "economics" but also human agency in such forms as associational activity, trends of thought, passage of laws, and the shaping of government – in sum, in the form of social movements and politics. Enterprise organizing in the marketplace is as much a part of a social movement and of politics when it is the activity of capitalists, as trade-union organizing in the market and farm-cooperative organizing in the market are parts of workers' and farmers' social movements and politics, respectively. Capitalists or partisans of capitalism invoked

9. In his classic study of social Darwinism, Hofstadter noted that its Spencerian version faded in American thought after the turn of the century, and that "As a conscious philosophy, social Darwinism had largely disappeared in America by the end of the [first world] war." Hofstadter, *Social Darwinism in American Thought*, rev. ed. (Boston: Beacon, 1955), pp. 201–204, quotation at p. 203. For the Wilson quotation, see Wilson, "The Making of the Nation," *PPWW*, 1, p. 318.

obedience to laws of the market or laws of economic evolution to explain, justify, and legitimize their interests, activity, and movements, in the same way that populists invoked obedience to natural rights, socialists, obedience to historical necessity, or evangelicals, obedience to God.

It is not in quantitative economics that we may find sufficient explanation of the emergence of corporate capitalism around the turn of the century; not in advancing or retarded rates of growth, productivity, unemployment, or profit; not in income shares, prices, debt, trade balances, monetary standards, or credit conditions; not in technologies of scale, market size, or market access; not in cycles of prosperity and depression; although all these were subordinate parts of the story and were invoked as reasons by contending movements for and against affirming corporate capitalism.[10] The explanation lies, rather, in the empirical record of the social relations within and among classes, the modes of consciousness, and the social movements, comprising, and relating to, the capitalist mode of production at the time.

The passage of capitalism from its competitive stage to its corporate stage, therefore, was not simply a matter of submission to "objective" laws of economic evolution, as the pro-corporate partisans would have it. Rather, their advocacy of changes in the law, policy, and government was, like the corporate reorganization of property and market relations itself, an integral component of the social-political movements effecting the corporate reconstruction of American capitalism.

Insofar as we think of changes in the economy as something that happens in the realm of "objective" conditions, and then of movements and reforms as "responses" by people, especially by people who are not capitalists, we have in effect adopted the evolutionary standpoint of pro-corporate partisans and, for that matter, of socialists. The standpoint adopted here, instead, is to think of capitalists as a social class to which social movements pertain as an attribute, just as with any other social class; and hence to think of changes in property and market relations as something that people are making happen; that is, to think of changes in the economy proper as the function of social movements. This would mean, as well, thinking of reforms in other spheres – in the law, policy, government, and other institutions – not only as "responses" to this or that "objective" circumstance but also as integral to the changes "happening" in the capitalist mode of production or economy. To put it another way, the evolution of capitalism from stage to

10. As this implies, a distinction is to be made between industrial concentration and corporate capitalism. See note 1 to this chapter, and Chapter 2, introductory section.

stage is part and parcel of what we think of in other contexts as the history of reform related to political-economic affairs, and therefore part and parcel of the history of social movements, not confined to, but indeed including, those involving capitalists in both their market and their extramarket activities.

The corporate reconstruction of capitalism in the United States, accordingly, is a historical event that requires explanation and interpretation: It cannot simply be taken as a "natural" outcome of economic evolution, as an "objective" consequence of techno-economic development, as a logical defensive reaction of capitalists to the depression of the 1890s, or as an organizational aspect of some broader search for order. Nor can the rise of corporate capitalism be properly understood as a "business" aspect of a society's response to industrialism. In dispelling parochialism with a comparative perspective, the concept "response to industrialism" has served a good purpose, portraying Americans engaged in a historical experience similar to that of other societies. In effect, however, the concept applies to the United States thinking drawn from modernization studies of twentieth-century nonindustrial societies; that is, it treats industrialism as an external force to which Americans responded. But industrialism was not only something Americans responded to; since at least the early nineteenth century, it was also something they were doing. Industrialism itself was, in an early phase, a "response" of many Americans to their own republican values; in all phases, a response to nature, the market, and the opportunities and insecurities of capitalism. Similarly, the corporate reorganization of industry was a way in which some Americans, particularly capitalists, were making industrialism respond to their changing position in, and to their changing ideas of, the market, or to their perception of the requirements of preserving capitalist property relations, or at least their own position as capitalist property owners.

Both capitalist industrialism and its corporate reorganization, in sum, are better understood not simply as an "external force" or an "objective" economic or organizational phenomenon but as a social movement, no less than populism, trade unionism, feminism, Afro-American equalitarianism, or socialism. Just as we treat these latter and their respective intellectual trends as political and social movements among farmers, workers, women, Afro-Americans, and others, so may we treat the corporate reconstruction of capitalism and the corresponding intellectual, legal, and legislative trends as political and social movements among capitalists and corresponding groups of intellectuals, reformers, politicians, and others. The tendency to regard "business" as economics or as economic history, or as consisting of "interests" and techno-economic structures and functions, in contrast to ideas and social movements, has obstructed the study of capitalists as a social class and as involved in social movements broader than, but directly related to, their property relations, no less than workers or farmers. It has largely confined the discipline of social history to noncapitalist classes and strata, and has narrowed the framework of research respecting capitalists to special studies of interest-group activity, business history, or the "business mind."[11]

Ascending and declining stages of capitalism

In designating the years 1890–1916 as a time of the corporate reconstruction of American capitalism it is intended to suggest a period of conflict within and between ascending and declining movements, corresponding with ascending and declining forms, or stages, of the capitalist property-production system. It was an era when critical components of the extant governmental system of power, including the legal order, fell

11. The concept of capitalists as a social class adopted here corresponds, although it may not be identical, with that of E. Digby Baltzell, *An American Business Aristocracy* (New York: Collier Books, 1962), chaps. 1–4 and passim, and Baltzell, *Puritan Boston and Quaker Philadelphia: Two Protestant Ethics and the Spirit of Class Authority and Leadership* (New York: Free Press, 1979), chap. 2, and passim, and of William A. Williams, *The Contours of American History* (Cleveland: World, 1961), with strong roots in Veblen and Marx. For a broad social, rather than narrow economic, conception of capitalists in the competitive stage of capitalism, see Philip Scranton, *Proprietary Capitalism: The Textile Manufacture at Philadelphia, 1800–1885* (Cambridge University Press, 1983), pp. 3–11, and passim. In his book *The Visible Hand* and earlier works (see Bibliography), Alfred D. Chandler, Jr., provides rich materials disclosing capitalists at work in the corporate reorganization of enterprise and the market. He tends, however, to treat that work in its techno-economic aspect without reference to broader social relations or modes of consciousness. The historical literature on the role of capitalists in the framing and passing of Progressive Era reform legislation has grown in quantity and substance since the leading works of Hofstadter (*Age of Reform*), Wiebe (see Bibliography), and Williams (*Contours*) were published in the 1950s and early 1960s. The present study is, in part, a further contribution to the genre. The prevalent tendency in the extant literature is to separate the capitalists' activity in the market from that in the larger society, with the latter portrayed as basically interest-group activity serving instrumentally to protect and legitimize the former. The effect is to maintain the dichotomy between "economics" and social movements and politics, or to reduce politics to interest-group pressure activity. Williams's conception in *Contours* is, however, in this respect integrative rather than dichotomous or reductionist. Cf. Richard L. Sklar, "On the Concept of Power in Political Economy," in Dalmas H. Nelson and Richard L. Sklar, eds., *Toward a Humanistic Science of Politics: Essays in Honor of Francis Dunham Wormuth* (Washington, D.C.: University Press of America, 1982).

out of phase with the changing pattern of authority in the property-production system and its expression in trends of thought.

The corporate-reconstruction movements sought to realize the emergent system of corporate-capitalist authority through a transformation of the legal order and the larger system of political power. In that quest, they proceeded in several spheres at once – in market and property relations, in the law and jurisprudence, in party politics, in government policy and legislation, in foreign-policy making, and in scholarly and popular modes of thought. Their efforts assumed the organizational forms of trade and civic associations, single-issue groups and committees, reform clubs, electoral party politics, lobbying, publications ranging from newsletters and newspapers to periodicals and books, and conferences and conventions – in short, organizational forms usually associated with social movements. Corporate capitalism, that is, had to be constructed. It did not come on the American scene as a finished "economic" product, or as a pure-ideal type; nor did it "take over" society and simply vanquish or blot out everything else. On the contrary, although tending toward relative decline and a permanent position of subordination, nevertheless, market relations, forms of thought, political movements, and cultural patterns associated with small-producer and proprietary enterprise remained widespread, influential, and strongly represented in party politics, Congress, and the judiciary, and at the state and local levels of politics and government. They continued to exert a large impact, moreover, in the national electoral arena and in national legislative forums. The large corporations and corporate-administered markets, for some time to come, lacked anything near full legitimacy in the minds of a considerable segment of the people and their political representatives.

The social relations, institutions, forms of thought, and policy preferences associated with corporate capitalism reached ascendancy in and through accommodations to, and modifications by, those on the decline and rooted in the past. Many corporations were themselves impregnated with attributes of the proprietary era – for example, in their being dominated by a strong personality, a "captain of industry" or "captain of finance," a figure like E. H. Harriman, John D. Rockefeller, Sr., J. P. Morgan, Sr., Elbert H. Gary, Henry Ford, or Henry O. Havemeyer. In reaching the peak of their power, however, at the head of large corporations (or investment banking houses specializing in corporate finance), these "Napoleons" of the market, as Cornell professor of political economy Jeremiah W. Jenks called them, prepared the way of their own decline as they exerted themselves on behalf of building bureaucratic organizations that rendered their style and authority increasingly dysfunctional and hence obsolete.[12] Similarly, within and among trade and civic associations, the conflict among variations of the corporate and proprietary outlook characterized the entire period. For example, within the National Association of Manufacturers (NAM) the "moderates," primarily concerned with foreign-market expansion and government measures fostering favorable industrial conditions, lost out to the proprietary manufacturers primarily concerned with opposing trade unionism. Within the American Asiatic Association, there was a continuous split between those who viewed international economic expansion as essentially a matter of markets for goods pure and simple, and those who viewed it as essentially a matter of corporate investment. Differences over government regulation, banking and currency reform, capital-labor relations, and social amelioration, divided opinion within and among such organizations as the National Civic Federation (NCF) on the one hand and the National Association of Manufacturers on the other; indeed, such differences divided capitalists within one and the same firm, corporation, bank, or investment banking house.

The sustained conflict integral to the rise and early development of corporate capitalism came increasingly to be defined by new patterns of consensus and hence differed from past conflict. Conflicts over regulation of the market, for example, proceeded within a new consensual framework, which by the 1890s was displacing the old consensus that

12. Jenks, *The Trust Problem* (New York: McClure, Phillips, 1900), pp. 73–74. Otto H. Kahn of Kuhn, Loeb & Co., called Harriman "The Last Figure of an Epoch," saying of him in January 1911, "His death coincided with what appears to be the ending of an epoch in our economic development. His career was the embodiment of unfettered individualism. For better or for worse – personally I believe for better unless we go too far and too fast – the people appear determined to put limits and restraints upon the exercise of economic power just as in former days they put limits and restraints upon the absolutism of rulers. Therefore, I believe there will be no successor to Mr. Harriman; there will be no other career like his." (Harriman worked closely with Kuhn, Loeb in his railway financing.) Otto H. Kahn, *Our Economic and Other Problems: A Financier's Point of View* (New York: George H. Doran, 1920) p. 12. Frank A. Vanderlip, from his position with the National City Bank as vice-president and then president, made similar assessments of Harriman and of J. P. Morgan, Sr. Upon Morgan's death in 1913, Vanderlip wrote to James Stillman, the bank's chief emeritus, that "there will be no other king; ... Mr. Morgan, typical of the time in which he lived, can have no successor, for we are facing other days." At the same time, Vanderlip and Stillman admired J. P. Morgan & Co.'s complex organization as a model to be followed by the National City Bank. Vanderlip assessed Harriman's individual capacities and talents as very great but far outstripped by the organizational needs of his railway properties. In general, Stillman and Vanderlip agreed on the need of corporate executives to subordinate their individuality to the requirements of complex organization. Vanderlip to Stillman, 4 Apr. 1913; Stillman to Vanderlip, 11 Jan. 1909, 19 Feb. 1909; Vanderlip to Stillman, 12 Feb. 1909, 28 May 1909, 24 Dec. 1910, FAV.

had favored the largely competitive domestic market. Manufacturers, bankers, farmers, workers, reformers, were variously reacting against the competitive market and its consequences. The anticompetitive consensus established the ground of conflict over the purposes, character, and methods of regulation, over how much and what kind of regulation could be left to arrangements among private parties in the market, and how much and what kind might be assigned to government.

Corporate consolidations, agricultural cooperatives, and trade unions constituted, in effect, regulatory trends in the private sector, each with roots in the past but now assuming a new significance. They involved or immediately called into play proposals for government regulatory roles, for it was a cardinal principle of the competitive market regime – no less ideologically powerful now than before – that regulatory authority could not be safely reposed in private hands free of public supervision. Conflicting proposals for government regulation of the market derived from small-producer fears of competition as well as of monopolistic oppression, from adversarial market interests such as those of shippers against carriers, from positive and defensive corporate initiatives, from investors in negotiable securities seeking greater stability in the capital markets – that is, from all manner of bourgeois sources within the market, as well as from intellectuals, social reformers, independent professionals, trade unionists, and political leaders of the various pro-corporate, populist, progressive, and socialist persuasions.

The pervasive conflict and the regulation that resulted from it constitute the realistic ground for interest-group interpretation of the period. Similarly, as the transition from competitive to corporate capitalism involved all classes, reform was not a matter of this class or stratum or that, but of all classes and strata; hence, historians could find in each class or social stratum *the* story of reform, and indeed there were in the Progressive Era myriad reform movements and reforms. Whatever their incongruities, however, regulatory laws and administrative practice tended, though far from consistently, to legitimize and recognize the new corporate order, its form of property, and its leading underlying assumptions. This is a measure of the corporate ascendancy and of the power of the corporate sector of the capitalist class; it registers the pro-corporate movement for change in the property-production system, or mode of production, that found expression in the market and in the legal, political, and intellectual spheres.[13]

13. Although the rise of corporate capitalism as a new stage in the history of capitalism was already a common theme by the early twentieth century, and has had its American chroniclers and theorists ranging from Jenks, Charles A. Conant, and Thorstein Veblen to Adolph A. Berle, Gardiner C. Means, and Alfred D. Chandler,

Jr., it may be fairly said that William A. Williams established the concept of corporate capitalism as an essential periodization of United States political, social, and intellectual, not only economic, history since the 1890s. Williams's phrase (*Contours*, pp. 343–478) was "The Age of Corporation Capitalism," and he dated the period from 1882 to the 1960s (and presumably beyond). Other historians, either independently or drawing upon Williams, have contributed works based upon such a periodization that touch both general interpretation and specific spheres of study. Severally and together, these works may be taken to indicate the fruitfulness of the periodization for historical inquiry. Some of the works apply the periodization more consistently than others, and some display a greater sensitivity than others toward the conflicts and complexities implicit in the periodization. Among the better-known and more frequently cited works in the genre, aside from Williams's, are the following (in approximate chronological order): Loren Baritz, *The Servants of Power: A History of the Use of Social Sciences in American Industry* (New York: Wiley, 1960); Martin J. Sklar, "Woodrow Wilson and the Political Economy of Modern United States Liberalism," *Studies on the Left* 1:3 (Fall 1960), reprinted in Ronald Radosh and Murray N. Rothbard, eds., *A New History of Leviathan* (New York: E. P. Dutton, 1972), pp. 7–65; Gabriel Kolko, *The Triumph of Conservatism* (New York: Free Press, 1963); Lloyd Gardner, *Economic Aspects of New Deal Diplomacy* (Madison: University of Wisconsin Press, 1964); David Eakins, "The Development of Corporate-Liberal Policy Research in the United States, 1885–1965" (Ph.D. diss., University of Wisconsin, 1966); Eakins, "Policy Planning for the Establishment," in Radosh and Rothbard, eds., *New History*, pp. 188–205; Ronald Radosh, "The Corporate Ideology of American Labor Leaders from Gompers to Hillman," *Studies on the Left* 6:6 (Nov.–Dec. 1966), pp. 66–87; James Weinstein, *The Corporate Ideal in the Liberal State, 1900–1918* (Boston: Beacon, 1968); Martin J. Sklar, "On the Proletarian Revolution and the End of Political-Economic Society," *Radical America* 3:3 (May–June 1969); Carl P. Parrini, *Heir to Empire: United States Economic Diplomacy, 1916–1923* (Pittsburgh: University of Pittsburgh Press, 1969); Alfred S. Eichner, *The Emergence of Oligopoly: Sugar Refining as a Case Study* (Baltimore: Johns Hopkins University Press, 1969); Joel Spring, *Education and the Rise of the Corporate State* (Boston: Beacon, 1972); Robert D. Cuff, *The War Industries Board: Business-Government Relations during World War I* (Baltimore: Johns Hopkins University Press, 1973); Eli Zaretsky, "Capitalism, the Family and Personal life," *Socialist Revolution* 3:1–3 (1973), republished as *Capitalism, the Family and Personal Life* (New York: Harper & Row, 1976); Stuart Ewen, *Captains of Consciousness: Advertising and the Social Roots of the Consumer Culture* (New York: McGraw-Hill, 1976); David F. Noble, *America by Design: Science, Technology, and the Rise of Corporate Capitalism* (New York: Knopf, 1977). Much of the labor history inspired by and including the work of Herbert G. Gutman (*Work, Culture and Society in Industrializing America* [New York: Random House, Vintage Books, 1977]) and David Montgomery (*Workers Control in America* [Cambridge University Press, 1979]) affirms and draws upon periodization in terms of corporate capitalism for United States history since the late nineteenth century.

The common periodization shared by these works nevertheless does not prevent their authors from differing significantly among one another politically, philosophically, and in matters of general and specific historical interpretation. See, e.g., Kolko's criticism of Williams and Weinstein and of his own earlier views as expressed in *Triumph*, in Kolko, "Intelligence and the Myth of Capitalist Rationality in the United States," *Science and Society* 44:2 (Summer 1980), pp. 130–154, at pp. 133–134, 134 nn. 4, 5. For critiques of the genre, inter alia, by opponents, see, e.g., Irwin Unger, "The 'New Left' and American History: Some Recent Trends in United States Historiography," *AHR* 72:4 (July 1967), pp. 1237–1263 (which contains, at p. 1252, a seriously distortive, although inadvertent, misquotation of Sklar, "Wil-

It does not follow from this, however, that the corporate reconstruction of law, politics, government policy, or administrative practice occurred overnight and all at once, in a unilinear manner, or "naturally," apart from social movements actively engaged in constructing and shaping the new corporate order. Nor does it follow that regulatory law and agencies were simply made, by manipulative ploy or otherwise, into the instruments of those corporate interests ostensibly regulated. The ascendancy of corporate capitalism proceeded on the basis of its accountability to, and accommodation of, smaller capital, and to a lesser extent accommodation of a changing working class. In the latter case it was on the basis not of a general collective bargaining system but of the open shop in most of industry, limited collective bargaining, particularly in railroads and the building trades for skilled workers, and the beginnings of regulatory legislation affecting conditions of labor. Regulation of business practices in general, moreover, was based on the principle of protecting property rights and the public interest, whether from competitive activity itself or from concentrated power within the market; regulation also embodied the intention of superseding the old competitive market while preserving or introducing mechanisms and incentives, including new kinds of inter-corporate competition, conducive to innovation and rising efficiency.

In the end, among the different views of what constituted legitimate property rights, the public interest, salutary innovation, and optimal efficiency, that which defined them in terms of regulating, affirming, and legitimizing the corporate-capitalist order came to dominate all the rest. It came to be identified in social thought with what was progressive and liberal in the nation's political life, with what in this study will be referred to as "corporate liberalism." This is an outcome, a "fact," however, that cannot be taken for granted but that needs to be explored and explained.

son"), and Alan L. Seltzer, "Woodrow Wilson as 'Corporate-Liberal': Toward a Reconsideration of Left Revisionist Historiography," *Western Political Quarterly* 30:2 (June 1977), pp. 183–212. Both critiques overestimate the agreement on matters of historical interpretation among authors of the genre, and both exaggerate the usefulness of the terms "New Left" and "Left Revisionist" in characterizing what is a rather significant diversity of thinking among the authors. See Ellis W. Hawley, "The Discovery and Study of a 'Corporate Liberalism'," *BHR* 52:3 (Autumn 1978), pp. 309–320. The authors of leading works associated more strongly with modernization theory – such as Wiebe, Samuel P. Hays, Louis Galambos, and Hawley, (especially "Herbert Hoover, the Commerce Secretariat, and the Vision of an 'Associative State,' 1921–1928," *JAH* 62 [June 1974], pp. 116–140) – would probably acknowledge without much hesitation the validity of the concept "corporate capitalism" for the purposes of economic analysis and economic history, and for some aspects of political and social history, but might not necessarily accept it for purposes of a comprehensive periodization.

In general, the emergence of the corporate reconstruction of American capitalism involved a pandemic conflict engendered by the larger conflict between two major forms of capitalist property and their corresponding modes of consciousness, or bewteen two historical stages of capitalist society: the proprietary-competitive market stage and the corporate-administered market stage, the one receding before but leaving its indelible marks upon the ascendancy of the other.

Class metamorphosis and corporate reconstruction

After the depression of the 1890s, the change in the organization of the capitalist property-production system crystallized quickly and involved massive amounts of property. Yet, for all the bitter and angry conflict it generated and for all its rapidity and hugeness of scale,[14] it proceeded relatively peacefully and within the framework of the existing political institutions. How come? It has not ordinarily occurred to historians to raise this question. The peaceful transition to corporate capitalism is generally taken for granted. But changes in property organization and ownership on so large a scale are not routine occurrences in history, and violence is a not uncommon accompaniment of such changes, as the Indian wars of the preceding decades and the Civil War scarcely four decades earlier had testified.

It must be said, first, that the nation's political life in the course of the change was not altogether peaceful or lacking in violence and coercive force. The disfranchisement, and the suppression of the citizenship rights, of Afro-Americans in the 1890s and early twentieth century, attended by legal and extralegal violence, narrowed the range of political democracy and substantially weakened populist or anti-corporate forces in the body politic. To some considerable extent, racism and racist violence played a facilitative role in the emergence of corporate capitalism.

Second, the 1890s saw the weakening of such trade unionism in industry as existed, from the effects both of the depression and of legal and extralegal violence against striking workers, as at Homestead in 1892, in the Pullman and railway strike of 1894, and in the western mining industry. It would seem, until further study indicates differently, that the curtailment of industrial union strength in the 1890s, and a decline in industrial workers' market power, served as a precondition of the corporate reorganization of American capitalism, and not that the corporate reorganization was itself a strategic capitalist reaction to a

---

14. See Chapter 2, notes 4 and 5 and related text, below.

presumably growing market power on the part of industrial workers.[15]

Third, the Spanish-American War and the three-year war of conquest in the Philippines, in the years 1898–1902, coinciding in time with most of the activity of the 1898–1904 merger wave, contributed to a political environment favorable to the corporate reorganization of industry. This effect was due in part to domestic economic expansion attributable to war-induced demand, and in part to the spread of chauvinistic or simply nationalistic sentiment, which strengthened the electoral hand of an incumbent president who favored the corporate reorganization of industry as a progressive national asset and was not inclined to turn the might of the national government against it.

All this said, nevertheless the corporate reorganization of American capitalism was a relatively peaceful affair. Unlike the great sociopolitical crisis of the 1850s and 1860s, which was resolved by a national reconstruction that required a civil war and revolution, the corporate reconstruction required neither civil war nor revolution, but rather political and economic reorganization and reform.

The crisis of the 1890s – political, economic, and social in its dimensions – did not involve, as did that of the 1850s and 1860s, an impasse or stalemate, where no move by a great class or stratum of society was in practice possible without destroying the extant state system, where neither side in the conflict could assert its interests and principles in a manner satisfactory to itself without rending the union and going beyond the terms of the Constitution.[16] The earlier crisis

15. It might be added that a rejuvenation and dramatic growth of trade unions coincided with the corporate merger movement of 1898–1904, although growth in union membership appeared less among unskilled and semiskilled industrial workers than among skilled and nonindustrial workers. See Chapter 4, note 62, and related text, below, and the chapter in general for discussion of the relation of trade unionism to intra-capitalist consensus on the corporate reorganization of industry. The support workers often received in the 1870s and 1880s from local capitalists in strikes against railways or large absentee-owned companies should not be generalized and read forward to the later 1880s and 1890s, when a change in the composition of the industrial working class and in bourgeois attitudes toward strikes and unions had produced considerably different circumstances. Nor should the intense competitive conditions among capitalists before the corporate reorganization, which drove down profits and prices and thereby enhanced the purchasing power of the wage dollar, be misconstrued as a shift in the balance of power in the market from capital to labor in the struggle over income shares. Capitalists' complaints that competition and lower prices in effect shifted income from capital to labor, especially during the depression of the 1890s, are better understood as indicative of real conditions in the ironic rather than in the iron-statistical sense. See Chapter 2, notes 14 and 43, and related text, below.

16. The word "crisis" has lately tended to come into excessive and indiscriminate use. Here, with respect to the Civil War era and the 1890s, the term is used in its strict

resulted in a colossal civil war that ultimately eliminated an entire property system, basically altered the class system, and reconstituted the nation-state with respect to both its structure and its relation to society. The crisis of the 1890s was entirely resolvable within the political system extant. The changes in political-economic affairs, in property ownership, in class relations, and in government ranged wide and deep; they were of the first significance; but they constituted a reconstruction without need of a civil war or revolution.

The crisis of the 1890s was of the fluid kind, not that of deadlock. No great class's or stratum's vital interests or development imminently threatened another's development or very existence; at least, whatever the rhetoric, no politically effective segment of any great class or stratum perceived itself to be so threatened. Each great class or stratum – capitalists, workers, farmers, professionals – had attained so large a degree of heterogeneity and itself was in such flux, that none could be solidly arrayed against the others. The balance of class and other social forces was, therefore, not unyieldingly fixed but asymmetrically fluid, tending to flow toward the further development of large-scale industrial capitalism and in the direction of its corporate reconstruction, without the disintegration of the political system. The corporate-tending sector of the capitalist class and pro-corporate sectors of other classes and strata could not simply impose their will on society. The very diversity of conditions and outlook within the capitalist class, as with the other classes and strata, obliged the pro-corporate sector of the capitalist class to proceed through compromise and accommodation with the proprietary and smaller capitalist sectors, as well as through alliances and alignments across lines of class and strata.

Where competitive capitalism and populist politics appeared, in the experience of the 1890s, to be disintegrative to large sectors of both the metropolitan and provincial populations, large-scale capitalism and the pro-corporate movement appeared to them to be reintegrative. In the latter respect, event matched anticipation. Corporate capitalism could subsume and make room for the interests and development of small producers, proprietary capitalists, the professions, a growing working class, and new middle-class strata. It could exploit and accommodate

---

sense as denoting a turning point, or critical juncture, resulting in decisive change, whether morbid or regenerative. Conflict as such, however intense or bitter, however intractable or morally reprehensible, does not necessarily constitute a crisis; it may well express normality or a method of preventing a crisis. On the impasse of the 1850s, see David M. Potter, *The Impending Crisis, 1848–1861* (New York: Harper & Row, 1976), chaps. 9–13, 16–18, and passim, and cf. Jonathan Arac, "The Politics of *The Scarlet Letter*," in Sacvan Bercovitch and Myra Jehlen, eds., *Ideology and Classic American Literature* (Cambridge University Press, 1986), pp. 247–266.

new technologies, new life-styles, new educational, scientific, and cultural institutions and patterns, on the basis of rising productivity and expanding production rooted in specialization, standardization, and economies of scale. In its very centralizing and standardizing characteristics, corporate capitalism was inclusive of social diversity in a way that proprietary-competitive capitalism was not and could not be. Its partisans, accordingly, called corporate capitalism progressive.

Corporate capitalism could make persuasive cross-class appeals, therefore, that small-scale competitive capitalism could not. To smaller capitalists it could offer coexistence with large capital, with more stable prices and markets, and with a large field for enterprise in real estate, banking and finance, construction, subcontracting, retailing, specialty production, and distribution of all kinds. Alternatively, it could offer to small capitalists a chance to merge with stronger firms or diversify their claim to a share in general profits of the capitalist economy, by exchanging reliance on one enterprise for stockholding in many. To smaller capitalists, professionals, and middle-class strata in general, corporate capitalism could also offer an outlet for savings and higher income without the headaches of management, as well as opportunity for employment and advancement based on "merit" without the obstruction of nepotism found in proprietary enterprise. To labor, corporate capitalism could offer greater stability of employment and better wages with higher productivity, as well as pensions, profit-sharing, recreational facilities, and even advancement from blue collar to white and prospective advancement up the corporate ladder. On the other hand, corporate capital could offer to smaller capital protection from trade unions in industry. By sustaining the open shop in their own plants, large industrial corporations helped keep trade unions weak in industry in general, thereby assisting smaller manufacturers in their battle against unions.[17]

As the foregoing suggests, the passage of capitalism from its competitive stage to its corporate stage involved a process in which the capitalist class was undergoing a corresponding metamorphosis, and while changing its composition and internal relations, it was also changing its relations with other classes and strata. The same may be said of workers and farmers, the professions, and others, but for present purposes, certain aspects of the internal relations of the capitalist class may be briefly pursued.

17. See Chapter 3, under "American corporations, European cartels," esp. notes 183 and 184, and related text; and Chapter 4, below, for discussion of the labor issue as important in the accommodation between smaller capital and large corporate capital.

By the last years of the 1890s, the changes in property and market relations associated with the appearance of large-scale enterprises in railroads and industry had created necessary techno-economic and social preconditions of a corporate reconstruction of capitalism. In particular, among the social preconditions, the changes had reached the point of generating a corporate sector of the capitalist class, of sufficient number and critical mass to form a political leadership poised to act within the class and in national politics. It was a leadership composed of capitalists recently engaged in organizing or directing corporate enterprise, and people from social strata with an interest in the emergent property relations or in their broader social effects or implications, among them lawyers, intellectuals, journalists, educators, clergy, engineers, and professional politicians, some of whom wore more than one hat at the same time or in succession.

It was a bipartisan class and political leadership oriented to corporate capitalism, beginning to displace or absorb the previous bipartisan leadership oriented to competitive capitalism. It first crystallized in the several years on either side of the turn of the century; provisionally, it may be said that it made its first relatively cohesive appearance in national politics at the Republican party national convention of 1896, the Gold Democratic party convention of 1896 in Chicago, and in the Indianapolis Monetary Convention of early 1897. Other associations in this period with a similar leadership significance might also be noted, such as the New York Reform Club, the sound money leagues, the Chicago Civic Federation, the National Civic Federation, the American Asiatic Association, some of the big city economic clubs and some state chambers of commerce, especially that of New York. The first McKinley administration represented an early stage in the bipartisan pro-corporate leadership's political development and in its policy-forming role in the executive branch of the federal government. Reference is made to McKinley's appointing, as his secretary of the treasury, Lyman J. Gage, the eminent Chicago banker and prominent Gold Democrat. Gage, in turn, brought into advisory roles on domestic and foreign fiscal and economic policies such other Gold Democrats as Charles A. Conant and Charles S. Fairchild, former secretary of the treasury in the first Cleveland administration.[18] The Republican side of the pro-corporate leadership was represented by John Sherman at State and John W. Griggs at Justice, as well as by Marcus A. Hanna as a close presidential adviser, and it was considerably strengthened with the accession at midterm of John Hay at State and Elihu Root at War.

18. On the bipartisan significance of the Gage appointment, see Herman H. Kohlsaat, *From McKinley to Harding* (New York: Scribner 1923), pp. 56, 58.

The Indianapolis Monetary Convention, its executive committee, and the monetary commission appointed by the latter, although obscure even in specialized monetary histories, played a key role not simply in monetary and banking reform history but also in the metamorphosis of the capitalist class, and particularly in the emergence of a corporate sector of the capitalist class to a position of leadership in national politics.[19] Bipartisan in political affiliation, this sector was, in its market activity, composed of capitalists from the major sections of the country associated with railways, newly emergent industrial corporations, and investment banking houses. In outlook, it was oriented not to narrow trade or special-interest issues alone but also to larger policy-formation related to the corporate reorganization of the economy, with specific emphasis on the realignment of the banking and currency system to accord with the needs of the corporate economy, on government regulation of the market, on tariffs and taxes, on recasting the nation's international relations, and on other such larger issues. Leading figures in this sector of the capitalist class intersected with one another in the leaderships of the Indianapolis and other policy-oriented reform associations, such as those just mentioned; several went on to serve as policymakers and implementers in the national administrations of the Progressive Era.

If we take into account the biographical and associational data respecting the individual capitalists involved in the leadership of such groups as the Indianapolis commission, the reform clubs, the civic federations, and others, a profile appears that indicates the integrative characteristics of both this emerging corporate sector of the capitalist class and the new corporate capitalism in its structural and associational aspects.[20]

At a time when bitter conflicts between small enterprisers and "the trusts" ranked among the more salient aspects of American national politics, the large railway and newly organized industrial, commercial,

19. In a current study in progress I explore matters of capitalist-class reformation in relation to the corporate reorganization of capitalism. I presented some of my preliminary findings, along lines presented briefly here, in my paper "Prosopography, Class, and Periodization: The Leadership of the Indianapolis Monetary Convention and Commission," delivered at the History Department Associates Forum, Northwestern University, Evanston, Illinois, 16 Feb. 1983. My thanks to Carl Parrini for sharing with me his research on the Indianapolis Monetary Commission. In attendance at my presentation were, among others, Robert H. Wiebe and James Livingston, and I am happy to thank them for their comments at the time.

20. The profile corresponds with what Baltzell (in *American Business Aristocracy*) refers to as the corporation-based intercity business aristocracy or upper class; I prefer to think of it as a corporate sector of what was at the time a heterogeneous capitalist class.

and financial corporations, although a major bone of that contention, also at the same time represented the countertendency, and in the long run the stronger one, of aligning strategic sectors of the small and middle-range bourgeoisie – including independent and salaried professionals – with large-scale corporate enterprise and hence with "big" capitalists. Aside from the ways, already noted, in which the large corporation offered the small and middle-range bourgeoisie new vocational and income-earning opportunities, it also, in the process, began to knit together in close association – not before accomplished by the competitive regime – "big city" capital and smaller hinterland capital. The large corporation was, therefore, both socially and sectionally integrative.

Quantitatively significant as the demographic movement off the farms in this period indubitably was, it should not obscure the qualitative significance of the movement of middle-class fathers and sons away from their immediate proprietary-business ties, or physically from small hometowns, to corporate ties or to the big city via corporate merger or recruitment. For many Americans, the corporation became the new frontier of opportunity that the western lands had once symbolized. In this sense, bureaucracy in the corporate form in the private economy represented a new bourgeois freedom; it "democratized" and nationalized previously segmented and hierarchic layers of the capitalist class, with new integrative patterns of hierarchy and new avenues of entry, enrichment, authority, and ascent toward the top or at least to greater affluence. For all the outcries against "big business," "the trusts," and the "soulless" corporation, emanating from agrarian populists and middle-class reformers, the large bureaucratic corporation offered opportunities of social mobility for middle class people, new and sturdier ladders of success, than the family-based farm or other business. Hence, the large corporation has enjoyed if not a heartfelt popularity, then at least a love-hate deference and attraction, among large sectors of the rural and urban middle classes.[21]

21. The evidence adduced by business historians and political scientists of the disproportionate bourgeois origins of top corporate leadership, although a salutary antidote to mythical exaggerations of trans-class mobility in the United States, substantiates what may be the more historically significant point: namely, the large corporations' broadening base of support among the smaller and middle-range bourgeoisie and professional strata, achieved through their recruitment of middle-class fathers and sons into white-collar and professional occupations, and into lower, middle, and top management positions, as well as through the new opportunities they afforded for profitable investment of family savings. The ideological and political implications of this reorientation of middle-class interests and loyalties, particularly in understanding Progressivism and corporate liberalism, would well repay further research and study. Although disproportionately less, quantitatively, a

The large corporation in transportation, communications, industry, distribution, and finance (including the larger investment banking houses) accelerated the growth of a kind of consciousness within the sphere of private enterprise formerly – and, in other countries, somewhat more persistently – lodged more decisively with government: namely, the long-term and wide-ranging "development" outlook, but in this case as integral to successful private enterprise as well as to national progress. Large corporations became centers of development planning, ranging from horizontal and vertical integration of productive and distributive facilities to complex production and flow scheduling, land settlement, resource allocation, income distribution, credit extension, and urban siting and planning. The development outlook involved the deployment and synchronization of expertise in everything from marketing and technological engineering to the invention of sophisticated instruments of long-term investment and the practice of skillful, subtle – and not so subtle – diplomacy in dealing with investors, suppliers, customers, employees, and officials of all levels of government at home and increasingly abroad. For many, accordingly, the corporate environment raised their ideological horizon from that of the short-term, the single-interest, and the provincial, to the long-term, the multi-interest, the national, and the international.

It was characteristic of the transition from competitive to corporate capitalism in the United States that although family alliances and family-based wealth continued to be no less important than before, the families actively involved in engineering the transition shifted their base of income, power, and prestige from the proprietary enterprise to the bureaucratic corporation, usually multifunctional and multilocational in operation, and to the diversified investment portfolio. The source of the family wealth, including that among the large number of families retaining proprietary enterprises, increasingly transferred out of the fixed base of the closely held firm to the fluidity and broad-ranging flow of negotiable securities. The family income and influence found an extended reach and a more secure matrix in the more generalized capital-

qualitatively similar impact on working-class and farm families by corporate recruitment undoubtedly made its mark, and likewise invites further research and study. On origins of top corporate leadership, see, e.g., W. Lloyd Warner and James Abegglen, *Big Business Leaders in America* (New York: Atheneum, 1963), pp. 11–33; Mabel Newcomer, "The Chief Executive of Large Corporations," *Explorations in Entrepreneurial History* (Oct. 1952), pp. 13–14; Frank W. Taussig and C. S. Joslyn, *American Business Leaders* (New York: Macmillan, 1932); William Miller, "American Historians and the Business Elite," *JEH* 9 (Nov. 1945); William Miller, ed., *Men in Business: Essays in the History of Entrepreneurship* (Cambridge, Mass.: Harvard University Press, 1952).

ist property right represented by corporate securities, as against having the larger part of the family's income eggs in one or two closely held proprietary baskets or individually held parcels of land or real estate. This not only broadened the income base but also, in effect, socialized the risk by diluting it with limited liability. It exerted a socializing impact of another sort on the outlook and interests of growing numbers of capitalists. Not only were those who remained engaged in proprietary business interested in government regulation to protect their continued coexistence with large corporations in the marketplace, but as players and investors in necessarily impersonal capital markets, the bourgeoisie in general became interested in government regulation on behalf of stability and fair play.

The process of transformation from the proprietary to the corporate form of capitalist property in the Untied States involved a considerable continuity of family position, while at the same time opening avenues to higher eminence and income to new families of middle and lower rank. In the case of many of the leading corporate executives in the years around the turn of the century, their lives, family roots, associations, and careers bridged the period of proprietary capitalism in the antebellum and post–Civil War years, and the period of corporate reorganization in the later 1880s to 1900s. Many of them were of "old stock" families with American forebears dating back to the seventeenth and eighteenth centuries. Those who arrived in America in the nineteenth century were often from family backgrounds that facilitated quick liaisons with "old stock" or well-established families: The Horatio Alger myth had a certain resonance for such men as these. Many were frequent travelers between the United States and Europe and had international, especially transatlantic, familial, social, and business relationships, which facilitated the orientation to international operations of large corporations. Some of the more prominent northerners had been active in antislavery or unionist politics in the Civil War era, and they personified the tradition that combined patriotic nationalism with business enterprise, a tradition that gave them great self-confidence as leaders, or stewards, of their society; a tradition associated with avidity for change, and one that lent to capitalism, and particularly to "big business," the ideological prestige of representing liberty, opportunity, national greatness, and, in short, American Progress. The southerners who joined the corporate procession, whatever their antebellum background, tended strongly to rank among the "Redeemers" that C. Vann Woodward so well depicted, bound up with the region's post–Civil War railroad, industrial, and commercial development, such as it was, some of them with immediate interests in international trade (in textiles and in agricultural and extractive commodities), and many with strong ties to northern corporate capital.

The corporate reconstruction, accordingly, was less a process of displacement of one bourgeois stratum by another than of an evolving adaptation of older prominent families and the continuous accretion of newer families, in both metropolis and province, to the corporate overhaul of market and property relations. Frictions and irritations there were, of the snobbery and bigotry kind, but not such as to obstruct the process as a whole. Many proprietary capitalists themselves changed their business organization to the corporate form, while many others were quick to join in the advantages of corporate reorganization initiated by larger capitalists, promoters, or financiers. In general, although it calls for further research, this process of class evolution and reintegration helps account for the celerity and relative thoroughness with which centralization directly through the form of corporate consolidation spread in the United States after the depression of the 1890s. The movement among capitalists composing this emergent corporate sector of the capitalist class amounted to a wholesale transformation of the system of capitalist property-ownership in commanding sectors of the economy; it was a movement in which capitalists were engaged in reconstructing the industrial-capitalist order, remaking "industrialism," or making industrialism "respond" to new forms of capitalist property relations. The widespread participation of proprietary capitalists in the corporate transformation, whether in primary or secondary roles, must count as part of the explanation of how it was that such a tremendous overhaul of property ownership transpired both so quickly and so peacefully.

Many corporate capitalist executives functioned as directors or officers of two or more enterprises, often both financial and nonfinancial, at the same time, so that they acquired an inter-sectoral and more generalized economic outlook along with diverse economic, social, and political associations than was, or had been, the case with proprietary capitalists. Many of them functioned on a broader social stage as leaders in commercial bodies, civic associations, reform clubs, and party politics. They were active as well, often as officers, in the institutional spheres of religion, culture, higher education, philanthropy, and organizations for inter-regional projects or development. In these capacities, they drew into close association with politicians and with leaders in the liberal professions, who themselves, in turn, became closely associated, personally, politically, socially, and professionally with corporate leaders and institutions. In such ways are the threads of class woven into the cloth of sociopolitical leadership. The capitalists in question are to be understood, in other words, not simply as personifications of "interests," but under the dignity of class: They were people of power, prestige, and leadership in the society at large.[22]

The rise of a corporate sector of the capitalist class brought with it, in the sphere of party politics, a realignment among the higher circles that paralleled, and ultimately fostered a policy-making coherence in, the voter realignment reshaping the major parties from the mid–1890s to the early years of the new century.[23] In the upper echelons of power and wealth, the class metamorphosis contributed strongly to a regrouping of people and ideas around the issues of money and banking, tariff reform, administered markets, government regulation, and international affairs that transcended older political divisions and reconciled free-trade Gold Democrats, mugwumps, and regular Republicans in a common front against agrarian populism and socialistic radicalism on the left, and against laissez-faire provincialism on the right.

On the one hand, capitalists in large corporations operating in major sectors of production and trade had changed from the entrepreneur-debtor outlook to the administrator-investor outlook, strengthening a growing consensus, reaching from metropolis to hinterland and intersecting business, political, and intellectual circles, in favor of government regulation of the market, central banking, downward tariff revision, and international trade and investment. On the other hand, captains of industry and finance joined reformers, moralists, and professionals in wanting "efficient" government, standing above the "corruptions" of party politics; they wanted government bureaucracies, like those of the better-managed corporations, based solely on merit instead

22. As this implies, I find in my own research that no useful or meaningful distinction is to be made respecting broader outlook or activity, ranging from economics and politics to philanthropy and culture, between "finance" capitalists and "industrial" capitalists. It is also my view, implicit in all I have written here but have reserved for argument, if necessary, elsewhere, that "corporate capitalism" is a more historically accurate naming of the postcompetitive stage of capitalism than "finance capitalism." Corporate capitalism represents the intermeshing of nonfinancial and financial capital.

23. Cf. Robert D. Marcus, *Grand Old Party: Political Structure in the Gilded Age, 1880–1896* (New York: Oxford University Press, 1971), pp. 245–250; Samuel P. Hays, "Political Parties and the Community-Society Continuum," in William N. Chambers and Walter D. Burnham, eds., *The American Party Systems* (New York: Oxford University Press, 1967), pp. 152–181, esp. pp. 154–155, 166–173; Burnham, "Party Systems and the Political Process," in ibid., pp. 277–307, esp. pp. 298–301; Burnham, *Critical Elections and the Mainsprings of American Politics* (New York: Norton, 1970), chaps. 1 and 4, pp. 1–10, 71–90; Paul Kleppner, "The Political Revolution of the 1890s: A Behavioral Intepretation," in David Brody, ed., *Essays on the Age of Enterprise, 1870–1900* (Hinsdale, Ill.: Dryden Press, 1974), pp. 273–287; and Kleppner, *The Cross of Culture* (New York: Free Press, 1977), last chapter.

of on clientage, patronage, or immediate popular demands, especially as government was assuming a greater role in administering the conduct of social life and business practices. They wanted a "government of laws, not of persons," conducive to a favorable investment environment, techno-economic progress, inter-class cooperation, and social stability – in short, "clean government" and "social efficiency."

In one type of manifestation, the political realignment extended outside and across party lines: for example, in such nonpartisan associations as the Indianapolis Monetary Commission, the New York Reform Club, sound money leagues, and the National Civic Federation; or in a bipartisan coalescence, in which such Gold Democrats as Conant and Gage cooperated in elections and in policy formation with McKinley- and then Progressive Republicans, and served in their administrations. In another type of manifestation, the regrouping expressed itself within each of the two major parties, with some Gold Democrats deserting altogether to the Republican party, and others, such as Conant, George Foster Peabody, Alton B. Parker, and Woodrow Wilson, remaining either to wrest control of their party from Bryanites or populists, or to domesticate the latter with the sticks of chastisement and disfranchisement, and the carrots of reform.

The corporate regrouping within the capitalist class pointed to another major characteristic of politics in the Progressive Era: namely, the shifting of national policy formation and legislative initiative increasingly away from party and congressional leaderships, arenas most sensitive to electoral politics, to "nonpartisan" bodies of experts – from the universities, the professions, and newly organized civic associations – cooperating closely with the executive branch and selected senior members of Congress.[24]

The longer-term reintegrative tendencies of the capitalist class's metamorphosis involved substantial socioeconomic realignment; at the same time, therefore, it proceeded as a function of a continuing intra-class division and conflict. Capitalists divided among themselves as between metropolitan and provincial, corporate and proprietary, big and small, shippers and carriers, creditors and debtors, and so on; they differed over such policy matters as monetary and banking reform, the tariff and

---

24. Cf. Marcus, *Grand Old Party*, pp. 258–259. It was in the years from the 1890s to 1914 that many of the associations prominent in policy-forming activity were first organized or assumed a political significance different from before. Among the newly formed may be noted the Indianapolis Monetary Commission, the National Association of Manufacturers, the American Asiatic Association, the Pan-American Union, the National Civic Federation, the Sound Money League, the United States Chamber of Commerce, the National Foreign Trade Council.

taxation, government regulation of the market, and capital-labor relations. "Business," that is, was not a monolithic entity, and certainly not
in a period of major intra-class, and hence inter-class, realignment. Even
without reference to such a special circumstance as a general class-
metamorphosis, intra-class divisions, with coalitions across class lines,
are, after all, what normal politics are largely about, and, in particular,
they were what the politics of the corporate reconstruction of American
capitalism was largely about in the Progressive Era, except that the
divisions and coalitions were undergoing realignment. To the extent
that party politics in the mid-1890s and in subsequent years were not
altogether "normal," insofar as they converged upon a "critical
realignment,"[25] they divided not primarily along "pro-business" versus
"anti-business" lines but along lines of conflict that were restructuring
the divisions within the capitalist class and other classes, as well as the
coalitions across class lines among capitalists, workers, farmers, professionals, reformers, and politicians.

In summary, the crisis of the 1890s was a fluid one in which a deep
economic depression was accompanied and followed by social and
ideological turbulence and political realignment in the society at large,
as well as by upheavals and realignments within the immediate sphere
of business activity itself, involving bankruptcies, reorganizations, consolidations, and ownership changes, affecting both property-owning
and working classes. Just as new class configurations and leaderships
were emerging among farmers, workers, professionals, and other
middle-class strata, so within the capitalist class: Out of the crisis there
crystallized an emergent class leadership reconstituting itself on the
basis of large corporate wealth, organization, and power, and attaching
to itself leaders and service savants from other social sectors – smaller
business, politics, the law, the academy, the press, science and engineering, the churches.

It was a leadership, however, whose growing ascendancy in significant spheres of power and authority within society and in relation to
higher political circles and executive branches of government remained
as yet unmatched, as the new century opened, by a commensurate
entrenchment in the sphere of popular politics and the representative
and judicial branches of government. The disparity between the rapidly
growing socioeconomic power and the more slowly growing political
power, legitimacy, and programmatic cohesion of the rising corporate
sector of the capitalist class underlay the time lag between the pro-

25. See note 23, above.

mulgation of pro-corporate reform objectives and their realization in law and institutions. That disparity also lay at the heart of national politics, including the politics of reform, in the Progressive Era.

Corporate capitalism and American liberalism

The antitrust debates came to the center of national politics in the Progressive Era because they were, in essence, about the passage of American society from the proprietary-competitive stage to the corporate-administered stage of capitalism – whether the passage should be permitted, and if so, on what terms. The debates, that is, were about the very fundamentals of American society, not simply over particular interests as they might be affected by competition, consolidation, or restraint of trade. Hence, it was not merely coincidental that it took an extended length of time – about twenty-five years – to attain a resolution of the trust question, and that, by the same token, the end of what we call the Progressive Era virtually coincided with this resolution. The Progressive Era, in other words, corresponded with the period that constituted the first phase in the corporate reconstruction of American capitalism.

A decisive reason for the corporate-capitalist ascendancy over the proprietary-competitive order was the general disenchantment of small producers and smaller capitalists themselves with the competitive market. They might call for imposition of competition among railroads and big industrial corporations, if not government ownership or command, but they wanted the right to curtail competition among themselves, just as capitalists in general preferred the imposition of competition among workers but its curtailment among themselves. Such a double standard, however, was untenable in principle, as not only Theodore Roosevelt but also William McKinley and Marcus A. Hanna were quick to point out; and however much it was sustained in practice against workers for a long time to come, it could not be made a basis of public policy and positive law with respect to relations among capitalists and property owners.

The conflict of small-producer and corporate capitalism, then, proceeded within a new, widening consensus hostile to the old competitive market and receptive to its replacement by administered markets. The question then became: Administered by whom, for what purposes, and for whose benefit? To facilitate or to stifle corporate capitalism's development? To protect and nurture, or to limit and supersede, the small producer? Or to achieve a mutual accommodation between corporate capital and smaller capital? Was the administering, or regulating, of the market to be done by government, by private parties, or by both?

These questions about the market related directly to the central principle of the American political tradition, namely, the supremacy of society over the state: Government and law were to adapt to, and serve, the freely developing society, so that society commanded the state, not the state the society. As shaped by strong republican imperatives since the Revolution, this tradition posited the society as one characterized by equal liberty for all full citizens and special privilege or monopoly power for none. Government's very purpose was to serve and guarantee such a society. Where public utility warranted or necessitated monopoly, the latter would, in principle, operate only as the creature of government and thereby be compelled to behave as if under competitive discipline, that is, with fair and equal treatment for all with whom it dealt, and at lowest cost consistent with property rights. If markets were to be administered, or regulated, by private parties exercising their contractual liberties, state intervention would inevitably be called upon to guard against, remedy, or effectively nullify special privilege or monopoly power. With the spread of administered markets throughout the economy, would not such intervention pose the danger of the state's ultimately assuming command of the market? Given the large extent to which market relations and society were coterminous under modern conditions, could the state increasingly command the market without ending up commanding the society as well?

The antitrust debates, then, were about basics: Were the central principles of the American political tradition compatible with anything other than small-producer, competitive capitalism? In particular, could they be reconciled with corporate capitalism and administered markets? If large-scale industry in the form of corporate enterprise was the progressive outcome of socioeconomic evolution, were traditional American political principles compatible with progress? In essence, could corporate capitalism and the American liberal tradition be mutually adapted the one to the other?

As it emerged in the Progressive Era, corporate liberalism was the prevalent ideology of the general movement seeking to transact the corporate reconstruction of the political-economic order on the basis of the mutual adaptation of corporate capitalism and the American liberal tradition. It sought, that is, to affirm administered markets and the growth of regulatory government without embracing a totalistic statism – or a corporate state. For this purpose, the distinction between positive government and statist command became crucial.

Given the diversity within classes and strata and the strong tendencies toward, or the necessity of, accommodation and alignments among them, corporate liberalism expressed the cross-class character of the movement for corporate capitalism. Accordingly, corporate liberalism emerged not as the ideology of any one class, let alone the corporate sector of the capitalist class, but rather as a cross-class ideology expressing the interrelations of corporate capitalists, political leaders, intellectuals, proprietary capitalists, professionals and reformers, workers and trade-union leaders, populists, and socialists – all those who could, to a greater or lesser extent, identify their outlook, or their interest in administered markets and government regulation, with the rise, legitimation, and institutionalization of the corporate-capitalist order, and hence with the dominant position in the market of the corporate sector of the capitalist class.[26] Corporate liberalism, in other words, was not, in its origins, a benefaction bestowed upon society by a sector of the capitalist class endowed with an enlightened disposition, nor by any other middle or upper class or stratum. It was instead the expression of a hierarchic but pluralistic web of class and political relations engaged in reconstructing American capitalism. Hence, as a cross-class, cross-strata construction, corporate liberalism manifested itself not monolithically but in several tendencies, among which we may identify three major variants that were at once mutually complementary and in conflict with one another, and that oscillated on the left toward a quasi statism and on the right toward regulatory minimalism.

The three major variants of corporate liberalism that emerged in American national politics during the Progressive Era and attained some degree of well-defined clarity by 1910–1912, were: (1) a statist-tending corporate liberalism on the left associated with Theodore Roosevelt; (2) a regulatory corporate liberalism on the center left, associated with Woodrow Wilson; and (3) a minimalist-regulatory corporate liberalism on the center right, associated with William Howard Taft. It was from this three-way progressive split that sprang the major divisions of twentieth-century American politics with respect to political-economic policy formation. The story, at least in part, of the origins of these variants in economic thought and in juristic, legislative, and political phases of the antitrust debates, is the burden of the chapters that

---

26. To work a variation on Marx, the "ruling ideology" in a society in normal, nonrevolutionary times is not necessarily the ideology of the "ruling class," but may be a cross-class, cross-strata outlook that is expressive of the evolving property-production system and its class hierarchy. In revolutionary times, it may be that of the cross-class, cross-strata coalition transacting a destruction of a property-production system, and its replacement by another.

follow; suffice it here to note their leading distinguishing characteristics.

The touchstone of difference among the corporate-liberal variants resided in the distinction each made between positive government and statist command, as it related to preserving society's supremacy over the state. That distinction, in turn, rested upon the distinction, in principle, between a public utility, or a "natural monopoly," on the one hand, and the economy in general, on the other. The position taken on the two distinctions together turned, ultimately, on the position taken on the definition or redefinition of property rights and human rights.

Among the corporate-liberal variants it was generally agreed that a public utility might be commanded by the state, either by outright government ownership or by direct government dictation of operating terms, rendering the enterprise an instrument of public policy. Such state command applied to a public utility, however, was not to be applied to the general economy. The public utility principle stood as an acceptable exception to the rule, or, in more positive terms, as a necessary exception that safeguarded the rule of a relatively autonomous market, precisely by protecting and insulating the market from monopoly power, by turning the public utility, or natural monopoly, into a common asset. With the state's command of the market limited to public utilities, the general economy, although subject to regulatory policing and modification, would remain relatively autonomous, society would remain effectively free of state domination, and property rights would remain secure.

The position associated with Roosevelt would extend the public utility principle to the economy as a whole wherever large corporations with market-administering power appeared. Although private ownership was to be retained, property rights would have to give way to public policy seeking to secure greater social equality and to fulfill a broader conception of human rights. The result would be a public-service capitalism under state direction, which would include public provision for distributive justice. Such a public-service – or public utility – economy would amount to a state-directed corporate capitalism in which self-seeking capitalists would be transformed into public-service capitalists. Apart from its large-corporate sector, the market, though regulated, would remain free of outright state direction. The people in all their sociopolitical relations would remain protected in the exercise of their liberties. Society as a whole, that is, would secure its free development by using the state to direct its corporate sector.

Whatever the intent, a state-directed corporate capitalism combined with political democracy and equalitarian goals would generate strong tendencies toward a corporate or a socialist state: that is, in the one case, a privately owned corporate economy under state command where the enterprise operated as an agent of public policy but owned its assets and accrued its revenues as private property; or, in the other case, a government-owned corporate economy under state command. The former could readily phase into the latter as private capital withdrew from one investment sphere after another, or was expelled by an activist state or by the pressure of popular politics. In either case, the state might end up in command of society in large part or in whole.

With such statist dangers in mind, those who came to adhere to the regulatory liberalism associated with Wilson distinguished much more finely between positive government and statism, and for that purpose they drew the line much more heavily between public utilities and the general economy. Large-scale corporate enterprise, in this view, did indeed endow the private property involved in it with a public character and affected it with a public interest, but to define it as a public utility and hence as subject to state direction would place the dominant components of the market under state direction; because the market coincided with so large a proportion of society, it would place the state in virtual command of society.

With respect to the general economy apart from public utilities, accordingly, the Wilsonian variant of liberalism affirmed the principle of administered markets under the primary management of the corporations and other private parties engaging in contractual relations, subject to secondary government regulation. On that basis, positive government, in both regulatory and distributive functions, supplementary to and corrective of market relations, might develop to the farthest limits, and might in the process modify property rights in the interest of expanded human rights, depending on the times and circumstances. Society would still retain the decisive initiative and continue to render the state its servant.

The Wilsonian variant accepted a larger degree of socioeconomic inequality than the Rooseveltian, at least in the latter's overt rhetoric, but they both sought to affirm corporate capitalism on the basis of accommodating smaller capital, farmers, workers, professionals and other complementary strata, while preserving the supremacy of society over the state. The Wilsonians, however, believed that the Rooseveltian way would lead to statist command of society, whatever the intent. The Rooseveltians believed that the Wilsonian way would, in effect, give state validation to corporate domination of society and to an inequality of economic and political conditions corrosive, if not entirely destructive, of democracy, the deep class divisions implied by such conditions might well result in the very statism that all abhorred. Here resided the basic difference between Roosevelt's New Nationalism and Wilson's New Freedom.

The Taft variant of corporate liberalism recognized the public utility principle, and agreed with the Wilsonians on the need to distinguish public utilities from the general economy in shaping government-market relations, but it doubted that the Wilsonian any more than Rooseveltian variant could, in practice, stop short of state command of the economy and society and, ultimately, the abrogation of capitalist property rights. While affirming corporate capitalism, the Taft variant therefore insisted upon the least government regulation of the market consistent with policing it against unfair or monopolistic practices and with modifying or correcting market outcomes injurious to the national interest or the general welfare. To the Taftians, traditional capitalist property rights needed no significant modification and were to be considered basic to, not in conflict with, human rights.

The major corporate-liberal variants rested upon – indeed, they arose from – the broader consensus they shared in an evolutionary positivist outlook that affirmed corporate capitalism as the natural historical outcome of, and progressive successor to, proprietary-competitive capitalism. Large-scale corporate capitalism, in this view, was best suited to sustaining the nation's development as a modern society, as an instrument both of progressive integration at home and of expansion abroad – the latter deemed to be essential to the disposal of surplus goods and capital, to the efficient operation of large-scale enterprise, and, more broadly, to the economic growth that would keep open a place in the market for smaller capital, as well as underwrite the costs of social reform. Government policy and the law respecting both domestic affairs and foreign relations would need to be adapted to the necessities and capacities of the rising corporate order, not only because market relations required an appropriate political and legal order for their optimum operation, but also because the subjection of market relations and economic power to the law was essential to a properly working political democracy. The rule of law validated society's supremacy over the state precisely by subjecting private power as well as state power to the law.

The general welfare and the public interest, according to the corporate-liberal consensus, ranked as the paramount objectives of the law and public policy relating to market relations. This meant, in the corporate stage of capitalism, a growing role for positive government in both regulative and distributive functions, but by and large in a manner consistent with the greatest possible preservation of private initiative and private-property ownership as against state direction and state ownership. On this basis, upper- and middle-class leadership could preside over progressive reform as the alternative to reform or revolution from below. Party politics could be sustained as a mode of inter-class alignment and cooperation rather than its being permitted to divide along class lines, with all the apocalyptic implications.

The corporate-liberal consensus formed the ground of political complementarity and conflict among its variants and assured their interaction within the limits of normal constitutional politics. In the United States, as in other countries, conventional political conflict has depended upon its grounding in a larger consensus, in the absence or breakdown of which it has verged upon or fallen into pervasive violence or civil war. This does not mean, however, that under normal circumstances political differences have been unreal or insignificant. If, as Louis Hartz incisively observed, American politics has often been a romance in which the quarrel preceded the embrace, nevertheless the outcome of the trust question arrived at by 1914 can be considered a "ceremonial solution" only if we assume that the alternative it offered to populist trust-busting or state ownership or command was ceremonial.[27] The substantive significance of adapting corporate capitalism and the American liberal tradition, the one to the other, was anything but a ceremonial accomplishment, however commonplace it may seem from hindsight – unless Providence is liberal and America is God's country.

It is through the continuing play of political differences that a consensus upon which they rest may itself evolve to new phases and meanings, or pass into an entirely different consensus, whether by evolutionary or revolutionary means. The Progressive Era yielded a powerful and highly stable consensus, in corporate liberalism as the prevalent outlook of the

---

27.   Hartz, *The Liberal Tradition in America: An Interpretation of American Liberal Thought Since the Revolution* (New York: Harcourt Brace & World, 1955), pp. 139–140. The term "ceremonial solution" is Hofstadter's in *Age of Reform*, p. 245. In that work, Hofstadter also argued (p. 252) that the antitrust debates, involving as they did "the very question of who was to control the country," were "so momentous in their character and so profound ... and the material results were by comparison so marginal, so incomplete," that it must be concluded that "the men who took a conservative view of the needs of the hour never lost control," and that "the Supreme Court stood with them," and that the presidents and congressional leaders were "quite reliable." For all the revisionist historiography on the Progressive Era in the thirty years or so since Hofstadter's book appeared, these particular assessments of his remain prevalent in the literature and in the classroom – a tribute to Hofstadter's power and persuasiveness as both a historian and a writer. The materials presented in the following chapters may indicate the need, and justification, of some revision in these matters.

general movement for the corporate reconstruction of American capitalism. That consensus framed the political divisions, in the three major variants sketched above, that in their own evolving interactions and alterations, dominated, shaped, and reshaped mainstream American politics and its prevalent consensus for much of the twentieth century.

PART I

The market and the law

2

Metamorphosis in property and thought

Introduction

The crisis of the 1890s in the United States centered upon a breakdown of production and exchange relations that telescoped a cyclical depression within a secular decomposition of the competitive market regime.[1] The cyclical and secular trends together yielded a combined economic crisis – the last great depression of competitive capitalism. The disruption of goods and capital markets during the depression years of 1893–1897 obstructed the financial arrangements necessary for the corporate reorganization of industry that had only begun to acquire momentum in the several years before the Panic of 1893. The short-term, cyclical crisis, however, although disruptive of the corporate reorganization process, heightened the sense of urgency among capitalists, political leaders, and intellectuals about the need to overcome the long-term crisis of the competitive regime.

In a market society like the United States at the time, protracted economic derangement brought on a simultaneous social, political, and cultural crisis of the broadest dimensions. Though manifested in many spheres of social life – in sectional conflict, in capital-labor relations, in race relations, in literature and thought – the crisis assumed its general expression in the great political battle between the partisans of the older

---

1. On the use of the word "crisis" here, see note 16 to Chapter 1.

small-producer, proprietary enterprise and the partisans of the corporate reorganization of the political economy; or, in populist terms, the republic of small producers against the trusts and the money lords, the masses against the classes.

The combined cyclical and secular crisis distinguished the depression of the 1890s from those of the 1870s and 1880s. In essence, previous cyclical crises spontaneously interrupted and reactivated existing market relations. The combined crisis of the 1890s, however, entailed an alteration of market structure and property ownership that reverberated in the alteration of the nation's party politics, legal order, social thought, government policies, and foreign relations.

The long-term corporate transformation of property and market relations had emerged only inchoately in the late 1880s and early 1890s, its development arrested by the crash of 1893 and the ensuing years of depression. Corporate reorganization of industry initially developed in response to the intensification of competition that had accompanied the extraordinary growth, during 1879–1893, in railways and industry, savings and investment, and industrial concentration. The 1880s was the decade of the most rapid economic growth in post–Civil War United States history, as measured by per capita rate of growth of reproducible tangible wealth, especially in manufacturing and railways, by amount of savings and investment funds, and by growth of per capita income. Savings continued in the 1890s at a volume only a little less than that in the 1880s; in both decades, the level of savings in constant and current dollars was on the order of about three times its average during the previous three decades from 1850 to 1880. During this period of rapid growth, industrial concentration, as distinguished from corporate consolidation and reorganization, proceeded within the framework of both the competitive market and the proprietary organization of enterprise. Competitive concentration is to be distinguished from corporate capitalism. By intensifying competition among firms in the domestic market and assembling great aggregations of production capacity in fewer units, concentration in the 1880s and 1890s served as a precondition of the corporate reorganization of the economy. Although the corporate form of enterprise long predominated in railroads, and although a few large corporations had arisen in industry by the early 1890s, corporate capitalism as a system of property relations and administered markets cannot be said to characterize the political economy as a whole before 1898–1900. Concentration by itself may be big business, but it is not yet corporate capitalism.[2]

2. On rapid growth and high levels of savings in the 1880s and 1890s, see Milton Friedman and Anna Jacobson Schwartz, *A Monetary History of the United States, 1867–1960* (Princeton: Princeton University Press, 1963), pp. 92–93; Raymond W.

The number of corporate consolidations in industry began to increase noticeably during the late 1880s and early 1890s. In response to rising activity in corporate finance in the industrial sector, the New York Stock Exchange in 1885 installed a department of unlisted securities. But it was not until May 1892 that it established its stock exchange clearinghouse, a facility considered unnecessary in the past, when transactions in railway and government securities dominated the New York capital market. The Panic of 1893 and the ensuing depression, however, though forcing railroad corporations into receivership and reorganization, interrupted the corporate reorganization of the industrial sector. During the depression years, monetary disorder, the great battle of the standards, and the upheaval in party politics further inhibited attempts at corporate finance in industry. By early 1898, the number of prominent industrials traded on the New York Stock Exchange – about twenty – was no greater than it had been in 1893.[3]

Then came the avalanche of corporate reorganization in industrial enterprise. "The real trust movement," noted the contemporary author-

Goldsmith, *A Study of Savings in the United States* (Princeton: Princeton University Press, 1955), 1, pp. 83–84; Robert E. Gallman, "Gross National Product in the United States, 1834–1909," in *Output, Employment and Productivity in the United States After 1800, Studies in Income and Wealth by the Conference on Research in Income and Wealth* (New York: National Bureau of Economic Research, 1966), 30, pp. 10–11; Harold G. Vatter, *The Drive to Industrial Maturity: The U.S. Economy, 1860–1914* (Westport, Conn.: Greenwood, 1975), pp. 240–243. On competitive concentration and the distinction between concentration and corporate capitalism, see William F. Willoughby, "The Concentration of Industry in the United States," *Yale Review* 7 (May 1898), pp. 72–94; Willoughby, "The Integration of Industry in the United States," *QJE* 16 (Nov. 1901), pp. 94–115, esp. pp. 96–97; Edward S. Meade, "Financial Aspects of the Trust Problem," *Annals* 16 (Nov. 1900), pp. 6–12.

3. Meade, "Financial Aspects," p. 1: "the panic [of 1893] brought the incipient movement toward consolidation to a sudden end." On the initial merger wave in industry from the late 1880s to 1893, and its interruption in the depression years 1893–1897, see ibid., 1–3; Meade, *Trust Finance* (New York: D. Appleton, 1903; 2d ed., 1906), pp. 1–2; Alfred D. Chandler, Jr., *The Visible Hand: The Managerial Revolution in American Business* (Cambridge, Mass.: Harvard University Press, 1977), p. 332; Chandler, "The Large Industrial Corporation and the Making of the Modern American Economy," in Stephen E. Ambrose, ed., *Institutions in Modern America: Innovation in Structure and Process* (Baltimore: Johns Hopkins University Press, 1967), pp. 71–101, at p. 82; Glenn Porter, *The Rise of Big Business, 1860–1910* (New York: Crowell, 1973), pp. 74–78; Lance E. Davis, "The Investment Market, 1870–1914: The Evolution of a National Market," *JEH* 25:3 (Sept. 1965), pp. 386–387, 393; Thomas R. Navin and Marian V. Sears, "The Rise of a Market for Industrial Securities, 1887–1902" *BHR* 29:2 (June 1955), pp. 126–127; Vincent P. Carosso, *Investment Banking in America: A History* (Cambridge, Mass.: Harvard University Press, 1970), p. 79; J. Laurence Laughlin, "Our Monetary Programme," *Forum* 20 (Feb. 1896), pp. 664–665; Charles A. Conant, "Securities as a Means of Payment," *Annals* 14 (Sept. 1899), p. 43; Charles Hoffmann, *The Depression of the Nineties: An Economic History* (Westport, Conn.: Greenwood, 1970), pp. 248–252, 264, 268 n. 15.

ity Edward Sherwood Meade in 1900, "dates from 1898. Two years have sufficed to reorganize the manufacturing industries of the United States." Estimates of the precise value of the capitalization in the consolidations of 1898–1904 vary. The magnitude of change may be validly conveyed by the familiar and often repeated estimate that by 1904, about 300 industrial consolidations with an aggregate capitalization of about $7 billion had precipitated out of the merger activity since the late 1880s. The suddenness and swiftness of the transformation, however, may be better grasped by noting that of these consolidations, more than three-fourths, or 236, with a capitalization of about $6 billion, or more than 85 percent of the total, were incorporated after 1 January 1898 – 170 under New Jersey law. What is more, consolidations accounting for about one-half the total value of capitalization in all the years from 1898 through 1904 occurred in less than two years' time, during 1899 and 1900, that is, before the organization of the United States Steel Corporation (1901), which was capitalized at just under $1.4 billion.[4] Without the Steel Corporation, the proportion is

4. Meade, "Financial Aspects," pp. 1–2 (quotation is at p. 1); Meade, *Trust Finance*, chap. 1; see also, John Moody, *The Truth About the Trusts: A Description and Analysis of the American Trust Movement* (1904; Westport, Conn. Greenwood, 1968), pp. 486–487; Conant, "Securities," p. 43. Cf. Howard N. Ross, "Economic Growth and Change in the United States under *Laissez-Faire: 1870–1929*," in Frederic C. Jaher, ed., *The Age of Industrialism in America: Essays in Social Structure and Cultural Values* (New York: Free Press, 1968), pp. 41, 42; Goldsmith, *Saving*, Tables V-20 (p. 499), V-23, V-24 (pp. 502–505); Ralph L. Nelson, *Merger Movements in American Industry, 1895–1956* (Princeton: Princeton University Press, 1959), pp. 4, 37, 78, 91–93, 102; Naomi R. Lamoreaux, *The Great Merger Movement in American Business, 1895–1904* (Cambridge University Press, 1985), pp. 1–13, Table 1.1, p. 2, and pp. 87–117, 139–158; Alfred S. Eichner, *The Emergence of Oligopoly: Sugar Refining as a Case Study* (Baltimore: Johns Hopkins University Press, 1969), pp. 1–25; Henry R. Seager and Charles A. Gulick, Jr., *Trust and Corporation Problems* (New York: Harper Bros., 1929), pp. 60–61; Chandler, *Visible Hand*, pp. 331–339; Thomas C. Cochran and William Miller, *The Age of Enterprise: A Social History of Industrial America*, rev. ed. (New York: Harper & Row, 1961), pp. 190–191. See also G. Warren Nutter and Henry A. Einhorn, *Enterprise Monopoly in the United States, 1899–1958* (New York: Columbia University Press, 1969), pp. 43–44; and Ralph L. Nelson, *Concentration in the Manufacturing Industries in the United States: A Midcentury Report* (New Haven: Yale University Press, 1963), pp. 1–14, esp. pp. 9–10. The latter two works together show that the degree of concentration of industrial production achieved by corporate reorganization and combination by 1904 changed little during the next half century, although there was some increase in concentration, in terms of market share, among the top fifty manufacturing corporations from 1947 to 1954 (Nelson, *Concentration*, pp. 96–99). Nutter and Einhorn (*Enterprise Monopoly*, pp. 43–44), for example, show that in every census year from 1904 to 1939 the top 184,230 plants accounted for at least 99 percent of the aggregate value of manufactured products, and that of these, the top one-tenth, or 18,423 plants, accounted for just over 75 percent of the aggregate value of manufactured products throughout the same period.

much higher. The value of the property transactions in the corporate reorganization of industry, even discounting watered stock, duplications, and failed issues, was the equivalent of about one-fifth of the nation's gross national product in 1900; it was the equivalent of more than the value of slave property in the United States in 1860. In more immediate industrial terms, Simon Newcomb Dexter North, chief statistician for manufactures of the United States Bureau of the Census, as early as April 1900 estimated the "reorganization of the manufacturing business, through combination and consolidation" as representing a gross capitalization equal in value to the total capital employed in all manufacturing industries as reported in the census of 1890.[5]

Property

In the course of the history of the United States, the law and jurisprudence have adapted to and reinforced the changing forms and requirements of private property, property rights, and the market in the context of incessant capitalist development. The law has also placed limits on property rights on behalf of the public interest and the general welfare as determined by public policy. The long-term tendency of the law, however, has been to favor those emergent property forms, property rights, and contractual obligations that were suited to, or associated with, developmental change embracing productive, distributional, or organizational innovation, as against older property forms, vested rights, or contractual obligations anchored in past or obsolescent market or production relations.[6]

5. S. N. D. North, "The Federal Census of Manufactures, 1900," a paper read before the National Association of Manufacturers, Boston, 25 Apr. 1900, p. 2–4. North was at the time a counselor of the American Statistical Association of Boston, of which Carroll D. Wright was the president and Henry Carter Adams a vice-president. Claudia D. Goldin estimated that the value of slave property in the United States in 1860 stood at about $2.7 billion in current dollars and that it was the equivalent of about 64 percent of U.S. GNP ($4.2 billion) in 1860. "The Economics of Emancipation," *JEH* 33:1 (Mar. 1973), pp. 66–85, at pp. 73–74. See also, for the same estimate, following Goldin, Gerald Gunderson, "The Origin of the American Civil War," *JEH* 34:4 (Dec. 1974), pp. 915–950, at p. 917. U.S. GNP, in current dollars, was about $18.7 billion in 1900 and about $21.5 billion in 1902. Hoffmann, *Depression*, Table 2, p. xxix. Although the value of assets undergoing corporate reorganization and consolidation in these years represented only about one-third the magnitude of the value of slave property as a percent of GNP, it nevertheless remains an impressively large figure.

6. Thorstein Veblen, *The Theory of Business Enterprise* (1904; New York: Mentor, 1958), esp. chap. 8: "Business Principles in Law and Politics," pp. 128–143; John R. Commons, *Legal Foundations of Capitalism* (1924; Madison: University of Wisconsin Press, 1957), pp. 6–7, 11–46 and passim; James Willard Hurst, *The*

From the late 1880s to 1914, both public and private law underwent changes suited to the protection, and hence the extension, of the emergent corporate reorganization of capitalist enterprise. But the adaptation proceeded along two not entirely concurrent lines, that of the law of property and contractual liberty, and that of the law of restraint of trade. The law of property and contractual liberty converged rather directly with the corporate reorganization of business enterprise, but the law of restraint of trade negotiated an indirect route with sharp turns and long delays before arriving at an adaptive destination. For about fifteen years, until mid-1911, with the United States Supreme Court's decisions in the American Tobacco and Standard Oil cases, the corpo-

Legitimacy of the Business Corporation in the Law of the United States, 1780–1970 (Charlottesville: University Press of Virginia, 1970); Hurst, *Law and the Conditions of Freedom in the Nineteenth-Century United States* (Madison: University of Wisconsin Press, 1956); Hurst, *Law and Economic Growth: The Legal History of the Lumber Industry in Wisconsin, 1836–1915* (Cambridge, Mass.: Harvard University Press, 1977); Hurst, *Law and Markets in United States History: Different Modes of Bargaining Among Interests* (Madison: University of Wisconsin Press, 1982), esp. chap. 1; Stanley I. Kutler, *Privilege and Creative Destruction: The Charles River Bridge Case* (Philadelphia: Lippincott, 1971); Harry N. Scheiber, "The Road to *Munn*: Eminent Domain and the Concept of Public Purpose in the State Courts," in *Perspectives in American History 5* (1971), pp. 329–402; Scheiber, "Federalism and the American Economic Order, 1789–1910," *Law & Society Review* 10:1 (Fall 1975), pp. 57–118; Lawrence M. Friedman, *A History of American Law* (New York: Simon & Schuster, 1973), pt. 2, chaps. 3, 5, 6, and pt. 3, chaps. 1, 4, 5, 8, 9; William E. Nelson, *Americanization of the Common Law: The Impact of Legal Change on Massachusetts Society, 1760–1830* (Cambridge, Mass.: Harvard University Press, 1975), esp. chaps. 1, 8; Morton J. Horwitz, *The Transformation of American Law, 1780–1860* (Cambridge, Mass.: Harvard University Press, 1977); Tony A. Freyer, *Forums of Order: The Federal Courts and Business in American History* (Greenwich, Conn.: JAI Press, 1979); G. Edward White, *The American Judicial Tradition: Profiles of Leading American Judges* (New York: Oxford University Press, 1976), esp. chaps. 2–7; Bernard Schwartz, *The Law in America: A History* (New York: McGraw-Hill, 1974); Stephen B. Presser, "'Legal History' or the History of Law: A Primer Bringing the Law's Past into the Present," *Vanderbilt Law Review* 35:4 (May 1982), pp. 849–890, esp. pp. 858–862, 879–883. The generalization in the text refers, of course, to nonslave property; slave property involves a different order of historical phenomenon and is subject to different generalization. Cf. Mark V. Tushnet, *The American Law of Slavery, 1810–1860: Considerations of Humanity and Interest* (Princeton: Princeton University Press, 1981); Robert Cover, *Justice Accused: Antislavery and the Judicial Process* (New Haven: Yale University Press, 1975); Paul Finkelman, *An Imperfect Union: Slavery, Federalism, and Comity* (Chapel Hill: University of North Carolina Press, 1981); A. E. Keir Nash, "Reason of Slavery: Understanding the Judicial Role in the Peculiar Institution," *Vanderbilt Law Review* 32 (1979), pp. 8–218; Eugene D. Genovese, *Roll, Jordon, Roll: The World the Slaves Made* (1974; New York: Random House, Vintage Books, 1976): "The Hegemonic Function of the Law," pp. 25–49; Genovese, "Slavery in the Legal History of the South and the Nation," *Texas Law Review* 59:5 (May 1981), pp. 969–998.

rate reorganization of American capitalism proceeded within an incongruent legal order, the law in part expediting, and in part obstructing, its progress.

With respect to the law of property and contractual liberty, the Supreme Court, beginning with the landmark Santa Clara decision of 1886, extended to corporations, at first to their stockholders as associated property owners, ultimately to the corporation itself as a "natural entity," the legal status of a person within the meaning of the Fifth and Fourteenth amendments of the United States Constitution. On that basis, in a series of decisions from 1886 through the 1890s and early years of the twentieth century, the Court endowed corporations with the rights and privileges it ascribed to the meaning of contractual liberty. Judicial construction thereby protected corporations against deprivation by either federal or state government of their life, liberty, assets, or earnings, without due process of law. In vesting corporate property with a claim to liberty similar (though not identical) to that enjoyed by white male persons, however, the new jurisprudence also sustained the older legal tradition under which corporations, as peculiarly the creatures of the law, were to remain responsible before the law and hence subject to public policy and judicial process. In the series of cases from 1886 to the end of the century, the Court established a legal doctrine of substantive and procedural due process, which further elaborated the reformulation of liberty attached to corporate property. In effect, with the limited liability of the stockholder it combined the limited liability of the corporation in the face of the legislative and executive powers of government. In addition, from the older meaning of property as the ownership, disposal, and exchange value of tangible things, the Court extended the exchange-value dimension to embrace a larger concept of property. It defined property to include the pursuit, and therefore the legal protection, of intangible value, or earning power — that is, the right to a reasonable return on investment in intangible assets (for example, "goodwill") as well as in tangible assets. Property and the liberty that went with it, accordingly, embraced both the use value of physical things and the exchange value of tangibles and intangibles. As John R. Commons summarized the revised judicial view:

> The definition of property is changed from physical things to the exchange-value of anything, and the federal courts now take jurisdiction. ... [The] cases ... have turned on a double meaning of property, and the transition is from one of the meanings to both of the meanings. ... One is Property, the other is Business. The one is property in the sense of Things owned, the other is property in the

sense of exchange-value of things. One is physical objects, the other is marketable assets.[7]

The redefinition of property at law to embrace intangibles and their exchange value facilitated the corporate reorganization of industrial property ownership. The corporate reorganization required proprietors to surrender ownership of their physical units or assets in exchange for securities that, as equities, were claims upon a share of earnings. Upon that claim, in turn, rested the exchange value of the securities. That value found itself enhanced in the market in proportion as the consolidated prestige, goodwill, and reinforced market power, of previously separate enterprises, raised the putative earning power of the new corporation. The legal protection of the value of intangibles as essential to property rights, along with the Court's strengthening of limited stockholder liability in its "natural entity" doctrine, reduced the risk and enhanced the value of corporate stock, and thereby facilitated the exchange of tangibles for securities and hence the separation of operational control from legal ownership characteristic of the corporate form of property. What is the same thing, the Court's redefinition of property solidified the legal ground for the liquidification of property, the transferability or negotiability of titles-to-ownership, and hence of titles to earnings or gains, through the conversion of capital from fixed tangibles into fluid intangibles. In short, it provided a secure legal environment for the capital market in industrials. It thereby combined the requirement of huge fixed investment, which imposed capital immobility upon the firm, with fluidity of ownership, which bestowed capital mobility upon the individual capitalist. Without such legal security, the corpo-

---

7. Commons, *Legal Foundations*, pp. 11–18 (quotation at pp. 17, 18); also Morton J. Horwitz, "*Santa Clara* Revisited: The Development of Corporate Theory," *West Virginia Law Review* 88 (1985), pp. 173–224; Hurst, *Legitimacy*, pp. 65, 68–71; Veblen, *Theory*, p. 130; Freyer, *Forums*, pp. 99–120; Friedman, *History*, p. 455. The leading Fourteenth Amendment cases recognizing the corporation as a person at law were *Santa Clara County* v. *Southern Pacific Railroad*, 118 U.S. 394 (1886), *Pembina Mining Co.* v. *Pennsylvania*, 125 U.S. 181 (1888), *Minneapolis & St. Louis Railroad Co.* v. *Beckwith*, 129 U.S. 26 (1889), *Charlotte, Columbia & Augusta Railroad* v. *Gibbes*, 142 U.S. 386 (1892), and *Gulf, Colorado & Santa Fe Railway Co.* v. *Ellis*, 165 U.S. 150 (1897); see Justice Harlan's reaffirmation and citation of cases, *Smyth* v. *Ames*, 169 U.S. 466, at 522 (1898). Cf. *San Mateo County* v. *Southern Pacific Railroad*, 13 Fed. 722 (1882), Justice Field, sitting on circuit, delivering the decision of the lower court; argued before the Supreme Court but not decided, at 116 U.S. 138. The leading cases, from 1890 to 1898, elaborating the revised view of property and liberty included *Chicago, Milwaukee & St. Paul Railway Co.* v. *Minnesota*, 134 U.S. 418 (1890), *Interstate Commerce Commission* v. *Cincinnati, New Orleans, and Texas Pacific Railway Co.*, 167 U.S. 479 (1897), *Allgeyer* v. *Louisiana*, 165 U.S. 578 (1897), and *Smyth* v. *Ames*, 169 U.S. 466 (1898).

rate reorganization of capitalist property ownership in industry and commerce might well have come more slowly, and would have been difficult and halting, even if not impossible.[8]

Concurrent with the change in the legal concept of property in the late 1880s and the 1890s, the federal law regulating the market increasingly superseded state law as an ever-growing number of firms extended business operations across state lines and also into foreign markets. The Interstate Commerce Act of 1887 and the Sherman Antitrust Act of 1890, by inaugurating regulative and judicial processes for the determination of the range and limits of the disposal of property in interstate and foreign trade and commerce, installed a rudimentary legal framework at the federal level for the corporate reorganization movement. In the railway rate and the due process cases, the Supreme Court further nationalized the law of property along with the law of the market. Its rendering of the Fifth and Fourteenth amendments went beyond the Thirteenth amendment's negative nationalization of property in its abolition of slavery, by stipulating positive federal standards of property rights and imposing them upon both the federal government and the states. The Sherman Act itself explicitly defined corporations as persons at law within the specfic provisions of the act.

State law contributed to the nationalizing trend in accommodating corporate reorganization of property ownership. New Jersey, Delaware, and New York, in the years 1886–1898, followed by other states, passed general incorporation laws that authorized corporations to own real estate and other assets, including the stock of other corporations, both within the chartering state and in other states. The New Jersey laws also exempted corporations from state taxation, and they left to the corporations' discretion the ratio of debt to value of assets and the amounts of common and preferred stock to be issued. The new state laws extended to capital in general, and on a routine basis, corporate powers and privileges previously reserved for such special purposes as railways or public-service undertakings, but with fewer and fewer restrictions. In sum, state legislation and both federal and state judicial

---

8. On the essential importance of intangibles, especially in the form of preferred and common stock, to the corporate reorganization of industrial property, see, e.g., Veblen, *Theory*, chap. 6: "Modern Business Capital," pp. 68–86; Jeremiah W. Jenks, *The Trust Problem*, 5th ed. (1900; New York: Doubleday, Doran, 1929), pp. 80–84, 99–101; Meade, "Financial Aspects," pp. 21, 22, 24–26, 40–41, 44–45. The rise of the market for industrial securities in large volumes dates from 1898. On making assets liquid and its facilitating the transfer of property from proprietary ownership and control to corporate stock-ownership, see Davis, "Investment Market," p. 387, and Navin and Sears, "Rise of a Market," p. 127. Cf. Porter, *Rise of Big Business*, pp. 74–79.

construction, from the late 1880s onward, increasingly gave to corporations stronger standing as "natural entities" with contractual and due
process rights of persons, weakened *ultra vires* restrictions on corporate
action, strengthened the limited liability of shareholders to the point of
rendering shareholder liability negligible, and in these ways and in
others facilitated and extended the negotiability of corporate securities
and hence the rise of a national capital market in industrials.[9] Precisely
in these tendencies, however, state law and judicial construction effectively placed the activity of corporations that availed themselves of
interstate holdings, and that accordingly engaged more intimately in
interstate trade and commerce, more firmly within the jurisdiction of
the commerce power of the federal government.

The legal redefinition of property, and the nationalization of the law
of property and the market, in a manner favorable to the corporate
reorganization of capitalist property ownership, were not a fortuitous
imposition of some *lex ex machina*; neither were they preordained by
the Constitution, nor the result of a willfully activist, "conservative" or
pro-corporation, Supreme Court. Indeed, legal revision in this period
was not uniformly favorable to the corporate reorganization of enterprise. With respect to the law of restraint of trade, in particular, as we
shall see in some detail in Chapter 3, the Supreme Court from 1897 to
1911, in its construction of the Sherman Antitrust Act, rendered the law
as positively forbidding corporate-administered markets, a rendering
that conflicted with its pro-corporate rulings in the law of property and
contractual liberty.

Legal revision, including its inconsistencies, arose from the conflicts
and contracts in the market among property owners and other parties.
It resulted from the litigative and legislative activity of capitalists,
lawyers, legislators, and many others, and only then from decisions by

9. Horwitz, "*Santa Clara* Revisited"; Hurst, *Legitimacy*, pp. 45, 69–70, 73, 148–149,
    156; Freyer, *Forums*, pp. 101–102, 104, 112; Adolph A. Berle, Jr., and Gardiner C.
    Means, *The Modern Corporation and Private Property* (New York: Macmillan,
    1933), pp. 136–137, 203–206; Schwartz, *Law in America*, pp. 132–133; Fried-
    man, *History*, pp. 454–455, 457–459; Porter, *Rise of Big Business*, pp. 71–72. In
    practical terms, the state laws permitted replacement of the trust device, placed in
    jeopardy by judicial decisions in the late 1880s and early 1890s, by the holding
    company device, or by the outright merger of assets under one corporate entity. In
    addition, the Supreme Court's decision in *St. Louis & San Francisco Railway Co.* v.
    James, 161 *U.S.* 545 (1896), extended to holding companies the rights of interstate
    intercorporate stock-ownership that it had upheld earlier for operating companies in
    United States v. *E. C. Knight Co.*, 156 *U.S.* 1 (1895). Freyer, *Forums*, p. 112. See
    also Link, *Wilson*, 1, p. 134; William R. Compton, "Early History of Stock
    Ownership by Corporations," *George Washington Law Review* 9 (1940), p. 125,
    and William Cary, "Federalism and Corporate Law: Reflections upon Delaware,"
    Yale Law Review 83 (Mar. 1974), pp. 663–705.

judges, who acted upon the corresponding legislation and litigation brought before them in cases. Legal revision was, in short, the outcome of an evolving social movement and the opposition it aroused. The movement had emerged by the late 1880s; although stalled by the depression of the 1890s, on the whole, it gained momentum and developed in the course of the 1890s. It was the emergence and rise of this great social movement that made the decade of the 1890s the "watershed" of American history that historians take it to be. Populism was not the only great social movement of the 1890s; on a lesser scale, so was the movement for socialism; but on a comparable, and ultimately larger, scale, so was the movement for corporate capitalism. Indeed, the first two would scarcely be intelligible, at least in the same form and substance, apart from the third. It was in the conflict of these movements, as the nation passed from the proprietary-competitive to the corporate-administered stage of capitalism, that the law of restraint of trade – the trust question – became a major point of contention and a paramount issue in national politics in what historians refer to as the Progressive Era. It was that conflict that made the accommodation of the law to corporate capitalism something less than a tidy, linear affair.

The market

In general, the movement for legal revision respecting property and the market embodied an emergent view of public policy among capitalists, intellectuals, and political leaders to the effect that neither market efficiencies, nor protection of property rights, nor satisfactory labor relations, nor social stability in the larger sense, could be expected from the regime of unrestricted competition among atomized units. The competitive market, left to itself, yielded not the harmonies of Frédéric Bastiat, not the equilibriums of Jean-Baptiste Say, not the steady accumulation and investment of capital, not a balancing of supply and demand at high levels of employment of labor and resources, but market disorganization, "wastes of competition," business failures, recurrent depressions, strikes and lockouts, social distemper, and political upheaval.

This revised view of the market was attaining an embodiment in law and jurisprudence while also finding expression in the 1890s in the thinking as well as the market behavior of capitalists, in theoretical trends among economists, and in policy-forming thought of political leaders.

By the mid-1890s, in the midst of the third long depression in three successive decades, a revulsion against the unregulated market spread among the bourgeoisie in all major sectors of the economy. Whatever their programmatic differences, farmers, manufacturers, bankers, and merchants, in addition to already disenchanted railway capitalists, found a common ground in the idea that unregulated competitive market activity resulted in production of goods and services in excess of effective demand at prices that returned reasonable earnings to producers of normal efficiency. The watchword was "overproduction."[10]

The view that overproduction had become chronic contradicted the central principle of classical political economy, Say's Law of Markets. Say's Law held that under freely competitive conditions, production and demand must generally balance each other at relatively full employment, with imbalances occurring only episodically and serving as corrective signals restorative of equilibrium. Abbreviated: Production creates its own demand.[11] Wide agreement on the abrogation of Say's Law by the reality of overproduction nevertheless generated sharp difference over the causes of overproduction and its remedy.

By 1896, national public opinion about the market had regrouped into two major tendencies, one associated with a small-producer, or populist, outlook, the other with the emergent corporate-capitalist outlook. A socialist outlook, influential among workers, intellectuals, feminists, reformers, and farmers as well, formed a significant tendency in its own right, but also as a component of both the populist and corporate-capitalist outlooks. Each of the two major tendencies, then, had its left-center-right configuration; each was in some ways affected by the other. Although the populist stream contained many currents, the main current attributed market disparities to factors exogenous to the market, that is, to a just market, defined as one that sustained the natural right of the small producer to remain an independent agent in the market. These exogenous factors, which populists identified with illegitimate monopolistic or corrupt political power, disrupted market harmonies by such devices as limiting the supply of money and credit, overvaluing the monetary unit, artificially fixing rates or prices, corner-

10. For example, in 1898, John Bates Clark brought out an American edition of Karl Rodbertus's *Theory of Crises* (1850–1851) under the title *Overproduction and Crises* (New York: Burt Franklin, 1898). In his Introduction (pp. 1–18), Clark wrote (pp. 1–2): "The modern world regards business crises much as the ancient Egyptians regarded the overflowing of the Nile.... The most available reasons that can be assigned for business crises are vaguely expressed in simple terms, such as 'overproduction', 'inflation,' 'speculation,' and 'liquidation.' ... the one that most nearly satisfies the public mind is *overproduction*." Clark's emphasis.

11. Cf. Samuel Hollander, *The Economics of David Ricardo* (Toronto: University of Toronto Press, 1979), chap. 2, "The Law of Markets," pp. 67–97, esp. pp. 79–95; Thomas Sowell, *Say's Law: An Historical Analysis* (Princeton: Princeton University Press, 1972), esp. chaps. 1, 5, 7.

ing land or real estate, or imposing unfair tariffs or other taxes. The populist remedy lay in laws against such devices and in restoring the market of small producers, if necessary by direct government intervention and regulation, even selective government ownership, to aid the small producer and to prevent the concentration of private market power or the private centralization of wealth.

The emergent corporate outlook took form in response to competitive market conditions in the industrial sector, broadly taken, but also, in the immediate political circumstances, in response to the "nonindustrial" populist challenge. The corporate outlook rejected exogenous theories of market disharmonies, including conservative and populist monetarist views that attributed disequilibriums to excessive and deficient money supplies, respectively. Although it insisted on the need for a sound currency and emphasized the disruptive impact of a defective currency on markets, the corporate outlook conceived overproduction as a chronic tendency inherent in modern industrial capitalist development. Concentration of productive capacity, in this view, was the inevitable concomitant of modern industrial methods; its development during the 1880s and 1890s intensified competition, which in turn induced further concentration. Concentration under competitive investment and marketing conditions resulted in the growth of production capacity beyond effective demand at prices that yielded adequate returns to capitalists, often at prices insufficient to cover costs. Hence, the progressive development of industrial capitalism under the competitive market mechanism, not exogenous factors, disrupted market harmony and brought on recurrent crises. All industrial capitalist countries during the late nineteenth century, it was noted, regardless of their monetary, banking, or tariff systems, regardless of patterns of land ownership or income distribution, suffered from overproduction and recurrent crises.

Capitalists in the United States, as elsewhere, came to such conclusions from their own experience. By the 1890s, their complaints that overproduction was destroying profit and causing depressions had become legion. Unrestricted competition rendered nugatory their contractual liberties, unless liberty of contract included the liberty to restrict competition; they accordingly resorted to the latter liberty with rising frequency. As John R. Commons noted, "while liberty of access to markets on the part of an owner is essential to the exchange-value of property, too much liberty of access on the part of would-be competitors is destructive of that exchange-value."[12] The competitive market had, in effect, converted many industrial capitalists into public servants

---

12. Commons, *Legal Foundations*, p. 17.

working without profit (though not without income), an outcome fore-
told by the more rigorous strands of classical political economy but of
small comfort to capitalists. The Industrial Commission reported in
1900: "Among the causes which have led to the formation of industrial
combinations, most of the witnesses [largely capitalists] were of the
opinion that competition, so vigorous that profits of nearly all competing establishments were destroyed, is to be given first place."[13] In the
same year, Edward S. Meade observed that although "the stronger
firms" earned some margin of profit, "even under competitive conditions, and in periods of depression," nevertheless "this margin is hardly
attained"; the manufacturers want "to stop this worrisome struggle,
whose benefits are nearly all of them gained by the consumer in low
prices. ... They want a larger profit without such a desperate struggle
to get it." In short, noted Meade, "The manufacturers are tired of
working for the public."[14]

The widening movement among capitalists to restructure and regulate
the market along noncompetitive lines forced economists and policymakers in the United States to find new theoretical explanations of the
market that would accord with the empirical record and at the same
time offer a practical guide to policy. Already in 1886, Carroll D.
Wright, in his first annual report as United States Commissioner of
Labor, had listed "overproduction" as a cause of industrial depressions
that was widely cited among capitalists and informed observers. In
1889, the eminent free-trade economist David Ames Wells, in his influential book, *Recent Economic Changes*, made "overproduction" central to his discussion of modern industrial tendencies and recurrent
crises. A decade later, Wright was writing in detail about overproduction, or excess production capacity, as a chronic fact of economic life in
the United States and in all the leading industrial capitalist countries.
By then, economists were joining farmers, capitalists, workers, and
political leaders in acknowledging "overproduction" as an established
fact, or at least as an established issue in national politics.[15]

13. U.S. Industrial Commission, I: *Preliminary Report on Trusts and Industrial Com-
     binations*, H.R. Doc. No. 476, pt. 1, 56th Cong., 1st Sess., 1 Mar. 1900 (Washing-
     ton, D.C.: Government Printing Office, 1900), "Review of the Evidence," pp. 9–38,
     at p. 9: "Competition the Chief Cause."
14. Meade, "Financial Aspects," p. 12. On combination and corporate reorganization as
     a response to intensified competition, see ibid., pp. 10–13, 17; Meade, *Trust
     Finance*, chap, 1; Willoughby, "Integration," pp. 94–115; Chandler, "The Large
     Industrial Corporation," pp. 76–80; and Chandler, *Visible Hand*, pp. 287–344.
15. Carroll D. Wright, *Industrial Depressions*, First Annual Report of the [U.S.] Com-
     missioner of Labor, March 1886 (Washington, D.C.: Government Printing Office,
     1886; New York: Augustus M. Kelley, 1968), pp. 279, 286–289. Wright also noted
     (p. 276) that industrial depressions occurred alike in countries with or without

What remained to be elaborated, however, was a theory that could explain the relation between competition and overproduction, and between overproduction and the tendency toward corporate consolidation, without disowning capitalism, validating populism, or embracing socialism.

Thought: Hadley and Jenks

A new theory of the capitalist market, one focusing upon disequilibrium, began to emerge in the 1880s, and took substantial form in the 1890s, among American economists.[16] It explicitly rejected Bastiat's harmonies and Say's Law of Markets, including its more sophisticated restatements by John Stuart Mill, W. Stanley Jevons, J. E. Cairnes, and the European marginal utility theorists; it substituted a concept of the business cycle as generated by the periodic disequilibrium of production and demand.[17] From 1896 to 1901, well before Veblen's *Theory of Business Enterprise* (1904), Arthur Twining Hadley of Yale University, Jeremiah Whipple Jenks of Cornell University, and Charles Arthur Conant, the nonacademic scholar and financial journalist, took a leading role among those with senior policy-making influence in laying the theoretical foundations for the break with the classical model of the competitive market.[18]

sound currency and banking systems and regardless of protectionist or free-trade policies. Wright, "The Relation of Production to Productive Capacity," I, II, *Forum* 24 (Nov. 1897, Feb. 1898), pp. 290–302, 660–675. David Ames Wells, *Recent Economic Changes, and Their Effect on the Production and Distribution of Wealth and the Well-Being of Society* (New York: Appleton, 1889).

16. By the early 1890s, British economists were contending that United States economists had forged ahead of them in studying modern economic conditions. In 1892, Section F (Economic Science and Statistics) of the British Association for the Advancement of Science appointed a committee to investigate economic studies at home and abroad. Known as the Gonner Committee, for its chairman, E. C. K. Gonner, its members were William Cunningham, H. S. Foxwell, John Neville Keynes (the father of John Maynard Keynes), Henry Higgs, F. Y. Edgeworth, L. L. Price, and J. Shield Nicholson. The committee worked for two years; in reports in 1893 and 1894, it praised economists in the United States for their recognition of the need for inductive inquiry and training, noting that in the United States economics was connected with political science, sociology, and history. For this account, see Joseph Dorfman, *The Economic Mind in American Civilization*, Vol. 3: *1865–1918* (New York: Viking, 1959), pp. 241–242.

17. Ibid., pp. 123–133, 164–195, 254–264, 310–311.

18. Hadley, Jenks, and Conant are singled out here because of their influence and their interrelation. They all served as advisers to Theodore Roosevelt from time to time, Jenks rather steadily, during the period stretching from the 1890s through the years of Roosevelt's presidency. In the 1880s, Hadley was commissioner of labor statistics of the State of Connecticut. With the publication in 1885 of his book *Railroad Transportation: Its History and Its Laws* (New York: Putnam), he became one of

The classical model, as expressed in Say's Law, held that as supply created its own demand, so demand in turn guided supply toward a volume and a price level that cleared markets at normal profit and relatively full employment. It was, Hadley wrote, a "commercial theory," not an industrial theory. It neglected the real conditions of supply under the regime of large-scale industry. Rising investment in fixed capital meant that capital was far from perfectly mobile and that it could not adjust to insufficient demand without an insolvency that conflicted with expectations of ownership and reward bound up with property rights. Large fixed investment put a premium on economies of scale, and, as Andrew Carnegie explained in what came to be known as "Carnegie's law of surplus," every manufacturer preferred to lose one dollar by running full and holding markets through selling at lower prices than to lose two dollars by running less than full or close down and incur the risk of losing markets, defaulting on interest payments, and falling into bankruptcy. Four years before Carnegie made this point in print, Hadley had already noted, in his treatise *Railroad Transportation* (1885), that the idea of competition, in which prices tended to be proportional to cost of production, approximated reality in Ricardo's time but not in an era of growing fixed investment. "It very often involves worse loss to stop producing than to produce below cost." In

the nation's leading authorities on railroad (and hence corporate) operations and finance. Hadley went on to become professor of politcal economy at Yale University and a founder and editor of the *Yale Review*. In 1899 he became president of Yale University, and he continued in that position until 1921. He served also as a director of several large corporations, including the New York, New Haven and Hartford Railway, the Atchison, Topeka & Santa Fe Railway, and the First National Bank of New Haven. As an eminent economist and university president with practical business experience and knowledge, Hadley was "consulted by the great business-men of the country." He was a director of the precursors of the Brookings Institution, and he became a trustee of Brookings upon its founding in 1927. Quotation from John Hays Hammond, *The Autobiography of John Hays Hammond*, 2 vols. (New York: Farrar & Rinehart, 1935), 1, p. 36. In his Preface (Mar. 1896) to his major work, *Economics: An Account of the Relations Between Private Property and Public Welfare* (New York: Putnam, 1896), Hadley acknowledged Irving Fisher, his colleague at Yale and fellow editor of the *Yale Review*. Conant's treatise *A History of Modern Banks of Issue* (see note 27, below) and Hadley's *Economics* were both published in the same year, 1896, by G. P. Putnam's Sons. George H. Putnam, president of the publishing house, was a leader in the gold-standard and banking-reform movements, as was Conant. In subsequent essays from 1896 to 1901, Conant often cited Hadley's books, especially with respect to disequilibrium. Conant and Jenks were closely associated in 1901 to 1904 in policy-making work for the Departments of State and War under Hay and Root during the McKinley and Roosevelt administrations (see notes 45 and 58, below). In *The Theory of Business Enterprise* (1904), Veblen drew upon Hadley and Jenks. See Carl P. Parrini and Martin J. Sklar, "New Thinking About the Market, 1896–1904: Some American Economists on Investment and the Theory of Surplus Capital," *JEH* 43:3 (Sept. 1983), pp. 559–578.

self-defense, capitalists in "nearly every industry employing fixed capital on a large scale" entered a pool or other noncompetitive arrangement. The result was either monopolistic restriction of production and higher prices, or, failing that, declining prices and overproduction – excess capacity and output in relation to remunerative effective demand – and the bankruptcy of many producers in spite of all their efforts to avoid it, attended in either case by unemployment of capital and labor. The real market price diverged from the "normal price," that is, the price, as Hadley defined it, that returned to the producer of average efficiency at full employment the current average rate of return under conditions of free competition.[19]

The rise and development of industrial capitalism, in this view, had rendered the classical theory in this respect obsolete. Hadley drew upon marginal utility concepts and terminology in his analysis, but insofar as marginal utility embodied the older commercial theory dressed in new terms, he regarded it as no less obsolete than the classical theory. "The 'Austrian' theory of value," he observed, "is nothing more than the commercial theory carried out to its logical conclusion." The classical doctrine of reciprocal demand, developed "in popular form" by J. E. Cairnes and "with scientific accuracy" by Léon Walras, he noted, "ceases to work smoothly" when with rising investment in fixed capital, an interval of time elapses between production and sale. "We can no longer say without much reserve that 'a market for products is products in the market.'" Hadley granted that the theory of reciprocal demand as "set forth by Jevons, and carried out in detail by the Austrian school of economists," had in the past explained the connection of utility and price under "the existing commercial system," and had elucidated "the psychological motives" that determined price when personal contact characterized the relation between buyers and sellers. But in an era of large fixed investment, high-volume production, rapid turnover, and impersonal markets, the Austrian school's theory "seems to belong rather to the domain of psychology than of economics, and to have a very remote application to the practical problems of business and legislation."[20] Modern industrial capitalism tended toward a chronic

19. Hadley, *Economics*, pp. 87–90; Hadley, *Railroad Transportation*, pp. 68–70; Andrew Carnegie, "The Bugaboo of the Trusts," *North American Review* 148 (Feb. 1889), pp. 141–150, esp. pp. 141–142. Cf. Joseph F. Wall, *Andrew Carnegie* (New York: Oxford University Press, 1970), pp. 584–586, 625.
20. Hadley, *Economics*, pp. iii–iv, 78–80, 79–80, n. 2, 87–90, 93 n. 1. Hadley also denied (pp. 69–70) that an average judgment as to a rational calculation of utility governed economic activity. He argued that obsolescent custom and convention representing "an average absence of judgment" about utility governed most people's economic activity, and, citing Simon Patten, he pointed to the success of advertising

disparity between production and consumption, expressed in periodic crises, or depressions.[21]

Jeremiah W. Jenks, professor of political economy at Cornell University, served prominently as an expert adviser and scholar with the Industrial Commission established by Congress in June 1898. By 1898–1900, he was acting, as well, as a principal adviser to New York Governor Theodore Roosevelt, especially in matters of corporations and corporation law. Jenks shared Hadley's view of the market under the conditions of modern industrial capitalism.[22] On the basis of his work with the Industrial Commission and confidential consultations with corporation executives, investment bankers, and speculators, among others, Jenks affirmed a concept of the market that decades later in a more sophisticated and elaborate theoretical form would become the theory of imperfect or monopolistic (or oligopolistic) competition associated with Edward H. Chamberlin and Joan Robinson and the Cambridge school.[23]

as additional substantiation of his contention. Cf. N. B. de Marchi, "Mill and Cairnes and the Emergence of Marginalism in England," in R. D. Collison Black, A. W. Coats, and Craufurd D. W. Goodwin, eds., *The Marginal Revolution in Economics: Interpretation and Evaluation* (Durham, N.C.: Duke University Press, 1973), pp. 78–97; also, in *Marginal Revolution*, R. D. C. Black, "W. S. Jevons and the Foundation of Modern Economics," pp. 98–112, and William Jaffé, "Léon Walras' Role in the 'Marginal Revolution' of the 1870s," pp. 113–139.

21. Hadley, *Economics*, chap. 6: "Combination of Capital," pp. 151–179, also pp. 294–296. More than ten years earlier, in 1885, Hadley had already denied the applicability of "the theory [of competition] of Ricardo" to modern industrial conditions. He categorically stated that "In the case of industries with large permanent investment, the law [of competition] is not merely imperfect or bad in practice, it is false in theory." *Railroad Transportation*, chap. 4, "Competition and Combination in Theory," pp. 63–81, at pp. 69–70, 70 n. 1, also pp. 74, 76.

22. For Jenks's leading role in the Industrial Commission and his relation to Theodore Roosevelt, see S. N. D. North (a member of the Commission), "The Industrial Commission," *N. Am. Rev.*, 168 (June 1899). p. 718; Jenks, *Trust Problem*, pp. 3–9, 235–240, 244n; Mary O. Furner, *Advocacy and Objectivity: A Crisis in the Professionalization of American Social Science, 1865–1905* (Lexington: University Press of Kentucky, 1975), pp. 248–249, 248 n. 31, 249 n. 33, 270–271. Jenks also acted as a principal academic adviser and member of the National Civic Federation throughout the early years of the twentieth century. See Chapter 4, below.

23. Jenks, *Trust Problem*, pp. 3–5. As expert adviser to the Industrial Commission, Jenks wrote the report on the effect of industrial combination on prices, at *Preliminary Report on Trusts and Industrial Combinations*, I, pp. 39–57; he wrote the report on statutes and decisions of federal, state, and territorial law (with the assistance of Herbert A. Heminway), at *Trusts and Corporation Laws*, II, H.R. Doc. No. 476, pt. 2, 56th Cong., 1st Sess. (Washington, D.C.: 1900) pp. 3–264; and the report on prices of industrial securities, at *Trusts and Industrial Combinations*, XIII, H.R. Doc. No 182, 57th Cong., 1st Sess. (Washington, D.C.: 1901), pp. 913–945. Jenks played a leading role in the Chicago Civic Federation's Chicago Conference on Trusts in 1899, and there began his close advisory association with NCF executive director Ralph Easley. The Chamberlin and Robinson works are: Edward H. Cham-

Jenks had no qualms about designating the new corporate consolidation as "capitalistic monopolies," because the power to make prices, whether exercised by one firm alone or shared with others, constituted a monopoly power. The emergence of corporate consolidations in recent years had been transforming the nature of the market. Unlike Hadley and Conant, Jenks rejected marginal utility theory altogether in his book *The Trust Problem* (1900), on the grounds that it was applicable to competition among small units but not to the operations of large corporations. He nevertheless concurred with Hadley and Conant in the view that the economists' "normal price" did not pertain to the marketplace of the large corporation.[24]

Although large corporations effected beneficial managerial and integrative economies, their principal purpose, in Jenks's view, was to regulate, and thereby restrict, the competition in investment and marketing that caused excess production at diminishing returns and the consequent instabilities in prices, profits, and employment that underlay the boom-bust cycle of competitive capitalism. Their market power putatively enabled the corporate consolidations to moderate such instabilities by limiting the access to the market of competing investment and by adjusting supply to demand at remunerative prices. They sought to keep prices and discernible returns on investment below the level at which new competitive investment would be induced to enter the industry. The large corporations, that is, sought to determine prices and returns on the supply side, as against leaving their determination to the demand side, as had been the case under the competitive regime. Jenks viewed this corporate regulation of the market, if not abused and if prudently regulated by government, as a progressive advance over the old competitive market: It tended toward the amelioration, although not the elimination, of depressions by stabilizing prices and profits and hence the employment of capital and labor. The corporate reorganization of industry placed a socially beneficial and economically efficient control upon the market.[25]

berlin, *The Theory of Monopolistic Competition* (Cambridge, Mass.: Harvard University Press, 1933); Joan Robinson, *The Economics of Imperfect Competition* (London: Macmillan, 1933). See also Gardiner C. Means, *The Corporate Revolution in America: Economic Reality vs. Economic Theory* (New York: Collier Books, 1964).

24. Jenks, *Trust Problem*, pp. 70, 76, 18–20, 141–142.
25. Ibid., chaps. 1, 2, 4. Like Hadley, Jenks favored government regulation, especially in the form of requiring publicity of corporate accounting, to enforce normal oligopolistic prices and returns, and, as an alternative to the discipline enforced by the older competitive mechanism, to ensure efficiency and continuing innovation. As New York governor and as president, Roosevelt consistently advocated publicity in this sense as an essential element in his regulatory policy proposals. See also, on publicity

Thought: Conant

Among those in senior advisory and policy-making positions in the United States around the turn of the century, it was Charles A. Conant who translated these new ideas about the market into an explicit concept of the business cycle that subsumed the overproduction question within the broader theory of oversavings, or of surplus capital. A prominent nonacademic scholar, financial journalist, and Massachusetts Gold Democrat, whose family line went back to John Winthrop's Massachusetts Bay Colony, Conant by the late 1890s had acquired an international reputation as an economist and a banking and monetary authority. From 1889 to 1901, he was Washington correspondent of both the *New York Journal of Commerce and Commercial Bulletin* and the *Springfield Republican* (Massachusetts). He was also international financial editor of the New York *Bankers Magazine*. In 1897–1901, he served as executive adviser to Hugh H. Hanna, chairman of the executive committee of the Indianapolis Monetary Convention, and as adviser and secretary of the Indianapolis Monetary Commission, which played a major role, in cooperation with the McKinley administration and especially with Secretary of the Treasury Lyman J. Gage, in effecting passage of the Currency (Gold Standard) Act of 1900. In the next several years, he served the McKinley and Roosevelt administrations in making and implementing international economic policy in the Philippines, Latin America, and China; in this connection, he served with Jenks and Hanna on the Commission on International Exchange (CIE) of 1903–1904, which was appointed by President Roosevelt and made directly responsible to Secretary of State Hay. In 1902, Conant became treasurer of the Morton Trust Company of New York, one of the nation's largest investment banking houses and a leading financial intermediary in the corporate reorganization movement. Throughout the period of the late 1890s and early years of the twentieth century, Conant was a prominent leader of the movement for central banking that culminated in the Federal Reserve Act of 1913. In general, Conant counted among that growing group, including such persons as George Foster Peabody, Walter Hines Page, Paul Samuel Reinsch, Carter Glass,

of corporate affairs, Hadley, "The Good and the Evil of Industrial Combination," *Atlantic Monthly* 79 (Mar. 1897), pp. 377–385, esp. p. 383. On discouraging competitive entry, cf. Chandler, *Visible Hand*, p. 334; Joe S. Bain, *Barriers to New Competition* (Cambridge, Mass.: Harvard University Press, 1956); and William G. Shepherd, "Bain's Influence on Research into Industrial Organization," in Robert T. Masson and P. David Qualls, eds., *Essays on Industrial Organization in Honor of Joe S. Bain* (Cambridge, Mass.: Ballinger, 1976), p. 3, note e: Shepherd here refers to Chamberlin and Robinson as among Bain's "immediate predecessors."

and Woodrow Wilson, who were Gold Democrats without being Cleveland Democrats. That is to say, they were progressives, and neither Bryan Democrats nor laissez-faire Bourbons.[26]

Conant's book *A History of Modern Banks of Issue*, published in 1896, contained four chapters aggregating 100 pages (out of a total of 575) on crises during the nineteenth century, including a general chapter on "Crises and Their Causes."[27] There and in a series of essays published from 1896 to 1901, Conant placed crises within the broader context of the business cycle. The business cycle, he observed, was peculiar to modern capitalist society, which combined industrial production and rapid transportation and communication with highly developed systems of credit. These accelerated the pace and enlarged the size of transactions, extended and intensified competition, and facilitated the operation of industry on an increasingly larger scale. The capitalist economy, in Conant's view, progressed and developed in and

26. Conant was born in Winchester, Massachusetts, in 1861; he died in Havana, Cuba, in 1915 (from what was thought to be stomach cancer), while on a mission for the Wilson administration to reform Cuban monetary and banking affairs. Conant's neglect by historians may be explained by four factors. (1) He was not a university economist; he had no graduate students, except for presidents, cabinet secretaries, U.S. senators and representatives, and capitalists, who were not prone to acknowledge their sources or assemble festschrifts. (2) He was a Democrat in a Republican era, and he died during Wilson's first term. (3) He left no collection of papers or letters for scholarly use; they are to be found scattered among collections of other notables, such as Root, Hay, Aldrich, Taft, Vanderlip; among business publications, such as the *Bankers Magazine*, the *Wall Street Journal* (for which he wrote unsigned editorials), the *Journal of Commerce*, etc.; and, as letters, memoranda, testimony, and state papers, in government publications and the National Archives. (4) He is erroneously taken to be eccentrically "Marxist." This is an understandable, if egregious, presentist error that usually, however, historians are careful to avoid. The only extended treatment of Conant's thinking by a historian is the sixteen-page chapter in David Healy, *United States Expansionism: The Imperialist Urge in the 1890s* (Madison: University of Wisconsin Press. 1970), chap. 11: "Charles A. Conant: The Implications of Commercial Struggle," pp. 194–209. It contributes much valuable information and accurate formulations about Conant's thought and role. See Davis Rich Dewey, "Charles Arthur Conant," *Dictionary of American Biography* 4 (1930), pp. 334–335; *National Cyclopaedia of American Biography* 65 (1910), p. 227; *Who Was Who, 1897–1942*, p. 294; Parrini and Sklar, "New Thinking About the Market," and notes 58, 59, below.
27. Conant, *A History of Modern Banks of Issue: With an Account of the Economic Crises of the Present Century* (New York and London: Putnam, 1896), chap. 19, pp. 453–466; the other chapters, 20–22 (pp. 467–553), deal with the crises of the nineteenth century, with chap. 22 devoted to the crisis of 1893. The book went through six editions over the next thirty years, each edition bringing the materials up-to-date. The last edition appeared posthumously in 1927, edited by Marcus Nadler, who added two new chapters on banking. All editions were published by Putnam's. Conant's other major treatise, published in two volumes by Harper Bros., New York, in 1905, while Conant was with the Morton Trust Company, was *The Principles of Money and Banking*.

through the rhythm of successive cycles, each one setting the stage for the next. As capitalism integrated national markets into a world market, the business cycle tended to become global and national cycles tended toward synchronization. Crises were the normal downside of the cycle. They recurred with periodic regularity along with the cycle; they were universal to all industrial capitalist societies, regardless of differences in banking and currency systems, tariff policy, income distribution, government intervention, or other secondary features and circumstances. Crises were unavoidable, and indeed therapeutic, but they could be subjected to countercyclical management, ameliorated, and thereby rendered curative and beneficial rather than destructive and lethal to modern economic life. Cycles and crises marked a society's development and progressive evolution as a modern civilization.[28]

Like Hadley, but in greater detail, Conant analyzed the immobility of fixed capital, rapidity of turnover, and, drawing upon Eugen Böhm-Bawerk, the element of the time interval between production and sale, as factors that invalidated the classical equilibrium model of the market. As the cycle went into its upswing, rising prices and profits, along with easy money and low interest rates, induced new fixed investment in additional plant, which ultimately yielded redundant plant and excess goods beyond immediate demand at prices that returned enough to cover capitalization. Then came the crisis of declining prices, tight money, rising interest rates, liquidation, and depression, which prepared the ground for the next upswing. Hence, production did not create its demand in the old sense, if it ever had. Equilibrium, not disequilibrium, was episodic. Competitive investment, moreover, in new laborsaving plant with greater efficiency and lower costs per unit of output, resulted in continuous value transformations, which the competitive market

28. Conant, *History* (1896), pp. 460–461; Conant, "Crises and Their Management," *Yale Review* 9 (Feb. 1901), pp. 374–398, passim. (It is not without significance that this article was published in *Yale Review*.) This view of the cycle as inhering in capitalist development became the basis of modern business-cycle studies. Wesley Clair Mitchell, a student at the University of Chicago of J. Laurence Laughlin – who worked with Conant on the Indianapolis Monetary Commission in 1897–1898 and wrote the commission's final report – went on to become the founder of academic business-cycle studies. Mitchell took many of his cues from Veblen. They were both at Chicago in the late 1890s; Laughlin had earlier brought Veblen with him from Cornell and installed Veblen as managing editor of his *Journal of Political Economy*. In this journal, Conant published two of his leading articles in 1899 and 1900 ("The Development of Credit," *JPE* 7:2 [Mar. 1899], pp. 161–181, and "The Distribution of Money," *JPE* 9 [Dec. 1900], pp. 47–75). Cf. Roy W. Jastram, *The Golden Constant: The English and American Experience, 1560–1976* (New York: Wiley, 1977), pp. 85–86, on the business cycle as a modern phenomenon, emerging distinctively in the early nineteenth century, and on Mitchell's concurrence in this view.

translated into the secular trend of declining prices and declining rates of profit characteristic of the last quarter of the nineteenth century. The more rapid turnover in the production process invalidated Mill's famous law that demand for commodities is not demand for labor. Conant argued that with large fixed investment, revenues from the sale of goods served as operating capital for the continued employment of labor. Hence, a break in the chain of production and sale, or downward competitive pressures on price, could throw the market into disequilibrium at rising rates of unemployment of both capital and labor.[29]

Conant identified the abiding source of the break in the chain of supply and demand as excess savings itself, whether held out of the investment stream or poured into it. In either case, savings resulted in supply in relative excess of demand for a period of time sufficient to break the market equilibrium.[30] With the development of machine production, banking and credit, and capital markets, oversaving and its concomitant of overinvestment in redundant plant became, throughout the developed capitalist world, not simply a cyclical phenomenon but a secular condition. The steady generation of geometrically rising savings, hence potential investment funds, made capital shortages episodic and capital congestion chronic. "Too much of the product of labor has been devoted to the creation of new equipment of doubtful or at least postponed utility"; "so large a part of the earnings of society has been set aside in recent years for investment that the equilibrium between production of finished goods and the effective demand for them has been broken."[31]

29. *History* (1896), chap. 19; "Crises," pp. 375–376, 381–382; Conant, "The Economic Basis of 'Imperialism,'" *N. Am. Rev.* 167 (Sept. 1898), pp. 328–330; Wall, *Carnegie*, pp. 317–322 (on investment in more efficient plant during depressions). Cf. James H. Thompson, "Mill's Fourth Fundamental Proposition: A Paradox Revisited," *History of Political Economy* 7:2 (Summer 1975), pp. 174–192.
30. "Economic Basis," pp. 328–330.
31. "Crises," pp. 380–382; Conant here cited Wilhelm Roscher and John Bates Clark's Introduction to Rodbertus. Conant's "mentor" above all was probably Paul Leroy-Beaulieu, the eminent French political economist well known on both sides of the Atlantic, particularly his 1879 work, *Essai sur la Repartition des Richesses*. See. e.g., "Economic Basis," p. 333. Conant knew and drew upon John A. Hobson's earlier work. See, e.g., Conant's reference to Hobson's "interesting book" *The Evolution of Modern Capitalism*, at Conant, "The United States as a World Power. I. The Nature of the Economic and Political Problem," *Forum* 29 (July 1900), pp. 608–622, at p. 615. The difference between Hobson's and Conant's oversavings analysis, in essence, was that Hobson's, as presented in *The Physiology of Industry* (1889, with A. F. Mummery) and *Evolution* (1894), was a distribution, or underconsumption, theory, whereas Conant's was a production, or investment, theory. Conant denied the possibility of raising consumption to the point of sustained market equilibrium within the framework of a private investment system. See note 47 and related text, below.

"Overproduction," then, was only the surface manifestation of a deeper-lying condition, an effect of surplus capital from oversaving. Nor could surplus capital be understood as occurring in discrete cases of "misdirected investment" or "misdirected production" resulting merely in temporary or partial disproportionalities.[32] Misdirected production was not simply sectoral or episodic, but universal and chronic because of sustained excess savings. A balance of production and demand under modern conditions would be possible only (1) at the cost of restricting production at unacceptable levels of unemployment, which would also sacrifice economies of scale to an effort at sustaining acceptable rates of return, both equally undesirable; or (2) by producing at full capacity and lowering prices, which would yield high levels of employment and investment but at unacceptably low returns on capital, in effect sacrificing rates of return to the maintenance of maximum efficiencies of scale. Something like the latter, under the whip hand of competition, but resulting all the same in recurrent depressions with high levels of unemployment, characterized the economies of the industrial nations from the 1870s through the 1890s.[33] In either case, surplus capital remained the problem. In (1), surplus capital appeared as idle capacity and idle money funds; in (2), as scarce funds and excess production capacity competing against itself to the destruction of profit.

"Misdirected production," therefore, was not simply a matter of erroneous but remediable judgments by capitalists in the present about the future. It was the result of unavoidable, deliberate, and rationally calculated decisions of capitalists in a competitive system of high fixed investment, where running full, even at lower prices, incurred less loss than cutting back or shutting down. It was the normal outcome of rational capitalist response to the business cycle: Capitalists put more capacity into use when rising prices and rising rates of return signaled a demand for greater output. During a depression, on the other hand,

32. John Bates Clark (e.g., Introduction to Rodbertus, *Overproduction and Crises*, pp. 2–5, 12–18), like Laughlin, held, in accordance with classical and the Austrian version of neoclassical theory, that there could be no "universal overproduction." Conant responded ("Crises," p. 382), citing Hadley (*Economics*, p. 294), that in terms of real needs and wants this was true, but not in terms of effective demand at prices covering capitalization and returning an adequate rate of profit. Conant claimed that Clark admitted as much in saying (Introduction to Rodbertus, p. 17): "It is in the relations of present to future – in speculative and inaccurate estimates of incomes that are about to be – that there lie influences that cause goods to be created for which, in time, there is no effectual demand."

33. See note 14 and related text, above. Hence, the large body of literature then and since on the "long depression" of the 1870s–1890s in the British, western European, and American economies. Cf. Veblen, *Theory*, chap. 7, pp. 87–127, esp. pp. 118–122; David S. Landes, *The Unbound Prometheus: Technological Change and Industrial Development in Western Europe from 1750 to the Present* (Cambridge University Press, 1969), pp. 230–237.

when costs were low, those capitalists with access to investment funds installed new and more efficient plant, thus placing themselves in position to undersell their competitors and take their markets when the cycle resumed upward.[34] "Misdirected production," therefore, inhered chronically in the business cycle itself, so long as prices were competitively determined and investment response to market cycles remained uncontrolled.

The movement toward an administered market under the auspices of the corporate reorganization of industry, in this view, represented the response of a progressive industrial capitalism to the competitive market under the conditions of surplus capital. Assuming a commitment to continuing industrialization, it offered an alternative to economically ruinous and politically dangerous depressions as well as to statist dictation in the marketplace. The corporate reorganization, however, rested on two fundamental premises: The regulation of investment in the operation and expansion of productive capacity made sense (1) only if price could be administered (not necessarily absolutely controlled), which presupposed sufficient centralization of authority to limit or regulate production, credit access, and marketing; and (2) only if − to counteract excessive unemployment, the vitiation of economies of scale, and the intensification of the oversaving implicit in the limitation of productive investment − the sphere of enterprise, particularly the sphere of investment, could be extended beyond national limits to capital-scarce areas, beyond the limits of the domestic investment, employment, and marketing system. It followed that the condition of a viable national corporate investment system was its globalization in an international investment system. Abbreviated, the formula ran: concentration, integration, expansion.[35]

34. For example, between 1892 and 1898, Illinois Steel Corporation paid only one dividend whereas it nearly doubled its plant capacity. Carnegie also followed the policy of expanding plant capacity at low cost during depressions. Meade, "Financial Aspects," p. 11; Carnegie, "Bugaboo," pp. 141−142; Wall, *Carnegie*, pp. 317−322, 584−586, 625.

35. Cf. Sidney Sherwood, "Influence of the Trust in the Development of Undertaking Genius," *Yale Review* 8 (Feb. 1900), pp. 362−372. A leading American marginal utility advocate, Sherwood of Johns Hopkins University designated the "Trust" (the large integrated corporation) as "the American solution" of the world-market problem. (Ibid., p. 372.) Conant cited and quoted Sherwood's article, including this phrase, in his "The United States as a World Power. II. Her Advantages in the Competition for Commercial Empire," *Forum* 29 (Aug. 1900), pp. 673−687, at 679; see also Conant, "The United States as a World Power. I.," pp. 608−622, and Conant, "The Struggle for Commercial Empire," *Forum* 27 (July 1899), pp. 427−440, and "Recent Economic Tendencies," *Atlantic Monthly* 85 (June 1900), pp. 737−742. These and other essays are reprinted in Conant, *The United States in the Orient: The Nature of the Economic Problem* (Boston: Houghton Mifflin, 1900; reissued Port Washington, N.Y.: Kennikat Press, 1971).

The international dimension, then, was integral to the corporate reorganization of the property-production system. Jenks noted the connection between the domestic and international dimensions in the testimony of corporate capitalists before the Industrial Commission. The large corporations required international outlets for goods and investment. At the same time, they were better equipped than small, unintegrated, and capital-scarce enterprises to compete in foreign markets and to make foreign investments that depended upon the transfer and management of capital in enterprises abroad. The thinking associated with Hadley, Jenks, and Conant, then, went beyond simple overproductionism to a theory of the corporate reordering of capitalism, or to an economic theory predicated on the business cycle and crises, the administered domestic market, and the globalization of the investment system.[36]

Marginal utility Americanized

Like Hadley, Conant embraced the language and concepts of marginal utility, but not the equilibrium theory of the Austrian school and its British counterparts.[37] On American soil, marginal utility took corporate root and yielded a hybrid grain of thought. Conant, again like Hadley, and in a Marshallian manner, did not treat marginal utility theory as mutually exclusive of a labor theory of value if modified in

36. In his review of Conant's *United States in the Orient*, John Bates Clark, in noting Conant's "major premise" to be the superabundance of capital, granted that he "seems to avoid the ancient fallacies about universal overproduction." Clark cited as the "chief weakness" of Conant's work the "failure to recognize" the benefits of "increasing capital," especially in making possible rising wages in the long run. Actually, in his writings. Conant both recognized and emphasized such benefits. Nevertheless, and of particular significance in the present context, Clark cited as among the "merits" of Conant's book "the vigor and general soundness of its plea for outlets for exportation and, in particular, its recognition of the fact that the opening of foreign countries means not only a chance to sell goods with profit, but a chance to invest our own capital with an even larger and more permanent profit." Clark, review of Conant, *United States in the Orient*, Brooks Adams, *America's Economic Supremacy*, and Josiah Strong, *Expansion Under New World Conditions*, in *PSQ* 16 (Mar. 1901), pp. 142–144 (quotations at pp. 142, 143). For Jenks, see, e.g., *Trust Problem*, pp. 74–76. Cf. Mira Wilkins, *The Emergence of Multinational Enterprise: American Business Abroad from the Colonial Era to 1914* (Cambridge, Mass.: Harvard University Press, 1970), pp. ix–xii, and chap. 3, pp. 35–69.

37. Conant frequently cited University of Glasgow Adam Smith Professor of Political Economy William Smart, the principal transmitter into the English language of Austrian school works in the 1890s, and a leading expositor of marginal utility theory who nevertheless emphasized the problems of market disequilibrium. In particular, Conant drew upon Smart's *Studies in Economics* (London: Macmillan, 1895). At the time he wrote *Studies*, Smart was a lecturer at Glasgow; he later became Adam Smith professor.

form as a cost of production theory: Marginal utility explained the determination of current prices and profits by supply and demand; labor theory explained long-term trends in capital-labor ratios, that is, in costs and social efficiencies.[38]

For Conant, insofar as marginal utility stressed the determining impact of the "last" unit on the general price and profit level, it reinforced the emphasis on the surplus not only of goods but also of capital (savings, investment funds, plant), and the focusing of policy-planning on the disposal of the surplus, that is, of supply beyond effective demand at prices yielding an adequate rate of return. Insofar as it stressed diminishing returns with rising supply, marginal utility demonstrated the declining rate of profit as dictated by the superabundance of capital, and the need for investment abroad in capital-scarce areas as a method of countering the declining rate of profit. Conant, for example, cited Böhm-Bawerk in arguing that marginal utility theory, in applying "to the earnings of capital the law of diminishing returns," demonstrated the need for international investment, not simply for the higher returns normal to investment in capital-scarce areas, but to maintain higher levels of profits in the United States. As Conant stated it, "capital becomes less productive in earning power where it is abundant, because less productive use can be found for the excess above a certain limit. And it is the excess which fixes the rate for all." On this question, marginal utility theory corroborated, in different language, the same point made by classical political economists from Smith and Ricardo to John Stuart Mill and Marx.[39]

In effect, marginal utility provided the theoretical ground for the pro-capitalist break with the competitive mechanism as the regulator of the market. Its supply and demand curves offered a model with which the firm might plan as a price-maker – instead of merely as a price-taker – virtually inconceivable on the basis of the classical competitive model.

38. Cf. Hadley's remark in his Preface to *Economics* (p. iv): "There is no general work in the English language which deals at all comprehensively with these problems of modern economics. As long as Marshall's book [*Principles*] remains incomplete there is nothing which attempts to do for ... to-day that which Mill did with such signal success for ... half a century ago." His book, Hadley stated, attempted to cover "the field thus left open." And see ibid., chap. 5, pp. 121–150, esp. pp. 123–124. Cf. Craufurd D. W. Goodwin, "Marginalism Moves to the New World," in Black, Coats, and Goodwin, eds., *The Marginal Revolution*, pp. 285–304.
39. Conant, "Economic Basis," p. 334. Cf. Eugen V. Böhm-Bawerk, *The Positive Theory of Capital*, trans. William Smart (London: Macmillan, 1891), pp. 28, 336, 361, 401; Maurice Dobb, *Theories of Value and Distribution since Adam Smith: Ideology and Economic Theory* (Cambridge University Press, 1973), pp. 198–200; Dobb, "The Falling Rate of Profit," *Science & Society* 23:2 (Spring 1959), pp. 97–103, at pp. 97–100.

That is, marginal utility validated the operational possibility of separating prices from costs. Or, in language more faithful to marginal utility concepts, it validated the redefinition of cost as the going price, the price the firm could make, and make stick – "based not on the cost . . . but on the market price," understood as "the maximum price" the market would bear, as Elbert H. Gary and George W. Perkins would advise the McCormicks about the pricing policy of the International Harvester Company and its relations with the United States Steel Corporation.[40] Accordingly, marginal utility laid the basis of a strategy for intervening against falling prices and the falling rate of profit, by adjusting production to demand and, where possible, by raising demand (whether, for example, through advertising or foreign trade and investment) to maintain prices and rates of return. Rising prices, moreover, could absorb a portion of disposable income that might otherwise go into savings free of centralized control. In short, marginal utility served as a theoretical basis of replacing the competitive with the administered market within the framework of private property and a highly developed industrial capitalism. It converted an economic reality productive of unmanageable abundances into an economic calculus suited to the restoration and management of relative scarcities.[41]

In the specific circumstances of American politics, marginal utility as conveyed by such thinkers as Conant and Hadley also provided what could be represented as authoritative scientific grounds for an assault against populism on two crucial fronts, that of the trust question and that of the money question. In conjunction with general evolutionary explanations for large-scale enterprise, centered on modern technology, credit, and competitive concentration, Conant could apply marginal utility's focus upon the diminishing returns yielded by a rising supply of capital in arguing that it was not monopolistic power that disrupted

40. See "Synopsis of the Effort to Amalgamate into I.H.Co.," n.d. (ca. 1903), IH-Archives #200, Stanley McCormick Files, McCormick Collection, State Historical Society of Wisconsin, Madison. Cf. William Smart, *An Introduction to the Theory of Value, on the Lines of Menger, Wieser, and Böhm-Bawerk* (1891; 3d ed., London: Macmillan, 1914), pp. 67–68; Chandler, *Visible Hand*, p. 350; Helen Kramer, "Harvesters and High Finance: Formation of the International Harvester Company," *BHR* 38:3 (Autumn 1964), pp. 283–301. Maximum price meant not necessarily the highest price but the highest price consistent with long-range objectives concerning investment and rates of return.
41. Cf. Smart, *Theory of Value*, pp. 16–18, 24–25, 34, 80–81; William Fellner, *Emergence and Content of Modern Economic Analysis* (New York: McGraw-Hill, 1960), pp. 144–146, 146 n. 1; Chandler, *Visible Hand*, pp. 339, 377; Ronald L. Meek, *Smith, Marx, and After: Ten Essays in the Development of Economic Thought* (London: Chapman & Hall, 1977), pp. 174–175.

the competitive market and caused market disequilibrium, as populists would have it, but market disequilibrium inhering in the competitive market under modern industrializing conditions that caused capitalists to resort to consolidations. Far from being unnatural, the "trusts," in other words, were the natural outcome of the naturally evolving market. With respect to the money question, Conant invoked marginal utility theory as certifying the necessity of the gold standard in a highly developed economy like that of the United States, according to "the law that the object most useful for a given purpose in any community will gradually exclude the use of other objects." Conant argued accordingly, as well, that marginal utility substantiated the rejection of the quantity theory of money of the silverite populists. The "quantitative theory of money," as he put it, "is opposed to the law of marginal utility, which is one of the most important laws affecting the employment of money, ... which makes it impossible that other conditions should remain the same when the supply of money is increased or decreased." Indeed, like Hadley and J. Laurence Laughlin, Conant held that productivity along with supply and demand fundamentally determined prices, and that, if anything, the price level determined the quantity of money in circulation (modified by velocity), rather than vice versa.[42]

On a broader plane of social-political policy, marginal utility, by stressing the point at which capital (machinery and technique) replaced labor as the cheaper factor of production, and by validating the international extension of investment, reinforced the emphasis on rising productivity and global expansion as the means of sustaining rising real wages without diminishing rates of return – that is, without income redistribution.[43] Imperialism and reform went hand in hand.

In a similar manner, marginal utility theory could claim to reconcile large-scale corporate capitalism, and its increasing socialization and standardization of production and exchange, with American individuality. The old, classical political economy, although arising from the soil of individual enterprise, based its analysis on calculating returns to classes or groups – land (rent), capital (interest), and labor (wages).

42. See, e.g., Conant, "The Law of the Value of Money," *Annals* 16:2 (Sept. 1900), pp. 13–35, at pp. 15, 26–27, 29, 31.
43. Conant held that under the competitive system, depressions and declining profits in effect redistributed income from the manufacturer to labor and professionals in the form of rising real purchasing power of the wage and salary dollar. *History* (1896), p. 463; to the same effect, Meade, "Financial Aspects," p. 12. This added further to swelling savings by increasing the portion of available disposable income above consumption needs or wants, if not among wageworkers then among professionals and the salaried.

Ironically, the economic theory of self-interest submerged the individual in the collectivity with a fate determined by an invisible hand. By placing emphasis on marginal wants, preferences, and effort, marginal utility, while serving the needs of large-corporate production scheduling and marketing strategy, at the same time resurrected the individual from the crypt of the group. Reward, or equity, in the marginal utility market was to be allocated not simply by class, or group, or collectivity, but also, variably, to individuals according to their skills, aptitudes, and attainments, as the latter differed in scarcity and market demand, or in marginal value. There was room, after all, in the highly industrialized, large-scale economy, even more so than before, for uniqueness, initiative, creativity, for personality, preference, difference – for the individual: room and reward. The market would return to each factor of production its true worth, but a factor need not be a group – it could be an individual; and true worth need not be an impersonal average – it could be differentially determined by individual effort. Large-scale efficiencies and American individuality could shape the nation's future together.

Conant, Keynes, and Marx

The corporate reorganization of industry was, in the pro-corporate view of things, a necessary response to the problem of oversaving and surplus capital – a response that was consistent with private property and capitalism and that did not renounce or retard large-scale production. But corporate reorganization on a large scale of operations was not by itself a solution of the problem of the surplus. It intensified the problem in certain decisive ways: It raised prices, or made them less elastic, and thereby limited demand in relation to capacity; it restricted the flow of savings into competitive investment, but at the same time it facilitated the concentrated accumulation of investment funds in corporate treasuries, and it mobilized investment funds through the creation of organized capital markets for negotiable securities and through the activity of investment banking houses and trust companies, which grew in number and size with the emergence of corporate capitalism. The corporate reorganization may be said to have treated, without curing, the malady of "overproduction" from the diagnostic standpoint of the capitalist property system; precisely in so doing, it reinforced the tendency toward oversaving and the generation of surplus capital, in the absence of vigorous international expansion of the investment system. It thereby made the disposal of the surplus and access to growing international investment outlets an all the more urgent question of policy both in the private sector and in government.[44]

The new thinking about the market that emerged in this period may suggest to some that it "anticipated" John Maynard Keynes and represented a kind of pro-capitalist "Marxism of the ruling class." To understand it in these ways, however, is to embrace a presentist error with respect to Marx that reads back into the past ideological divisions that arose later, and an anachronistic error with respect to Keynes that ignores substantial connections and continuities between earlier and later thought. It misreads and distorts the historical context of both the earlier and the later thought.

Educated at King's College, Cambridge, and a protégé of Alfred Marshall, Keynes knew the broad contemporary currents of thought critical of the competitive market and the classical conventional wisdom, of which the works of Hadley, Conant, and Jenks on the American side of the Atlantic were a part. Keynes's father, John Neville Keynes, was a member of the Gonner Committee of the British Association for the Advancement of Science, which in 1893 and 1894 reported on what it considered the advanced state of American economic thought. It is therefore plausible to assume that Keynes, like other British economists, was alert to American economic writings. More specifically, Keynes knew Conant's work. Conant published in the *Economic Journal* (London), as did the young Keynes, who became its editor in 1911. In these years, as a secretary in the British India Office, Keynes was deeply involved with Indian currency and financial affairs. Britain was in the process of putting the Indian rupee on the gold-exchange standard to facilitate British investment in India and India's international payments. Keynes's first major treatise was his study *Indian Currency and Finance*, published in 1913. Separately or together, Conant and Jenks in these years were engaged in official missions for

---

44. See, e.g., Conant, "Economic Basis," pp. 333–334; Conant, *United States in the Orient*, pp. 126–128; Conant, "Securities as a Means of Payment," *Annals* 14 (Sept. 1899), pp. 25–47; Conant, "The World's Wealth in Negotiable Securities," *Atlantic Monthly*, Jan. 1908, pp. 102–103; Conant, *Wall Street and the Country: A Study of Recent Financial Tendencies* (1904; Westport, Conn.: Greenwood, 1968), chaps. 3, 4, pp. 83–116, 205–235. On overcapacity throughout the 1896–1914 period, see Hoffmann, *Depression of the Nineties*, chap. 1, pp. 9–42; Solomon Fabricant, *The Output of Manufacturing Industries, 1899–1937* (New York: National Bureau of Economic Research, 1940), pp. 44–46. The papers and letters of the National City Bank's Frank A. Vanderlip, in this period, are strewn with references to and discussions of excess capacity, surplus capital, and idle investment funds, e.g., Diary of European Trip, 1901 and Vanderlip to James Stillman, 8 May 1908, 18 Feb. 1909, 26 March 1909, 11 Feb. 1910, 13 May 1910, 29 Sept. 1911, 9 Feb. 1912, 24 May 1912 (to cite just a few), all in FAV.

the United States government and in work with American investment bankers relating to currency reform in Asia and Latin America, including the Philippines, China, Mexico, Panama, and Nicaragua. In 1910, Keynes explicitly stated his agreement with the analysis of Chinese currency reform – an analysis that focused on the problem of surplus capital and the need for a system of international investment facilitated by a gold-exchange standard – contained in the official report prepared by Conant and Jenks (along with Hugh H. Hanna) in their work as the members of the Commission on International Exchange for the Department of State in the opening years of the twentieth century. In recording his agreement, Keynes specifically cited the pages of the report that included the emphasis on chronic surplus capital in the industrial nations as requiring the expansion of the international investment system into capital-scarce countries like China.[45]

45. Keynes, "A Memorandum on a Currency System for China" (Feb. 1910), in *The Collected Writings of John Maynard Keynes*, 15, ed. Elizabeth Johnson (New York: Macmillan, 1971), pp. 60–65, esp. at pp. 62–63, citing pp. 14–24 and 103–117 of [Charles A. Conant, Hugh H. Hanna, and Jeremiah W. Jenks] U.S. Commission on International Exchange, *Stability of International Exchange: Report on the Introduction of the Gold Exchange Standard into China and Other Silver Using Countries* (Washington, D.C.: Government Printing Office, 1903). Also U.S. Commission on International Exchange, *Report on the Introduction of the Gold Standard into China, the Philippine Islands, Panama, and Other Silver Using Countries* (Washington, D.C.: Government Printing Office, 1904); Conant, *A Special Report on Coinage and Banking in the Philippine Islands*, 25 Nov. 1901, Appendix G in U.S. Department of War, in *Annual Report of the Secretary of War, 1901* (Washington, D.C.: Government Printing Office, 1901); U.S. Department of War, *Report on Certain Economic Questions in the English and Dutch Colonies in the Orient*, by Jeremiah Jenks, Bureau of Insular Affairs, War Department Doc. No. 168, Sept. 1902 (Washington, D.C.: Government Printing Office, 1902); also, e.g., relating to Conant's policy-forming role, Conant to Secretary of the Treasury Lyman J. Gage, 16 Oct. 1900, Gage to Root, 8 Nov. 1900, Conant to Clarence R. Edwards (chief of the Division of Insular Affairs, War Department), 9 July 1901, Root to William Howard Taft (civil governor of the Philippines, Manila), 23 July 1901, all in U.S. War Department, National Archives, Record Group 350; and Taft to Root, 14 Oct. 1901, Papers of Elihu Root, Library of Congress, Washington, D.C. Cf. Parrini and Sklar, "New Thinking." On the Gonner Committee, see note 16, above. On international currency reform, see also J. C. Coyajee, *The Indian Currency System, 1835–1926* (Madras: Thompson & Co., 1930), pp. 49–143; Edwin W. Kemmerer, *Modern Currency Reforms: A History and Discussion of Recent Currency Reforms in India, Porto Rico, Philippine Islands, Straits Settlements and Mexico* (New York: Macmillan, 1916), pp. 3–152 and passim. In October 1903, Kemmerer, who had been Jenks's graduate student at Cornell University, became the first chief of the Division of the Currency of the Philippine civil government under Taft, administering the gold-exchange standard program worked out by Conant in 1901–1903. Currency reform encompassed banking, fiscal, tax, budgetary, and legal reform as integral to monetary reform in the narrow sense. Kemmerer dedicated his *Modern Currency Reforms* "To my former teacher and colleague Jeremiah Whipple Jenks, who first directed my interest to the field of modern currency reforms" (Frontispiece). On Conant's association with Taft in Philippine affairs, see note 58, below.

The chief difference between Conant and the later Keynes lay not in the analysis of the causes of disequilibrium, but in the remedy. The difference was a matter of time and circumstance that did not pertain to the early twentieth century. Conant saw a remedy in the corporate regulation of competition, in investment imperialism, and in counter-cyclical central banking policy. He was prominent throughout this period in writings and activity relating to all three areas. In the movement for central banking, his *History of Modern Banks of Issue* (1896) and other writings played an influential role, as did his frequent testimony before congressional committees; he served as executive adviser to the Indianapolis Monetary Commission in the closing years of the 1890s and the opening years of the new century, later as a member of the New York Chamber of Commerce's special currency and banking committee (1906), and with the National Monetary Commission as an adviser to its chairman, Senator Nelson W. Aldrich, in the work eventuating in the Federal Reserve System.[46]

By the 1930s, the devastation of World War I and the subsequent breakdown of the international investment system appeared to have rendered the imperialist remedy excessively dangerous, if not obsolete, and the internationalist remedy in general moot. Keynes offered the remedy of fiscal policy as a complement to central banking policy, in order to repair the tendency toward insufficient demand, or over-capacity, or oversaving. Keynes offered it in a spirit – which Conant had acknowledged as being not without some validity – considerably favorable to income redistribution if not socialism. In 1898, Conant had cited "state socialism" as a possible solution to the surplus capital

46. Cf. Parrini and Sklar, "New Thinking." For Conant's work with the Indianapolis Monetary Commission, see Conant, "Plans for Currency Reform," *Review of Reviews* (Jan. 1898), pp. 43–52; Papers of Robert Stewart Taylor (member of the IMC, Fort Wayne patent lawyer, bar leader, and counsel to General Electric Corporation, et al.), Indianapolis State Library, Indianapolis, Ind.: e.g., Conant to Taylor, 17 Nov. 1897, Herman H. Kohlsaat to Taylor, 11 Dec. 1897, Jules Guthridge to Taylor, 4 Jan. 1898 (Guthridge, an Indiana journalist, served Hanna as secretary of the IMC and then as secretary of the CIE). Concerning Conant's continuing involvement in the movement for central banking, see, e.g., Conant testimony (16 Feb. 1901), U.S. House of Representatives, Committee on Banking and Currency, *Hearings and Arguments*, "Currency Responsive to the Needs of Business," H.R. 13303, 56th Cong., 2d Sess. (Washington, D.C.: Government Printing Office, 1901), pp. 87–105; Conant et al., *The Currency: Report of the Special Currency Committee of the Chamber of Commerce of the State of New York, Submitted to the Chamber October 4, 1906* (the other members of the committee included Jacob Schiff, Lyman J. Gage, Frank A. Vanderlip, A. Barton Hepburn, Isidor Straus, Dumont Clarke, and John Claflin); Conant, "The Functions of Centralized Banking," *Bankers Magazine* 89 (Oct. 1914), pp. 388–398. Conant wrote *The Banking System of Mexico* (1910) and the *National Bank of Belgium* (1910) for the National Monetary Commission.

problem, but he rejected it as inconsistent with capitalist property relations, with dynamic growth, and with liberal antistatism. He had also considered and rejected the "underconsumptionist" proposal to raise demand by redistributing income from investors to consumers. He rejected it on the ground that the reduction of already declining rates of return on capital would inhibit investment and aggravate the problem of unemployment, and that in any case, rising demand could not keep pace with rising savings short of a stationary state or socialism. Conant also recognized war as a way of absorbing surplus capital, but he rejected it as a wasteful form of consumption as well as morally inappropriate. Conant did, however, believe that a mix of social democratic reform at home and imperialist expansion abroad, in the framework of the general corporate regulation of the market (including central banking), could prove effective in alleviating capital congestion and hence in moderating the business cycle without jeopardizing continuing progressive economic and social development. He predicted that United States politics in the twentieth century would increasingly turn upon the conflicting but complementary claims of social democracy and imperialism.[47]

As for Marx, a critique of the competitive market had never been unique to him, and by the late nineteenth century economic writings in Britain, Europe, and the United States were brimming with it. So were the thoughts and complaints of countless capitalists. In this respect, as in others, pro-socialist and pro-capitalist thought shared a common ground. By social origins and vocation, Conant was conversant with, and readily drew upon, the thinking of capitalists and politicians and the implications of general economic conditions. As a journalist and scholar, he also drew widely upon British and European economic thought that ranged from the writings of Paul Leroy-Beaulieu in France and Léon Walras in Switzerland, to those of Walter Bagehot, W. Stanley Jevons, John A. Hobson, and William Smart in Britain, Georges de Laveleye in Belgium, Eugen Böhm-Bawerk in Austria, and Wilhelm Roscher in Germany.

The critique of the competitive market cut across ideological and class lines; it divided marginal utility theorists themselves. But the United States historical context was probably of decisive relevance in turning pro-capitalist American writers so explicitly and resolutely

---

47.   Conant, "Economic Basis," pp. 337–338; "The Future of Political Parties," *Atlantic Monthly* 86 (Sept. 1901), pp. 365–373. In 1909, Conant recommended to Senator Nelson W. Aldrich the adoption of a federal tax on corporate profits; in that year, Congress passed such a tax. Conant to Aldrich, 22 Apr. 1909, Nelson W. Aldrich Papers, Library of Congress, Washington, D.C.

against the competitive market model. In Britain and western Europe, pro-capitalist economic thought in the late nineteenth century developed with a strong defensive sensibility toward working-class political movements heavily rooted ideologically in the socialist tradition, especially that associated with Marx.[48]

In the United States, class relations and hence the political and ideological situation in the 1890s were different. Although the working class was assuming a position of growing importance in political life, national politics did not yet center upon capital-labor relations, nor were industrial workers sufficiently organized in trade unions to pose a serious threat to capitalists' power over labor in the market. The dominant national political alignments arrayed some groups within the large and diversified bourgeoisie against others, with the also large and diversified working class for the most part dividing its support among them in an auxiliary role. In the United States around the turn of the century, populism, representing powerful strands of the small-producer outlook, was the principal political antagonist of the corporate capitalist movement. The new concept of the market, based on a mix of marginal utility and a modified labor-value theory, provided a persuasive refutation of two of the populists' major arguments, namely, the quantity theory of money as the explanation of declining prices and profits, and the "antimonopolist" explanation of market disequilibrium.[49] In comparison with the populists' contentions, Marx's thought appeared to American pro-corporate theorists to be urbane, sophisticated, and modernistic. His theory of money was "sound," rejecting as it did the quantity theory, and equally sound were his theory of value transformations and crises under the impact of competition and rising productivity, his time-interval analysis of market disequilibrium, and his affirmation of large-scale enterprise as the inevitable evolutionary result of progressive capitalist development. The American pro-corporate theorists tended to greet Marx and Marxian socialist economic theory with equanimity as something of an ally in their conflict with those

48. Cf. Smart, in his Preface to Wieser's *Natural Value*: "The general reader ... will probably find the most suggestive matter ... in the attacks on Socialist theory." Friederich von Wieser, *Natural Value*, trans. Mrs. Mallock, ed. with a Preface and Analysis by William Smart, (1893; New York: Augustus M. Kelley, 1971), p. v.
49. Prevalent populist thought glorified labor as the source of all value, but when it got down to cases, it embraced a monetary and "monopolistic" theory of prices. The rejection of the quantity theory of money (really, the quantity-of-money theory of prices) was common to gold-standard advocates in the United States, Britain, and continental Europe in the late nineteenth century. Cf. Albert E. Feavearyear, *The Pound Sterling; A History of English Money*, 2d. ed. (Oxford: Clarendon Press, 1963), p. 310.

whom they regarded as primitive agrarians and provincial antimodernizers – "retrogressors," as Woodrow Wilson, and "rural tories," as Theodore Roosevelt, called the populists.[50]

Corporate capitalism and imperialism

The theory of surplus capital as the motive cause of modern capitalist imperialism originated neither with John A. Hobson or Vladimir I. Lenin, nor with Rudolf Hilferding or Rosa Luxemburg. There is no distinctive Marxist theory of imperialism, modern capitalist or otherwise. Marx's own discussion of eighteenth- and nineteenth-century "colonization" differed little from the view of international capitalist market- and settler-expansion generally held among knowledgeable observers of his times, with roots in mercantilist thought, as well as in that of Smith, Malthus, and Ricardo; in particular, Marx followed Wakefield and Merivale, the British writers – although, of course, critically – with respect to nineteenth-century "colonizing." By 1900, when modern capitalist imperialism was just getting under way, Marx had been dead for more than fifteen years. He was undoubtedly highly intelligent, an exemplary scholar, even remarkably foresighted in certain telling ways, but he was not a fortune-teller, at least not a seriously committed one as he got on in years.[51]

50. Hence, in his *Economics*, where Hadley headed each chapter with a list of selected readings, he placed two readings at the head of chap. 5, "Investment of Capital," W. J. Ashley's *English Economic History* and Marx's *Das Kapital* (the S. Moore and E. Aveling translation). About the latter he noted only that "This book ..., in the closing sections of the first volume, gives the socialistic view of the events and processes described in this chapter" (p. 121). Conant did not cite Marx in his *History* or in his essays before 1900; after that, in three places, he cited or quoted Marx matter-of-factly as an authority on monetary and banking theory. E. R. A. Seligman, in 1907, distinguished Marx's theory of the declining rate of profit based on the organic composition of capital from simple overproduction theories, and he praised "the socialist scholars" as having "undoubtedly made valuable contributions to the discussion of the problem" of modern crises, although they had not, he believed, understood "business enterprise and capitalization." Seligman, "The Crisis of 1907 in the Light of History," Introduction to *The Currency Problem and the Present Financial Situation*, a Series of Addresses Delivered at Columbia University, 1907–1908, ed. E. R. A. Seligman (New York: Columbia University Press, 1908), pp. xii, xiii. On the warmer reception and greater appreciation of Marx among American economists, coinciding with the spread among them of marginal utility theory, cf. Dorfman, *Economic Mind*, 3, pp. 238, 253.
51. This does not detract from the fact that Marx's theory of capital accumulation, crisis, and surplus capital was consistent with and suggestive of the theory of modern capitalist imperialism in question here. Otherwise, on matters discussed in the text, see Marx, *Capital*, Vol. 1 (Moscow: Foreign Languages Publishing House, n.d.), chap. 33, pp. 765–774; Shlomo Avineri, ed., *Karl Marx on Colonialism and Modernization* (New York: Doubleday, Anchor Books, 1968), esp. pt. 2; Bernard

The theory of modern capitalist imperialism as a function of surplus capital generated by mature industrial capitalist society was an American theory before it was a twentieth-century British or European theory; it was a pro-imperialist and pro-capitalist theory before it was an anti-imperialist or anti-capitalist theory. In short, it was a "bourgeois theory" before it was a "Marxist theory." By the latter 1890s, the bourgeois press and journals in the United States and Europe were filled with discussion of the idea of the relation between surplus capital and modern imperialism. In a more rigorous, theoretical form, its comprehensive statement was laid out, published, and in place in the United States (1898–1900), two to four years before Hobson's *Imperialism* (1902), and more than fifteen years before Lenin's *Imperialism* (1916).[52] The major works were Conant's, in the sphere of econo-

Semmel, *The Rise of Free Trade Imperialism: Classical Political Economy, the Empire of Free Trade, and Imperialism, 1750–1950* (Cambridge University Press, 1970), chap. 9, pp. 203–229; Tom Kemp, *Theories of Imperialism* (London: Dennis Dobson, 1967), pp. 19–24; Eric Stokes, "Late Nineteenth-Century Colonial Expansion and the Attack on the Theory of Economic Imperialism: A Case of Mistaken Identity?" *Historical Journal* 12:2 (1969), pp. 285–301; Norman Etherington, "Reconsidering Theories of Imperialism," *History and Theory* 21:1 (1982), pp. 1–36.

52. Wolfgang J. Mommsen, *Theories of Imperialism* (German ed., 1977; New York: Random House, 1980), p. 9, notes "an almost constant element in bourgeois thought before 1914 that the capitalist economy needed overseas markets and investment opportunities and that it might be necessary to obtain them by imperialist means," but having reported this finding, he remains within the limits of the traditional understanding of the subject and does not pursue its implications. Hobson's *Imperialism: A Study* first appeared in 1902; chap. 6, "The Economic Taproot of Imperialism," originally appeared as an article of the same title in *Contemporary Review* 82 (Aug. 1902), pp. 219–232. In that chapter (p. 76 of the University of Michigan Press edition, [Ann Arbor 1965], edited with an Introduction by Philip Siegelman), Hobson states: "Indeed, the conditions alike of cutthroat competition and of combination attest the congestion of capital in the manufacturing industries which have entered the machine economy ... No one acquainted with trade will deny a fact which all American economists assert, that this is the condition which the United States reached at the end of the century, so far, as the more developed industries are concerned. Her manufactures were saturated with capital and could absorb no more." In his Introduction, Siegelman (p. xii) quotes in agreement Richard Koebner and Helmut Dan Schmidt, *Imperialism: The Story and Significance of a Political Word, 1840–1960* (Cambridge University Press, 1964), pp. 252–253: "Imperialism as a political and economic theory first emerged during and immediately after the Boer War. It originated in England." To which Siegelman immediately adds: "It originated, in fact, from Hobson's pen." This is representative of what has long been the commonly held view. (See also, e.g., to the same effect, D. K. Fieldhouse, "'Imperialism': An Historiographical Revision," *EHR*, 2d ser., 14:2 [1961], pp. 187–209.) It does not seem, however, to be accurate, nor is it based on an adequate empirical inquiry, as it ignores the American record completely. The theory of modern capitalist imperialism as a question involving surplus capital "originated" in the United States by 1898 before the Boer War and before it "originated" in England. It originated in the United States as a pro-capitalist and

mic theory as such; and, in the sphere of political-science theory as such, University of Wisconsin Professor of Political Science Paul Samuel Reinsch's *World Politics*, published in 1900.[53]

Both Conant and Reinsch — Reinsch in greater political detail — formulated the basic strategy of the "Open Door" as an alternative to war, in terms of the need for a worldwide investment system as against a globally segmented one; in terms, that is, of shares instead of spheres, or shares in world development instead of spheres of interest or closed annexationist empires. But the distinguishing feature of the theory was the emphasis on investment expansion as differentiating modern capi-

pro-imperialist theory before it originated as an anticapitalist and anti-imperialist theory. If any pen is to be cited, it was Conant's, although he would most likely have cited Paul Leroy-Beaulieu's as far back as 1879 (*Essai sur la Repartition des Richesses*; see note 31, above). The search for one "originator" in matters of this sort is usually less than fruitful and, in this case, profoundly misleading. For his part, Lenin, in his *Imperialism*, was in essence doing little more than educating his readers "up to" the point reached years before by the "bourgeois" scholars and writers, and placing it within a political framework of his own. If there was anything original in Lenin's work, it was that political framework, not the theory of imperialism as such. See, e.g., Lenin's "Notebooks on Imperialism," *Collected Works*, Vol. 39 (Moscow: Progress Publishers, 1968), pp. 40–41, 207, 208, 212–213, 368, 375, 377, for bibliographical listings of, among many others, Conant, Jenks, Reinsch, Leroy-Beaulieu, W. T. Stead, T. Roosevelt, David Starr Jordan; not that Lenin necessarily read the listed works of these authors, but his listing indicates their routine inclusion in a well-known international literature in the early twentieth century. Cf. Kemp, *Theories of Imperialism*, pp., 64–66, 84–85. See also Parrini and Sklar, "New Thinking"; Norman Etherington, "The Capitalist Theory of Capitalist Imperialism," *History of Political Economy* 15:1 (Spring 1983), pp. 38–62.

53. Reinsch, *World Politics at the End of the Nineteenth Century, As Influenced by the Oriental Situation* (New York: Macmillan, 1900), esp. pt. 1, "National Imperialism," pp. 3–82, and esp. chaps. 1, 2, pp. 3–47. In four years, the book went through as many printings, all by Macmillan; the first was dated May 1900; the second, September 1900; the third, February 1902; the fourth, July 1904. Reinsch (p. vi) acknowledged University of Wisconsin colleagues, Professors Richard T. Ely, Charles Kendall Adams, Frederick J. Turner, and Charles H. Haskins, "for helpful suggestions as to the subject matter." For Jenks's use of Reinsch's book as a text in his classes at Cornell, Jenks to Reinsch, 25 Jan. 1901: "I have made so much use of your book, 'World Politics,' in one of my classes in Politics ..." Paul S. Reinsch Papers, Correspondence, 1892–1908, State Historical Society of Wisconsin, Madison. See also Reinsch's article for Walter Hines Page's newly founded magazine, *World's Work*: "The New Conquest of the World," *World's Work* 1:4 (Feb. 1901), pp. 425–431. By 1905, Reinsch had become one of the leading – perhaps the leading – American authority on modern colonial government and administration, with his books *Colonial Government: An Introduction to the Study of Colonial Institutions* (New York: Macmillan, 1902) and *Colonial Administration* (New York: Macmillan, 1905). Reinsch advised the Departments of State and War frequently, especially on Latin American affairs in the 1900s; he also made himself respected as a leading authority on China and on Asian culture and affairs in general. President Wilson appointed Reinsch his minister to China in 1913. Like Conant, Reinsch was a Democrat. Hobson (*Imperialism*, p. 146) quoted from *World Politics* and cited Reinsch as "an able writer."

talist imperialism from older territorial, settler, or commercial (goods-market) forms of imperialism, pre-capitalist and capitalist alike. Conant supplied the economic explanation, based on business-cycle and crisis theory. Reinsch elaborated the political explanation; that is, he explained how investment expansion differed basically from the older commercial and other forms of expansion in requiring new international political relations between investing and host societies, and among rival investing societies.[54]

The older commercial, territorial, or settler imperialism, if it did not displace or exterminate the host society in whole or in part, touched it only peripherally or superficially in its immediate and near-term impact. Modern capitalist-investment imperialism, in contrast, went to the very heart of the host societies' internal affairs from the outset, transforming basic class relations, social structures, and political institutions. Hence, it brought with it colossal and rapid upheavals in the host lands and in world politics, unprecedented in human history. Investment imperialism required extending capitalist (or modern) property relations, and the appropriate sociopolitical environment for capitalist property relations, into noncapitalist societies. It required "modernizing" the host government's fiscal, budgetary, and taxation systems; the host society's laws of property and contract along with its judicial administration; the host society's class structure in the direction of the commoditization of land and the creation of a wage-earning working class. It required the introduction and spread of secular and instrumental modes of consciousness at the expense of religious and traditionalist modes, through the institutions of education, media of communication, and otherwise. Investment imperialism required, as well, the tying of the host society's monetary and banking system into the international monetary, banking, and investment system, so that transfers of capital, foreign exchange, and repatriation of profits could proceed smoothly and routinely. In all these requirements, the large corporations and investment banking houses, both in their private operations and in their cooperation with government, were the chosen, if the only existent and conceivable, instrumentalities. The domestic and international dimensions of the corporate reorganization of capitalism were inseparable.

The precondition of establishing and sustaining modern capitalist imperialism in the nonindustrial societies, as distinguished from mere trade or discrete investments, was state-to-state relationships (whether within a colonial structure or between nominally independent states), in

---

54. See in particular Reinsch, *World Politics*, pt. 1, pp. 3–82, and Reinsch, *Colonial Government*, chaps. 5, 6, pp. 57–91, upon which is based the summary in the next paragraph of the text.

which the investing country's government adopted the goal of "modernizing" (or "civilizing") noncapitalist societies as a matter of state policy, that is, as a matter of national interest, and worked with the corporations and banks to reorient the host society's government, laws, and social relations to this end. Conant, like Reinsch, understood these things, referring to them in his published essays and dealing with them at greater depth in his state papers. The same may be said for Jenks, who dealt with such matters in his report to the War Department of 1902 on English and Dutch colonies in the Orient, and who by 1901 was already teaching Reinsch's book in his courses at Cornell. In the American view, as represented by Conant and Reinsch, the process as a whole, if it did not follow the ancient Roman model of universal empire or the more recent British and European colonial models (or the most recent Russian or Japanese patterns) of oppressive annexationism or national and cultural chauvinism, would bring development, progress, and modern civilization to the noncapitalist societies of the world – precisely by transforming them into capitalist societies. Conant and Reinsch advocated, and the United States Open Door policy attempted to implement, what would later be shrewdly analyzed by Karl Kautsky as "ultra-imperialism" (an analysis for which Lenin polemically denounced him) – that is, a policy of international cooperation among the great capitalist powers in allocating shares in the development of the nonindustrial world, in accordance with each capitalist nation's production and investment capacity. That, of course, would give the greatest single share (and world leadership, at least as *primus inter pares*) to the United States. The alternative to such inter-imperialist cooperation, Conant and Reinsch warned, was war.[55]

Historians who have looked first for trade and investment statistics as indicating the "economic" impetus for "political" imperialism have only half the story, and often half the story backward. Similarly, historians who find small foreign investments in a noncapitalist country, but a large amount of political activity there by an industrial country's government, and who conclude from this that the industrial country lacked surplus capital or that its government was "politically" or "ideologically" rather than "economically" motivated, uniformly fail to

---

55. Karl Kautsky, "Der Imperialismus," *Die Neue Zeit* 2:21 (Sept. 11, 1914); Conant, "Economic Basis," pp. 337–340; Conant, "The United States as a World Power. I.," pp. 608, 622; Reinsch, *World Politics*, pp. 39–40, 60–61, 69–70, 360–362. Cf. Brooks Adams, "Reciprocity or the Alternative," *Atlantic Monthly*, Aug. 1901, and, drawing upon Adams's article, Theodore Roosevelt, Message to Congress, Dec. 1901, at William A. Williams, ed., *The Shaping of American Diplomacy* (Chicago: Rand McNally, 1964), 1, pp. 424–426.

understand the question.[56] But that misunderstanding flows rather inevitably from an interpretive framework that compartmentalizes the political or ideological or cultural "factor" and the economic "factor" into discrete spheres. Surplus capital could not be invested on a large and sustained basis in countries not undergoing political modernization. Their lack of modernization, or resistance to it, hindered the industrial countries' solution of their surplus-capital problem – and throwing capital away in excessively risky investment environments was no alternative solution. Hence the need for political (or diplomatic) advance work. Secretaries of State John Hay, Elihu Root, Philander C. Knox, William J. Bryan, and Robert Lansing, as well as presidents McKinley, Roosevelt, Taft, and Wilson, understood all this very well. "Missionary" diplomacy was the very essence of rationalism in the strict sense of modernization theory.[57] It was the other side of the same coin occupied by "dollar diplomacy" and struck in the name of the Open Door and the new capitalist imperialism.[58]

56. Fairly representative of what might be called such inverted economic determinism is the following formulation: "Mahan, Conant, [Brooks] Adams, and the businessmen and politicians who dominated American thinking at the end of the 19th century were firmly convinced that the United States suffered from an overproduction of goods and a surplus of capital. In their view a radical expansion of foreign trade was the only feasible alternative to economic stagnation. On the basis of this analysis, which McKinley and his advisers shared, theorists of imperialism urged a variety of policies that would aid American commercial domination of the Far East. Yet neither commerce nor investments expanded at the expected rate." Of course, there was no "expected rate," and the thinking associated with Conant was not a stagnation thesis; far from it. It assumed continuing growth and development in and through the chronic tendency toward the decline in the rate of return on investment and toward relatively high levels of unemployment of capital and labor. It assumed, further, that if the latter conditions persisted without amelioration, not stagnation, but revolution would most likely result. The quotation is at the very interesting and valuable work by Marilyn B. Young, *The Rhetoric of Empire: American China Policy, 1895–1901* (Cambridge, Mass.: Harvard University Press, 1968), p. 229. Also along the same lines, in general interpretation, see Paul A. Varg, *The Making of a Myth: The United States and China, 1897–1912* (East Lansing: Michigan State University Press, 1968), and Varg, "The Myth of the China Market, 1890–1914," *AHR* 73:3 (Feb. 1968), pp. 742–758.

57. As Bryan was to put it while secretary of state, "The doctrine of universal brotherhood is not sentimentalism – it is practical philosophy." *Journal of the American Asiatic Association* 14:1 (Feb. 1914), p. 13. See Martin J. Sklar, "Woodrow Wilson and the Political Economy of Modern United States Liberalism," at Radosh and Rothbard, eds., *New History*, pp. 7–65, at pp. 36–38. For a study that comprehends the "missionary" perspective by a historian attuned to modernization theory, see Jerry Israel, *Progressivism and the Open Door: America and China, 1905–1921* (Pittsburgh: University of Pittsburgh Press, 1971), esp. Introduction and chap. 1, pp. xi–xxiv, 3–30.

58. For a fascinating glimpse of the absorption of the new thought by political leaders and administrators, see, e.g., William Howard Taft's discussion of the interrelations of institutional modernization, development, and capital investment in the Philip-

In comparison with the public and official writings of Conant, Jenks, and Reinsch, Hobson's *Imperialism* and Lenin's *Imperialism* are less informed and relatively unsophisticated. But in this respect, historians have generally ignored the American record and in particular the role of Conant and Jenks as advisers, policy formulators, and policy implementers in the years around the turn of the twentieth century, and the writings of Reinsch between 1900 and 1905.[59] The result has been both

pines, in his testimony as the United States civil governor of the Philippines, before the Senate Committee on the Philippines (Sen. Henry Cabot Lodge, chairman), in January–February 1902. Conant, having been sent there by Secretary of War Root, worked closely with Taft in Manila in 1901 on establishing a Philippine monetary and banking system suited to facilitating Philippine development through international capital investment. Taft returned to the United States to work with President Roosevelt and Secretary Root in persuading Congress to ratify legislation affecting the government and development of the Philippines, including the currency and banking legislation drafted in 1901 by Conant. Conant cooperated with Taft and the others in this work, lobbying with members of Congress and testifying before congressional committees. In the course of his testimony, Taft stated that the "Secretary of War was good enough to send us Mr. Conant, who is a banking expert" and that "the advantages that a country like England or a country like the United States would get from colonies of all descriptions are not confined to mere trade between the colonies and are not measured by the mere cost of administration of the colonies. The opportunities for investment under a secure government, under a friendly government, and the extension of those investments for the benefit not only of the islands or the colonies where the investments are made, but also for the benefit of the investors, is one exceedingly great, and I do not know any place in which it is better shown than it is in the book of Mr. Conant on the United States in the Orient." U.S. Senate, Committee on the Philippines, *Hearings*, "Affairs in the Philippine Islands," Sen. Doc. No. 331, pt. 1, 57th Cong., 1st Sess. (Washington: Government Printing Office, 1902), pp. 232, 408. For testimony by Conant in January 1902, see e.g., U.S. House of Representatives, Committee on Insular Affairs, *Hearings*, "Coinage System in the Philippine Islands," 57th Cong., 1st and 2d Sess., 1901–1903 (Washington: Government Printing Office, 1903), pp. 491–510, 511–530, 531–553, 554–555. Also, U.S. Department of War, Conant's *Special Report on Coinage and Banking* . . . (1901), pp. 31–33; Conant to Root, 11 Dec. 1901, Conant to Edwards, 13 Dec. 1901, 19 Dec. 1901, 3 Jan. 1902, 16 Jan. 1902, 25 Jan. 1902, 12 Mar. 1902, Vanderlip to Conant, 23 Jan. 1902, Joseph French Johnson to Conant, received 25 Jan. 1902, all in U.S. Department of War, NA RG 350/3197. See also note 45, above.

59.   See Parrini and Sklar, "New Thinking." In the 1930s, a memory trace of Conant's importance remained among scholars; cf., e.g., the statement by William L. Langer in the first footnote of his reappraisal of John A. Hobson's *Imperialism*: "I strongly suspect that Hobson . . . took over the idea [of surplus capital] from the very bourgeois American financial expert, Charles A. Conant, whose remarkable article, 'The Economic Basis of Imperialism,' . . . is now forgotten, but deserves recognition." Langer, "A Critique of Imperialism," *Foreign Affairs* 14 (1935–1936), pp. 102–119, at p. 102 n. 1. Cf. also, e.g., Albert K. Weinberg's references to Conant as an "expansionist" economist in his 1930s book, *Manifest Destiny: A Study of Nationalist Expansionism in American History* (Baltimore: Johns Hopkins University Press, 1935; Chicago: Quadrangle, 1963), pp. 275, 395, 424, 458. Neither Langer nor Weinberg indicated a knowledge of Conant's policy-making role or of his larger intellectual significance. Cf. Healy, *Expansionism*, pp. 194–209; M. B.

an inadequate understanding of United States foreign policy in general (and in particular, with respect to China) in the period 1896–1914, and a rather thorough, if essentially Euro-centered, misunderstanding of the "intellectual history" of the theory of modern capitalist imperialism.[60]

Conclusion

By the last years of the nineteenth century, a sophisticated body of new thought on property and the market had begun to crystallize in the nation's political and intellectual life. It affected judicial doctrine and hence the law of property, and it exerted an immediate impact on domestic and foreign policy-making. The new trend in legal doctrine and in political-economic theory alike represented the movement among those sectors of capitalists, political leaders, and intellectuals engaged in, or favoring, the corporate reorganization of the property-production system, that is, the supersession of the competitive-proprietary regime by a new corporate-administered order. The small-producer forces, however, were far from vanquished; with powerful fortresses in the political parties, in Congress, and in the ideas and values of a large part of the population, including influential sectors of the intelligentsia, they made a strong and protracted stand, particularly in the law of the market, as distinguished from the law of property. The great conflict between the small-producer and the pro-corporate forces shifted after 1896 from the monetary "Battle of the Standards" to the field of "Antitrust."

Young, *Rhetoric*, pp. 226–229; Etherington, "Reconsidering Theories," pp. 25–26, and "Capitalist Theory," pp. 46–47. For perceptive, if brief, remarks on the thinking of Conant and Reinsch and its political influence, see Akira Iriye, *Pacific Estrangement: Japanese and American Expansion, 1897–1911* (Cambridge, Mass.: Harvard University Press, 1972), pp. 68–71.

60. Langer, however, was aware of the role of what he called the "thoroughly bourgeois writers" in the United States in the origins of the theory of modern capitalist imperialism, but that awareness became submerged in predominantly Euro-centered scholarship and did not become part of the canon. Langer, *The Diplomacy of Imperialism, 1890–1902* (New York: Macmillan, 1935), 1, p. 68. Cf., e.g., the reference to "C. A. Conan" [sic] in Koebner and Schmidt, *Imperialism*, pp. 236–237, and more recently W. J. Mommsen's discussion of Conant under the theme of "Older Theories of Imperialism" (chap. 1), where he cites Conant as an anti-imperialist who published in British radical journals. Mommsen, *Theories of Imperialism*, pp. 10–11. By and large, American scholars professing themselves Marxists have followed the Euro-centered standpoint of prevalent scholarship. Cf. notes 51, 52, above.

3

The corporate reconstruction and the antitrust law

Introduction: The market and the law

The modern capitalist market is a realm of contracts and property rights, that is, a realm of law. In a capitalist society, to say "market" or "business" is to say "the law." As capitalist market relations develop, the law tends increasingly to permeate society, not only the public sphere of legislation and administration but also the private sphere of day-to-day relations in and out of the market. In proportion as market relations mature, the law displaces religion, just as the courts displace the church, and lawyers and judges, the clergy, in the regulation of everyday life. In the American vernacular as early as the mid-seventeenth century, the people go from God to cod. Hence, to understand property, to understand market relations, to understand politics, in a capitalist society and especially in a capitalist republic such as the United States, it is not sufficient, but it is certainly necessary, to understand the law – or, more precisely, the interrelations of property, class, the market, and the law.

There can be no modern capitalist market, as a sustained and stable system of social relations essentially coterminous with society as a whole, apart from the complex development and the certainty of the law. The law is the Latin of the market, just as the language of money and prices is the Vulgate. Certainty, here, does not mean changeless rigidity, but a consistency of logic and reasoning, which, though rooted in precedent, may also depart from it in adapting to, or providing for, changing conditions. Certainty means, in other words, a logic, whether instrumentalist or formalistically rational, that yields as reasonable predictability in both the constancy and the variability of the law. The whole structure of equity, credit, debt, liability, and obligation – the whole network, that is, of contractual relations and property rights that constitute a viable private investment marketplace – rests upon the foundation of known law and reliable judicial process.[1] Capitalist property and contractual relations did not originate in the law, but once having emerged, those relations will have laid a firm legal foundation or, in not so doing, signify and suffer distorted, arrested, and incomplete development, lacking sufficient roots in the institutions and commanding values of the society and hence vulnerable to erosion and decay.

The developing capitalist market brings with it not only "economic laws," in the form and substance of the discipline of political economy, or economics, but also a government subject to law – constitutionalism, written or unwritten – and a government administering the law, both public and private, without regard to person, in the marketplace. The modern capitalist market without the law is as little feasible as the church without religion. The courts are the church, the law the canon of everyday life, jurisprudence the theology. This is as true of laissez-faire capitalism as of regulated capitalism, less so of mercantilist than of modern liberal capitalism.

The rise, development, and stability of the capitalist order go hand in hand with the rise of a suitable legal order, which, however varied in other respects, is characterized by public legislation, open courts, universally accessible judicial process, endless litigation, lawyers, lawyers, and more lawyers. The modern capitalist market is a realm of law twice over. It is a realm of property based on exchange value, money, and contracts, or "economics"; as a realm of property it is, like other forms of society, a realm of law of class domination and its related arts of power, politics, and ideology; as a realm of economics, unlike other forms of society, it is a realm of law of contract, tort, money, and all the other accoutrements of the market. With the development of the

---

1. Cf. Max Weber, *Economy and Society: An Outline of Interpretive Sociology*, ed. Guenther Roth and Claus Wittich (New York: Bedminster, 1968), 2, pp. 880–900, esp. pp. 883, 890; *Max Weber on Law in Economy and Society*, ed. Max Rheinstein (Cambridge, Mass.: Harvard University Press, 1954), chap. 6, esp. p. 105, and pp. 304–305; David M. Trubek, "Max Weber on Law and the Rise of Capitalism," *Wisconsin Law Review* no. 3 (1972), pp. 720–753; Harold J. Berman, *Law and Revolution: The Formation of the Western Legal Tradition* (Cambridge, Mass.: Harvard University Press, 1983), pp. 545–548.

market beyond a simple commercial stage, toward the growing pro-
letarianization of labor and a rising multiplicity of complex contractual
relations, only the idiot or the powerless goes into the market without a
lawyer, and without political clout – something workers learned after
most capitalists had. The idea of a politically innocent capitalist market,
or an apolitical capitalist market, is a contradiction in terms.

There is no society more "political" than the "market society," that
is, capitalist society. The more economic a society becomes, the more
political it is bound to be. The more producers are drawn into the
market, the more they are drawn into politics. By the same token, the
"legal mind," in the secular mode, legalism, constitutional and legal historicism, philosophy of law, rise and develop with the bourgeoisie and
capitalist society. A legalistic mentality, whether in a judge or a politician, represents a characteristic mode of consciousness of a developed
or developing capitalist society. Coke and Blackstone were as historically integral to the flowering of capitalist society as coke and coal were to
the flourishing of the iron and steel industry and of steam-power technology, historically so central to the development of modern capitalism.
The symbolism of the jurists' names seems almost providential.

It is no accident that the American Declaration of Independence so
largely reads like, indeed is so largely, a lawyer's bill of indictment, nor
that lawyers and legalistic thought played so large a role in the founding
of the nation as well as in the nation's political life thereafter.
The American Revolution – not the French – was the quintessential
bourgeois revolution, on behalf of the quintessential market society.
De Tocqueville knew his subject in noting that in the United States,
lawyers were the surrogate aristocracy, "the highest political class," and
that the spirit and language of the law permeated the entire society.[2]
Lawyers and property owners, not pamphleteers and "ideologues" (like
Tom Paine), dominated or ultimately determined the founding politics
of the new American nation, as they have dominated the practice of the
nation's politics throughout its history. Commentators ever since have
erroneously supposed the "nonideological" character of American politics. It was a nation "born free" – in the binding rites of contract and
sanctity of the law, the Constitution being the highest contract, the
highest law. The Shaysites and whiskey rebels, the Natty Bumppos and
Billy Budds, of American history were not to forget it. If the courts
became the sacred temples of modern commerce, something more than
forums of order, the justices, the judges (not for nothing ritually robed),

---

2. Alexis de Tocqueville, *Democracy in America*, 2 vols. (1840; New York: Knopf,
   1945), 1, pp. 278–280; but see Perry Miller's reservations in Miller, *The Life of
   the Mind in America* (New York: Harcourt Brace & World, 1965), p. 114.

and the lawyers became, respectively, the college of cardinals, the bishops, and the priesthood, clothed in temporal power and presiding (in good Protestant fashion without a pope, though with a supreme synod) over many things, but whatever else, over the sanctity of lawful contracts, the disposal of property, and the rules of behavior in the market.

The law, in sum, is not some "reflection" of, or "superstructure" hovering above, capitalist property and market relations; it is an essential mode of existence and expression of those relations. When those relations are undergoing substantial change, so will the law, resulting in an evolutionary course of development, or, if change in the law is obstructed, in lawlessness and political disruption, if not in revolutionary upheaval. The process of change will be expressed in significant conflict in the spheres both of the market and the law, and hence in politics. The law becomes a major terrain of contest, as existing property and market relations come into conflict with emergent property and market relations (or relations of production). When the law falls into incongruity with emergent market and property relations, the ensuing politics that intervene to change the one or the other signify the conflict between established and emergent property and market relations, in this case, the United States in 1890–1916, between proprietary-capitalist and corporate-capitalist property and market relations.

In the period 1890–1916, proprietary-capitalist property and market relations came into conflict with, and were being displaced or transformed by, emergent corporate-capitalist property and market relations. As the law of market relations in its legislative and juristic phases became a major field of the conflict, and hence a central question of national politics, the law of money and banking, of railroad regulation, of labor organization, of restraint of trade, and of other market relations, came to center stage. All these involved the question of regulating, or administering, the market. Although the law of property accommodated rather promptly and without significant resistance to corporate instruments of property ownership and control, the law of restraint of trade became a storm center of political contention, and before the turn of the century it fell out of phase with the emergent corporate reorganization of the market, thereby posing a threat to the value and stability of corporate property. The politics of the trust question centered upon the law of restraint of trade.

The drafting of the Sherman Antitrust Act (1889–1890) and its subsequent early enforcement and judicial construction (1890–1911) became a critical field of contest among advocates of small producers, proprietary-capitalist property and corporate-capitalist property, and correspondingly between those favoring a regulated market suited to preserving and strengthening proprietary capitalism and those favoring a regulated market suited to encouraging, protecting, and legitimizing corporate capitalism. Cutting across these differences were those over the role of government, and the role of such private parties as pools, cartels, cooperatives, or corporations in the regulation process, as well as differences over the broader question of the state-society relation.

Once the law of restraint of trade and the emergent corporate-administered market were brought into correspondence on a sustained and stable basis, the trust question receded from the center of American politics, a major achievement of the Wilson administration. After 1914, with the passage of the Federal Trade Commission and Clayton Antitrust acts, which in effect gave legislative and administrative embodiment to the Supreme Court's "Rule of Reason" decisions in the Standard Oil and American Tobacco cases of 1911, the trust question remained a large issue at law but became, and has ever since remained, a peripheral, or minor, however histrionic, issue in national party politics. The respective regulatory roles of government and private parties, and the state-society relation, remain, of course, central political questions, but detached from the antitrust issue as such.

Legal historians have shown the need to understand the relation of changes in the law to changes in the uses and conceptions of property and to economic development in a market society. Their work has been particularly rich and effective in their study of eighteenth-century and antebellum nineteenth-century United States history (see note 6, Chap. 2). By and large, however, historians (legal as well as others) have understood the Sherman Act and its early judicial construction within the limits of such static conceptions as competition versus monopoly (or combination), centralization versus decentralization, protection of a consumer interest in efficiency, prevention of undue wealth transfers, and the trade-production distinction rooted in constitutional principles of dual (federal vs. state) jurisdiction. In so doing, they have shed much light on the subject, but they have ignored and obscured some things as well.[3] The Sherman Act and its early judicial construction invite study

3. See, e.g., Hans B. Thorelli, *The Federal Antitrust Policy: Origination of an American Tradition* (Baltimore: Johns Hopkins University Press, 1955); Donald Dewey, *Monopoly in Economics and Law* (Chicago: Rand McNally, 1959); William Letwin, *Law and Economic Policy in America: The Evolution of the Sherman Antitrust Act* (New York: Random House, 1965); Eliot Jones, *The Trust Problem in the United States* (New York: Macmillan, 1926); Oswald W. Knauth, *The Policy of the United States Towards Industrial Monopoly* (New York: Columbia University Studies, 1914); Robert H. Bork, "Legislative Intent and the Policy of the Sherman Act," *Journal of Law & Economics* 9 (Oct. 1966), pp. 7–48; Robert H.

from a historical standpoint, such as that employed with good effect by legal historians in other cases, and specifically from the standpoint of changes in the market and in uses and conceptions of property accompanying the passage of the United States political economy from the proprietary-competitive stage to the corporate-administered stage of capitalism.[4]

The redefinition of property at law and the reconceptualization of the market among capitalists and intellectuals around the turn of the century intersected with the continuing conflict in the courts over the law of the market governing restraint of trade. In the jurisprudence of antitrust law, the legal conflict, and to a large extent the ideological and political battle, between the small-producer and corporate outlook played itself out in a seesaw contest that extended over twenty-five years (1890–1914) before arriving at a definitive result. Both sides of the conflict, in their respective variations, had ready access to the courts and had fellow partisans at the bar and bench.

Little controversy attended the redefinition of property at law. The new thinking about market disequilibrium, cycles, and crises went forward in scholarly journals and high policy-making circles, somewhat removed from popular political discourse; but it overflowed into popular channels in debates over unemployment, overproduction, farm prices, foreign markets, money and banking, capitalism and socialism.

Lande, "Wealth Transfers as the Original and Primary Concern of Antitrust: The Efficiency Interpretation Challenged," *Hastings Law Journal* 34 (Sept. 1982), pp. 67–151; Charles W. McCurdy, "The *Knight* Sugar Decision of 1895 and the Modernization of American Corporation Law, 1869–1903," *BHR* 53 (Autumn 1979), pp. 304–342; Naomi R. Lamoreaux, *The Great Merger Movement in American Business, 1895–1904* (Cambridge University Press, 1985), chap. 6, pp. 159–186; Donald G. Morgan, *Congress and the Constitution: A Study of Responsibility* (Cambridge, Mass.: Harvard University Press, 1966), chap. 7, pp. 140–159.

4. Cf. Alfred D. Chandler, Jr., *The Visible Hand: The Managerial Revolution in American Business* (Cambridge, Mass.: Harvard University Press, 1977); J. Willard Hurst, *The Legitimacy of the Business Corporation in the Law of the United States, 1780–1970* (Charlottesville: University Press of Virginia, 1970); Morton J. Horwitz, "*Santa Clara* Revisited: The Development of Corporate Theory," *West Virginia Law Review* 88 (1985), pp. 173–224; Carl P. Parrini and Martin J. Sklar, "New Thinking About the Market, 1896–1904: Some American Economists on Investment and the Theory of Surplus Capital," *JEH* 43: 3 (Sept. 1983), pp. 559–578; Martin J. Sklar, "Woodrow Wilson and the Political Economy of Modern United Stated Liberalism" (1960), in Ronald Radosh and Murray N. Rothbard, eds., *A New History of Leviathan* (New York: Dutton, 1972), pp. 7–65: Alfred S. Eichner, *The Emergence of Oligopoly: Sugar Refining as a Case Study* (Baltimore: Johns Hopkins University Press, 1969); David F. Noble, *America by Design: Science, Technology, and the Rise of Corporate Capitalism* (New York: Knopf, 1977); William A. Williams, *The Contours of American History* (Cleveland: World, 1961), pt. 3, pp. 343–478.

The antitrust debates resounded in Congress and the state legislatures, proceeded in dramatic and well-publicized cases at law, and flooded the broader arena of popular politics. The courts did not produce legal doctrine on restraint of trade with the consistency and general agreement that characterized their revision of the definition of property. On the contrary, with respect to the law of restraint of trade, the partisans of a corporate-administered market, after initial victories in the courts in the 1890s, found the advocates of the small-producer outlook counterattacking and prevailing in Supreme Court majorities from 1897 to 1911. For almost fifteen years after 1897, the corporate reorganization of industry proceeded not only amid widespread popular hostility but also, as it pertained to the regulation of the market, within an incongruous legal order.

In effect, the revised law of property and the new thinking about the market established legal and intellectual grounds for the corporate reorganization of property ownership. Together they set the stage for the emergence of corporate market administration. But the law of restraint of trade, from 1897 until 1911–1914, obstructed and inhibited the development of the administered market regime envisioned by partisans of the corporate reorganization. The resulting incongruity of the legal order, combined with continuing popular hostility to corporate power, bred a sense of insecurity among corporate capitalists and underlay their complaints that political uncertainty hindered economic prosperity.

Apart from legislation that strengthened railroad regulation, in which a powerful consensus among farmers and capitalists favored "ganging up" on the railroads and making them contribute external economies to industry, agriculture, and foreign trade, there never were, in the years after 1890 and before 1914, majorities in Congress bold enough either to enact bills that might so much as appear to favor large corporations, or to enact bills that might dismantle them. The conflict, therefore, went forward extralegislatively, in the press, in party politics, in the courts, and, especially after the establishment of the Bureau of Corporations in 1903, in a running controversy between the executive and the judicial branches of the federal government. Its resolution came in part with the Supreme Court's Rule of Reason decisions of 1911 in the Standard Oil and American Tobacco cases, and definitively with the passage of the Federal Trade Commission Act of 1914. From 1897 to 1911, however, the pro-small-producer majority in the Supreme Court and the pro-corporate-policy orientation of the federal executive engaged in continual conflict. An understanding of this conflict is essential to understanding the antitrust debate of the early twentieth century, and to this understanding the law of restraint of trade as it zigzagged its way through the courts is, in turn, essential.

Before the Sherman Act

The enactment by Congress, on 2 July 1890, of the Sherman Antitrust Act focused the conflict between the small-producer and corporate outlooks on two basic questions: (1) Did liberty of contract include the liberty of private parties to restrict competition, and thereby, to that extent, the authority to regulate interstate and foreign trade and commerce? (2) Had Congress reserved to itself, to the exclusion of private parties, the power to regulate the interstate and foreign market, and in so doing made the restriction of competition by private parties in interstate commerce an unlawful restraint of trade? In the ensuing controversy, the resolution of the question at law turned on the technical-legal meaning of the common law with respect to restraint of trade, and on whether the Sherman Act was to be construed as having embodied, or rather as having superseded, the common law, which permitted reasonable restraints of trade. Pro-corporate partisans, of necessity, argued in and out of court that the Sherman Act enacted the common law, that is, gave the common law a statutory embodiment at the federal level. Small-producer partisans argued that the Sherman Act superseded the common law and thereby made restriction of competition as such by private parties, in interstate and foreign commerce, a criminal restraint of trade.

In the United States before the passage of the Sherman Antitrust Act, the common law as it had developed in Great Britain and the United States constituted the preeminent legal authority in matters of restraints of trade and monopoly. By 1890, twenty-one states and territories, most of them in the South and West, had incorporated provisions against restraints of trade in their constitutions or statutes. Many of these measures were first enacted only as late as 1888–1890. Although varying in particulars, these laws and constitutional provisions generally declared illegal those types of contracts and agreements that state courts had previously held to be void, unenforceable, or enjoinable at common law. Before 1890, however, as Hans B. Thorelli has noted, the states "made no determined attempts to enforce their laws," while "the limited number of state suits against the trusts . . . generally were based on common law doctrines or incorporation acts."[5]

5. Thorelli, *Antitrust Policy*, pp. 155, 156. Of the twenty-one states and territories, eight (Ark., Conn., Ga., Ind., Md., Mont., Wash., Wyo.) had constitutional provisions; seven (Iowa., Kans., Maine, Mich., Miss., Mo., Nebr.) had statutory mea-

By 1890, there existed no distinct federal body of common law on restraints of trade or monopoly. The states had for the most part occupied the field. Where federal courts assumed jurisdiction over cases of restraints of trade, they based their decisions upon precedent at common law made in British courts and in state courts in the United States. Because common-law precedent proved of fundamental significance in the drafting of the Sherman Act, and in the evolution of its judicial construction, it is necessary to examine what, at common law, the terms "restraint of trade," "monopolize," and "attempt to monopolize," as used in the Sherman Act, were taken to mean.[6]

With respect to agreements among parties to restrict competition among themselves (e.g., by one competitor selling out to another, or by agreements to control supply, limit output, fix prices, pool profits, or divide markets), it had become established at common law as early as 1831 with the case of *Horner* v. *Graves*[7] that such agreements were

sures; and six (Ky., N.C., N.Dak., S.Dak., Tenn., Tex.) had both. Cf. "Statutes and Digested Decisions of Federal, State, and Territorial Law Relating to Trusts and Industrial Combinations," prepared by Jeremiah W. Jenks, Expert Agent (with assistance of Herbert A. Heminway), in U.S. Industrial Commission, II: *Trusts and Industrial Combinations*, H. R. Doc. No. 476, 56th Cong., 1st Sess. (Washington, D.C. Government Printing Office, 1900), vol. 2, pt. 1, pp. 5–264.

6. Cf. U.S. Bureau of Corporations, Department of Commerce, *Trust Laws and Unfair Competition*, by Joseph E. Davies, Commissioner of Corporations, 15 Mar. 1915 (Washington, D.C.: Government Printing Office, 1916), p. 24: "The importance of the common law decisions becomes even more evident when it is perceived to what extent the courts, in deciding cases under both State and Federal Statutes, have cited such decisions." Also, ibid., p. 10. Hereafter cited as Davies, *Trust Laws*. Davies's statement represents the pro-corporate agrument; it also corresponds with the facts. President Wilson appointed Davies head of the Bureau of Corporations (commissioner of corporations) in 1913 and then appointed him first chairman of the Federal Trade Commission upon its establishment by Congress in 1914. On the relevance of common-law cases, particularly in state courts and in the absence of a distinct jurisprudence in federal courts, see Thorelli, *Antitrust Policy*, pp. 36, 53; also, Donald Dewey, "The Common-Law Background of Antitrust Policy," *Virginia Law Review* 41:6 (Oct. 1955), pp. 759–786, at 783. Cf. Dewey, *Monopoly*, chap. 11: "The Origins of AntiTrust Policy," pp. 139–157.

7. 7 Bingham 735. This was a British case. The common law of Britain and the United States was considered at the bar as a single body of jurisprudence. Although its development in Britain had by the late nineteenth century permitted greater freedom of contract at the expense of unrestricted competition than that in the United States, nevertheless principles established by British courts at common law were considered by United States courts to be as authoritative precedents upon which to render decisions as those established at common law in United States courts. See Circuit Judge William Howard Taft's review of common-law cases on restraint of trade, including *Horner* v. *Graves*, at *U.S.* v. *Addyston Pipe & Steel Co. et al.*, 85 *Federal Reporter* 279 (8 Feb. 1898); there, discussing *Horner* v. *Graves*, Taft cited British Chief Justice Tindal "as the highest English judicial authority on this branch of the law" (ancillary as against direct restraints). On the

legal unless, whatever their form, they directly and unduly or unreasonably restrained competition and were therefore detrimental to the public interest. Central to common-law doctrine were the procedural rule that each case be settled on its merits in the light of the facts, and the substantive rule, affirmed in *Horner* v. *Graves*, that "Whatever is injurious to the interests of the public is void, on the grounds of public policy."[8] In the course of the next sixty years, and particularly during the 1870s and 1880s, as pools, combinations, and consolidations multiplied, the courts in the United States elaborated this substantive common-law principle into a complex body of doctrine. Several leading court decisions in cases at common law during the 1880s indicate what at common law constituted invalid restraints of trade and monopoly by 1890 when Congress passed the Sherman Antitrust Act.

The well-known case of *Central Ohio Salt Company* v. *Guthrie*,[9] decided by an Ohio state court in 1880, concerned a pool of Ohio salt manufacturers and sellers formed for the purpose of regulating prices, dividing profits, and restricting production. The court, in refusing to enforce the agreement against a recalcitrant member, held that although it was settled at common law that all contracts restraining only a part of trade in a given line of business were not necessarily void as against public policy, contracts restraining trade completely were against public policy and therefore void. The court's opinion, however, was directed not against the right of the parties to the agreement to restrict competition among themselves but against what the court considered to be the agreement's clear intent and inevitable result, namely, the establishment of monopoly, that is, the attempt by the parties to prevent all competition on the part of others, over and above restricting competition

authority of British common-law precedent in United States courts, see also Thorelli, *Antitrust Policy*, pp. 19, 36–39, and Dewey, "Common-Law Background," p. 783. Hereafter, *Federal Reporter* will be cited: vol. no. *Fed.* page no.; this source is the official report of arguments and decisions in federal district and circuit court cases. *United States Reports* is the similar official report for U.S. Supreme Court cases, and will be cited: vol. no. *U.S.* page no.

8. Cf. Memorandum of Herbert Knox Smith, commissioner of corporations, prepared for U.S. Senate Subcommittee of the Committee on the Judiciary, *Hearings*, "Amendment of the Sherman Antitrust Law," 60th Cong., 1st Sess., 8 May 1908, in *Hearings Before Subcommittee of the Committee on the Judiciary, U.S. Senate, during 60th, 61st, 62nd Congresses, compiled for Consideration of H.R. 15657*, 63rd Cong., 2nd Sess., 1914 (Washington, D.C.: Government Printing Office, 1914), p. 331. Hereafter cited as H. K. Smith, *Memorandum* (1908). Like Davies's (note 6, above), Smith's statement was representative of the pro-corporate argument. Like Davies's, also, it was essentially accurate. See Eliot Jones, *Trust Problem*, p. 302, for discussion of *Horner* v. *Graves*.

9. 35 Ohio State 666.

among themselves. The court therefore refused to aid in the enforcement of the agreement.[10]

In the same year, 1880, in the Missouri case of *Skrainka* v. *Scharringhausen*,[11] the state court of appeals upheld an agreement among twenty-four quarry operators to sell through an exclusive sales agent that apportioned output and specified prices. The association had sued a recalcitrant member, who, having violated the agreement, refused to pay the prescribed fine. The court held that although the agreement constituted a restraint of trade, it was a valid restraint at common law, because it worked no "public mischief," did not tend "to deprive men of employment," nor "unduly raise prices, cause a monopoly, or put an end to competition." Indeed, said the court, "we know of no case in recent times in which a contract such as the one before us has been declared illegal."[12]

Two other leading cases at common law in the United States during the 1880s demonstrate the consistency with which the courts construed common-law principles: *Dolph* v. *Troy Laundry Machinery Company*[13] and *Central Shade-Roller Company* v. *Cushman*.[14] Although in these cases the courts based their decisions in part upon a distinction between articles of convenience to the public and articles of necessity, and in the Shade-Roller case in part upon the rights of patent ownership, they nevertheless invoked principles at common law pertinent to trade in general as well.

The Dolph case, decided in 1886, significantly by a federal court, concerned an agreement between the two leading manufacturers of washing machines in the United States. The companies entered the agreement for the purpose of avoiding deleterious consequences of competition between themselves and securing higher prices and greater profits. The Dolph company sued the Troy company to recover damages after the latter had terminated the contract prior to its expiration. The federal Second Circuit Court for the Northern District of New York sustained the Dolph company, holding the agreement valid. Judge William J. Wallace, for the court, ruled: "Assuming that, in entering into the contract, ... the only purpose in view was to promote the interests of the parties, and enable them to obtain from customers higher prices ..., it is not obvious how such a contract contravenes any

10. See discussion of this case by Justice John Marshall Harlan in his dissenting opinion in *U.S.* v. *E. C. Knight Co.*, 156 *U.S.* 27–28 (21 Jan. 1895); cf. Jones, *Trust Problem*, p. 304; Thorelli, *Antitrust Policy*, pp. 41, 42.
11. 8 Missouri Appeals Reports 522.
12. As cited and quoted at Jones, *Trust Problem*, pp. 308–309.
13. 28 *Fed.* 553–559.
14. 143 Mass. 353.

principle of public policy." The contract was legally valid. It "did not contemplate suppressing the manufacture or sale of machines by others ... and the law of demand and supply would effectually counteract any serious mischief likely to arise from the attempt of the parties to get exorbitant prices." The court held that it was "quite legitimate for any trader to obtain the highest price he can for any commodity in which he deals," and that is was "equally legitimate for two rival manufacturers or traders to agree upon a scale of selling prices for their goods, and a division of their profits." Nor was it "obnoxious to good morals, or to the rights of the public," that competitors "agree to consolidate their concerns and that one shall discontinue business ... for a specified period," as in the case at hand. Although the public might have to pay higher prices for the particular goods, it was not obliged to purchase them, for the agreement did not attempt to suppress competition from other producers. It therefore fell short of "a conspiracy between the parties to control prices by creating a monopoly."[15]

In 1887 a Massachusetts state court, facing essentially similar issues, upheld the Shade-Roller sales company against one of its constituent companies. The court decided that the contract did not restrain the production or sale of shade-rollers; its purpose was, by establishing price stability, to enlarge production. The court reasoned, moreover, that the contract "does not look to affecting competition from outside, ... but only to restrict competition in price between themselves [the parties to the contract]." It ruled that "A natural purpose and a natural effect [of the contract] is to maintain a fair and uniform price, and to prevent the injurious effects both to producers and consumers of fluctuating prices caused by undue competition. When it appears that the combination is used to the public detriment, a different question will be presented from that now before us." Even should such an agreement tend to raise prices, said the court, "it is one which the parties have a right to make. To hold otherwise would be to impair the right of persons to make contracts, and to put a price on the production of their own industry." The court therefore upheld the contract as neither an invalid restraint of trade nor a contravention of public policy, because it was beneficial to the parties and not necessarily injurious to the public.[16]

In the leading British case, *Mogul Steamship Company, Ltd.* v. *McGregor, Gow & Company*, decided in 1889,[17] the court held that

15. 28 *Fed.* 555–556.
16. Quoted and discussed at Davies, *Trust Laws*, pp. 53–57; Jones, *Trust Problem*, pp. 310–311; Thorelli, *Antitrust Policy*, p. 47.
17. 21 Q.B.D. 544, affirmed 1892, A.C. 25.

not only agreements restricting competition that affected part of a line of business or trade, but also those that covered a whole line of business or trade, were valid at common law, provided such agreements did not prevent outsiders from entering into competition and did not affect prices or supply in a manner deleterious to the public interest.

By the early 1890s, therefore, the general rule at common law with respect to restraint of trade stipulated that voluntary restraints among parties, whether partial or general, to maintain prices at a profitable level and to protect their business interests, were to be held reasonable and therefore valid, provided their intent or effect did not exceed such purposes, were not considered to be detrimental to the public interest, and did not include the physical prevention of, or a conspiracy to prevent, others from entering or remaining in the line of business or trade concerned – that is, did not restrain the trade of outsiders, or did not prevent or seek to prevent competition. The courts held freedom of contract essential to the public welfare and individual liberty, and considered unreasonable and therefore invalid and enjoinable at common law those restraints that interfered grossly with public welfare or violated another individual's liberty of contract or right to compete.[18]

All these cases, in one form or another, concerned pools or cartel-type agreements among independent, potentially competitive concerns. Before the enactment of the Sherman law, comparatively few corporate combinations as such were challenged in the courts. But between 1888 and 1892 several dramatic cases were brought in state courts by either state governments or private parties to contest the legality of certain corporate combinations effected by the trustee device. Because these cases included suits against such great aggregations of capital as the "Diamond Match Trust,"[19] the "Standard Oil Trust,"[20] the "Sugar Trust,"[21] and the "Whiskey Trust,"[22] they attracted public attention disproportionate to their importance in the development of restraint-of-

---

18. Cf. Judge Walter H. Sanborn's discussion of these and other common law cases in his opinion for the court in *U.S.* v. *Trans-Missouri Freight Association et al.*, 58 *Fed.* 71–72; among the other common-law cases, the leading ones included *Wiggins Ferry Co.* v. *Chicago and Alton Railroad Co.* (73 Missouri 389); *Gibbs* v. *Consolidated Gas Co. of Baltimore* (134 *U.S.* 396); and the British case *Nordenfelt* v. *Maxim Nordenfelt Co.* (A.C. 535). See also, H. K. Smith, *Memorandum* (1908), pp. 344–347; cf. Thorelli, *Antitrust Policy*, pp. 20, 30, 34, 35.

19. *David M. Richardson* v. *Christian H. Buhl and Russell A. Alger*, 77 Mich. 632 (1889). Alger became President McKinley's secretary of war in 1897, preceding Elihu Root.

20. *State* v. *Standard Oil Co.*, 49 Ohio State 137 (1892).

21. *The People of the State of New York* v. *The North Sugar Refining Co.*, 121 N.Y. 582 (1890).

22. *State* v. *Nebraska Distilling Co.*, 29 Neb. 700 (1890).

trade jurisprudence. But their impact upon the public, together with their large combinations of capital, impressed the problem of the concentration and consolidation of capital with the cognomen "the Trust Question." Similarly, these cases imprinted upon both contemporaneous and subsequent congressional legislation the popular title "Antitrust Laws," although most corporate combinations were not trusts.[23]

In the match, oil, sugar, and whiskey trust cases, the trustee devices were declared illegal, not because they constituted combinations or represented a particular method of combination as such, but on one or both of two other grounds. The first, having nothing necessarily to do with restraint of trade or with the common law, held that the particular corporations, in entering the trust agreements, had acted *ultra vires*, that is, had exceeded the powers granted them in their respective corporation charters issued by the states. The second, wholly consistent with, and an application of, common-law principles, held that the particular trusts had undertaken to establish monopolies in their respective lines of business, that is, to acquire the whole business for themselves by preventing outside competitors from pursuing trade or maintaining their independent existence.[24]

The basic principle of common-law doctrine on restraints of trade was "the well-established distinction ... between reasonable and unreasonable restraint of trade,"[25] reasonable restraints being valid and enforceable, unreasonable restraints being (if challenged) void and enjoinable. The general consistency with which courts in the United States construed the common law with respect to restraint of trade did not mean that their decisions in cases were similarly consistent or routinely predictable. In some cases, judges refused to apply the test of reasonableness or ignored it altogether in rendering decisions. In most cases concerned with restraint of trade, judges applied the common-law test of reasonableness to declare contested contracts and agreements invalid. The minority of cases in which judges upheld restraints as valid, however, embraced as broad a range of practices as in the larger number of adverse cases, and the types of practices upheld were similar. Beyond this, and perhaps of greater significance, although most courts in the United States applied the common law with less leniency toward restraint of trade than was customary in British courts, still in the majority of cases – and, what is more important, in the leading and precedent-setting cases – courts in the United States recognized the test of reason-

23. Jones, *Trust Problem*, pp. 311–317.
24. *Cf.* Thorelli, *Antitrust Policy*, pp. 80, 50, 161; Jones, *Trust Problem*, pp. 311–317; Davies, *Trust Laws*, pp. 58–69.
25. H. K. Smith, *Memorandum* (1908), p. 332.

ableness as integral to common-law doctrine on restraints of trade and applied it accordingly.[26]

By 1890, the line between "reasonable" and "unreasonable" did not lie in the distinction between restrictions of competition that were general or universal and those that were partial or local.[27] Accordingly, the intent or effect of the restraint, rather than the fact of the restraint or its form or extent, figured as the controlling consideration at common law, and the standard for judging the intent or effect was its reasonableness or unreasonableness. In short, restriction of competition did not necessarily constitute an unreasonable (invalid) restraint of trade.

Let us now summarize and indicate some of the implications of what at common law the terms "restraint of trade," "monopolize," and "attempt to monopolize," were taken to mean at the time Congress enacted the Sherman law.

Invalid restraints of trade at common law were those contracts, agreements, or combinations that were unreasonable and therefore void, unenforceable, and enjoinable at the bar; those that were reasonable remained valid and enforceable. A reasonable restraint accorded with "public policy," or with the "public interest" or "public welfare."[28]

It should not be supposed that judges could seize capriciously upon these latter concepts to render decisions simply in accordance with their personal predilections or biases, whether corrupt or honest. For the concepts themselves embodied principles enunciated in common-law precedents and strictures. These, in turn, were rooted in the dogma of natural liberty as it had developed and as it had infused the common law by the latter part of the nineteenth century. Indeed, the common law, by this period, may be described as the juristic hypostatization of the dogma of natural liberty, as the two had evolved *pari passu* in Britain and the United States.[29]

26. Cf. Thorelli, *Antitrust Policy*, pp. 40, 44.
27. H. K. Smith, *Memorandum* (1908), 342–344; Davies, *Trust Laws*, 29–31, discussing *Diamond Match Co. v. Roeber*, 106 N.Y. 473 (1887) and *Watertown Thermometer Co. v. Pool et al.*, 51 Hun. 157: N.Y. (1889).
28. H. K. Smith, *Memorandum* (1908), pp. 330–331; Thorelli, *Antitrust Policy*, pp. 19, 40–47; George Stuart Patterson, "The Case of the Trans-Missouri Freight Association," *American Law Register and Review* n.s., 36 (May 1897), pp. 307–321, esp. pp. 314–320 for review and discussion of British and U.S. (including state) cases, particularly with reference to the centrality of public policy in determining reasonableness.
29. Cf. Thorstein Veblen, *The Theory of Business Enterprise* (1904: New York: Mentor, 1958), pp. 128–129, 130. See also pp. 133–134, 215 n.9 and chap. 8: "Business Principles in Law and Politics," pp. 128–143.

At common law, the public interest required an expansion of production and trade. But expansion was assumed to be most assuredly achieved by the guarantee of liberty of private contract and the rights of private property, two fundamental precepts of the natural liberty doctrine. Under these conditions, it was assumed, individuals who pursued their personal interests and entered into contractual relations best served the expansion of production and trade with increasing efficiency and at lower cost to the community.[30] Accordingly, restraints of trade (restriction or regulation of competition) were held reasonable and valid at common law, and therefore enforceable, under the following conditions: when such restraints, not otherwise unlawful, were purely ancillary to legitimate agreements or contracts (whether among competitors or noncompetitors) for the purchase, sale, or production of goods, services, or plant; or when contracts or agreements involving nonancillary, but direct, restraints undertook to maintain prices at levels guaranteeing fair returns on invested capital or, in other words, sought to maintain against what might otherwise become "destructive" or "ruinous" competition the remunerative nature of market activity; and when restraints did not restrict production of goods or rendering of services, or raise prices, to a point considered dangerous to the public welfare; and when they did not seek, or actually result in, an unwarranted prevention of others from entering into the particular line of business, or from competing. If contested, a contract, agreement, or combination found to exceed these bounds thereby stood as unreasonable and void. Nevertheless, at common law an unreasonable restraint that did not itself include an unlawful act or conspiracy was neither criminally punishable nor liable to civil suit for damages: It was void, nonenforceable, or enjoinable, should its validity be successfully contested in court.[31]

The particular forte of the common law was that it left wide discre-

---

30. Cf., e.g., the Ohio court's decision in *Central Ohio Salt*, which stated in part (35 Ohio State 672): "Public policy, unquestionably, favors competition in trade to the end that its commodities may be afforded to the consumer as cheaply as possible, and is opposed to monopolies, which tend to advance market prices, to the injury of the general public." See Justice Harlan's discussion in his dissent in *E. C. Knight*, 156 *U.S.* 27–28; Taft's decision for the lower federal court in *Addyston Pipe*, 85 *Fed.* 279; H. K. Smith, *Memorandum* (1908), p. 341; and Davies, *Trust Laws*, pp. 35–36, discussing, inter alia, *Hubbard* v. *Miller* (27 Mich. 15, 1873).

31. H. K. Smith, *Memorandum* (1908), pp. 330–331. " . . . a contract in restraint of trade, even though avoidable and unenforceable, had none of the elements of a tort." Ibid., p. 331. Also, Dewey, "The Common-Law Background," pp. 784–786, and at p. 786: "The enforcement of contracts imposing 'direct' restraints on trade turned upon their 'reasonableness.' The tort action afforded no relief to victims of unfair competition no matter how blatant."

tion with the courts to judge each case on its merits, for it thereby permitted flexibility among private parties in regulating the market and in developing new market relations with changing circumstances. At the same time, judicial discretion had to be founded upon definite principles embodied in common-law precedent that safeguarded both the public interest and the rights of property and liberty of contract. In the United States, the inviolability of lawful contractual obligations and of lawful contractual liberty frequently came into conflict; but within the framework of judicial resolution of the conflicts, contractual liberty had in general not only attained protection at common law but had also acquired further reinforcement by federal constitutional guarantee,[32] including the Fifth and Fourteenth amendments as construed by the courts.[33]

"Monopolize," or "attempt to monopolize" originally had two meanings at common law as it had evolved in Britain: first, the sole possession on the part of a person or group of persons of a market or branch of industry or trade that derived from royal grant or "letters patent"; second, such sole possession or attempt at such possession that derived from or involved any or all of the practices designated as badgering, forestalling, engrossing, and regrating.[34] The first type of monopoly had become a thing of the past in Britain by the late nineteenth century; in the United States it had never been relevant after independence. Although state legislatures had conferred monopoly

32. Veblen, *Theory*, p. 131: "[In the United States] the metaphysics of natural liberty, pecuniary and other, was embodied in set form in constitutional enactments. It is therefore involved in a more authentic form and with more incisive force in the legal structure of this community than in that of any other. Freedom of contract is the fundamental tenet of the legal creed, so to speak, inviolable and inalienable; and within the province of law and equity no one has competence to penetrate behind this first premise or to question the merits of the natural-rights metaphysics on which it rests.... The citizen may not be deprived of life, liberty, or property without due process of law, and the due process proceeds on the premise that property rights are inviolable."

33. Cf. Justice Rufus W. Peckham's celebrated definition of the term "liberty" as protected in the Fifth and Fourteenth amendments, in his opinion of 1 Mar. 1897 for a unanimous Supreme Court in *Allgeyer* v. *Louisiana* (165 *U.S.* 578–593, at 589): "The liberty mentioned in that amendment means not only the right of the citizen to be free from the mere physical restraint of his person, as by incarceration, but the term is deemed to embrace the right of the citizen to be free in the enjoyment of all his faculties; to be free to use them in all lawful ways; to live and work where he will; to earn his livelihood by any lawful calling; to pursue any livelihood or avocation, and for that purpose to enter into all contracts which may be proper, necessary and essential to his carrying out to a successful conclusion the purposes above mentioned."

34. U.S. Senate, Committee on Interstate Commerce, *Trusts in Foreign Countries*, compiled by Fred A. Johnson (Washington, D.C.: Government Printing Office, 1912), p. 139.

rights upon favored corporations, by the mid-nineteenth century general incorporation laws in the states, and such judicial doctrine as that embodied in the Charles River Bridge case of 1837, made even this practice one of diminishing significance. With respect to the second type of monopoly, in Britain the penal statutes on badgering, forestalling, engrossing, and regrating were repealed in 1772 (12 George III, ch. 71); the common law was thereby left unaided, and in 1844 its repeal with respect to these practices prohibited further suits against them (7, 8 Victoria, ch. 24).[35] The theory that underlay these repeals held that unmitigated freedom of contract and the resultant operations of the market would nullify any advantages or evil consequences from an attempt at monopoly, that the practices formerly prohibited "tended to fructify and develop trade" rather than restrain it, that "the course of trade could not be made free by obstructing it, and that an individual's right to trade could not be protected by destroying such right."[36]

In the United States, the practices signified by the terms "badgering," "forestalling," "engrossing," and "regrating" were not significantly relevant in judicial procedure at common law,[37] in view, perhaps, of the apparently vast expanse of the domain and therefore of the market. The steady expansion southwestward and westward of the national boundaries before the Civil War, and of people and enterprise after it, along with a supply or concentration of capital relatively insufficient (at least until the late nineteenth century) to permit any one person or group of persons to acquire sole control over such huge commercial horizons, seemed to render the danger of badgering, forestalling, engrossing, or regrating all the more remote and irrelevant.

Accordingly, in both the United States and Britain, "monopolize" and "attempt to monopolize" came to mean the preventing or attempting to prevent others from entering, or competing in, a market or line of business, by a person or group of persons, corporate or otherwise, who sought thereby to control prices and supply. A contract, agreement, or combination to restrict competition in prices, sales, or production, that

35. Ibid., p. 139; Davies, *Trust Laws*, pp. 2–3; Thorelli, *Antitrust Policy*, pp. 14, 16–17; Arthur M. Allen, "Criminal Conspiracies in Restraint of Trade at Common Law," *Harvard Law Review* 23 (1910), pp. 531, 534 (here will also be found succinct legal definitions of forestalling, engrossing, and regrating).

36. Chief Justice Edward D. White, for the Supreme Court, in *Standard Oil Co. of N.J. et al. v. United States* (221 U.S. 55, 56), in *Federal Anti-Trust Decisions, 1890–1917*, 4 (1917), pp. 125, 126 (hereafter cited as vol. no. *FAD* page no.). Cf. Davies, *Trust Laws*, p. 2: ". . . as long as the fundamental laws of property and of trade contemplate and favor a system of individual activity and free contract the power of competition will assert itself to a wide extent, even though monopolistic agreements are not prohibited."

37. Thorelli, *Antitrust Policy*, p. 52.

did not operate to close the channels of trade to others, was therefore not guilty of "monopolizing" or "attempting to monopolize." For example, a corporation, company, partnership, or entrepreneur might acquire sole possession of a market or of the production of a line of goods through skillful enterprise, superior efficiency, and the like without "unduly" affecting prices or production. Although a monopoly by dictionary definition and in eocnomic theory, such market power did not constitute a monopoly at common law unless in achieving or seeking to maintain its position it undertook to prevent others from trying their hand at competition if they so chose. Monopoly at common law, therefore, was a special case of an unlawful restraint of trade, a manifestation, a form, or a consequence, of an unreasonable restraint of trade.[38] Nor was it considered an unreasonable restraint for one competitor to buy out the plant of another if done in the course of normal expansion or the quest of greater efficiency. Here again, "monopolize" or "attempt to monopolize" at common law was liable neither to criminal prosecution nor to civil suit for damages, but was merely void, unenforceable, or enjoinable as against public policy.

The common law, then, was not intended to protect weaker or inefficient competitors from stronger or more efficient competitors, nor even to compel competition. Indeed, as Hans B. Thorelli has well said, the common law "never proved a very effective means in actually throttling monopoly, much less in fostering competition. In fact, it may well be questioned whether it ever purported to do so."[39] Rather, by the late nineteenth century it was intended to safeguard the right of individuals freely to enter the market and make contracts, and to let the operations of the market determine the outcome.

The achievement of "bigness" per se was not unlawful, nor was the restriction of competition among capitalists to preserve or enhance the profitability of the trade or production in which they were engaged.

38. See, e.g., Chief Justice White in *Standard Oil*, 221 *U.S.* 61, 62, at 4 *FAD* 131; Holmes's dissent in *Northern Securities* Co. v. *United States*, 193 *U.S.* 197–411, at 404. Cf. Myron W. Watkins, *Industrial Combinations and Public Policy: A Study of Combination and the Common Welfare* (Boston: Houghton Mifflin, 1927), p. 236: "... the difference between 'restraints upon trade' as that phrase came latterly to be understood and attempts to monopolize was a difference only of form or degree. Monopolization was simply the more far-reaching, the more pervasive, the more permanent scheme for controlling the market." Also, Thorelli, *Antitrust Policy*, pp. 39–40, 53; Richard S. Harvey and William F. Notz, *American Foreign Trade as Promoted by the Webb–Pomerene and Edge Acts* (Indianapolis: Bobbs-Merrill, 1921), p. 27.
39. Thorelli, *Antitrust Policy*, p. 51; to similar effect, Paul H. Rubin, *Business Firms and the Common Law: The Evolution of Efficient Rules* (New York: Praeger, 1983), pp. 21–22.

Should a group of entrepreneurs, companies, partnerships, or corporations enter into voluntary agreements among themselves on such matters as ownership, prices, production, or sales in order to guarantee a fair return on their invested capital, or should business concerns buy the plants of competitors for purposes of expansion or increased efficiency, they would not thereby be engaging in "unfair" or "unreasonable" restraints of trade or monopoly, unless in so doing they undertook to prevent others from competing – that is, placed involuntary restraints on others – or overstepped their bounds by imposing intolerable burdens upon the public, for example, in the form of outrageous prices or the withholding of necessaries of life. The overriding principle at common law in the United States was not unrestricted competition, but the natural liberty principle of freedom of contract: that is to say, the right to compete, not the compulsion to compete.[40]

The Sherman Act

By the late 1880s, it had become increasingly evident, and a commonplace at law, that liberty of contract neither implied nor yielded unfettered competition. The market activity of capitalists brought the two principles into growing conflict. Common-law doctrine, in upholding both liberty of contract and the right to compete, permitted reasonable restrictions of competition among contracting parties.[41]

On its face, the Sherman Antitrust Act, in a manner similar to state antitrust laws, superseded the common law procedurally in two respects: (1) It made restraints of trade that were held to contravene public policy criminally illegal, as misdemeanors, punishable by the government. (2) It rendered such restraints liable to private, civil suits for treble damages.[42] The question remained whether the Sherman Act

40. The freedom-of-contract principle might be limited by "public policy" as well as by the "police power" of the state (to safeguard the health, safety, morals, and welfare of the community) and by the power to regulate commerce constitutionally endowed upon state legislatures and Congress. But freedom of contract was considered a vital element of the general welfare and public policy in the U.S. legal and political tradition. "The only principle (attested habit of thought) which may contest its primacy in civil matters is a vague 'general welfare' clause; and even this can effectively contest its claims only under exceptional circumstances. Under the application of any general welfare clause the presumption is and always must be that the principle of free contract be left intact so far as the circumstances of the case permit." Veblen, *Theory*, p. 131. Veblen here overstates his case, neglecting the force of the commerce clause, the "necessary and proper" clause, and the doctrine of "public policy" itself.
41. For Veblen's differing view, see *Theory*, pp. 130, 131.
42. Cf. *In re Greene*, 52 *Fed*. 104–119, at 111 (4 Aug. 1892). "The act of July 2, 1890 ... goes a step beyond the common law, in this: that contracts in restraint of

sustained or superseded the common law substantively, that is, whether or not it enacted the common-law distinction between reasonable and unreasonable restraints of trade in determining the validity or illegality of contracts, agreements, and combinations. The great debate over the meaning of the Sherman Act within the federal judiciary revolved around this question from 1890 until the matter was definitively settled in 1911 with the Supreme Court rulings in the Standard Oil and American Tobacco cases.

Section 1 of the Sherman Act declared illegal "every contract, combination in the form of trust or otherwise, or conspiracy, in restraint of trade or commerce" among the states or with foreign nations, and held every person convicted of a violation guilty of a misdemeanor punishable by fine or imprisonment or both. Section 2 declared "Every person who shall monopolize, or attempt to monopolize, or combine or conspire with any other person or persons, to monopolize any part" of interstate or foreign trade or commerce, guilty (upon conviction) of a misdemeanor and subject to the same punishment.[43]

The significant terms for judicial construction were "restraint of trade," "monopolize," and "attempt to monopolize." They all had acquired meaning at common law and were for that reason appropriated for use in the Sherman Act. In the ensuing years the Supreme Court justices who favored strict prevention of restrictions of competition, whether reasonable or unreasonable, argued that the Sherman Act had superseded common law both procedurally and substantively. This group, a majority between 1897 and 1911, was led by Justice John Marshall Harlan. The justices who insisted upon the distinction between reasonable, legal restrictions of competition, and unreasonable, illegal restrictions, argued that the Sherman Act constituted merely a federal statutory embodiment of the common law. This group, led by Justice (later Chief Justice) Edward Douglass White and, after 1902, also by Justice Oliver Wendell Holmes, Jr., represented the minority view from 1897 until 1911.[44]

> trade, while unlawful, were not misdemeanors or indictable at common law. It adopts the common law in making combinations and conspiracies in restraint of ... trade and commerce criminal offenses, and creates a new crime." Also, *U.S.* v. *American Tobacco Co. et al.*, 164 *Fed.* 711, at 3 *FAD* 443–444; and H. K. Smith, *Memorandum* (1908), pp. 330, 331.
>
> 43. Act approved and signed by President Benjamin Harrison, 2 July 1890, *Congressional Record*, 51st Cong., 1st Sess., 2 July 1890, vol. 21, p. 7, p. 6922 (26 U.S. Stat. 209). The word "person," or "persons," included corporations and associations (sec. 8). Section 3 extended the provisions of section 1 to the internal and external trade of territories of the United States.
>
> 44. The two groups were not identical in composition in every ease. But Harlan and White were usually to be found on opposite sides in Sherman Act cases, with

The Sherman Act was considered by its principal authors and floor managers in the United States Senate – Republican senators John Sherman of Ohio, George F. Hoar of Massachusetts, and George F. Edmunds of Vermont – as a federal enactment of the common law with respect to restraints of trade and monopoly.[45] In three of the first four cases brought under the act against business concerns by the federal government, and finally disposed of in the lower federal courts between 1890 and 1897,[46] the courts construed the act's meaning according to the precedent and interpretation previously established at common law. That one of the four cases stood apart mirrored, in the lower courts, the division of opinion within the federal judiciary soon to become manifest in the Supreme Court. By and large, these decisions reinforced the view that the Sherman Act essentially constituted federal enactment of the common law on restraints of trade and monopoly. The question nevertheless awaited definitive settlement by the Supreme Court.

The common-law intent of the framers of the Sherman law is evident in its legislative history. It originated as a bill from the Senate Finance Committee, drafted by Sherman, the committee's chairman. Sherman's version, first introduced in the Senate on 4 December 1889, was reintroduced amended in detail on 21 March 1890. It would have made illegal "all arrangements, contracts, agreements, trusts, or combinations" among citizens of different states or territories or foreign countries, "made with a view or which tend to prevent full and free competition" in imported goods or in goods "of growth, production, or manufacture" in the United States or its territories, or "in the transportation or sale" of goods. It also declared illegal all arrangements, contracts, agreements, trusts, or combinations "made with a view or which tend to advance the cost to the consumer." All such acts were declared to be "against public policy, unlawful, and void," and liable to civil suit for double damages by injured parties. Sherman's bill would have directed

justices David Josiah Brewer, Henry Billings Brown, Rufus W. Peckham, and Chief Justice Melville Weston Fuller often joining Harlan, and justices Stephen Johnson Field, George Shiras, Jr., Horace Gray, and, later, Holmes often concurring with White. As an example of changeability, although Fuller and Peckham joined Harlan in the Trans-Missouri and Joint Traffic cases, Peckham writing the decisions, they joined White and Holmes in the Northern Securities case.

45. See notes 52–62 to this chapter and related text.
46. See notes 64–72 to this chapter and related text. Not until 1895 did the Supreme Court render its first decision in a Sherman Act case involving a combination of capital, that of *U.S. v. E. C. Knight Co. et al.* (156 U.S. 1); in the same year, the Court rendered its decision in the case *In re Debs*, involving a combination of labor. But in neither case did the Court attempt a comprehensive interpretation of the meaning of the Sherman Act. It did not undertake to do so until the next Sherman Act case reached the Court in 1897, that of *U.S. v. Trans-Missouri Freight Association* (166 U.S. 290).

and empowered the United States attorney general, United States district attorneys, and the federal courts to put a stop to all the proscribed practices through judicial process. The Senate Finance Committee subsequently deleted Sherman's original provision of a fine of up to $10,000 and imprisonment of up to five years, or both, for convicted persons, including not only officers, trustees, and stockholders of corporations, but also anyone acting as their "agent" or "attorney."[47]

On the same day, 21 March, that Sherman introduced the revised bill, Senator John H. Reagan, the Texas Democrat who as a representative had co-authored with Senator Shelby Cullom (Republican-Illinois) the Interstate Commerce Act of 1887, and who was justly known as a champion of farmers' sentiments in the effort to regulate railroads, introduced as a substitute to Sherman's bill an ostensibly far more stringent bill expressing militant agrarian hostility to the market power of associated capital. Reagan's bill, which the Senate would later defeat, defined a "trust" as "a combination of capital, skill, or acts by two or more persons, firms, corporations, or associations of persons," involved in interstate or foreign commerce, for any of the following purposes: (1) to "create or carry out any restrictions in trade"; (2) to "limit or reduce the production or to increase or reduce the price" of goods; (3) to "prevent competition in the manufacture, making, purchase, sale, or transportation" of goods; (4) to "fix a standard or figure whereby the price to the public [of any goods] shall be in any manner controlled or established"; (5) to "create a monopoly in the making, manufacture, purchase, sale, or transportation" of goods; (6) to undertake in agreements or contracts in any form "not to manufacture, sell, dispose of, or transport [goods] ... below a common standard figure" or "to keep the price ... at a fixed or graduated figure, or ... establish or settle the price ... so as to preclude free and unrestricted competition among themselves and others ... or ... to pool, combine, or unite in any interest they may have ... that its [a good's] price may, in any manner, be so affected." Any person convicted of participation in such a "trust" was to be "deemed guilty of a high misdemeanor," subject to fine up to

47. *Cong. Rec.*, 51st, 1st, 21 Mar. 1890, vol. 21, pt. 3, pp. 2455, 2463; Joseph B. Foraker, *Notes of a Busy Life* (Cincinnati: Stewart & Kidd, 1916), 2, pp. 170–171. The Senate Finance Committee eliminated the criminal feature of the bill, including penalties, to meet the criticism that the courts would not uphold a criminal statute that did not precisely define the nature of the offense, a rule the terms, preventing "full and free competition" and advancing "the cost to the consumer," could not meet. Procedurally, therefore, the committee invoked the common-law remedial device of making the offenses "unlawful, and void," as "against public policy," although not punishable, except that the Justice Department and the courts were directed and empowered to enforce the law by judicial process, and that injured parties could sue for double damages.

$10,000, "or imprisonment at hard labor" up to five years, or both; "each day" of violation was to be held "a separate offense."[48]

Reagan's bill, though more penally severe, did not differ in essential principle from Sherman's bill; but it did differ in specifying offenses left implicit in Sherman's bill and in making those offenses criminal acts punishable by fine and imprisonment. Both bills expressed the extreme atomistic idea of the competitive marketplace peculiarly evocative of the commercial farmer's predicament, and perhaps that also of the self-employed, especially rural or small-town, working proprietor. However much these small entrepreneurs might have preferred price-making and production-controlling power for themselves, through cooperation or in some other way, it was beyond their reach. If they could have no such power, they wanted no others to have them, for it made the market a place of unequal advantage and hence unjust. The language of Sherman's bill, no less than that of Reagan's, reflected the widely popular small-producer outlook aimed at enforcing the competitive mechanism against any attempts by metropolitan capitalists to regulate production or prices, and particularly any attempt by capitalists to acquire price-making power.[49] In this sense, Sherman's original bill was, potentially, a radical anti-corporate measure; it would have superseded rather than embodied the common law. Taken literally and strictly enforced, it would have placed the corporate reorganization of the market beyond the pale of the law. Sherman's bill, like Reagan's, moreover, would probably have made most, if not all, practical business relations beyond the level of the solitary proprietor at least legally suspect when not positively criminal. Making "full and free competition" compulsory, aside from revolutionizing the Anglo-American law of the market, in effect would have outlawed the developed metropolitan market – on the assumption that such a law, once passed, could or would be enforced at all.

Sherman, however, did not intend his proposed legislation to carry such implications or consequences. His intent, rather, was twofold: (1) As an astute national political leader, he sought to reconcile metropoli-

---

48. *Cong. Rec.*, 21:3, p. 2456. On 8 Apr. 1890, the Senate rejected Reagan's bill, 13 yeas, 36 nays, 33 absent. Ibid., 21:4, p. 3151. On Reagan's role in the drafting of the Interstate Commerce Act, see George W. Hilton, "The Consistency of the Interstate Commerce Act," *Journal of Law & Economics* 9 (Oct. 1966), pp. 87–113, at 103–107.

49. A substitute amendment offered unsuccessfully by Republican Senator John Ingalls of Kansas, in a gesture for votes needed for reelection in the heavily populistic Kansas legislature, would have regulated trading in options and futures in agricultural commodities and punished speculative abuses. *Cong. Rec.*, 21:3, pp. 2462–2463. Cf. David J. Rothman, *Politics and Power: The United States Senate, 1869–1901 (New York: Atheneum, 1969), p. 173*

tan and provincial forces within the Republican party and in the body politic at large; (2) as one who affirmed modern industrial, or business, development, he sought a uniform law to govern the national market as it was evolving toward its corporate reorganization. He thought this dual objective might be accomplished by drafting a law that drew upon the "free market" language satisfactory to bourgeois agrarian and provincial (or "populist") opinion, but that would remain subject to common-law construction by the courts. This intent appeared clearly in his major address on the Senate floor, on 21 March 1890, in support of his bill.

Sherman noted that the urgency of Congressional action had become apparent to the Senate because the people "are feeling the power and grasp of these combinations, and are demanding of every [state] Legislature and of Congress a remedy for this evil, only grown into huge proportions in recent times. They had monopolies and mortmains of old, but never before such giants as in our day. You must heed their appeal," he warned the Senate with no little exaggeration, "or be ready for the socialist, the communist, and the nihilist." More realistically, Sherman reminded his colleagues: "Society is now disturbed by forces never felt before. The popular mind is agitated with problems that may disturb social order." Among these, "none is more threatening than the inequality of condition, wealth, and opportunity" that had emerged "within a single generation" from "the concentration of capital in vast combinations to control production and trade and to break down competition."[50] His bill, said Sherman, was "an honest effort to declare

50. *Cong. Rec.*, 21:3, p. 2460. Whatever their other differences, Democratic and Republican senators widely agreed on the urgency of the trust question. Cf. statements by Democratic senators George G. Vest of Missouri and James Z. George of Mississippi, both critics of Sherman's bill. Vest: "... no one can exaggerate the importance of the question pending ... or the intensity of feeling which exists, especially in the agrricultural portions of the country in regard to it.... I appreciate fully the significance of the remark of the Senator from Ohio when he says that unless relief is given, to use the language of Mr. Jefferson, 'worse will ensue.'" Ibid., p. 2463. George: "The country calls on us loudly for relief; the Senate is being pressed now, urged now to go on with this bill, because we ought to take some step, make a beginning to show that we are opposed to trusts." Ibid., 21:4, p. 3148. It should not be inferred from Sherman's remarks that he believed equality possible. Although he understood, and rendered a healthy respect for, the popular appeal of the equalitarian expectation in American political life, he regarded the United States as no different in this respect from other civilizations based on private property. As a political leader, he often deferred publicly to American exceptionalist pretensions, but privately he observed: "Undoubtedly the tendency of all civilizations is to make the rich richer and the poor poorer, with sudden fluctuations and changes in life beyond the control of prudence and care, but these have always existed and always will exist in any society where property is protected. Labor becomes more abundant and cheaper, property increases and the

a rule of action." Although the Senate was "always conservative," yet it had "always been ready to preserve, not only popular rights in their broad sense, but the rights of individuals as against associated and corporate wealth and power."[51]

Nevertheless, the bill was meant, Sherman explained, to regulate, not to abolish, large corporations or prevent their further development. Combination of capital in large corporations provided the vehicle of progress in transportation and production under modern conditions. He acknowledged – in fact, he said, "I assert" – that not only "the tendency of all combinations of corporations," but also "the inevitable effect of them," was "to prevent competition and to restrain trade," something that "must be manifest to every intelligent mind." But such a tendency was not necessarily illegal or dangerous to the public interest. On the contrary: "The combination of labor and capital in the form of a corporation to carry on any lawful business is a proper and useful expedient, especially for great enterprises of a quasi public character, and ought to be encouraged and protected as tending to cheapen the cost of production"; Sherman also cited "the vast development of our railroads and the enormous increase of business and production of all kinds" as attesting to the "good results of corporate power." As devices that "have enabled individuals to unite to undertake great enterprises only attempted in former times by powerful governments," he noted, "Corporations tend to cheapen transportation, lessen the cost of production, and bring within the reach of millions comforts and luxuries formerly enjoyed by thousands." Accordingly, "Experience has shown that they are the most useful agencies of modern civilization."[52]

The question, then, was how to reconcile a policy that would encourage and protect corporations, which as agencies of modern civilization inevitably restricted competition and restrained trade, with the plain terms of Sherman's bill. Sherman's answer was (1) that the terms were to be understood not literally but as shaped by the common-law tradition, which distinguished between unlawful and lawful restraints of

fortunate few enjoy the greater share of the blessings of life. He would be a wise man who could change this course of civilization, and a very bold one to try to do it." Sherman to W. Sprague, 15 Jan. 1884, quoted at H. Wayne Morgan, *From Hayes to McKinley: National Party Politics, 1877–1896* (Syracuse, N.Y.: Syracuse University Press, 1969), p. 42.

51. *Cong. Rec.*, 21:3 (21 Mar. 1890), p. 2460. Invoking the older natural liberty tradition, Sherman also said in this connection: "It is the right of every man to work, labor, and produce in any lawful vocation and to transport his production on equal terms and conditions and under like circumstances. This is industrial liberty and lies at the foundation of the equality of all rights and privileges." Ibid., p. 2457.

52. Ibid., pp. 2460, 2457.

trade and restrictions of competition, and (2) that the federal courts would so construe the bill's terms. As he put it, the bill "does not announce a new principle of law, but applies old and well recognized principles of the common law to the complicated jurisdiction of our State and Federal Government." The bill would enable the federal courts to invoke the common law on restraints of trade; it "would be construed liberally" by the courts, not literally. The courts "will distinguish between lawful combinations in aid of production and unlawful combinations to prevent competition and in restraint of trade."

Citing recent litigation involving the Standard Oil Trust, Sherman stated, "I accept the law as stated by Mr. [Samuel C. T.] Dodd," general counsel of Standard Oil, "that all combinations are not void, a proposition which no one doubts." Hence, Sherman explained, "It is the unlawful combination, tested by the rules of common law and human experience, that is aimed at by this bill, and not the lawful and useful combination." In aiming "only at the unlawful combinations," the bill "does not in the least affect combinations in aid of production where there is free and fair competition," that is, where "corporate rights granted to one are open to all," as under the general incorporation laws of the states, and where a corporation, however large, did not improperly prevent others from competing or did not contravene the public interest. The bill, in sum, "has for its single object to invoke the aid of the courts of the United States . . . to supplement the enforcement of the established rules of the common and statute law by the courts of the several states." Sherman reasoned that because "it is difficult to define in legal language the precise line between lawful and unlawful combinations," that distinction "must be left for the courts to determine in each particular case. All that we, as lawmakers, can do is to declare general principles, and we can be assured that the courts will apply them so as to carry out the meaning of the law, as the courts of England and the United States have done for centuries."[53]

Other pro-corporate senators, while entirely agreeing with Sherman's legislative intent, doubted with good reason that the bill as drawn could accomplish it. The bill's leading phrases, "full and free competition" and "advance the cost to the consumer," although possibly gratifying small-producer and popular anti-corporate sentiment, were not particular matters of concern at the common law and, at any rate, did not have the settled meaning at common law that "restraint of trade" and "monopoly" had. Sherman's assurances notwithstanding, there was no

53. Ibid., pp. 2456, 2459–2460, 2457, 2460.

guarantee that the courts would construe the bill as simply embodying common-law doctrine and precedent. There was, indeed, the strong possibility that the courts would construe the bill as superseding the common law and would refuse to risk the appearance of usurping the legislative function by reading into a law a meaning that could not be held beyond doubt to have been intended by Congress.

To the trained legal mind, there were other grave defects in Sherman's bill. Its imprecision had made it necessary to reduce it from a criminal to a civil statute and hence to delete criminal penalties for violations; it thereby made the Senate appear to be treating the "trusts" with a leniency regarded as impolitic in view of the intensity of popular opinion. But perhaps most important from the legal standpoint were two other aspects of the bill: (1) The Supreme Court might well find in the phrases "full and free competition" and "cost to the consumer" an unconstitutional deprivation of property and liberty without due process; and (2) the Supreme Court might find that the phrase "growth, production, or manufacture" exceeded federal jurisdiction over interstate and foreign commerce by encroaching upon the jurisdiction of the states. This latter defect was particularly salient in light of the Court's decision as recently as 1888, delivered by Justice Lucius Q. C. Lamar, in the case of *Kidd* v. *Pearson*, which sharply and clearly distinguished between Congress's authority to regulate interstate and foreign commerce on the one hand, and the states' authority to regulate property ownership and production on the other.[54] This defect also needlessly jeopardized pro–states' rights southern support for the bill.

In summary, the bill as drawn by Sherman would probably not have fulfilled his common-law intent. It might also be found in whole or in part unconstitutional by the courts. Hence senators who as members of the Senate Judiciary Committee were more conversant than Sherman with legal and constitutional subtleties, or who as southerners and New Englanders were particularly sensitive to constitutional issues since the Civil War and Reconstruction eras (James Z. George of Mississippi,

---

54. *Kidd* v. *Pearson*, 128 *U.S.* 1 at 20–22 (decided 22 Oct. 1888). Justice Lamar held that giving Congress authority to regulate manufacture (or production) would invalidly insert Congress's authority into state and local jurisdictions. Lucius Quintus Cincinnatus Lamar, the prominent post–Civil War Mississippi "Redeemer" and exponent of North–South reconciliation, served as President Cleveland's secretary of the interior, 1885–1888, and, on appointment by Cleveland, as justice from 1888 to 1893. See also *Coe* v. *Erroll*, 116 *U.S.* 517 (1886). Cf. Charles W. McCurdy, "American Law and the Marketing Structure of the Large Corporation, 1875–1890," *JEH* 38:3 (Sept. 1978), pp. 631–649; Morgan, *Congress*, chap. 7, pp. 140–159, at pp. 142–148, 150.

John T. Morgan of Alabama, Edmunds of Vermont, and Hoar of Massachusetts) took leading roles in the effort to replace Sherman's bill with the version that ultimately passed.[55]

Sherman had earned wide and genuine respect as a skilled and popular national political leader and as an expert in financial and currency matters, but, as he was the first to concede, he was no great lawyer or expert in legal and constitutional affairs.[56] Whether for that reason or for political reasons, neither he nor the Finance Committee was able to produce a substantially different bill. In an extraordinary action, the Senate, on motion of senators George and Morgan, took the bill away from Sherman and the Finance Committee, and referred it to the Judiciary Committee.[57]

Within two weeks, on 8 April 1890, the Judiciary Committee unani-

55. Discussion on the constitutional issue of federal versus state jurisdiction, as well as the question of common-law intent, punctuated the entire Senate floor debate on 21 Mar. 1890. *Cong. Rec.*, 21:3, pp. 2455–2472. E.g., Vest (p. 2463): "... What we want is one thing, what we can do is another; and for Congress to pass a law which will be thrown out of the Supreme Court under the terrible criticism that any such law must invoke is simply to subject ourselves to ridicule and to say to our constituents that we are powerless to enact laws which will give them relief. This bill, if it becomes law, must go through the crucible of a legal criticism which will avail itself of the highest legal talent throughout the entire Union. It will go through a furnace not seven times but seventy-seven times heated, because the ablest lawyers in this country, it goes without saying, are on the side of the corporations and of aggregated wealth."

56. E.g., Sherman's statement on the Senate floor during debate on his bill: "Indeed, as I lost the suit of my first client some thirty-five years ago, when I entered public life, I am not very familiar with the practice of the courts ..." Ibid., p. 2604 (25 Mar. 1890). Cf. Hoar's remark on the Senate floor, on 8 April: "I suppose no member of this body who remembers the history of the processes by which this bill reached the shape in which it went to the Judiciary Committee will doubt that the opinions of Senators themselves, of able and learned and experienced lawyers, were exceedingly crude in this matter." Ibid., 21:4, p. 3146.

57. Ibid., 21:3, pp. 2604, 2610–2611, 2731. Sherman acquiesced in the move, but he noted on the Senate floor, "it is a very unusual proceeding in the Senate of the United States, very rarely resorted to, to refer the action of one committee to another. It is not a wise proceeding to take at any time. ... Such a course would create controversies and contention and rivalry between committees. ... As a general rule, such a proposition ought not to be made; but in this particular case I appeal to every Senator to say whether it would be wise to do it." Sherman feared that referral to the Judiciary Committee might be intended as a way of killing the bill without putting senators on record as having voted against a popular measure: "If it is proposed to kill this measure, let it be done in a fair and legitimate way." Ibid., p. 2604. Democratic Senator Zebulon Vance of North Carolina, in extended and witty remarks, expressed the same fear, referring to the Judiciary Committee as one of "the receptacles where we deposit our dead," and where a bill "sleeps the last sleep known to the literature of this Senate," offering in the process "the strains of that familiar old hymn: Hark! from the tombs a doleful sound; /Mine ears attend the cry./Come, living men, and view the ground/Where your bills must shortly lie. (Laughter)." Ibid. (25 March 1890), p. 2610.

mously reported a substitute bill in exactly the version ultimately passed by Congress, which became known as the Sherman Antitrust Act. Sherman immediately declared his support for the bill.[58] It would be more accurate to call the law the Edmunds Antitrust Act. A leading Republican senator since 1866, Edmunds had by 1890 earned the reputation as the Senate's foremost constitutional authority; in earlier years, he had ranked in this respect second only to Senator William Pitt Fessenden of Maine. As chairman of the Judiciary Committee, Edmunds drafted the bill in its essential provisions. With contributions also by committee members William M. Evarts (Republican of New York, formerly secretary of state under Hayes), Hoar, George, and John Ingalls of Kansas, the Judiciary Committee pointedly centered the legislation in its operative clauses on the common-law terms, "restraint of trade" and "monopolize, or attempt to monopolize."[59]

Managing the new bill on the Senate floor, Edmunds and Hoar reemphasized and amplified its common-law intent, with which, they held, the bill's explicit terms were now made consistent. For example, Senator John E. Kenna of West Virginia inquired of Edmunds whether the committee intended to make it an offense "if an individual . . . by his own skill and energy, by the propriety of his conduct generally, shall pursue his calling in such a way as to monopolize a trade." Edmunds

---

58. Ibid., 21:4 (8 Apr. 1890), p. 3145. The Senate passed the bill on that day, 8 April, by a vote of 52 yeas, 1 nay, 29 absent. The House passed the bill, with substantial amendments of its own, on 1 May. It required two conferences before both houses agreed to the Senate bill, exactly as drafted by the Senate Judiciary Committee and passed by the Senate, which then became law on 2 July 1890. Ibid., 21:4, p. 3153; 21:5, pp. 4086–4096; 21:7, p. 6922.

59. Text of bill as reported by the Judiciary Committee, ibid., 21:4 (8 Apr. 1890), p. 3145. Edmunds drafted sections 1 (restraint of trade), 2 (monopolize), 3 (territories), 5 (giving federal courts general subpoena power), and 6 (forfeiture of property involved in violations); Evarts contributed the phrase "in the form of trust or otherwise" in sections 1 and 3; George drafted section 4 (giving federal circuit courts primary jurisdiction, and the attorney general and U.S. attorneys authority to initiate prosecutions); Hoar drafted section 7 (treble damages); Ingalls drafted the eighth (and last) section (defining "persons" to include corporations and associations). See Foraker, *Busy Life*, 2, pp. 160–171; William A. Robinson, "George Franklin Edmunds," *Dictionary of American Biography* 6 (1931), pp. 25–26; Francis E. Leupp, "The Father of the Anti-Trust Law," *Outlook* 99 (30 Sept. 1911), pp. 271–276; Albert Henry Walker, "Who Wrote the Sherman Law?" *Central Law Journal* 73 (13 Oct. 1911), pp. 257–259; Thorelli, *Antitrust Policy*, pp. 212–214; and Letwin, *Law and Economic Policy*, p. 94, and 94 n. 9. The Judiciary Committee's bill, and the act as passed, restored the legislation to its original status as a criminal statute, with violations made misdemeanors punishable by up to $5,000 fine and up to one year imprisonment, or both, as against $10,000 and five years in Sherman's original bill and in Reagan's bill; it permitted suit by injured parties for treble damages, instead of the double damages allowed in the Sherman bill.

replied, "It is not intended by it and the bill does not do it. Anybody who knows the meaning of the word 'monopoly,' as the courts apply it, would not apply it to such a person at all; and I am sure my friend must understand that." Hoar spelled it out. He had had, he said, "that precise difficulty in the first place with this bill," but the committee members unanimously agreed that "'monopoly' is a technical term known to the common law ... which has a clear and legal signification, and it is this: It is the sole engrossing to a man's self by means which prevent other men from engaging in fair competition with him."[60] Hence, the words "monopolize, or attempt to monopolize," were meant to signify not an actual monopoly in economic or lay terms, not bigness or market power as such, but a form of "restraint of trade" resulting from invalid methods intended to drive others out of business or to prevent others from entering business. Accordingly, in the bill as a whole, Hoar stated, "We have affirmed the old doctrine of the common law in regard to all interstate and international commercial transactions, and have clothed the United States courts with authority to enforce that doctrine." Indeed, "The great thing that this bill does, except affording a remedy [and making violations criminal offenses], is to extend the common-law principles, which protected fair competition in trade in old times in England, to international and interstate commerce in the United States."[61]

To leave nothing undone in establishing the common-law meaning of the act, after the Senate passed the bill, it amended the title in a manner which, although seeming trivial to the untrained eye, made a basic, if subtle, difference. The title was changed from "A bill to declare unlawful trusts and combinations in restraint of trade and production" to "A bill to protect trade and commerce against unlawful restraints and monopolies."[62]

60. Edmunds added, "This subject was not lightly considered in the committee, and ... we studied it with whatever little ability we had..." Senators Kenna, Edmunds, and Hoar, *Cong. Rec.*, 21:4 (8 Apr. 1890), pp. 3151–3152.
61. Ibid., 21:4 (8 Apr. 1890), pp. 3146, 3152. Cf. Edmunds: "... the committee, I think unanimously, ... thought that if we were really in earnest ..., as a new line of legislation, we would frame a bill that should be clearly within our constitutional power, that we should make its definition out of terms that were well known to the law already, and would leave it to the courts ... to say how far they could carry it or its definitions as applicable to each particular case as it might arise." Ibid., p. 3148. Cf. also remarks of Representative David B. Culberson of Texas, who managed the bill for the House Judiciary Committee on the House floor: "Now, just what contracts, what combinations in the form of trusts, or what conspiracies, will be in restraint of the trade or commerce mentioned in the bill will not be known until the courts have construed and interpreted this provision." Ibid., 21:5 (1 May 1890), p. 4089.
62. Ibid. 21:3 (21 Mar. 1890), p. 2455; 21:4 (8 Apr. 1890), p. 3153. By deleting

It is plain, then, that the distinction between reasonable and un-reasonable, lawful and unlawful, restraints of trade and monopoly and that the corollary distinction between "good" and "bad" combinations (or "trusts"), were not the sudden inventions of political leaders like Theodore Roosevelt, or of the Supreme Court majority that delivered the Rule of Reason decisions of 1911. Rather, by 1890, those distinctions already constituted a well-established juridical principle embodied in the common-law doctrine on restraint of trade and monopoly. The authors of the Sherman Act intended the distinctions to be construed as essential to the act's meaning.[63]

Judicial construction, 1890–1897

Given the common-law distinction between reasonable and unreasonable restraints of trade and the legislative intent of the Sherman Act's framers, it was neither surprising nor an act of judicial legerdemain, though it was significant, that for the most part the lower federal courts, from 1890 to 1897, interpreted the law accordingly. For exam-

"production," the title also reflected the constitutional concern of not asserting federal authority in a jurisdiction held to be reserved to the states. Cf. Morgan, *Congress*, p. 148. Cf. also George Stuart Patterson, "Trans-Missouri Freight Association," p. 316, noting that American courts had consistently held invalid restraints of trade at common law to be those that were unreasonable as against public policy: "Is not the title of the act in harmony with this view? It reads: 'An act to protect trade and commerce against unlawful restraints and monopolies'; not an act to protect trade against any restraint whatsoever, but an act to protect trade against unlawful restraints – that is, unreasonable ones – and it is submitted that the title of the act can be used as an aid to the construction of the body of the statute..."

63. Cf. Knauth, *Policy of the United States*, p. 33; Davies, *Trust Laws*, p. 10; "Speech of Senator Hoar, delivered in the Senate, Tuesday, January 6, 1903," at Senate Subcommittee of the Committee on the Judiciary, *Hearings*, "Amendment of the Sherman Antitrust Law," 60th, 1st (28 Apr. 1908), p. 232. Hereafter cited as *Hearings* (1908): Cf. also concurring opinion of Judge Hook, *U.S.* v. *Standard Oil Co.*, 173 *Fed.* 196–197, at 3 *FAD* 725–726; and as to the significance of the statute's title, Justice Holmes's dissent in the Northern Securities case, at 193 *U.S.* 405. See also Thorelli, *Antitrust Policy*, p. 571. Thorelli's interpretation (pp. 570–571) tends to identify congressional and judicial opinion concerning liberty with that concerning competition; at another level, it identifies competition in the economic sense with competition in the legal sense. His interpretation of the meaning of the Sherman law and of its jurisprudence is, accordingly, different from that offered here. His work, nevertheless, is comprehensive, a gold mine of information, and although written more than twenty-five years ago, it remains unsurpassed as a source on federal antitrust policy and still the starting point among secondary works for scholars interested in the subject. Without detracting from the value of Thorelli's work, this comment is nevertheless intended to suggest the need for fresh studies of the law of property and the market in the late nineteenth and early twentieth centuries, based also on the work of Commons, Veblen, Jones, Hurst, Dewey, and Letwin, to which this study is offered as a preliminary contribution.

ple, in the case of *United States* v. *Nelson et al.*,[64] which concerned an agreement among lumber dealers in the Midwest to advance the price of pine lumber fifty cents per thousand feet in five states (Illinois, Iowa, Minnesota, Missouri, and Wisconsin), the Eighth Circuit court in the District of Minnesota, on 10 October 1892, dismissed the indictment, construing the Sherman Act on common-law grounds. Judge Rensselaer R. Nelson held that "In order to administer the law, the court must determine what is an unreasonable and unlawful restraint of trade" and "whether a contract is injurious to the public." The judge noted further that "In all cases at common law, it must be made to appear that the acts complained of threatened the interests of the public, and this is true whether the remedy sought to be applied is by civil or criminal proceedings." Accordingly, the court ruled unobjectionable "a mutual agreement between several dealers" to "raise the price," in the absence of "fraudulent or coercive means resorted to for the purpose of restraining other dealers." Since the parties to the agreement did not resort to such means, "competition in the commodity would soon bring the price down."[65] The restriction of competition among the lumber dealers did not constitute an unlawful restraint of trade.

Similarly, in the "Whiskey Trust" cases of 1892, *United States* v. *Greenhut et al.*[66] and *In re Greene*,[67] the federal courts adhered to the framers' intent in construing the law. The Distilling and Cattle Feeding Company, incorporated in Illinois and controlling more than seventy previously competing distilleries in Illinois, Ohio, and New York, accounted for about 75 percent of all distillery products manufactured and sold in the United States.[68] In *Greenhut*, brought by U.S. attorney Frank D. Allen in federal district court in Massachusetts against the company, represented by Elihu Root and Richard Olney, among others, Judge Thomas L. Nelson threw out the indictment. He held that since the indictment, brought under section 2 of the Sherman Act, alleged a monopoly of manufacture and sale of distilled spirits without stating a monopoly of trade or commerce among the states or with foreign nations, it was insufficient.[69] In effect, Nelson's decision followed *Kidd* v. *Pearson* and presaged the subsequent Supreme Court decision in *E. C. Knight*. In *In re Greene*, basing his decision explicitly on the assumption that the Sherman Act embodied the common law, Judge Howell

64. *52 Fed.* 646–648.
65. *52 Fed.* 646–647.
66. *50 Fed.* 469–471 (decided, 16 May 1892).
67. *52 Fed.* 104–119 (decided, 4 Aug. 1892).
68. *50 Fed.* 470; *52 Fed.* 108, 109.
69. *50 Fed.* 471.

Edmonds Jackson, who was to be elevated within the year to the Supreme Court by President Harrison, ruled for the Circuit Court of the Southern District of Ohio that when Congress "adopts or creates common-law offenses, the courts may properly look to that body of jurisprudence for the true meaning and definition of such crimes, if they are not clearly defined in the act creating them." In construing the Sherman Act, therefore, "recourse must . . . be had to the common law for the proper definition of these general terms." Judge Jackson decided on these grounds that no unlawful restraint of trade or monopoly had been committed, because the contracts in question placed no restraint on the former owners of the distilleries absorbed by the company from reentering, nor on outsiders from entering or remaining in, the distillery industry.[70]

In the same year, 1892, indictments were brought against the officers of the National Cash Register Company under sections 1 and 2 of the Sherman Act, charging them with conspiracies to restrain the trade of their competitors and to monopolize the industry by driving competitors out of business. The indictments further alleged that the company's officers had resorted to "fraud and misrepresentation, deceit, threats, intimidation, obstruction and molestation, and other unlawful, oppressive, and vexatious means." On 28 February 1893, Judge William L. Putnam for the circuit court in Massachusetts quashed the major part of the indictment. He allowed to stand only those counts containing "allegations of an intent to engross, monopolize, and grasp [the market], and of means clearly unlawful, and adapted to accomplish this intent."[71] Before the case could be tried, the company reached agreement with those of its competitors at whose instigation the case had been brought, taking them into the combination on advantageous terms. In November 1894, Richard Olney, now attorney general, suspended proceedings against the enlarged combination.[72]

70. 52 *Fed.* 108, 109, 111, 112–113, 116, quotation at p. 111. Justice Jackson served on the Supreme Court, 1893–1895.
71. *U.S.* v. *Patterson et al.*, 55 *Fed.* 605–642, at 638–642, and 59 *Fed.* 280–284.
72. Thorelli, *Antitrust Policy*, p. 389. In this case, Elihu Root, as assistant U.S. attorney, appeared with U.S. Attorney Frank D. Allen for the government. 59 *Fed.* 280. The fourth case brought under the Sherman law against a combination of capitalists and finally decided in the lower federal courts between 1890 and 1897 was that of *U.S.* v. *Jellico Mountain Coke and Coal Co. et al.*, 43 *Fed.* 898–899 (3 Oct. 1890; Sixth Circuit Cout of the Eastern District of Tennessee; temporary injunction denied pending trial), and 46 *Fed.* 432–437 (4 June 1891, trial, Sixth Circuit). There, with Attorney General William H. H. Miller and Acting Attorney General William Howard Taft presenting the government's case, Judge D. M. Key for the court found the companies composing the Nashville coal exchange, operating mines chiefly in Kentucky and dealing in coal in Nashville, guilty of violating

In addition to the Sherman Act cases receiving final adjudication in the lower federal courts from 1890 to 1897, several cases were adjudicated in the lower courts but not finally disposed of until appeals to the Supreme Court resulted in decisions in 1897–1899. In these latter cases, as in the former, the lower federal courts explicitly placed upon the Sherman Act a common-law construction.

The case of *United States* v. *Trans-Missouri Freight Association et al.*, initiated in 1892, was a bill in equity filed in the circuit court of the Eighth Circuit in Kansas by the federal government against the freight association and its fifteen member railroads handling among them a substantial part of the traffic west of the Mississippi and Missouri rivers.[73] Brought under sections 1 and 2 of the Sherman law, the bill charged the railroads with fixing noncompetitive uniform rates and regulations for nearly all freights handled by them. On 28 November 1892, Judge John A. Riner in the court of the first instance dismissed the bill. He held that the Interstate Commerce Act had priority over the Sherman Act in railroad affairs, and that it did not compel unrestricted competition. Even under the Sherman Act, however, the association and its members were guilty of no violation because, he argued, their combination was a reasonable one. On the basis of an extensive review of common-law cases, Riner found "the question whether or not the contract is prejudicial to the public interest," and "whether the contract was reasonable," to constitute the principal test applicable under the Sherman law.[74]

Distinguishing between restriction of competition and unlawful restraint of trade, Riner held that "when contracts go to the extent only of preventing unhealthy competition, and yet at the same time furnish the

the Sherman Act, and he enjoined the companies from further violations. 46 *Fed.* 437. The only other case under the Sherman Act finally decided in the lower federal courts during this period was that against the Workingmen's Amalgamated Council of New Orleans, where the court, in 1893, upheld a temporary injunction against a general strike in New Orleans led by the union organization, Judge Edward C. Billings of the Fifth Circuit Court of the Eastern District of Louisiana, holding that the Sherman Act applied equally to combinations of labor and of capital; decision affirmed in Fifth Circuit Court of Appeals by judges A. P. McCormick and Harry T. Toulmin. 54 *Fed.* 994–1000 (25 Mar. 1893) and 57 *Fed.* 85–86 (13 June 1893).

73. 53 *Fed.* 440–459. The Freight Association, formed 15 Mar. 1889 (53 *Fed.* 443), included among its members: the Atchison, Topeka & Santa Fe Railroad; Chicago, Rock Island & Pacific Railway; Chicago, St. Paul, Minneapolis & Omaha Railway; Burlington & Missouri River Railroad in Nebraska; Denver & Rio Grande Railroad; Denver & Rio Grande Western Railway; Missouri Pacific Railway; St. Louis and San Francisco Railway; Union Pacific Railway; Utah Central Railway. 58 *Fed.* 60.

74. 53 *Fed.* 446–450.

public with adequate facilities at fixed and reasonable prices, and are made only for the purpose of averting personal ruin, the contract is lawful." He declared that the "rule of law" did not condemn a contract between competing railway companies, "which is made for the sole purpose of preventing strife, and preventing financial ruin to one or the other." Indeed, such contracts, not unrestricted competition, "benefit the public by preventing unjust discrimination among shippers, and providing equal facilities for the interchange of traffic, and thus avoiding many of the unfair and unjust results which often follow the unrestricted competition of rival companies." The judge argued further that the public interest was not served by competition that destroyed returns on investment by driving down rates or prices: "It cannot be said that the public is benefited by competition when that competition is carried beyond the bounds of reasonable prosperity to the parties engaged in it, for surely the citizen investing his capital, whether in railways or otherwise, is entitled to the benefit of a contract which affords to him only a fair protection for his investment, and which does not interfere with the rights of the public by imposing unjust and unreasonable charges for the service performed." So long as the freight association charged a "fair and reasonable" rate, defined as "no more than a fair compensation to the carrier" for services, "the public cannot complain." Accordingly, Judge Riner concluded, "The public is not entitled to free and unrestricted competition, but what it is entitled to is fair and healthy competition; and I see nothing in this contract which necessarily tends to interfere with that right."[75]

On appeal, the Eighth Circuit Court of Appeals, on 2 October 1893, by a two-to-one decision, affirmed the lower court. Like district judge Riner, circuit judge Walter H. Sanborn, writing the opinion of the divided court,[76] noted that the provisions of the Interstate Commerce Act of 1887 "establish beyond cavil that from that date the public policy of the nation was that competition between railroad companies engaged in interstate commerce should not go wholly unrestricted."[77] Similarly, Sanborn found it necessary to review British and United States common-law cases on restraint of trade and monopoly in order properly to interpret and apply the Sherman Act. On the basis of his survey of common-law authorities, Sanborn concluded that if the act "applies to and governs interstate and international transportation and

---

75.   53 *Fed.* 450, 451, 452, 453, 454–456.
76.   58 *Fed.* 58–100. Judge Sanborn was joined in his decision (pp. 65–83) by Judge Amos M. Thayer; Judge Oliver P. Shiras dissented (pp. 84–100).
77.   58 *Fed.* 75.

its instrumentalities, the contract and association here in question do not appear to be in violation of it."[78] For, he reasoned:

> From a view of these and other authorities, it clearly appears that when the anti-trust act was passed the rule had become firmly established in the jurisprudence of England and the United States that the validity of contracts restricting competition was to be determined by the reasonableness of the restriction. If the main purpose or natural and inevitable effect of a contract was to suppress competition or create monopoly, it was illegal. If a contract imposed a restriction that was unreasonably injurious to the public interest, . . . it was illegal. But contracts made for a lawful purpose, which was not unreasonably injurious to the public welfare, . . . had been uniformly sustained, notwithstanding their tendency to some extent to check competition.[79]

Brought at the request of the Interstate Commerce Commission, and at the direction of President Cleveland's attorney general, Judson Harmon, the case, *United States* v. *Joint Traffic Association*, involved the association established by thirty-one railroads that accounted for most of the interstate traffic between the Atlantic seaboard and Chicago and the Mississippi valley. The association established rates and regulated and apportioned the traffic among the railroads. The association's board consisted of nine managers, one each from the Baltimore & Ohio, the Erie, the Grand Trunk, the Chesapeake & Ohio, the Lackawanna, the Lehigh Valley, and the Pennsylvania railroads, and the New York Central system and the Wabash system. District Judge Hoyt H. Wheeler in the Second Circuit Court of the Southern District of New York on 28 May 1896 dismissed the bill against the association, and on 19 March 1897 the Second Circuit Court of Appeals sustained the lower court without filing an opinion.[80] Here again, the federal court applied a common-law construction of the Sherman Act and, referring in its decision to the decisions of the lower courts in the Trans-Missouri Freight case, upheld the defendants. Judge Wheeler ruled that the contract did "not provide for lessening the number of carriers; nor their facilities; nor for raising their rates, except expressly by its terms not contrary to law, and therefore not beyond what are reasonable," and that, therefore, the contract constituted "no unlawful restraint of commerce," and consequently, that it did not violate the Sherman Act.[81]

Upon government appeal to the Supreme Court, ex-Senator George F.

78.   58 *Fed.* 67–72, 83.
79.   58 *Fed.* 72–73.
80.   76 *Fed.* 895–898; 89 *Fed.* 1020.
81.   76 *Fed.* 897.

Edmunds, principal framer of the Sherman Act and, since his retirement from the Senate in 1891, a prominent corporate and constitutional lawyer practicing in Philadelphia, appeared among counsel for the Joint Traffic Association. He and his associates challenged the intervening Supreme Court five-to-four decision in the Trans-Missouri case, which reversed the lower courts and declared the Trans-Missouri association illegal. The eminent attorney Edward J. Phelps for the New York Central Railroad, and Edmunds for the Pennsylvania Railroad, argued that common-law construction was essential to the meaning of the Sherman Act, and that unless so construed the statute was unconstitutional. The Supreme Court's construction of the Sherman law in the Trans-Missouri case, they held, put the act "in violation of the provisions of the Constitution of the United States, since it deprives the defendants in error of their liberty and their property without due process of law, and deprives them likewise of the equal protection of the laws." The contract effected only a reasonable restraint of trade, and it could not be ruled illegal "without infringing the freedom of contract and the right of property, which the Constitution declares and protects."[82]

Decisions in two other leading cases in the period 1890–1897, the Addyston Pipe and E. C. Knight cases, both affecting manufacturers, reinforced judicial construction of the Sherman Act as limited in its meaning by common-law doctrine and by constitutional strictures on federal versus state jurisdiction. The cases also established the distinction between restriction of competition in the sphere of production and such restriction in the sphere of trade and commerce, the former being construed as only an indirect or ancillary restraint of the latter in the absence of conclusive evidence to the contrary. This distinction would govern Sherman Act jurisprudence, at least formally, even with the Harlan majority from 1897 to 1911.

United States v. *Addyston Pipe & Steel Co. et al.*, decided 5 February 1897 by District Judge Charles D. Clark in the Sixth Circuit Court of the Eastern District of Tennessee, concerned a pool of six relatively small manufacturers of cast-iron pipe producing and marketing in the South, Midwest, and West.[83] Defense counsel based their case directly

---

82. *U.S.* v. *Joint Traffic Association*, 171 *U.S.* 505–578: Phelps, pp. 527–535, at p. 532; Edmunds, pp. 535–545, at p. 544. Edmunds and Phelps had also served as defense counsel in the lower court, Edmunds on brief. 76 *Fed.* 895.
83. 78 *Fed.* 712–724. The companies were: Addyston Pipe & Steel Co., Cincinnati; Dennis Long & Co., Louisville, Ky.; Howard-Harrison Iron Co., Bessemer, Ala.: Anniston Pipe & Foundry Co., Anniston, Ala.; South Pittsburgh Pipe Works, South Pittsburgh, Tenn.; Chattanooga Pipe & Foundry Works, Chattanooga, Tenn. To-

on the common law, arguing that the manufacturers' association did not come within the purview of the Sherman Act because "in its purposes and mode of doing business," it did not "constitute a monopoly" and caused "no restraint of trade, such as would be unlawful at the common law." Suggesting at this late date that the Sherman Act, like the Interstate Commerce Act, was "new and experimental legislation," whose "constitutional validity" had been considered "doubtful" by many members of Congress at the time of its enactment, Judge Clark affirmed defense counsel's argument and dismissed the bill.[84] In reaching his decision, he relied heavily not on his personal asseverations, but on the common-law doctrine invoked by Judge (later Justice) Howell E. Jackson in *In re Greene* and by circuit court judge Walter H. Sanborn in the Trans-Missouri case. Beyond that, citing and quoting at length from both Justice Lamar in *Kidd* v. *Pearson* and Chief Justice Fuller in *E. C. Knight* to distinguish between state jursidiction over production and federal jurisdiction over interstate commerce, Judge Clark held the pool to have had no direct effect on interstate commerce and hence to lie beyond the reach of the Sherman Act.[85]

United States v. *E. C. Knight Company*, decided 21 January 1895, was the first Sherman Act case involving a large corporate consolidation to reach the Supreme Court. President Cleveland's attorney general, Olney, presided over the government's appeal from the decision of the Third Circuit Court in Philadelphia. The principal defendant, Henry O. Havemeyer's American Sugar Refining Company, had become known and excoriated in public discourse as "the Sugar Trust." The government alleged that, in violation of the Sherman Act, American Sugar's purchase of the stock and hence control of Philadelphia's four large sugar-refining corporations had resulted in a monopoly of refined sugar production in the United States, in restraint of interstate and foreign commerce.[86]

gether the companies were estimated in evidence to account for less than half the manufacturing capacity in cast-iron pipe of all companies operating in their territory, and for about 20 percent of total national capacity. 78 *Fed.* 713–714.

84. 78 *Fed.* 716, 724.

85. 78 *Fed.* 720–721, 723–724, 716–720, 720–723.

86. 156 *U.S.* 1–46. The case was argued for the United States by Solicitor General Lawrence Maxwell, Olney on the brief. John G. Johnson, the venerable Philadelphia lawyer, with John E. Parsons on brief, represented defendants. The government alleged that on or before 4 March 1892, the American Sugar Refining Company, incorporated in New Jersey, had obtained control through stock acquisition of four sugar-refining companies, all incorporated in Pennsylvania and operating refineries in Philadelphia: namely, E. C. Knight Co., Franklin Sugar Refining Co., Spreckels Sugar Refining Co., and Delaware Sugar House. These four accounted for one-third of total refined sugar output in the United States, so that in

Chief Justice Melville W. Fuller, delivering the opinion of the Court, dismissed the case on two grounds. First, citing and quoting at length from Justice Lamar's decision in *Kidd* v. *Pearson*, Fuller sustained the constitutional distinction between state jurisdiction over manufacturing or production and federal jurisdiction over interstate and foreign commerce. He noted that relief from monopoly within the states must rest with state jurisdiction, and that Olney's brief had not shown an unlawful restraint of interstate or foreign commerce as a direct and necessary consequence of the alleged monopoly in manufacture as such.[87] Second, invoking the traditional common-law distinction between direct and indirect or ancillary restraints of trade, and declaring accordingly that "Commerce succeeds to manufacture, and is not part of it," Fuller ruled:

> Contracts, combinations, or conspiracies to control domestic enterprise in manufacture, agriculture, mining, production in all its forms, or to raise or lower prices or wages, might unquestionably tend to restrain external as well as domestic trade, but the restraint would be an indirect result, however inevitable and whatever its extent, and such result would not necessarily determine the object of the contract, combination, or conspiracy.[88]

In his lone dissent, Harlan did not dispute, in principle, the two grounds stated by Fuller. He sought, rather, to show injury to the public implicit in the sugar combination, and the direct and necessary connection between monopoly in manufacture and restraint of interstate and

acquiring them, American Sugar had obtained control of most of the production of refined sugar in the United States. All five companies were defendants in the case. 156 *U.S.* 2, 8, 18. Both the lower federal circuit court and the circuit court of appeals dismissed the case. 60 *Fed.* 306; 60 *Fed.* 934. Cf. Eichner, *Emergence of Oligopoly*, pp. 169–171.

87. 156 *U.S.* 14–15, 11, 16. As Fuller stated: "The fundamental question is, whether conceding that the existence of a monopoly in manufacture is established by the evidence, that monopoly can be directly suppressed under the act of Congress in the mode attempted by this bill" (p. 11). "Slight reflection will show that if the national power extends to all contracts and combinations in manufacture, agriculture, mining, and other productive industries, whose ultimate result may affect external commerce, comparatively little of business operations and affairs would be left for state control." "Congress did not attempt [by the Sherman Act] ... to assert the power to deal with monopoly directly as such; or to limit and restrict the rights of corporations created by the States or the citizens of the States in the acquisition, control, or disposition of property; or to regulate or prescribe the price or prices at which such property or the products thereof should be sold; or to make criminal the acts of persons in the acquisition or control of property which the States of their residence or creation sanctioned or permitted" (p. 16). Cf. McCurdy, "*Knight* Sugar Decision," pp. 304–342.

88. 156 *U.S.* 12, 16.

foreign commerce.[89] But in this, he had little support from Olney's brief. The distinctions between state and federal jurisdiction, between production and trade or commerce, and between direct and indirect or ancillary restraints of trade, as laid down by Fuller in the Knight case, remained controlling from 1895 on, including during the period of the Harlan-led majority from 1897 to 1911, a majority that Fuller was to join. Monopoly of manufacture or production, or dominance therein, or predominant market power, as such, whether achieved by a corporation's stock ownership in other corporations or by other means lawful in themselves, was never considered by the Supreme Court as sufficient to constitute a violation of the Sherman Act. This held true in the period 1897–1911 as before and after. Except for Olney's brief in the Knight case, the federal government in no case under the Sherman Act brought suit solely on grounds of bigness or monopoly of production. In fact, authorities have held that the Knight case was improperly presented by the government. There was some contemporary suspicion that Olney, a prominent corporation lawyer in private life, who while attorney general made no secret of his disdain for the Sherman Act, mishandled the case, if not deliberately, then from an incapacitating predisposition.[90]

Though *E. C. Knight* sustained the "Sugar Trust," it is usually overlooked that Fuller's decision nevertheless strengthened the reach of both the Sherman Act and congressional authority in general in the regulation of the market. Denying an absolutist doctrine of liberty of contract or rights of property, and noting that "the power of Congress to regulate [interstate and foreign] commerce" was "exclusive" as against the states, Fuller held that "The Constitution does not provide that interstate commerce shall be free, but, by grant of this exclusive power

89.   156 *U.S.* 18–46. Harlan extensively reviewed state and pre–Sherman Act federal cases, discussing *Kidd* v. *Pearson* at length (pp. 34–36), and quoting from the Central Ohio Salt case (pp. 27–28).

90.   Cf. Jones, *Trust Problem*, p. 391; Thorelli, *Antitrust Policy*, pp. 383, 385, 388–389, 394–395; Davies, *Trust Laws*, pp. 74–76; Morgan, *Congress*, p. 417 n. 13; Harlan's view in his opinion for the Supreme Court, and Holmes in his dissent, in the Northern Securities case, 193 *U.S.* 329, 391. In this view of the case, Fuller's decision was more a critique of Olney's brief than a judgment on whether the operations of the American Sugar Refining Company actually constituted a violation of the Sherman Act. For a different and informative, though not completely convincing, view of Olney's role in this case and its handling by the federal government, see Letwin, *Law and Economic Policy*, pp. 117–122, including n. 2, pp. 122–123. For a more convincing analysis of *Knight*, suggesting that no improvement in the brief would have succeeded in changing the Court's decision, based as it was on a strict construction of dual jurisdiction between the federal government and the states, see McCurdy, "*Knight* Sugar Decision."

to regulate it, it was left free except as Congress might impose restraints." Congressional power extended not only to goods considered "necessaries of life" but also to "all articles of general consumption." The Sherman Act, furthermore, reached not only a contract or combination that effected "a complete monopoly" but also any such contract or combination that "really tends to that end and to deprive the public of the advantages which flow from free competition."[91] Fuller's decision also promulgated a constitutional ambiguity, which was later to affect policy-forming thought before it was mooted by the Rule of Reason decisions of 1911. In holding that Congress's power was "exclusive," Fuller implied that just as Congress could not constitutionally delegate authority to regulate interstate or foreign commerce to the states, so neither could it delegate such authority to private persons, nor could states authorize private persons to do what the states themselves could not. In sum, if competition were to be restricted in interstate or foreign commerce, at all, it must be effected directly and exclusively by the federal government. Or, only the national state could constitutionally administer the national market. Whatever the constitutional ambiguity, Fuller's *Knight* decision, as much as Harlan's dissent in the case, would serve as grounds upon which the Harlan-led majority would take its position in the leading cases of 1897–1899, a majority, it should be remembered, in which Fuller joined.[92]

Coup de jure

It was not until 1897, with its decision in the Trans-Missouri case, that the Supreme Court first construed the Sherman Act as recognizing no distinction between reasonable and unreasonable restraints of trade. The Court declared both types of restraint illegal, and thereby construed the Sherman Act as reversing or superseding the common law with respect to restraints of trade and monopoly, not only procedurally

91. 156 *U.S.* 11, 12, 16.
92. In this connection, Justice Peckham wrote the *Allgeyer* decision (1 Mar. 1897) with its classic definition of liberty (see note 33, above). But he also wrote the majority opinion in *Trans-Missouri* (22 Mar. 1897) and *Joint Traffic* (24 Oct. 1898), and the unanimous opinion in *Addyston Pipe* (8 Feb. 1898), in *Trans-Missouri* citing E. C. *Knight*, and in *Joint Traffic* and *Addyston Pipe* specifically distinguishing *Allgeyer* from the issues in those cases, holding that liberty as defined in *Allgeyer* was nevertheless limited by Congress's power to regulate interstate and foreign commerce. Congress's power, in turn, of course, remained subject to the constitutional protections of life, liberty, and property under the due process of the law. *Allgeyer*, at 165 *U.S.* 589; *Trans-Missouri* at 166 *U.S.* 325–326; *Joint Traffic*, at 171 *U.S.* 572; *Addyston Pipe*, at 175 *U.S.* 228–229. See notes 110, 111, and 180, and related text, below.

but substantively as well.[93] The high court, nevertheless, remained sharply and closely divided over such construction of the Sherman Act. From 1897 to 1911 the justices engaged in a running dispute among themselves, grouping variously around Justice Harlan on the one side and justices Edward D. White and (from 1902) Oliver Wendell Holmes, Jr., on the other, whenever they undertook to adjudicate cases brought under the Sherman Act. Central to the dispute, and around which the decisions, dissents, lawyers' arguments and briefs, always turned, stood the question of whether the Sherman Act was to be interpreted in the light of common law and therefore interpreted as permitting reasonable restraints of trade or whether the act had superseded the common law and thereby prohibited all restraints, reasonable or unreasonable.

The leading case, and the case in which the Supreme Court made its first comprehensive interpretation of the Sherman Act, was *United States* v. *Trans-Missouri Freight Association*, argued 8–9 December 1896 and decided on 22 March 1897.[94]

The railroads' attorneys, in accord with previous lower court decisions in Sherman Act cases, including the lower court decisions in this case by judges Riner and Sanborn, urged "with much amplification of argument" that the act reached only those contracts "unlawful at common law," and that it only meant "to declare illegal any such contract which is in *unreasonable* restraint of trade, while leaving all others unaffected." They argued "that when terms ... known to the common law are used in a Federal statute those terms are to be given the same meaning that they received at common law."[95]

But by a five-to-four decision, written by Justice Rufus W. Peckham, the Court rejected defense pleas and reversed the lower court. After affirming that the Sherman Act applied to common carriers, it held that since the law declared illegal "every contract" in restraint of interstate or foreign trade, it thereby superseded the common law and covered reasonable and unreasonable restraints alike. "By the simple use of the term 'contract in restraint of trade,'" wrote Peckham for the Court, "all contracts of that nature, whether valid [at common law] or otherwise, would be included, and not alone that kind of contract which was

---

93. Cf. H. K. Smith, *Memorandum* (1908), p. 348: "It will be observed that there was a period from 1890, when the [Sherman] law was passed, to 1897 (at which time the Supreme Court ruled the question of reasonableness or unreasonableness out of the matter entirely), during which time the consideration of the law in the more important cases practically inserted the word 'reasonable'..."
94. 166 *U.S.* 290–374.
95. 166 *U.S.* 327–328 (Peckham summarizing defense argument; Peckham's emphasis). Cf. Harlan's partial dissent in *Standard Oil* v. *United States*, 221 *U.S.* 87–89, at 4 *FAD* 152–154.

invalid and unenforceable [at common law] as being in unreasonable restraint of trade."[96] Although a contract in restraint of trade might "still be valid at common law," reasoned Peckham, "it is nevertheless a contract in restraint of trade, and would be so described either at common law or elsewhere." By passing the Sherman Act, Congress had made illegal all contracts in restraint of trade, "whether valid or otherwise ... and not alone that kind of contract which was invalid and unenforceable as being in unreasonable restraint of trade." Should the Court rule otherwise, Peckham concluded, it would amount to "a process of judicial legislation wholly unjustifiable" and hence it was something the Court "cannot and ought not to do."[97]

With the concurrence of justices Stephen J. Field, Horace Gray, and George Shiras, Jr., Justice Edward D. White wrote a sharply dissenting opinion insisting upon common-law construction of the Sherman Act. He denied the majority contention that at common law the words, "restraint of trade," embraced all contracts restraining trade, whether reasonable or unreasonable, and that the act had therefore proscribed all such contracts. White held that "only such contracts as unreasonably restrain trade are violative of the general law." Accordingly, he argued, "a brief consideration of the history and development of the law on the subject will not only establish the inaccuracy of this proposition, but also demonstrate that the words 'restraint of trade' embrace only contracts which unreasonably restrain trade, and, therefore, that reasonable contracts, although they, in some measure, 'restrain trade,' are not within the meaning of the words."[98] White's opinion in *Trans-Missouri* would, in essence, become the majority opinion fourteen years later, after he had succeeded Fuller as chief justice. Until then, however, in case after case brought before it under the Sherman Act, the Court, although closely divided, consistently maintained the position that all restraints of trade, whether reasonable or unreasonable at common law, were illegal.

The case of *United States* v. *Joint Traffic Association*, argued 24–25 February 1898, was decided by the Supreme Court on 24 October 1898, about a year and a half after its decision in the Trans-Missouri case.[99] Counsel for the defense, including ex-Senator Edmunds, had

96. 166 *U.S.* 311–313, 325–326, 327–328. Cf. Harlan, 221 *U.S.* 87–89. In 1895, Peckham had succeeded Howell E. Jackson on the Court. Concurring in Peckham's decision were Chief Justice Fuller and associate justices David J. Brewer, Henry B. Brown, and Harlan.
97. 166 *U.S.* 328, 340. Peckham quoted at length from the dissenting opinion of Judge Oliver P. Shiras in the lower appeals court. 166 *U.S.* 335–337.
98. 166 *U.S.* 344, 346.
99. 171 *U.S.* 505–578.

argued in the lower court that the Sherman Act must be construed as the embodiment of the common law, that otherwise the act would be unconstitutional, and that, accordingly, the Court's Trans-Missouri decision had been in error.[100] With White again dissenting, joined by Gray and Shiras, the Supreme Court by a five-to-three decision specifically rejected these contentions.[101] Peckham, for the Court, reaffirmed its Trans-Missouri decision, declaring that the latter had been "intentionally and necessarily decided." Noting that the two cases were essentially the same, and quoting from his decision in *Trans-Missouri*, Peckham stated that "while this is not strictly an application for a rehearing in the same case, yet in substance it is the same thing." He then pointed out that the Court had heard and reheard the Trans-Missouri case: "And now for the third time the same arguments are employed and the court is again asked to recant." In maintaining its initial decision, therefore, the Court had ruled uniformly on the question for the third successive time.[102] As Harlan was to state in his partial dissent in the Standard Oil case in 1911, these decisions "show so clearly as to admit of no doubt that this court, ... upon the fullest consideration, interpreted the Anti-Trust Act as prohibiting and making illegal ... *every* contract or combination, in whatever form, which was in restraint of interstate commerce, without regard to its reasonableness or unreasonableness."[103]

Subsequently, the lower federal courts "throughout the entire country" as well as the Supreme Court, enforced the Sherman law "according to the interpretation given in the *Freight Association* case."[104] The litigation in *Addyston Pipe* provides a pertinent illustration.[105] In February 1897, prior to the Supreme Court's Trans-Missouri decision, Judge Clark in the Sixth Circuit Court in Tennessee had dismissed the government's bill against the manufacturers' pool, relying heavily upon the Supreme Court decisions in *E. C. Knight* and *In re Greene* and on the lower court decisions by judges Riner and Sanborn in *Trans-Missouri*. The appeal reached the Sixth Circuit Court of Appeals in early 1898, after the Supreme Court's Trans-Missouri decision. Ruling for a unanimous appeals court, Judge William Howard Taft, on 8

100. 171 *U.S.* 527–545.
101. Field had died in 1897. Joseph McKenna succeeded to his seat in 1898 after the Court had heard argument in the case, and he took no part in it.
102. 171 *U.S.* 573–574.
103. *Standard Oil Co. of N.J. et al.* v. *United States*, 221 *U.S.* 91–94, at 4 *FAD* 156–158. Harlan's emphasis.
104. Harlan at ibid., 221 *U.S.* 90, at 4 *FAD* 155.
105. 78 *Fed.* 712–724 (5 Feb. 1897); 85 *Fed.* 271–302 (8 Feb. 1898); 175 *U.S.* 211–248 (4 Dec. 1899).

February 1898, reversed the lower court and held the pool in violation of the Sherman Act. Taft undertook an extensive review of British and American common-law cases to distinguish between direct and ancillary restraints, finding that the defendants' restraint of trade was a direct one. He noted that under the common law, contracts in unreasonable and direct restraint of trade were void, that the defendants' pool was an unreasonable direct restraint, but that whether reasonable or unreasonable, it must be ruled illegal, because in its intervening Trans-Missouri decision, the Supreme Court had held that "contracts in restraint of interstate transportation were within the statute, whether the restraints could be regarded as reasonable at common law or not."[106]

In addressing the question of direct and indirect restraints, Taft had, in effect, reaffirmed an area in which the common law could still aid in the construction of the Sherman Act. In the course of his ruling, he noted that a restraint of trade may be enforced, or remain legal under the act, when the covenant that embodies it is "merely ancillary to the main purpose of a lawful contract, and necessary to protect the convenantee in the enjoyment of the legitimate fruits of the contract, or to protect him from the dangers of an unjust use of those fruits by the other party."[107] With this point as central to the Addyston Pipe case, and given Taft's ruling that the contract in question was an unreasonable restraint, the Supreme Court sustained Taft and in doing so reached its first unanimous decision in a case based exclusively on the Sherman Act. Peckham once again delivered the opinion of the Court. In *Joint Traffic* the year before, he had already stipulated that "the statute applies only to those contracts whose direct and immediate effect is a restraint upon interstate commerce." Hence, he continued, "to treat the act as condemning all agreements under which, as a result, the cost of conducting an interstate commercial business may be increased, would enlarge the application of the act far beyond the fair meaning of the language used. The effect upon interstate commerce must not be indirect or incidental only."[108] In reiterating this principle,

---

106. 85 *Fed.* 278, 279–283, 302. Sitting with Taft in the circuit court of appeals and concurring in his opinion were Justice Harlan and Judge Horace H. Lurton, whom Taft as president appointed to the Supreme Court in 1909. Cf. also *United States* v. *The Coal Dealers' Association of California et al.*, 85 *Fed.* 262, 264 (1898), where it was held that whether a contract or combination "imposes only a fair and reasonable restraint upon trade and commerce" was irrelevant.
107. 85 *Fed.* 282.
108. 171 *U.S.* 568. Peckham here cited to the same effect the Court's decisions, on the same day as *Joint Traffic*, 24 Oct. 1898, in *Hopkins* v. *United States*, 171 *U.S.* 578, and *Anderson et al.* v. *United States*, 171 *U.S.* 604. *Hopkins* and *Anderson* are often ranked with other leading Sherman Act cases because they were brought under the act, but they are of subsidiary relevance to the construction of federal

Peckham now affirmed Taft's decision, except to hold that the defendants might combine for selling pipe *within* their own state, which action, Peckham held, federal law could not reach.[109]

In limiting the reach of the Sherman Act to direct restraints of interstate or foreign commerce, however, Peckham took the occasion of the Addyston decision to enlarge upon Fuller's *E. C. Knight* ruling regarding Congress's power to limit contractual liberty in regulating interstate or foreign commerce. Invoking the authority of Chief Justice John Marshall and specifically citing his landmark decision in *Gibbons* v. *Ogden* (1824), Peckham for a unanimous Court declared Congress's "power to regulate interstate commerce" to be "full and complete," not only as against the states but also with "no limitation" as against "private contracts" that might directly "regulate to any substantial

law on restraint of trade in general, to the construction of the Sherman Act in particular, and to the bearing of the two on corporate enterprise. In each case, the defendants were an unincorporated association of Kansas City livestock dealers organized in the form of a livestock exchange providing services to buyers and sellers, and in each case, the Supreme Court held that the association's business did not constitute interstate trade or commerce, but had only an ancillary effect on it, if any, and hence did not fall within the reach of the Sherman Act, a federal law. Peckham delivered the Court's decision in both cases. In each case, the Court held that there had been no restriction of competition or restraint of trade. In *Hopkins*, Peckham noted that the members of the Kansas City Livestock Exchange of Kansas City, Missouri, and Kansas City, Kansas, "still continued their individual business in full competition with each other," and the association itself conducted no business whatever; hence the case had no bearing at all on the controversy over reasonable and unreasonable restraints of trade in the form of combinations or otherwise. Peckham here also invoked the ancillary principle, for which usually *Hopkins* and *Anderson* are cited in relation to Sherman Act construction (*Hopkins* involved defendants residing in two states), noting that the Sherman Act "must have a reasonable construction," in the sense that it applied to direct restraints of interstate trade or commerce, not to any and all business arrangements that could be shown to affect or restrain interstate trade or commerce only "indirectly or remotely" (*Hopkins* v. *U.S.*, 171 *U.S.* 587, 590, 603). In *Anderson*, involving the Traders' Live Stock and Exchange of Kansas City, Missouri, Peckham delivered a similar decision, noting that "This suit is somewhat similar to the *Hopkins suit*, just decided" (171 *U.S.* 605, 615–616, 619). In each case, Harlan alone dissented, but without opinion, and McKenna took no part.

109.   175 *U.S.* 248. In otherwise affirming Taft's decision, the Court put particular emphasis on the distinction between direct and indirect restraints. In Peckham's words: "Congress . . . may enact such legislation as shall declare void and prohibit the performance of any contract between individuals or corporations where the natural and direct effect of such a contract will be, when carried out, to directly, and not as a mere incident to other and innocent purposes, regulate to any substantial extent interstate commerce." Peckham added: ". . . the power of Congress to regulate interstate commerce comprises the right to enact a law prohibiting the citizen from entering into those private contracts which directly and substantially, and not merely indirectly, remotely, incidentally and collaterally, regulate to a greater or less degree commerce among the States." 175 *U.S.* 228, 229.

extent interstate commerce."[110] More than this, Peckham continued, distinguishing the issues here from those he had addressed with respect to liberty in *Allgeyer*, "We do not assent to the correctness of the proposition that the constitutional guaranty of liberty to the individual to enter into private contracts limits the power of Congress and prevents it from legislating upon the subject of contracts" that directly and substantially affected interstate or foreign commerce. "Nor is any such limitation contained in that other clause of the Constitution which provides that no person shall be deprived of life, liberty or property without due process of law." Noting that in *Allgeyer* the Court had held "liberty" as found in the Constitution to be not "confined to the mere liberty of person" but to include as well "a right to enter into certain classes of contracts for the purpose of enabling the citizen to carry on his business," Peckham declared that nevertheless "it has never been, and in our opinion ought not to be, held that the word included the right of an individual to enter into private contracts upon all subjects, no matter what their nature and wholly irrespective (among other things) of the fact that they would, if performed, result in the regulation of interstate commerce and in the violation of an act of Congress." The liberty of the citizen did not include the right to make a contract directly and substantially restraining or regulating interstate or foreign commerce, a power that Congress reserved exclusively to itself and denied alike to the states and to private persons. Accordingly, Peckham concluded, "the provision regarding the liberty of the citizen is, to some extent, limited by the commerce clause of the Constitution."[111]

Subsequent cases brought in federal courts under the Sherman Act fell in line with the leading decisions in the Trans-Missouri, Joint Traffic, and Addyston Pipe cases of 1897–1899. In *Chesapeake & Ohio Fuel Co. v. United States*, the Sixth Circuit Court of Appeals in Cincinnati,

---

110. Peckham here also stated, "And when we speak of interstate we also include in our meaning foreign commerce." 175 *U.S.* 228.

111. 175 *U.S.* 228–229. Cf. also Peckham's further remarks (pp. 230–231): "Commerce is the important subject of consideration, and anything which directly obstructs and thus regulates that commerce which is carried on among the States, whether it is state legislation or private contracts between individuals or corporations, should be subject to the power of Congress in the regulation of that commerce." "The power of Congress over this subject seems to us much more important and necessary than the liberty of the citizen to enter into contracts of the nature above mentioned, free from the control of Congress, because the direct results of such contracts might be the regulation of commerce among the States, possibly quite as effectually as if a State had passed a statute of like tenor as the contract." Reiterated and reaffirmed by Harlan at *Northern Securities Co. v. United States*, 193 *U.S.* 197, at 330–332 (1904).

134 Corporate reconstruction and the antitrust law

in 1902, upheld the lower federal court's decision against the company. Relying on the three prior leading decisions, the three-judge panel unanimously ruled that "Congress has seen fit to prohibit all contracts in restraint of trade. It was not left to the courts the consideration of the question whether such restraint is reasonable or unreasonable, or whether the contract would have been illegal at common law or not. The act leaves for consideration by judicial authority no question of this character."[112] That same year, the Supreme Court ruled similarly in *Bement* v. *National Harrow Co.* While holding that restrictions of competition that resulted from patent rights were not illegal under the Sherman Act, Peckham for the Court, citing the three leading cases, stated, "It has been held by this court that the act included any restraint of commerce, whether reasonable or unreasonable."[113]

In two cases in 1904, the Supreme Court reiterated and reaffirmed its construction of the Sherman Act as determined in *Trans-Missouri, Joint Traffic,* and *Addyston Pipe.* In *Montague & Company* v. *Lowry,* the Court held that in spite of the defendant's contention that the trade had been so small as to be negligible, the contract was nevertheless a direct and substantial restraint of interstate trade and therefore illegal, since the Sherman Act prohibited all such restraints.[114] In the celebrated *Northern Securities Company* v. *United States,* Harlan, speaking for the closely divided Court, ruled that "the act is not limited to restraints of interstate and international trade or commerce that are unreasonable in their nature, but embraces *all* direct *restraints.*"[115] Again, in April 1908, in *Shawnee Compress Company* v. *Anderson,* the Court declared that "it has been decided that not only unreasonable, but all direct

112. 115 *Fed.* 610–624, at 619. This was the same court in which Taft had delivered his Addyston Pipe decision four years earlier. Judge William R. Day delivered the opinion of the court (8 Apr. 1902), with judges Lurton and Henry F. Severens concurring. In 1903, Day, who had been a close friend and political ally of McKinley and had served as McKinley's secretary of state in the interim between Sherman and Hay, was appointed to the Supreme Court by President Theodore Roosevelt. In 1911, Justice Day, as well as Justice Lurton, joined the White majority in restoring the common-law (Rule of Reason) construction of the Sherman Act.
113. 186 *U.S.* 70–95, at 92. Justices Harlan, Gray, and White took no part in the case. There was no recorded dissent.
114. 193 *U.S.* 38–48, at 44–48 (23 Feb. 1904). The case involved California manufacturers of and dealers in tiles, mantels, and grates. Peckham delivered the opinion of the court, with no recorded dissent.
115. 193 *U.S.* 197–411, at 331 (14 Mar. 1904). Harlan's emphasis. Harlan delivered the opinion of the court, in which he was joined by justices Brown, Day, and Joseph McKenna, with Brewer concurring in a separate opinion but holding that the Northern Securities corporation constituted an unreasonable restraint of trade. White and Holmes each delivered a separate dissent, each concurring in the other's, with Fuller and Peckham concurring in both dissents.

restraints of trade are prohibited, the law being thereby distinguished from the common law."[116] Two months earlier, in *Loewe* v. *Lawlor* – the famous Danbury Hatters' case brought by the company against the labor union for treble the damages incurred in the union's boycott campaign – the Supreme Court, citing *Trans-Missouri, Joint Traffic*, and *Northern Securities*, declared it settled that "the Anti-Trust Law has a broader application than the prohibition of restraints of trade unlawful at common law."[117]

It is plain, then, that at the end of the first decade of the twentieth century the federal courts since 1897 had consistently required that the Sherman Act be regarded as having superseded the common law with respect to restraints of trade and monopoly insofar as the critical distinction between reasonableness and unreasonableness was concerned. Although the Supreme Court remained sharply divided over this construction of the Sherman Act, nevertheless, as Commissioner of Corporations Herbert Knox Smith pointed out, "One of the few propositions upon which the entire court agreed was on the common-law distinction between reasonable and unreasonable restraint of trade."[118]

Even in the period 1897–1911, however, two traditional features of jurisprudence with respect to restraint of trade and monopoly remained in effect as implicitly embodied in the Sherman Act.

First, restraints of trade or restrictions of competition incidental to an otherwise lawful contract or agreement continued to be regarded as legal; or, in common-law terms, restraints ancillary to a valid contract or agreement were legal. For a contract to come within the ban of the statute it had necessarily, naturally, directly, and immediately to result in, lead to, or constitute a substantial restraint of trade.[119] But whereas at common law the court would then have proceeded to examine whether such a direct and substantial restraint was reasonable or unreasonable, under the Sherman Act during this period such inquiry stood moot: Any direct and substantial restraint constituted a prima facie violation of the law.

This distinction between direct and ancillary restraints arose from a long-established recognition that by the very nature of competition, each successful competitor restrained to a degree the trade of one or

---

116. 209 *U.S.* 423–435, at 434 (13 Apr. 1908). This was an appeal from the supreme court of the Territory of Oklahoma. Justice McKenna delivered the opinion of the court, with no recorded dissent.
117. 208 *U.S.* 274–309, at 297 (3 Feb. 1908). Chief Justice Fuller delivered the opinion of the court, with no recorded dissent.
118. H. K. Smith, *Memorandum* (1908), p. 342.
119. The word "substantial" was taken in its qualitative, not quantitative, sense.

more other competitors. Peckham for the Supreme Court had invoked this principle in the Joint Traffic decision.[120] Similarly, in writing the opinion of the Court in *Northern Securities* Harlan reiterated the principle that only direct restraints of interstate trade or commerce fell within the proscription of the Sherman Act.[121]

The second feature of traditional jurisprudence that the federal courts retained in construing the Sherman Act was the principle that a literal monopoly of manufacture or production achieved by a person or firm or corporation through superior efficiency, or through effective and otherwise lawful competition, or through expansion by the purchase of property, remained unobjectionable. At no time before the Rule of Reason decisions of 1911 did the Court construe either combination or bigness as such to be in violation of the Sherman Act. In this respect, the Rule of Reason decisions left previous judicial interpretation untouched.

The distinction between manufacture or production and trade or commerce, as affirmed in *E. C. Knight*, remained in effect at all times. For example, in its decision in the Addyston Pipe case, which is sometimes cited as having reversed *Knight*, the Supreme Court distinguished between the two cases. It pointed out that in the earlier case, although the American Sugar Refining Company had obtained "a practical monopoly of the business of manufacturing sugar," the Sherman Act "did not touch the case," because the combination "only related to manufacture and not to commerce among the States or with foreign nations." Peckham insisted on "the plain distinction between manufacture and commerce," holding that "a contract or combination which directly related to manufacture only was not brought within the purview of the act."[122] Indeed, as Peckham noted in his Joint Traffic decision, "the formation of corporations for business or manufacturing purposes has never, to our knowledge, been regarded in the nature of a contract in restraint of trade or commerce."[123] Not even Harlan disputed this principle, as may be seen in his Northern Securities decision for the Court.[124]

---

120. 171 *U.S.* 568; to similar effect, *Hopkins* v. *United States*, 171 *U.S.* 578–604, at 600, cited by Peckham at *Joint Traffic*, 171 *U.S.* 568. (See note 108, above.)
121. 193 *U.S.* 331.
122. 175 *U.S.* 238. Cf. Davies, *Trust Laws*, pp. 74–75; Jones, *Trust Problem*, p. 397.
123. 171 *U.S.* 567.
124. 193 *U.S.* 331: "... although the act of Congress ... has no reference to the mere manufacture or production of articles or commodities within the limits of the several States, it does embrace and declare to be illegal every contract, combination or conspiracy ... which directly or necessarily operates *in restraint* of trade or commerce *among the several States or with foreign nations*." Harlan's emphasis.

The distinction between manufacture or production and interstate trade or commerce was dictated less by logic or abstract principle than by historical and political circumstances in the United States, in particular the post-Reconstruction agreement to leave "domestic" (race) relations to the states, combined with the constitutional separation of state and federal jurisdictions,[125] but it also found some reinforcement in the common-law distinction between direct and ancillary retraints. In American jurisprudence, these elements of politics and constitutional and common law became mutually intertwined, and they reinforced each other to yield a greater protection to contractual liberty in practice than might otherwise have been the case. Accordingly, the purchase by one competitor of the plant or stock of another for the purpose of legitimate expansion or greater efficiency, although it might incidentally restrict competition, at no time before 1911, or thereafter, constituted a violation of the Sherman Act as construed by the federal courts.[126] Similarly, such a practice as "the sale of a good will of a business with an accompanying agreement not to engage in a similar [competing] business," noted Peckham in both his *Trans-Missouri* and *Joint Traffic* decisions, was to be construed as legal "within the meaning of the [Sherman] act."[127] "Monopolize" or "attempt to monopolize" were still taken to mean unfair methods designed to eliminate existing competitors or prevent the appearance of potential competitors.[128]

It would be inaccurate, then, to say that from the Trans-Missouri case of 1897 to the Standard Oil and American Tobacco cases of 1911 the Supreme Court and lower federal courts applied no "standard of reason" to the interpretation and enforcement of the Sherman Act. As Justice Peckham stated for the Supreme Court in 1898 in the Hopkins case, decided on the same day as *Joint Traffic*, "The act of Congress must have a reasonable construction or else there would scarcely be an agreement or contract among business men that could not be said to have, indirectly or remotely, some bearing upon interstate commerce

---

125. *Kidd v. Pearson*, 128 *U.S.* 20–22; *United States v. E. C. Knight Co.*, 156 *U.S.* 12, 16; also *Coe v. Erroll*, 116 *U.S.* 517. And see note 180, below.
126. Cf. *United States v. American Tobacco Co. et al.*, 164 *Fed.* 718, at 3 *FAD* 453; Davies, *Trust Laws*, p. 84.
127. *Trans-Missouri*, at 161 *U.S.* 329; *Joint Traffic*, at 171 *U.S.* 568.
128. Cf. *U.S. v. American Tobacco Co. et al.*, 164 *Fed.* 702, 709, at 3 *FAD* 429, 441; *United States v. Standard Oil Co. of N.J. et al.*, 173 *Fed.* 191, 195–196, at 3 *FAD* 717, 723–725. "... while unlawful means to monopolize and to continue an unlawful monopoly of interstate and international commerce are misdemeanors and enjoinable under [the Sherman Act]..., monopolies of part of interstate and international commerce by legitimate competition, however successful, are not denounced by the law, and may not be forbidden by the courts..." *U.S. v. Standard Oil*, 173 *Fed.* 191, at 3 *FAD* 717.

and possibly to restrain it."[129] Between 1897 and 1911 the Court, before declaring that a restriction of competition constituted a restraint of trade or an attempt to monopolize in violation of the Sherman Act, had always first to determine whether the contract, agreement, or combination in question (1) constituted a direct as against an indirect or incidental restraint, and (2) directly and substantially affected and restrained interstate or foreign commerce as against production or the purchase and sale of property as such.

In other respects, the majority view that reigned within the Supreme Court from 1897 to 1911 represented a substantial departure from traditional United States jurisprudence on restraints of trade and monopoly. The traditional jurisprudence had been in effect not only under common law before the enactment of the Sherman Act, but also for seven years thereafter. Contrary to Justice Harlan's partial dissent in the Standard Oil and American Tobacco cases of 1911,[130] it was his (and Peckham's), not White's (and Holmes's), construction of the Sherman Act that constituted new judicial doctrine, which "upset the long-established interpretation" of the courts. If anything, White's construction in the 1911 cases represented not an "upset" but a restoration.

For the traditional judicial doctrine that reasonable restrictions of competition in interstate trade were legal, the Court's majority had substituted the doctrine that no direct restrictions of competition were legal; for the traditional doctrine upholding the right to compete and contractual liberty as distinguished from a compulsion to compete, the Court's majority had substituted a doctrine that set compulsory competition against contractual liberty. As against calculative attempts by capitalists to regulate the market in order to maintain the remunerative nature of pecuniary pursuits, the Court now asserted the natural, impersonal rule of the unfettered market, enforced where necessary by government regulation of capitalists' behavior. Commerce, Harlan held, "must be allowed to flow in its accustomed channels, wholly unvexed and unobstructed by anything that would restrain its ordinary movement."[131] As he ruled for the Court in *Northern Securities*, "The natural effect of competition is to increase commerce, and an agreement whose direct effect is to prevent this play of competition restrains instead of promotes trade and commerce."[132] Hence "The constitution-

129. *Hopkins* v. *United States*, 171 *U.S.* 600.
130. *Standard Oil Co. of N.J. et al.* v. *United States*, 221 *U.S.* 83, 90, at 4 *FAD* 149–150, 155; *American Tobacco Co.* v. *United States*, 221 *U.S.* 191, at 4 *FAD* 243–244.
131. *Standard Oil Co.* v. *U.S.*, 221 *U.S.* 96, at 4 *FAD* 159–160.
132. *Northern Securities Co.* v. *United States*, 193 *U.S.* 331.

al guarantee of liberty of contract does not prevent Congress from prescribing the rule of free competition for those engaged in *interstate and international* commerce."[133]

Interwoven with the learned disputes in the federal courts over legal theory as it related to the Sherman Act were ideological differences among jurists over the desirable and just nature of the market and its relation to the "good society." Harlan and his like-minded colleagues gave judicial expression to the older natural-liberty doctrine of a market composed predominantly of independent, self-employed proprietors as the guarantor of economic welfare, social justice, and small-producer democracy. For them, this doctrine was self-evident, beyond the scrutiny of economic fact or historical inquiry, and to that extent it assumed the essential characteristics of what Veblen would have called metaphysical prescription.

It was a doctrine that, for them, transcended considerations of market efficiencies or lower costs to society for goods or services. Justice Peckham made this clear in his extended defense of the small enterpriser in his *Trans-Missouri* decision. Referring there to "combinations of capital, whose purpose in combining is to control the production or manufacture of any particular article, and by such control dictate the price at which the article shall be sold," Peckham argued that it was not "for the substantial interests of the country that any one commodity should be within the sole power and subject to the sole will of one powerful combination of capital." Beyond this, however, Peckham noted that the effect of such combination "being to drive out of business all the small dealers in the commodity and to render the public subject to the decision of the combination as to what price shall be paid for the article," it was, he insisted, "not material that the price of an article may be lowered," for the end result must be "unfortunate for the country by depriving it of the services of a large number of small but independent dealers who were familiar with the business and who had spent their lives in it, and who supported themselves and their families from the small profits realized therein." It was also "not so material," Peckham continued, that "they be able to find other avenues to earn their livelihood," because it was "not for the real prosperity of any country that such changes should occur which result in transferring an independent business man, the head of his establishment, small though

133. Ibid., p. 332; Harlan's emphasis. Also, *National Cotton Oil Co. v. Texas*, 197 *U.S.* 115, at 129 (1905). Cf. Peckham to same effect in *Joint Traffic*, at 171 *U.S.* 569, and in *Addyston Pipe*, at 175 *U.S.* 228–231. See notes 110 and 111, and related text, above.

it may be, into a mere servant or agent of a corporation for selling the commodities which he once manufactured or dealt in, having no voice in shaping the business policy of the company and bound to obey orders issued by others."[134] Sheer *obiter dicta* though it may have been, here was a classic statement of small-producer antipathy to corporate enterprise.

Justices White and Holmes and their like-minded colleagues rejected such doctrine as ill-suited to modern business conditions, as oblivious of the necessity of combination and consolidation in an industrially developed economy, as destructive of contractual liberty and profitable enterprise suited to modern technology, and hence as detrimental to social progress in an urban-industrial age. For them, contractual liberty, regulated in the public interest and adapted to modern business conditions, constituted the preeminent self-evident principle. Neither side in the dispute, it will be noted, embraced a doctrine of laissez-faire; both sides affirmed a strong regulatory role for government in subjecting the market to social policy, but for different purposes. There was, however, this further significant difference: To the Harlan side, only government, a presumably neutral agency outside the market, should regulate it; to the White–Holmes side, both government outside the market and capitalists within the market should share authority in regulating it.

In upholding their respective positions, Harlan and Peckham departed from traditional common-law jurisprudence to reestablish the earlier small-producer version of natural liberty, while White and Holmes invoked the traditional common law to vindicate new economic theory and a legal positivism suited to the mature industrial capitalism of the late nineteenth and early twentieth centuries. As common-law doctrine was not committed to unrestricted competition, it was peculiarly fitted to adjusting judicial process to the "common sense" of the market. Its juridical permanence, therefore, guaranteed the facilitating of change, the adaptation of the legal order to evolving economic conditions.[135] By interpreting the Sherman Act as having superseded, rather than as having embodied, common-law principles on restraint of trade and monopoly, Harlan and those in agreement with him were, in the view of those like White and Holmes, invoking a visionary theory that was as destructive of social stability in an industrial society as it was ill-suited to modern business conditions.

Justice Holmes made this argument forcefully in his *Northern Secu-*

134.   166 *U.S.* 323.
135.   Cf. Thorelli, *Antitrust Policy*, pp. 13, 51; Rubin, *Business Firms and the Common Law*, pp. 21–22.

rities dissent of 1904. He opened his opinion with the now famous aphorism "Great cases like hard cases make bad law." After insisting that "Contracts in restraint of trade are dealt with and defined by the common law," Holmes, author of the celebrated treatise on the common law, argued squarely in the common-law tradition that there was no restraint of trade or monopoly "until something is done with the intent to exclude strangers to the combination from competing with it in some part of the business which it carries on." The Sherman Act should "not be construed to mean the universal disintegration of society into single men, each at war with all the rest, or even the prevention of all further combinations for a common end." Such a construction of the Sherman Act "would make eternal the *bellum omnium contra omnes* and disintegrate society so far as it could into individual atoms. If that were its intent," Holmes objected, "I should regard calling such a law a regulation of commerce as a mere pretense. It would be an attempt to reconstruct society." Whatever might be "the wisdom of such an attempt," Holmes declared, "I believe that Congress was not entrusted by the Constitution with the power to make it and I am deeply persuaded that it has not tried."[136]

The judges on the federal bench were jurists first, social theorists second. Disagree as some might with the Supreme Court majority view from 1897 to 1911, as "true and upright" jurists, the lower federal judges nevertheless upheld the interpretation of the Sherman Act dictated by the high court's majority, while some of them prudently suggested from time to time that the remedy for unwise public policy lay with Congress, in the absence of a change in the Court's majority view itself. This attitude was perhaps nowhere more dramatically expressed than in the apparently pained decision handed down by the lower federal court against the American Tobacco Company in 1908, and similarly, although less dramatically, in the decision written in 1909 by Judge Sanborn of the lower federal court against the Standard Oil Company.

Sanborn had delivered a common-law construction of the Sherman Act in the Trans-Missouri case, which the Supreme Court subsequently

---

136.   193 *U.S.* 400, 404, 409, 407, 411. Holmes here also noted the significance of the Sherman Act's title in dictating its construction as the enactment of the common law. 193 *U.S.* 405. Holmes's opinion, of course, flatly contradicted the majority view that Congress had full constitutional power, under the commerce clause, to regulate interstate and foreign commerce as it saw fit, against both the states and the contractual liberty of private parties, as Harlan specifically ruled for the court in this case, reiterating Peckham's prior rulings. 193 *U.S.* 350–352. See notes 110, 111, and 122, above.

reversed. In the Standard Oil case, on 20 November 1909, he was obliged to reject the common-law distinction between reasonable and unreasonable combinations as no longer operative. Citing *Addyston Pipe, Joint Traffic, Hopkins,* and *Northern Securities,* Sanborn ruled that the parties to the combination "are presumed to intend the inevitable results of their acts, and neither their actual intent nor the reasonableness of the restraint imposed may withdraw it from the denunciation of the statute."[137] He further held that it was the "purpose" of the Sherman Act "to keep the rates of transportation and the prices of articles in interstate and international commerce open to free competition." Hence, any contract or combination that transferred "the control of such rates or prices ... from separate competitors and vested [them] in a person or an association of persons, necessarily restricts competition and restrains that commerce," in violation of the act.[138]

In the American Tobacco case, the Circuit Court of the Southern District of New York, on 7 November 1908, by a three-to-one majority, decided against the company in the suit brought under the Sherman Act.[139] Both the opinion of the court, delivered by Judge E. Henry Lacombe, and the separate concurring opinions of judges Walter C. Noyes and Alfred C. Coxe – the latter two having been appointed to the circuit court by Roosevelt – in essence amounted to an apology for interpreting the act as destructive of the corporation. They asserted, however, that they had no alternative in the face of persistent Supreme Court decisions, short of congressional alteration of the law, or modification by the Supreme Court itself of its construction of the law.[140]

Lacombe stated that the act was "no longer open to construction in

---

137. *U.S.* v. *Standard Oil,* 173 *Fed.* 177, 179–192, 179 (Circuit Court, Eastern District, Missouri), at 3 *FAD* 696, 699–719, 700. The court was unanimous, judges Adams and Van Devanter concurring in Sanborn's opinion, Judge Hook concurring in a separate opinion. Willis Van Devanter was appointed to the Supreme Court by Taft the next year, 1910, and served to 1937. In 1914, after the Rule of Reason decisions, Sanborn resumed his common-law view of the Sherman Act, holding the International Harvester Company to be a reasonable combination. Jones, *Trust Problem,* pp. 435–436.

138. 173 *Fed.* 184, at 3 *FAD* 707.

139. *United States* v. *American Tobacco Co. et al.,* 164 *Fed.* 700–728, at 3 *FAD* 427–470. Each of the judges of the majority wrote a separate opinion, with Lacombe's designated as for the court. Judge Henry G. Ward dissented.

140. With respect to possible modification of the Sherman Act by Congress, the judges may well have been referring to the Hepburn and other bills then pending in Congress. See Chapter 4, below. On the appointments of Noyes (1907) and Coxe (1902), see Rayman L. Solomon, "The Politics of Appointment and the Federal Courts' Role in Regulating America: U.S. Courts of Appeal Judgeships from T.R. to F.D.R.," *American Bar Foundation Research Journal,* No. 2 Spring 1984, pp. 285–343, at pp. 306–307, 311.

the inferior federal courts." In view of the decisions handed down by "successive majorities of the Supreme Court," he noted, the act "is to be construed as prohibiting any contract or combination whose direct effect is to prevent the free play of competition and thus tend to deprive the country of the services of any number of independent dealers however small." In a manner reminiscent of Justice Holmes's words, Lacombe continued, "As thus construed, the statute is revolutionary." He hastened to add, however, in deference to the Supreme Court, that he did not intend thereby to imply that the construction was incorrect in point of law. "The act may be termed revolutionary," he explained, "because, before its passage, the courts had recognized [as legal] a 'restraint of trade' which was held not to be unfair, but permissible, although it operated in some measure to restrict competition." Lacombe noted that "by insensible degrees, under the operation of many causes, business manufacturing and trading alike, has more and more developed a tendency toward larger and larger aggregations of capital and more extensive combinations of individual enterprise." He then cited with approval the contention that "under existing conditions," only thus could "production be increased and cheapened, new markets opened and developed, stability in reasonable prices secured, and industrial progress assured." The record in the case, he wrote, did not indicate that the company had increased the price of tobacco to the consumer, or had resorted to unfair competition or improper practices to drive out or absorb competitors. But all this, as well as the question of whether benefits had accrued to the public from the merger, was immaterial under the Supreme Court's construction of the law, which the lower court was bound to accept. That the merger involved contracts and combinations directly "in restraint of a competition existing" before was sufficient, held Lacombe, "to bring it within the ban of this drastic statute."[141]

The concurring opinions of judges Noyes and Coxe demonstrated the extent to which the construction of "this drastic statute" remained qualified by traditional doctrine on the distinction between direct and indirect restraints and by the technical-legal meaning of monopoly.[142]

---

141.   164 *Fed.* 701–703, at 3 *FAD* 429–431.
142.   For example, Judge Coxe emphasized that "The statute was not intended to strike down enterprise or to prevent the restraint of trade by destroying it. . . . it has never been held that the mere fact that a business is large and is extended over a wide territory renders its promoters amenable to the statute. Success is not a crime. . . . Prosperity is the premium which has always been awarded to earnest and intelligent endeavor. The statute was never intended to punish success or reward incompetency. . . ." 164 *Fed.* 709–710, at 3 *FAD* 441. In the same vein, Sanborn a year later in his *Standard Oil* decision. 173 *Fed.* 191, at 3 *FAD* 717,

But Noyes made it clear that given the Supreme Court's decisions, a combination with sufficient market power, derived from the merger of previously competing firms, to regulate supply and prices, however reasonably, in interstate or foreign commerce constituted an illegal restraint of trade under the Sherman Act. The American Tobacco Company, as Noyes explained, did not confine its operations to intra-state commerce. The Knight case was therefore not germane to its case: "In view of the world-wide business of these defendants," he ruled, "of the constant reaching out for new markets in new countries, of the many different industries in many different states involved, of the constant shipment of materials from state to state, and of the control of the disposition of the manufactured product, . . . the defendants are engaged in interstate commerce, and that which the combination directly affects is interstate commerce."[143]

Judge Noyes, however, found himself unable to contain his disagreement with the given construction of the Sherman Act, offering a not altogether discreet set of *obiter dicta*. Because his opinion illustrates the temper and character of arguments then being advanced from the bench by federal jurists who were chafing under the Harlan construction of the Sherman Act, it is worth quoting from at length. Noyes wrote:

> The modern tendency of business is toward cooperation, instead of competition. This tendency, while of earlier inception, has developed with phenomenal activity in this country during the past 20 years – especially during the past decade. Concentration of interests and unification of control have taken the place of separate and independent operation. Important industrial corporations, formerly competing, have been combined into greater companies of wider scope, and these, in turn, have been united into combinations with vast resources, embracing, as their fields of operation, whole branches of industry.
>
> And yet this economic development toward the elimination of competition has taken place in the face of statutes and judicial decisions declaring that "competition is the life of trade" and must be preserved. . . .
>
> Insofar as combinations result from the operation of economic principles, it may be doubtful whether they should be stayed at all

143.   164 *Fed.* 716, at 3 *FAD* 450–451. Judge Henry Ward, however, based his dissent both on *Knight* and on grounds, not formally in conflict with the Harlan majority in the Supreme Court, that the purpose of the combination was not to restrain trade or prevent competition, "although competition was incidentally prevented," but to increase volume and profits of the business "by intelligent economies." 164 *Fed.* 722–728, 726, at 3 *FAD* 459–467, 465. Ward was, like Noyes and Coxe, a Roosevelt appointee. Solomon, "Politics of Appointment," pp. 310–311.

by legislation. It may be that the evils in the existing situation should be left to the remedies afforded by the laws of trade. On the other hand, it may be that the protection of the public from the operations of combinations of capital – especially those possessing the element of oppression – requires some measure of governmental intervention. It may be that the present anti-trust statute should be amended and made applicable only to those combinations which unreasonably restrain trade – that it should draw a line between those combinations which work for good and those which work for evil. But these are all legislative, and not judicial, questions. It cannot be too clearly borne in mind that this court has nothing to do with the wisdom, justice, or expediency of the statute. Equally true is it that this court, in applying the statute, must follow the decisions of the Supreme Court. If the decisions of that court have been too broad, it is for that court alone to modify them. The only right and duty of this court is to take the statute as it finds it, and, as it finds it, apply it in accordance with the interpretation placed upon it by the highest tribunal. That this course may lead to results believed by many persons to be prejudicial to the public welfare cannot affect our action. This court can neither refuse to enforce a constitutional act of Congress nor ignore the decisions of the Supreme Court of the United States.

... Concede that the present statute goes too far. Concede, even, that no enactments are now necessary. Yet all must agree that conditions may arise in the future requiring legislative action which shall be both uniform and effective. Congress alone could take such action....[144]

Noyes's opinion is significant not only because it represented the view of a considerable body of federal jurists who regarded the Harlan construction of the Sherman Act as bad public policy, but also because it demonstrated the general agreement among jurists as to the meaning of the Harlan construction, whatever their opinion of it as a matter of policy. At the same time, on the other hand, Noyes's opinion represented what by 1910 had become a powerful current of opinion among corporate and political leaders, particularly "progressives" among them. In their view, the corporate reorganization of the property system and of the market constituted the modern mode of business enterprise, to which the law and public policy must adapt, by legalizing reasonable combinations and restrictions of competition while providing by legislation for appropriate government supervision.

144.   164 *Fed.* 711–712, 716–717, at 3 *EAD* 443–444, 451

Restoration

By 1911, the stage had already been set for the return to the common-law construction of the Sherman Act that the Supreme Court, in the Standard Oil and American Tobacco cases, was to declare. Not only had many federal judges expressed dissatisfaction with the public policy embodied in the prevailing construction of the Sherman Act, but also public criticism of that construction had been building throughout the period 1897–1911. The criticism came from economists, such political leaders as Theodore Roosevelt and William Howard Taft, capitalists, labor leaders, farm leaders, and not least of all from the Bureau of Corporations, established in 1903 as a "progressive" measure intended as a first step toward a more effective federal regulatory policy.[145]

The Supreme Court's decisions in the Standard Oil and American Tobacco cases, therefore, in restoring a common-law construction of the Sherman Act, did not rise as a phoenix from the void suddenly to proclaim a novel doctrine. On the contrary, the decisions had been presaged by traditional jurisprudence before 1897, by persistent minority opinions within the Supreme Court, and by qualifications and *obiter dicta* of judges in the lower federal courts after 1897. The Rule of Reason decisions came after a decade or more of demands by political leaders, corporate capitalists, government officials, and intellectuals in public forums, for a new policy to correspond alike with traditional jurisprudence and modern business conditions.

As Joseph E. Davies, the first chairman of the Federal Trade Commission, put it, "The decision of the United States Supreme Court in the Standard Oil case made it evident that the words 'restraint of trade' in the Sherman Act should be construed as declaratory of the common law so far as the meaning of that term was concerned. This view had been taken by the dissenting members of the Court in the Trans-Missouri case."[146] In technical-legal terms, the distinguishing characteristic of the Rule of Reason decisions of 1911 was not, as sometimes assumed, that now size or bigness no longer came under proscription. As already

145. See Chapter 4, below.
146. Davies, *Trust Laws*, p. 24. Also *Standard Oil Co. of New Jersey et al.* v. *United States*, 221 U.S. 57, 60–61, at *FAD* 127, 130–131: The Court's opinion, written by Chief Justice White, defined "monopolize" and "attempt to monopolize" as synonymous with "restraint of trade," that is, as a subtype, natural consequence, or intended effect of a restraint of trade. Hence the observation by Davies applies to the Sherman Act as a whole with respect to the meaning of the act's two prohibitive sections (sections 1 and 2). Cf. Gerard C. Henderson, *The Federal Trade Commission: A Study in Administrative Law and Procedure* (New Haven: Yale University Press, 1924), p. 6.

observed, never under the Sherman Act, even during 1897–1911, was size or bigness as such considered by the courts as a valid criterion for determining the illegality of a corporation or combination. Instead, in reestablishing the principle that common-law doctrine had been embodied in the Sherman Act, the Supreme Court rehabilitated the juridical principle that restriction of competition did not necessarily constitute or imply an illegal restraint of trade or attempt to monopolize. Private persons, including corporations, could lawfully restrict competition in the market; to that extent, private persons, and not the federal government alone, could lawfully regulate interstate or foreign commerce.

In essence the Court ruled definitively that the Sherman Act prohibited unreasonable restraints of trade and monopoly as defined at common law. Unreasonable restraints of trade or monopoly thus defined meant (1) unfair, oppressive methods designed to eliminate, damage, or destroy competitors; and (2) business practices, the purpose or necessary effect of which was to enhance or depress prices unduly, or affect trade or distribution or transportation unduly, that is, to the detriment of the public interest.

Accordingly, in the Supreme Court's Standard Oil decision, the corporation's offense was not its size or market power as such, but the intent and purpose "to exclude others" and to "drive others from the field and to exclude them from their right to trade and thus accomplish the mastery which was the end in view."[147] By the same token, the Court declared that its decision did not preclude "agreements between one or more of the subsidiary [Standard Oil] corporations" subsequent to the ordered dissolution.[148]

Consistent with common-law doctrine, the Court, moreover, made it explicit that freedom of contract and the right to compete ("the legitimate purpose of reasonably forwarding personal interest"), as distinguished from unrestricted competition, or the obligation to compete, constituted the controlling *desideratum* under the Sherman Act. By corollary, the Court went on to state that to compel unrestricted competition must necessarily infringe free trade, liberty of contract, and rights of property, precisely which, it insisted, the Sherman Act had been designed to protect:

> The statute under this view evidenced the intent not to restrain the right to make and enforce contracts, whether resulting from combination or otherwise, which did not unduly restrain interstate

147. *Standard Oil* v. *United States,* 221 *U.S.* 76, at 4 *FAD* 143.
148. 221 *U.S.* 80, at 4 *FAD* 147.

or foreign commerce, but to protect that commerce from being restrained by methods, whether old or new, which would constitute an interference that is an undue restraint.[149]

In this connection, in the American Tobacco case, the Court, reaffirming its Standard Oil decision, elaborated its view:

> Applying the rule of reason to the construction of the statute, it was held in the *Standard Oil case* that as the words "restraint of trade" at common law and in the law of this country at the time of the adoption of the Anti-Trust Act only embraced acts or contracts or agreements or combinations which operated to the prejudice of the public interests by unduly obstructing the due course of trade or which, either because of the evident purpose of the acts, etc., injuriously restrained trade, that the words as used in the statute were designed to have and did have but a like significance.... In other words, ... the words restraint of trade should be given a meaning which would not destroy the individual right to contract and render difficult if not impossible any movement of trade in the channels of interstate commerce – the free movement of which it was the purpose of the statute to protect.... Indeed, the necessity for not departing in this case from the standard of the rule of reason which is universal in its application is ... plainly required in order to give effect to the remedial purposes which the act ... contemplates, and to prevent that act from destroying all liberty of contract and all substantial right to trade, ... thus causing the act to be at war with itself by annihilating the fundamental right of freedom to trade which, on the very face of the act, it was enacted to preserve.[150]

In subsequent cases, the Supreme Court followed through consistently with concrete applications of the meaning of its Rule of Reason

149. 221 *U.S.* 58, 60, at 4 *FAD* 128, 129. See also the Court's statement that implicit in the principles embodied in common law and in the Sherman Act lay the "instinctive recognition of the truisms that the course of trade could not be made free by obstructing it, and that an individual's right to trade could not be protected by destroying such right"; that "freedom to contract and to abstain from contracting and to exercise every reasonable right incident thereto became the rule in the English law"; and that U.S. law "simply followed the line of development of the law of England." 221 *U.S.* 55–56, 58–59, at 4 *FAD* 125–126, 128. Harlan (221 *U.S.* 83–106, at 4 *FAD* 149–168) concurred in part and dissented in part, concurring with the dissolution of the company, dissenting in the Court's reasoning.

150. *American Tobacco Co.* v. *United States*, 221 *U.S.* 179–180, at 4 *FAD* 233–234. Chief Justice White again delivered the opinion of the Court, with Harlan again concurring in part and dissenting in part, as in the Standard Oil case. The Standard Oil decision came down 15 May 1911, the American Tobacco decision on 29 May 1911; Harlan died the following October.

decisions. Less than a year after the American Tobacco decision, a unanimous Supreme Court, without Harlan, who had died in the interim, in the case of *United States* v. *Terminal Railroad Association of St. Louis*, held that a combination unreasonably and therefore illegally in restraint of trade might, by modification of its provisions, become a lawful combination. Since the test of legality was the reasonableness of the restraint, the mere combining of several independent concerns, the Court held, did not necessarily constitute an illegal restraint.[151]

Again, in 1912, in the case of *Standard Sanitary Manufacturing Company* v. *United States*, the Supreme Court voided a patent agreement the company had entered into, but left the corporation itself untouched, although it comprised a consolidation, effected in 1910, of sixteen previously competing corporations, and controlled at least 50 percent of the nation's total production of bathroom fixtures. All that was necessary, the Court held, was the enjoining of certain unfair practices.[152]

One month after this decision, the Supreme Court in the Anthracite Coal Combination case, voided as unfair or unreasonable practices certain price and distribution pools among coal operators in Pennsylvania and New Jersey, but upheld as reasonable consolidations the acquisition in January 1898 by the Erie Railroad of the New York, Susquehanna and Western Company and in 1899 of the Pennsylvania Coal Company and its allied railroads, and the acquisition in 1901 by the Reading Company of a majority of the stock of the Central Railroad of New Jersey.[153]

The next year, 1913, in the case of *United States* v. *Winslow*,[154] a criminal suit brought by the government under the Sherman Act against the president and other officers of the United Shoe Machinery Company, the Supreme Court held in a brief and unanimous decision that although the corporate consolidation, effected in 1899, controlled 70 to 80 percent of the nation's total production of essential shoe manufacturing machinery, it did not in itself constitute a violation of the antitrust act, (1) because it represented a legal exercise of patent rights, (2) because "the combination was simply an effort after greater efficiency"

151.　224 *U.S.* 383–413, esp. at 410–413 (22 Apr. 1912). Justice Lurton delivered the opinion of the Court, with no dissent.
152.　226 *U.S.* 20–52 (18 Nov. 1912). Justice McKenna delivered the opinion of the Court, with no dissent.
153.　*United States* v. *Reading Co. Temple Iron Co.* v. *United States. Reading Co.* v. *United States* (known as *U.S.* v. *Reading Co.*), 226 *U.S.* 324–373, esp. at 371–373 (16 Dec. 1912). Justice Lurton delivered the opinion of the Court, with no dissent.
154.　227 *U.S.* 202–210 (3 Feb. 1913).

through integration of related processes, and (3) because the companies combined had not been competitors before the consolidation. The Court made it clear, as it was to do in the subsequent United States Steel case seven years later, that consolidation for the purposes of integration and the achievement of greater efficiency possessed no element of unreasonableness nor, therefore, of illegality under the Sherman Act. The statute, the Court explained, did not aim at "reducing all manufacture to isolated units of the lowest degree."[155] Five years later, the Court again upheld the United Shoe Machinery Company as a legal consolidation on essentially the same grounds, although here the question of patent rights assumed the central position in the outcome of the case.[156]

The case of *United States* v. *United States Steel Corporation et al.*,[157] decided by the Supreme Court in 1920 after ten years of litigation, delivered the coup de grace, in the series of cases from 1911 to 1920, to any remaining vestiges of the Harlan construction. As in its decision in the Shoe Machinery case, the Court, in upholding the lower court's decision in favor of United States Steel, reiterated the principle that a merger controlling all or a substantial proportion of an industry could not be construed, on that account, as in violation of the Sherman Act, provided it was not at the time harassing or oppressing its remaining rivals with unfair practices or excluding others from entering the industry. Finding that since the termination of the price-setting "Gary Dinners," which, the Court held, were illegal, the Steel Corporation had not resumed such practices, the Court pointed out that the desire for, and achievement of, integration and greater efficiency, which the Court recognized as an important element in the establishment of the corporation, in no way violated the Sherman Act. The Court therefore rejected

---

155.   227 *U.S.* 215–218, 217. Justice Holmes delivered the opinion of the Court.
156.   *United States* v. *United Shoe Machinery Co.*, 247 *U.S.* 32–91 (20 May 1918). Justice McKenna (pp. 35–67) delivered the opinion of the Court, with Justice Day dissenting (pp. 67–75), concurred in by justices Mahlon Pitney and John H. Clarke. Justices James C. McReynolds and Louis D. Brandeis took no part in the case. McReynolds had served as U.S. solicitor general in the prosecution of the earlier case. Brandeis had been counsel, organizer, and a director of the company from before the consolidation in 1899 to 1906, and thereafter attorney for the independent manufacturers who had pressed the government to bring the earlier case against the Company. Cf. [S. W. Winslow], *Brandeis and Brandeis* (Boston, 1912), pamphlet in State Historical Society of Wisconsin, Madison (the second "Brandeis" is printed backward and upside down).
157.   251 *U.S.* 416–466, at 8 *FAD* 527–571 (1 Mar. 1920). Justice McKenna delivered the opinion of the Court, concurred in by Chief Justice White and justices Van Devanter and Holmes. Justice Day dissented, concurred in by justices Pitney and Clarke. Justices McReynolds and Brandeis took no part in the case.

the government's plea for dissolution as contrary to the public interest, and it acquitted the corporation.[158]

In tone and content, the opinion of the Court had all the features of a lay polemic against the doctrine of unrestricted competition that had prevailed in the Court from 1897 to 1911. It argued that only a common-law, Rule of Reason construction of the act could guarantee contractual liberty, the right to compete, and the rights of property, the very objective of the statute; that the doctrine of unrestricted competition was, in its application, destructive of these and of competition itself. In pressing its argument, the Court took judicial notice of the movement toward integration of the steel industry from ore to finished product, which had obtained at and shortly after the turn of the century. Industrial integration, observed the Court, although perhaps not an absolute necessity, "had certainly become a facility of industrial progress." But, the Court objected, the government was "reduced to the assertion that the size of the Corporation ... is an abhorrence to the law," and that the corporation, through the power consequent upon its size, unduly and thus unlawfully restrained competition, "regardless of purpose." "To assent to that," the Court asked derisively, "to what extremes should we be led? Competition consists of business activities and ability – they make its life; but there may be fatalities in it. Are the activities to be encouraged when militant, and suppressed or regulated when triumphant because of the dominance attained?" It was "the inevitable logic of the Government's contention" that competition not only must be free, "but that it must not be pressed to the ascendancy of a competitor." The regression was admittedly extreme, "but short of it the Government cannot stop. The fallacy it conveys is manifest." Restoring the principle enunciated in *Trans-Missouri* by Judge John A. Riner in the lower court twenty-eight years earlier in his common-law rendering of the Sherman Act, that "the public is not entitled to free and unrestricted competition, but ... to ... fair and healthy competition,"[159] the Supreme Court had since 1911 come full circle in affirming that the act "does not compel competition nor require all that is possible."[160]

Dissolution proceedings and consent decrees, after the 1911 decisions, in cases that affected prominent corporate consolidations, as well as looser arrangements, consistently reinforced the meaning of the Sher-

158. 251 *U.S.* 417, 436–457, at 8 *FAD* 527, 544–563. Lower court decision, at 223 *Fed.* 55–179, at 6 *FAD* 1–182 (3 June 1915).
159. 53 *Fed.* 453.
160. 251 *U.S.* 442, 450–451, at 8 *FAD* 549, 556–557, 558.

man Act under the restored common-law construction. In dissolution proceedings the Supreme Court (1) invariably required that stock held by the "parent" corporation in its constituents be redistributed from the "parent" corporation itself to its stockholders, so that the constituent corporations would be left nominally independent; (2) seldom required atomizations of the constituent corporations, which themselves were often combinations; (3) prohibited the use of specified unfair practices in the future; but (4) did not prohibit the constituent corporations or the "parent" corporation from entering subsequent contracts of cooperation or association with one another or with others, which could be considered reasonable. The consent decrees entered into between the Department of Justice and various associations or corporate consolidations by and large prohibited particular practices and enjoined their repetition in the future. After the Rule of Reason decisions of 1911, and particularly during Woodrow Wilson's presidency, the consent decree or agreements informally negotiated by the Justice Department with corporations became a common method of settling antitrust cases.[161]

Among the corporations that submitted to consent decrees were the American Coal Products Company, the American Thread Company, S. F. Bowser & Company, the Burroughs Adding Machine Company, the Central West Publishing Company, the General Electric Company, the Otis Elevator Company, the American Corn Products Company, and the International Harvester Corporation. In Eliot Jones's words, "In no instance were the aforementioned companies required to submit to a physical dissolution [except that International Harvester and Corn Products were ordered to divest themselves of certain units]; the decree merely enjoined certain objectionable practices, though in a few instances it ordered the dissolution of a few subsidiary companies or the sale of some securities."[162]

Alongside the large corporation, the trade association developed in the first two decades of the twentieth century not simply as a lobbying or promotional agency but also as a device for regulating the market.

---

161. Cf. Jones, *Trust Problem*, p. 490: "In very few instances, if any, have these consent decrees involved the physical division of the plants or assets of the companies. Instead they have dealt with the future conduct of the trust or combination." Also Arthur S. Link, *Woodrow Wilson and the Progressive Era, 1910–1917* (New York: Harper & Row, 1954), p. 76.

162. For discussion and analysis of dissolution proceedings involving the Standard Oil Co., the American Tobacco Co., the Du Pont "Powder Trust," the United Shoe Machinery Co., the National Cash Register Co., and the "Beef Trust" (a pool among Armour, Cudahy, Swift, Morris, and Wilson corporations), and of consent decrees mentioned in the text above, see Jones, *Trust Problem*, pp. 445–498 (quotation is at p. 492).

The idea of the "new cooperation" took hold and found application in the corporation and trade association alike. By 1912, regional and national trade associations had emerged in most industries, some of them implementing the less formalized practice of exchanging information among companies about prices and costs, as well as about orders, inventories, and the like, for the purpose of stabilizing prices by modulating supply and reducing price competition. Consistent with the Rule of Reason doctrine, in a series of trade-association cases initiated after the 1911 decisions and decided in the early 1920s, the Supreme Court ruled that competitors might legally exchange price and other information if in so doing they did not explicitly agree to raise prices or to control production or distribution, and did not attempt to injure or exclude outside competitors by unfair practices.[163] Similarly, in 1919, the Supreme Court upheld the "resale price maintenance" device whereby manufacturers required dealers to maintain prescribed prices and refused to sell to those not complying.[164]

In effect and at law, the restored common-law construction of the Sherman Act in the decisions of 1911 and thereafter meant that unreasonable, and hence illegal, restraints of trade (of which "monopolize" or "attempt to monopolize" remained a subtype or a necessary or intended consequence) became synonymous not with the restriction of competition by private parties, but (a) with unfair methods of competition designed to oppress or eliminate competitors, and (b) with the use of market power to dictate prices or norms of trade or distribution deemed unreasonable, as prejudicial to the public interest. The two categories were doctrinally interrelated: Unfair practices were ipso facto against the public interest, which by definition included the right of enterprisers to compete unharassed by illegitimate means, while the "undue" fixing of prices, trade, or distribution constituted in itself an unfair practice obnoxious to the public interest. Accordingly, the remedy under the law resided not in the prohibition of combinations,

---

163. By the end of World War I, of about 1,000 trade associations operating on a nation-wide basis, more than 100 were experimenting with the "open-price policy" in the form of each member posting its prices with the association, which in turn circulated them, along with other pertinent information, in letters and periodicals. Thomas C. Cochran, *The American Business System, 1900–1955* (New York: Harper & Row, 1962), pp. 57–58, 61–62. In agriculture, farmers' cooperatives and exchanges designed to regulate supply and prices also emerged in the first two decades of the century. The Capper-Volstead Act of 1922 expressly exempted them from the provisions of the Sherman Act. Samuel P. Hays, *The Response to Industrialism, 1885–1914* (Chicago: University of Chicago Press, 1973), pp. 59–62.

164. *United States* v. *Colgate & Company*, 250 *U.S.* 300. Cf. Charles C. Rohlfing et al., *Business and Government*, 5th ed. (New York: Foundation Press, 1949), p. 113.

associations, or loose arrangements, but in the prohibition of unfair practices as determined in each case on its merits. Neither the size or market power of a business enterprise, nor reasonable arrangements among business units, whether competitors or not, to stabilize markets or guarantee profitability, nor the necessary effects of these conditions on the market or on the competitive capability of less favorably disposed business units, came under the ban of the Sherman Act as now construed.[165]

American corporations, European cartels

From 1890 to 1914, the corporate reorganization of industry in the United States and its corresponding legal order undertook a course of development different from that in Britain and continental Europe. In Britain, policy and law on restraint of trade and monopoly were concerned primarily with protecting investors and creditors against fraud and coercion in their exercise of contractual liberty. Accordingly, as embodied by Parliament in the Companies Consolidation Act of 1908, British law eliminated government restrictions on either competition or combination that was unaccompanied by fraud, violence, or other such coercive or injurious acts.[166] In the industrial nations of continental Europe, the laws permitted combination not detrimental to the public welfare, but provided, in varying degrees, for a modicum of governmental supervision or regulation. Whether the laws sanctioned combinations negatively by refraining from condemning them any more than any other contractual arrangement, as in France and Austria, or whether the laws actually recognized the validity of combinations and positively encouraged them, as in Germany, combinations flourished in the nations of continental Europe.[167] In Britain and continental Europe, combinations characteristically took the form of associations of independent firms in syndicates or cartels, in contrast to the United States, where they characteristically took the form, after 1897, in industry, of

165. Cf. Joe S. Bain, "Industrial Concentration and Anti-Trust Policy," in Harold F. Williamson, ed., *The Growth of the American Economy* (New York: Prentice-Hall, 1951), p. 625; Cochran, *Business System*, p. 57; Thorelli, *Antitrust Policy*, pp. 4–5. Cf. Robert L. Raymond, "The Federal Anti-Trust Act," *Harvard Law Review* 23, (Mar. 1910) pp. 353–379, at p. 375.
166. "Digest of Provisions of Great Britain Companies Consolidation Act, 1908," in U.S. Senate, Committee on Interstate Commerce, *Trusts in Foreign Countries* (1912), pp. 137–142, 139.
167. Francis Walker, "The Law Concerning Monopolistic Combinations in Continental Europe," *PSQ* 20:1 (Mar. 1905), pp. 13–41, 39; reprinted by the Senate Committee on Interstate Commerce in its 1911 report to the Senate at *Trusts in Foreign Countries*, pp. 62–80.

the corporate merger, although, it should be kept in mind, not to the exclusion of continuing widespread resort to looser forms of cooperation.

Contemporary observers in the United States and Europe assumed that the difference in the law went far to explain the difference in the forms of combination. In the United States, they believed, the Sherman Act under the Harlan construction appeared to be most effectively directed against restrictions of competition among independent firms, and that it thereby was driving capitalists into outright consolidation in large integrated corporations. In Britain and Europe, where the law placed no special ban upon cooperative arrangements among independent business units, capitalists preserved the autonomy of their enterprises by availing themselves of the cartel. As Francis Walker, a leading early-twentieth-century United States authority on "trust" laws in foreign countries, concluded, "It is undoubtedly true ... that except in America, there is no such thing as a cartel law proper." The Sherman Act under the Harlan construction, that is, was in this view essentially an anticartel law, being ineffective against corporate consolidations. Accordingly, Walker explained that for Europe as a whole, "industrial combinations seem quite as numerous as in America, and in some countries they are highly developed. They are usually called cartels. The European cartel corresponds to an American pool, but it is generally more highly organized. Consolidated organizations of business – trusts, fusions, mergers, etc. – are rarely found."[168] Or, as Robert P. Skinner, the United States consul general at Hamburg, reported, the German "trust" or cartel was usually a federation of firms in which each member retained its commercial identity while abandoning its freedom of action for a temporary contractual period. But in "the typical American trust, instead of this association of units with influence usually rated according to productive capacity, we observe generally the permanent ownership of a large part of the enterprise by a small group of persons in which there is ordinarily some dominating personal element."[169]

---

168. Ibid., pp. 38, 14; also at *Trusts in Foreign Countries*, pp. 78, 63. Walker served as a special examiner in the Bureau of Corporations, under Commissioner of Corporations Herbert Knox Smith, then in 1912–1913 as deputy commissioner under Commissioner Luther Conant, Jr. U.S. Bureau of Corporations, *Annual Report of the Commissioner of Corporations to the Secretary of Commerce for the Year Ended June 30, 1913*, 9 Feb. 1914 (Washington, D.C.: Government Printing Office, 1914), p. 3 (hereafter cited as Bureau of Corporations, *Annual Report*, year).

169. Robert P. Skinner, "Legal Operation of Trusts in Germany," in *Trusts in Foreign Countries*, pp. 116–117; see also, testimony of Jeremiah W. Jenks in 1908 before the subcommittee of the Senate Judiciary Committee, *Hearings* (1908), pp. 297–

In sum, the argument went that in Britain and elsewhere in Europe, where the "antitrust" laws were relatively lax, smaller business units survived as members of cartels and pools and the like. In the United States, however, with the strict Harlan construction of the Sherman Act deterring business units from entering looser forms of association for regulating competition, the smaller units found themselves increasingly defenseless against absorption or elimination at the hands of large corporate consolidations with superior efficiency and in command of greater capital resources. Pursuing this line of argument, pro-corporate advocates hammered at the Harlan construction from both sides at once. They insisted that the law must accommodate to and recognize the large corporations instead of seeking to destroy them; and, simultaneously in an appeal to small-producer sentiment, they argued that the legalization of reasonable restraints of trade was essential to the survival and prosperity of smaller business units. "In short, as a practical scheme for the handling of the present corporation problem," urged Commissioner Herbert Knox Smith in the Bureau of Corporation's report for 1908, "the sweeping prohibition of the antitrust laws has been altogether unsatisfactory." For, the "present law, forbidding all combination, . . . is now inflexible and indiscriminate. It takes no account of intent, methods, and results of combination.... In prohibiting combination agreements it has gone far to drive corporations directly to the most extreme and complete form of consolidation."[170] In the same vein, Theodore Roosevelt declared, "The small men must be allowed to co-operate under penalty of succumbing before their big competitors; and yet such co-operation, vitally necessary to the small men, is criminal under the present law."[171]

302, 312; also, remarks of Federal Trade Commission chairman Joseph E. Davies at the banquet of the National Foreign Trade Convention of 1916, describing the difference between the organization of United States and European foreign trade: Davies, "Cooperation in Foreign Trade," *Official Report of the Third National Foreign Trade Convention* (New Orleans, 27–29 Jan. 1916), p. 456; also, with respect to the German coal, iron, and steel industries, Special Report of Consul General Julius G. Lay, Berlin, Germany, 2, 16, Nov. 1915, in Federal Trade Commission, *Report on Cooperation in American Export Trade*, 2 vols. (Washington, D.C.: Government Printing Office, 1916), 2, p. 5; and with respect to combinations in British industry, Special Report of Consul General Robert P. Skinner, London, England, 20 Dec. 1915, at ibid., pp. 90–91.
170. Bureau of Corporations, *Annual Report* (1908), p. 5.
171. Roosevelt, "My Confession of Faith," before Convention of National Progressive Party, Chicago, 6 Aug. 1912, in George H. Payne, ed., *The Birth of the New Party, or Progressive Democracy. A Complete Official Account of the Formation and Organization of the Progressive Party* (Naperville, Ill.: Nichols, 1912), p. 256. Actually, as a description of the law as it then stood, more than a year after the Rule of Reason decisions of 1911, Roosevelt's statement was an anachronism in legal terms, although perhaps not in political terms.

Historians and other commentators in more recent times have largely yielded to this assessment of pre–1911 Sherman Act jurisprudence and of its decisive impact in reinforcing the trend toward outright corporate consolidation.[172]

There is a substantial cogency to this interpretation, but if taken as a sufficient one, it is, I believe, misleading. According to this prevalent view, at all stages of its development in the late nineteenth and early twentieth centuries – in the pre–Sherman Act years, in the period of the common-law construction of the Sherman Act, 1890–1897, in the period of the Harlan construction, 1897–1911, and thereafter – the law in the United States militated against cartel-type arrangements and fostered corporate consolidation. Thus, before 1890 common law and state law in cases on restraints of trade and monopoly had been applied most effectively and most frequently, according to Thorelli, "against relatively loose-knit business combinations" as represented by informal or formal pools, thereby inducing capitalists to resort to fusion and mergers as an alternative method of restricting competition. Successful state prosecutions of the trustee device only reinforced the trend toward direct corporate consolidation. With the Sherman Act of 1890 and the early decisions under it in *Greenhut, In re Greene,* and *E. C. Knight,* which sustained consolidations in manufacturing in cases brought under the act, capitalists and their lawyers, according to this view, took practical note of the "applicability of the federal antitrust law to cartel-type combinations," while interpreting the Knight decision by the Supreme Court "as a practical nullification of the law as far as tight combinations were concerned."[173] The strict Harlan construction of the

172. At an earlier stage of this study, I, too, accepted this view: It seemed convincing; it accorded with the fact of the corporate ascendancy; it made a nice irony on the adaptation of the law, in spite of itself and in spite of Harlan's intent, to the corporate reorganization of property relations and the market. But upon further study, I arrived at a different understanding of the matter, as presented in the foregoing exposition of this chapter and as indicated further in the text below.

173. Thorelli, *Antitrust Policy,* pp. 41, 48–49, 258–259. The contemporary authority Robert L. Raymond, while accepting this view of *Knight's* impact on lawyers' advice to clients, nevertheless noted in 1910, in the *Harvard Law Review,* how little basis there was for it in the actual terms of the decision: "Until the decision in the Northern Securities case it was the generally accepted belief among lawyers that . . . a combination in the form of a corporation was valid under the Act. . . . with one notable exception every case under the Act was concerned with a loose combination in which independent identities were maintained. The exception was the Knight case, the first great case under the statute, which dealt with a combination in corporate form. . . . It is interesting to note, however, certain facts connected with these decisions which might have lessened the confidence of lawyers as to the validity of the corporate combination. The decision in the Knight case was rested wholly on the point of interstate commerce. There is only a *dictum* by Fuller, C.J., expressing a doubt as to the possibility of remedy in the case of a real fusion. In later cases, where attempts were made to distinguish the Knight case no stress

act established in *Trans-Missouri*, *Joint Traffic*, and *Addyston Pipe*, only sustained and strengthened the impact of the law in directing capitalists and their lawyers to outright consolidation. As Thomas C. Cochran put it, concurring with Thorelli, although the Supreme Court seemed "loathe to apply the Sherman Act against big unified manufacturing companies," having ruled in *Knight* "that a monopoly of manufacture was not directly a restraint of trade," it ruled, on the other hand, in *Addyston Pipe* "that a contract between medium-sized companies governing conditions of interstate sales was a violation of the antitrust law."[174] Thus, the argument continues, precisely in the period of intense combination activity, 1898–1904, the strict construction placed upon the Sherman Act by the Harlan majority in the Supreme Court appeared to forbid loose agreements, associations, pools, or cartels, among independent firms, and certain methods of incomplete consolidation such as the trustee device and the "artificial" holding company, but not corporate merger or consolidation.[175] "This construction of the Sherman Act," as Joe S. Bain has summarized the prevalent view, "seems definitely to have encouraged firms to *combine* with their competitors rather than to agree with them to limit competition."[176] Or, as Cochran has formulated the same point, "The lesson seemed fairly clear. . . . Buying up of rivals and merging them into one big company was . . . legal, at least in manufacturing. But efforts by small companies to control markets by cartels or agreements were illegal." Indeed, Cochran adds, it was because of this judicial construction that "the Sherman Act has been referred to as the 'mother of trusts.'" With this in mind, Wendell Berge, a former chief of the

was laid on the fact that the combination in that case was in corporate form." Raymond, "Federal Anti-Trust Act," pp. 376–377.

174. Cochran, *Business System*, p. 54; cf. Thorelli, *Antitrust Policy*, pp. 258–259. See notes 86–92 and related text, above.

175. The decision in *Northern Securities* (1904), which invalidated the holding company of that name, is sometimes mistaken as a reversal of *E. C. Knight* and as imposing a ban on the holding company device as such. Aside from the point that if there were any reversal of *Knight* at all, it occurred in *Trans-Missouri* (see notes 180–182 and related text, below), *Northern Securities* involved railroads, not manufacture, and the creation of a third corporation solely to own the stock and thereby control the interstate traffic of two other railroad corporations. Thorelli properly concluded that "the significance of the *Northern Securities* case as a 'new departure' in the antitrust field on the whole has been exaggerated." *Antitrust Policy*, p. 433. Although the Northern Securities decision had dramatic political impact, it laid down no new principles and established no precedent beyond that established in the three leading cases of 1897–1899. Without invalidating the holding company device as such, the decision did demonstrate that the Sherman Act as construed by the Court reached tight corporate consolidations no less than loose forms of restraints of trade. Cf. Raymond, "Federal Anti-Trust Act," pp. 373–375.

176. Bain, "Industrial Concentration," p. 625. Bain's emphasis.

Justice Department's Antitrust Division, similarly remarked that if the Sherman Act "were passed today, I am quite sure it would be called an 'Anti-Cartel Act.'"[177]

In the United States, the movement among capitalists to restrict competition and to reorganize production and marketing did embrace the form preeminently of the large-scale corporation, although it would be a mistake to think that after *Knight* and the Sherman Act cases of 1897–1899 it did not also include a multitude of contractual and associational arrangements of the looser sort. Still, the large corporation as a form of business organization particularly suited to the consolidation and integration of industrial and marketing processes progressed farther, faster, and sooner in the United States than in the other industrial capitalist countries.[178] The law did play an important role in that development, but not the role attributed to it by the prevalent view. The course of Sherman Act jurisprudence did not constitute the decisive cause of the corporate reorganization of industry in the United States. The development of the law – in its legislative and judicial phases – constituted, rather, a major arena in the construction of, and in the conflict over, the corporate reorganization, the effective causes of which lay elsewhere.

At the national level, American jurisprudence on restraint of trade and monopoly from before 1890 to 1914 did not undergo a unilinear development. It went through four stages, the third of which differed in

177. Cochran, *Business System*, p. 54; Wendell Berge, *Cartels* (1946), p. 2, quoted at Saul Chesterfield Oppenheim, *Cases on Federal Anti-Trust Laws, Including Restraints of Trade at Common Law: Trade Regulation* (St. Paul, Minn.: West Publishing, American Casebook Series, 1948), p. 781. For a similar view, cf. Robert A. Brady, *Business as a System of Power* (New York: Columbia University Press, 1943), p. 191. Following prevalent authority, Robert L. Heilbroner repeats this general interpretation of the Sherman Act at *The Making of Economic Society* (Englewood Cliffs, N.J.: Prentice-Hall, 1962; 3d ed., 1970), pp. 109–110.

178. Cf., e.g., Sidney Sherwood, "Influence of the Trust in the Development of Undertaking Genius," *Yale Review* 8 (Feb. 1900), pp. 362–372; Sherwood, "The Function of the Undertaker," ibid. 6 (Nov. 1897), pp. 233–250; William F. Willoughby, "The Concentration of Industry in the United States," ibid. 7 (May 1898), pp. 72–94; Willoughby, "The Integration of Industry in the United States," *QJE* 16 (Nov. 1901), pp. 94–115; Luther Conant, Jr., "Industrial Consolidations in the United States," *Quarterly Publications of the American Statistical Association*, n.s., no. 53 (Mar. 1901), pp. 1–20; E. S. Meade, "Financial Aspects of the Trust Problem," Annals 16 (Nov. 1900), pp. 6–15; S. B. Saul, "The American Impact on British Industry, 1895–1914," *Business History* 3:1 (Dec. 1960), pp. 19–38; W. Arthur Lewis, "International Competition in Manufactures," *AER* 48:2 (May 1957, Supplement), pp. 578–587; E. H. Phelps Brown with S. J. Handfield-Jones, "The Climacteric of the 1890s: A Study in the Expanding Economy," *Oxford Economic Papers*, 4:3 (Oct. 1952), pp. 266–307, esp. pp. 279–289; Richard B. DuBoff, "The Introduction of Electric Power in American Manufacturing," *EHR*, 2d ser., 20:3 (Dec. 1967), pp. 509–518.

basic principle from the other three: (1) pre–Sherman Act common law; (2) common-law construction of the Sherman Act, 1890–1897; (3) the Harlan, non-common-law construction, 1897–1911; (4) the Rule of Reason restoration of common-law construction from mid–1911. That business reorganization included the resort to tight combination in all these periods, whatever the differences in the law as construed by the courts, would seem to deny the law the decisively causative role. The following tentative conclusions, based upon the foregoing inquiry, are offered to describe the relation of the law to the course of business reorganization.

In the common-law period before the Sherman Act and in the period of the common-law construction of the act from 1890 to 1897, the American law permitted reasonable restraints of trade in the form of pools or cartels as well as in the form of tight combinations. With differences in application and jurisdictional variations in detail, American law was, in essence, no different from British common law or continental European law in this respect. Most combinations that fell afoul of the law in these years were loose because before 1898 there were as yet few large corporations, other than railways, with the power to regulate the interstate market and even fewer large intercorporate consolidations. The situation in the United States, that is, was similar to that in Britain and continental Europe. There, too, most cases that invalidated agreements or combinations involved the looser sort. In the United States, moreover, the common law and state laws rather quickly proved effective against the trustee device, which in the 1880s and the early 1890s was the method capitalists frequently used in seeking tighter forms of combination on a very large scale. The exemption of manufacture or production as such from the reach of the Sherman Act did not make consolidations immune to state laws, or to the Sherman Act if they unlawfully restrained interstate trade. Insofar, it might be added, as the exemption rested on the ancillary principle of the common law itself, rather than on that of dual federal-state jurisdiction, it did not distinguish the American from the British law. In general, then, by 1897, American law placed no greater inhibition upon loose than upon tight combination. It permitted reasonable restraints of trade, of both the loose and tight variety, as defined at common law. But this marked a distinction, not between American and British or continental European law but between American law up to 1897 and American law in the period following, to 1911.[179]

179. Cf. Dewey, "The Common-Law Background," p. 786: "The cases ... indicate neither a hardening of judicial attitudes ... over the years nor any significant difference between English and American doctrines during the nineteenth century." Also, McCurdy, "*Knight* Sugar Decision."

If, in the earlier period, the law generally permitted reasonable restraints of trade of both the loose and the tight kind, in the latter period.
of the strict Harlan construction it generally forbade both kinds equally.
From the outset of its non-common-law construction of the Sherman
Act, in its Trans-Missouri decision of 1897, before the merger wave set
in, the Supreme Court clearly affirmed the act's effectiveness against
tight combinations, in holding illegal any "combination of capital"
whose control of "production or manufacture" gave it the power to
"dictate the price" of an article. Indeed, as Peckham here specified for
the Court, "Manufacturing or trading companies may also affect prices
by joining together in forming a trust or other combination, and by
making agreements in restraint of trade and commerce, which when
carried out affect the interests of the public." From which it followed,
Peckham ruled, that "The results naturally flowing from a contract or
combination in restraint of trade or commerce, when entered into by a
manufacturing or trading company . . ., while differing somewhat from
those which may follow a contract to keep up transportation rates, are
nevertheless of the same nature and kind, and the contracts themselves
do not so far differ in their nature that they may not all be treated alike
and be condemned in common." With its Trans-Missouri decision,
then, the Court combined Fuller's affirmation in *E. C. Knight* of Congress's plenary power to regulate interstate commerce with Harlan's
dissenting argument in *E. C. Knight* that contracts or combinations
respecting property or intra-state trade conditions might be held directly
and necessarily to restrain interstate trade or commerce, and thus be
reached by the Sherman Act. In this latter principle, the Court's majority in *Trans-Missouri* tacitly reversed, or at least superseded, Fuller's
dictum in *E. C. Knight* that "Commerce succeeds to manufacture, and
is not part of it," and along with it Fuller's sharp separation of the
sphere of production or property ownership from that of interstate
trade. That Fuller joined the majority in this reversal made it all the
more definitive and authoritative.[180]

If still there remained doubt as to the Sherman Act's applicability to
tight combinations, aside from *Joint Traffic* and *Addyston Pipe*, which

---

180. *United States* v. *Trans-Missouri Freight Association*, 166 U.S. 322, 323, 324; see
notes 87–92, 138, 141–143, and related text, above. Although it bears further
inquiry, it might be noted here that *Plessy* v. *Ferguson* (163 U.S. 537), decided in
1896, a year before *Trans-Missouri*, by validating the states' control of race
relations even where they might touch interstate commerce, in effect cleared the
way for the Court's majority, including Fuller, to recede from the strict distinction
between the police power (or "production") and interstate commerce that had been
maintained in *Knight* (following *Coe* v. *Erroll* and *Kidd* v. *Pearson*), without
jeopardizing the legal structure of racial segregation then being installed in the
southern states.

reiterated and reaffirmed *Trans-Missouri*, the Supreme Court's Northern Securities decision of 1904, and the lower federal court decisions in the Standard Oil and American Tobacco cases in 1908–1909, conclusively demonstrated the law's effectiveness against corporate consolidations, no less than against pools or cartels. The distinction between production and commerce, in the applicability of the Sherman Act, made no practical difference because under the Court's construction, if interstate or foreign commerce were involved, it was only necessary to show a direct connection between consolidation and (1) public injury, or (2) unfair practices, or (3) suppression of competition, or (4) a power to control prices or in any other way to regulate trade, to bring the consolidation within the reach of the law and subject it to dissolution. Alternatively, the basic purposes of consolidation would be defeated if, after consolidating, the corporations doing so, even if not dissolved, were to be prohibited effectively from regulating prices or investment in interstate and foreign commerce. The Sherman Act's applicability to tight as well as loose combinations was, after all, what the controversy over the Harlan construction was all about. It ran for almost fifteen years.[181] It was not the law as judicially construed that facilitated or

181. Note, for example, Herbert Knox Smith's assessment of the issue, which he made for the Bureau of Corporations in early 1905 while he was serving as deputy commissioner to Commissioner of Corporations James R. Garfield: Citing "the very common misinterpretation of the Knight case," Smith observed that "the legal point actually decided merely was that production does not *necessarily* imply interstate commerce. The Court did not say, nor did it decide, that there is never any connection between production and commerce." Smith's emphasis. H. K. Smith, "Memorandum on Paper by James H. McIntosh on the Power of Congress to Regulate Industrial Corporations" (Paper read before the Nebraska Bar Association, 9 Jan. 1903), 18 Feb. 1905, BC, G.F. 2480. Cf. Raymond's 1910 summary in the *Harvard Law Review* of the Sherman Act's meaning as construed by the Supreme Court in cases decided by it under the act since 1897 ("Federal Anti-Trust Act," pp. 373–375): "It is now proposed to state the definitely binding rules of law to be drawn from these decisions. As a general summary the following is ventured: Any combination which directly restrains interstate trade is illegal. Trade is restrained by the ending or limiting of competition among the members of the combination as well as when the business of others is injured; it is not necessary that competition of outsiders be destroyed or affected. The restraint need not be unreasonable. The actual effect of the transaction on prices is not a determining factor; it is sufficient if a power to raise prices is acquired or increased. This power need not be broad enough to cover the whole country; indeed, its possible exercise may embrace only comparatively narrow limits.... As there is no rule as to what constitutes a direct restraint, each case stands on its own basis.... If the restraint is direct, the fact that it is reasonable is of no avail. The decisions in the Trans-Missouri Freight case and in the Joint Traffic case expressly decide that even a reasonable restraint of interstate commerce is invalid under the Act. In both the majority and minority opinions in the former case, the reasonableness of the restraint in question was expressly accepted as a fact. In the Northern Securities case this principle, laid down in the Freight cases, was recognized as law by all the

encouraged corporate consolidation; it was, rather, business and political policy – the decisions of capitalists and their lawyers in the private sector, and the decisions of the executive branch of the federal government under presidents McKinley and Roosevelt, and up to a point under Taft, not to prosecute or to prosecute selectively.[182] The courts could only act upon cases brought before them.

The causes of the large corporation's emergence as the characteristic form of market regulation in the United States, then, lie somewhere outside the realm of judicial construction, and, rather, in the realm of property and market relations and of politics. The work of such scholars as Alfred D. Chandler, Jr., has offered a substantial but as yet incomplete part of the explanation. Chandler and others have observed that outright corporate consolidation had the advantage of facilitating a centralization of authority that could engage in vertical as well as horizontal integration and subject the enterprise as a whole, if not to a single operational management, then to a more coordinated or unitary financial control. Because consolidations were not vulnerable to subsequent disaffection by recalcitrant constituents once the agreement had been closed, as were cartels or pools, consolidations obviated not only repeated disruptions of regulatory efforts but also, to a significantly larger extent, court intervention from private suits. The question remains, however, why these factors operated more powerfully in the

judges with the exception of Brewer.... The reasoning of the [Northern Securities] decision ... seems to be broad enough to cover any corporate combination when combination is the vital feature of the transaction. Whether a combination depends for its success on the real economic values lying in the fact of combination or merely on its power to control the situation is, under the law, immaterial. The best possible trust, if it represents a combination, is illegal.... it appears not only possible but probable that every great combination in the country is liable to prosecution and dissolution under the Anti-Trust Act." Whether or not this statement of the law is essentially accurate, and I think it is, it is important in indicating what by 1910 respected legal opinion – and hence the opinion of many corporate-capitalists as advised by their counsel – believed the law to be.

182.   See Chapters 4 and 5, below. Cf. Raymond ("Federal Auti-Trust Act" pp. 375, 377): "Clearly as this conclusion follows from the decisions discussed ["that every great combination in the country is liable to prosecution and dissolution"], it involves such tremendous consequences as to be accepted only with extreme reluctance. Moreover the fact itself is extraordinary ... [that] business and law have got into what it is little exaggeration to call an *impasse*.... [In practice,] the government showed no disposition to enforce the law as thus newly construed against the many corporations which might fall within its prohibitions.... It has not done so. The tremendous significance of the American Tobacco Company and Standard Oil Company decisions in the United States Circuit Court lies in the message conveyed that the law is to be enforced rather than in any addition to existing law. It can hardly be endured that the law remain in its present state. The logic of events is certain to bring about a change either by continued judicial construction or by legislation."

United States than in Britain and continental Europe, something the
state of the law cannot explain. Among the reasons, the following seem
worthy of consideration.[183]

The expanse of the nation and the market, and the diversity of the
capitalist class, along with the multiplicity of legal jurisdictions, made
enforcement of cartel-type agreements difficult and often impossible.
The incomparably greater "impersonality" of the market in the United
States among capitalists and their families, in contrast with Old World
conditions, critically weakened the discipline of deference and honor.
Handshakes counted for little and even contracts could often be disre-
garded or broken with impunity.

By the late nineteenth century, the capitalist family in the United
States had come to base its wealth and status much less than in Britain
and continental Europe on a particular enterprise in a particular place.

183. For what follows, with respect to this explanation, cf. Willard L. Thorp, *The
Integration of Industrial Operation*, Census Monograph no. 3, Department of
Commerce, Bureau of the Census (Washington, D.C.: Government Printing Office,
1924), pp. 91, 94, 96, 267, and passim; National Industrial Conference Board,
*Mergers in Industry: A Study of Certain Economic Aspects of Industrial Consolida-
tion* (New York: NICB, 1929), p. 190 and passim; Brown with Handfield-Jones,
"Climacteric," pp. 280–281; Frank A. Vanderlip, "The Americanization of the
World," An Address Delivered Before the Commercial Club of Chicago, 22 Feb.
1902 (Chicago: Rand McNally, 1902; 15 pages), especially pp. 4–7, 10; James B.
Dill, "Industrials as Investments for Small Capital," in American Academy of
Political and Social Science, *Corporations and the Public Welfare* (New York:
McClure, Phillips, 1900), pp. 109–119, especially p. 115; George W. Perkins,
"The Modern Corporation," in E. R. A. Seligman, ed., *The Currency Problem and
the Present Financial Situation* (New York: Columbia University Press, 1908), pp.
155–170, esp. pp. 157–160; H. W. Macrosty, "Business Aspects of British
Trusts," *Economic Journal* (London), 12 (Sept. 1902), pp. 347–366; Macrosty,
review of *American Industrial Conditions and Competition. Reports of British Iron
Trade Commission* (London: British Iron Trade Association, 1902), *Economic
Journal* 12 (Sept. 1902), pp. 367–370; Evelyn Hubbard, "American 'Trusts' and
English Combinations," *Economic Journal* 12 (June 1902), pp. 159–176; Charles
M. Schwab, "What May Be Expected in the Steel and Iron Industry," *N. Am. Rev.*
(May 1901), pp. 655–664; P. L. Payne, "The Emergence of the Large-Scale
Company in Great Britain, 1870–1914," *EHR*, 2d ser, 20:3 (Dec. 1967), pp.
519–542, esp. pp. 532–539; Lance E. Davis, "The Capital Markets and Industrial
Concentration: The U.S. and U.K., A Comparative Study," *EHR*, 2d ser., 19:2
(Aug. 1966), pp. 255–272; Davis, "The Investment Market, 1870–1914: The
Evolution of a National Market," *JEH* 25:3 (Sept. 1965), pp. 355–399; Thomas
R. Navin and Marian V. Sears, "The Rise of a Market for Industrial Securities,
1887–1902," *BHR* 29:2 (June 1955), pp. 105–138; John A. James, "Structural
Change in American Manufacturing, 1850–1890," *JEH* 43:2 (June 1983), pp.
433–459, esp. pp. 449–451; Margaret G. Meyers, *The New York Money Market*
(New York: Columbia University Press, 1931); Nelson, *Merger Movements*, p.
136; Dewey, *Monopoly*, pp. 53–55; Eichner, *Emergence of Oligopoly*, pp. 8–9;
Chandler, *Visible Hand*, pp. 484–500, and passim; Lamoreaux, *Great Merger
Movement*, chaps. 2, 3, pp. 14–86. Also see Chapter 1, under "Class Metamorpho-
sis and Corporate Reconstruction."

Size of money income and income-yielding assets (if not disrespectable), rather than prestige of management in a firm and at a place, counted most in the quest for sustained power and status, not to mention sustained wealth. Those capitalist families in the United States that put firm and place above income and investment mobility put themselves at high risk of falling on hard times and hence by the wayside as well. The intensity of competition, both in marketing and in technological innovation, made it difficult for the single firm to keep up with ever new developments year in and year out. Merging into a large corporation with broader access to, and some centralized control over, marketing and innovation, and with a relatively more stable earning power combined with limited liability, offered stronger inducements than the insecurities of the autonomous firm, whether competing alone or entering ephemeral or unreliable cartels. Family tradition, and with it nepotism, exerted a less powerful impact on business organization and management in the United States than they did in the Old World. In eroding family-centered enterprise and nepotistic impulses along with it, bureaucracy of the modern capitalist type reinforced family-centered wealth and security within the higher circles of the capitalist class. This, however, was not without its trickle-down effect upon a broader segment of the bourgeoisie.

Given the expanse of the domestic market, and the ready access to it made possible by railway and telecommunication, the feasible optimum scale of industrial enterprise in the United States in nonspecialty products far exceeded that in Britain and continental Europe, and the intensity and impersonality of competition in the United States made the feasible increasingly mandatory. Medium-sized plant in the United States was often larger by some multiple than the largest in Britain or the rest of Europe. The railway played another role, more social than purely logistical, in contributing to a class cohesiveness across enterprise and distance, which facilitated consolidation on a large scale. By bringing together capitalists of diverse backgrounds and places on railway boards of directors, and by easing and quickening intercity and intersectional travel, the railway countered American market impersonality with sociability and associative relations that strengthened common class identities and business trust, in aid of assembling enterprise consolidations on a large scale of operation.[184]

With respect to financial requirements, the larger scale of enterprise

---

184. Some of my preliminary findings on the associative role of railways in the class reformation process, along lines indicated here in the text, were presented in my paper "Prosopography, Class, and Periodization: The Leadership of the Indianapolis Monetary Convention and Commission"; see note 19, Chapter 1, above.

called for a greater concentration of capital funds particularly conducive to or requiring corporate organization. The magnitude of requisite funds usually exceeded the resources of a family or group of families and their enterprises, and, given the atomized structure of commercial banking in the United States, was not attainable from banks through ordinary credit channels. Indeed, in contributing to those conditions that restricted the credit capacities of local banks, the bourgeois-populistic opposition to central banking, which prevailed until the Federal Reserve Act of 1913, may be counted, paradoxically, as a potent additional cause of corporate reorganization of capitalist property ownership in industry.

For these various reasons, among others, the resort to the corporate form of enterprise based upon negotiable securities and limited liability as a mode of property ownership became increasingly more compelling in the United States than in Britain and continental Europe, and its extension to intercorporate combination a familiar routine. Protected in part by law and otherwise by executive policy, the property form matched inducement and need with effective and available market instrumentalities.

The corporate-liberal alternative

If the state of the law on restraint of trade cannot be said to have caused the resort to tight combinations of capital in the United States, it nevertheless played an important role of a different sort. The Harlan construction of the Sherman Act placed the corporate reorganization of industry in jeopardy to an incongruous legal order. On the one hand, the law of restraint of trade represented a menacing counterattack of the small-producer and anti-corporate populist forces against corporate regulation of the market. On the other hand, the law of property as promulgated in the Supreme Court's construction of liberty and due process protected the corporate form of property as such; this the small-producer partisans could not gainsay without hazarding a serious challenge to private-property rights in general, and their own in particular. Yet, if enforced by a populist president and attorney general with broad-ranging prosecutions, the Sherman Act under the Harlan construction threatened to prevent the corporate form of property from fulfilling its raison d'être, that is, from actuating corporate-directed regulation of the market. Given the intensity of popular animosity toward the large corporations, there was always the risk that even nonpopulist presidents and political leaders, either from legalistic principle or from pursuit of electoral success, might enforce, or "play politics" with, the Sherman Act, or enact other disabling legislation at the expense of corporate power.

The crux of the matter was that the Harlan construction held the law to prohibit any substantial regulation of the interstate or foreign market by private persons, that is, by any agency other than the federal government. It faced two ways at once: toward unrestricted competition, and toward exclusive regulation by the nation-state. Potentially, then, it placed the corporate reorganization of industry beyond the pale of the law, and by the same token it intensified those tendencies that forced the trust question – the corporate reconstruction of the economy – into the center of American party politics. The twofold objective of the pro-corporate movement was to change the law and get the corporation question "out of" politics. This twofold objective the Rule of Reason decisions of 1911, coupled with the Federal Trade Commission (FTC) Act of 1914, eventually accomplished, but not without about fifteen years of protracted, sharp, and bitter political conflict that culminated in the temporary splitting of one of the two major parties.

The Rule of Reason decisions of 1911 and after applied to an economy dominated by corporate consolidations, not, however, because of the Sherman Act but because of the corporate movement among capitalists along with pro-corporate political policy of the federal executive. In restoring a common-law construction of the Sherman Act, and thereby establishing an "antitrust" doctrine essentially similar to the relatively "lax" doctrine of Britain and continental Europe, the Rule of Reason legalized corporate consolidations as well as cartelization on a "higher basis." With respect to the latter, it sanctioned looser types of arrangements among large corporations no less than among smaller units for the restriction of competition, through such informal devices as trade associations or price leadership, or, less frequently, through formal contract, so long as such arrangements could be construed as reasonable and not contrary to the public interest.

It is, then, inaccurate to claim that had the Rule of Reason operated throughout the period after the enactment of the Sherman Act, it would have preserved a smaller-business organization of industry in the United States instead, coming when it did, of legitimizing and regulating the "new cooperation" among large corporate enterprises, to which myriad smaller business units were obliged to adjust. But with the Rule of Reason decisions, as Thomas C. Cochran observed, the federal law now "served to define certain rules for 'monopolistic' competition." Or, following Chandler's phrase, the law now accorded with the replacement of the Invisible Hand by the Visible Hand. Large corporations could share a market and regulate investment and prices, as well as production, so long as they did not contravene the public interest by overtly rigging unreasonable prices, or by taking unfair action to destroy existing competitors or prevent new ones from entering the field. Now that great corporations dominated industry, the laws "dictated a live-and-let-live policy among the largest firms, since attempts to devour each other might lead to prosecution."[185] As opposed to conditions in Britain and continental Europe, cartelization proceeded in the United States with a diffidence, largely through informal arrangements. The huge corporations provided the basic structure for the restriction of competition and regulation of the market, subject to government supervision, desired by those in predominant control of the nation's industrial processes. The "new cooperation" sprang from the new corporatization.

In summary, from 1890 to 1920, and beyond, judicial construction of United States federal law on restraint of trade passed through three distinct periods: (1) that of common-law construction, from 1890 to 1897; (2) that of the superseding of common-law construction, from 1897 to 1911, during which the Sherman Act was held to prohibit reasonable as well as unreasonable restrictions of competition in interstate or foreign commerce; and (3) that of the restoration of common-law construction, beginning with the Rule of Reason decisions of 1911. The restoration rested, however, upon a new basis: an economy reorganized along corporate lines. It came to apply both to corporate consolidations and to looser arrangements among corporations and other business entities. Precisely in this application, based upon common-law construction, the law, while regulating corporate administration of the market to keep it within the bounds of reasonableness and the claims of the public interest, sanctioned and legitimized it. That, however, is only one part of the story. Another part resides in the way and the form in which the corporate reorganization found sanction and legitimacy and, here in particular, in the role of the common law in reaching the denouement.

To construe the Sherman Act as having embodied the common law was in effect to assign to judge-made law a leading authority in regulating the market, and to give it legislative sanction. That, in turn, meant permitting private law, and hence private parties, to determine to a large extent the regulation of the market, within a framework of judi-

---

185.   Cochran, *Business System*, p. 58; cf. U.S. Attorney General, Report of the Attorney General's National Committee to Study the Antitrust Laws, Stanley N. Barnes and S. Chesterfield Oppenheim, co-chairmen (Washington, D.C.: Government Printing Office, 1955), pp. 5–11, 80–81; Brady, *Business as a System of Power*, pp. 191, 195–196, and chap. 6 in general, pp. 189–220.

cial process, that is, substantially through contractual relations and contractual law. Hence, the common-law construction of the Sherman Act embodied the policy of allocating to private parties the primary role, the initiative, in regulating the market, and to government, through executive oversight and judicial process, a secondary, reactive role. It meant, in the specific historical context of the time, a policy of permitting and regulating a corporate-administered market.[186] Conversely, to construe the Sherman Act as having superseded the common law was in effect to hold that only the federal government, through public law, that is, through legislation and executive administration, could regulate the market – either to the exclusion, or with only a secondary role, of private parties and private law. Because it was politically all but certain that Congress in the years 1897–1911 could not be brought to pass legislation expressly permitting corporations or other private parties to regulate the market, nor could Congress be brought to repeal, amend, or supplement the Sherman Act, the Court's construction of the Sherman Act as having superseded the common law meant that either American business in interstate and foreign commerce must remain entirely and compulsively competitive, or it must be regulated, if at all, by the federal government to the exclusion of both the states and private parties. The alternatives, in short, were unrestricted competition or statist command.

Although it expressed pro-small-producer proclivities, the Court's position was neither doctrinally laissez-faire in substance nor anti-regulation in intent. On the contrary, in his decisions for the Court in *Trans-Missouri*, *Joint Traffic*, and *Addyston Pipe*, Justice Peckham, who had delivered *Allgeyer*, substantially qualified the latter's liberty and due process principles, in effect, and indeed explicitly, subordinating them to Congress's power to regulate the interstate and foreign market. The Court's position in these cases, and in all subsequent Sherman Act cases until the Rule of Reason decisions of 1911, held that the Sherman Act superseded the common law and thereby made illegal reasonable as well as unreasonable restraints of trade. Its position was, therefore, that Congress had, under the commerce clause of the constitution, full power to regulate interstate and foreign commerce, and to limit liberty to the extent thereby implied; that in enacting the Sherman law, Congress had decided to retain exclusive power to regulate the

186. On common law and private party regulation, cf. Morton J. Horwitz, "The Emergence of an Instrumental Conception of American Law, 1780–1820," *Perspectives in American History 5* (1971), pp. 285–326, at p. 288; G. Edward White, *The American Judicial Tradition* (New York: Oxford University Press 1976), pp. 113–115.

interstate and foreign market by forbidding such regulation to private parties (the states being constitutionally excluded); and that for the duration, until it might decide otherwise, Congress had chosen to exercise its regulatory power through the hidden hand of unrestricted competition. Such, in the Court's view, was the public policy enacted by Congress.

Put somewhat differently, the Sherman Act as construed by the Court took regulatory authority out of the market, where one-dollar-one-vote ruled, and placed it in the political arena, where (theoretically) one-person-one-vote ruled. Hence, just as with the national banking and currency laws (before the Federal Reserve Act of 1913), which kept ultimate control of the money supply in the hands of the national state (Congress and the Treasury Department), subject to electoral politics, and out of the control of private parties, so with the law regulating commerce and industry: Regulation was to remain lodged with the federal government and forbidden to private parties; it was to remain "politicized," that is, subject to electoral politics and public law.

The Court's construction of the Sherman Act readily reached tight corporate consolidations, as well as those of the looser sort, as its Trans-Missouri decision indicated, and as the Northern Securities case, and the decisions of the lower federal courts in the American Tobacco and Standard Oil cases, clearly demonstrated. Hence, the construction of the Sherman Act by the Court from 1897 to 1911 put the nonstatist corporate reconstruction of American capitalism, then in process, beyond the pale of the law. The corporate reorganization of the economy in those years went forward within the framework of an incongruent legal order. Because the law and the market in a modern capitalist society are so intimately interrelated, the legal incongruity directly translated itself into a political conflict that became central to national politics.

The generally held view that the Supreme Court in the 1890s and early years of the twentieth century assumed the policy-making role with respect to restraint of trade has been well summarized by J. Willard Hurst: "Inertia, slow perception of fast-moving business change, and ignorance of what to do about it figured in Congress's failure to generalize policy fast and effectively concerning the concentration of private industrial and financial power; within the context of lagging and vague legislation the United States Supreme Court thus became the principal maker of antitrust policy."[187]

187. J. Willard Hurst, "Legal Elements in United States History," *Perspectives in American History* 5 (1971), pp. 3–92, at p. 71. Elsewhere in the same essay (p. 15),

As indicated earlier in this chapter, however, it does not seem to be historically accurate to describe Congress's action in passing the Sherman Act in 1890 as either laggard, inept, or ineffective. By 1890, corporate consolidation on a scale large enough to regulate the market was still in an inchoate state in industry, finance, and commerce; even among railroads, where "natural monopoly" added to the regulatory capacities of large-scale corporate organization, competition still raged. The states retained full power, unequivocally affirmed by the United States Supreme Court, to break up inter-firm combinations domiciled within their respective jurisdictions.[188] Passage of the Sherman Act in 1890, then, should be viewed as a rather prompt response of the federal legislative branch to constituents' opinion and to changing conditions. The drafting of the bill was, indeed, a matter of multifaceted contention and negotiation among small-producer and pro-corporate partisans, and it was further complicated by the constitutional law of federal-state jurisdiction, but the result, the act as passed, was neither vague nor inept. Its terms, rather, constituted a sophisticated embodiment of a definite policy of permitting and regulating, through judicial process, corporate combination and enterprise.[189]

It is, of course, the Supreme Court's (and in general the judiciary's) routine and proper function, within the United States constitutional system, to interpret the meaning of a law in cases brought before it.

Hurst offers a guideline that I have tried to follow and with which I fully agree: "A history of anti-trust law proper might stick to the Sherman and Clayton Acts and rulings of the courts and the Federal Trade Commission. But a history of the law's relations to market structure and procedures and of the results for resource allocation must invite some economic theory and economic history, as well as materials from political science and sociology." Cf. Hurst, *Law and Markets* in the United States (Madison: University of Wisconsin Press, 1982), chap. 2, esp. pp. 73–74. For a more recent statement of the generally held view, see e.g., Morton Keller, "The Pluralist State: American Economic Regulation in Comparative Perspective, 1900–1930," in Thomas K. McCraw, ed., *Regulation in Perspective: Historical Essays* (Cambridge, Mass.: Harvard University Press, 1981), pp. 56–94, at p. 69.

188. McCurdy, "*Knight* Sugar Case"; Morgan, *Congress*, chap. 7.
189. Cf. Morgan, *Congress*, p. 149, for an evaluation of Senate debate and deliberation on the Sherman Act as having been of a "high caliber" and at a "high level" of thought and legal expertise (also at p. 157, and chap. 7, passim). The famous statement of Republican Senator Orville H. Platt (Conn.) that "the whole effort has been to get some bill headed 'A bill to punish trusts' with which to go to the country" (*Cong. Rec.*, 21:3, p. 2731) has been cited time and again as evidence of the fraud or ineptness of the Sherman Act. But Platt, who in Senate debate argued in favor of permitting reasonable restraints of trade, made that statement about, and during the debate on, Sherman's original bill, not the Judiciary Committee's bill, that is, not the act as passed, which he voted for. Cf. Letwin, *Law and Economic Policy*, p. 53 n. 3; Bork, "Legislative Intent," p. 23, 23 n. 43; Thorelli, *Antitrust Policy*, pp. 197–199, 201.

Judicial interpretation, however, is not necessarily equivalent to policy-making. From 1890 to 1911 (and thereafter), the Supreme Court acted as the principal interpreter of the meaning of the Sherman Act, and it is in that sense accurate to say that from 1890 to 1897, it shared with Congress and the executive branch the role of a "principal maker" of policy. But from 1897 to 1911, the principal maker of government policy on the trust question was neither Congress nor the Supreme Court (or the judiciary), but the executive. Presidents McKinley, Roosevelt, and (to a lesser extent) Taft refused to accept the Court's non-common-law construction of the Sherman Act as sound policy, and by controlling the prosecutorial process and, in Roosevelt's case, by establishing a rival, executive, agency (the Bureau of Corporations), and entering extralegal understandings with corporate executives, they took determination of antitrust policy away from the judiciary and, in the face of Congress's inability to act, lodged it with the executive.[190] The Rule of Reason decisions of 1911 together with the legislation of 1914 (FTC and Clayton acts) during the first Wilson administration restored a stable equilibrium of policy-making sharing among the three branches of the federal government, along with an effective clarification of the law.

In the meantime, however, although the Executive assumed the principal policy-making role on the trust question from 1897 to 1911, nevertheless, throughout this period the Executive and the Court were at loggerheads and engaged in a running battle over the nature of policy with respect to the regulation of the market. This made for uncertainty of the law, the bane of commerce, and hence for a crisis, or at any rate a crisis psychology, in the market and in politics that made the resolution of the trust question the single most important issue in the nation's politics. Corporate executives, investment bankers, small enterprisers, labor unionists, could not know for certain where they stood with respect to the law of market relations and practices, in the near or far future, and therefore in the present as well: The Court's majority might change; the next election might bring a president with a different policy, or a Congress ready to act in an unwanted way.

Under pressure to resolve the crisis of the legal order, President Roosevelt came, in effect, to accept the Court's definition of the alternatives, namely, either a freely competitive market or statist regulation. In an evolving but by no means premeditated policy, first through executive action via the Bureau of Corporations (established 1903), then

190. On the extralegal understandings, see Robert H. Wiebe, "The House of Morgan and the Executive, 1905–1913," *AHR* 65:1 (Oct. 1959), pp. 49–60.

through introduction of the Hepburn amendments to the Sherman Act in 1908, and culminating with Roosevelt's public statements and writings, private policy-planning, and presidential campaigning over the next four years, Roosevelt ultimately sought to legalize the corporate reorganization of the economy under direct state command: a statist solution, although not necessarily the equivalent of a corporate state in either practical or strict theoretical terms (see Chapter 5 under "Roosevelt"). His efforts proved unsuccessful, and many earlier supporters of the policy backed off as they perceived more clearly the statist implications of Roosevelt's position. President Taft opposed the statist solution, as did Woodrow Wilson. This was the essence of the difference in policy between Roosevelt and Taft, as it was between Roosevelt's New Nationalism and Wilson's New Freedom – not the Tweedledee, Tweedledum of "regulated monopoly" versus "regulated competition."

In restoring the common-law construction of the Sherman Act, in its Rule of Reason decisions of 1911, the Supreme Court laid the juridical basis of what may be called the corporate-liberal solution of the trust question, that is, of a nonstatist accommodation of the law to the corporate reorganization of capitalism, a solution that Taft and Wilson affirmed and sought as presidents, in different ways, to strengthen and develop, with ultimate success, Wilson with considerably greater political success than Taft. It was a solution capped by the legislation of 1914. Historians have long noted and often puzzled over the suddenness with which the trust question thereafter receded from the center of national politics, if not disappearing altogether. Some have thought that the American people grew tired of the issue or that the legislation of 1914 lulled them into complacency. With the Rule of Reason decisions of 1911 and the legislation of 1914, however, the American people (or the major American political forces) had not become tired with, or complacent about, the issue; they had settled it. It was a settlement, that is, sufficiently satisfactory to the major concerns and interests among them, however unsatisfactory it may have been to the concerns and interests of historians.

Conclusion

For its normal functioning and development, capitalism requires both certainty and predictability in the sociopolitical environment, and particularly in the law and the legal order. At the same time, capitalism requires openness to rapid change ("development," "growth"). Hence, the law must provide for the play of continuous change on a field of

relative certainty and predictability. The strength of common-law jurisprudence lay precisely in its flexibility composed of these two virtues
intertwined. That is, judge-made law, based on precedent and rational-
instrumental reasoning rooted in experience, has allowed for both predictability and change. By its very nature, moreover, it is a predictability
and change that has corresponded in general with the outlook, values,
and interests of the litigants (with all the conflicts, contradictions, or
inconsistencies implied therein), and hence with those propertied and
contracting parties making regular use of the courts. Judge-made law in
a capitalist society, then, has normally tended to express, arbitrate, and
enforce the social dominance of capitalist property and capitalists as a
class, but in the United States in particular it has tended ultimately to
validate that form of capitalist property and those capitalists that were
ascending in the market and the society at large.

This result has been a matter not of a special American teleology of
Progress but of capitalists deploying their liberty in aid of their interests,
and knowing in their bones if not in their heads that the market is as
much a realm of law and politics as of economics. The common law
and, even better, its legislative embodiment, as in the Sherman Act
properly construed, have thereby facilitated change as American capitalism has developed, while validating the certainty and security of capitalist property and social relations as such. It has had one other virtue: It
has sustained the principle and practice of a large autonomy of the
market from party politics and state command, and hence the principle
and practice of the supremacy of society over the state. Capitalists in
America have long understood that politics are not limited to, or simply
coterminous with, party politics and the state. As long as the capitalists
in general feel secure in their dominance in society, they may be expected to affirm, and act to sustain, the supremacy of society over the
state. It was a sense of insecurity along these lines within a sector of the
corporate wing of the capitalist class in the early twentieth century that
led some of them to back, or flirt with, Roosevelt's statist tendency. In
the end, they came back to the common law, which has been peculiarly
suited to serve as a powerful ally of the liberal form of capitalism, while
no less amenable to serve, in a similar manner, the needs of a liberal
form of socialism.

The corporate-liberal alternative,[191] as embodied in the Rule of

191. On corporate liberalism as an interpretive, or periodizing, concept, see M. J. Sklar,
      "Woodrow Wilson"; Alan L. Seltzer, "Woodrow Wilson as 'Corporate-Liberal':
      Toward a Reconsideration of Left Revisionist Historiography," *Western Political
      Quarterly* 30:2 (June 1977), pp. 183–212; Ellis W. Hawley, "The Discovery and
      Study of a 'Corporate Liberalism'," *BHR* 52:3 (Autumn 1978), pp. 309–320; Kim

Reason decisions and as fleshed out in the legislation of 1914 and since, accomplished two basic conditions: It "depoliticized" the market in the sense of removing the regulation of the market from determination by electoral politics or by the exclusive or paramount power of the state. Second, apart from common carriers, public utilities, or "natural monopolies," it assured primary regulation of the market by private parties and private law, that is, by private parties subject to judicial process, while assigning to the state, in its legislative and executive capacities, the secondary role through regulatory laws authorizing prosecutory action or administrative policing, but again, subject to judicial review, and in either case, judicial review based on common-law doctrine and precedent.

The adaptation of the legal order to corporate capitalism was an integral phase of the corporate reconstruction of American capitalism in general. It stands as a signal achievement of the Progressive Era. The adaptation was based, in part, upon the recognition of the corporation as a person at law, both in constitutional constructions of the Supreme Court and in the Sherman Act itself and subsequent antitrust legislation. The adaptation was also based upon the ultimate judicial construction of the Sherman Act as embodying the common law and the shaping of subsequent antitrust legislation by such construction. Antitrust law and jurisprudence represented one among a number of areas in the adaptation of the law to corporate capitalism, areas that included transportation and communication, banking, labor, agriculture, and foreign relations. Neither in its realization nor in its form was the adaptation a foregone conclusion. It was an outcome of political contention stretching over twenty-five years (and beyond), a contention that saw the rise of significant populist and socialist party-politics, the temporary splitting apart of both major parties (the Democrats in the 1890s, the Republicans in 1910–1914), and more lasting political realignments. It was, finally, an outcome of a great social movement for corporate capitalism that rejected a statist for a liberal form.

McQuaid, "Corporate Liberalism in the American Business Community, 1920–1940," in ibid., pp. 342–368; Robert M. Collins, "Positive Business Responses to the New Deal: The Roots of the Committee for Economic Development, 1933–1942," in ibid., pp. 369–391; James Weinstein, *The Corporate Ideal in the Liberal State, 1900–1918* (Boston: Beacon, 1968); David Eakins, "Policy-Planning for the Establishment," in Radosh and Rothbard, eds., *New History*, pp. 188–205; M. J. Sklar, "On the Proletarian Revolution and the End of Political-Economic Society," *Radical America* 3:3 (May-June 1969), pp. 1–41, esp. pp. 12, 5–11; and, from a different standpoint, R. Jeffrey Lustig, *Corporate Liberalism: The Origins of Modern American Political Theory, 1890–1920* (Berkeley: University of California Press, 1982).

PART II

Politics

4

The politics of antitrust

Introduction

The trust question was the corporation question. The great antitrust debates of the late 1890s and the early years of the twentieth century, including the measures proposed and adopted, were, in essence, debates about the role and power of the large corporations in the market and in society at large, and debates about the corresponding role and power of government in relation to the emergent corporate order. The great question of the day, as Woodrow Wilson defined the issue on more than one occasion, "we sum up under the general term of the corporation question, the trust question." Accordingly, "We state our problem for statesmen by saying that it is the problem of the corporation."[1]

Beneath the outer layers of controversy over doctrines of competition and monopoly, the antitrust debates consisted at their core of two major questions: Was the corporate reorganization of the marketplace inevitable or desirable? and, What measures were necessary and proper in adapting the law and administrative policy to the corporate reorganization?

Although interrelated, the two questions posed different issues. The one challenged the rise of corporate capitalism; the other assumed and affirmed it. But in politics the debates did not proceed in separate channels that corresponded with logical distinctions. Their intermixture

---

1. Woodrow Wilson, "Politics (1857–1907)," *Atlantic Monthly* 100 (Nov. 1907), PPWW, 2, pp 19–20 and Wilson, "The Tariff and the Trusts," Address at Nashville, Tenn., 24 Feb. 1912, ibid., p. 410.

has proved a source of confusion to participants and commentators alike. Compounding the confusion, national political leaders, especially presidents and presidential aspirants, whatever their personal policy inclination, could not easily avoid entering debate on both questions, while seeking support from all sides of each. Partisans of the corporate reorganization found themselves necessarily arguing on two fronts at once: against small-producer or populist advocates who opposed large-corporate power in principle, and against one another over the proper adaptation of law and policy. Similarly, opponents of the corporate reorganization found themselves not only arguing against its advocates but at the same time unable to avoid being drawn into the debates over adaptive law and policy. Hence, it has always been difficult for commentators to distinguish arguments over methods of regulation from arguments for and against regulation itself, or for and against "big business."

In the calmer realm of legislation and policy-making, as in that of public controversy, the antitrust debates centered upon the role of the large corporation and the relation of government to the market. The leading individuals and groups were not disputing competition versus monopoly, nor laissez-faire versus regulation, as such. By the opening years of the new century, whatever the rhetoric, in substance no significant segment of organized opinion advocated a return to the old competitive market or the preservation of laissez-faire prohibitions on regulatory intervention by the federal government. By 1900, Cleveland Democracy and Republican mugwumpery were already antiquities.[2] Partisanship to the small-producer marketplace was not equivalent to

2. Although often left unexplicit, this is to be inferred from the empirical evidence and general formulations in works as widely divergent in interpretation as Louis Galambos, "The Emerging Organizational Synthesis in Modern American History," *BHR* 44 (Autumn 1970), pp. 279–290; Samuel P. Hays, *The Response to Industrialism* (Chicago: University of Chicago Press, 1957), esp. chaps. 3, 7; Richard Hofstadter, *The Age of Reform* (New York: Random House, Vintage Books, 1955), esp. chaps. 3, 6; Gabriel Kolko, *Railroads and Regulation* (Princeton: Princeton University Press, 1965); Kolko, *The Triumph of Conservatism* (New York: Free Press, 1963); Albro Martin, *Enterprise Denied: Origins of the Decline of the American Railroads, 1897–1917* (New York: Columbia University Press, 1971); James Weinstein, *The Corporate Ideal in the Liberal State, 1900–1918* (Boston: Beacon, 1968); Robert H. Wiebe, *Businessmen and Reform: A Study of the Progressive Movement* (Cambridge, Mass.: Harvard University Press, 1962); Wiebe, *The Search for Order, 1877–1920* (New York: Hill & Wang, 1967), esp. chaps. 5–7; William A. Williams, *The Contours of American History* (Cleveland: World, 1961), pt. 3, pp. 343–478. Cf. L. Galambos, "The Agrarian Image of the Large Corporation, 1879–1920: A Study in Social Accommodation," JEH 28 (Sept. 1968), pp. 341–362; Richard H. K. Vietor, "Businessmen and the Political Economy: The Railroad Rate Controversy of 1905," *JAH* 64:1 (June 1977), pp. 47–66.

favoring the old competitive discipline, nor was partisanship to large corporate enterprise equivalent to rejection of government regulation.

Although the popular catchwords of the great debates included "monopoly," "trust," "combination," and "competition," the specific issues that the leading participants invariably found themselves obliged to address took form in response to such questions as: Should corporations be permitted to regulate the market at all, and if so, to what extent? What methods might corporations use? How large might they grow? In view of Congress's constitutional power to regulate interstate and foreign commerce, where should corporate regulation of the market end and the federal government's regulation begin? To what extent might Congress in effect delegate its authority to private parties? What methods might the federal government undertake in regulating corporations? How far should government go in supervising corporate practices? Should its reach, for example, extend to monitoring contracts and setting prices? How should regulatory authority be distributed among the executive, legislative, and judicial branches? Implicit in all these questions was the larger question of how far, if at all, the organization of the political economy should be permitted to go toward statism, that is, toward state command of investment, prices, and contractual relations. The position taken on these questions, more than on doctrinal principles of monopoly, combination, or competition, located public figures on the political spectrum of the trust question and, indeed, often determined their attitude toward such doctrinal ideas. More often than not the attitudes were not clear-cut, because few if any had rigorously defined their answers to these questions; hence the political spectrum of the trust question was indeed a continuously shifting and sliding one.

The basic issues bore a distinctly modern imprint. The broad consensus on the necessity of a visible hand to regulate the market – on the displacement of the competitive by an administered market – established the ground of differences over whose hand was to do the administering, how, and to what extent. In the market proper, beginning with railroads and spreading to industry, the large-corporate hand was trumping all the others. The Interstate Commerce Act of 1887 and the Sherman Act of 1890 represented attempts to find an alternative alike to unchecked private market power and to statist dictation of the market. Each law permitted private administration of the market under government policing, with both the private sector and government made subject to adversarial, rationalistic, and flexible processes of judicial review. The laws embodied the assumption that judicial process would guard against arbitrary private or public power, protect property rights, and at the same time secure the public's interest in growth and progress through efficiency and innovation. They represented as well the principle of the high priority of contractual liberty as a limit on powers of the state in the organization and operation of the market.

In the first decade of the twentieth century, however, the Elkins Act (1903), the Hepburn Act (1906), and the Mann–Elkins Act (1910), coupled with prosecutions or threatened prosecutions of railway pools and combinations under the Sherman Act, subordinated the hand of the corporation to that of the state in the railway sector. With the Sherman Act cases of 1897–1899, moreover, the law as construed by the Supreme Court and applied to the economy as a whole stipulated either the restoration of the invisible hand of unrestricted competition in interstate and foreign commerce, or the intercession of the visible hand of the nation-state to the exclusion of any other – that is, either the old competitive laissez-faire or a new statism.

The Court's position thereby set the Sherman Act in conflict with other pro-corporate law and policy: with the railroad law and policy originally embodied in the Interstate Commerce Act; with the Court's own adaptation of due process to protect the corporate form of business organization and secure the value of corporate, intangible property. Not least, the Court's decisions placed enforcement of the Sherman Act in conflict with the broader policy of permitting a primary corporate market power subject to a secondary government regulation and judicial process, that is, in conflict with the corporate reorganization of the market short of effective statist dictation. An image of a supposedly conservative, pro–big business Supreme Court that obstructed anti-corporate regulatory efforts little corresponds with the record. It makes difficult, if not impossible, an adequate understanding of the conflict between the legal order and the rising corporate order, and hence of a large part of the political history of this era.

The conflict in policy and law may be defined as follows: Neither the executive branch nor Congress was prepared to impose upon the market the law as construed by the Court; neither branch wished to require unrestricted competition, and each was either unwilling or unable to undertake statist command. This conflict added its peculiar dimension to, and became an integral part of, the antitrust debates. From 1897 to 1911, always interwoven with the questions of corporate power and government-market relations were those of enforcing, evading, or modifying the law as construed by the Supreme Court. Presidents William McKinley, Theodore Roosevelt, and William Howard Taft disagreed with the public policy implied by the Court's construction of the law. Roosevelt and Taft sought to restore antitrust law to its pre–1897 common-law meaning and to establish corresponding regulatory policy and procedures. Toward the latter part of Roosevelt's presidency, however, and for some time thereafter, Roosevelt became convinced that justice, social efficiency, and popular politics dictated a statist direction of the market as the condition of its corporate reorganization. In this ironic sense, Roosevelt ultimately acceded to the Court's construction of the law. Indeed, as the following narrative will indicate, Roosevelt skillfully deployed the Court's literalist construction of the Sherman Act as leverage to promote the attainment of a statist command of the market. Even after the Court's 1911 decisions, he continued to propose a statist alternative alike to unrestricted competition and to mere government regulation of a corporate-administered market.

In restoring the common-law construction of the Sherman Act in 1911, the Supreme Court set the stage for a nonstatist resolution of the debates that would sanction the corporate administration of the market subject to government regulation and judicial review. American liberalism made its nonstatist adjustment in this way to the demise of the competitive market, but not before a prolonged and perplexing conflict that opened a fissure between the political-economic and legal orders and split the Republican party in the election of 1912.

In the absence of attention to detail, to the specific content of the antitrust debates and their necessary relation to the course of Sherman Act jurisprudence, it is difficult to avoid a superficial characterization of the leading participants as pro or anti "business," "competition," or "regulated monopoly." Such shibboleths neither define essential differences among principal leaders such as Roosevelt, Taft, and Wilson, nor signify much more than a play on words. Thus, for example, astute observers have dismissed differences between Roosevelt and Wilson as a matter of Tweedledee versus Tweedledum, although their disagreements were, in fact, of considerable significance. In particular, as we have come to learn during the past half century, differences over how to administer the market are as politicially, economically, and culturally significant as differences over whether to administer at all. Indeed, the differences over how have constituted a large part of the politics of industrial, and industrializing, societies in modern times.

By the early years of the twentieth century in the United States, for a public figure to declare against "monopoly" was really beside the point, if not a deliberate method of evading or obscuring the issue. At law, "monopoly" had a technical-legal meaning that denoted not bigness, or sole possession of a market, or even total ownership of a resource, each of which was of major concern to large sectors of the public, but the overt suppression of competition by "unfair" means for the attainment of undue ends — something that might not be related to bigness or sole possession of a market, and that no one professedly approved. Virtually every qualified observer, not least capitalists themselves, agreed that literal monopoly, except where "natural" as in railroads or public utilities, was undesirable, and at any rate was unattainable in the absence of "unfair" practices or patent protection. There was no significant dissent from the view that government regulation of natural monopolies and government prevention of unfair practices were necessary and desirable.

In the courts, the antitrust debates proceeded explicitly in the form of disputes on the relation of the common law to federal legislation, and they were permeated with the technical-legal terms appropriate to juridical discourse. Out of court, the debates proceeded in a mixture of legal and lay language where terms such as monopoly, competition, restraint of trade, trusts and combinations, assumed meanings different from or less precise than, those prevailing in the courts or in professional economic thought. Although the multiple possible meanings of such terms made them particularly suited to the arts of political persuasion, the debates in substance always addressed themselves to the rise of the large corporation as the dominant form of business organization, how to deal with it, and what it meant for the relation of government to the market and to society as a whole.

Bureau of Corporations v. U.S. Supreme Court

The first federal executive agency established to monitor industry, as distinguished from transportation and banking, was designated not a bureau of industry but, significantly, the Bureau of Corporations. Congress created the bureau in the act of 14 February 1903 that established the new cabinet-level Department of Commerce and Labor, with the bureau as a sub-unit.[3] From its inception, the bureau engaged in a running dispute with the Supreme Court over proper policy for regulating the market. It consistently campaigned for the restoration of a common-law construction of the Sherman Act, permitting reasonable restraints of trade. As a central part of its argument, the bureau devoted much of its public reports and internal studies to interpreting the emergence of the large industrial corporations as the natural and inevitable result of economic evolution, and to formulating proposals for

---

3. U.S. Bureau of Corporations, *Report of the Commissioner of Corporations*, 21 Dec. 1904 (58th Cong., 3d sess., H.R. Doc. No. 165), p. 7. This was the first annual report of the commissioner of corporations; hereafter the commissioner's annual reports will be cited as *Ann. Rep.* (year).

defining allowable corporate behavior and for adjusting and institutionalizing the relation between the corporation and the state.[4]

The bureau had its immediate origins in the work and recommendations of the Industrial Commission, which Congress had established in the act of 18 June 1898 in response "to the general public concern which developed in the late nineties over the rapid growth of industrial consolidations."[5] Composed of United States representatives, senators, and presidential appointees, the commission displayed in its work the extent to which policy-forming opinion had already come to define the trust question as the corporation question. In its preliminary report of 1900, the commission recommended systematic and mandatory publicity of corporate affairs to guarantee responsible corporate management, to protect investors, and "to encourage competition when profits become excessive thus protecting consumers ... and to guard the interests of employees by a knowledge of the financial condition of the business." In its final report of 1902, the commission recommended that Congress enact a federal license law under which no corporation could engage in interstate or foreign commerce without obtaining a license from a federal bureau of industry. The agency would have the authority, subject to judicial review, to refuse or withdraw the license if the corporation in question violated the terms of the license or other federal law. To attain and keep a license, a corporation would be further required to publish, under oath and subject to government inspection and verification, properly audited annual reports of its assets, liabilities, profits, and losses.[6]

Roosevelt took a leading initiative in the framing and passage, a year later, of the legislation that established the bureau. Among those active in reorganizing industry along large-corporate lines, George W. Perkins of J. P. Morgan & Company, a friend and political supporter of Roosevelt since his New York gubernatorial term, played a major role, in close cooperation with the president, in mobilizing business support for the establishment of the new cabinet department and its bureau. The bureau's authority, however, did not include a licensing power; it did not extend beyond investigatory duties. Roosevelt insisted upon and got provisions designed to enlarge the presidential prerogative in dealing with large corporations. The bureau could publish its findings only upon the president's approval and subject to the president's censorship.

4. See esp. ibid., pp. 38–40, and *Ann. Rep.* (1909), p. 3.
5. Ibid. (1912), p. 5; U.S. Industrial Commission, I: *Preliminary Report on Trusts and Industrial Combinations*, 56th Cong., 1st Sess., H.R. Doc. No. 476, pt. 1, 1 Mar. 1900 (Washington, D.C.: Government Printing Office, 1900).
6. *Ann. Rep.* (1904), pp. 47–48; ibid. (1912), p. 14; Industrial Commission, *Preliminary Report*, pp. 5–7, 36–37, and *Final Report*, 19 (1902), pp. 619 651.

The law, on the whole, made the bureau responsible to the president; it was to report to the president, not to Congress; it was to function, and in practice so it did, as an instrument of presidential discretion. The bureau's investigations, buttressed by the power of subpoena, were expected to aid the president in shaping public opinion and in recommending to Congress regulatory legislation, and thereby strengthen presidential leverage in monitoring and influencing corporate behavior. Although Congress gave these powers to the executive branch, it nevertheless rejected proposals from some of its own members for automatic submission by interstate corporations of annual reports to the bureau, and for giving the bureau positive regulatory powers. In this respect, Congress's action accorded generally with Roosevelt's own views. The president at this time wanted to move, but slowly, in a manner he could control, and as a basis for further action, the nature of which he could largely determine. Roosevelt got from Congress essentially the bureau he wanted. Congress endowed the president with greatly expanded powers of information gathering and oversight, and hence of moral jawboning and policy-making initiative in affairs of the market but, with Roosevelt's approval, refrained from mandating the executive with new regulatory authority.[7]

Just as Jeremiah W. Jenks, Roosevelt's adviser on corporations and trusts, had played a leading role in the Industrial Commission's work and in shaping its reports, so two Roosevelt loyalists and personal friends – "Roosevelt progressives" – James Rudolph Garfield of Ohio and Herbert Knox Smith of Connecticut, directed the Bureau of Corporations over most of its years in existence, Garfield as commissioner of corporations, the bureau's head, from its establishment in 1903 until his appointment by Roosevelt as secretary of the interior in 1907, Smith as Garfield's deputy from the outset and as his successor as bureau head from March 1907 to mid–1912, that is, from the latter part of Roosevelt's elected term through most of President Taft's.

7. See analysis of the bureau's functions as provided by the law of 14 Feb. 1903, in *Ann. Rep.* (1914), pp. 6–7, and text of the law creating the bureau in ibid., pp. 17–18. For Perkins's role, T. Roosevelt to George W. Perkins, 26 Dec. 1902 and 26 June 1903, and Perkins to Roosevelt, 12 Aug. 1905, all in GWP. Of the two pens President Roosevelt used in signing the bill into law, he gave one to Perkins in recognition of his activity on behalf of the legislation. (Roosevelt to Perkins, 26 June 1903, GWP.) In his letter to Roosevelt of 12 Aug. 1905 (GWP), Perkins congratulated the president on his pro-regulation speech of the previous day, stating that his (Perkins's) belief that "the regulation and supervision of great corporations ... ought to come and *must* come, sooner or later, was what impelled me to do everything in my power to help in the fight we made to establish the Department of Commerce and Labor." (Perkins's emphasis.) Cf. Wiebe, *Businessmen and Reform*, pp. 45–47. On the bureau's and the president's powers, see also Arthur M. Johnson, "Theodore Roosevelt and the Bureau of Corporations," *MVHR* 45:4 (Mar. 1959), pp. 571–590.

Under their direction, and in accord with Roosevelt's views, the bureau's general position, like the earlier recommendations of the Industrial Commission, stood in fundamental opposition to the Supreme Court's literalist construction of the Sherman Act. It favored the affirmation and regulation of corporate combinations, and the recognition in law of the common-law distinction between reasonable and unreasonable restraints of trade.

The bureau matched its adversarial posture toward the Court with efforts at formulating positive regulatory policy. On the one hand, it proceeded in its investigatory activity to distinguish reasonable from unreasonable combinations ("good trusts" from "bad trusts") and fair from unfair business methods. On the other hand, Garfield and Smith developed detailed legal, economic, and administrative thinking with respect to proposals for federal incorporation, registration, or licensing of corporations, and for executive as against judicial regulation of the market. It was in dealing concretely with methods of regulation that Garfield and Smith had to grapple with statist implications of the various regulatory proposals, and found themselves not free from doubt and ambivalence over the framing of appropriate policy.

Nevertheless, they lost no time in publicly taking the offensive against the Supreme Court. The bureau's first annual report argued that the term "antitrust" had been "loosely used," because in reality antitrust legislation could be "divided into two classes of subject matter, the one which is aimed at the prohibition of monopoly and the restraint of trade, and which is properly 'anti-trust,' and the other, which is aimed at improper rebates, discrimination, and unfair competition, and which has no necessary connection with combinations." Of the two classes of legislation, the bureau rejected the first as having been proved impracticable and unsound, representing as it did the law already in place because of Supreme Court decisions. "The theory of the first class of 'anti-trust' legislation," said the bureau, "is the prevention of monopoly and the maintenance of a condition of competition." With few exceptions, this legislation had been "singularly futile," for it was "an attempt to stop the operation of strictly economic law by statutory enactment." As a matter of policy, the bureau insisted, "The attempt to maintain a state of competition by prohibiting all combination, reasonable or unreasonable, is wrong in principle." In contrast, the second class of legislation had "no necessary connection with combinations or trusts"; it rested on "an entirely different principle," and it was therefore "fundamentally correct." It aimed neither at "the restraint of combination" nor "the maintenance of competition," but simply at "regulating the *methods* of competition." In acknowledging the passage of economic development beyond the classical — and neoclassical —

model of the competitive market, the second class of legislation would adjust public policy and the law of the land to the modern laws of economics, that is, to the practice of those capitalists engaged in the corporate reorganization of the market and property. Such legislation would base itself on "the irresistible tendency toward combination" and seek "to make certain that combination is reached only through just, fair, and proper means." In recognizing that "the tendency to combine can not be stopped by statute," and that the proper object of policy was "to see that this process shall be attended with as little injustice as may be," the second class of legislation was "correct in theory." The bureau, in summary, held from its inception that combination in the form primarily of the modern corporation had become "an industrial necessity, and hence will be engaged in despite penal legislation." With equal consistency, the bureau coupled this theme with the recommendation that Congress "provide a method by which reasonable combination may be permitted."[8]

For its own part the bureau developed suggestions involving the establishment of federal inspection and supervision of the larger corportions through federal incorporation, licensing, or registration, along lines considered by the Industrial Commission. Federal incorporation, instead of state incorporation, of corporations engaged in interstate or foreign commerce had been widely proposed as a form of licensing during the proceedings of the Industrial Commission. In serving as both Roosevelt's adviser and the commission's expert on "trusts and industrial combinations," Jenks had opposed federal incorporation while he was with the commission "on the ground that it was altogether too centralizing in its tendency"; but later, at about the same time that Congress was passing the bill establishing the Department of Commerce and Labor, Jenks advised Roosevelt in favor of a proposal for voluntary federal incorporation of large corporations as the basis for permitting those choosing federal incorporation to engage in reasonable restraints of trade. This proposal and variations upon it, involving licensing or registration instead of incorporation, were to circulate in Congress and the federal executive, in the bureau as well as in the White House, over the next decade, and would become in particular the basis of the Hepburn amendments to the Sherman Act, introduced in Congress in 1908 without success.[9]

8. *Ann. Rep.* (1904), pp. 40–41, 38–39; ibid. (1905), p. 8 (emphasis in original).
9. Jenks to Roosevelt, 2 Feb. 1903, TR. On the widespread and persistent desire among capitalists for uniform federal standards as against the multiplicity of state laws and jurisdictions, as well as against political tendencies in some states toward stringent anti-corporate policies, see, e.g., Charles G. Dawes, "Trusts and Trade

Whether the law should provide for incorporation, licensing, or registration, the bureau proposed that it be so drawn as to distinguish between reasonable and unreasonable restraint of trade, "lessen the possibilities of unfair and dishonest competition," and still leave to the courts a large role in determining "the questions of the reasonableness of combination, of conspiracies in restraint of trade, of monopolistic control." The intended effect would be to permit a corporate-administered market under government supervision that would protect individuals and enterprises against abuses of market power and thereby guarantee "equality of opportunity" without "equality in results."[10]

In its annual reports, the bureau repeatedly made explicit one of the major objectives implicit in its general policy: A licensing law or its equivalent, in requiring publicity of corporate affairs, would yield accurate information, "so that the people ... may form an intelligent opinion ... and not be driven to extreme and unwise action by the clamor of those who assail all great corporate interests because some have done ill." Hence, the bureau's policy "to cooperate with, not antagonize, the business world" sought "to secure conservative action, and to avoid ill-considered attack upon corporations charged with unfair or dishonest practices."[11]

In viewing the great corporation as the characteristic institution of modern industrial organization, vital to continued economic progress, the bureau emphasized the need to direct popular animosity toward miscreant individuals who misused or abused corporate power and away from the corporation as an institution. Appropriate legislation like a federal license law "will restore individual responsibility and prevent the corporation from being the hiding place of the irresponsible, dishonest, or corrupt manager." If the individual "can hide behind a corporation, can conceal his acts ... [and] escape personal responsibility," unscrupulous persons would use the corporation "as an agency for imposition, fraud, and corruption." As Smith put it in an internal bureau memorandum, "The modern corporate system ... has one of its greatest defects in that it necessarily reduces greatly the old personal responsibility that went with an individual or partnership business." For effective regulation, "we must be able to place the real responsibil-

Combinations," delivered at annual meeting of Merchants' Club of Boston, 17 Oct. 1899 (Washington, D.C.: Judd & Detwiler, 1899), esp. pp. 6–7; George W. Perkins, "The Modern Corporation," in Edwin R. A. Seligman, ed., *The Currency Problem and the Present Financial Situation* (New York: Columbia University Press, 1908), esp. p. 165.

10. *Ann. Rep.* (1905), pp. 8–9; ibid. (1906), p. 6.
11. Ibid. (1906), pp. 6–7; ibid. (1904), p. 36.

ity for corporate management." Regulatory law "must affect *real*, not fictitious, interests," if necessary, by making stock ownership "as public as land titles" or by having it placed on the record "in a confidential form, so that we can deal directly with individuals." "The real and ultimate responsibility for a corporation's acts cannot be fairly determined unless we know the person or persons controlling its policy," that is, not only the directors and officers but also the stockholders "who elect these officers." Hence, open the corporation's books and records to "proper public inspection," the bureau argued in its official reports, and "the danger of such wrongs will be reduced to a minimum." Suggesting the text for future theorists, the bureau expected that with "the individuals who control it" known, and "personal responsibility for its actions" fixed, "the corporation is not then soulless." Or, as George W. Perkins, in 1910, told students and faculty of the Harvard Graduate School of Business Administration, "Indeed, there is even hope that a corporation might, after all, have a soul."[12]

The bureau's emphasis on publicity of corporate affairs and the fixing of individual responsibility for corporate behavior was no nostalgic exercise over a lost individualism. Aside from the objective of identifying illegal or unethical behavior with the individual rather than with the institution, the bureau's position addressed three other concerns: (1) finding a replacement for the competitive investment and price mechanism as the spur to cost efficiency and innovation, and as a guarantor of fair prices and reasonable returns; (2) enforcing management accountability and responsibility to investors, consumers, workers, and the public; (3) securing the confidence of the small and medium investor in the corporation – and hence in the stock market – as a safe investment outlet for savings and as an equitable allocator of property income. Publicity within the framework of federal registration or licensing seemed to go far toward attaining all these objectives.[13]

In general, although not necessarily in detail, the bureau's legislative recommendations, as well as its overall outlook, coincided with the

12. Ibid. (1906), p. 6. Herbert Knox Smith, "Stock Ownership" (Memorandum), 29 May 1906, BC, G.F. 1132. Smith's emphasis. Perkins, "Some Things to Think About," address at the Graduate School of Business Administration, Harvard University, 15 Apr. 1910, p. 11.

13. Industrial Commission, *Preliminary Report*, pp. 5–6; Jenks, *Trust Problem*, pp. 3–9, 235–240 (app. B), pp. 244–279 (app. D); Arthur Twining Hadley, "The Good and the Evil of Industrial Combinations," *Atlantic Monthly* 79 (Mar. 1897), pp. 377–385, at p. 383; also, along these lines, Theodore Marburg to Ralph M. Easley, 17 Apr. 1908, and R. D. Silliman to President William Howard Taft, 6 Mar. 1909, enclosed in Silliman to Easley, 16 Apr. 1909, NCF.

policies of President Roosevelt. As the president altered policy so did the bureau,[14] regardless of divergent personal inclinations of Garfield and Smith. Upon Smith's becoming commissioner in 1907,[15] the bureau in accord with the president placed increasingly greater emphasis on the need to supplant judicial process under the Sherman Act with administrative licensing or registration of corporations by the bureau or a successor interstate trade commission. Although moving to the Interior Department as secretary, Garfield remained in close touch with the bureau's work, and he and Smith consulted and worked together and with Roosevelt regularly in formulating regulatory policy.

The bureau had since its establishment based a large part of its investigatory activity on the kind of voluntary cooperation it had developed with corporations like United States Steel and International Harvester. These corporations, under the leadership of Perkins, Elbert H. Gary, and Cyrus McCormick, had submitted their affairs in detail to the close scrutiny of the bureau and held themselves ready to cease or modify objectionable practices or contracts, in return for which the bureau, with the president's approval, informally guaranteed them against litigation under the Sherman Act by the Department of Justice.[16] From this experience, the bureau expected that under a licensing or registration system, a federal regulatory agency might guide and counsel corporations in the arrangement of their affairs to conform with fair methods of competition, reasonable restraints of trade, and sound managerial standards, and if need be use its licensing or registration power, including the threat of prosecution under the Sherman Act, to discipline or punish misbehaving corporations or their officers or stockholders.

In the meantime, however, the advisory and protective relations that the bureau had established with cooperative corporations entirely

14. Johnson, "Theodore Roosevelt and the Bureau"; Robert H. Wiebe, "The House of Morgan and the Executive, 1905–1913," *AHR* 65:1 (Oct. 1959), pp. 49–60, esp. pp. 52–56; William Letwin, *Law and Economic Policy in America: The Evolution of the Sherman Antitrust Act* (New York: Random House, 1965), pp. 240–247. Cf. Ralph M. Easley to Charles G. Dawes, 11 Nov. 1907, Easley to Herbert K. Smith, 15 Jan. and 5 Feb. 1908, Easley to Henry W. Taft, 2 Mar. 1908, Easley to Nicholas Murray Butler, 2 Mar. 1908, Easley to Edgar A. Bancroft, 2 Mar. and 21 Mar. 1908, Bancroft to Easley, 13 Mar. 1908, all in NCF; and Roosevelt to N. M. Butler, 29 Aug. 1903, Roosevelt to Philander C. Knox, 10 Nov. 1904, Roosevelt to Paul Morton, 2 Jan. 1907, Roosevelt to Henry Higginson, 11 Feb. 1907, all in TR.

15. As a prominent Roosevelt Progressive, Smith in July 1912 resigned as commissioner of the bureau to run, unsuccessfully, for governor of Connecticut on the Progressive party ticket, and in the process to support Roosevelt's presidential bid.

16. Cf. Wiebe, "The House of Morgan."

lacked either legislative sanction or judicial standing. They amounted to the assumption of extralegal executive action in evasion of the law as construed by the Supreme Court. Although the administration's policy might be characterized as a selective enforcement of the law, it amounted, in essence, to presidential legislation. Roosevelt did not refrain from joining the issue publicly, stating that his administration had been enforcing the Sherman Act according to the criteria of reasonableness and public interest, rather than in accordance with the Court's rendering of the law. As he told Congress in his special message of 25 March 1908, in requesting legislation that would in effect validate, post facto, executive practice: "It may well be remembered that all of the suits brought by the Government [during Roosevelt's presidency] under the antitrust law have been in cases where the combination or contract was in fact unfair, unreasonable, and against the public interest." Beginning with his annual report for 1907, and following Garfield's lead, Smith challenged the Supreme Court directly. Invoking as a matter of conventional wisdom the axiom that the trust question was essentially the corporation question, Smith attacked the Court's ban on corporate restriction of competition. "It is not the existence of industrial power, but rather its misuse, that is the real problem," he held. "Corporate methods, not corporate existence, is the question at issue." Or, as the bureau's next annual report reiterated, "the real issue is, what are the intent, methods, and effect of a given combination or corporation? What a great corporation does and how it does it is of far more practical importance than the mere question whether it is legally a combination or not." The corporation that acquired or sustained its power "simply because it gives better service to the public by fair and open means justifies itself," whereas the corporation that succeeded through the "active destruction of the success of competitors by unfair methods" condemned its methods as "the evils to be prevented." This position was an altogether proper statement of desirable policy, but as a statement of the law it flew in the face of the Supreme Court's ruling that if a corporation by its practices or contracts directly and substantially regulated interstate or foreign commerce, it thereby, under the Sherman Act, illegally arrogated to itself powers reserved exclusively to Congress.[17]

Confronted with the Court's recalcitrance on antitrust law, and following Roosevelt's lead, the bureau intensified its call for the establishment of a federal administrative agency – a trade commission – that

17. *Ann. Rep.* (1907), pp. 5, 6–7; ibid. (1908), pp. 4–5; *Cong. Rec.*, 60th Cong., 1st Sess., 42:4, p. 3854.

would diminish judicial process and expand administrative supervision in the regulation of interstate corporations. The commission's methods were to be corrective, preventive, and advisory "rather than penal," in dealing with corporations as institutions. Criminal prosecutions were to be reserved for cases of individuals suspected of violating laws against unfair competition. Many "leaders of industry" and "most of the large corporations" under investigation by the bureau were volunteering their "cooperation and assistance," Smith reported; "the time is ripe" for a regulatory system that "will afford a permanent practical ground for contact and cooperation between the Government officials charged with this work on the one hand and corporate managers on the other."[18]

In response to the Supreme Court's strong reaffirmation of its literalist construction of the Sherman Act, in *Loewe* v. *Lawlor* and *Shawnee*, the bureau in its 1908 annual report once again attacked the law of the land. Smith restated the bureau's basic premises that unrestricted competition no longer suited modern industrial conditions, that old-style competition could not, in any case, be expected from the voluntary behavior of capitalists, and that to impose competition by the coercion of law would prove a dangerous anachronism. "There is an irresistible movement toward concentration in business," the bureau argued. "We must definitely recognize this as an inevitable economic law. We must also recognize the fact," Smith went on, not a little disingenuously in view of the administration's refusal to enforce the law as judicially interpreted, "that industrial concentration is already largely accomplished, in spite of general statutory prohibition." This was a rather candid acknowledgment by the government, and by one of its expert authorities no less, that the corporate reorganization of capitalism was proceeding or was "already largely accomplished" outside the law and in violation of it. But it was not more than President Roosevelt stated publicly in his annual messages to Congress of both 1906 and 1907, where he noted that "the law as construed by the Supreme Court is such that the business of the country can not be conducted without breaking it." The law "provides that its own infraction must be the condition precedent upon business success." The remedy lay not in undoing the corporate reorganization but in revising the law. As the bureau put it, "the aim of new legislation should be to regulate, rather than to prohibit combination." It was an "obvious absurdity" to attempt both at the same time. If, therefore, the government "elects to regulate combination, it must logically permit at least a reasonable degree thereof," and it must "recognize in law what has already become

18. *Ann. Rep.* (1907), pp. 5–6.

an accomplished fact." Economic evolution, including the organization of business and the shape of the market, could not be determined by legal standards; on the contrary, the law must be adjusted to the dictates of economic evolution. The Sherman Act as then judicially construed must be superseded. "Our present law, forbidding all combination, therefore needs adaptation to the actual facts." It should be made to apply not to combination or restraint of trade as such, but to "the intent, methods, and results of combinations," with the practical object of keeping "business opportunity and the highways of commerce ... equally open to all," by preventing "fraud, special privilege, and unfair competition." This meant, the bureau concluded, that "we must recognize concentration, supervise it, and regulate it," not passively through the courts primarily but "positively, through an active federal agency" that guaranteed, so far as possible, government "cooperation with corporate interests."[19]

The bureau continued to recommend penal laws that would define and prohibit "specific forms of unfair competition." Their purpose would be to prevent not monopolistic combinations but "the misuse of monopoly powers" by individuals. "Efficient publicity" would serve as the "strongest means" for implementing the system of government supervision of corporate affairs. The bureau emphasized its proposal that the system of federal supervision rest on the larger corporations' voluntary filing with the trade commission of regular reports, which should disclose their capitalization, management, and contractual relations. Compulsory filing would be reserved for extreme cases. The bureau doubted the need for compulsion, because many leaders of large corporations had already entered cooperative liaison with the bureau and expressed willingness to place themselves within such a system as the bureau recommended. "A system of practical publicity with cooperation," explained the bureau, "will obtain that requisite for all wise measures, reliable information." It would "involve no drastic action" but rather "forestall such action." In bringing together "the Government and the corporate manager in conference and cooperation," the system would "serve to adjust continuously the complex and changing relationship between our business forces and the public welfare." As a result, forecast the bureau, "unjust prejudice" would abate, "the standing of our corporate securities, both at home and abroad," would rise, "public confidence" in the "fairness and openness" of corporate management would grow, and not least of all, "Extreme and sweeping

19. Ibid. (1908), pp. 4–8. Annual Message, 3 Dec. 1907, *Cong. Rec.*, 60th, 1st, 42:1, p. 69 (first quotation from Roosevelt is his quotation of his own words in his 1906 message).

attacks on all corporate business [would] ... thus be greatly lessened as the misconception of the real facts disappears."[20]

By the midpoint of Roosevelt's second presidential term, the bureau had developed a program that included the following ends and means. It sought the adaptation of the law to an administered market, and the legitimation of the corporate reorganization of the economy. Because the corporation had become "the accepted machinery" for managing and controlling the nation's "dominant commercial forces," intelligent and progressive policy required not the attempt to return to the regime of unrestricted competition with its recurrent boom-bust cycle, as stipulated by the Court's construction of the law, but rather, the affirmation of large corporations with their market-administering powers, and the ordering of their affairs to place "a premium on business efficiency, business honesty, and commercial service to the public."[21] For these purposes, the bureau recommended publicity of corporate affairs through a licensing or registration system administered by a federal executive agency; this system would replace the old competitive mechanism as the spur to efficiency, innovation, and ethical practices. It would, in sum, install a regulatory system based on routine corporation-government "conference and cooperation."

The "cooperation" theme, coupled with federal licensing or registration, had potentially statist implications. It raised the question of how to construct a regulatory system of corporation-government cooperation without making government the direct instrument of powerful capitalists, or without making capitalist enterprises the mere agencies of the state. This was not necessarily a new question, but under modern historical conditions either case could yield a version of a corporate-state regime, or the strong basis for one, as distinguished from a regulatory or welfare state.

The statist implications at first emerged indirectly in deliberations on questions of federal-state jurisdictions, judicial review, and due process, and then directly in questions of government power and dictation in the market. In both manifestations, Roosevelt's views took a statist route, along which neither Garfield nor Smith were eager to go. They posted roadside warnings, but Roosevelt pushed strenuously ahead, and his two junior colleagues were progressive troopers who followed their leader even against their own judgment, expecting that they could reroute him from time to time, or at the last turn.

---

20. *Ann. Rep.* (1908); ibid. (1909), p. 5; ibid. (1910), pp. 3–7; ibid. (1911), pp. 3–4.
21. Ibid. (1908), pp. 9–10; ibid. (1909), p. 3; ibid. (1910), p. 6.

The indirect manifestations of concern over statist implications of regulatory proposals were already apparent by 1906–1907, as Smith and Garfield wrestled with the concrete framing of an incorporation or licensing law that might be sent to Congress. The attendant issues of jurisdiction, due process, and judicial review raised questions of centralized power and executive-administrative controls over the market that could unwittingly, even if not by design, result in state command.

The proposal for federal incorporation, which initially enjoyed wide favor during the Industrial Commission's proceedings, arose in part out of a fear that regulation of interstate commerce might have fallen into a limbo between state and federal jurisdictions, reachable by neither, given the Supreme Court's decision in the Knight case. The states, it was said, created the agent, the operating corporation, but could not regulate the agent's market activities beyond the state's borders; the federal government, on the other hand, could not effectively deal with the interstate market activities because it could not touch the agent.[22] The Supreme Court had already laid this argument to rest, and Smith was not deterred by it. He had in his memorandum of 1905 pointed out "the very common misinterpretation of the Knight case." The Court had not held "that there is never any connection between production and commerce," but only "that production does not necessarily imply interstate commerce." If any doubt remained after the cases of 1897–1899, the Court in the Northern Securities case of 1904, as Smith noted in another memorandum in early 1906, made it clear that persons could not do something, even if legal in itself, such as enter articles of incorporation chartered by a state, "as a means of evading a federal law." Indeed, in still broader terms, the Supreme Court had ruled in *Addyston Pipe* as elsewhere, and Chief Justice Fuller explicitly reaffirmed in *Champion* v. *Ames* (while dissenting in the case but agreeing with the majority on this point), that, in Fuller's words, "Congress could prohibit the performance of contracts, whose natural effect, when carried out, would be to directly regulate interstate and foreign commerce."[23] It might be added, as well, that under the Sherman Act's conspiracy clause, contracts, agreements, and acts legal in themselves were still reachable if part of a conspiracy to violate the law.

22. Smith, "Stock Ownership," BC, G.F. 1132; also Secretary of Commerce and Labor Charles Nagel to William C. Adamson, chair, House Committee on Interstate and Foreign Commerce, 27 June 1911, BC, G.F. 5596.
23. Smith, "Memorandum on Paper by James H. McIntosh . . .," 18 Feb. 1905, BC, G.F. 2480; Smith, "Important Features of Federal License Law, Memo., – Jan. 10, 1906," BC, G.F. 095–2; Fuller at *Champion* v. *Ames*, 188 *U.S.* 367 (23 Feb. 1903), citing *Addyston Pipe and Steel Co.* v. *U.S.*, 175 *U.S.* 211; to same effect, Harlan for the Court in *Champion*, at 175 *U.S.* 353, 355–356. *Champion* was not

Smith rejected federal incorporation on other grounds – that it might be unconstitutional, that it might prove ineffective or unwieldy, or that it might result in inordinate federal government power. On constitutional grounds, Smith advised Roosevelt, federal power to regulate interstate commerce did not reach the form of organization of corporations established under state law, and the federal government could neither prevent states from chartering corporations nor debar corporations, simply for being state-chartered, from engaging in interstate commerce. Federal incorporation could therefore not be made compulsory as a condition of engaging in interstate commerce, and if voluntary, might be ineffective.[24]

Supposing these constitutional obstacles absent, federal incorporation, if applied to the thousands of corporations engaged in interstate commerce, big and small alike, could bury the regulatory agency in mountains of paperwork and might well become little more than a formality without real regulatory effect. Alternatively, it could lead to ever growing centralized federal power and politicization of the market, as Congress might add more and more conditions in the granting of corporate charters, and as the executive regulatory agency might find itself obliged to intrude in myriad everyday contract relations, including those involved in the issue, marketing, and classification of securities. Because a system of federal incorporation would necessarily include the authority to deny or revoke the corporation charter for cause, and to police compliance with charter conditions, the executive officer and agency administering the system would exercise enormous power, in the process of which they would be constantly making decisions of a judicial or quasi-judicial nature. This would result either in dangerous, if not unconstitutional, violations of due process rights, or in the smothering of the system under an avalanche of litigation. In general, Smith feared, "under the exercise of such an extreme power the Federal Government could undoubtedly usurp substantially all the present state powers and rights and could go to the extreme of regulating state forms of taxation, contract, and execution of documents, and even private rights of individuals."[25]

a Sherman Act case (it is widely known, and listed in *United States Reports*, as the "Lottery Case"), so that the opinions given here on this point, both the majority and the dissenting, assume a particular significance as representing a settled principle of law, whatever the specific statute under which a case might be brought.

24. Smith to William Loeb, Jr., secretary to the president, Oyster Bay, N.Y., 5 Sept. 1907, in reply to Loeb to Smith, 22 Aug. 1907, stating that the president requested Smith's views on these matters as raised in a letter to Roosevelt from William Shaw of Boston, BC, G.F. 1125.

25. Smith to Loeb, 5 Sept. 1907, BC, G.F. 1125.

Federal licensing or registration of corporations as a condition of their engaging in interstate commerce did not pose the jurisdictional problem attached to federal incorporation, but it raised essentially the same questions of government power and due process, and gave Smith and Garfield similar second thoughts.

In 1906–1907, the bureau deliberated continually on a possible federal license law, and by mid–1906 it had under consideration a draft Federal License Act. The proposed law would bring within the jurisdiction of the Bureau of Corporations only larger corporations with an interstate trade of $10 million or more per year, and only such larger corporations in basic or staple industries tentatively listed to include petroleum and its products, beef and dressed meats, sugar, flour, tobacco, coal, iron, steel, farm implements, lumber, and paper. In order to determine jurisdiction, however, the commissioner of corporations would have the power to examine the books, accounts, and records of all corporations engaged interstate commerce, and require from them any other necessary information, including sworn statements and reports.[26]

Corporations coming within the act would receive a federal license or franchise to engage in interstate trade, without which they would be barred from interstate trade. As a further condition prerequisite to obtaining the license, a corporation would be required a file with the commissioner an initial report stating its name, state of incorporation, location of principal office, with a copy of its charter or articles of incorporation and bylaws; also, the nature of its business, the names and addresses of officers, directors, and executive committee members, and the amount and classifications of its authorized and outstanding capital stock. The initial report would then be updated by annual reports that would, in addition, provide full information on the corporation's assets, liabilities, and indebtedness, the amount of annual interstate business transacted, and all stock held by and in other corporations with the names of the other corporations. The corporation and its individual officers, directors, agents, and employees would be subject to fine or imprisonment for noncompliance with the registration provisions. Subsequently, the commissioner or a designee would have at all times access to all books, records, accounts, and papers of licensed corporations.

Upon notice and hearing, the commissioner could revoke or suspend the license, in whole or in part, in case of a corporation's noncom-

---

26. Smith, "Important Features …," BC, G.F. 095–2, and "Federal License Act," 24 May 1906, BC, G.F. 4472–2.

pliance with registration provisions, and the commissioner, subject to appeal to the secretary of commerce and labor, could revoke or suspend license completely or, at the commissioner's discretion, for a given period or in a given territory (market) or over specified routes, if it was found that the corporation had been employing unfair methods of competition. Attempts to evade licensing through holding companies, purchasing or selling agents, or otherwise, would also be illegal and grounds for being barred from interstate trade. A corporation engaging in interstate commerce after its license had been revoked or suspended would be guilty of violation of the law, and both the corporation and its officers, directors, agents, or employees would be punishable by fine, subject to remission or mitigation by the commissioner before final adjudication in the courts. Common carriers would also be required to give information in aid of determining the extent of a given corporation's interstate trade. All acts of the commissioner and of the secretary of commerce and labor would be appealable to United States district court, but the findings of either officer would be *prima facie* evidence as to the truth of matters of fact. State courts would have no jurisdiction over licensed corporations' franchises, and states would be prohibited from hindering, hampering, taxing, or interfering with the use of the franchise; licensed corporations could remove or transfer suits to United States courts without state interference. The commissioner, finally, would have the authority to make, amend, alter, or repeal all necessary regulations, and these regulations, upon approval of the secretary of commerce and labor, would have the force of law.[27]

This proposed law would establish, in effect, a system of federal incorporation through licensing and registration, it would provide for thorough disclosure of large corporate affairs, and it would repose vast power in the hands of a federal executive agency and its officers. It was the kind of program Roosevelt had by 1906–1907 come strongly to favor. If anything, the draft bill provided for less executive power and more judicial review in the regulation of the market than Roosevelt would have preferred. The drastic power to forbid for cause engagement in interstate trade had earlier been recommended by the Industrial Commission, and it would seem to be warranted by the Supreme Court's repeated affirmation of Congress's plenary power, consistent with rules of due process, to regulate interstate and foreign commerce.

Smith favored the publicity and oversight provisions of the proposed law, but he raised questions touching matters of policy, due process, and judicial review that went to the heart of the bill, namely, the

27. "Important Features," and "Federal License Act."

commissioner's power to revoke or suspend licenses for violation of federal law. "I don't like this provision, and yet I don't know how to get away from it." On policy, Smith noted that the "practical trouble will be that the onus of enforcing the anti-trust law, the economic value of which is nil," will fall upon the commissioner. In other words, aside from being "swamped with innumerable applications and complaints throughout the country," the commissioner would become the chief enforcer of precisely the policy that ought to be changed. The commissioner would be called upon by complainants to take "action against corporations on the ground of unlawful combination," resulting in endless investigations and litigation, "all of which would disturb business greatly, and would, in my opinion, have no good result." Smith therefore advised, "I should be inclined to dodge this issue by leaving out the enforcement of the anti-trust law from the various objects of the federal-license law, and by frankly stating that the enforcement of that law is peculiarly the duty of the Department of Justice." Indeed, if necessary, "I would go as far as to say that I didn't believe in the anti-trust law anyhow, rather than have the responsibility of enforcing it." On the basis of this criticism, the draft law was changed from providing for suspension or revocation of license due to violation of the Sherman Act or federal laws in general, to suspension or revocation due specifically to noncompliance with registration regulations or to engagement in unfair methods of competition.[28]

On the questions of due process and judicial review, Smith noted that the revocation and suspension powers would oblige the commissioner "to exercise a difficult and dangerous discretion, often apparently arbitrary, or else to provoke an immense amount of litigation by revoking the licenses of a lot of corporations and forcing them to appeal from his decisions." Such powers were "too great to be placed for determination in the hands of any one man." Smith recommended a clear separation of administrative and judicial functions that would "restrict the actual power of the Commissioner for the revocation or suspension of license to a small class of well-defined cases," preferably to cases of noncompliance with registration regulations, where the commissioner's "determination of the offense was purely a ministerial act." For all other cases of alleged violations of the law, the commissioner, upon complaint or at the commissioner's own initiative, might present the cases to the courts, "leaving to the courts all jurisdiction as to revocation or suspension of licenses." If Smith were to have his preference, he would entirely divorce the commissioner from punitive powers (except with respect to

28.   "Important Features," and "Federal License Act."

registration): "Dont expressly give Commissioner power or duty to report offenses," he urged. "Leave him free."[29] That is, free to let disclosure and registration procedures work their discipline on corporate behavior within the framework of business-government cooperation, but without strong tendencies toward executive coercion or dictation.

Roosevelt was prepared to go much farther, and he pressed his aides accordingly for draft legislation that went beyond their own proclivities. Approaching the end of his term, the president wanted at least to introduce, if not to pass, legislation on regulating the market before he left office. He might thereby influence the terms of subsequent legislative debate whoever resided in the White House. In late October 1907, he sent over to Garfield – who was now secretary of the interior but still a principal presidential adviser on business regulation – a draft bill for Garfield's deliberation and counsel.[30] Along with the earlier draft license bill, it affords a good view of the direction Roosevelt's policy-thinking was taking on the eve of the movement for the Hepburn amendments to the Sherman Act. In this later draft bill, Roosevelt returned to the idea of outright federal incorporation, in spite of Smith's previous warnings about its constitutional vulnerability. It was a bill drawn for introduction in the United States Senate. It stated its purpose to be "To provide for the incorporation controlled and governed of associations organized to carry on business, enter into or become a part of interstate commerce."[31]

Whereas the draft licensing bill dealt with unfair methods of competition, this bill was designed to give the secretary of commerce and labor complete control over the business conduct and the capitalization of corporations engaged in interstate trade, with far-reaching control over their investment function. Under its terms, the condition of engaging in interstate commerce would be the filing of articles of association with the secretary of commerce and labor and their certification by the secretary; certified articles would then be received in the courts as *prima facie* evidence of the facts stated therein. The corporation would have to supply information similar to that required in the license bill, and in addition, the names of all shareholders and the amount of stock held by each. In its articles of association, the corporation would have to "consent and agree to subject itself, and to conform, to all needful rules and regulations" prescribed by the secretary "for the conduct of its

---

29. "Important Features." ("Dont" in original.)
30. Rudolph Forster, acting secretary to the president, to Garfield, 28 Oct. 1907, enclosing draft bill, "A Bill," JRG, F. 41: National Incorporation, Box 128.
31. "A Bill," ibid.

business," and to submit its books and records to examination by the secretary or designees upon request, and render to the secretary, "whenever required," complete information on its "financial condition and manner of conducting business." The corporation would "at no time issue new stock in excess of the cash value of its assets," and any new stock could be issued only in "such sum as shall be approved" by the Secretary, "upon a valuation made by him."[32]

In short, every corporation organized under the act would "at all times be under the supervision and control of the Secretary of Commerce and Labor." No certified corporation could issue stock except as authorized by the secretary, and in no case in excess of the value of its assets, except that the secretary could authorize issue of additional stock to enlarge or extend or improve the business, provided however that the secretary would see to it that the proceeds were "used for the purposes for which such stock was authorized." A certified corporation would have to submit to the secretary annual reports fully stating gross and net earnings, improvements or additions, their cost, value of assets, expenditure of receipts, "and such other information ... as may be required" by the secretary. Whenever the amount of outstanding stock should exceed the value of assets, the secretary would require the corporation to call in all stock and issue new stock in lieu thereof in an amount not exceeding the value of assets, and each stockholder would be required to surrender the old stock and receive the new issue in an amount proportionate to the old holdings. Upon any delinquency, the secretary would "by order annul and cancel" the certificate of incorporation. This would effect "a dissolution of such corporation," except that any legal action by or against it would proceed as if it were not dissolved. To administer the law, the secretary would appoint "a sufficient number of competent accountants and appraisers" to investigate "the condition of all associations organized under the provisions of this act."[33]

Here was a blueprint, however crudely drawn, for a centralized executive ministry of economics lodged in the Department of Commerce and Labor. Combined with such measures as those in the proposed licensing act, it would establish the framework of state command of the nation's major business enterprise. Note that the incorporation bill made no provision at all for judicial review, consistent with Roosevelt's own views, although an exclusive executive administration without recourse to the courts would have been impossible without

32. Ibid.
33. Ibid.

modification of the constitutional order. The great emphasis on stock issue reflected Roosevelt's repeated denunciation of stock speculation, watering, and fraud. It signified his determination to make government the arbiter of corporate combination and growth, to restrain thereby tendencies toward redundant capacity by heading off speculative stock issue, to guarantee the safety of the stock market as an outlet for savings, and, at the same time, to assure a degree of competition among separate corporate enterprises sufficient to yield innovation, efficiency, managerial excellence and accountability, fair prices, and reasonable returns: in one word, Progress.

The scheme, taken as a whole and precisely as drafted, had little chance of immediate adoption, but it revealed Roosevelt's intent, for which there was a potentially growing popular support among a people who had come to trust government more and big business less. The presidential intent looked toward an executive agency, as free as possible from judicial restraint, with powers of command over the business operations in general, and the investment activity in particular, of corporate enterprise, backed up by the power of summary dissolution of delinquent corporations. The state would not simply police or regulate the economy; rather, particularly as the law underwent further elaboration and refinement over the years, corporations would become agents, "controlled and governed," of the state and of public policy. Representing as it did the president's long-term outlook, the draft legislation went beyond objectives or methods that the American body politic could be expected to absorb in the near term. A superb politician, Roosevelt was prepared to take what he could get if it was pointed in the same general direction as his own.

The movement for Sherman Act revision

By 1907, dissatisfaction with the Supreme Court's interpretation of the Sherman Act reached into the ranks of virtually every organized grouping in the marketplace. No more than large-corporate capitalists did trade unionists or small producers (whether farmers, manufacturers, or merchants) want to be bound by the choices dictated by the Supreme Court, namely, either unrestricted competition or statist direction. Sentiment on all sides wanted the legalization of reasonable restraints of trade subject to government regulation. But the contending groups could not reach agreement on which restraints were to be presumed reasonable, on the method and extent of government regulation, or, consequently, on how to accomplish a legislative revision of the Sherman Act.

With congressional action foreclosed by insufficient consensus on positive legislation, the Supreme Court in effect continued unilaterally to determine the meaning of federal antitrust law, while the executive persisted in its policy of permitting business practices violative of the law as judicially construed. No lawyer could counsel with certainty exactly what the law, in practice, allowed or forbade. The next election, if not merely a change in political winds, might alter executive policy. What the Justice Department countenanced today it might prosecute tomorrow. The Supreme Court majority might change. Accordingly, the law that governed all manner of business practices, including basic contractual relations, remained obscure – and a market without clarity and stability of law is like a terrain with a sudden loss of gravitation, where everyone becomes disoriented and no one knows up from down.[34]

In a major effort at resolving the conflict of policy and law, the National Civic Federation in 1907–1908, in close liaison with the Roosevelt administration, undertook to mobilize public opinion on a scale sufficient to induce congressional action in favor of legalizing reasonable restraints of trade. The Civic Federation represented one segment of that broad range of opinion, which although divided on the corporate reorganization of the economy, nevertheless favored some degree of private and government regulation of the market. The outlook articulated by the leaders of the Civic Federation combined an unequivocal affirmation of large-corporate administered markets with an advocacy of a strong government regulatory role.

The federation's active leaders consisted of prominent figures from a

---

34. The inhibitive impact of the uncertainty of law on market activity was a continuous theme among capitalists from the turn of the century to 1914. Typical, for example, is the statement in 1908 by Henry R. Towne, president of Yale & Towne Manufacturing Co. and president of the Merchants' Association of New York, at the House Judiciary Committee subcommittee hearing on the Hepburn amendments to the Sherman Act: "We business men are profoundly concerned with this question. We object to our present position. . . . what we wish is a standard. The law should be known and fixed in advance for business as for everything else, so that business men may make their plans on a solid foundation, guided by their legal advisers as to what the consequences and the intent of the law is." U.S. House of Representatives, Committee on the Judiciary, *Hearings on House Bill 19745, An Act to Regulate Commerce, etc.*, Subcommittee No. 3, 60th Cong., 1st Sess. 6 April 1908 (Washington, D.C.: Government Printing Officer, 1908), pp. 153–154, 155 (hereafter cited as House Hearings, 1908). Similarly typical along these lines, but more concretely indicative, are private discussions in National City Bank president Frank A. Vanderlip's correspondence with James Stillman and others over deferment of investment programs by railways and manufacturing corporations pending clarification of the antitrust law. E.g., Vanderlip to Stillman, 3 Feb. 1910, 3 June 1910, 17 Oct. 1911; Stillman to Vanderlip, 16 Sept. 1910; Vanderlip to Lyman J. Gage, 28 Feb. 1910; all in FAV.

cross section of economic, political, intellectual, religious and cultural elites: capitalists prominent in railways, communications, industry, commerce, and investment banking; former and current senior officers of the federal government; eminent members of the legal profession; national officers of farmers' organizations and trade unions; prominent publishers and journalists; high-ranking clergy; and university presidents and professors.[35]

35. In late 1907 the NCF's officers were: president: August Belmont; vice-presidents: Samuel Gompers, Nahum J. Bachelder, Ellison A. Smyth, Benjamin I. Wheeler; Treasurer: Isaac N. Seligman. Its executive council, the inner leadership, separate from the larger executive committee, consisted of the officers; Ralph M. Easley, chair of the executive council; and the chairs of the standing committees. In 1907 these were: John Mitchell (trade agreement committee), Charles A. Moore (welfare), E. R. A. Seligman (taxation), Seth Low (conciliation), William H. Taft (public employees' welfare), Nicholas Murray Butler (industrial economics), Melville E. Ingalls (public ownership), and Franklin MacVeagh (immigration). The executive committee was organized in such a way as to regroup the various social sectors represented in it into three larger groupings conceived as constituting the society as a whole – capital, labor, and the public (with farmers categorized as part of the public). As of October 1907, the executive committee members included, in each of the three categories, the following persons:
   1. "On the part of the Public": *government*: ex-president Grover Cleveland, ex-secretaries of the interior Cornelius N. Bliss and David R. Francis, U.S. Attorney-General Charles J. Bonaparte; *capital*: Andrew Carnegie and V. Everit Macy (each listed as "Capitalist"), Isaac N. Seligman and James Speyer (each listed as member of his respective investment house); *agriculture*: Nahum J. Bachelder (master, National Grange) and John M. Stahl (president, Farmers' National Congress); *religion*: Roman Catholic Archbishop John Ireland of St. Paul, Minn., and Episcopal Bishop Henry C. Potter of New York City; *higher education*: Benjamin Ide Wheeler (president, University of California, Berkeley), Charles W. Eliot (president, Harvard University), Nicholas Murray Butler (president, Columbia University); and Seth Low, "Publicist."
   2. "On the Part of Employers": *industry*: Henry Phipps (director, U.S. Steel and International Harvester, formerly longtime partner and close associate of Carnegie), William A. Clark (president, United Verde Copper Co.), Clarence H. Mackay (president, Postal Telegraph-Cable Co.), M. H. Taylor (president, Pittsburgh Coal Co.), Samuel Mather (president, Pickands, Mather & Co., director of Lackawanna Steel, brother-in-law of John Hay), Charles A. Moore (president, Manning, Maxwell & Moore), Ellison A. Smyth (president, South Carolina Cotton Manufacturers' Association), Dan R. Hanna (of M. A. Hanna & Co., Cleveland), Marcus M. Marks (president, National Association of Clothing Manufacturers), Otto M. Eidlitz (chairman of Board of Governors, Building Trades Employers' Association); *railroads*: Lucius Tuttle (president, Boston & Maine Railroad), Frederick D. Underwood (president, Erie Railroad), Melville E. Ingalls (chairman, C.C.C. & St. Louis Railway, part of the New York Central system), H. H. Vreeland (president, New York Central Railway Co.); *finance and banking*: August Belmont (president, August Belmont & Co.), Franklin MacVeagh (president, Franklin MacVeagh & Co., Chicago, became President Taft's secretary of the treasury); *journalism and publishing*: Frank A. Munsey ("Publisher"), Charles H. Taylor, Jr. (ex-president, American Newspaper Publishers' Association).
   3. "On the Part of Wage Earners": *American Federation of Labor unions*: Samuel Gompers (president, AFL), John Mitchell (president, United Mine Workers

At this time, the investment banker and leading Democrat August Belmont was approaching the end of his more than three years (1904–1907) as president of the federation, having succeeded its first president, Senator Marcus A. Hanna (1900–1904) upon the senator's death. Seth Low, the former president of Columbia University, eminent New York progressive reformer, recent mayor of New York City, friend and political ally of Roosevelt and of New York Governor Charles Evans Hughes, and a member of the federation's executive council, was about to succeed Belmont as president of the organization, beginning 1 January 1908. Under the adept direction of its executive council chair, Ralph M. Easley, the federation represented an impressive aggregation of inter-class power, civic authority, and bipartisan prestige. It exerted an especially large influence with executive branches of government at federal, state, and local levels. For all this, however, the Civic Federation strikingly lacked a commensurate popular legitimacy in the nation at large, or a positive law-making influence in Congress. In other words, the power and authority exerted by these corporate and pro-corporate leaders in various strategic spheres of society far exceeded their power and authority in electoral and legislative politics. Hence, many among them and their allies outside the federation thought of themselves as an embattled progressive vanguard in a nation still largely misled and distracted by crisscrossing currents of harmful opinion, whether retrograde, uninformed, or radical.[36]

In organizing and sponsoring the National Conference on Combina-

of America), Daniel J. Keefe (president, International Longshoremen, Marine and Transportworkers Association), William D. Mahon (president, Amalgamated Association of Street Railway Employees of America), William J. Bowen (president, Bricklayers' and Masons' International Union), James O'Connell (president, International Association of Machinists), John F. Tobin (president, Boot and Shoe Workers Union), Joseph F. Valentine (president, Iron Moulders' Union of North America), James M. Lynch (president, International Typographical Union), William Huber (president, United Brotherhood of Carpenters and Joiners of America), James Duncan (general secretary, Granite Cutters' International Association of America), Timothy Healy (president, International Brotherhood of Stationary Firemen), Denis A. Hayes (president, Glass Bottle Blowers' Association of United States and Canada); *railway brotherhoods*: A. B. Garretson (grand chief conductor, Order of Railway Conductors), Warren S. Stone (grand chief, International Brotherhood of Locomotive Engineers), P. H. Morrissey (grand master, Brotherhood of Railroad Trainmen), J. J. Hannahan (grand master, Brotherhood of Locomotive Firemen).

36. For more detail on activities and thinking of National Civic Federation leaders, see Weinstein, *Corporate Ideal*, Marguerite Green, *The National Civic Federation and the American Labor Movement, 1900–1925* (Catholic University of America Press, 1956), and Gordon M. Jensen, "The National Civic Federation: American Business in an Age of Social Change and Social Reform, 1900–1910" (Ph.D. diss., Princeton University, 1956).

tions and Trusts, which convened in Chicago on 22–25 October 1907, the Civic Federation sought a broad base, upon which to press Congress for revision of the Sherman Act to permit reasonable restraints of trade. The federation leaders planned to attract delegates from the widest possible spectrum of the social order, although not necessarily of political opinion, representing not only large and small capital, corporate and otherwise, but also labor, agriculture, civic and professional associations, and state and local government. Although the Civic Federation at this time was seriously engaged in action on many other policy fronts – such as taxation, industrial economics, welfare, capital-labor conciliation, and so on – it gave the conference, concerned as it was with the basic law of the market, the highest priority. The conference was, noted Easley, "the most important and biggest thing we have undertaken."[37]

The 1907 conference bore some resemblance to the 1899 Chicago Conference on Trusts, which had been sponsored by the federation's predecessor, the Chicago Civic Federation. Easley and Jenks played leading roles in the earlier conference, as they did in the later one. The dominant theme of both conferences emphasized the need to accept and regulate large corporations. Both conferences, in effect, served as platforms for attacks upon the Supreme Court's literalist construction of the Sherman Act. At the 1899 conference, speakers as different from one another in general outlook as W. Bourke Cockran and William Jennings Bryan advocated regulation through such devices as federal incorporation or licensing and publicity of corporate affairs, a program similar to that of the Industrial Commission and to that subsequently given prolonged consideration by Garfield and Smith at the Bureau of Corporations.[38] The 1907 conference sought objectives similar in intent if not in detail, and its leaders worked closely with the Bureau of Corporations. Not far beyond these similarities, however, the resemblance between the two conferences ended.

The earlier conference yielded a dominant theme valuable for influencing policy, but it did not exclude the airing of the most diverse views and differences. Delegates to that conference, ranging in opinion

---

37. Easley to Jenks, 31 May 1907; Easley to Louis D. Brandeis, 4 Sept. 1907 (quotation is from latter) NCF.
38. Civic Federation of Chicago, *Chicago Conference on Trusts: Speeches, Debates, Resolutions, List of Delegates, Committees, Etc.,* 13, 14, 15, 16 Sept. 1899 (Chicago: The Civic Federation of Chicago, 1900); speeches by Cockran and Bryan at pp. 462–494, 496–514; other speakers included Henry C. Adams, Charles J. Bonaparte, Edward W. Bemis, John Bates Clark, Samuel Gompers, Laurence Gronlund, George Gunton, Joseph Nimmo, Jr., Francis G. Newlands. Cf. R. I. Holaind, "The Chicago Trust Conference," *Annals* 15 (Jan. 1900), pp. 69–80, and pp. 70–72 for discussion of Jenks's leading role at the conference.

from laissez-faire capitalism to single-tax populism and Marxian socialism, reflected the panoply of political opinion that characterized public
discourse in the United States at the time. The delegates' ideological
diversity attested to an openness to free expression still strongly in-
grained as a basic value among politically active Americans at the turn
of the century, including those who led the Chicago Civic Federation.
(Or if it did not reflect their own personal openness, then it reflected
that which they felt obligated publicly to display.) At the close of the
1899 conference, a group of delegates dissatisfied with its results immediately began to organize the National Anti-Trust Conference, which
convened five months later, on 12 February 1900. The sponsors of this
splinter conference included smaller entrepreneurs like M. L. Lock-
wood, president of the American Anti-Trust League, and populists,
Silver Democrats, Silver Republicans, and socialists, such as Senator
Richard F. Pettigrew of South Dakota, ex-Governor John Peter Altgeld
of Illinois, Ignatius Donnelly of Minnesota, Henry Demarest Lloyd of
Illinois, General James B. Weaver of Iowa, and Governor Charles S.
Thomas of Colorado. The conference heard socialist, single-tax, and
agrarian-populist speeches. It rang with appeals for the more rigid
enforcement of the Sherman Act as it stood. It passed resolutions in
favor of government ownership of public utilities and measures to
prevent what it called the imminent danger of a banking and money
monopoly. In contrast to the conference of 1899, this conference of
1900 gave little attention to publicity and corporation licensing laws.[39]

No such schism would issue from the 1907 conference. Delegate
selection and agenda planning were both carefully controlled. The 492
delegates who convened in Chicago on 22 October 1907 consisted of
appointees of the governors of thirty-nine states and four territories,
official representatives of 105 commercial, manufacturing, professional,
labor, agricultural, and civic associations, and specifically invited classes
of individuals, including presidents of selected colleges and universities,
officers of industrial, railway, and other corporations, state attorneys
general, presidents of state bar associations, and members of the
National Civic Federation and the civic federations of St. Louis, Cleveland, Chicago, and New England. Seth Low, for example, attended the
conference as a representative of New York State, appointed by Governor Hughes, as a representative of the New York Chamber of Commerce, and also as a member of the federation's executive council.
Specifically not invited to the conference, unlike in 1899, were nation-

---

39. Hans B. Thorelli, *The Federal Antitrust Policy: Origination of an American
Tradition* (Baltimore: Johns Hopkins University Press, 1955), pp. 337–339.

ally prominent political leaders, particularly prospective presidential candidates as well as United States senators and representatives. The invitations policy accorded with the broader objective of taking the trust question out of politics and hence ostensibly keeping politics out of the trust question, so that the recommendations of the conference might be presented to the public and to Congress as nonpartisan, nonpolitical, and simply the best product of the most expert and disinterested thinking in the country, or, as Easley put it to Smith, not without an informed touch of irony, as emanating from "the most representative conference ever held under the auspices of our organization 'or any other.'"[40]

As for the agenda, Easley and the federation leadership, beginning in the earlier part of 1907, engaged in continuous correspondence and meetings among themselves and with prospective delegates to predetermine the outcome. They sought to endow a wide diversity of social and economic groups with a single voice in favor of revising the antitrust law. By the end of May, they had succeeded in limiting the conference agenda to three major topics: (1) corporations as the modern form of business organization; (2) government power over corporations, including the question of federal and state jurisdiction; (3) the nature and limits of regulation. Together with delegate selection planning, the agenda predisposed the conference to the adoption of resolutions asking

---

40. Easley to Smith, 12 Oct. 1907, BC, G.F. 324–1; Robert H. Fuller (secretary to Gov. Hughes) to Low, 28 Aug. 1907, Low to Fuller, 30 Aug. and 4 Sept. 1907, Low to Hughes, 30 Aug. 1907, Low to George Wilson (secretary, N.Y. Chamber of Commerce), 26 Oct. 1907, all in SL, Box 32, File G-H, Box 33, File A-E. Easley to Jenks, 31 May 1907, Easley to William D. Foulke, 15 Oct. 1907, Easley to William C. Brown, 31 Oct. 1907, Easley to Alabama Governor Braxton B. Comer (transmitting proceedings and resolutions of conference), 23 Jan. 1908, Gertrude Beeks (Easley's secretary) to Easley, cable, 17 Oct. 1907, and letters, idem., 17, 18 Oct. 1907, all in NCF. Presidential candidates whom Easley specifically mentioned as not being invited were Bryan, La Follette, Hearst, Fairbanks, Cannon, "and the rest" (Easley to Foulke, 15 Oct. 1907, NCF). Among the groups and associations invited to send delegates were, for example, the American Economic Association, American Bar Association, National Grange, Farmers' National Congress, National Farmers Union, American Federation of Labor, railway brotherhoods, National Board of Trade, American Bankers Association, National Association of Manufacturers and its affiliate the Citizens Industrial Association of America. See also *Proceedings of the National Conference on Trusts and Combinations*, under the auspices of the National Civic Federation, Chicago, 22–25 Oct. 1907 (New York: National Civic Federation, 1908), p. 14; and testimony of Seth Low at U.S. Senate Subcommittee of the Committee on the Judiciary, *Hearings*, "Amendment of the Sherman Antitrust Law," 60th Cong., 1st Sess. (1908), in *Hearings Before Subcommittee of the Committee on the Judiciary, U.S. Senate, during 60th, 61st, 62nd Congresses, Compiled for Consideration of H.R. 15657*, 63rd Cong., 2d Sess., 1914 (Washington, D.C.: Government Printing Office, 1914), pp. 207, 208 (hereafter cited as Senate Hearings, 1908).

Congress to amend the Sherman Act to permit reasonable restraints of trade. As part of the agenda planning, the federation leaders worked with Smith at the bureau in lining up papers to be presented at the conference, coordinating those of Isaac N. Seligman and Low, for example, to support that of Smith. This took some care, for, as Easley acknowledged to Smith, "Certainly it would be, as you say, rather indelicate for you to be criticising the Sherman Anti-Trust Law," and hence the alternative topic title Smith suggested for his paper, "'A System of Supervision of Corporations' will be much better."[41]

The Civic Federation leaders anticipated as the one major source of disharmony the conflict between small-manufacturer delegates – especially those associated with the National Association of Manufacturers – and labor-union delegates, a conflict based on the manufacturers' campaign to enforce the Sherman Act against union strikes and boycotts, and labor's determination to exempt unions from the Sherman Act. This small manufacturer-labor conflict loomed as the most dangerous obstacle to forging a consensus on Sherman Act revision; the manufacturers viewed the Court's Sherman Act literalism as a potent weapon against unions, a view with which Gompers and the other labor leaders entirely agreed. Through prior consultations with Gompers and the mineworkers' John Mitchell, among the labor delegates, and with prestigious reformer-delegates like attorneys Louis D. Brandeis of Boston and Frederick N. Judson of St. Louis, the federation leaders sought to avoid or at least contain the conflict at the conference. In early September 1907, for example, Easley informed Brandeis that "Mitchell, Gompers and the labor men" had been conferring on the conference program, and that a session of the conference "will be devoted to the labor combinations and the union smashers will be on hand"; the labor leaders "want you to help them wipe up the floor, so to speak, with [the

41. Easley to Smith, 12 Oct. 1907, BC, G.F. 324–1. On agenda planning in general, also, e.g., Easley to Jenks, 31 May 1907, Easley to Cornelius N. Bliss, 9 Oct. 1907, Easley to Charles G. Dawes, 11 Nov. 1907, all in NCF. The title Smith finally settled upon was "Administrative Regulation of Corporations." *Proc. Conf. on Trusts*, pp. 5, 288–298. The Introduction to the published *Proceedings* emphasized the contrast between the relative homogeneity of views among the 1907 conference delegates and the great diversity of views among the 1899 conference delegates, although the number of delegates at the later conference was more than twice that at the earlier. Of the proceedings of the 1899 conference, it noted, "So diverse are the views therein expressed," that although the conference's committee on resolutions "made an earnest effort to find common ground upon which all could stand," it "failed to do so." "But what could not be accomplished in 1899 might be possible in 1907." It turned out that "The conference of 1907, though larger in numbers, was much more of a unit in sentiment.... there was no important element antagonizing [i.e., antagonistic to] the trust and combination as such." Ibid., pp. 9, 14.

NAM's] Van Cleave, Parry and Post." Easley added, "You know we have always counted on you and Judson of St. Louis to perform that important service." Planning such as this succeeded in muting the conflict at the conference. But it amounted to a temporary deferment; the small manufacturer-labor conflict would ultimately play a substantial role among those forces that stalled attempts at Sherman Act revision for the next several years.[42]

The conference itself, however, marked a success for the federation's objectives. Too large and diverse to define and adopt a specific regulatory plan, the conference was nevertheless sufficiently cohesive to arrive at a strong declaration in favor of reasonable restraint of trade under some kind and degree of government regulation. In essence, its unanimously passed resolutions affirmed a broad political consensus for the administered market, as against the old competitive regime, and for a corresponding adaptation of the law. In this respect, the conference resolutions did get specific; they called for administered markets in the four major sectors of the economy: railroads, industry, agriculture, and labor.

The conference assembled in the midst of the Panic of 1907. The Knickerbocker Trust Company of New York closed its doors on 23 October, the second day of the conference. The delegates, however, carried on with their work in the midst of the trying distractions and produced the resolutions that, generally phrased, even evasive as they were, fulfilled the federation's immediate goals.

The conference's resolutions committee, chaired by federation member Albert Shaw, editor of the *Review of Reviews*, and composed of fifteen members at large appointed by Shaw, plus a member from each state delegation (a committee of fifty), produced a compact text rather shrewdly calculated in its wording to appeal to Democrats and Republicans, to party regulars and insurgents, to manufacturers, farm and labor leaders, to those who favored and those who disdained the Sherman Act, as well as to those of small-producer and large-corporate sentiment. In so doing, the resolutions emphasized the importance of the law to property and market relations, to broader political stability, and not

---

42. Easley to Brandeis, 4 Sept. 1907, NCF. David M. Parry and James W. Van Cleave were, respectively, past and current presidents of the NAM; Charles W. Post, the cereals manufacturer, was active in the NAM and was current president of the anti-union Citizens Industrial Association of America. All three were leaders in the national campaign to apply the Sherman Act against union strikes and boycotts and other collective bargaining techniques. Frederick Newton Judson was the prominent reform Gold Democrat and attorney of St. Louis, married to Jennie W. Eakin (granddaughter of Felix Grundy), and professor of constitutional law at Washington University Law School.

least, in this latter respect, to assuring a popular belief in the compatibility of the large-corporate regime with republican traditions.[43]

In its more general sections, the resolutions praised the enforcement of the Sherman Act under presidents Harrison, Cleveland, McKinley, and Roosevelt as having "accomplished great national results in awakening the moral sense of the American people and in asserting the supremacy and majesty of the law, thus effectually refuting the impression that great wealth and large corporations were too powerful for the impartial execution of the law." The regulatory experience with both the Sherman and Interstate Commerce acts, in dealing with "grave abuses in the management of railroads and corporations," had "rendered more secure all property rights, resting, as they must, under a popular government, on universal respect for and obedience to law." But now, as this experience itself had revealed, "the necessity" had arisen for new legislation, "which shall maintain all the Sherman Act was intended to secure and safeguard interests it was never expected to affect." Such new legislation should be so framed, declared the resolutions, valiantly squaring the circle, as to adapt the law to large corporate enterprise and at the same time "preserve individual initiative, competition, and the free exercise of a free contract in all business and industrial relations."

Translated, this meant that with respect to railroads, "Immediate legislation is required," in accordance with recommendations of President Roosevelt and the Interstate Commerce Commission (ICC), "permitting agreements between railroad corporations on reasonable freight and passenger rates," subject to the "approval, supervision, and action of the Interstate Commerce Commission." With respect to labor, agriculture, and industry, new legislation should provide for the "modification of the prohibition now existing [under the Sherman Act as construed by the Supreme Court] upon combinations," as follows:

1. National and local organizations of labor and their trade agreements with employers relating to wages, hours of labor, and conditions of employment.

43. "Report on National Conference on Trusts and Combinations," *National Civic Federation Review*, Feb. 1908, p. 20, copy at SL, Box 106: NCF, Trust Miscellaneous Data, no. 1; *Proc. Conf. on Trusts*, pp. 219–220, 451–456. The fifteen resolutions committee members appointed by Shaw included Low, Gompers, Charles H. Smith (president, Illinois Manufacturers' Association), John M. Stahl (Farmers' Congress), Franklin MacVeagh, William Jay Schieffelin (the New York merchant), John F. Crocker (president, Boston Chamber of Commerce), and Prof. J. Laurence Laughlin of the University of Chicago. Among the seven others, five were labor leaders (heads of the longshoremen, carpenters, machinists, cigarmakers, and typographers unions).

2. Associations made up of farmers, intended to secure a stable and equitable market for the products of the soil, free from fluctuations due to speculation.

3. Business and industrial agreements or combinations whose objects are in the public interest as distinguished from objects determined to be contrary to the public interest.

For the purpose of framing new legislation, the resolutions called upon Congress, "without delay," not itself to move to the work, but to establish "a non-partisan commission," representative of "the interests of capital, of labor and of the general public," which should "consider the entire subject of business and industrial combinations" and their regulation, including the advisability of federal license or incorporation plans. Such a commission should formulate its proposals and report them to Congress. In the meantime, in a strong endorsement of the Bureau of Corporation's publicity work and its recommendations for extending it, the resolutions stated that the "examination, inspection and supervision of great producing and manufacturing corporations, already begun by the Department of Commerce and Labor and accepted by these corporations, should be enlarged by legislation requiring, through the appropriate bureaus of the Department . . ., complete publicity in the capitalization, accounts, operation, transportation charges paid, and selling prices" of all such corporations, the operations of which were "large enough to have a monopolistic influence"; this matter of size and market power, in turn, should be "determined and decided" by a classification system to be devised by the proposed commission. Having passed the resolutions unanimously, the delegates mandated the Civic Federation to present them to President Roosevelt and to Congress, as well as to arrange for legislative lobbying on their behalf.[44]

The Civic Federation now had the credentials to proceed as the representative of accords issuing from an intricate web of negotiations among major constituents of a market undergoing corporate reconstruction – constituents in railways, industry, commerce, agriculture, and labor, with their professional and political allies, seeking to define their roles in an administered market and to adapt the law and public policy accordingly.[45]

44. Ibid., pp. 453–456, 464. The resolutions also favored leaving the question of federal-state jurisdiction to the Supreme Court, and opposed any attempt to repeal the Sherman Act pending new legislation. See also Low, at Senate Hearings, 1908, p. 208. Also, on the resolutions, Easley to Dawes, 11 Nov. 1907, NCF. They were printed in full, the day after the conference adjourned, at *New York Times*, 26 Oct. 1907.

45. The NCF's involvement with market constituents extended also to those seeking

The day following the conference, on 26 October, Low reported privately to both Hughes and Roosevelt. As a New York reform governor of presidential timber, following in the steps, most recently, of Roosevelt and Cleveland, Hughes could view the resolutions with satisfaction. They pointed to reform without either preempting on attractive position or forcing him to commit himself for or against any specific program. Low thought the governor would therefore find the resolutions "well conceived." Given "your own general attitude" to the question of business regulation, "I feel confident" that the course taken by the conference "will commend itself to your judgment." While the conference "spoke with some assurance as to the next step immediately needed in the matter of railroads," Low noted, it dealt with industry in general terms, calling only for legalizing reasonable restraints of trade and "the appointment of a Commission, so that action ... might be taken with more knowledge." Considering the great number and diversity of the conference delegates, Low observed, "It signifies a great deal ... that the resolutions adopted should have been unanimously supported by such a body."[46]

To Roosevelt, Low was more explanatory of his own role at the conference and somewhat apologetic about its outcome. Roosevelt wanted more than another investigating commission (the Bureau of Corporations had been investigating for over four years), more than publicity, more than a general endorsement of reasonable restraints of trade, more than a green light for further regulatory action on railroads and only an orange for industry. None of this gave the president anything new, no less support for regulatory legislation before the end of his term. It was during these same weeks that he was pressing Smith and Garfield for draft legislation providing for strong license or incorporation measures that he might send to Congress in the upcoming session.

banking and currency reform in the direction of central banking. E.g., Easley told Charles G. Dawes: "As the American Bankers' Association helped us in our Trust Conference, we are trying to return the compliment by helping them out on the things they want. Mr. A. Barton Hepburn [president of the Chase National Bank, active in the ABA, and prominent leader in the movement for central banking] will help us arrange the program [on currency reform scheduled for the upcoming NCF annual meeting]. It may be that we can agree on some good strong resolutions urging currency reform." Dawes, the Chicago Republican leader and banker (president, Central Trust Co. of Illinois), active in the ABA, and prominent in the central banking movement, had been instrumental in arranging strong ABA participation in the NCF's trust conference. Easley to Dawes, 11 Nov. 1907, B. F. Blye (private secretary, Office of the President, Central Trust Co. of Illinois) to Easley, 27 Sept. 1907, NCF.

46. Low to Hughes, 26 Oct. 1907, SL, Box 33, File F-H.

Low wrote "My dear Theodore" that he was "confident you will be pleased with the spirit" of the resolutions, although he expressed no such confidence about their letter. Rather, Low hoped "that you will also agree with the Conference that, outside of the railroad situation, it is better to get more light before we act." Roosevelt had undoubtedly been informed of what had transpired at the conference and knew of "the very strong effort," as Low referred to it, "made in the Committee on Resolutions to get a definite pronouncement in favor of licensing all corporations engaging in inter-State commerce." Low acknowledged that "I am perhaps as much responsible as anybody for having this included in the matters to be looked into before action is taken" – that is, having the resolution sidetracked for that calling for a commission. In explanation, Low first reaffirmed, although not without equivocation, his own support for a license system, but then stated that he did not think the country, or the conference, was ready for it. "Personally, I wrote to Mr. Garfield when he first made his report in favor of a Federal license, expressing my sympathy with the proposition," Low wrote, "and I have never seen any occasion, so far, to change my personal view." But the problem, he told Roosevelt, was that the question had not been "sufficiently thought out by the people at large to make it wise to attempt so radical a departure in all our business methods without further discussion and consideration." This view was widely held among the conference delegates; hence, Low thought it best to push strongly, in the resolutions committee, for further inquiry by commission rather than risk the divisiveness of "a definite resolution committing the Conference to that [license] idea," and jeopardize the consensus that was achieved in favor of reasonable restraints of trade across the board.[47]

Low here appealed to the president's sure political instinct, but he also anticipated his disappointment, and perhaps his resentment at the license plan's being labeled "radical." Low concluded his report with a sweetener, knowing that Roosevelt was drawing sharp criticism from some quarters as bearing a large responsibility for the economy's travail because of his "attacks" on business. "Whatever may be the immediate consequences of the financial disturbance ..., I am sure," Low wrote, "that the ultimate outcome will vindicate your wisdom in making the National Government stand for righteousness at all hazards." More particularly, at the Chicago conference "there was absolutely no difference of opinion on this point."[48] Two days after Low wrote this report

---

47. Low to Roosevelt, 26 Oct. 1907, SL, Box 33, F. N-Z.
48. Ibid.

to Roosevelt, the president added some sweetener of his own: He sent over to Garfield the drastic draft incorporation bill. Within the next two weeks, on 8 November, he conferred with Low at the White House.[49]

At about this time, in early November 1907, the Civic Federation's executive council began the work of assembling a committee to present the conference resolutions to the president and to Congress by early December. It started by making a list of "one hundred of the most representative citizens." Roosevelt, for his part, prepared to work with the federation and perhaps in the process to push it beyond the position of the conference resolutions. Having already decided to recommend to Congress the need for legislation, Roosevelt told Easley that (in Easley's words) "he thinks the Committee can do a lot of good in helping to back up his recommendations for amendments to the Sherman Act, which will be almost identical with what we are proposing." In fact, the president's proposals went well beyond the conference resolutions. Aware of this, and aware also of Congress's reluctance to do anything that even appeared favorable to the large corporations, or openly to oppose a substantial proposal to regulate them, Roosevelt stressed the importance of bringing visible multiclass pressure on Congress, especially from popular sources with large numbers of votes and strong pro-regulation opinion. Roosevelt urged Easley to "make the labor and agricultural representation [on the Federation committee] as strong as we can possibly get it."[50]

In his annual message to Congress of 3 December, Roosevelt urged Congress to pass legislation corresponding with, but going well beyond, the conference resolutions. He recommended that the Sherman Act "be so amended as to forbid only the kind of combination which does harm to the general public." Any such amendment, however, was not to be passed by itself, but only as "accompanied by," or as "an incident of, a grant of supervisory power to the government over these big concerns engaged in interstate business." Specifically, the president recommended, "Reasonable agreements between, or combinations of, corporations should be permitted, provided they are first submitted to and approved by some appropriate government body." For the purpose of implementation, Roosevelt contended that because Congress had "the power to charter corporations to engage in interstate and foreign commerce," it should enact a general federal incorporation law under which a federal board or commission would predetermine whether the applicant

49. Acting Secretary Forster to Garfield, 28 Oct. 1907, with enclosure, "A Bill," JRG; Low to Roosevelt, 4 Nov. 1907, Loeb to Low, 6 Nov. 1907, SL, Box 33, F. N-Z, I-M.
50. Easley to Dawes, 11 Nov. 1907, NCF.

for a federal charter stood in violation of federal law, and enforce compliance thereafter. If Congress preferred, it might enact a license law instead of an incorporation law, "or a combination of the two might be tried." In addition, he recommended legislation to reinforce the coexistence of large corporate and smaller capitalist enterprise, and to assure the stock market's performing as a safe investment outlet for the savings of the middle strata of professionals and bourgeoisie as well as of the upper strata. He called for laws to prohibit such specific forms of "unhealthy competition" as pricing at a loss to drive out competitors, injuring suppliers or customers by devices such as exclusive tying contracts, and such other methods particularly lethal to smaller enterprises, and he called for laws against the defrauding of investors and the gouging of consumers that went with overcapitalization.[51]

In sum, the president's program consisted of permitting reasonable restraints of trade, expanding the requirements of corporate disclosure, preventing business practices especially injurious to smaller enterprise and to middle-income investors and consumers, and establishing a system of federal license or incorporation – or the legalization of the corporate administered market, but only under strong state control.

The Civic Federation leaders thereupon framed their legislative strategy with reference to the president's position. The day following the message, the eminent Chicago railway attorney, prominent Republican, active federation member, and general counsel of the International Harvester Company, Edgar Addison Bancroft, wrote to Easley about how to proceed. As Harvester's lawyer, Bancroft acted also as something of a diplomat. He had to deal with the Bureau of Corporations and maintain good relations between the Harvester corporation and Smith, Garfield, and the Roosevelt administration. He began with cordial praise of the president's message. It "fully vindicates the wisdom of the Trust Conference, and goes as far as any resolutions could well have asked." But, although Bancroft assumed the president had "no such purpose," he warned that Roosevelt's recommendations "could be worked out most oppressively to interstate commerce corporations." Bancroft therefore proposed that the committee of one hundred should "interpret the recommendation of the Trust Conference in the light of the President's message," that is, "instead of asking for a commission," it "adopt the President's suggestion and ask for constructive legislation" to amend the Sherman Act, "so that it will apply only to injurious and

---

51. Annual Message of 3 Dec. 1907, *Cong. Rec.*, 60th, 1st, 42:1, pp. 67–85, at pp. 68–70. Cf. "Federal License Act," and inserted therein Smith's handwritten memo on unhealthy methods of competition, BC, G.F. 4472–2, and "A Bill," JRG. Roosevelt's proposals drew in part on these two draft bills.

unreasonable trusts and restraints of trade." Beyond this, Bancroft advised leaving "to a future congress the more difficult questions of federal incorporation, or federal license coupled with federal taxation and supervision." It was "essential," urged Bancroft, to act now "to destroy what the President so well describes as the immorality of the existing anti-trust law." Hesitation might lose for some time to come the chance of congressional action "of a statesmanlike character," while seizing the opportunity at hand could make the conference "bear fruit – and important fruit – much earlier than its resolutions expected."[52] In short: Walk with the president past the conference resolutions, and steal the march.

The federation's executive council was not prepared simply to bypass its obligation to the conference to work for a commission. It therefore combined the commission proposal with Bancroft's suggestion of seizing upon Roosevelt's message to seek legislation revising the Sherman Act to permit reasonable restraints of trade. At an expanded strategy meeting in New York City on 15 January 1908, the Civic Federation leaders unanimously agreed, as Easley reported to Smith, to attempt to secure at the current session of Congress "definite amendments of the Sherman Act," or at any rate "to help get as much as could be obtained," and at the same time to "urge the commission idea to cover the remainder." The meeting also unanimously agreed that the federation should "under no circumstances . . . take any steps that were not in harmony with the administration view," Easley reassured Smith, and that it not "in any way, seem to lead in any effort that might be made" to change the law, but "that we should follow" the lead of the administration.[53]

The federation's executive council now also finalized the composition of the committee of one hundred, deciding to assign to it at least one member from each of the organizations that had sent delegates to the conference. In groups or singly, they were to go to Washington and confer with administration officials and lobby members of Congress. In

52. Bancroft to Easley, 4 Dec. 1907, NCF. Bancroft was a partner in the Chicago law firm of Scott, Bancroft & Stephens, with Frank Hamline Scott and Redmond D. Stephens. He was kin of the historian George Bancroft.
53. Easley to H. K. Smith, 15 Jan. 1908, NCF. Those in attendance at the meeting, given as a luncheon by Columbia University president Nicholas Murray Butler, were: Butler, Low, Bancroft, Albert Shaw, Easley, Talcott Williams, Henry L. Higginson, Elbert H. Gary, Francis Lynde Stetson, Henry Phipps, August Belmont, Isaac N. Seligman, James Speyer, William A. Clark, James M. Beck, Walker D. Hines, Victor Morawetz, Samuel Mather, Charles S. Hamlin, Charles A. Moore, V. Everit Macy, William Jay Schieffelin, Theodore Marburg, Mahlon N. Kline, Walter Breed, Theodore M. Taft, Marcus M. Marks, and P. Tecumseh Sherman.

keeping with Roosevelt's advice that labor and agriculture be strongly visible in the general campaign, the executive council appointed as a three-member directorate of the larger committee the federation's new president, Seth Low, and vice-presidents Samuel Gompers, president of the American Federation of Labor (AFL), and Nahum J. Bachelder, former governor of New Hampshire and currently head of the National Grange. In the following days the committee of three consulted in Washington with Roosevelt, and also with Garfield and Smith, whom Roosevelt had set to work on a draft of an administration bill. The committee also conferred with other administration officials and with leaders of the House and Senate.[54]

The stage was set, then, for an administration–Civic Federation coalition, united by the desire to accommodate the law to the corporate reorganization of property and the market but divided over exactly how to do so. The federation grouping urgently wanted Sherman Act revision, and they were seeking to draw upon presidential power, prestige, and political leadership for a leverage with public opinion and Congress that they otherwise lacked. Roosevelt was prepared to enlist the intelligence, expertise, energy, and momentum of the federation-led movement to introduce legislation into Congress. He was not about to support simple amendment of the Sherman Act to permit reasonable restraints of trade without measures for strong government control of property and market relations, and he would not let himself be used for such permissive purposes; rather, he intended to be the user of those who would use him. In spite of the differences, there was ample basis for the coalition that emerged. The federation grouping did not oppose, and many within it positively favored, some form of government regulation of the market by a federal executive agency. In general, it represented the view that regulation was the appropriate complement, or the necessary and proper price, of the legalization of reasonable restraints of trade.

Roosevelt, for his part, was prepared to accept less than his maximum if it did not preclude further progress in the right direction. As party leader and as president, he was also in the position of being able to scuttle any legislation he found unacceptable, while benefiting the cause as a whole by having provoked national debate among the American people at a time when they were strongly receptive to vigorous government regulation and control of "big business." The president

---

54. The committee met with Roosevelt at the White House on the morning of 28 Jan. 1908. Easley to Smith, 15 Jan. 1908; Easley to Bachelder, 20 Jan. 1908; Easley to Loeb, 21 Jan, 1908; Loeb to Easley, 22 Jan. 1908; Easley to Roosevelt, 6 Feb. 1908, all in NCF.

held one other trump card: The Civic Federation had found itself in the position of following his lead; within that framework he had the commitment of powerful corporate capitalists and their attorneys, as well as of smaller capitalists and intellectuals, a commitment that they could not easily disown and that was tied into a committee whose directorate Roosevelt himself might have selected, consisting as it did of a compliant political ally, Low, a labor leader, Gompers, and a farm leader, Bachelder. The president was in the better position, therefore, to use rather than be used.

On the basis of a long talk with Senator Nelson W. Aldrich on 9 January, Easley had advised the Civic Federation leaders, and later he similarly advised the directorate of three, that "While it is not likely that any positive amendments to the Sherman Anti-Trust Act will be considered" at the current session of Congress, "the idea of a Commission, such as is recommended in our resolutions, seems to be very well received" by many members of Congress. "One strong argument I find in favor of this proposition," Easley noted, "is that it would largely have the effect of taking the trust question out of politics." Aldrich, accordingly, believed that a commission bill could pass Congress at the current session. Not much more was possible, in his opinion, in view of the upcoming elections, but it would be wise nevertheless, the Senator thought, and as was subsequently agreed to at the New York strategy meeting, to draft an amendment to the Sherman Act and thereby initiate deliberation on such a measure, while being prepared to settle at this session for a commission.[55]

By mid-January, the federation's general strategic perspective stood essentially as Easley summarized it to Talcott Williams, an active federation leader and the editor of the newspaper the *Philadelphia Press*: "I am fully mindful of the fact that neither political party desires to put itself on record as proposing any amendment at this session of Congress which would look to be favorable to trusts or combinations, and yet, the responsibility for any action can be placed on the President, who, in his recent message, recommended an amendment to the Sherman law, so as to permit the making of *reasonable agreements*." Accordingly, the Civic Federation committee would suggest to Congress a bill "construed as a temporary expedient," immediately amending the Sherman Act "by inserting the words '*in direct and unreasonable restraint of trade*,'" but providing for "the appointment of a commission to go into the entire

---

55. Easley to Dawes, 10 Jan. 1908, Easley to Bancroft, 10 Jan. 1908, Easley to Bachelder, 20 Jan. 1908, NCF.

question" and to report to Congress in the next session "its recommendations for a complete and scientific revision of the Federal Anti-Trust Laws." Such a bill, Easley reasoned, could be accepted in Congress as a not more "serious amendment to the present Sherman Act ... than that already recommended by the President." It would "command considerable support, especially from the different trade organizations representing all classes throughout the country," while placing Congress in a favorable light by showing that its intent "was to study the Anti-Trust question in all its bearing upon present business conditions, but in the meantime, to grant the relief which practically all parties agree is necessary and fair."[56]

The federation's position, as defined here by Easley, meant seeking the simple amendment of the Sherman Act to legalize reasonable restraints of trade, and deferring all other change in the law to a time when Roosevelt would be out of office. Roosevelt, however, had already made it clear that he supported the amendment of the Sherman Act to permit reasonable restraints of trade only if simultaneously combined with rigorous regulatory measures. The federation and Roosevelt positions resembled two sides of a cone moving away from the vertex.

In the course of their lobbying efforts in Washington in January, Civic Federation leaders encountered a fairly widespread opinion among members of Congress, implying a discomfort with the president's regulatory proposals, that legislation could best be expedited if the federation itself drafted a bill and arranged for its introduction in Congress. In the meantime, the President prepared a special message to Congress on government regulation of the market; he summoned Low, Gompers, and Bachelder to the White House on 28 January for consultation, and on 31 January, he formally submitted the message.[57]

The president tendered a short treatise on the need for affirming the

---

56. Easley to Talcott Williams, "Confidential," 18 Jan. 1908, NCF. Easley's emphasis. In 1912, Williams became the first director of the Columbia University School of Journalism, established in that year with an endowment of $2 million from Joseph Pulitzer. *National Cyclopedia of American Biography* 15, pp. 306–307.

57. Elkins to Easley, 29 Jan. 1908, Easley to Elkins, 5 Feb. 1908, NCF. Low, at Senate Hearings, 1908, p. 208, stated that Senator Stephen H. Elkins, chair of the Senate Committee on Interstate Commerce, had advised the federation committee that "if we wanted the matter considered we must prepare a bill"; the committee, Low added, had received the same advice from leaders of the House, including Iowa Republican William P. Hepburn, chair of the House Committee on Interstate and Foreign Commerce. On the meeting at the White House, Easley to Loeb, 21 Jan. 1908, Loeb to Easley, 22 Jan. 1908, NCF, and Low to A. Barton Hepburn, 27 Jan. 1908, SL, Box 34 F 1-1. Cf. Arthur M. Johnson, "Antitrust Policy in Transition, 1908: Ideal and Reality," *MVHR* 48:3 (Dec. 1961), p. 424, 424 n. 34.

administered market under the active direction of the national government. The message, which caused something of a political sensation, ranged from the labor market and labor law to railway and industrial regulation. It emphasized the duties as well as the rights of property and wealth. It argued the necessity of equal opportunity and equal enforcement of the law with respect to all classes. It indulged in an extended rebuttal of attacks on the administration by officers of the Standard Oil Company and the Santa Fe railway, stung by their conviction in federal court of illegal rebate agreements. In this concrete context of publicly taking two corporate giants to the woodshed, Roosevelt warned against "law-defying wealth," on the one hand, and "vindictive and dreadful radicalism," on the other, as lethal to republican institutions, and then made the case for preserving private enterprise as against state ownership, precisely by subordinating the market to public policy through rigorous regulation by the national government. Roosevelt regarded the message as perhaps the last to be delivered by him that the political world would seriously consider, because the words of viable candidates in the coming election would hereafter eclipse his. He therefore attached more than ordinary importance to it. The message, according to Roosevelt, "caused a great flutter in the dove cote," but it expressed "my deep and earnest convictions." He told his son, "All my advisers were naturally enough against my sending it in, for councils of war never fight," but it was "on the right track and . . . says what ought to be said and . . . the ultimate effect will be good."[58]

With respect to railways, the message advocated, as Roosevelt had in previous messages and in many other utterances, traffic associations to establish uniform rates and operations, but under the complete control of the Interstate Commerce Commission, which was to have the power to determine rates, routes, regulations, and practices, as well as control over all railway expenditure and finance, including the issue of stocks and bonds. Railways would remain privately owned, but public agents: "the fundamental idea that these railways are public highways must be recognized." As to industrial corporations, Roosevelt reaffirmed the recommendations of his annual message, but he now addressed the immediate political situation, with the effect of heading off any attempt at an amendment of the Sherman Act solely to restore it to its common-law meaning. He stated that the "extraordinary growth of modern industrialism has rendered the common law" by itself "inadequate to deal with the new conditions." Simply to restore the common-law meaning of the Sherman Act would "permit a return to the utter lack of

58. T. Roosevelt to Kermit Roosevelt (Groton School), 2 Feb. 1908, TR.

control" by government or the public over "the great corporations." Congress must therefore provide for a "thoroughgoing and satisfactory control ... by the action of the National Government," involving "continuous supervision over the acts" of the large corporations. He would therefore support no restoration of common-law principle to the terms of the Sherman Act without simultaneous provision for a system of executive regulation. "The law should correct that portion of the Sherman Act which prohibits all combinations ..., whether they be reasonable or unreasonable," he stated, "but this should be done only as part of a general scheme to provide for the effective and thorough-going supervision by the National Government of all the operations of the big interstate business concerns." The "general scheme" referred to Roosevelt's incorporation or license proposal of his annual message of December 1907.[59]

Three days later, on 3 February 1908, the Supreme Court's decision in *Loewe* v. *Lawlor* came down and shifted the whole configuration of forces in Roosevelt's direction – for a fleeting moment only, but long enough to illuminate the ideological landscape in its shape at the time and as it would evolve for the next several years.

The Danbury Hatters' case involved a private suit for treble damages brought under section 7 of the Sherman Act by the hat company, headed by Dietrich Loewe, of Danbury, Connecticut, against the United Hatters of North America, the union headed by Martin Lawlor. In a struggle against the manufacturing company for union recognition, the union had been directing a boycott campaign against the sale of the company's fur hats. The Supreme Court found the union and its individual members liable for payment of the immense sum, for that time, of about $250,000 in damages because of the boycott. Chief Justice Fuller, for the Court, in a unanimous opinion uncharacteristic of major Sherman Act cases, held that the act applied with as equal force to combinations of farmers and laborers as it did to those of capital, that the union sought "to unionize" the shops of fur hat manufacturers, "with the intent thereby to control the employment of labor in the operation of said factories," and, citing *Trans-Missouri, Joint Traffic*, and *Northern Securities*, that whether such union combinations might be reasonable or not, "the Anti-Trust Law has a broader application than the prohibition of restraints of trade unlawful at common law."[60]

---

59. Special Message of the President, 31 Jan. 1908, *Cong. Rec.*, 60th, 1st, 42:2, pp. 1347–1353, at pp. 1348, 1352.
60. *Loewe* v. *Lawlor*, 208 *U.S.* 274–309, at 297, 307–309 (3 Feb. 1908). The required payment was treble the assessed $80,000 in damages, plus costs, altogether about $232,000. Local union members' homes and personal bank

Led by Gompers, the top officers of the AFL unions and the railway brotherhoods mobilized themselves quickly and vehemently against the Court's decision. They called an emergency protest conference, which convened in Washington later in March and was attended by leaders of all AFL unions and railway brotherhoods, and by some farm leaders. The labor leaders understood the Court's ruling to mean that because all direct restraints of interstate trade, however reasonable, were forbidden by the Sherman Act, and because trade unions were not to be distinguished from enterprises-for-profit, not only were boycotts illegal, but so were strikes and union contracts with employers that provided for union recognition and that set wages and conditions over a period of time rather than leaving them to management's discretion or permitting them to fluctuate freely and competitively with market conditions. In *Loewe* v. *Lawlor*, the Court had indeed cited as improper the union's intent to unionize the shop and interfere with the management prerogative. To the union leaders, the Supreme Court had made the Sherman Act a lethal weapon against labor. Under it, labor markets could not be administered by private contract, at least by private contract to which a labor union was a party. At stake, they believed, was not simply the boycott as one of many possible weapons in labor's arsenal, but the survival of the union shop, of collective bargaining, and hence of trade unionism itself. They had no doubt that American workers would not passively acquiesce in such a dispensation but would respond defiantly with civil disobedience, violent self-defense, and political unionism as in England, if not revolutionary unionism and politics.[61]

accounts were attached until the company settled with the AFL for a payment of $235,000 from the national AFL treasury. Two months after the *Loewe* decision, in *Shawnee Compress Co.* v. *Anderson*, the Supreme Court, again unanimously, reaffirmed and reiterated its position, declaring, "it has been decided that not only unreasonable, but all direct restraints of trade are prohibited, the law being thereby distinguished from the common law." Justice McKenna delivered the Court's opinion. 209 *U.S.* 423–435, at 434 (13 Apr. 1908).

61. For these views, see text of conference resolutions, presented by a committee of delegates, led by Gompers, to Speaker of the House Joseph G. Cannon (Republican-Illinois) in his House building office on 19 March, and exchange between Gompers and Cannon, entered into the *Congressional Record* by Cannon at 60th, 1st, 42:4, 23 Mar. 1908, pp. 3765–3768. In the verbal exchange, Gompers told Cannon that under the Court's interpretation of the Sherman Act, "there is not anything that a labor organization can do or that the laborers can do in an associated effort, even if they be unorganized prior to the dispute, but which is unlawful. It is indeed true that under the decision our very organized existence is unlawful.... Such a condition of affairs, of course, we regard not only as unfair and improper, but intolerable." Gompers then warned Cannon that "If we can not conduct our movement as we have conducted it heretofore, ... to develop this spirit of self-restraint and respect [for the law] – if these are outlawed, then there is no use, there is no place, for the men of the American labor movement where they

The larger context of capital-labor relations makes more understandable the strong sense of crisis pervading the minds and the political actions of American labor leaders on the heels of *Loewe* v. *Lawlor*. This was a period of impressive trade-union growth, of massive capitalist counterattack, and of ominous judicial setbacks for labor. Trade-union membership grew from just under 800,000 in 1900 to more than 1.8 million by 1905, and to more than 2 million by 1910, or from 7.8 percent of non-farm workers in 1900 to 14.3 percent by 1905, dropping back to 12.5 percent by 1910, although at the higher absolute number.[62] The employer counteroffensive, led most vociferously by the National Association of Manufacturers but involving the larger corporations also, centered on seeking to sustain and extend the open shop and to keep unions out of industry as much as possible. Aside from their private security forces, the blacklist, and other direct methods of coercion and intimidation, employers resorted to the aid of the state, in some instances to the use of local or state police, more generally to court-supported union-breaking through yellow-dog contracts, lockouts, injunctions, and, most recently, to suits for treble damages under the Sherman Act against strikes and boycotts. *Loewe* v. *Lawlor* came on the crest of this employers' anti-union offensive, as a great victory for capital and a bitter defeat for labor. Labor had lost on the issue of state regulation of hours of work in *Lochner* v. *New York* (1905), and it was in the midst of losing on the yellow-dog contract and the boycott in, respectively, *Adair* v. *U.S.* (1908) and *Buck's Stove and Range Co.* v. *Gompers* (1908). Although the Supreme Court tended to divide closely in Sherman Act cases involving business, it tended, as in *Loewe* v. *Lawlor*, toward unanimity in turning the act against labor. Judicial process in general, and the Sherman Act in particular, posed an incomparably greater threat to labor than to capital. By and large, the Sher-

can exercise any influence whatever for rationalism, for development, for progress upon lawful lines. . . . It is a matter . . . of . . . whether the labor movement, as we understand it and as we have tried to conduct it, shall be lawful and proper and recognized for its social effect and for its support of republican institutions, as you and all of us understand them, . . . or whether this discontent shall find its expression in another form, whatever that may be." Cannon replied that he did not think the Court's decision carried such far-reaching implications, and he issued a counterwarning: "I am not in sympathy in respect to one thing that you say, namely, that you can not speak as to what may happen. I think I can. I believe this Caucasian race of yours and mine is competent in the United States for self-government." Ibid., pp. 3767, 3768.

62. Stanley Lebergott, *The Americans: An Economic Record* (New York: Norton, 1984), p. 386, Table 29.5; for similar, although not identical, numbers and percentages, see Harold G. Vatter, *The Drive to Industrial Maturity: The U.S. Economy, 1860–1914* (Westport, Conn.: Greenwood, 1975), pp. 290–292, esp. Table 22, p. 291.

man Act might affect the personal security of capitalists, or their business entities or practices, only as and when the federal government brought suit. But without government action at all, employers could bring Sherman Act cases for treble damages against unions and, with the injunction, attain instant relief for themselves and swift retribution or destruction to the unions.

Worker militancy was going head to head against employer obduracy, and the law seemed rather to exacerbate than to conciliate class conflict. *Loewe* v. *Lawlor* struck Gompers and his like-minded colleagues among labor leaders as an American Taff Vale. In England, Parliament had in 1906 removed the disabilities imposed by Taff Vale on labor, but in the United States no relief seemed to be in sight. The legal situation was working to make untenable the "business unionism" doctrines, and hence the leadership position, of Gompers and his colleagues, in the American labor movement. Within the AFL itself, the call for an end to party-neutral politics and for the establishment of an American labor party was now growing stronger. Should the larger political-legal system continue to line up with capital against labor, American workers, Gompers warned, might increasingly resort to political unionism as in England, and to revolutionary politics reaching beyond electoral activity and respect for the law. Roosevelt had repeatedly warned against such a trend and urged ameliorative action by Congress, including modification and restriction of the use of judicial injunctions against strikes, and exemption of unions and farm organizations from the Sherman Act as currently construed, most recently in his messages of December 1907 and January 1908. Gompers and other labor leaders had been sounding the theme as well for some time, and they now continued to do so with added fervor.[63] Amendment of the Sherman Act became a matter of the highest priority.

In the heightened sense of urgency provoked by *Loewe* v. *Lawlor*, Gompers immediately told Low, on the day after the Court's decision became public, that the judicial construction of the law was of such "far reaching consequence and importance" that the trade unions were now prepared to go to Congress, in an "appeal for redress," to seek the outright amendment of the Sherman Act exempting unions from its reach.[64]

On the next day, William Jennings Bryan, already the odds-on favor-

63. See, e.g., the labor conference resolutions and the Gompers–Cannon exchange, at *Cong. Rec.*, 60th, 1st, 42:4, pp. 3765–3768; the comparative discussion of Taff Vale by Gompers is at p. 3766. Cf. Stephen J. Scheinberg, "Theodore Roosevelt and the A.F. of L.'s Entry into Politics, 1906–1908," *Labor History* 3:2 (Spring 1962), pp. 131–148.

64. Gompers to Low, 4 Feb. 1908, NCF. Cf. Easley to Charles W. Eliot (president,

ite to become once again the Democratic party's presidential candidate in the 1908 elections, told Easley that in view of the Court's decision, which restricted unions and farmers' organizations alike, "he would be in favor of repealing the Sherman Act entirely" and replacing it with a federal license law or some other such law effectively regulating the large corporations.[65] In effect, at least provisionally, Bryan had come to a position close to that of Roosevelt. Bryan astutely understood the implausibility of a simple exemption of unions or farm organizations from the Sherman Act. Even if, as was doubtful, Congress could be brought to pass a special exemption for farmers or workers, the Supreme Court in its present frame of mind, he advised, would strike it down as unconstitutional. Because a repeal of the Sherman Act without replacing it with effective regulatory legislation was altogether out of the question, Bryan was ready to throw his support to new legislation substantially amending the Sherman Act, or replacing it, in the direction of permitting reasonable restraints of trade, while providing for stringent government regulation of interstate commerce.[66]

Harvard University, and NCF executive committee member), 16 Mar. 1908, NCF: "... the recent Supreme Court decision on the boycott matter is so far reaching that the unions fear it will unsettle all of their collective bargaining propositions; also they fear it will serve to prevent them from striking on the ground that a strike on a railroad would be construed as an interference with the Interstate Commerce Commission [*sic*]. While all the inferior courts have held that strikes were legal, no one knows what position would be taken now that the Supreme Court of the United States has held as it did in the case referred to." Also, cf. Easley to Bancroft, 16 Mar. 1908, NCF: "[There is] great danger under the recent Supreme Court decision of its being held illegal for an organization, especially a railroad organization, to strike as such strikes would undoubtedly have the effect of restricting Interstate Commerce. I think no one would object to the unions, as well as the employers, having the right to strike or lockout. The courts have always granted that right, but under this new decision no one knows what action would be taken and therefore labor interests are not being protected." Labor's fears as to the far-reaching implications of the Court's decision in *Loewe* v. *Lawlor*, although well-founded in logic and technical-legal reasoning, proved unwarranted in practice. It cannot be excluded, however, that labor's vigorous response to the Court's decision may have itself played a significant role in assuring that less hostile judicial outcome. Nevertheless, for the better part of the next thirty years, labor remained subject to the Sherman Act and to the disabling impact of the yellow-dog contract, the blacklist, and the injunction.

65. Easley to Smith, 5 Feb. 1908, and, to the same effect, Easley to Gompers, 6 Feb. 1908, and Easley to Roosevelt, 6 Feb. 1908, NCF.

66. Easley to Gompers, 6 Feb. 1908, NCF. Also, Easley to Roosevelt, 6 Feb. 1908, NCF: "I saw Mr. Bryan yesterday and got some points on his attitude that I want to give you. He is ready for a repeal of the whole Sherman Act under certain conditions." Easley spoke with Bryan in New York City: Easley to Bryan (Hoffman House, Broadway and 28th St., New York City), 4 Feb. 1908, NCF, asking for an appointment to discuss the matter, which "had been made a little more important by the Supreme Court decision yesterday on the boycott case." In effect, Easley was acting as liaison between Bryan and the president.

The labor leaders, similarly, came by degrees to understand that although they might publicly advocate a simple exemption of unions from antitrust law, on the grounds that "labor power" was a human faculty and not "a commodity,"[67] they could not expect to attain such an exemption by a direct legislative establishment of a special status for labor, but only indirectly within the framework of a statute that applied more broadly to business and the market.

The Hepburn bill

In the new climate of leadership opinion crystallized by *Loewe* v. *Lawlor*, Easley drew the conclusion, first suggested the previous December by Bancroft but laid aside, that it was now possible to bypass the trust conference resolution calling for a commission, and proceed directly to seeking revision of the Sherman Act. The conditions had emerged, Easley thought, for a bipartisan, multiclass coalition in favor of revision, sufficiently potent to move Congress. The coalition potentially included not only corporate capitalists, professionals, and intellectuals, not only regular Republicans and Democrats in Congress, but also trade unionists, farm leaders, and, of particular importance, congressional Bryan Democrats and therefore quite plausibly insurgent Republicans as well. As Easley wrote to Smith on 5 February, informing him of Bryan's views, "The Supreme Court decision Monday very materially changes the situation.... Let's get everything done at this session [of Congress] that we can. If necessary for this [NCF lobbying] delegation to go further than the Trust Conference, it can act for the Civic Federation." Easley added, "Of course, this is my personal opinion and I am giving it to you in confidence." But one week later, Easley spoke authoritatively for the Civic Federation in informing Roosevelt that a Civic Federation legislative drafting committee was meeting, and that the executive committee would meet on 20 February, to put the Civic Federation "squarely behind any measures that can be secured at this session of Congress." The NCF lobby would present itself as representing the federation rather than as representing the trust conference. "In other words," Easley explained to Roosevelt, "our delegation will be in position to ignore the commission idea embodied in the resolutions adopted at Chicago."[68]

67. The labor conference resolutions handed to Speaker Cannon emphasized this point, using the quoted terms. See *Cong. Rec.*, 60th, 1st, 42:4, p. 3765.
68. Easley to Smith, 5 Feb. 1908, Easley to Roosevelt, 12 Feb. 1908, and cf. Easley to Roosevelt, 6 Feb. 1908, all in NCF. Low, at Senate Hearings, 1908, p. 208, testified that the NCF drafting committee went beyond the conference's resolutions

The turn of events placed the initiative with Roosevelt. It favored the early introduction of legislation in Congress that would combine Sherman Act revision with executive regulation.

The president already had Smith and Garfield working in Washington on a draft bill that would provide for a license or incorporation system under the Bureau of Corporations and Department of Commerce and Labor. In New York at the Civic Federation, after both the chair of the Senate Committee on Interstate Commerce, Senator Stephen H. Elkins of West Virginia, and the chair of the House Committee on Interstate and Foreign Commerce, Representative William P. Hepburn of Iowa, had joined other congressional leaders in January in recommending that the federation prepare a bill, Low enlisted Roosevelt's friend and adviser, and federation activist, Jeremiah W. Jenks, in the work of drafting legislation corresponding with the trust conference resolutions. The Cornell professor of political economy was also at this time serving as the president of the American Economic Association, and as a member of the special Dillingham commission on immigration, to which Roosevelt had appointed him in early 1907. Jenks now shifted the drafting agenda, in response to the new situation, to the preparation of a bill to amend or replace the Sherman Act, without the trust conference's commission proposal. In the drafting work, Jenks and Low stayed in continuous touch with Elkins and Hepburn on Capitol Hill, with Garfield and Smith at the executive offices, and with Roosevelt at the White House. Roosevelt brought into the drafting process Attorney General Charles J. Bonaparte and Secretary of State Elihu Root. During February, Jenks worked in committee in New York City with Low, George W. Perkins, and the eminent corporation lawyers and active federation members Francis Lynde Stetson, a principal counsel to J. P. Morgan & Company, and Victor Morawetz, who was then also serving as a vice-president of the recently chastised Atchison, Topeka & Santa Fe Railway. Jenks's committee, in turn, consulted singly and in conference with Elbert H. Gary, Nicholas M. Butler, Bancroft, Henry L. Higginson, August Belmont, James Speyer, Isaac N. Seligman, among others.[69]

To coordinate the drafting work, Smith shuttled between Washington and New York, conferring with the Jenks committee in New York and

---

    in deciding "to submit a bill that contemplated action rather than to suggest the postponement of action by the appointment of a commission."

69. Elkins to Easley, 29 Jan. 1908, Easley to Elkins, 5 Feb. 1908, Easley to Smith, 5 Feb. 1908, Easley to Roosevelt, 6 Feb. 1908, Easley to S. B. Carvalho (*N.Y. American*), 7 Feb. 1908, Easley to Henry W. Taft, 2 Mar. 1908, all in NCF. For names of some others consulted, see note 53, above

with Gompers and other labor leaders in Washington. On 15 and 20 February 1908, his conferences in New York with Low, Perkins, Stetson, and Jenks resulted in a first draft of a bill, and on 23 February he attended an all-day conference with the labor leaders in Washington, which Jenks attended also. The parleying culminated in a conference in New York on 27 February, attended by the Jenks committee and other Civic Federation leaders, Gompers and other labor leaders, and, on behalf of the administration, Smith and U.S. Commissioner of Labor Charles P. Neill. The conference reached unanimous agreement on an amended provisional draft bill, but, as also agreed, it remained subject to approval by President Roosevelt and by the AFL executive council. Smith brought the draft bill back to Washington. The next night, 28 February, a full cabinet meeting discussed the bill with the president at the White House, found it generally satisfactory as a working draft, and authorized Smith so to inform the federation committee and leadership. This Smith did the following day, 1 March, upon his return to New York for further consultations. A week later, on 6–7 March, Low conferred in Washington with Roosevelt, Senator Elkins, Representative Hepburn, cabinet members, and with Gompers and other labor leaders, concerning arrangements for the bill's introduction into Congress and the scheduling of hearings.[70]

In the meantime, Roosevelt in late February and early March maneuvered the Civic Federation into the frontline position of proud parent of

---

70. Stetson to Garfield, 15 Feb. 1908, Smith to Garfield, 17 Feb. 1908, Garfield to Stetson, 19 Feb. 1908, Garfield to Smith, 19 Feb. 1908, all in JRG, Box 128, F. 45. Text of provisional first draft: "Anti-Trust 20 Feb. '08," ibid. In attendance at the Washington conference with labor leaders on 23 February were: Gompers, Daniel J. Keefe (president, International Longshoremen's Association and AFL vice-president and executive council member), James P. O'Connell (president, International Association of Machinists and AFL vice-president and executive council member), Frank Morrison (secretary, AFL executive council), for labor; Jenks for the NCF; Smith and Neill for the administration. All of these then attended the New York conference on 27 February, joining the following, who also attended: P. H. Morrissey (grand master, Brotherhood of Railway Trainmen), D. L. Cease (editor, *Railroad Trainmen's Journal*), Low, Talcott Williams, Albert Shaw, Alton B. Parker (Democratic party presidential candidate in 1904 and current president of the American Bar Association), Gary, Perkins, Stetson, and Morawetz. The names of those attending the conferences are in Easley to Bancroft, 25 Feb. and 2 Mar. 1908, NCF. One of the NCF's objectives in these conferences was to persuade the labor leaders that they could not expect to attain relief for unions from the Supreme Court's Sherman Act literalism apart from a broad legislative amendment or replacement of the act. According to Easley, the Washington meeting went round the clock in a "24 hour conference" without conclusive results, but the larger New York meeting was "the most successful conference we have had and a unanimous agreement was reached on the amendments." Easley to Bancroft, 2 Mar. 1908, NCF.

the bill. He thereby had a bill that might effectively raise regulatory issues of his choosing, without making it an administration measure that could strain relations with Congress, embarrass him or compromise his position on the issues if it failed, or damage Roosevelt Republicans in the approaching national elections.

It is apparent that by this time, Roosevelt had assessed the political situation and concluded that legislation satisfactory to himself, if any at all, was not likely in the current session of Congress. Even should Bryan publicly and specifically endorse a bill of Roosevelt's choosing, which was doubtful, congressional Democrats would be reluctant to hand a Republican administration credit for a toughening of the antitrust laws on the eve of a presidential election. Roosevelt's interest, then, came to lie less in passing a law than in exerting the educational impact of debate and in establishing a record that might bind his successor or at least strongly influence the terms of future legislative deliberations.

Roosevelt accordingly placed the Civic Federation in the position of taking the lead publicly as the originator and sponsor of the bill, and not in that of merely seeming to be following the president's lead. When Low asked Smith whether the bill was to be introduced "as an administration measure to be supported by the Civic Federation, or whether as a Civic Federation measure to be supported by the government," Smith referred the matter to Garfield, to whom he confided that he assumed the bill "will probably be supported by the administration, but whether the President desires to have it known pointedly that it is practically his measure or not is the question." Garfield then advised Stetson that "it would be better to have the bill presented to Mr. Hepburn and Mr. Elkins by the Civic Federation Committee, with such statement regarding the attitude of the Executive as Mr. Smith might be authorized to make." The Civic Federation now followed the president by honoring his request to appear publicly to be leading him. As Easley reported to Butler, Roosevelt "is anxious to have it go in as a Civic Federation proposition and he will do all he can to help it." So it went. Roosevelt kept his options open, and the "Civic Federation proposition" that came to be known as the Hepburn amendments to the Sherman Act was neither a Civic Federation bill nor a Hepburn bill, nor a purebred Roosevelt bill, but a hybrid of hybrids with strong Roosevelt characteristics.[71]

The bill joined together legislative proposals from four major sources:

71. Stetson to Garfield, 15 Feb. 1908, Smith to Garfield, 17 Feb. 1908, Garfield to Stetson, 19 Feb. 1908, JRG, Box 128, F. 45. Easley to Butler, 2 Mar. 1908, Easley to Bancroft, 25 Feb. and 2 Mar. 1908, Easley to William A. Clark, 8 Mar. 1908, NCF.

the Civic Federation, the trade unions, the Bureau of Corporations (Smith and Garfield), and Roosevelt. Congressional input was conspicuous by its absence. In its original version of 20 February, which served as a working draft, the bill was a mild registration-publicity measure, with a minimal Roosevelt and a maximum NCF–bureau imprint. It would have directly amended the Sherman Act's terms to prohibit only "unreasonable" or "unfair" restraints of trade or monopolies. It would have provided for railways and industrial corporations to register with the Interstate Commerce Commission and the Bureau of Corporations, respectively, by submitting detailed information about their officers, structure, finances, debt, and stock issues and by providing the federal agencies with continuing access to their books, records, accounts, and papers. Registered corporations could then submit their contracts and agreements to the commission or the bureau (and secretary of commerce and labor) for approval as reasonable and fair, and hence for exemption from government or private suits charging restraint of trade or monopoly. If disapproved, such contracts and agreements could be prosecuted, or challenged by private parties, under the Interstate Commerce Act or Sherman Act, as the case may be; similarly for contracts or agreements not submitted, and for those of unregistered corporations. Trade unions, farm organizations, and other not-for-profit associations could register and thereby be exempted from the Sherman Act merely by submitting a statement of name, officers, bylaws, and location of principal office; they need not file their contracts or agreements. All information, including copies of contracts and agreements, would be placed on public record and be made freely available to public scrutiny. Railroads would be exempt from the Sherman Act; their regulation would be entirely under the Interstate Commerce Act, as amended, and by the Interstate Commerce Commission. All actions and decisions of the commission and of the bureau were to be subject to judicial review.[72]

The bill, in sum, would have combined the restoration of the Sherman Act to a common-law construction with registration and publicity. Registration would be voluntary; the resulting publicity would therefore extend only to those corporations choosing to register. Those corporations choosing not to register would still benefit from the bill's legalization of reasonable and fair restraints of trade, and they might prefer the risk of a suit or prosecution, which they might well win, to registration. Even disapproval of a contract or agreement by the Interstate Commerce Commission or the Bureau of Corporations would not void it but

---

72. "Anti-Trust, 20 Feb. '08" (first version of bill), JRG, Box 128, F. 45.

would simply make it liable to judicial process. This provision, together with the voluntarist feature, satisfied Smith's and Garfield's concerns about federal-state jurisdiction, due process, and inordinate state power over the market, but the bill did not satisfy their desire for a stronger system of government regulation.

The exemption of trade unions from the Sherman Act gave the labor leaders only part of what they sought: The exemption was not outright, but contingent upon registration, although a perfunctory one, and it still did not exempt "unreasonable" or "unfair" contracts or agreements, including the boycott, nor did it exempt strikes from injunctions nor protect workers from yellow-dog contracts or blacklists. The Civic Federation came closest to what it wanted – legalization of reasonable restraints of trade with mild government regulation. Roosevelt, for his part, had a draft bill to work with, but one that in its initial shape offered government protection of the corporate reorganization of the economy with only minimal executive regulation. In the next week, 21–28 February, two revisions quickly followed, strengthening the registration powers of the commissioner of corporations and the secretary of commerce and labor by making more comprehensive the information required of registered corporations, and, most significantly, making exemption of reasonable and fair restraints contingent upon registration.

During the same week, however, emboldened by the president's acceptance of the bill's initial version of 20 February as the working draft, a draft strongly shaped by the Jenks-Stetson-Morawetz committee at the Civic Federation, Stetson and Morawetz submitted a revision that reverted to the initial draft, making the common-law meaning of the Sherman Act absolute and further weakening the government's regulatory authority. In a letter dated 26 February, accompanied by a print of the revised bill, and sent simultaneously to secretaries Root and Garfield, to Low, to American Bar Association president and Democratic party leader Alton B. Parker, and to Gary, Stetson explained that upon reconsideration of the bill that had emerged from conference, he had become "dissatisfied with the sufficiency of the legal basis for the bill," and concerned "as to the possibility of its surviving the test of destructive criticism in Congress." He therefore "invoked the able and valued assistance" of Morawetz, from which "has resulted the bill of which I enclose a proof copy." The principal features of the revised bill were as follows: The Sherman Act was to be "unqualifiedly" amended with the words "unreasonable" and "unfair," thereby "relieving from the condemnation of that law all fair and reasonable contracts made by any corporation, association or person, whether or not registered under

the act." Thereafter, the "Executive Department" would be "forbidden
to institute any suit or proceeding" against any registered corporation
respecting any contract or agreement filed with and not disapproved by
the Interstate Commerce Commission or commissioner of corporations.
If disapproved, the contract or agreement would be subject "to the
attack of the courts and to condemnation if unfair or unreasonable,"
but not if found fair and reasonable.[73]

The Stetson–Morawetz revision also provided for a general amnesty
for all contracts and agreements made before passage of the bill, provided they were those of registered corporations and that they were filed
with and not disapproved by the Interstate Commerce Commission or
the commissioner of corporations. Although the Stetson–Morawetz revision included other points, these were the important ones, along with
a restoration of the Sherman Act's applicability to railroads, the motive
for which Stetson candidly explained: "With these points secured, it has
seemed to Mr. Morawetz and to me unnecessary to attempt to take
railroads out of the Sherman Anti-trust Law – an attempt which in our
judgment would be certain in Congress to encounter hostile suspicion
and perhaps mortal resistance."[74]

The Stetson–Morawetz revision sought to accomplish precisely what
Roosevelt strongly opposed, namely, legalization of reasonable restraints of trade without strong government regulation. Although Stetson
claimed that the proposed immunity from prosecution for approved
contracts or agreements "would be amply sufficient to induce corporations to register and to make public their trade agreements,"[75] it was
just as likely that corporations would prefer to take their chances in the
courts, rather than submit to registration, and attain judicial sanction of
their contracts or agreements as reasonable restraints of trade. This
would leave regulation of the market largely in the hands of the judiciary with a limited or minimal executive role.

Garfield immediately went to the heart of the matter. Under the
proposed Stetson–Morawetz revision, the Sherman Act, he noted,
would be "amended *flatly and for all purposes*, by inserting the words
'unreasonable or unfair.' This is a particularly new and radical
change.... It departs from my original plan, which was to amend the

73.	Stetson to Root et al., 26 Feb. 1908, enclosing "4th. [Revise:] V. M. [Victor
	Morawetz] Anti-Trust 26 Feb., '08," and attached therewith, "5th. [Revise.] V. M.
	Anti-Trust 27th Feb., '08," at JRG, Box 128, F. 45. A copy of Stetson's letter,
	marked "Copy for Information" and sent in other copies to all those who had
	attended the NCF strategy meeting of 15 January, is at NCF. See also Easley to
	Henry W. Taft, 2 Mar. 1908, NCF.
74.	Stetson to Root et al., 26 Feb. 1908, JRG.
75.	Ibid.

Sherman law only for the benefit of the corporations which should be registered."[76] In other words, under Garfield's plan, and in accordance with Roosevelt's intent, both reasonable and unreasonable restraints of trade by nonregistered corporations were to remain illegal, so that although in form registration was to be voluntary, in substance it would be virtually compulsory.

Roosevelt now inserted himself directly into the drafting process, and he played his trump, that is, the federation's commitment to follow his lead and the general agreement among those engaged in the drafting work that everything was to be subject to White House review and approval. During the first three weeks of March, Roosevelt personally and through Smith and Garfield orchestrated a complex series of negotiations among federation leaders, capitalists, trade unionists, farm leaders, and administration officials. The bill went through at least eight revisions beyond the Stetson–Morawetz revisions of 26 and 27 February – or at least thirteen in all, before it reached the final draft of 21 March that went to Congress two days later. Roosevelt dominated the drafting and revising work through ongoing consultations with Garfield, Smith, Low, and others, capped by a major White House conference on 11 March, presided over by Roosevelt and attended by Root, Bonaparte, Garfield, Smith, Stetson, Morawetz, Low, and Gompers, but by no members of Congress, although senators Aldrich and Elkins, and representatives Cannon and Hepburn, were consulted or kept apprised. Easley indicated Roosevelt's commanding role to Bancroft when he noted that unanimous agreement had been reached on draft revision number ten among federation, business, labor, and other leaders at their Victoria Hotel conference in Washington of 6 March, "but when they got over to the White House [on 11 March] so many changes were proposed that it practically had to be redrafted ... to meet the desires of the President."[77]

76. Garfield, "Memorandum on the Anti-Trust Bill, Draft of February 27," 28 Feb. 1908. Attached: "V. M. Anti-Trust 26 Feb., '08." Garfield's emphasis. JRG, Box 128, F. 45.
77. Smith to Garfield, 9 Mar., 13 Mar., 16 Mar., 17 Mar. 1908, with attached revised drafts of bill, JRG, Box 128, F. 45. Easley to Bancroft, 16 Mar. 1908, NCF, referring to draft revision no. 10 of the bill and to the fact that no draft had remained the same over twenty-four hours, something more of an exaggeration than a fact, but figuratively accurate. Also, *Philadelphia Record*, 12 Mar. 1908, *New York Times*, 13 Mar. 1908, *New York Journal of Commerce*, 14 Mar. 1908, give accounts of the White House conference of 11 Mar.; the clippings of the stories are at BC, G.F. 5563. Successive drafts with notations, memos, and covering letters or notes are at JRG, Box 128, F. 45. The twelfth revision ("Anti-Trust. 12th Revise. 17 March '08") is essentially the same as that dated 21 March but not otherwise numbered, which was the version as introduced in Congress by Hepburn

With each revision, the registration provisions and the regulatory authority of the executive branch became stronger, and the bill as a whole, although not entirely what Roosevelt wanted, came more and more to reflect his views. The disposal of suggestions by Root and Bonaparte will serve to illustrate the trend.

Root favored government regulation of business and shared many of Roosevelt's views on the matter, but he sought to place definite limits on executive power over market relations. At draft revisions numbers nine and ten, on the latter of which unanimous agreement had been reached by the conferees apart from Roosevelt, Root had inserted a section to provide that approval by the commissioner of corporations and secretary of commerce and labor, or by the Interstate Commerce Commission, of a "contract, agreement, or combination, as being fair and reasonable and not contrary to the public interest, shall be conclusive evidence to that effect in any action or suit, prosecution or proceeding," brought under the Sherman Act, "and shall be *prima facie* evidence to that effect."[78] The intended effect of Root's proposal would be to put a limit on the government's supervision and control of business practices by making the administrative finding of the commissioner of corporations or the Interstate Commerce Commission permanently binding, and therefore, fortified against further attack by the government or by private parties. It would also enhance the judiciary's role as a protector of reasonable restraints. Root's proposal did not survive the White House conference of 11 March. Roosevelt wanted a continuing, alterable, and paramount executive supervision of the market, so that a contract, combination, or agreement found reasonable at first might still be condemned if at a later time the Department of Justice or the Bureau of Corporations or the Interstate Commerce Commission determined it to be unreasonable or contrary to the public interest.

Bonaparte's views in this respect were closer to the president's. His advice, accordingly, strongly influenced the final shape of the bill. Bonaparte favored a strong executive power over the market, and as the government's principal law officer he was obliged to suggest how to accomplish that objective in a manner consistent with constitutional law.

on 23 Mar. 1908. It bears Smith's handwritten notation at the top of its first page, "Introduced Mar. 23 1908." The final draft, then, may be considered the "13th Revise." Cf. Low, at House Hearings, 1908, pp. 149–151, where in response to a question by Representative Charles E. Littlefield as to whether the bill was the result of twelve to thirteen drafts, Low replied, "Yes, sir."

78. "Anti-Trust. 9th Revise. 9 March," and Smith to Garfield, 9 Mar. 1908; "Anti-Trust. 10th Revise. 10 March," and Smith to Garfield, 13 Mar. 1908, enclosing 10th Revise, JRG, Box 128, F. 45.

To begin with, Bonaparte saw the Sherman Act in its literalist construction by the Supreme Court as an asset to strong government control of the market, because its impact in practice depended on executive enforcement policy, while its stringency created a large receptivity to executive regulation. Hence he wryly counseled Roosevelt, in referring to the White House conference of 11 March, that "I think the outlawry of modern business methods and labor organizations by the anti-trust law, on which our friends dwelt so much at our recent conference, is theoretical rather than practical; and it would be more nearly in accordance with entire accuracy to describe the [dire] consequences of retaining the law without amendment ... as possible or, at most, probable, rather than certain."[79] The anxiety over the possible or probable becoming the certain exerted a salutary pressure in favor of legal revision. Bonaparte favored retaining the Sherman Act's prohibition on all restraints of trade. That is, he opposed writing into the law an explicit distinction between reasonable and unreasonable restraints, as this would make the law vague and open to legal manipulation, especially by corporations' well-paid attorneys, and it would expand judicial at the expense of both legislative and executive authority in the regulation of the market.

He suggested, therefore, the following provisions: Let registration of corporations be made voluntary in form, to comply with constitutional strictures concerning federal-state jurisdiction and due process, and, for the same purpose, let registration procedures and all administrative decisions by the executive agencies be subject to judicial review. Those constitutional obligations having been met, the executive authority (the bureau or the ICC), Bonaparte advised, "should decide whether the contract ought to be licensed." If it decides against license, the Department of Justice "should not have any discretion" but should be required to prosecute, "whatever any other authority might think of its 'reasonableness,' 'fairness,' or other characteristics." In the case of a contract that seemed "harmless when filed," but "should turn out, by subsequent development, to be contrary to equity or the public welfare," the licensing authority "could revoke the license" upon notice and hearing, subject to judicial review. "This is what I understood you to suggest," Bonaparte told Roosevelt, "with respect to the revocation of the contracts at the time of the conference, and the idea impressed me, at the time, as a very happy one," as it would leave full authority with the executive and avoid "a hopelessly cumbrous and ineffective

79. Bonaparte to Roosevelt, 17 Mar. 1908, TR (Series 2), advising Roosevelt on his upcoming special message to Congress of 25 Mar. in support of legislation along the lines of the Hepburn amendments to the Sherman Act.

practice" of resorting to "suits in equity to do away with the effect of an improvident approval of a contract."[80]

In its final draft, as sent to Congress, the bill was, as Garfield later noted, "necessarily a compromise measure," having been "the result of many conferences in which the representatives of all interests took part."[81] The Stetson–Morawetz permissive view and the Smith–Root concern for state-federal jurisdiction, due process, and limits on governmental regulatory power, were reflected in the inclusion of the provisions for amnesty, judicial review, and Department of Justice discretion in prosecuting disapproved or nonregistered contracts, combinations, or agreements. Labor and farm organizations were accorded a perfunctory registration as compared with that required of corporations, but not outright exemption from the Sherman Act. The Roosevelt–Bonaparte view, however, gave the bill its basic shape: There was to be no amendment of the terms of the Sherman Act in its prohibitory sections; legalization of reasonable restraints was to be strictly contingent upon executive registration and approval; and the Bureau of Corporations, the Interstate Commerce Commission, or the Department of Justice could at any time withdraw approval and move to prosecution. Finally, power to control the registration process was shifted upward from the commissioner of corporations and the secretary of commerce and labor to the president.

The bill was not all that Roosevelt might have wanted, but what began in late February as a mild registration-publicity measure with permissive legalization of reasonable restraints of trade, ended in late March as a strict license bill providing for stringent state direction of the market. If, as would be said several years later of the Clayton Antitrust Act, it went into Congress as a lion and came out as a tabby cat, in this case, it was rather the reverse: The bill started with the Civic Federation as a pussycat and came out of the White House as a roaring king of the jungle.

On 23 March, Representative Hepburn, whose name adorned the act of 1906 that enlarged the powers of the Interstate Commerce Commission, received the bill as the chair of the House Committee on Interstate and Foreign Commerce, and he introduced it into the House, where, although referred to the Judiciary Committee, it became known as the Hepburn amendments to the Sherman Act. As a congressional leader extending a courtesy to his own party's president, and as a progressive midwestern Republican who in general favored greater government

---

80. Ibid.
81. Garfield to Henry Corning, 7 May 1908, JRG, Box 128, F. 45.

regulation of business, Hepburn lent the considerable prestige of his name to the bill. But he had nothing to do with either its drafting or its legislative processing. It is doubtful that he favored the bill, of which, as the *New York Journal of Commerce* reported, he was "the putative 'author,'" but which he had "received like the Commandments."[82] In a similar vein, the Civic Federation, in accord with Roosevelt's wishes, publicly claimed parentage of the bill; Low and Jenks at the congressional hearings represented it, although with some difficulty and hedging, as a federation bill;[83] and scholars since have so regarded it.[84] But the bill, compromises and all, was basically the administration's, more precisely Roosevelt's.

On 25 March, Roosevelt sent another special message to Congress, supplementing his special message of 31 January. In explicitly noting the introduction of the bill in Congress, he called for the passage of legislation similar to that embodied in the Hepburn bill, but he refrained from giving the bill itself an outright endorsement, declaring that "I do not pretend to say the exact shape that the bill should take," and that "the suggestions I have to offer are tentative." He then outlined and recommended provisions similar to those in the bill, but in words heavily colored by Bonaparte's advice, including an outright declaration against changing the terms of the Sherman Act's prohibitory sections.[85]

82. *New York Journal of Commerce*, 27 Mar. 1908, as reported by Henry Parker Willis from Washington. Clipping at BC, G.F. 5563.
83. In the House, the bill received the designation *H.R. 19745*. In the Senate, Senator William Warner (Republican-Missouri) introduced the bill as *S. 6440* on 1 Apr. 1908; there it was sent to the Senate Judiciary Committee and was commonly referred to as the Warner bill. *Cong. Rec.*, 60th, 1st, 42:4, 23 Mar. 1908, pp. 3769–3770, and 42:5, 1 Apr. 1908, p. 4212. At the hearings, under questioning as to the bill's origins, Low and Jenks ambivalently maintained the fiction of a Stetson-Morawetz-NCF authorship but acknowledged a broader range of authorship without, however, referring to the president. Opponents of the bill were happy to stigmatize it as the work of Wall Street lawyers. See e.g., House Hearings, 1908, Jenks at pp. 78, 80–81, Low at pp. 11, 149–151, and Senate Hearings, 1908, Low at p. 208, Jenks at p. 297. Also, Low's circular letter of 30 Mar. 1908, NCF, in explanation of the Hepburn bill, stating ambiguously that the bill had been "prepared under the auspices of the National Civic Federation."
84. In addition to the work of other leading scholars dealing with the Hepburn bill, this applies as well to the interpretation to be found in my dissertation, which I here state to be in error, as I was still following the traditional view at the time of its writing. Sklar, "The Corporate Reconstruction of American Society, 1896–1914: The Market and the Law," University of Rochester, 1982 (Ann Arbor, Mich.: University Microfilms International, 1983), esp. pp. 172–201.
85. Special Message of the President, 25 Mar. 1908, *Cong. Rec.*, 60th, 1st, 42:4, pp. 3853–3854. Cf. Easley to Bancroft, 21 Mar. 1908, NCF, written "in confidence," informing Bancroft that Roosevelt was "strongly behind this Bill" and would send a message to Congress the day following its introduction in the House by Hep-

The Civic Federation was now the parent of a bill it had not conceived, and the chief organizer of support, at the congressional hearings, for a presidential measure that the president would not specifically endorse. Low was a good soldier placed in dubious battle. Three days after he had delivered his special message, Roosevelt wrote Low, to console as much as to inspire him, "I think we have what is in substance a very good bill. You have done admirable work for the public, my dear fellow – as usual."[86] Words very much like what a commander in chief might say to a selfless lieutenant.

It served Roosevelt's purpose to have the bill introduced in Congress and to have hearings begun, but without committing his administration or himself personally to the bill as such. His judgment that no legislation on the subject was likely to pass in the current session was borne out by the bill's immediate referral in both houses to their judiciary committees, where bills often went for prolonged scrutiny unto death. But the president was of serious purpose. On an issue of such importance to himself and to the nation, he had not expended so much of his own efforts and those of his attorney general, his secretaries of state and interior, and numerous business, civic, and legal notables – hours upon hours of drafting work, consultations, meetings, conferences, and travel between New York City and Washington – in a frivolous endeavor. Roosevelt wanted to inaugurate serious public debate, on terms defined largely by him, about the government-market relation in accommodating the law to the corporate reorganization of the economy. He wanted to do so in such a way as strongly to influence its outcome without risking a political defeat for himself or courting a setback for his views. The bill, bearing Hepburn's name and debuting as the offspring of the Civic Federation, successfully served that purpose. Congress readily cooperated with the president in introducing and holding hearings on a bill that was not meant to come to a vote. As Henry Parker Willis, successor to Charles A. Conant as Washington correspondent of the *New York Journal of Commerce*, reported soon after the bill's introduc-

burn. Also, Bancroft to Easley, 27 Mar. 1908, NCF, two days after the special message: "... the President's special message ... is clear, strong and conclusive; and is by far the strongest, most accurate and statesmanlike utterance on the combination question that has ever been given to the public. No man of public affairs hitherto has ever dared to talk straight on this subject; and very few of them have ever been able to see as straight, as the President has from the very beginning." Bancroft's ringing compliment of the president did not lead him to testify in favor of the bill, nor did it prevent him from expressing criticisms of it.

86. Roosevelt to Low, 28 Mar. 1908, at Elting E. Morison, ed., *The Letters of Theodore Roosevelt* (Cambridge, Mass.: Harvard University Press, 1952), p. 984 (hereafter cited as *Letters*).

tion, congressional Democrats and Republicans who had "devoted some genuine attention to the bill" stated that it was "really intended" for the purpose "of testing opinion and affording a basis for discussion."[87] Let us now consider in some detail the provisions of what the *Journal of Commerce* called, in the headline to Willis's report, this "drastic" and "extreme measure."

The Hepburn bill would have amended the Sherman Act by adding to it new sections providing for the following:[88]

A business corporation engaged in interstate or foreign commerce might register with the Bureau of Corporations by filing with the commissioner, under regulations determined by the president, a statement of its "organization . . ., its financial conditions, its contracts, and its corporate proceedings." The bill further authorized and directed the president "from time to time" and "in his discretion," to "make, alter, and revoke, regulations prescribing what facts shall be set forth . . ., and what information thereafter shall be furnished . . ., and he may prescribe the manner of registration and of cancellation of registration." Earlier drafts had given these registration and cancellation powers to the commissioner of corporations, subject to the approval of the secretary of commerce and labor; now the president was to exercise these powers directly, and virtually absolutely.

Having registered, a corporation might file with the bureau its contracts or combinations. If the commissioner, with or without "notice or hearing . . . as the Commissioner may deem proper," failed within thirty days of the filing to enter an order declaring the contract or

87. Willis, dateline Washington, D.C., 26 Mar. 1908, *New York Journal of Commerce*, 27 Mar. 1908, clipping at BC, G.F. 5563. Also, *Philadelphia Record*, 12 Mar. 1908 (reporting on White House conference of 11 Mar.): ". . . what is certain is that a powerful conservative element of the Republican party, represented by the Judiciary Committees of Congress, is unfriendly" to the president's proposals "and above all to the centralizing scheme. . . ." To insist on passage of the bill would "create a wide rift in the Republican party in the midst of the Presidential election. For this reason Mr. Roosevelt, who is the ablest politician this generation has produced, will not persist obstinately to the end in a course that would menace the certain defeat of his own favorite candidate for President." Clipping at BC, G.F. 5563. This last reference was to Taft, whom, as his absence from the Pertinent documents would seem to indicate, Roosevelt kept away from the drafting and political work related to the bill.
88. Text of the bill, *H. R. 19745*, at House Hearings, 1908, pp. 3–6; identical to print, "21 March '08." [13th Revise.], at JRG, Box 128, F. 45. The only significant difference between the House and Senate versions of the bill lay in the section relating to labor, with the Senate bill overtly addressed to reaffirming the common-law ban on labor boycotts by declaring legal strikes or combinations for "any purpose not unlawful at common law." Henry M. Hoyt (U.S. solicitor general) to Theodore Marburg, 21 Apr. 1908, NCF

combination to constitute "an unreasonable restraint" of trade, the corporation could continue a party to the contract or combination and be exempt from federal prosecution on account of it under the Sherman Act, "unless the same be in unreasonable restraint of trade." The bill, then, contained Bonaparte's open-ended proviso, rendering corporations subject to continuing supervision and potential punitive action by the executive even with reference to contracts or combinations previously approved. Common carriers might receive the same exemption, subject to the same open-ended proviso, by undergoing a similar registration and filing process with the Interstate Commerce Commission. Any contract or combination not so filed, whether a reasonable or unreasonable restraint, remained fair game for prosecution by the Department of Justice under the Sherman Act.

Under the bill's provisions compulsion followed upon voluntarism. A registered corporation could not pick and choose which of its combinations to file with the commissioner. Once registered, if a corporation failed to file with the commissioner all current and subsequent combinations or consolidations made by it with other corporations or associations, its registration would be canceled and with it all benefits and immunities under the act.

Although pending prosecutions or suits were not to be affected, there was to be a general amnesty and immunity from federal prosecution or private suit for all past contracts or combinations in reasonable restraint of trade, and after one year from passage of the act for all past contracts and combinations, whether reasonable or unreasonable, provided they were filed with the Bureau of Corporations (or Interstate Commerce Commission). But this amnesty would apply only to corporations that had registered under the act and that had not had their registration canceled.

The bill would have prohibited private suit for damages based on action before the act's passage, unless commenced within one year from the act's passage. In a related provision favored by labor leaders, especially in the wake of *Loewe* v. *Lawlor*, the bill would have reduced from treble to single the damages originally provided for in section 7 of the Sherman Act.

Trade unions and other associations not for profit might register and receive the benefits of the act by filing with the commissioner of corporations a statement disclosing no more than their charter, bylaws, principal place of office, and the names and residences of their officers and standing committees. The bill exempted trade unions, and other corporations or associations not for profit or without capital stock, from filing their contracts or combinations as a condition for maintaining their registration and obtaining the benefits and immunities of the act. In this and in the much less rigorous registration requirements for unions and for unincorporated entities ("without capital stock"), the bill provided for differential treatment between capital and labor, and between corporate capital and smaller business (including farmers and farm organizations), granting them greater leniency, indeed making their registration little more than a formality.

With respect to capital-labor relations, the bill further stipulated that the Sherman Act was not to be construed "to interfere with or restrict any right of employees to strike for any cause or to combine or to contract" among themselves or with employers for "peaceably obtaining ... satisfactory terms" of labor or "satisfactory conditions of employment." This provision protected the right of workers to strike and engage in collective bargaining agreements, against doubts raised by *Loewe*, but it was not intended to protect the boycott, although the wording was ambiguous and might have been interpreted as permitting the boycott. The bill also provided that the Sherman Act was not to be construed "to interfere with or to restrict any right of employers for any cause to discharge all or any of their employees or to combine or to contract with each other or with employees for the purpose of peaceably obtaining labor on satisfactory terms." This provision protected the right of employers to impose yellow-dog contracts and the open shop and to engage in lockouts, but it was not intended to protect blacklisting, although here also the wording was ambiguous and might have lent itself to a contrary interpretation.

The bill provided for only a minimal measure of judicial review. A corporation could challenge in federal court an order of the commissioner of corporations that canceled or otherwise adversely affected the corporation's registration. But the commissioner's, or ICC's, rulings as to the unreasonableness of contracts or combinations filed were not made subject to judicial review.

At the same time, it should be remembered, the government would have reserved the right, at any time, to reverse its judgment and prosecute under the Sherman Act a filed contract or combination, as unreasonable, even though it had been previously approved. The exemption against prosecution, then, was not made unequivocal or absolute by the bill, but amounted, in effect, to an executive declaration of presumptive legality, which might at any time be revoked. The prosecutorial loophole vastly expanded administrative discretion over corporate behavior, subjecting corporations to the one-two punching power of the Bureau of Corporations (or ICC) and the Department of Justice, and hence, ultimately, of the president. What the bill gave with one clause toward establishing certainty of the law in favor of reasonable restraints of trade, it took back with the other.[89]

Although the bill did not include provisions for government control of investment such as contained in the proposed incorporation measure that Roosevelt had sent over to Garfield back in late October, it represented a stringent license system with extraordinary executive powers. It gave expression to basic objectives that Roosevelt had come to hold and that he had begun to formulate publicly, in attenuated form, most recently in his three successive messages to Congress of 3 December 1907, 31 January, and 25 March, 1908. As the *New York Times* commented, upon the bill's introduction in Congress, the measure was "intended to enable President Roosevelt to accomplish by indirection what he very well knows he could not get by the express authorization of Congress, the power to regulate and control all corporation business of the country by a system of registration or license, a power which he has repeatedly asked Congress to confer upon him."[90]

The basic objectives may be summarized as follows: (1) to legalize

89. For other interpretations of the Hepburn bill and the politics relating to it, which differ from that offered here, see Letwin, *Law and Economic Policy*, pp. 248–249; Kolko, *Triumph*, pp. 134–138; Wiebe, *Businessmen*, pp. 80–81; Wiebe, "Business Disunity and the Progressive Movement, 1901–1914," *MVHR* 44:4 (Mar. 1958), pp. 664–685; Wiebe, "House of Morgan and the Executive," pp. 49–60; Johnson, "Antitrust Policy in Transition," pp. 415–434; Weinstein, *Corporate Ideal*, pp. 78–82; Naomi R. Lamoreaux, *The Great Merger Movement in American Business, 1895–1904* (Cambridge University Press, 1985), pp. 170–173. These interpretations, which are representative of the generally held view, explain the bill as an attempt to "weaken" the Sherman Act, and they explain conflict over the bill as revolving essentially around interest-centered differences between "big business" and "little business." None of these treatments examine the specific provisions of the bill and their implications, nor the bill's drafting history, nor the concrete debate, in and out of the hearings, over the bill's provisions, except in a casual and essentially unanalytical way. Kolko's account rests on substantial primary documentation, and it contributed much new information at the time of its writing, but it is insufficient in range to disclose an adequate understanding. Letwin's account rests entirely on Johnson's, a pioneering work at the time of its publication, which stated categorically that the Hepburn bill was "an effort to weaken" the Sherman Act (p. 426). Lamoreaux's account rests essentially on Johnson and Kolko. Weinstein's assessment of the bill and its politics rests on Wiebe and on an earlier, unpublished inquiry of mine, which, however, in this matter, rested on Wiebe. Of the older sources, and with respect to the questions at issue here, Wiebe's and Johnson's *MVHR* essays and Wiebe's *AHR* essay are the most valuable and remain important sources.

90. "Amending the Anti-Trust Act," *New York Times*, 24 Mar. 1908. The *Times* also noted that the bill "faithfully follows the lines" of Roosevelt's "famous message" of 31 January, to amend the Sherman Act to permit reasonable combinations and restraints but (quoting the President's words) "'only as a part of a general scheme to provide for this effective and thoroughgoing supervision by the National Government of all the operations'" of the large corporations. Clipping at BC, G.F. 5563.

reasonable restraints of trade, that is, to legalize the large-corporate organization of the economy; (2) to subject this legalized economic order to stringent federal regulation, direction, and control; (3) to provide for the exercise of this government authority by powers of constant administrative supervision lodged in an executive agency, which might engage in close consultation and cooperation with compliant corporate managers, who would become in increasing measure well-paid public servants rather than old-style capitalists; and (4) to replace judicial process with legislation and executive administration as far as it was constitutionally possible, in determining the structure and operation of the market.

On the matter of executive as against judicial authority, Roosevelt was particularly adamant. As he told Low when complimenting him on his "admirable work for the public": ". . . as you know, my desire is to strengthen the hand of the executive in dealing with these matters, and not to turn them over to what I regard as the chaos and inefficiency necessarily produced by an effort to use the courts as the prime instrument for administering such a law." Or, as he told another correspondent at about the same time, explaining his refusal to permit the bill directly to amend the Sherman Act to prohibit only unreasonable or unfair restraints of trade without qualification, "I want full power given to the *Executive* officers in the matter of the Sherman Antitrust Law." That law was not wise, but "it would be much more unwise to amend it by leaving the matter to be fought out after the event before the courts, or by giving the courts any original power in the matter." Hence, he would "keep the bill in that respect just as it is."[91]

In formal terms, the bill made registration and the concomitant filing of contracts and combinations voluntary. In practical terms, however, once having registered, a corporation's filing of contracts and combinations became compulsory. The very act of registration required the filing of contracts and all manner of other information, the latter of which was to be defined and alterable at the pleasure and discretion of the President of the United States. It could be expected, moreover, that virtually all corporations engaged significantly in interstate commerce

---

91. Roosevelt to Low, 28 Mar. 1908, and Roosevelt to John Carter Rose, 30 Mar. 1908, *Letters*, 6, pp. 983–984. Roosevelt's emphasis. It may be noted here that E. E. Morison's short account of the Hepburn bill, at ibid., p. 926 n. 2, is in error, in describing it as an attempt to establish "a kind of consent decree system" and in confusing Roosevelt's opposition to the Stetson–Morawetz proposal with his attitude toward the bill as introduced. This confusion of the Stetson-Morawetz proposal with the actual bill carries over into the work of all the other scholars cited here, including Wiebe, Johnson, Kolko, Weinstein, and my own previous work ("Corporate Reconstruction," pp. 172–201, and 335 n. 57), and it is in error.

would feel compelled to register, given the powerful inducement of government approval of contracts and combinations, their consequent quasi exemption from legal process, and hence the greater certainty of business conditions thereby accruing. It was also to be expected that a government seal of approval combined with rigorous supervision would bring relief from intense popular hostility to large corporations. Not least, furthermore, corporate executives and their attorneys might well regard registration as effectively compulsory, because failure to comply voluntarily would immediately arouse popular distrust, journalistic inquiry, and political attention. But perhaps most compelling, it would expose not only their unreasonable but also their reasonable contracts, combinations, or agreements to threat of prosecution, with little hope of their judicial vindication in the face of the Supreme Court's current, and repeatedly reaffirmed, construction of the Sherman Act. Hence the decisive significance of Roosevelt's resolve, with Bonaparte's advice and support, to leave the terms of the Sherman Act's prohibitory sections untouched, whereby all restraints of trade remained illegal unless brought within, and approved under, the registration system. In sheer market terms, not to register would place a corporation at a serious competitive disadvantage as against its registered rivals.

The *Journal of Commerce* did not fail to see all these implications. "The effect . . . is to give the registered corporations or associations the benefit of the distinction between unreasonable [and reasonable] . . . restraint of commerce . . . and to deny it to all that are not registered, leaving the latter to be crushed out by legal proceedings, . . . the executive power at Washington being the judge. The coercive effect of such legislation," the *Journal* noted, "is obvious. No corporation or association could afford to engage in interstate commerce without being registered." Any that "ventured to do so would be subject to the assumption that it was unlawful." Therefore, the *Journal* concluded, the "manifest aim" of the bill was "to establish by indirection a system of registration for corporations" that would "coerce them into submitting to it, without ostensibly making it compulsory." The *Journal's* assessment typified that of a large segment of the press.[92]

92. "Amending the Sherman Act," *New York Journal of Commerce*, 25 Mar. 1908; to similar effect, e.g., Willis, ibid., 27 Mar. 1908; *New York Herald*, 26 Mar. 1908, *New York Sun*, 27 Mar. 1908, *Philadelphia Record*, 12 Mar. 1908. Also, *Wilkes-Barre* (Pa.) *Leader*, 27 Mar. 1908: "What tremendous power this gives the Executive is obvious. The affairs of the railroads and industrial combinations must be spread out for his inspection, and his discretion as to cancellation will enable him to bring, as a pressure upon them, the threat of casting them to the wolfish mercies of the Sherman law, under which, if literally enforced, no combination could live." Clippings at BC, G.F. 5563.

Because once registered, moreover, a corporation must file all its combinations, just about all significant contracts, combinations, and agreements among enterprises that represented the dominant forces in the economy would become subject to the review, alteration, approval, or condemnation of the federal executive through the officers and staff of the Bureau of Corporations and the Interstate Commerce Commission. The *New York Sun* put it as follows, about what it called "really a most remarkable proposition." As the bill "would subject the validity of all contracts in restraint of trade to the fiat" of an executive department, "the validity of every important trade combination would practically be dependent upon the will and approval of the President." Willis offered a similar judgment as to the bill's scope if passed: It "would mean the absolute control of interstate industrial business by one man [the commissioner of corporations] subject to the veto or oversight of one other man [the president]." Or, as the *New York Times* tersely commented, the bill would "confer upon the President the power of control over the country's business."[93]

On the assumption of effective implementation had they become law, the bill's provisions would have made the federal executive not simply a regulator, but an active partner, of corporations in the administration of the market. The legislative basis would have been laid for making the Bureau of Corporations, along with the Interstate Commerce Commission, the arbiter of contracts and arrangements that determined not only corporate structure and capital formation but also, either directly or indirectly, prices of goods and services. The Bureau of Corporations, and by extension the Department of Commerce and Labor, would have been placed in position to become a vast centralized planning and administering agency, working in tandem with corporate enterprise, but having in the last analysis final authority. The judicial process provided for in the bill, and that invoked under constitutional authority, if not resulting in crippling, dismantling, or striking down the legislation, gradually would have created the norms of due process legitimizing and institutionalizing what would amount to a state-directed corporate capitalism.

The leading figures in the pro-corporate movement grouped around

93. *New York Sun*, 27 Mar. 1908; Willis, *Journal of Commerce*, 27 Mar. 1908; *New York Times*, 24 Mar. 1908. Also, *Macon* (Ga.) *Telegraph*, 18 Mar. 1908; also, *New York World*, 24 Mar. 1908: "It is an extraordinary programme President Roosevelt proposes for the control of the country's business." And [?] (R.I.), *Times*, 25 Mar. 1908: "If the Sherman law is amended, as the President would have it amended, the theory of Government ownership of railroads would be replaced by a condition of Presidential ownership of all corporations," Clippings at BC, G.F. 5563.

the Civic Federation, including capitalists and corporate lawyers, did not view their efforts at legislative revision as a ploy to evade government regulation of business. Their intent, in this respect, was to accommodate both public opinion and the law to the large-corporate organization of enterprise and the corresponding transformation of the competitive into the administered market. To attain this objective, they were willing to accept, and they undertook the initiative to construct, a plan of government regulation of corporate affairs; but the direct participation of the government in marketplace decision-making, a participation centered in extraordinary executive powers, as provided for by Roosevelt's bill, was more than they had bargained for. They believed that in the American body politic at that time the condition of legalizing the corporate-administered market (reasonable restraints of trade) was corporate accountability effected by a system of government regulation consisting of a mix of administrative oversight and judicial process, but they were not ready for the comprehensive government supervision and direction provided for in the bill.

Behind the scenes, Stetson and Morawetz worked with members of Congress to return the bill to the basis upon which they had tried to place it in their drafts of late February, namely, to combining outright legalization of reasonable restraints of trade with a mild registration-publicity plan. Roosevelt emphatically opposed and rejected their efforts and made this plain to Low in no uncertain terms.

In response to a letter from Low of 30 March, enclosing a letter from Morawetz, sounding out the president about his supporting a reversion to the Stetson–Morawetz draft or something along those lines, Roosevelt immediately warned Low that he would fight any such attempt and, if necessary, veto it in the unlikely event of its passage by Congress. He told Low that although he would not now categorically "say that I would veto a measure inserting the word 'reasonable,' ... my present impression is that I should do so." He further warned that "certainly before any such measure passed I should be obliged to send a message to Congress" pointing out its inadequacy "and emphasizing the fact that while it would accomplish certain good results, it would undoubtedly do a great deal of mischief." Referring to Morawetz's lobbying, Roosevelt commented, "I am afraid that the Congressmen with whom Mr. Morawetz talked are more or less covertly against every form of proper control of the great corporations and simply represent the reactionary feeling." Making it plain that he would gladly take up the cudgels, he added, let them "come out openly and give their names and make their arguments, and meet openly what I shall say in my message as to their proposals." But in that event, "I might be forced to veto the bill on the ground that it did more harm than good."[94] A week later, Roosevelt warned Low still more strongly: "The more I think over it the more I believe that to pass the bill on the Stetson–Morawetz line would be worse than passing nothing." Not only would it be "ruinous politically," because it would inevitably be popularly perceived as designed to release the "big corporations" from effective regulation, but "what is more important, it would represent a very grave setback in the movement for corporation control – a movement which I believe essential to the well-being of the country." Then, delivering the coup de grace, Roosevelt added, "Incidentally, I do not believe there would be the slightest chance of passing it."[95]

Roosevelt reaffirmed his support of the bill as it was: "By this bill in substantially the present form we offer the big corporations ... what they have profest to want; that is, the chance to go into proper combinations without molestation." If, therefore, "they choose to back and fill," and if they "won't recognize the need of action," then "the blame for the continuance of the present system will rest upon them and upon no one else." Similarly with "the labor men," who were dissatisfied with the bill's failure to sanction the boycott, end the blacklist, or give unions unqualified exemption from the Sherman Act. Roosevelt hereby also put Low and his associates on notice that he intended to stay his strategic course of using the current legal situation as leverage for ultimately, if not in the short run, attaining strong government powers over the market, and as the alternative to that, keeping the pressure on by offering nothing. To underline that strategic point, he reminded Low that Bonaparte "does not really favor the bill," for reasons "the direct reverse of those that make Stetson and Morawetz lukewarm"; that is, "his chief objection is to the insertion of the word 'reasonable.'"[96]

Roosevelt also took this occasion to reassert his determination to place regulatory powers with a comprehensive executive authority, and to remove it as far as possible from the judiciary. "My own position, as you know," he told Low, "has never varied. I believe we should not forbid all combinations, good or bad; but I emphatically believe that

---

94. Roosevelt to Low, 1 Apr. 1908, *Letters*, 6, pp. 986–987.
95. Roosevelt to Low, 9 Apr. 1908, ibid., p. 997.
96. Ibid. Cf. *New York Times*, 24 Mar. 1908: "Presumably the President, seeing his opportunity, insisted upon shaping the amendment to accomplish his purposes, as the condition of giving to it his support.... The insertion of the word 'unreasonable' before the word 'restraint' would take the mischief out of the [Sherman] act, and sufficiently amend it. So simple a process, however, would not confer upon the President the power of control over the country's business," and hence "would very likely fail to receive the support of Mr. Roosevelt, and might therefore fail." Clipping at BC, G.F. 5563.

the power should be put in the hands of some branch of the Executive
..., and that this power should be greater than merely to obtain
publicity.... I am unalterably opposed to the folly of trying to leave a
measure like this to be determined in the first instance by the courts ...
and the only proper way, to meet the matter is by lodging supervisory
power in some branch of the Executive." Here, Roosevelt cited as the
appropriate analogy for industry the type of regulation of railroads
represented by the Interstate Commerce Commission: "The Interstate
Commerce Commission has done excellent work, and it would have
been fatal to have adopted the plan of putting their work on the courts
instead of on an administrative body." There was not "the slightest
warrant," he believed, "for the objections raised against this course."[97]

It was, indeed, precisely the bill's implicit extension, to industry and
business in general, of the regulatory regime applied to railroads or
public utilities, that alarmed capitalists and others interested in legal
revision, including particularly those who favored government regulation. As Willis reported from Washington within days after introduction of the Hepburn bill, both Democrats and Republicans in Congress
were appalled – "'too absurd to be considered'" was the "almost
unanimous opinion"; "extreme and impossible." "The universal objection ... to the new bill is the immense increase that would be given by
it to the Executive power," which in the judgment of lawyers in
Washington "would be very much greater than that bestowed upon the
Interstate Commerce Commission" over railroads. The bill would give
the executive "practically the power to say what concerns are within the
law" without having "to wait for the co-operation of the courts." Such
unprecedented power over the economy in general "would not only be
much more extreme than that over the railroads, but it would be much
more highly centralized."[98]

Neither such criticism in and out of Congress, nor the qualms expressed by the bill's ostensible friends, deterred Roosevelt from viewing
the bill as a responsible and moderate measure, and from pressing Low

97. Roosevelt to Low, 1 Apr. 1908, *Letters*, 6, pp. 986–987.
98. Willis, *Journal of Commerce*, 27 Mar. 1908, clipping at BC, G.F. 5563. Willis also
     reported: "No such direct personal control, according to members [of Congress]
     familiar with the history of our industrial legislation, has ever been attempted in
     the United States with reference to any branch of business." Cf. *New York Sun*, 27
     Mar. 1908: "The President proposes a change in our statutory law relating to
     contracts which we venture to say is without a precedent in American legislation.
     ... The question of reasonableness ... is essentially judicial in its nature, and yet
     it is proposed by Mr. Roosevelt that the decision ... shall be confided to an
     administrative officer ... no such extraordinary and far reaching power has ever
     yet been conferred upon any single officer in the history of the American Govern-
     ment." Clipping at BC, G.F. 5563.

and the Civic Federation to honor their commitment to appear as the bill's sponsor and to go through with supporting it at the congressional hearings.

In response to the strong tide of criticism of the bill's statist implications, Low sought in a circular letter of 30 March to minimize the extent to which the bill represented a novel departure from traditional government-market relations and from traditional restraints upon executive authority. But he concluded his appeal by emphasizing that public opinion, and hence Congress, was not ready for a simple amendment of the Sherman Act permitting reasonable restraints of trade; such a bill would be regarded in the popular mind as a sellout to big business. He then characterized the Hepburn bill, as if apologetically, although not without warrant from Roosevelt's own words in his message of 25 March, as "a tentative effort" designed "to deal with the problem in a way that may be accepted, and may be effective." Low was undoubtedly right, as so indeed was Roosevelt, about the implausibility of expecting Congress to pass a simple amendment of the Sherman Act permitting reasonable restraints of trade. On 25 March, Republican Senator Joseph Benson Foraker of Ohio, a venerable and respected solon, introduced a bill, along Stetson–Morawetz lines, that would simply and directly have amended the Sherman Act to provide that nothing in the antitrust law "shall hereafter be construed or held to prohibit any contract, agreement, or combination that is not in unreasonable restraint of trade or commerce with foreign nations or among the several states." The bill received negligible attention and less support in Congress. It died in the Senate Judiciary Committee.[99]

The underlying assumption of the logic in support of the Hepburn bill was that only a truly competitive market could be "left alone" by government, whereas a market that consisted increasingly of entities with monopolistic – that is, price-making – powers, must be subjected to government controls on behalf of the public interest as well as on behalf of economic efficiencies. Accordingly, just as "natural monopolies" such as railways and utilities must be placed under government supervision in everything from capitalization and contractual relations to rates

---

99. Low, Circular Letter of 30 Mar. 1908, NCF. Sent to those who had engaged in drafting work and had been preparing to give their support at congressional hearings. The Foraker bill was introduced as *S. 6331. Cong. Rec.*, 60th, 1st, 42:4, 25 Mar. 1908, p. 3852. At the Senate Judiciary Committee hearings, Joseph Nimmo, past president of the National Statistical Association, raised a lonely voice of support for the bill. Senate Hearings, 1908, pp. 203, 231–243. For press support of Foraker's bill or legislation along its lines, see, e.g., *New York Times*, 24 Mar. 1908, and *New York Sun*, 27 Mar. 1908 (explicitly supporting the Foraker bill), clippings at BC, G.F. 5563.

(or prices), so with industrial and other large corporations. In short, industry would have to undergo "ICC-ization." Insofar as a few corporate capitalists and like-minded civic or political leaders, such as Perkins, Gary, Carnegie, Low, and Roosevelt, held this view or sympathized with it, they had arrived at, or close to, the point of regarding large capitalist enterprise as, in effect, public utilities, no longer as purely private enterprise, and corporate executives not only as capitalists but also as public servants. It was a view that implied favoring at one and the same time the preservation of the advantages of private ownership with its initiative and munificent rewards, and the establishment of a legal-administrative framework of service to public policy and the general welfare. Whether realistic or utopian, it was the viewpoint of capitalist noblesse oblige seeking to combine established personal wealth with dedication to public service; it was not that of the capitalist entrepreneur-on-the-make. In American English, it was the viewpoint of the public-service capitalist.

In this view, enlightenment meant acceptance of large-corporate enterprise as progressive and beneficial, but embedding it in appropriate law and judicial precedent and subjecting it to state direction. Property ownership and its rewards might remain private on condition that the structure and distributive function of the market were subjected to public policy determined and enforced by the state. The state was to become not merely a regulator but a partner with corporations in the market, and as a partner with sovereign power, ultimately, if it chose, the senior partner. In a political democracy the state's eventual senior partnership was a strong likelihood. The chief benefits to be obtained from such an arrangement, in the eyes of corporate leaders such as Perkins and Gary, whether or not they comprehended or acknowledged all the implications, were the certainty of law governing the market, the legalization of the administered market in place of the old competitive market, the consequent stabilization of prices and employment, or, in other words, the countercyclical management and moderation of the business cycle, and in the broadest terms, the attainment of class harmony in a political economy that reconciled the dynamism of capitalist property ownership with a social-democratic public policy, and the entrepreneurial initiative of capitalist property owners with public service.[100] State direction would stand in for the competitive mechanism

100. For thinking along these lines, see, e.g., Roosevelt, messages to Congress of 5 Dec. 1905 and 3 Dec. 1907 (quoting the former), *Cong. Rec.*, 60th, 1st, 42:1, p. 68, and his special message of 31 Jan. 1908, ibid., 42:2, p. 1349; Perkins, "The Modern Corporation" (1908), in Seligman, ed., *The Currency Problem*, pp. 155–170; Perkins, "Some Things to Think About," 15 Apr. 1910; John Wanamaker, "The

in turning private vices into public virtues. One might say, the idea was to infuse the body of capitalism with the spirit of socialism.

The defeat of the Hepburn bill

Immediately upon its introduction into the House on 23 March, the Hepburn bill drew an avalanche of criticism that continued until, within a matter of weeks, it irretrievably buried the bill in committee. The American body politic instinctively, as it were, rejected this statist transplant at the heart of the nation's vital functions. The hostilities cascaded from all sides – from the press, as already indicated, from Congress, commercial bodies of large and small cities alike, manufacturers' associations, agricultural bodies, lawyers, and, of not least significance, from large-corporate executives both aligned and nonaligned with the Civic Federation.

Upon the public airing of the bill's provision for unusual executive power and unprecedented government participation in the market, the presumed broad coalition crumbled.[101] On the one hand, although the

Evolution of Mercantile Business," in American Academy of Political and Social Science, *Corporations and the Public Welfare* (1900), pp. 123–135, and William H. Baldwin, "The Interest of Labor in the Economies of Railroad Consolidation," ibid., 139–149. Also, testimony of Perkins before the Senate Committee on Interstate Commerce, 1911 (62d Cong., 1st Sess.), and of Gary and Carnegie before the special Committee on Investigation of the United States Steel Corporation, 1912 (62d, 2d), in Edwin C. Rozwenc, ed., *Roosevelt, Wilson and the Trusts* (Boston: D. C. Heath, 1950), pp. 64–79. Cf. Wiebe, "Business Disunity," p. 683. Also, referring to Perkins's "Modern Corporation," Perkins to Roosevelt, 8 Feb. 1908, and Roosevelt to Perkins, 11 Feb. 1908, GWP.

101. The heavy stream of hostile comment that flowed within the two weeks from the White House conference of 11 March to the first days after the bill's introduction in the House had as its major line of criticism that the bill represented an attempt at aggrandizing executive power on behalf of an unwarranted and extreme form of government interference in the market, as already indicated in text and notes, above. A representative sampling of such opinion expressed in the press is at BC, G.F. 5563, particularly *Macon* (Ga.) *Telegraph*, 18 Mar. 1908, *New York World*, 24 Mar. 1908, *New York Times*, 24 Mar. 1908, *New York Journal of Commerce*, 25 and 27 Mar. 1908, *New York Herald*, 26 Mar. 1908, *New York Sun*, 27 Mar. 1908, *Wilkes-Barre Leader*, 27 Mar. 1908, *Baltimore Sun*, 26 Mar. 1908, *Springfield* (Mass.) *Union*, 29 Apr. 1908. See also for similar opinion the telegrams and letters from manufacturers and other capitalists, at House Hearings, 1908, pp. 8–9, 432–470. Noteworthy also, and rather emblematic, is the letter to Herbert K. Smith from Richmond, Va., attorney Wyndham R. Meredith, who had served on the trust conference resolutions committee, and who after requesting from Smith and receiving a copy of the bill as introduced in Congress, wrote Smith in dismay of his opposition to the bill: "The President knows that as a 'Roosevelt Democrat,' I heartily approve proper regulation of corporations which ... will prevent illegitimate growth through unfair and illegal favoritism and discrimination. Beyond this I cannot go, believing as I do, that any attempt to 'fix' rates &c.,

various leaderships agreed on the objective of legalizing reasonable restraints of trade, they remained far from agreement on positive legislation, and even farther from accepting the necessity, desirability, or propriety of the Hepburn bill's method of accomplishing it. After *Loewe* v. *Lawlor*, moreover, the manufacturers organized in the National Association of Manufacturers and its affiliates decided to stand pat with the Sherman Act as the strategy best suited to strengthen them against trade unions and to protect them against large corporate power in an administered market. On the other hand, in spite of theories just then issuing from such social scientists as Moisei Ostrogorski, Robert Michels, and Max Weber that in mass democratic politics, charismatic, bureaucratic, or organizational elites displaced their constituencies in the effective wielding of power, in this case, at least, even those elite figures who had engaged in the negotiations that fashioned the bill and had come personally to favor the bill in its parts, if not in whole, nevertheless in finding their constituencies divided or opposed, felt compelled in their public comportment to remain silent, waffle, or openly oppose the bill.

As head of the National Grange, for example, Nahum J. Bachelder – himself a Civic Federation executive officer who only a few weeks before had served on the three-member lobbying committee with Gompers and Low – found it necessary to maintain public silence on the bill and to refrain from testifying on its behalf at the congressional hearings. In apology, he told Low, "I am frank to say that I think the organization which I represent will be divided upon this question and that I would have no authority to speak for it in this matter.... I must be loyal to the organization which I represent and not overstep the bounds which are fixed for me."[102] By and large, the other farm leaders acted

is an unwise interference with economic and social forces that can best adjust themselves, and any interference with which is bound in the long run to prove disastrous." Meredith to Smith, 23 Mar. 1908, Smith to Meredith, 24 Mar. 1908, Meredith to Smith 26 Mar. 1908 (quotation from latter), BC, G.F. 5589–3.

102. Bachelder further explained to Low: "The National Grange, unlike the Federation of Labor, does not delegate the right to speak for it to its executive officer, and I could not appear in favor of this or any other measure unless the organization had passed upon it. It is with sincere regret that I write you this, for I have great admiration for your leadership in civic matters." Bachelder to Low, 31 Mar. 1908, NCF. Bachelder, like Gompers, was at this time a vice-president of the NCF. The Hepburn bill was a Civic Federation–sponsored measure, yet Balchelder could not act in support of it. With public support for the bill from farm organizations negligible or nil, Easley urged Gompers to persuade leaders like the president of the National Farmers Union, Charles S. Barrett (a member of Roosevelt's Country Life Commission), to testify in support of the bill at the hearings, especially as Roosevelt had emphasized that he regarded the support of farm leaders as crucial to the success of the measure. "We must get those people in with us," Easley told

similarly, either refraining from supporting the bill, or explicitly opposing it.

Gompers and the other AFL and railway union leaders were able to
proceed more flexibly, but they, too, acted under organizational con-
straint. In public, they pressed for more than the Hepburn bill offered,
namely, for the outright exemption of trade unions and farm organizations from the Sherman Act, while at the same time they gave a general
endorsement of those of the bill's measures that applied to corporations, without specifically supporting or even discussing any of the
pertinent provisions. Behind the scenes, they assured Low of their
support of the bill as the best that could be expected under the circumstances, although it was questionable that such muted and qualified
support had much value.

The earlier drafts of the bill, in the two weeks following the 27
February New York meeting, contained wording that came closer than
did the final version to the exemption of unions from antitrust law that
the labor leaders wanted. At the White House conference of 11 March,
however, the many changes in the bill that Roosevelt stipulated as the
condition of his support included a rewording that, while recognizing
the legality of unions and strikes, kept unions within the reach of the
Sherman Act. This wording appeared in the bill as introduced in the
House. As Easley reported to Bancroft, when the drafting group went to
the White House, "labor lost about all it had gained in the bill."[103] It
was a few days later that the leaders of more than one hundred AFL
and railway unions convened in Washington in response to Gompers's
earlier call to deal with the Danbury Hatters' case crisis. The delegates
drew up a petition to Congress for the redress of grievances. A committee led by Gompers presented it on 19 March to Republican Speaker of
the House Joseph G. Cannon. Among other things, the petition called

Gompers. "The President, as you will note, has made them very prominent in his
message." Easley to Gompers, 26 Mar. 1908, NCF.
103. Easley to Bancroft, 16 Mar. 1908, NCF. Close as he was to International Harvester
and U.S. Steel interests and to executives such as Perkins and Gary, Bancroft was a
leader in negotiating support for the bill, in its earlier versions, among Illinois and
midwestern capitalists. But after the White House conference of 11 March, Bancroft wrote to Easley from Chicago that press reports of the conference were
"rather disquieting to our friends here. They are suspecting that the labor elements
are getting the 'long end' of the bargain, and that there will be little or nothing for
business interests in the proposed changes." Bancroft to Easley, 13 Mar. 1908,
NCF. In his letter of 16 March Easley was able to reassure Bancroft on the labor,
although not the business, end of the matter; he pointed out that the results of
the White House conference were in fact "just the reverse" of the impression
conveyed by the press, in that there "was no effort to give the unions the right to
boycott, sand bag, or commit murder as some of the papers have put it." Easley to
Bancroft, 16 Mar. 1908, NCF.

for the outright exemption of unions and farm organizations from the Sherman Act. Not surprisingly, Cannon gave the labor leaders little reason to expect such action from Congress.[104]

Business opinion, buttressed by strong academic and legal opinion not then regarded as necessarily anti-union, was adamant against anything that might be construed as legalizing the boycott weapon in the hands of labor. In nonbusiness circles, and to a lesser extent in business circles, the strong opposition to the union boycott weapon went hand in hand with an equally strong opposition to the employer blacklist, so that it had become obligatory in public discourse, even among NAM-aligned manufacturers, to couple opposition to the boycott with opposition to the blacklist, while in principle accepting as legitimate such practices as strikes, lockouts, and yellow-dog contracts. This opinion, as Roosevelt knew, had to be satisfied if the objectives embodied in the bill with respect to corporations were to have a chance of sustained, serious consideration by a politically effective cross section of public opinion. Gompers and the other labor leaders wanted the blacklist and the yellow-dog contract outlawed, and trade unions free to strike and boycott as necessary to protect workers' human and economic rights; but they also understood that, as yet at least, public opinion would not go beyond outlawing the blacklist along with the boycott. "At no time," as Easley reported, "has there been any idea in the minds" of Roosevelt, Gompers, and Low of seeking to legalize the boycott. Roosevelt told Smith that if the wording of the bill as introduced in the House inadvertently permitted either the boycott or the blacklist, he would without question agree to the appropriate change.[105]

Accordingly, the labor leaders, as Easley observed, "have not broken with us in any way, excepting at this time they feel that they must ask for more than what our Bill grants them. The leaders understand perfectly well that it would avail them nothing to secure the Amendment they have asked for [for] two reasons; First, that it is likely to be declared unconstitutional; Second, that it would leave them under the common law which would not very materially improve matters for them." They well knew, moreover, "that the President would not sign a Bill to which there was any doubt as to its constitutionality, should such a Bill get that far," but they understood equally well "that Congress

---

104. See note 61 and related text, above.
105. Roosevelt to Smith, 14 Apr. 1908, TR. Also, Garfield to Corning, 7 May 1908, JRG, Box 128, F. 45: "The President has never for one moment stood for any law or approved of any suggestion that looked toward the legalizing of either the black-list or the boycott ... and he stated to the representatives of the Civic Federation that he would not approve any bill that contained such provisions."

would not likely pass any Bill of that character." They had decided, nevertheless, upon pushing in public for exemption because, in light of the NAM-led campaign against unions, the Supreme Court decision, and workers' indignation and related trade-union politics within the AFL and the railway brotherhoods, there were "political reasons why it is important for them to stand on that proposition at this time." At the hearings, therefore, Gompers will "strongly take the grounds that the business of the country is entitled to the relief that it asks in these Bills and he will heartily approve all of the provisions of our Amendment excepting the ones relating to labor.... In the end, however, they will support our Bill as the best that they can secure at this time." Gompers's testimony at the hearings played out this pattern precisely. In so doing, Gompers gave away nothing in return for influential support for some of labor's objectives. He knew, as did everyone else, that the bill had little prospect of passing. In general, Gompers and many other labor leaders regarded corporate concentration, in industry as in railways, as progressive, inevitable, and not necessarily disadvantageous to union organization, and he affirmed the propriety and benefits of superseding the unrestricted competitive market with an administered one, regulated by the government, that stabilized prices, wages, and employment. The administered market with the appropriate legal environment would be most conducive to the spread of collective bargaining. The position Gompers took at the hearings was consistent with one he had long been espousing. He backed reasonable restraints of trade and large-scale enterprise under government regulation, without defending the bill's specific provisions, and devoted almost all of his testimony to defending labor's rights and arguing the case for exemption of unions from the Sherman Act.[106] His support for the bill gave him an effective platform. Because, however, he and other labor leaders offered what

106. Easley to Bancroft, 21 Mar. 1908, NCF. *Railway Trainmen's Journal* editor D. L. Cease, who had participated with Gompers and other labor leaders in the drafting work, in urging a Detroit associate to line up support for the bill among local manufacturers and the Detroit Board of Commerce, stated: "The Administration is behind this bill in every possible way, and [so are] many of the largest corporations, including the United States Steel and a number of the railroads. Organized labor will be behind it also before we are through with the hearings. (This is confidential.)" Cease to O. W. Mulkey (Penobscot Bldg., Detroit), 8 Apr. 1908, NCF (Cease's parenthesis). Cf. T. C. (Easley's secretary) to Low, 20 Apr. 1908, NCF: "Mr. Gompers handled himself in very good shape yesterday [at the hearings]." Also, Ralston (AFL attorney) to Gompers, 13 Mar. 1908, Ralston to Easley, 13 Mar. 1908, NCF. Gompers's testimony is at House Hearings, 1908, pp. 47–65, 509–521, 644–665. Cf. Gompers, "The Control of Trusts," *Chicago Conference on Trusts*, 1899, pp. 329–330: "... the state is not capable of preventing the legitimate development or natural concentration of industry."

amounted to a qualified endorsement of the bill, and because important farm organizations either did not support or openly opposed it, the bill's meager chances in Congress were further seriously eroded.

It was the determined opposition of smaller manufacturers across the country, however, that proved decisive in creating the congressional climate of opinion that buried the bill in committee and prevented it from becoming a basis for the normal legislative negotiation and re-drafting that usually accompanied a viable bill. Neither major party claimed a monopoly on the loyalties of smaller manufacturers. Never-theless, in the North they counted as a venerable and potent constituen-cy of the Republican party, as they did in the South of the Democratic party. Neither party's leaders or officeholders could ignore their senti-ments. They concentrated and conveyed their opposition to the bill through such nationwide organizations as the National Association of Manufacturers and the closely aligned American Anti-Boycott Associa-tion and National Citizens Industrial Association, as well as through their state manufacturers' associations and their party connections in the several states and congressional districts.[107]

107. The more than one hundred telegrams and letters recorded in the transcript of the House hearings (House Hearings, 1908, pp. 8–9, 432–470) came mostly from smaller manufacturers and, in the vast majority, opposed the bill. Three major themes dominated the communications: (1) that the bill would permit boycotts, blacklisting, and unjustified strikes, and accord to labor unwarranted power to restrain trade; (2) that the bill would give inordinate power over the market to government, especially to the executive branch and its bureaucratic officers; (3) that if passed, the bill would be the ruin of the Republican party in the upcoming national elections. The following are typical. From Farel Foundry and Machine Co., Ansonia, Conn., 16 Apr. 1908: "... we strenuously object to the discrimina-tion in treatment of corporations and voluntary associations and to the autocracy vested in the Commissioner of Corporations." From Landers, Frary & Clark, New Britain, Conn., 16 Apr. 1908: "Kill the Hepburn bill. It toadies to labor unionism and gives to the Bureau of Commerce [sic] powers of the Spanish inquisition. Kill it." From the New York State and Northern Pennsylvania Stove Manufacturers' Association, Albany, N.Y., 13 Apr. 1908: "[We are] in urgent opposition to the Hepburn amendment ... as being dangerously subversive of the interests of American industries, employers, and employees." From Winn & Hammond, De-troit, Mich., 14 Apr. 1908: "As employers of labor, we must protest against the passage of the bill, particularly those sections that ... legalize strikes, picketing, boycott, and other combinations most injurious to honest, law-abiding capital and labor." From the Merchant Tailors' Exchange of Philadelphia, Pa., 14 Apr. 1908: "We desire to enter our protest.... The bill takes away from the judiciary many functions hitherto exercised by them and confers them upon executives.... it exercises stringent supervision of the rights of corporations to make contracts or combinations.... The bill legalizes ... all forms of malicious strikes ... legalizes the boycott ... legalizes the black list." From the Davis Sewing Machine Co., 4 Apr. 1908: "If the Hepburn bill ... is passed, we believe, the people will repudiate the Republican party at the next election." From the W. P. Callahan Co., 4 Apr. 1908: "Passage of the Hepburn bill will kill the Republican party next fall, we fully believe, and it should." And, from the Dayton Manufacturing Co., Dayton, Ohio, 4 Apr. 1908: "For God's sake spare us such legislation."

By the end of January 1908, the Civic Federation leaders had been working with leaders of the National Association of Manufacturers and other manufacturers' groups over an extended period of time in efforts to change the Sherman Act to permit reasonable restraints of trade. The manufacturers had been well represented at the trust conference in Chicago the previous October. Prominent among them were figures such as Charles H. Smith, president of the Illinois Manufacturers' Association, which Easley, Low, and Bancroft regarded as a leading opinion-making force among the country's manufacturers. Smith had served on the resolutions committee of the conference, alongside Gompers and other labor leaders, in formulating the resolutions in favor of changing federal antitrust law. Similarly, James M. Beck, attorney to National Association of Manufacturers' president James W. Van Cleave and to the American Anti-Boycott Association and other anti-union associations, attended the Civic Federation strategy meeting of 15 January, which unanimously agreed to seek revision of the Sherman Act. Beck continued thereafter as a member of one of the federation's committees concerned with revising the antitrust law.[108]

The smaller manufacturers' strong anti-unionism, however, divided them from the NCF-aligned capitalists, civic leaders, and intellectuals over the application of the law to trade unions. This, in turn, colored their attitude toward revising the antitrust law. Like the NCF-oriented approach, their view by and large favored government regulation of large corporations; it favored relief, at least for themselves, from the Supreme Court's interpretation of the Sherman Act as dictating unrestricted competition; it favored the legalization of reasonable restraints of trade for capital. But, in contrast to the NCF orientation, smaller manufacturers opposed such legalization if it might deprive employers of the injunction weapon against strikes and other union activity, if it might weaken the prohibition on boycotts, or if it might facilitate or encourage unions' organizing or collective bargaining leverage. The Supreme Court's decision in *Loewe* v. *Lawlor*, on 3 February 1908, drove this wedge of disagreement on antitrust law deeper into the councils of capitalists.

In early February, soon after the decision, Beck and Charles Smith told Easley that, personally, "they are in favor of pushing through a bill at this session [of Congress] that will give all hands relief" from the

---

108. Easley to Gompers, 12 Feb. 1908, Easley to Roosevelt, 12 Feb. 1908, NCF; and see note 53, above. As head of Buck's Stove and Range Co. of St. Louis, Van Cleave had earlier, in 1907, won injunctive relief against an AFL-led boycott campaign, resulting subsequently in the conviction of Gompers, John Mitchell, and Frank Morrison for contempt of court upon their refusal to obey the injunction. Beck served as Van Cleave's attorney in the case. In his own business affairs, Charles H. Smith was president of the Western Wheeled Scraper Co. of Aurora. Ill.

Sherman Act as currently construed by the Court. In the flush of *Loewe* v. *Lawlor*, however, organized labor's opponents, Easley found, were "insisting that the President and Attorney-General Bonaparte follow up the Supreme Court decision." Sentiment was building among manufacturers and other employers to the effect that "now that the Sherman Act had knocked out the unions, it had better be let alone, and that employers would rather be inconvenienced by that Act than to get the unions 'out of the hole' they are now in." Beck and Smith disavowed personally holding such views themselves, but, under bonds of accountability imposing constraints upon their action similar to those upon the farm and labor leaders, they warned against attempting to pass legislation either exempting unions from the Sherman Act in whole or in part, or treating unions more leniently than business.[109]

The sentiment among manufacturers in favor of turning the Sherman Act against labor much more decisively determined their legislative priorities than their desire, real as it was, for a change in the law as it applied to themselves. When, furthermore, the Hepburn bill as finally introduced in Congress provided, quite apart from the objectionable license features, for differential treatment in the registration of labor organizations as against business, and in so doing appeared to encourage trade-union action and organization, the manufacturers turned resolutely against the bill. To the smaller manufacturers, the issue of differential treatment covered considerable ground; it included, for example, any treatment such as provided for in the bill that might even seem to weaken the injunction or the ban on the boycott, or that might conceivably vitiate the Sherman Act as a weapon against unions.[110]

109. Easley to Gompers, 12 Feb. 1908, Easley to Roosevelt, 12 Feb. 1908, NCF.
110. For example, the Illinois Manufacturers' Association stipulated that the bill be changed to make no discrimination between business and labor organizations in conditions of registration. "All interests should be treated exactly alike, regardless of the object of the corporation." The bill should also be changed to declare that nothing in the Sherman Act should be construed "to interfere with or restrict" the workers' right to make agreements among themselves or with employers as to wages, conditions, or hours, nor "to interfere with or restrict" the employers' right "for any cause to discharge any or all of their employees," or to make agreements with employees or their associations or with employers or others regarding wages, conditions, or hours. Fred W. Upham (president, Illinois Manufacturers' Association) to Low, 24 Apr. 1908, NCF. (Upham had recently succeeded Smith as president of the association.) This meant, of course, that workers were to have the right to have a union, a right they already had, but there was to be no change in the law validating injunctions against strikes or the banning of boycotts, thereby effectively continuing to prohibit or restrict workers' implementing collective coercive action against employers. At the same time, on the other hand, it meant that employers were to continue to have the right to implement singly or collectively coercive measures against workers, namely, the lockout, the yellow-dog contract, the open shop, and in practice, if not in law, the blacklist.

Within days of the bill's introduction into the House, the Illinois Manufacturers' Association's special committee on the proposed legislation returned an adverse report, which the Association's executive committee immediately approved. "They object," reported Bancroft from Chicago, "on the ground that an unfair preference and discrimination is made in favor of labor organizations, and against corporations for profit; ... not that the regulations ... should be the same ..., but that the power of the Department [Bureau of Corporations] over such associations, and the right to as full publicity as to their acts ..., should be as ample as toward business corporations." Bancroft added that he saw "no good answer to this contention."[111] A few days later, Charles Smith informed Low that because of opposition to the bill among the members and directors of the Illinois Manufacturers' Association, he could not testify at the hearings.[112]

The National Association of Manufacturers and the American Anti-Boycott Association undertook the major share of presenting the manufacturers' position against the Hepburn bill at the congressional hearings. They warned that the bill would in effect accomplish the legalization of the boycott, which even many of labor's professed friends opposed; and they rang the defense of the "little man" against the trusts, praising the Sherman Act as an exemplary law that ought to be enforced as it stood and that ought not to be tampered with. Amendment of the Sherman Act to permit reasonable combinations, they now argued, would sow judicial confusion and make impossible the protection of the smaller manufacturers against great corporate combinations.[113]

111. Bancroft to Easley, 27 Mar. 1908, NCF.
112. C. H. Smith to Low, 1 Apr. 1908, NCF. Many among the members and leaders of the Illinois Manufacturers' Association may be presumed to have had social or business relations with those (including Bancroft, Gary, Perkins, et al.) associated with Chicago-area International Harvester and U.S. Steel interests, and hence with the NCF. The Civic Federation was, of course, a major presence in Chicago in its own right, and Bancroft, by late March and early April, was still expressing qualified support for the bill "as a decided improvement upon the present law." Bancroft to Low, 27 Mar. 1908, NCF. This may explain why the manufacturers' association's leaders decided to abstain from testifying, rather than actively testify against the bill. E.g., Upham to Low, 21 and 24 Apr. 1908, NCF.
113. Attorney James A. Emery testified for the National Association of Manufacturers and through it, as he stated, for about 135 other "industrial, manufacturing, and commercial" associations. Emery had served as Dietrich Loewe's attorney in the Danbury Hatters case. Attorney Daniel Davenport, who assisted Emery in the hatters case, appeared for the American Anti-Boycott Association. As could be expected, they both also opposed the pending Foraker bill. Their testimony is at Senate Hearings, 1908, pp. 243–275 (Davenport), and pp. 276–282 (Emery), and at House Hearings, 1908, pp. 470–495, 665–693 (Emery), and pp. 223–241, 273–336 (Davenport); the list of organizations represented by Emery is at House

The animating impulse behind the manufacturers' position was the labor question. Had it not been, they might have found good reasons for seeking to amend or defeat the Hepburn bill, but they would not have taken a position – in favor of standing pat on the Sherman Act – that before *Loewe* v. *Lawlor* (for example, at the trust conference the previous October, and at the NCF strategy meeting in mid–January, 1908), they had not been advocating. Although smaller manufacturers genuinely feared the unregulated power of large corporations, they did not necessarily want to abolish them, nor to go back to the unrestricted competition dictated by the Supreme Court's interpretation of the Sherman Act. They wanted to be able to engage in reasonable combinations themselves, and they wanted, in addition to judicial process, rigorous regulation of the practices of the large corporations by an agency of the federal executive – practices such as differential pricing, discriminatory buying and selling, and tying contracts, which might eliminate the smaller enterprises from the market altogether and hence prevent their coexistence with large corporations in an administered market. There was even strong sentiment among smaller manufacturers for subjecting what they regarded as monopolistic corporations like Standard Oil to detailed regulation, including the setting of prices, similar to ICC jurisdiction over the railroads.[114]

To attain any of these objectives as a matter settled in the law would require, minimally, a reversal of its position by the Supreme Court or

Hearings, pp. 663–664, and by Davenport at p. 223. Henry B. Martin of the American Anti-Trust League opposed the Hepburn and Foraker bills from the populist left, as it were, arguing like Emery and Davenport for the enforcement of the Sherman Act as it stood, but calling for the total exemption of labor unions from the antitrust laws. Ibid., pp. 336–364, and Senate Hearings, 1908, pp. 353–361. Cf. Johnson, "Antitrust Policy," pp. 429 n. 52, 432.

114.   This characterization of small-manufacturer opinion is based on the testimony cited in note 113; on telegrams and letters from manufacturers at House Hearings, 1908, pp. 8–9, 432–470; on communications to Herbert K. Smith from capitalists at BC, G.F. 5589, 5590, 4414; on responses to the Hepburn bill in NCF records, including, e.g., C. W. Shoemaker (treasurer, The Cumberland Glass Manufacturing Co., Bridgeport, N.J.) to Low, 7 Apr. 1908, Upham to Low (enclosing suggested amendments of the bill formulated by the directors of the Illinois Manufacturers' Association), 24 Apr. 1908, and "Report of the Committee of the Commercial Club of Richmond, Indiana," 13 Apr. 1908, approved by the directors and members of the club; and on James W. Van Cleave to Secretary of Commerce and Labor Oscar M. Straus, 1 Apr. 1908, enclosing National Council for Industrial Defence (Van Cleave, chairman, and Emery, general counsel), "An Analysis of the Proposed Amendments to the Sherman Anti-Trust Act," by Emery, at BC, G.F. 5589–5. There were those who favored the Hepburn bill, e.g., Thomas F. Parker (president, Momaghan Mills, Greenville, S.C.) to Low, 1 Apr. 1908, NCF, but their opinions were distinctly in the minority of those on record.

legislation to amend or supplement the Sherman Act. The decision to stand pat with the Sherman Act at this time, therefore, reflected a tactical maneuver in the smaller manufacturers' war with organized labor, a war in which their allies included many large corporations as well. This was the basic motive that underlay the manufacturers' position on the Hepburn bill as expressed at the hearings. As Herbert K. Smith summarized the situation to Low in the midst of the hearings on the bill, the manufacturers' position represented "not the real opposition to the principles of the bill," but one that "really centers around the labor question." Whatever else in the bill "that crowd" opposed, Smith explained, "their real interest . . . lies wholly in . . . a desire to (1) maintain the Sherman Law in statu quo, so that they may make full use of the Danbury Hatters case against the labor unions, and (2) to see at least that the amendment of the law does not allow any more leeway to labor unions than possible." At the hearings, Jenks made the same point publicly: "One reason why some of these manufacturing corporations are opposing the bill so vigorously," he told the Senate Judiciary Committee's panel, "is that they feel that if it were put through it might, in the long run, take from them some of the advantages that they think they have under the present Sherman antitrust act in their contests with trade unions."[115]

115. Smith to Low, 13 Apr. 1908, BC, G.F. 5589–10; Jenks, at Senate Hearings, 1908, p. 319. Also, Easley to Gompers, 26 Mar. 1908, NCF, commenting on their having encountered Van Cleave in Washington, probably in the corridors of the House office building: "It was fortunate, I think, that we ran into Mr. Van Cleave just as we did; he was caught off his guard and gave himself away completely. He was so excited he could scarcely express himself intelligently; one interesting point was his statement that 'it' would never get out of the committee. Whether he meant the Littlefield sub-committee or the full [House Judiciary] committee, I do not know, but, as they Van Cleave, Emery, Davenport & Littlefield are working so closely together, it may be surmised that it was semi-official." Representative Charles Edgar Littlefield, Republican of Maine, had succeeded to Nelson Dingley's seat upon the latter's death in 1899; he was the chairman of the subcommittee of the Judiciary Committee holding hearings on the Hepburn bill. He had in the past been a leading advocate of amending or supplementing the Sherman Act, having introduced a bill in the 57th Congress (1903–1904) to ban discriminatory rates and prices by common carriers and corporations, to require interstate corporations to file reports with the ICC on penalty of losing the right to engage in interstate commerce, and to require the ICC to publish annual lists and summaries of these reports. His bill, which did not pass, paralleled provisions of the Elkins Act and the act establishing the Bureau of Corporations, both passed in 1903. Roosevelt and Attorney General Philander C. Knox opposed Littlefield's bill as (in Roosevelt's words) "too drastic." Littlefield also introduced a bill in the House in late 1905 that would have empowered the Bureau of Corporations to require corporations to submit information on bonds issued, outstanding amount of authorized capital stock, the division of shares among common and preferred, their par value, and

Smaller manufacturers viewed themselves as caught in a potential scissors of two powerful forces: large corporations able to make prices and pass on costs or absorb them in economies of scale, on the one side, and trade unions able to make the price of labor, on the other. This presented them with a likelihood of being cut out of the administered marketplace. They were not opposed to replacing the competitive market with the administered market, nor, for the most part, to large enterprise as such – which, at any rate, many of them aspired to become. They therefore focused their energies on detaching or dulling the labor blade of the scissors. In practical terms, the condition of the corporate reorganization of the market, from their standpoint, was the open shop. In more general historical terms, the prior condition of organized labor's integration into the corporate order was the working out of a modus vivendi between large-corporate and smaller capital that would permit their coexistence and mutual prosperity.

The Hepburn bill marked an early and dramatic stage in intra-capitalist negotiations that would continue over the next thirty years before organized labor was ultimately accorded a subordinate place in the corporate order. The tactics of the smaller manufacturers on the Hepburn bill were embedded in a larger outlook; they were not simply a matter of mindless reaction or shortsighted opportunism. Rather, smaller manufacturers had drawn conclusions from their understanding of the calculus of power and survival in the changing conditions of the market society. Herbert K. Smith referred to the National Association of Manufacturers' having fought the Hepburn bill "on the side issue of the boycott," and as having "gone mad on a minor issue."[116] But although the boycott in particular and labor's organizational strength in general were indeed minor to the regulatory purposes of the bill as intended by either Smith or Roosevelt, they remained basic issues to smaller manufacturers and to a broad cross section of capitalists as well, and until the arrival at some arrangement on the labor issue, acceptable to larger and smaller capitalists, or invulnerable to their opposition, there could be no legislative resolution of the trust question. As this implies, what some historians refer to as "corporate liberalism," in designating the rise of the regulatory state, is not accurately to be

dividends. The Judiciary Committee reported the bill favorably, but it died in the House. Littlefield was therefore no Sherman Act standpatter, but he *was* a congressional ally of the NAM and its anti-union campaign. Johnson, "Roosevelt and the Bureau," pp. 573–574; Thorelli, *Federal Antitrust Policy*, p. 548; Jenks, at House Hearings, 1908, p. 96, discussing Littlefield's 1905 bill.
116. H. K. Smith, "Memorandum," 24 Aug. 1908. BC, G.F. 4414–9.

understood as originating in an alignment of corporate capital and organized labor (or "big business" and "big labor") against little capital and others, but on the contrary, in an accommodation between large-corporate and smaller capital, negotiated over time and registered in a consensus eventually embodied in government policy and the law, on the basis of which trade unionism and collective bargaining on a systemic scale was later, in turn, accommodated – some thirty years later.[117]

The smaller manufacturers, however, were not alone in their anxiety over the bill's implications for capital-labor relations. A broader range of business opinion, as typified by the New York Board of Trade and Transportation, objected to the bill on grounds that, aside from the bill's providing for inappropriate federal government control over interstate commerce, it would discriminate in favor of trade unions in its registration provisions, it would so exempt trade-union actions from the Sherman Act as "practically to nullify" *Loewe* v. *Lawlor*, it would for all practical purposes legalize both the labor boycott and the employer blacklist, and it would also legalize "agreements which, by controlling the cost of production or the output of labor, might establish most oppressive restraints of trade." The bill would thereby contribute to strengthening labor's hand in the market and exacerbating rather than pacifying capital-labor conflict.[118] Representative of an influential current of reform opinion that intersected with business opinion but also extended well beyond it, Moorefield Storey, the eminent Boston lawyer and civic leader, opposed the bill on similar grounds. Referring to the bill's labor provisions, he told Low that he opposed "any attempt to make a distinction between combinations of labor and combinations of capital," and that he therefore did not approve in general "the attempt to relieve labor organizations from the provisions of the Sherman Act," and in particular the prospect that the bill could "be interpreted to

117. See Epilogue, below. The view of corporate liberalism's origins rejected here as erroneous is sometimes associated with New Left historiography, although it also expresses the outlook of a strand of ideology current then and since among smaller capitalists, professionals, and white-collar employees, who have pictured themselves and "the poor" and "the unorganized" as the victims of a "big business," "big labor," "big government" alliance.

118. New York Board of Trade and Transportation, "Petition to the members of the United States Senate and House of Representatives," 8 Apr. 1908, at BC. G.F. 5589–7. Also, Frank S. Gardner (secretary, N.Y. Board of Trade and Transportation) to Low, 2 Apr. 1908, and Theodore Marburg to Easley, 17 Apr. 1908 (reporting that the Baltimore Board of Trade had acted to oppose the Hepburn bill), both in NCF; and Roosevelt to H. K. Smith, 14 Apr. 1908, TR, (reiterating his opposition to the boycott and blacklist and his agreement to any necessary change in the wording of the bill affecting either practice). Cf. Johnson, "Antitrust Policy," p. 429; Wiebe, *Businessmen*, p. 81, Kolko, *Triumph*, pp. 135–136.

justify a sympathetic strike [boycott] such as the courts have condemned."[119]

For its part, the National Association of Manufacturers did not confine its attack on the Hepburn bill to the labor issue. It joined in taking up what emerged as the issue of universal concern, not only to all sectors of business but also among the most diverse shades of political and legal opinion. It was the issue that, over the long term, and once a capitalist consensus on the labor question had been reached, would exert the decisive impact on shaping the positive content of antitrust law, namely, the extent to which the Hepburn bill provided for a statist direction of the economy and inordinate executive power in wielding that direction. This issue, as we have seen, had already filled the press by the time congressional hearings began.

The National Council for Industrial Defense (NCID), an umbrella group of 130 industrial associations organized by the National Association of Manufacturers and headed by NAM president Van Cleave, denounced the bill as "the most dangerous and diabolically ingenious measure yet proposed to Congress" affecting the nation's business. Van Cleave told Secretary of Commerce and Labor Oscar S. Straus that it represented "the attempt to turn over the interstate commerce of the country, practically 95 percent of its total business, to the discretionary control of administrative bodies." The NCID's general counsel, James A. Emery (also general counsel of the NAM), stated officially for the NCID that under the bill, corporations must comply "with every request for information of any character required by the Executive," that judicial functions would be inappropriately conferred upon executive officers, and that "the country's business" would thereby be "placed under the control of individuals of vast power, easily misused with the best of intentions, and capable of the most frightful abuse." Emery's official statement also noted that the bill was "alleged to be the outcome" of White House conferences that included representatives of the Civic Federation, labor, "and counsel for several of the larger industrial and transportation corporations," and if so, it presented "the suspicious spectacle of powerful industrial organizations who cannot be blind to the dangers of this bill, yet would risk commerce, industry and personal and property rights in the doubtful scale of some ulterior advantage." There was little of substance to this latter charge, but an insinuation of "Trust" support for the bill could not hurt the cause of the bill's opponents.[120]

119. Storey to Low, 2 Apr. 1908, NCF.
120. Van Cleave to Straus, 1 Apr. 1908, and enclosure, NCID, "An Analysis of

A wide cross section of opinion expressed itself along similar lines of criticism. Storey wrote to Low that he "very distinctly opposed" the bill, not only on grounds of the labor issue but also because "it gives to a bureau officer altogether inordinate and dangerous power."[121] Civic Federation executive officer William A. Clark, president of the United Verde Copper Company, reported of Wall Street and Washington opinion that the bill had "given rise to a great deal of criticism"; particularly, "the recommendation to allow the President so much discretion is obnoxious to a good many." A large number of capitalists and lawmakers "seem to be opposed to the license system," and, Clark confided, "I do not know but what the objections ... are pretty well founded."[122]

From the state of Washington, A. H. Perry, a smaller manufacturer, wrote to Low at length explaining why he could not, at Low's request, urge the United States senators or representatives from his state to support the bill. As a delegate to the Chicago conference the previous October, he said, he could not recall a "crystallized sentiment" or "a consensus of opinion" in favor of such a bill. The bill would, in effect, "usurp the functions of the courts by executive officials." It would, in the process, "place in the hands of the Chief Executive and his Administration an equivalent to absolute control and direction of all corporations and combinations in ... trade and commerce as well as common carriers." Perry said that although he believed in "the centralization of the power of government to a great extent," the bill "goes too far," as it would authorize an administration so inclined to "aggrandize to itself a mighty power," and thereby serve as a "weapon" and "an all powerful adjunct" to an administration with "any tendency toward a bureaucratic government ... to carry out its purpose." By concentrating power and information in an executive agency engaged in cooperation with managers of favored corporations, the bill would make it "possible for the great corporations to become greater while the smaller corporations would be destroyed." If, Perry concluded, the power vested in the Interstate Commerce Commission over railroads may be considered

Proposed Amendments to the Sherman Anti-Trust Act," by Emery, BC, G.F. 5589-5. The bill's opponents had nothing to lose in portraying it as the product of a bargain among big business interests, trade unions, and government officials, but one should be wary of regarding such statements as that by Emery as evidence of such a bargain, or as evidence that the line of division over the bill fell between big business and little business.
121.   Storey to Low, 2 Apr. 1908, NCF.
122.   Clark to Easley, 25 Mar. 1908, NCF.

excessive, the bill "exalts this power [over all business] to the point of finality."[123]

Urban commercial associations, representing the gamut of mercantile, manufacturing, transportation, financial, and small- as well as large-corporate interests, took the lead at the congressional hearings and in public debate in opposing the bill's statist features, while at the same time urging the need for amending the Sherman Act to permit reasonable restraints of trade and establish some degree of appropriate federal regulation of business practices. Among these associations, the New York Board of Trade and Transportation and the Merchants' Association of New York assumed a prominent, and intellectually representative, role.

The New York Board of Trade, as its president, William McCarroll, stated, agreed that experience had "demonstrated defects in the Sherman law," in need of correction, "but measured by its effect upon the evils it was intended to mitigate," the Hepburn bill "is as dangerous and ill-advised a piece of legislation as has been attempted in Congress." The board understood the bill "to reflect the views" of the president and of representatives of the AFL and the Civic Federation, McCarroll noted, and its authorship was credited to NCF president Low, who was publicly advocating it. "In view of the high character of those who are responsible for the measure, any suggestion of ulterior purpose will not be entertained"; it could therefore "only be assumed that they have failed to analyze its provisions, or realize their possible effect, as fully as the importance of the measure would seem to have demanded." The effect, the board's committee on legislation stated, "will be to practically establish the Federal licensing of corporations, for which the President has contended but has not, thus far, been able to secure by direct legislative provision."[124]

The bill, moreover, the board contended, would endow the president with "sole power to name the terms upon which corporations or associations formed for profit may obtain registry and the consequent benefits," and it would give "to the Commissioner of Corporations alone judicial power to decide questions upon which the Supreme Court of the United States has never yet reached a unanimous decision." In essence, accordingly, the bill, if passed, would improperly concentrate

123. A. H. Perry (Marcus, Wash.) to Low, 15 Apr. 1908, NCF. Perry favored permitting reasonable restraints of trade, but now believed it best to keep the Sherman Act as it was, with perhaps supplementary regulatory legislation guarding against abuses and unfair practices.
124. New York Board of Trade and Transportation, "Petition," 8 Apr. 1908, BC, G.F. 5589–7.

legislative and judicial functions in the executive branch, in conferring upon "the Executive departments of the Government power to exercise arbitrary control over the commerce and industries of the United States." The board urged the defeat of the Hepburn bill. At the same time, however, it stated its support for an amendment of the Sherman Act to exempt "such agreements which are in justifiable restraint of interstate trade and have a reasonable or laudable purpose," and it recommended, as had the Chicago conference, "that the whole matter be referred to a Commission, to consist of Senators and Members of Congress together with political economists and business men to be appointed by the President."[125]

At the beginning of April 1908, the board of directors of the Merchants' Association of New York informed Low that it favored the amendment of the Sherman Act, but not the Hepburn bill, and that accordingly, at a special meeting, it had appointed a committee, headed by the association's president, Henry R. Towne, president of the Yale & Towne Manufacturing Company, to appear at the congressional hearings to oppose the bill.[126]

On 9 April, the board of directors met again, unanimously adopted a resolution in opposition to the Hepburn bill, and decided to initiate a national mobilization by sending the resolution, with a letter urging similar action and the exertion of pressure on Congress, to business organizations and trade publications throughout the country. The Merchants' Association emphasized the need to amend the Sherman Act in order to permit reasonable restraints of trade and to establish a federal regulatory agency. But it opposed the statist features of the bill. In line with the resolutions adopted at the Chicago conference and with the New York Board of Trade's position, it called for, and it urged the other business organizations to call for, the establishment by Congress of a commission to study the whole antitrust question and recommend suitable legislation.[127]

The association's letter – also sent to House Judiciary subcommittee chair Charles E. Littlefield, Republican of Maine, and to Senate Judiciary Committee chair Clarence D. Clark, Republican of Wyoming –

125. Ibid.
126. S. C. Mead (secretary, Merchants' Association of New York) to Low, 1 Apr. 1908, NCF. The Merchants' Association was not a merchants' association. Its membership consisted of "some 1,200 corporations, firms, and individuals, representing almost every interest, manufacturing, mercantile, banking, law, and other professions." Towne, at House Hearings, 1908, p. 152.
127. The letter is reproduced in "Concerning the Amendments to the Sherman Anti-Trust Law of 1890," *Bulletin of the Merchants' Association of New York*, No. 47, April 13, 1908, copy in NCF.

struck a note of extraordinary urgency, stating that the issues involved in the pending bill were "of profound importance to the manufacturing, mercantile and transportation interests" of the country, and that these issues, "with the possible exception of legislation relating to National finances [that is, currency and banking], involve more far-reaching consequences than any other legislation which has been enacted or discussed since the close of the Civil War." The implication, worthy of note, was that the issues in each case involved a reconstruction of American society. The letter went on to argue that while the sponsors of the bill were "actuated by a sincere purpose to modify and improve" the nation's antitrust law, and "to promote the public weal," the bill, if enacted, would make "the present situation . . . still worse by introducing further perplexities, uncertainties and untried methods opposed to the spirit of our constitutional system and the past usages of our people."[128]

The association's accompanying resolution noted that the courts had interpreted the Sherman Act "as prohibiting all restraint of interstate commerce by combinations either of labor or capital," but that both before and since the passage of the Sherman Act in 1890, "it has been the established and increasing usage of our people, in relations affecting labor, industry, commerce and transportation, to avail of contracts and agreements for purposes of mutual benefit which frequently, in greater or less degree, involve some measure of restraint of interstate commerce." Accordingly, the opinion had become widespread among Americans that the Sherman Act ought to be amended "to sanction combinations and agreements which are in justifiable restraint of interstate commerce and which have a reasonable or a laudable purpose, while regulating or forbidding those which are unreasonable." It was "essential," the resolution further stated, that "by carefully collating, classifying and analyzing" the facts, "some measure or standard be determined upon and incorporated" in legislation, "which would enable the courts to differentiate between reasonable and unreasonable contracts." On this basis, the resolution called, as had the New York Board of Trade, for the defeat of the Hepburn bill and for the establishment by Congress of a commission "to investigate the matter at issue . . . and to embody their conclusions in a report which shall include specific recommendations concerning further legislation." At the hearings, the Merchants' Association opposed the Hepburn bill, but it also recorded its strong support for the amendment of the Sherman Act to permit reasonable restraints of trade and provide for publicity of corporate

128.   Ibid.

affairs through a federal administrative agency. In proposing that Congress establish an investigatory commission to define standards of reasonableness and unreasonableness, the association called for the precise definition of the corporation practices to be subject to federal regulation, these standards and practices to be specified in federal legislation, which was to include the establishment of a federal interstate trade commission for its administration and enforcement.[129]

It is evident that the position of the Merchants' Association, like that of the New York Board of Trade and a broad cross section of business opinion, was not one of standing pat on the Sherman Act, nor was it antiregulatory in any sense. Rather, it sought the legalization of reasonable restraints of trade under a system of regulation combining executive administration and judicial process, with terms and administrative powers defined with some precision in explicit legislation. It was a position that wanted government regulation, but not state direction, of the market.

At the House Judiciary subcommittee hearings, Towne elaborated the objections to the statist implications of the Hepburn bill. He argued that the bill offered executive fiat, and not the legislated certainty of law needed by the market. "Instead of fixed and definite laws we would have a set of rules made by . . . the President, subject to change without notice by him . . . at pleasure. In brief we would have personal government and instability in place of law and order." The principle here was that in its administrative functions, the executive would make the law as well as enforce it, rather than being subject to law made by Congress and interpreted, and to that extent enforced, by the judiciary. In commanding basic market functions, the executive branch of the state would also begin to rise above society as manifested in its representative and judicial organs, as well as in its civil, economic transactions. Accordingly, after analyzing the effective compulsion built into the registration and filing provisions of the bill, Towne noted that they meant "the substitution of a bureaucracy for the judiciary as the source of authority and control and decision in regard to all of the vast interests at stake." Basic decisions on contracts and combinations were to be made by the commissioner of corporations, subject to the approval of the secretary of commerce and labor. It was "obvious in advance," Towne reasoned,

129. "Resolution in Opposition to the Hepburn Amendments to the Sherman Anti-Trust Act," Unanimously Adopted by the Board of Directors of the Merchants' Association of New York, April 9th, 1908, in NCF; and brief filed on behalf of the Merchants' Association of New York by Nathan Bijur at Senate Hearings, 1908, pp. 282–296. Also, House Hearings, 1908, pp. 152–165 (Towne) and pp. 241–273 (Bijur).

"that the vast volume of documents to be received and the infinite number of questions which would arise ..., would be beyond the power of any one person to deal with, and that, therefore, in practice the work would of necessity be distributed among a number, probably a vast number, of clerks and other subordinates of the Commissioner." Each of these bureaucrats would then "in effect have the power of deciding ... whether the business operations of the parties concerned were reasonable or unreasonable, and whether they should be sanctioned or forbidden." For these and similar reasons, Towne concluded, the bill "would seem to be revolutionary and contrary to the fundamental principles on which our Government has been based."[130]

Representing western and midwestern cattle raisers at the hearings, S. H. Cowan of Fort Worth, Texas, an attorney and former judge, pursued the statism issue in further detail. As a spokesman for those with a keen interest in the regulation of the railroads to assure themselves favorable rates and terms, Cowan stated that "the great farming and stock raising interests" of the country strongly opposed permitting further combinations among railroads and large corporations, because they would only "pillage the people," but for purposes of regulation, he emphasized the distinction between public utilities, such as railroads, and business in general. "The public-service corporation is a different thing. We have always held that we can legally deal with a public-

---

130. Towne, at House Hearings, 1908, pp. 152–165. In the course of his testimony, Towne made clear the Merchants' Association's general agreement with the National Civic Federation on the necessity to revise the Sherman Act to permit reasonable restraints of trade, including "combinations to control prices." He also told the subcommittee, in distancing his position from that of Emery and Davenport of the National Association of Manufacturers and the American Anti-Boycott Association, "May I say that the Merchants' Association of New York appreciate most highly the work of the Civic Federation, and are convinced of their sincerity." Ibid., pp. 163, 165. Towne also pointed to the potential for corruption: "The plan just indicated is suggestive of a national 'bargain counter,' where those desiring to conduct their business on certain lines must apply and negotiate for permission, where the decision would be vested in a minor governmental employee, and where opportunities and inducements for corrupt practices would be rampant." Ibid., p. 162. Also, on the potential for corruption, *New York Times*, 24 Mar. 1908: "[A President might be] possessed of the ambition to succeed himself or to name his successor, ... [and he] would be under the greatest of temptations to issue indulgences, ... to powerful corporations from whom campaign favors might be expected, or to present a stern and forbidding countenance to those known to be reactionary opponents of his policies." To similar effect, *New York Journal of Commerce*, 25 and 27 Mar. 1908, *New York Herald*, 26 Mar. 1908. *Macon* (Ga.) *Telegraph*, 18 Mar. 1908: "These are not the days when the Websters and the Calhouns in the Senate, and the Alexander Stephenses in the House, were stronger than the occupants of the executive mansion, and held the latter strictly to account. Then the Government was republican in essence as well as in form; now it verges toward empire and one-man power more and more."

service corporation" in such a way as to appoint "an agent of the government" to regulate its "price or point of profit" and to prevent its engaging in "unreasonable restraint of trade." But to apply such regulation to "private business" would be to "shake the foundations of the Government as to the ownership of property" and shred "the legal fabric upon which all our industries are built." It would amount to "putting in the control of the Government the question as to whether you shall manufacture this or that, or whether you shall sell this or that, because you reach the point of saying whether a man shall be permitted to manufacture it and sell it at a certain price, so long as he is in combination with some other concerns who do the same thing." Littlefield here interjected that in the case of public-service corporations, "The Government, in other words, acts through the corporation, and ... has the right and power and responsibility, in fact, as to regulating the prices to be charged for the services rendered." Cowan agreed, and then noted that if the government were empowered to determine the reasonableness of a contract or combination, and if the reasonableness turned at least in part on whether the enterprise "is charging an unreasonable price or making an unreasonable profit," then, Cowan concluded, "there is no end to the regulation of your business by the Government authority." For, he explained, "You go from the point of unreasonable restraint of trade to its elements, namely, its price and profit. You go from that to the cost of production, and you go from that to the cost of the elements of the production, the labor and the materials." Hence, in Cowan's view, and as Littlefield suggested, the Hepburn bill would extend the public-service principle to all business sectors, in effect transforming the bulk of private enterprise, and the market as a whole, into a public-service agency or the agent of public policy as defined by the government.[131] This view was the same in essence as that of the New York Board of Trade and the Merchants' Association, and it was fairly representative of a broad cross section of business, legal, and journalistic opinion.

In the face of almost universal opposition to the bill, Low found himself in an awkward position. In spite of his political influence and personal prestige, Low, the bill's ostensible sponsor, was unable to marshal any substantial support for the bill at the hearings, either from

131. Cowan, at House Hearings, 1908, pp. 175, 184–185, 187. Cowan represented, at the hearings, the American National Livestock Association (Denver), the Cattle Raisers' Association of Texas (Fort Worth), and the Iowa Corn Belt Meat Producers' Association. Henry C. Wallace, editor of *Wallace's Farmer* of Des Moines, Iowa, was the secretary of the Iowa association. See Wallace to Cowan (telegram), 9 Apr. 1908, printed at House Hearings, 1908, p. 175.

his own organization, the Civic Federation, or from other quarters. The entire elaborate plan for filling the hearings with the testimony of favorable witnesses disintegrated. As the loyal soldier, he labored mightily, to little avail, through March and April, in New York and Washington, on behalf of the bill.[132] In mid–April, he at length remonstrated with Roosevelt for some support from the administration for what was really the president's bill. He reported to Roosevelt that not only had such important business organizations as the New York Board of Trade and the Merchants' Association passed resolutions "condemning the bill," but that he had "found it absolutely impossible to get any lawyer who will undertake its defense." The "philosophical lawyers," including the eminent corporation attorneys Joseph H. Choate and ex-Senator John C. Spooner (Wisconsin), from whom support was expected in the bill's earlier versions, were "objecting to it as to the precise point which seems to you essential." In order to produce at least one prestigious lawyer for the bill, Low suggested that Roosevelt have Frank B. Kellogg, the Minnesota attorney then serving as Bonaparte's special assistant in the Sherman Act prosecution of Standard Oil, testify at the hearings. More than that, Low urged, "the time has come when Mr. Knox Smith, or some one representing the Administration, ought to appear for the bill." For, he reminded the president, "So far as the business element is concerned, most of our difficulties come from our effort to carry out your views, and from some things that I hear, I believe that this is also the case with the Congress." Low acknowledged

132. In addition to his political influence, referred to earlier in this chapter, Low's personal prestige was indicated by his unanimous election as president of the Economic Club of New York, the previous June, an honor he declined due to the press of his other obligations. The club's executive committee included A. Barton Hepburn, Edwin R. A. Seligman, Stuyvesant Fish, James Speyer, John Claflin, Norman Hapgood, John Bates Clark, Henry Clews, Rollo Ogden, Edward B. Whitney, and Bainbridge Colby. J. W. Beatson (acting secretary, Economic Club) to Low, 6 June and 8 June 1907, and Low to Beatson, 10 June 1907, SL, Box 32, F. D-F. On Low's preoccupation with the bill in March and April 1908: Jacob Riis to Low, 12 Mar. 1908, Low to Riis, 16 Mar. 1908, Low to Walter E. Clark, 26 Mar. 1908, Low to Carl Kelsey, 28 Mar. 1908, in reply to Kelsey to Low, 27 Mar. 1908, all in SL, Box 34, F. A-B, C, R-S. Aside from himself, Low could produce as witnesses for the bill at the House hearing, only Gompers and Garretson (Railway Conductors), Theodore Marburg, William Jay Schieffelin (National Wholesale Druggists' Association), and Jenks, none of whose testimony, however, addressed the issues raised by the bill's major critics. House Hearings, 1908, Gompers at pp. 47–65, 509–521, 644–652, Garretson at pp. 657–663, Marburg at pp. 65–78, Schieffelin at pp. 31–44, Jenks at pp. 78–149, 521–546, 559–631. Also, Marburg to Smith, 7 May 1908, with enclosure, "Amendment of the Sherman Anti-Trust Law," by Marburg, before the American Academy of Political and Social Science, Philadelphia, 11 Apr. 1908, and Smith to Marburg, 13 May 1908, and Jenks to Smith, 9 May 1908, BC, G.F. 5589–12, 5589–8.

that Roosevelt had "said what you could" in the special message to
Congress of 25 March, but, he plaintively queried, "is it not time now
for the Administration to defend a policy which is so essentially its
own?"[133]

Roosevelt referred Low's letter to Herbert Knox Smith and, unper-
turbed, held to his course of at one and the same time refusing to recede
from supporting the measures and objectives embodied in the bill, while
keeping himself and his administration at a long arm's length from the
bill itself in Congress. To Smith, Roosevelt calmly noted that the New
York Board of Trade's opposition was "primarily aimed" at that aspect
of the bill that "practically licenses interstate commerce corporations,
thus submitting them to the control of the Federal Government." He
found that "interesting," because, "In other words the chief objection
. . . to the bill is to that measure which it is of most consequence to
have enacted into law; our aim is to secure . . . [illegible word] Federal
control of these corporations."[134]

Roosevelt kept the administration's identification with the bill at
the hearings to the bare minimum. Bonaparte at first deferred making
a statement on the bill at the hearings and then refused to do so
altogether, referring the House Judiciary Committee instead to Smith.
Roosevelt authorized Smith to submit a memorandum on the bill to the
House and Senate judiciary committees and to testify as necessary.

133. Low to Roosevelt, 11 Apr. 1908, BC, G.F. 5589–10. Roosevelt had suggested to
      Low that he invoke Kellogg's aid, but Roosevelt now did nothing to get Kellogg to
      the hearings. Roosevelt to Low, 9 Apr. 1908, *Letters*, 6, p. 997. Kellogg did not
      testify. Smith recommended to Low that he produce Kellogg or Stetson at the
      hearings, preferably Stetson, but given Stetson's position, that was quite out of the
      question. Smith to Low (telegram), 14 Apr. 1908, BC, G.F. 5589–10. In his letter
      to Roosevelt of 11 April 1908 (ibid.), Low also stated, "I think the large interests,
      such as Judge Gary represents, are still loyally behind our bill," and the "objection
      comes from the mercantile element as distinguished from the corporation element."
      In fact, the "corporation element" was deeply divided over the bill, at best, and
      people like Gary showed their "loyalty" by not testifying at the hearings. Perkins,
      Carnegie, Speyer, and the Boston banker Henry Lee Higginson privately expressed
      support for the bill to Easley or Smith. It is possible that they were prepared for a
      public-service capitalism, but it is also possible, and more likely, as suggested by
      their correspondence or distance from the bill's drafting, that, as McCarroll of the
      Merchants' Association had suggested, except for Perkins they did not give much
      attention to the actual terms of the bill. Speyer to Easley, 23 Mar. 1908, Carnegie
      to Easley, 24 Mar. 1908, Higginson to Easley, 24 Mar. 1908, all in NCF. Also,
      Carnegie to Low, 13 Apr. 1908, at House Hearings, 1908, pp. 654–655, which
      was entirely irrelevant to the actual terms of the bill. And Perkins to Smith, 18 Apr.
      1908, as well as Smith to Perkins, 20 Apr. 1908, BC, G.F. 5589–8.
134. Roosevelt to Smith, 14 Apr. 1908, TR, ser. 2 (also at *Letters*, 6, pp. 1007–1008).
      Roosevelt added: "The second objection is as to the legalization of the blacklist
      and the boycott. Here I agree with them, and would favor a modification of the
      bill."

Smith delayed as long as possible both his appearance at the hearings and the filing of his formal memorandum. By the time he did so, toward the end of April and early May, the bill was not merely dead but buried.[135]

The testimony in favor of the bill by Low, Smith, Jenks, and others was noteworthy for its advocacy of allowing reasonable restraints of trade, regulating against unreasonable restraints, and providing for publicity of corporations' affairs, and more noteworthy for its reticence or complete silence on federal licensing and the actual terms of the bill itself. Indeed, having recognized that the president intended to deliver no significant administration support for the bill at the hearings, Low in late April submitted to the Littlefield subcommittee a substitute bill drawn along the Stetson–Morawetz lines that Roosevelt had strongly

135. Bonaparte to Jenkins, 31 Mar. and 8 Apr. 1908, at House Hearings, 1908, pp. 433, 440. Marburg to Easley, 17 Apr. 1908, NCF, reporting Bonaparte's opinion that the bill had no chance of passing. Smith did not testify before the House Judiciary subcommittee until 25 April, toward the end of the hearings, three weeks after they had begun. He did not file his memorandum with the House committee until 1 May, and with the Senate Committee until 5 May. Smith to Loeb, Jr., 13 Apr. 1908, Smith to Low, 13 Apr. 1908, Smith to Littlefield, 1 May 1908, Low to Smith, 4 May 1908, Smith's secretary to Low, 4 May 1908 and 5 May 1908, Jenks to Smith, 9 May 1908, Smith to Marburg, 13 May 1908, BC, G.F. 5589–9, 10, 11, 12. The House Judiciary Committee requested a memorandum on the bill from Attorney General Bonaparte. Instead, Roosevelt directed Smith to prepare the memorandum "to state the position of the Administration on the bill," as Smith informed Low, "and the purposes, legal and practical, upon which the position is based." This kept the statement of the administration's position at the subcabinet level. Moreover, although the bill had been introduced on 23 March, Roosevelt did not so direct him, Smith claimed, until the first week of April, and the commissioner was still working on the memorandum toward the end of the month. To this reason for delay in his appearance at the hearings, Smith added another in his explanation to Low, namely, that the administration's ends "would be best served by having me appear at a time subsequent to Mr. Davenport's day in court," because otherwise, although from the administration's standpoint the labor issue was "incidental" to the bill's purposes and a "minor question," the newspapers would "reduce the whole matter to a somewhat undignified and sensational discussion between the Administration and the National Manufacturers' Association on the labor question," which would be "quite disastrous," and they would entirely ignore "whatever I might say on the much more important questions, to wit, the corporate issues and business matters." Smith to Low, 13 Apr. 1908, BC, G.F. 5589–10, Smith's memorandum is printed in House Hearings, 1908, directly after his testimony of 25 April (pp. 372–411) at pp. 411–432 (reprinted at pp. 693–715, 1 May), and in Senate Hearings, 1908, along with the transcribed proceedings for 8 May, at pp. 330–351. Typescript copy, "Memorandum on H. R. 19745 . . .," at JRG, Box 128, F. 45. This was the detailed survey of antitrust jurisprudence and its common-law background, which noted the legality of reasonable restraints of trade in American law until the Supreme Court's decisions of 1897–1899. See Chapter 3, above.

denounced, that is, permitting reasonable restraints across the board.[136]

In his testimony, as in his memorandum, where he stated that "like all other branches of law, the law of combinations must keep pace with economic conditions and be developed to fit modern facts," Smith urged the restoration of the common-law construction of the Sherman Act to permit reasonable corporate combinations, and the establishment of a system of publicity of corporate affairs under administrative supervision. He emphasized the importance of voluntary registration and of keeping the commissioner's decisions in the registration process clearly nonjudicial in nature by separating nonapproval of contracts from discriminatory or prosecutory treatment. Invoking President Roosevelt's message of 31 January, but not of 25 March, Smith declared that the bill was "drawn to accomplish these essential purposes."[137]

The disparity between Smith's asseverations and the terms of the Hepburn bill was so obvious that Davenport, in attendance after having completed his own testimony, inquired of Smith "whether you are addressing yourself to the printed bill or the proposed substitute prepared and submitted by Mr. Low?" Littlefield's efforts to prod Smith into defending or explaining the registration measures, their effectively compulsory character, and the enlarged executive powers provided by the plain terms of the bill and their practical implications, resulted in little more, in substance, than Smith declaring, "The thing I am interested in is the publicity feature. Anything that would relieve me personally of any exercise of executive [or judicial] functions as to what is reasonable would be a great pleasure to me personally."[138] Smith's own reservations about statist tendencies in Roosevelt's regulatory proposals, strongly reinforced by the public criticisms of the Hepburn bill, resulted in a memorandum and testimony that were evasive or ineffective in supporting the bill, if not in essence a repudiation of the measure.

In this respect, Jenks's testimony had basically the same impact. Jenks appeared at the House and Senate hearings officially on behalf of the

---

136. House Hearings, 1908, pp. 373–374; Low's testimony at pp. 10–31, 149–152, 495–505, 653–656.
137. Smith, "Memorandum," at House Hearings, 1908, pp. 430, 414, and at typescript copy, JRG, pp. 38, 7. In his *Annual Report* for 1908, p. 9, Smith characterized the bill essentially as having "proposed to modify the present sweeping prohibition against all combination," and as having "recognized ... the propriety of reasonable combinations."
138. House Hearings, 1908, pp. 373–374, 411.

Civic Federation, but as the current president of the American Economic Association, and as an expert known to be a close adviser of Roosevelt and an appointee to important presidential commissions in recent years, the Cornell professor's views carried more than ordinary weight. At the House hearings in April, Jenks, in the course of Towne's testimony, interjected that "the interpretation of the bill by the Merchants' Association of New York is not a fair interpretation," and he would "later on ... attempt to show wherein it is not."[139] There was nothing in Jenks's prolonged testimony, however, that refuted Towne's assessment of the plain terms of the bill. Jenks spent most of his time before the Littlefield subcommittee explaining the need for a regulated as against a competitive market and allaying fears about the bill's implications, but without dealing specifically with the meaning of the bill's express terms. He spent the rest of his time sparring with Littlefield, Emery, and Davenport on the labor issue.[140]

At the Senate hearings in early May, before the Judiciary subcommittee chaired by Minnesota Republican Knute Nelson, Jenks made no effort to defend the bill's specific provisions but confined himself to discourses on economics and economic history, and on the general need to adjust the law to the rise of large corporate enterprise by restoring the Sherman Act to its initial common-law construction.[141] Jenks's testimony was significant not for the bill itself but for its expressing in a conspicuous public forum essential components of the general pro-corporate argument.

Pointing out that although "there are various forms, ... in the main what we call trusts now are simply giant corporations," Jenks explained that his NCF committee considered it "desirable that Congress in any legislation which it should undertake should recognize changes in the economic conditions of the country by fitting the legislation to those economic changes." The law should adjust to such basic conditions, not seek to impede or nullify them. This required, Jenks continued, the rejection of the previously "accepted principle that we ought to leave competition as free and as unrestricted as possible." For, he explained, elaborating his own, the NCF committee's, and Roosevelt's underlying outlook, "The events of the last fifteen or twenty years in the United

---

139. Ibid., p. 164.
140. Ibid., pp. 78–149 (6 Apr.) pp. 521–546 (25 Apr.), pp. 559–631 (30 Apr.); for the sparring, see, e.g., pp. 114–115, 134–137.
141. Cf. Jenks to Smith, 9 May 1908, urging Smith to file his memorandum with the Senate subcommittee: "I trust you will do so; otherwise, our showing from the legal side will be weak. I made no attempt whatever to uphold that end yesterday, devoting all my time to the economic phases of the matter." BC, G.F. 5589–9.

States seem to me to show conclusively that we can not rely upon the principle of free competition to bring about the best industrial condition." The large-corporate reorganization of industry provided the structure for investment planning and pricing capable of yielding countercyclical stability as against the boom-bust roller coaster. This structure, in turn, required government regulation, including publicity of corporate affairs, to prevent abuses and guarantee the working of the economy in the public interest and for the general welfare.[142]

Jenks then presented an analysis of how the regime of free competition itself had nurtured the development of "monopoly in nearly all the leading lines of industry," how capitalists seized upon combination to avoid the "wastes of competition" and the decline of profits, and to take advantage of technological innovation and the more efficient management rendered possible by centralized control. He reiterated the pro-corporate argument that the Sherman Act itself had forced industrial and financial leaders to organize "single great corporations," and that consequently the organization of industry in the United States, characterized by great corporations, differed from that in Britain and continental Europe.[143]

Without referring to its provisions in detail, Jenks praised the bill on the grounds that by providing for publicity of corporate affairs, it would bring corporate operations out into "the open" and thereby prevent unfair, fraudulent, or dishonest practices, and foster investment and pricing efficiencies. At the same time, the bill would restore the common-law distinction between "reasonable" and "unreasonable" combination, thereby establishing recognition in the law of the econom-

---

142. Senate Hearings, 1908, p. 297. In addition to Nelson, the other members of the subcommittee were: Chauncey M. Depew (Republican-New York), William P. Dillingham (Republican-Vermont), Augustus O. Bacon (Democrat-Georgia), and James P. Clarke (Democrat-Arkansas). Senator Bacon was already on record as strongly against the Hepburn bill's enlargement of executive powers: "This usurpation of executive power has been going on so openly, so unblushingly and so boastfully that we have almost come to disregard it. I am so indignant that I can hardly find words in which to express that indignation." *Macon* (Ga.) *Telegraph,* 18 Mar. 1908, clipping at BC, G.F. 5563.

143. Senate Hearings, 1908, pp. 297–302, 312. Somewhat incredulously, Senator Nelson asked Jenks: "Your theory, then, is that the Sherman antitrust [act] has tended to breed these monopolies?" Jenks: "Absolutely that.... By attempting to prevent all organizations, that act has forced them into greater organizations and has tended to breed monopoly." Ibid., p. 302. Why the Sherman Act could not reach "greater organizations" even if not preventing all of them, if the Justice Department brought suit, Jenks did not explain. More accurately faithful to the prevailing technical-legal logic, Jenks reminded the Senate subcommittee that while the resulting great corporations evaded "the spirit" of the Sherman Act, they did not, by virtue of their size alone, necessarily violate "the letter of the law." Ibid., p. 301.

ic necessity of industrial concentration and centralization of control. "To us it has seemed," Jenks stated, "that if we were to put into the statute the words 'reasonable or unreasonable' we should find the courts taking the meaning of those words held in the common law."[144] In effect, and in a manner similar to Smith's testimony before the House subcommittee, Jenks's praise related less to the Hepburn bill than to the Low substitute drawn along Stetson–Morawetz lines, which was not officially before the Senate subcommittee.

The full Senate Judiciary Committee, in January 1909, returned an adverse report on both the Hepburn and Foraker bills. Senator Nelson wrote the report.[145] A midwestern progressive, the senator was no Sherman Act standpatter. In 1893, as governor of Minnesota, he had called a midwestern conference on trusts, and as a United States senator in 1903, he had been instrumental in the enactment of the amendment to the Department of Commerce and Labor act that established the Bureau of Corporations as an instrument of executive power. It was he who inserted the wording, insisted upon by the president and drafted by Attorney General Philander C. Knox, that made the bureau primarily a presidential agency by stipulating that it report exclusively to the president, not to Congress, and that the president alone decide which of the bureau's reports, or parts thereof, were to be made public.[146]

Now, however, responding to the massive outpouring of business opinion against the bill's statist implications, in particular the aggrandizement of executive power, Nelson emphasized the bill's inconsistency with traditional constitutional principles of due process of law and checks and balances, noting that it would confer upon "a mere bureau head" both a judicial and a legislative function in the "power of granting immunity" to the law. Nelson extended the due process argument, holding that insofar as the Sherman Act was a criminal and penal statute, to inject into it the "indefinite and uncertain" criteria "of whether an agreement or combination is *reasonable* or unreasonable" would render the act "to that extent, utterly nugatory and void, and would practically amount to a repeal of that part of the act." The courts, Nelson stated, had consistently held that a criminal statute must precisely define the crime in question to protect individuals from arbitrary procedures and trials.[147]

144. Ibid., pp. 302–303, 320.
145. Senate Committee on the Judiciary, Adverse Report, "Amending Antitrust Act," *Senate Report No. 848*, 60th, 2d, 26 Jan. 1909 (to accompany S. 6440). (Hereafter cited as Adverse Report.)
146. Johnson, "Roosevelt and the Bureau," p. 575; Thorelli, *Federal Antitrust Policy*, pp. 551–554.
147. Adverse Report, at Senate Hearings, 1908, p. 486. Nelson's emphasis. Cf. Letwin,

In his memorandum, Smith had shown persuasively and with detailed citation of cases, that the terms "reasonable" and "unreasonable" as they related to restraint of trade had precise meanings at common law as laid down over the years by the federal courts, and that therefore, consistent with Supreme Court decisions relating to similar questions of word meanings in other criminal matters, their use in the Sherman Act would not compromise its standing as a criminal statute.[148] Beyond this, however, neither the Bureau of Corporations nor innumerable proponents of amending the Sherman Act – large-corporate and otherwise – concealed their intent ultimately to transform the antitrust laws from criminal and penal to preventive and corrective civil statutes, just as many of these, including the president, did not conceal their intent to supplement or supplant judicial procedure with administrative supervision.[149]

With respect to civil suits under the Sherman Act, Nelson argued that "while the same technical objection does not apply . . ., the injection of the rule of reasonableness or unreasonableness would lead to the greatest variableness and uncertainty in the enforcement of the law. The defense of reasonable restraint would be made in every case and there would be as many different rules of reasonableness as cases, courts, and juries." He therefore concluded that to amend the Sherman Act as proposed "would be to entirely emasculate it," for all practical purposes as both a criminal and civil statute. He now sang the praises of standing pat with the Sherman Act as a law that was "clear, comprehensive, certain and highly remedial," and that was "in every respect a model law." But it was the political situation that really mattered with respect to the Sherman Act: "To destroy or undermine it at the present juncture, when combinations are on the increase, and appear to be as oblivious as ever of the rights of the public would be a calamity." It was this last point, rather than the cogency of Nelson's technical-legal argument that, in reflecting the prevalent mood in Congress, proved invulnerable to refutation. Congress wished neither to do anything even appearing to weaken the Sherman Act nor to adopt Roosevelt's proposals for strengthening the federal government's regulatory authority over the market. Nelson's report fit the bill – that is, the Foraker bill or the Stetson–Morawetz draft, but it served the purpose of rejecting the

---

Law and Economic Policy, p. 250. The question of the act's meeting the requirements of a criminal statute in the Anglo-American legal tradition had come up in the congressional debates on the Sherman Act in 1890. See Chapter 3, above.
148. Smith, "Memorandum," Senate Hearings, 1908, pp. 347–349; typescript, at pp. 34–38, JRG.
149. E.g., Commissioner of Corporations, *Ann. Rep.*, 1907, p. 6.

Hepburn bill. It completed the charade: Just as Low, Smith, and Jenks praised, so Nelson's report now denounced, what were in effect provisions of the other proposals. Roosevelt, for his part, opposed all efforts at passing a bill simply permitting reasonable restraints of trade combined with mere publicity, and he recognized that his strong measure could not at this time succeed. In postponing the bill indefinitely, leaving it to die in committee, the Senate Judiciary Committee Republicans gave Roosevelt what he wanted with little political cost – a bill that opened debate around issues Roosevelt wanted aired, with no negative vote on the floor of Congress that might hurt the cause.[150]

In the course of the period from the Civic Federation's trust conference in October 1907 to the debates over the Hepburn bill in early 1908, a consensus forming since the turn of the century had crystallized and come to encompass a cross section of capital, union labor, and farm groups, as well as influential circles of intellectuals, professionals, and political leaders. The common outlook favored (1) the legalization of reasonable restraints of trade; (2) effective federal regulation of interstate commerce to prevent unreasonable restraints and unfair methods of competition; and (3) the establishment of some federal administrative agency clothed with authority to carry out such regulation. But there was as yet no agreement on how to translate these objectives into positive legislation.

Aside from a general and amorphous, but intense, popular hostility to "the trusts," which deterred politicians from taking any action that might appear either to favor big business or to put the government in bed with it, dissension over two fundamental elements of market regulation obstructed a legislative consensus at this time and for the next several years. Differences especially among capitalists, but among many others as well, over (1) the rights and immunities of trade unions, and (2) the role of the state, in administering the market, prevented the drafting of regulatory legislation acceptable to a congressional majority.

The Hepburn bill failed to embody or attain sufficient accord on either count. In all likelihood, no bill that succeeded on the one but not the other could expect enactment by Congress at any time during the Progressive Era. Aside from the relatively narrow band of opinion

150. Adverse Report, at Senate Hearings, 1908, pp. 486–487. Nelson's report assumes its significance less from its actual content than from the fact that Justice Harlan, in his partial dissent in the Standard Oil decision of 1911, quoted in full the passages quoted in part here to substantiate his argument that not only the Supreme Court but also Congress, from 1897 to 1911, consistently rejected proposals to restore the common-law Rule of Reason to the meaning of the Sherman Act. 221 U.S. 97–98, at 4 *FAD* 160–161.

associated with Roosevelt, there was little support along the spectrum of politically effective opinion, whatever the popular state of mind, for the statist version of market administration represented by the Hepburn bill. Having been maneuvered by the president into the awkward position of ostensibly supporting a bill that went well beyond what the NCF constituency had been prepared to support, the federation's leadership found itself relieved to be let off the hook by the bill's dignified demise in congressional committee. As Easley commented in the autumn of 1908, the Civic Federation would "take the matter up again and begin *de novo*," but not until "after the election," that is, with Roosevelt out of the presidential picture; for, he noted, "the shape it [the bill] finally got into was such that the [NCF] committee was glad it did not pass."[151]

Neither the major organizations of capitalists, big and small alike, nor those of a broader segment of the public, including farmers and trade unionists, favored direct government participation in shaping the market, outside the market relations of "natural monopolies" such as railroads and public utilities, or the degree of executive power implied in provisions of the Hepburn bill. The Supreme Court's decision in *Loewe* v. *Lawlor*, by making labor and farm organizations more palpably vulnerable to the Sherman Act and hence more avid for reform of the law, activated a cross-class alignment for revision of the Sherman Act to permit reasonable restraints of trade. The Court's decision, however, at the same time, deepened the division among capitalists over the application of the law of restraint of trade to labor relations, and as a deterrent to legislation it was this division that proved the more potent force.[152] Thereafter, the Civic Federation leaders recognized that a modus vivendi on the trade-union question would have to be reached within the ranks of capital as a condition of viable legislation.[153] The division over the labor question combined with the strong aversion to the statist features of the bill to dissolve support for the measure from the moment it was introduced.[154]

---

151. Easley to E. R. Bacon (2 Wall St., New York City), 17 Oct. 1908, NCF.
152. The Supreme Court's decision in *Shawnee Compress Co.* v. *Anderson*, 209 *U.S.* 423–435, reaffirming *Loewe* v. *Lawlor*, became public in the midst of the hearings on the Hepburn bill, on 13 Apr. 1908.
153. E.g., Bancroft to Easley, 24 Nov. 1908, NCF, discussing the prospects of a new bill's gaining the support of the Illinois Manufacturers' Association: "You know fully the position of that organization and the necessity of having any proposed bill clear on the secondary boycott question."
154. For different interpretations of the major factors in the bill's defeat, see Wiebe, *Businessmen*, p. 81; Weinstein, *Corporate Ideal*, p. 80, which repeats and quotes from Wiebe's conclusions; and Kolko, *Triumph*, pp. 135–138. All of these accounts fall in with the prevalent view, rejected here, of the Hepburn bill as a

The rejection of the Hepburn bill closed out the Roosevelt presidency's efforts at market regulation, but it opened a new phase of legislative activity seeking the accommodation of the legal order to the administered market. The bill itself represented a plan of accommodation by resort to statist means – that is, by means of a government-corporation partnership in regulating the market that would authorize the government's assumption of the senior partnership and the commanding force. In a capitalist society like the United States at the time, in which the market so largely allocated power and composed, limited, or permeated the people's basic social relations, such government authority carried with it the implication of reversing the traditional subordination of the state to society (or to capitalist social relations), and making the state the master of society: Who commands the market commands the society. Instead of taking the trust question – the regulation of the market – "out of politics," that is, taking it out of, or rendering it heavily insulated from, electoral and party politics, as many advocates of government regulation had hoped, the Hepburn bill would have placed electoral and party politics at the center of market relations, and market relations at the center of party politics. In making market administration the direct responsibility of the state in its executive and legislative functions, the bill would have placed it among the constant and major overt issues of American electoral politics. Given no serious interference with such political democracy as then prevailed, the politics of market administration could reasonably be assumed inevitably to yield a state-ridden capitalism or to invite an easy demarche to a state-directed socialism. The Hepburn bill, therefore, not only closed out the Roosevelt presidency's regulatory initiatives but also opened the debate on a broad public front on the role of the state in the administra-

Roosevelt–NCF measure supported by a powerful sector of corporate capital and designed to relax government regulation of the market or give the large corporations greater market freedom or power. These accounts also confuse the Stetson–Morawetz draft with the Hepburn bill itself. In general, the prevalent view as expressed in these works is that the labor issue united capitalists against the bill, while the regulatory provisions of the bill divided capitalists largely along the lines of small versus large capital. The view here is that the labor issue divided capitalists over general legislative strategy with respect to antitrust law, and the specific regulatory provisions of the Hepburn bill united capitalists against it. Johnson, in his "Antitrust Policy," pp. 415, 433–434, thought the opposition to the Hepburn bill reflected a conflict between the reality of the rise of large-scale enterprise and the older ideal of free competition. There is little, if any, evidence, however, that the influential opponents of the bill had any interest whatever, or expressed any such interest, in resuscitating an ideal of free competition. Like many others, Johnson mistakenly equated a view favoring small-unit capitalism with one favoring free competition.

tion of the market, a debate that could not be extricated from legislative politics without being resolved by positive legislation.

Between Roosevelt and Wilson

The Hepburn bill served to intensify serious debate – in the press, in Congress, and in countless business, farm, labor, and civic organizations – on the government-market relation. It did so on terms that Roosevelt had largely determined, that would strongly influence subsequent legislative deliberation, and that would bind his successor's administration through most of its tenure. What this meant specifically was that until the last months of Taft's presidency, and until the later stages of the legislative process that finally yielded the Federal Trade Commission and Clayton acts, federal license or incorporation proposals with strong statist implications dominated efforts at drafting legislation.

In the autumn of 1908, after Taft's election victory, the Civic Federation resumed its efforts at amending the Sherman Act, in consultation with persons close to or about to join the incoming adminstration. Members of two prominent New York law firms, both with offices in the same building at 40 Wall Street, provided strong connecting links: attorney general–designate George W. Wickersham and the president-elect's brother Henry W. Taft of Strong & Cadwalader; and former judge Reuben D. Silliman of Choate & Larocque, a friend of the Tafts and a reform-minded attorney close to Low, Easley, and the Civic Federation.

By December 1908 the Civic Federation leaders decided against presenting a new bill at the current session of a lame-duck Congress. Instead, it appointed a committee to draft legislation for submission to organizations throughout the country and, after revision, to the newly elected Congress at the next session. The committee members were Low, Henry Taft, Silliman, attorney Frederick N. Judson of St. Louis, and patent attorney and AT&T executive Frederick P. Fish of Boston. Wickersham at first kept in close touch with this committee, to which his law partner, the president's brother, belonged. The committee produced a draft bill that would have reverted to the Stetson–Morawetz plan for legalizing reasonable restraints, and to the trust conference's and New York commercial organizations' proposals that Congress establish an investigatory commission. Neither President Taft, Roosevelt's protégé and successor-designate, nor Wickersham, however, were interested in pursuing a course that appeared less stringent than Roosevelt's regulatory program. Upon its inauguration, accordingly, the Taft administration moved to keep the Civic Federation at arm's length. Wickersham stipulated that the federation and the administration proceed independently, each preparing its own draft legislation, on the basis of which they might from time to time confer and cooperate. In line with this policy, Commissioner of Corporations Smith, whom Taft kept at his post, also distanced himself from the federation's renewed efforts. By the spring of 1909, therefore, the federation's committee receded from drafting a bill, and instead it decided to circulate a questionnaire to corporations, business associations, labor and farm organizations, and professional and civic groups, and after studying the responses, either to draft a bill or turn over the information with recommendations to Wickersham and Secretary of Commerce and Labor Charles Nagel, those members of Taft's cabinet "who were especially interested in the preparation of a bill for the forthcoming Congress," and with whom, the committee flattered itself, it was "working in close harmony."[155]

The federation committee's efforts yielded no significant results over the next two years. In that period, public debate and congressional committees continued to grapple with the search for regulatory legislation, while the Republican party's insurgent–regular breach deepened in legislative and polemical battles over Cannon's speakership powers in the House, the tariff, the corporation tax, postal savings, the Ballinger–Pinchot affair, and the Mann–Elkins Act that extended and strengthened the ICC's regulatory powers over railroads. The midterm congressional elections of 1910 gave the Democrats a sweeping victory, enough to take control of the House, in which most of those Republicans losing their seats were regulars whom Taft supported, while insurgents, whom Roosevelt backed, for the most part held on to theirs.[156]

155. Easley to E. R. Bacon, 17 Oct. 1908, Easley to Wickersham, 17 Nov. 1908, Wickersham to Easley, 18 Nov. 1908, Bancroft to Easley, 24 Nov. 1908, William C. Breed to Easley, 17 Dec. 1908, Easley to Marshall Cushing, 11 Jan. 1909, Silliman to Taft, 6 Mar. 1909, Wickersham to Silliman, 5 Apr. 1909, Silliman to Wickersham, 7 Apr. 1909, Wickersham to Silliman, 9 Apr. 1909, Silliman to Easley, 16 Apr. 1909, Easley to Samuel Mather, 3 May 1909 (quotation is from this letter), Judson to Low, 10 May 1909, Easley to Pierre S. du Pont, 11 May 1909, all in NCF.

156. James Holt, *Congressional Insurgents and the Party System, 1909–1916* (Cambridge, Mass.: Harvard University Press, 1967), pp. 16–43; Kenneth W. Hechler, *Insurgency: Personalities and Politics of the Taft Era* (New York: Columbia University Press, 1940), pp. 27–82, and passim. Cf. Paolo E. Coletta, *The Presidency of William Howard Taft* (Lawrence: The University Press of Kansas, 1973), pp. 101–120; William H. Harbaugh, *Power and Responsibility: The Life and Times of Theodore Roosevelt* (New York: Farrar, Straus & Cudahy, 1961), pp. 377–398; Henry F. Pringle, *The Life and Times of William Howard Taft: A*

The popular mood and the political situation, therefore, appeared distinctly unfavorable to mild trust legislation along Stetson–Morawetz or similar lines, and rather strongly insistent upon measures like those Roosevelt had been urging.

In early 1911, at its annual meeting, the Civic Federation authorized Low, still its president, to form a new committee on the trust question. In June 1911 he appointed the committee, which included himself as chair: James R. Garfield (now in private law practice); Talcott Williams (soon to become, the following March, the first director of the Columbia University School of Journalism, endowed by Joseph Pulitzer); William Dudley Foulke, the Indiana progressive newspaper editor (*Richmond Item*); Leo S. Rowe, University of Pennsylvania political science professor; Frederic J. Stimson, dean of the Harvard Law School; Walter George Smith, prominent Philadelphia attorney and president of the Conference of Commissioners on Uniform State Laws; and Samuel Untermyer, the New York reformer and attorney who would shortly begin to serve as general counsel of the Pujo House committee investigation of the "Money Trust." The NCF committee was one with diverse views, but also, once again, with strong Roosevelt ties, through Low, Garfield, and Foulke. Foulke, a longtime friend and adviser of Roosevelt's, was currently working with the former president in the drafting of new regulatory legislation. The committee, in turn, appointed a legislative drafting subcommittee consisting of Low, Williams, and two non-committee members, namely, Roosevelt's friend and adviser Jenks, and the eminent economist John Bates Clark. The federation groups now oriented themselves to work with, or seek to influence, the Senate Committee on Interstate Commerce, which was chaired by insurgent Republican Moses E. Clapp of Minnesota, and included insurgent Republican senators Robert M. La Follette of Wisconsin and Albert E. Cummins of Iowa, as well as Democrat Francis G. Newlands of Nevada. Newlands, who was then drafting regulatory legislation of his own, succeeded Clapp as chair after the 1912 elections and presided over the work in the Senate that would at length produce the Federal Trade Commission Act of 1914.[157]

Whatever had been the mood in Civic Federation circles in late 1908 and early 1909, by the spring of 1911 the drafting subcommittee now

Biography, 2 vols. (New York: Farrar & Rinehart, 1939), 1:538–555, 2:557–581; Pringle, *Theodore Roosevelt, A Biography* (New York: Harcourt Brace, 1931), pp. 525–544.

157. Low to Dear Sir, 3 June 1911, Low to Dear Sir, [?] Oct. 1911, Easley to Dear Sir, 31 July 1911, Low to Dear Sir, 8 Nov. 1911, Low, Clark, Jenks, Williams to [Dear Sir], [ca. Feb. 1912], Walter G. Smith to Low, 24 Mar. 1913, all in SL, Box 106, NCF, Trust Miscellaneous Data, #1 and #2 (hereafter cited as NCF, TMD).

found itself unable to depart from a registration-license scheme resembling the provisions of the Hepburn bill. The larger committee was divided, with a strong opinion against such a measure well represented and favoring instead the legalization of reasonable restraints of trade coupled with a provision for publicity. As Judson had put it earlier, in support of a bill along Stetson–Morawetz lines, the law "should be construed as applying only to contracts and combinations unenforceable at common law," which would allow "the largest liberty of business association, subject to the requirement of publicity ... for the prevention of abuses."[158] But by the time the subcommittee began its work, in June 1911, the Supreme Court had already handed down its Rule of Reason decisions in the Standard Oil and American Tobacco cases, rendering superfluous an amendment of the Sherman Act to legalize reasonable restraints of trade. Given the state of popular opinion and the impact of Roosevelt's past position on the trusts, reinforced by his current pronouncements and arguments in the *Outlook* and elsewhere, not to mention Senator La Follette's strong presidential campaigning and a notable rise in a socialistic tide of opinion, a mere publicity measure could not command political credibility. Low now told the committee members, "It is proposed to consider the whole question in the light of the recent decisions of the Supreme Court of the United States."[159]

The drafting subcommittee of Low, Clark, Jenks, and Williams proceeded in the fall of 1911, with some deference to the divided opinion within the larger committee, by preparing another questionnaire and sending it "to some twenty thousand representative men – manufacturers, farmers, wholesale and retail merchants, lawyers, bankers, political eoncomists, labor leaders, officials of Chambers of Commerce and Boards of Trade ... [and] to all classes of organizations directly affected by existing legislation." The formulating, circulating, and processing of the questionnaire resulted in a draft bill by February 1912.[160]

158.　Judson to Low, 10 May 1909, NCF; to similar effect, W. G. Smith to Low, 24 Mar. 1913, SL, Box 106, NCF, TMD, #2.

159.　Low to Dear Sir, 3 June 1911, SL, Box 106, NCF, TMD, #1.

160.　Low to Dear Sir, 8 Nov. 1911, with enclosure, "Questionnaire," BC, G.F. 324–1; also typescript copy of letter dated Oct. 1911 (no day), and Questionnaire, dated 31 Oct. 1911, with handwritten emendations, at SL, Box 106, NCF, TMD, #1; and Low, Clark, Jenks, Williams to [Dear Sir], [ca. Feb. 1912], SL, Box 106, NCF, TMD, #2. See *The Trust Problem: Replies of 16,000 Representative Americans to a Questionnaire Sent Out by Department on Regulation of Industrial Corporations of the National Civic Federation*, compiled and edited by Henry Mann (New York: National Civic Federation, 1912), which consists of a short introduction (pp. 5–8) and about six hundred pages of excerpts, without analysis, from the replies,

The draft bill elicited debates within the larger committee and among a wider NCF circle over the desirability and feasibility of devising a regulatory system based upon the license-registration model. By this time, effective political opinion in the country at large divided similarly: It generally agreed with the proposition, long urged by Roosevelt, that regulation of the market could not be left to the courts alone, but must be administered to a large degree by an executive agency in the form of an interstate trade commission; but it disagreed over whether the powers of a trade commission must include those of a license-registration authority. The anti-license position was represented, for example, by the proposed interstate trade commission bill of the Chicago Association of Commerce; the pro-license position by Senator Newlands's proposed trade commission bill, which he introduced in Congress in July 1911.[161]

The NCF drafting subcommittee, not surprisingly, given its closeness to both Roosevelt and Newlands, produced a pro-license bill. Any predisposition in that direction on the part of Jenks and Williams may well have been reinforced by Clark. As one of America's leading mar-

classified by occupation. The introduction stated (p. 5) that the Civic Federation had sent out 30,000 questionnaires, in two series, one to capitalists and officers of commercial, labor, and other organizations, the other to educators, editors, political economists, lawyers, publicists, and statisticians. It summarized the replies by noting their general agreement that "the principle embodied in the Sherman Law is in accord with almost universal popular sentiment and that the people are determined that 'big business' shall be controlled and regulated." Less universally agreed upon, according to the introduction, but representing "a considerable majority of manufacturers, merchants, bankers, lawyers, educators and editors, and a large proportion of labor representatives," was the idea of establishing a system of federal licensing or incorporation of enterprises engaged in interstate commerce. On the other hand, "a large percentage of the replies" favored an interstate trade commission, "but comparatively few express themselves in favor of control of prices by the commission," while a "'return to old competitive methods in business' is overwhelmingly rejected as not feasible – practically an acknowledgment that combination has come to stay." Ibid., p. 8. Some historians have cited the NCF questionnaire and replies as evidence of widespread business support for a license or incorporation plan along lines proposed by Roosevelt (e.g., Kolko, *Triumph*, p. 256; Weinstein, *Corporate Ideal*, pp. 87–88), but taken in the detailed historical context, and as indicated by the quotations above, it is more accurate to understand them as expressing a broad consensus in favor of trade commission regulation that might include a license or incorporation feature, but not a degree of government control of the economy then envisaged by Roosevelt.

161. Chicago Association of Commerce, "Resolutions, Report of Committee and Form of Bill, Prepared for and adopted by this Association ... upon the question of Anti-Trust Legislation," n.d., at SL, Box 106, NCF, TMD #1. Newlands bill: S. 2941, 62d, 1st, 5 July 1911, at Senate Committee on Interstate Commerce, *Federal Trade Commission*, Senate Report No. 597, 63d, 2d, Calendar No. 518, 13 June 1914, app., pp.15–19, filed at SL, Box 105, NCF, Trust Bills #1, hereafter cited as Sen. Rep. 597 (1911).

ginal utility economists, Clark had since the turn of the century argued that the large corporation was the inevitable outcome of economic evolution; that it was essential to American competition with British and other European rivals for foreign markets and investment outlets; that its superior efficiencies, if not obstructed by unfair practices or unreasonable restraints of trade, would distribute to each factor of production a just recompense at fair prices and proper returns; and that to assure that outcome, in the absence of the old-style competition among myriad small enterprises, and as an alternative to a stultifying socialist nationalization of ownership, the national government must closely regulate the large corporation through a strong executive commission.[162] Apart from his marginal utility axioms, Clark's views were, in these respects, similar to those of Jenks and Roosevelt.

The subcommittee's draft bill would expand the Bureau of Corporations into an interstate trade commission. All large corporations, defined as those with a gross annual revenue of $10 million or more, as revealed in their tax returns under the corporation tax law of 1909, and estimated to number between two hundred and five hundred, would be required to receive a federal license from the commission as a condition of engaging in interstate or foreign commerce. The commission would have the power to revoke license for cause. Large corporations would be required to register with the commission, submitting prescribed information, supplemented by annual reports. They would then be required to submit to the commission for its approval or disapproval their "trade agreements," defined as "any agreement relating to or affecting competition," that is, for all practical purposes, all their agreements, contracts, and combinations. The commission's power to revoke license and its rulings on agreements would be subject to judicial review. The filing of the agreements, whether approved or disapproved, would exempt the corporation from criminal prosecution, thereby making the Sherman Act to that extent a civil rather than a criminal statute. All other corporations and businesses with annual revenues under $10 million might voluntarily file their trade agreements with the commission for approval or disapproval, and in so doing be relieved of criminal liability without having to apply for a license. In the months following the bill's drafting, spanning the presidential election campaign of 1912, Wilson's victory, his inauguration and first several months in office, the drafting subcommittee circulated the draft bill among capital-

---

162. Clark, *The Distribution of Wealth* (1899); discussion of his views at Joseph Dorfman, *The Economic Mind in American Civilization*, vol. 3: 1865–1918 (New York: Viking, 1959), 3, pp. 188–195; see also Clark, "Education and the Socialistic Movement," *Atlantic Monthly*, Oct. 1908, pp. 433–441.

ists, lawyers, experts, and other interested persons for comment and debate, received written responses, held conferences, and revised the bill.[163]

Sent out in February 1913, on the eve of Wilson's presidential inauguration, the bill sharpened debate over the extent of state dictation of corporate structure and operations in a proper regulation of the market. It tended to clarify, on the one hand, a consensus of opinion in favor of establishing an interstate trade commission in the federal executive, and, on the other hand, a basic division of opinion between those favoring a commission presiding over and administering a license-

---

163. Copies of bill, with handwritten and typed emendations by Marburg, Jenks, Low, and others; Low, Clark, Jenks, Williams to [Dear Sir], [ca. Feb. 1912]; H. K. Smith to Low, 27 Apr. 1912, estimating the number of the larger corporations at 200 to 500; "Letters re Trust Bill Examined by Committee, March 26, 1913," dated various days in March 1913, and more letters, dated in March, April, and May 1913; all in SL, Box 105, NCF, Trust Bills, #2 and #3, and Box 106, NCF, TMD, #1 and #2. As an example of conferences held on the bill: "Invited to Trust Luncheon at Midday Club, March 18, 1913," SL Box 106, NCF, TMD, #1. In addition to Low, Clark, Jenks, Williams, and Easley, those on the list of invitees included: Edgar A. Bancroft, August Belmont, George B. Cortelyou, James R. Garfield, John Hays Hammond, Adolph Lewisohn, V. Everit Macy, Marcus M. Marks, Ogden L. Mills, Gilbert H. Montague, George W. Perkins, J. G. Schmidlapp, Isaac N. Seligman, Francis L. Stetson, Henry W. Taft, Samuel Untermyer, Theodore N. Vail.

In sending out the draft bill, the subcommittee requested from recipients their opinion on two collateral proposed amendments of the Sherman Act, which, they stated, were "not absolutely essential" but were "formulated for the purpose of helping to determine whether public opinion wishes to prevent monopolizing in trade and industry, at all costs." The first amendment would provide for the forfeiture to the United States, for seizure and condemnation, in full or in part, of any property owned by a person and "used or intended to be used in or in connection with any business" in a monopolizing enterprise, or in an attempt to monopolize, or in a conspiracy to monopolize. The proceedings were to be similar to those provided by law for seizure and condemnation of property illegally imported into the United States. Section 6 of the Sherman Act provided for forfeiture, seizure, and condemnation of goods in transit in interstate or foreign commerce that were involved in a restraint of trade or monopoly. This provision in the proposed bill would presumably render the entire enterprise forfeit to the United States government for seizure and condemnation. The second amendment, intended to remove "all doubt, if there be now any such doubt" in the wake of the Rule of Reason decisions, "that 'restraint of trade,' as used in the statute, is not the equivalent of 'restraint of competition,'" would add to the Sherman Act's prohibition of restraints of trade and monopoly the words "if it shall impair the efficiency or potentiality of competition." "In other words," the subcommittee explained, the trade commission "must be empowered to exercise discretion in determining whether a given trade agreement is or is not repugnant to the Sherman Law." Respondents generally opposed the first proposed amendment as extremely drastic; and although not objecting to the second, many doubted the likelihood that Congress could be brought to pass it. The proposed amendments and quotations from the subcommittee's discussion of them are at Low, Clark, Jenks, Williams to [Dear Sir], [ca. Feb. 1912], SL, Box 106, NCF, TMD, #2.

registration system, and those favoring a commission that might gather information and disseminate publicity but whose authority extended no farther than policing the market against unfair practices and unreasonable restraints of trade, without a license-registration system.

Expressing the latter view, for example, in late March 1913, soon after Wilson's inauguration, Walter George Smith, member of both the larger NCF committee on trust legislation and the federation's executive committee, wrote to Low at length. Having considered the draft bill for over a month since receiving it from the subcommittee, Smith said, "I have been hesitant about reaching any hard and fast conclusion upon this important subject," but although satisfied that the bill "expresses the idea ... clearly and distinctly" of creating an interstate trade commission "with the powers and duties" for which it provides, Smith now felt it necessary to state "My doubt ... as to the wisdom of passing any such acts." He acknowledged the existence of "the strongest tendency towards governmental regulation of business" in the country's recent politics and public opinion, a tendency in favor of making government, in the words Smith quoted from an editorial in the *Philadelphia Public Ledger* of 23 February, "'the active and intimate supervisor of trusts under a licensing system.'" Smith agreed with the editorial, however, "that the plan would surely create a great bureaucracy 'with the result that the government would be perpetually in multifarious business, while the business [interests] would ultimately own the government.'"[164]

The Philadelphia lawyer was "well aware of the inconvenience at present existing" in business transactions from "the doubts and uncertainties" as to the meaning of the law, but in considering the various current trade commission proposals, including that of the subcommittee, he had concluded that "the remedy to my mind is worse than the disease." A distinction must be made, he urged, between public utilities and general business enterprise. "The arguments to be drawn from the success of the interstate commerce [commission] law I do not think apply to private business. Public service corporations, such as railroads," Smith argued, "present problems different from those arising from private business corporations engaged in interstate commerce." Hence, Smith advised, with the Supreme Court's Rule of Reason decisions of 1911 in mind, "it would be better to await the effect on business of the interpretations of the Sherman Act that are gradually being given by the Supreme Court ... before resorting to government regulation of all interstate commerce [corporations] employing capital

164. W. G. Smith to Low, 24 Mar. 1913, SL, Box 106, NCF, TMD, #2.

of $10,000,000 or over." Accordingly, "the policy adopted by the last [Taft] administration, and which is being followed out by the present [Wilson] one, of a firm, consistent enforcement of the Sherman Act interpreted by the rule of reason, will meet the difficulties of the case."[165] In other words, as Smith saw it, judicial regulation of the market through enforcement of the Sherman Act as now reconstrued by the Supreme Court, was the alternative to state direction of the market resulting in either government control of business, on the left, or business control of government, on the right.

Smith therefore advised strongly against "any license law at present." That kind of legislation, he held, represented a dangerous departure from traditional American principles of government-market relations. "Until we give up entirely our traditional views of the scope of the Federal Government's sphere of action," he wrote, "I do not see how we can urge the enactment of such legislation as that embodied in the Sub-committee's bill." More specifically, Smith argued, fearing more the potential outcome to the left than to the right, "It may be that we shall be forced to come eventually to a licensing of interstate commerce," but as licensing alone did "not succeed in attaining the object" expected by the public, it would very likely be "followed by a regulation of prices." The license system and its implications, therefore, amounted to "a far step towards a socialized state," Smith concluded, "and I do not believe in it."[166]

With such considerations in mind, Wall Street attorney Gilbert H. Montague, who was also prominent in the affairs of the Merchants' Association of New York, wrote to Low two weeks later, in opposition to the subcommittee's draft bill, and in support instead of a new nonlicense draft bill that Morawetz was currently presenting to the Senate Interstate Commerce Committee. "My feeling is," he stated to Low, "that ... you and the [NCF] Committee will become convinced that the license feature is not essential to an effective Interstate Trade Commission."[167] In detaching the trade commission idea from the license idea, Montague's formulation represented a redefinition of the alternatives more politically practical than those preferred by Walter G. Smith, and one that would ultimately find implementation in legislation.

The subcommittee, however, could not yet bring itself to renounce the license system in some form, but the response to its draft bill led it

165. Ibid. As will be remembered, the $10 million standard in the bill referred to annual revenues, not, as mistakenly stated by Smith, to capital employed.
166. Ibid.
167. Montague (40 Wall Street, New York City) to Low, 7 Apr. 1913, SL, Box 106, NCF, TMD, #2.

to revise the bill to tone down the license-registration requirements. By mid-December 1913, it had produced a new draft that removed from the license authority of an interstate trade commission the comprehensive powers over all "trade agreements" that had been the centerpiece of the earlier draft. Earlier drafts had also provided for refusal or revocation of license on account of interlocking directorates between competing firms or between shippers and common carriers, on account of discriminatory prices or buying or selling practices, on account of state incorporation laws insufficiently rigorous in barring improper business practices, and on account of the trade commission's finding on its own, and without judicial process, any violation of the Sherman Act or of decrees issued by courts upon convictions under the act. Except for those relating to discriminatory pricing and practices, these provisions were cut from the subcommittee's later draft of mid-December.[168]

Low, Clark, Jenks, and Williams circulated the draft bill once again, with a covering letter in which they blended an appeal to those who favored a tough regulatory measure with an appeal to those who wanted eased conditions for large corporations, certainty of law, and a moderate provision for regulation and publicity.[169] In general, the subcommittee's position now represented some movement away from that of Roosevelt and toward what would emerge as that of Wilson. The bill still provided for a licensing scheme that applied compulsorily to the two hundred to five hundred large nonfinancial corporations with $10 million or more in annual gross revenues, not including common carriers but including pipelines. It still provided, also, for voluntary filing of agreements with the commission by smaller businesses. The Bureau of Corporations would be detached from the Department of Commerce (a new, separate Department of Labor having been established in 1913), and transformed into an independent interstate trade commission consisting of seven commissioners. As the condition of engaging in interstate or foreign trade, the large corporation must register with the commission, giving detailed information and submitting annual reports

168. "Confidential. Proposal for a Bill ..." Handwritten at top of first page: "Criticisms of Theodore Marburg. Brussells" (Marburg was serving as U.S. minister to Belgium, on appointment by President Taft); "Confidential. Proposal for a Bill ..." Handwritten at top of first page: "Mr. Low's copy." Low excised these provisions on his copy, although Marburg retained them and on the margin next to some of them had handwritten, "Highly important." SL, Box 105, NCF, Trust Bills, #2. Also, "Confidential. Dec. 8, 1913. Proposal for a Bill ..." Handwritten at top of first page: "S.L.'s copy" [Low's copy], and "Confidential. Dec. 16, 1913. Proposal for a Bill ..." SL, Box 105, NCF, Trust Bills, #3.
169. Low, Clark, Jenks, Williams to Dear Sir, 9 Dec. 1913, SL, Box 105, NCF Trust Bills #3.

as prescribed by the commission, make all its accounts, books, and records freely accessible at all times to the commission, and appear before the commission to give testimony as the commission might require, for all of which purposes the commission was to have full subpoena powers. The commission could refuse or revoke license for violation of the Sherman Act or other laws, or for discriminatory pricing or buying or selling practices. A licensed corporation would have to submit to the commission for its approval any increase in capital stock, including an increase associated with a merger, and if a corporation made such increase without the commission's approval, it would be subject to forfeiture of license. The commission could issue cease and desist orders against discountenanced practices, and order payment of damages to injured parties. Failure to comply with any orders, or with registration requirements, would result in cancellation or revocation of license.[170]

The trade commission could specify the forms of accounts and records to be kept by a licensed corporation, and the corporation could not keep another set of accounts or records. Violations of the law were made punishable by fines and/or imprisonment. The commission could act on complaints or initiate its own investigations and actions. Its findings would be *prima facie* evidence in court. It could recommend prosecutions to the attorney general under the Sherman Act or the trade commission act, and it could initiate prosecutions itself. The commission, serving the courts as a master in chancery, might lend advice concerning, and also supervise, the enforcement of convictions under the Sherman Act or other statutes relating to restraint of trade, including measures of dissolution or reorganization of corporations, and it could in the process appoint receivers or sell property involved. All of the commission's orders or decisions were to be subject to judicial review.[171]

In their covering letter, Low, Clark, Jenks, and Williams emphasized similarities between the draft bill and the Interstate Commerce Act, including the fact that some sections and phrases of the bill were taken verbatim from the act. This was to suggest the toughness of the bill, as representing "an effort to apply to general commercial business the methods of regulation which have worked so well as applied by the Interstate Commerce Commission to the regulation of common carriers." The subcommittee particularly cited the bill's provision for the

170. "Confidential. Dec. 8, 1913. Proposal for a Bill ...," and "Confidential. Dec. 16, 1913. Proposal for a Bill ...," SL, Box 105, NCF Trust Bills #3.
171. Ibid.

revocation of license in case of discriminatory pricing, buying, or selling, so that just as the ICC had been enabled "to put an end to rebating and every other unfair practice in railroading," so the trade commission would be enabled "to smoke out and put an end to any unfair practice in connection with ordinary commercial business." Nevertheless, the bill would not give the trade commission price-making powers (to parallel the ICC's rate-making powers), nor would it require, as in previous proposed bills and in earlier drafts of this bill, the submission of all agreements, contracts, and combinations for the commission's approval. On the other hand, the bill did retain commission power to disapprove increases in capital stock, including those involving mergers, and hence authority in the area of investment strategy.[172]

The subcommittee stated that in preparing the bill it had acted upon two assumptions: that the Sherman Act "will remain on the statute books substantially unchanged," and that as recently interpreted by the Supreme Court in the Rule of Reason decisions, the Sherman Act "forbids restraint of trade but not necessarily all restraint of competition." In an accurate reading of judicial construction, the subcommittee explained the second assumption to mean that the Sherman Act was "specifically aimed at all restraint of competition which is brought about either by monopolizing or by unfair practices," but the law "does not assume that restraint of competition and restraint of trade are synonymous terms."[173]

This led the subcommittee to the conciliatory aspect of the bill: securing publicity and establishing certainty of the law in the market. The bill would "secure publicity on the widest scale." In the process, it would not only deter business malpractice but relieve business of the risk of civil or criminal penalty by authorizing the federal commission to "give to the business man the benefit of its findings as to the legality" of current or proposed operations, with the opportunity to revise those the commission disapproved. The commission, therefore, "far from being an agency of the arbitrary control of business," would act as "an agency to help business men to determine whether what they are doing, or proposing to do, is probably lawful or unlawful." By placing the largest corporations under the license authority of a federal commission, and inviting smaller businesses to file their contracts and agreements voluntarily, the bill would contribute toward establishing a uniform law of trade in place of a "governmental chaos" of multiple state incorporation laws. By "seeking to put an end to all competition that is

---

172. Low, Clark, Jenks, Williams to Dear Sir, 9 Dec. 1913, SL, Box 105, NCF Trust Bills #3.
173. Ibid.

unfair," the bill would help secure for both capital and the public throughout the nation "the benefits of such competition as is fair."[174]

In summary, by early 1914 the Civic Federation subcommittee had moved closer, although by no means all the way, to a legislative position that the Wilson administration was moving toward and would adopt in the Federal Trade Commission legislation passed later that year. The subcommittee's position, as embodied in the bill, stood somewhere between Roosevelt and Wilson. The bill still retained a relatively strong license feature, with provision for government authority over some investment activity. But it would also have limited a trade commission's direct control of business transactions, as compared with previous draft bills, and expanded its sphere of indirect supervision through its counseling of corporations, its enforcing the Sherman Act as construed in the Rule of Reason decisions, and its monitoring against unfair methods of competition. In these latter respects, the bill resembled the Federal Trade Commission act as finally passed.

At the Bureau of Corporations, Herbert Knox Smith continued in the post of commissioner under the new president. His uninterrupted tenure signified Taft's policy, from the outset of his term to his break with Roosevelt, of maintaining continuity with the previous administration in the matter of regulating the market, as in other matters. Taft himself, in his public statements and in his official messages to Congress, through 1911, continued to recommend and support proposals for a trade commission with license or incorporation powers as the preferred method of market regulation. Although at Interior he replaced Garfield, who had been important in regulatory policy-planning under Roosevelt, with Richard A. Ballinger, Taft appointed as secretary of commerce and labor, presiding over the bureau, Charles Nagel, who was a strong advocate of regulating the market through an executive trade commission administering a license or incorporation system. Similarly, Taft's attorney general, George W. Wickersham, favored rigorous federal regulation of large corporations, both by judicial enforcement of the Sherman Act and by trade commission coupled with federal incorporation or license.[175]

174. Ibid.
175. H. K. Smith to Garfield, 15 Apr. 1911, JRG, Box 120, Special Correspondence File: Herbert Knox Smith. 1911 (hereafter cited as Box 120: SCF). Also, e.g., Nagel to William C. Adamson (chair, House Committee on Interstate and Foreign Commerce), 27 June 1911, and Taft to Nagel, 27 June 1911, BC, G.F. 5596; Wickersham, address, Duluth, Minn., 19 July 1911, at Sen. Rep. 597 (1914), app., pp. 27–28. As a St. Louis corporation lawyer, Nagel had been counsel to the brewery capitalist Adolphus Busch. Cf. Pringle, *Life and Times*, 2, pp. 156–177; Coletta, *Presidency*, pp. 50, 153–165.

The Taft administration, then, presented a congenial environment to a Roosevelt loyalist intent upon promoting the former president's regulatory policies. Herbert Knox Smith remained the loyalist, but with an intent on regulatory policy that had for some time diverged from that of Roosevelt. Smith and Garfield stayed in close touch with Roosevelt, Smith from within the Taft administration and Garfield from his private law practice in Cleveland, Ohio, but their reservations concerning the implications of federal license-registration or incorporation powers had grown stronger in the course of the Hepburn bill debates and continued to do so in the ensuing months. As early as toward the end of 1908, for example, New York attorney and NCF associate William C. Breed reported to Easley that he had had a long talk with Smith in Washington and had found that "his ideas are very much softened over those held by him last year."[176] The softening was, rather, a matter of his expressing to others the misgivings about due process, centralized power, and government direction of business operations, which he previously had been expressing confidentially to Garfield and Roosevelt.

Into the eleventh hour of his presidency, Roosevelt continued to solicit Smith's counsel on federal incorporation. As in the past, so, for example, in the case of a draft bill Roosevelt sent over to him for comment in January 1909, Smith advised against it.[177] Smith once again addressed the complex constitutional question of the proper line between federal jurisdiction and state police power. He advised that carefully drawn, federal chartering of production corporations could stand the constitutional test if based not on a principle of production with intent to engage in interstate commerce, but on the principle of production as "a necessary incidental to commerce and thus a 'necessary and proper' part thereof." Nevertheless, he cautioned that federal incorporation touched an area in which the "constitutional powers of Congress" were still "not sufficiently clear," and that it would involve a "disturbance of State powers of police and taxation," which, being "extremely great," would raise formidable opposition to federal regulation in such form or ensnare it in protracted legal dispute. Having disposed of the constitutional issue, Smith proceeded on policy grounds to argue against federal incorporation of general business enterprise, citing the need to distinguish between public service and general business corporations, and the dangers of centralized national power. As

176. William C. Breed to Easley, 17 Dec. 1908, NCF.
177. William Loeb, Jr., to Smith, 23 Jan. 1909, enclosing a copy of a federal incorporation bill, and stating, "The President wishes you to send him a report on this as soon as possible." Smith to Roosevelt, 25 Jan. 1909. Both at BC, G.F. 5553–2.

Smith put it, although national policy might "come to a system of Federal incorporation of railroads and carriers ... not very far in the future, I do not think that we are yet in any position where we can attempt to establish a *general* Federal incorporation law for all corporations." It was, he thought, "sufficient for the Federal Government to consider the best method of regulating corporations organized under State charters," for federal incorporation would represent an "advance toward centralization ... [which] would be certainly too sweeping to be approved by present public opinion."[178]

In the next several months, with Roosevelt away on safari, and with legislative efforts respecting regulation of business other than common carriers relatively quiescent, Smith's thinking about the government-market relation settled more and more firmly upon distinguishing public service from general business enterprise, and indirect regulation of the market through publicity and monitoring from direct government management of market transactions. In the process, he became less sure of what he thought might constitute appropriate regulatory legislation, with doubts even about the desirability of establishing an independent trade commission to replace the Bureau of Corporations.

His state of mind by early 1910 may be viewed in an exchange of letters with the prominent corporation lawyer Charles P. Howland of the Wall Street law firm of Howland, Murray & Prentice.[179] Howland wrote that aside from the constitutional questions, government regulation of the market under modern conditions raised the prospect that "the processes of centralization in a country of such great extent as ours may easily be carried too far." Noting that "the bureaucratic administrations of [the European] continental countries do not extend over such a [large] country as ours," Howland feared that the officials of "a central government naturally desire to exercise and extend the central power," and that in the United States "there is a continuous tendency in that direction." Measures intended "to check the savagery and licentiousness of current business methods or of ruthless individuals seem to be excellent expedients," Howland acknowledged, but taken together with the size and power of large corporations, "they tend to further economic and governmental centralization, and in the long run create further dangers." The centralizing tendency was "likely to lead to inevitable results," such as those "outlined in a suggestive book by Mr.

178. Smith to Roosevelt, 25 Jan. 1909, BC, G.F. 5553–2. Smith's emphasis.
179. The law firm, at 33 Wall Street, New York City, consisted of partners Howland, George Welwood Murray, E. Parmalee Prentice, and William E. S. Griswold; letterhead, Howland to Smith, 4 Mar. 1910, BC, G.F.? (Stamped "Bureau of Corporations, Answered APR 13 1910").

Brooks Adams 'Civilization and Decay,' – a book whose conclusions are not to be dismissed, whatever one thinks of some of his premisses." "That the centralizing tendency itself is inevitable would be a discouraging admission," thought Howland, but he hoped, "not a necessary one."[180]

Smith, too, was troubled by the centralizing tendency and the implications of a government-directed economy. He was no less concerned, at the same time, with the economically and socially deleterious effects of concentrated market power represented by the large corporations. The question was, how to make market power socially responsible, politically benign, and economically efficient, without resort to direct state ownership or control.

Smith pondered Howland's letter for well over a month, along with the lawyer's recent *Columbia Law Review* article, "Monopolies: The Cause and the Remedy," in which Howland advocated limiting the size and power of corporations by legislation restricting the amount of their capitalization and forbidding intercorporate stockholding. As "a private citizen," the commissioner wrote in reply, he might agree with Howland's remedy, but as a government official who gave "practically all my time to considering the facts of corporate business," and who was responsible for formulating "constructive policy which shall be immediately practicable," he must look to "the 'next step,' without attempting, even to myself, to lay down any final result or ultimate system." He had come to the conclusion at this point that the "next step" should not go beyond "centralized publicity, organized on a permanent basis, and made efficient by such treatment as will make the facts of corporate business available for the man in the street."[181]

This was not "a final step," but it had the virtue of not constituting "any such positive regulation of business operations as would, in the complexity of those operations, make possible serious mistakes," while providing for "that primary essential for avoiding mistakes, to wit, complete and accurate information." Publicity would improve the standing of "meritorious corporate securities," as the ICC's supervision "has already done for railroad securities." But "most important of all," Smith stated, "effective publicity" would exert "a restraint upon improper methods of business," because public opinion, "when intelligent

---

180. Ibid. Punctuation and spelling as in original. Brooks Adams's book was *The Law of Civilization and Decay: An Essay on History*, originally published by Macmillan in 1896.

181. Smith to Howland, 15 Apr. 1910, BC, G.F.? (Stamped "Bureau of Corporations, Answered APR 15 1910").

and concentrated, is a very effective force." The restraint of public opinion would subject corporations to "the effectiveness of potential competition," the principle that underlay the common-law concept of restraint of trade, as well as Jenks's concept of profit discipline guiding the behavior of "capitalist monopolies," and in which, Smith now told Howland, "I do have more faith than you." Publicity, Smith held, combined with laws keeping "the highways of commerce ... equally open," and eliminating "all forms of rebates, discriminations and unfair competition," would assure that "the struggle becomes a purely evolutionary one for the survival of the fittest, with a perfectly fair field."[182]

Smith's choice of words should not be misread as indicating some "social Darwinist" nostalgia for the old competitive regime; that would have made him a strange ally of Roosevelt's indeed. Rather, he was groping for a way to reconcile large-scale enterprise with efficiency and public acceptance without resorting to a state-directed market. "That some degree of control should be exercised by the Government over corporate operations seems to me entirely justifiable," he wrote. The "community" established corporations, giving them "great and peculiar powers and exemptions not granted to the individual." The community therefore was "responsible" for any resulting evil, and was "entitled to restrain and limit its creatures." Indeed, Smith noted, as Howland, too, had observed in his article, "our large corporations are now exercising in many cases what might be called a quasi-governmental function," with the danger that the "old distinction between private and public service corporations is practically disappearing." If a railroad was, as all admitted, "a public service corporation," then "if one can only buy one's oil or tobacco or other staple from one particular corporation, is not that concern also in essence a public service company?" And would not the same classification apply to corporations "based on the ownership of a natural monopoly, such as the supply of minerals, water power, forests or lands"? The principle of potential competition would not apply in such "special cases." Smith acknowledged his deep state of perplexity. "I would not at present venture to offer any suggestion"; he would not "assume the position of dogmatizing on this subject." On the contrary, he confessed, "When it comes to arriving at conclusions that I am willing to stand by, I am filled with misgivings." Requesting that his words be treated "as confidential," he told Howland, "Practically the only general conclusion that I have reached, of which I am certain, is

182. Ibid.

the desirability of a definite system of Federal publicity," through which "our citizens should be educated not only in the 'three R's,' but also in the essential facts of finance, production and distribution."[183]

With the quickening of legislative activity on business regulation, after the congressional elections of 1910, Smith entered into advisory consultations with Senator Francis G. Newlands of Nevada, who now, as the senior Democratic member of the Senate Interstate Commerce Committee, was taking a leading role in the drafting of an interstate trade commission bill. By the spring of 1911, Newlands had emerged as a proponent of legislation that would combine the establishment of an interstate trade commission with a federal license system, that is, legislation very much similar in content to that favored by Roosevelt, but about which Smith and Garfield had been entertaining serious doubts.

In mid-April 1911, Smith reported to Garfield that Senator Newlands favored the commission idea, that the administration had not "gotten away" from the "Wickersham Federal incorporation idea," that Secretary Nagel "has spoken in favor of it a number of times recently," and that although the incorporation proposal "hasn't a ghost of a show in Congress," nevertheless, "as long as that still has any life in it, it is pretty hard to take up anything else." Smith was trying to move Newlands away from supporting a commission with strong powers over the market, and toward something, instead, "along the lines of a publicity bill," that is, a Bureau of Corporations with expanded authority for developing information and publicity of corporations' affairs. In one respect, "I think he has come over to our point of view," Smith informed Garfield, "namely, that prosecution and publicity must be kept separate." But the Senator was "still desirous of creating some sort of a board or commission in connection with this Bureau," on the grounds that "it would give the Bureau's work a stronger standing with the public, even in the matter of publicity, while, of course, if any judicial functions are added, it would give such decisions greater weight." Smith's "difficulty," he told Garfield, was that "the Senator seems still set on the board idea; I want to keep his support for the publicity feature, and I don't know quite how the thing will work out yet."[184]

---

183. Ibid. Also, Smith to Leo S. Rowe, 25 May 1912, BC, G.F. 6161, criticizing the deep-rooted American belief in individualistic self-interest, and stating the need for "positive collective action by the body politic" in economic and business affairs as the condition of "national advance." Cf. Nagel to Adamson, 27 June 1911, BC, G.F. 5596, for similar views on the need for federal power over interstate corporations.
184. Smith to Garfield, 15 Apr. 1911, JRG, Box 120: SCF.

Smith pointed out to Newlands that "the question is thus reduced to the problem whether it is desirable at the present time to give to this Bureau any judicial functions, or, in fact, to have the Government exercise any such functions as to industrial corporations at present." Smith was "inclined to answer this in the negative," for two reasons, one, involving the distinction between public service and general business, and the other, the potential of a commission with judicial functions to develop directive powers over the market. With respect to the first reason, Smith argued that he did not think "that we are yet in a position to exercise such functions" in the economy at large. Smith emphasized to Newlands "the distinction between the I.C.C. and this Bureau"; the ICC's judicial functions applied to "a comparatively simple set of conditions" common to "one business, thoroughly standardized all over the country," which although "controlled by different corporations," nevertheless dealt in "only one commodity (or service)," and, not of least importance, was "affected by the peculiar characteristics of a public service business." In contrast, "the case of industrials" presented a situation in which "business facts are extremely diverse" and were "in no way standardized." It would be a "very difficult and perhaps an impossible thing" to attempt "even to standardize their accounting." The relation of costs to earnings "varies with varying circumstances to a degree to which it does not in the railroad business," and although "some of the great industrials are practically public service companies, the vast majority are not."[185]

As his second reason, Smith objected "to the imposition of judicial functions in the shape of any board," because he had become convinced that "no matter how innocuous might be the functions" given to a commission, once a bill to establish such a commission were introduced, "it would serve as a peg upon which to hang amendments of a very radical sort before its passage, giving very broad and drastic judicial powers." Hence, although Smith might favor a bill to establish a commission with "some very modest judicial functions, if I were sure it would go through in that shape," he feared that given the temper of public opinion in current circumstances, "on the contrary, ... it would probably be developed into something very impractical and very drastic."[186]

In the following month, May 1911, the Supreme Court handed down its Rule of Reason decisions in the Standard Oil and American Tobacco cases. Smith and Garfield applauded them as restoring the Sherman Act

185. Ibid.
186. Ibid.

to the meaning for which they had long contended. As Smith wrote to Garfield, "I am satisfied that the [Standard Oil] decision establishes exactly the distinction that you and I have always insisted upon as being necessary to make this law workable."[187]

The decisions materially changed the political situation, in their sharpening the sense of urgency among those concerned with drafting regulatory legislation. Anti-corporate populists in Congress responded to the decisions in outrage, demanding the rewriting of the law to smash all large corporations. As Smith complained to Garfield, "The radical element, representing those who have extreme faith in anti-trust legislation generally, are very much disturbed by the [Standard Oil] decision, and some dozen bills have already been introduced, in substance amending the Sherman law so that it shall cover all combinations 'whether reasonable or unreasonable.'"[188]

Both Roosevelt and the National Civic Federation leaders saw the Court's decisions and the reactions to it as enhancing political receptivity to renewed legislative initiatives. The Civic Federation's committees on trust legislation swung into action, as we have seen, and Roosevelt now took up the drafting of new legislation in earnest, in consultation with Garfield, Gifford Pinchot, and Foulke, the latter of whom was serving on the NCF's trust legislation committee.

President Taft, for his part, welcomed the Court's common-law construction of the Sherman Act as judicially sound, and also as laying the basis for an alternative to a state-controlled economy, which he opposed in principle and would oppose politically, in public, as his break with Roosevelt became irrevocable.[189] The Court's decisions permitted Sherman Act prosecutions against any and all of the great corporations – something that would appeal to "radicals," satisfy liberals and conservatives opposed to state direction of the economy by an administrative bureaucracy, and undercut Roosevelt – without threatening the large-corporate organization of the economy as such. In aid of this position, Taft needed to head off legislation that might restore the non-common-law construction of the Sherman Act. A bill providing for a commission with authority limited largely to publicity with moderate policing powers would well serve the purpose. Smith had been restrained from engaging in bill-drafting activity over the previous two years of the Taft administration; he now received a green light from

187. Smith to Garfield, 23 May 1911, JRG, Box 120: SCF.
188. Ibid.
189. See Chapter 5, under "Taft."

Secretary Nagel "to take up with Senator Newlands and others my original suggestion for a voluntary publicity act."[190]

Smith now moved into close consultations with Senator Newlands. Smith wanted legislation that would authorize the bureau to expand its publicity functions, with their presumed corrective impact on corporations' behavior, by providing for registration of the larger corporations with the bureau. Smith had come to oppose the establishment of an independent trade commission with quasi-judicial and prosecutorial powers. He considered the registration process, by itself, as sufficient, through information and publicity, to exert a restraining discipline against corporations' engaging in unfair or inefficient practices. He continued to believe, as he had since the Hepburn bill debates, that registration should not be encumbered with a license system. That is, he believed that revocation of registration, a power he wanted the bureau to have, should not bar a corporation from engaging in interstate commerce, nor should it be tied to any authority vested in the bureau to initiate punitive or judicial proceedings. If Smith had his way, the bureau would have no judicial function; registration would therefore not impinge upon a property right subject to due process protections. Revocation of registration would simply signify that the affected corporation would lose its standing as being approved by the federal government, and its practices might thereby become especially vulnerable to critical public attention, political attack, or Department of Justice prosecution. Most important, in Smith's mind, the registration system he favored would avoid the state direction of market transactions implied in the proposals for an administrative commission with license or incorporation powers. His system, in other words, would reconcile government regulation with a relatively free market, free not in the old competitive sense but in the new corporate-administered sense. Private parties would be vested with the primary authority to regulate the market – reasonably, subject to government monitoring. In this essential respect, Smith's position was closer to Taft's than to Roosevelt's. It also placed him at odds with Newlands, who favored an

---

190. Smith to Garfield, 23 May 1911, JRG, Box 120: SCF. Smith complained that he was "afraid it is now a little too late; that a good many Congressmen will have been committed to some such foolish amendment to the Sherman law as I have just suggested [i.e., restoring a non-common-law meaning to the act]. Nevertheless, I am going to see what I can do." He added: "It does seem too bad that I could not have been allowed during the last two years to work out this proposition and at least get it into shape. I might now have been able to do something with it. But starting now from the beginning, it is a pretty hopeless proposition, I am afraid." Ibid.

administrative commission with intrusive powers. As a Democrat, however, Newlands was open to suggestions less strongly identified in public opinion which Republican presidential initiatives, and he was sensitive to the states' rights proclivities of his southern party colleagues that made them antagonistic to federal powers connected with license or incorporation proposals.

Toward the end of May, Smith could report a growing meeting of minds with the Senator. "Our sole point of difference," he informed Garfield, "is that he still sticks on the commission idea." Newlands had, however, "apparently given up, under my urgency, the really dangerous feature of that idea, namely, the proposal to give the commission positive directory powers over industrials." Smith had argued to Newlands the case for "the very actual influence that the Bureau would have over industrial corporations through the simple fact of registration and the power to deny or revoke such registration," and Newlands "seemed impressed with the idea, and with the possibility that this would be quite a sufficient power without giving any positive control over business transactions." Newlands, however, turned just such power into a reason for a commission. He "took me up along my own line and said that if this power through registration was so strong . . ., it was almost too great a power to be exercised by one officer [the commissioner of corporations], subject to political pressure," and that therefore there would have to be "some sort of a commission to exercise the power of admission to and revocation of registration." Smith confessed that the senator had "thus rather turned the force of my own remarks upon me," and he was "almost driven to admit that there was something in his proposition as so stated." He was trying now, he said to Garfield, "to scratch around and get some sort of a form of bill that will meet his general idea without injuring the efficiency of the Bureau or establishing an increasingly powerful judicial branch thereof."[191]

At this time, Roosevelt was conferring with Garfield, Pinchot, and Foulke in New York, and, as Garfield informed Smith, they "discussed very fully the corporation question." Pinchot was to see Smith in Washington, "and explain the matter in detail." The matter was Roosevelt's sustained partisanship to strong government direction of the market and a plan drafted for that purpose by Foulke, which Roosevelt approved as a basis for further drafting. "T.R. feels very strongly," Garfield reported to Smith, "that in order to obtain the necessary support to compel Congressional action, we must present a more concrete proposition for direct federal control than ever before."[192]

191. Ibid.
192. Garfield to Smith, 24 May 1911, JRG, Box 120: SCF.

Foulke's plan would combine the stringent license-registration system as provided for in some of the preliminary NCF draft bills with other market-regulating and enforcement powers of earlier incorporation bills Roosevelt had favored. The latter powers, as described by Garfield, would give the Bureau of Corporations or a new trade commission the authority to prosecute any corporation or person for "being or exercising a monopoly." Upon conviction, the corporation would "immediately become subject to the control" of the commission, "exactly as the railroads are now subject to the jurisdiction of the Interstate Commerce Commission." This control would give the commission "the right to enforce regulations governing methods of competition," including, "if necessary, prices." Private parties could also institute judicial proceedings against an alleged monopolistic corporation, and if the latter were convicted, the commission would assume the same control over it as in the case of proceedings initiated by the commission. The commission would have the further power "to declare any particular corporation a monopoly, and as a result of such declaration the corporation would become subject to the jurisdiction above explained," the corporation having the right to judicial appeal.[193]

Garfield tried, to no avail, to dissuade Roosevelt from supporting the Foulke plan. "As you know," he wrote to Smith, "I have always likened the power that the Commissioner should exercise to the power now exercised by the Comptroller of the currency, rather than the Interstate Commerce Commission." Garfield reported that he had "told T.R. that I was not at all clear about the wisdom of adopting in full Mr. Foulke's suggestions." Garfield fell back on advocating a milder registration-license alternative, arguing to Roosevelt "that complete publicity, resulting in registration, with the power of the Commissioner to revoke the license, subject to proper appeal to the Courts, is advisable." Roosevelt rejected this as inadequate: "T.R. feels that under the present conditions, and because of the appeals to the Court, this method would not be strict enough." Garfield reminded him "that under the Foulke scheme an appeal to the Court is likewise necessary, but T.R. felt that the appeal under those circumstances was not as objectionable as the other."[194]

Smith and Garfield continued to work along with Roosevelt, Pinchot, and Foulke, particularly with respect to a general strategy for introducing new regulatory legislation in Congress, now that, in Smith's words, "Things seem indeed to be getting active on this matter of legislation for

193 Ibid
194. Ibid.

corporate regulation." Roosevelt and Pinchot preferred to have Republican insurgents like senators Robert M. La Follette of Wisconsin and Albert B. Cummins of Iowa, introduce the new legislation, in cooperation with Democrats like Newlands and George E. Chamberlain of Oregon, but they also agreed with Smith's emphasis on the need "to regard Senator Newlands's feelings in the matter," as his support "will tend to bring with it some other Democratic votes in the Senate, and just at present there seems considerable prospect of a combination of Democrats and Insurgent Republicans in the Senate" on regulatory legislation. With respect to the substance of legislation, however, as against the strategy of its introduction, Smith concentrated his efforts on drafting bills in cooperation with Newlands, who himself was "very broad-minded" about working in a bipartisan spirit with the other senators.[195]

Smith stated flatly to Garfield, "I cannot say that I like the Foulke plan," reiterating that what he wanted was publicity coupled "with Federal registration and the right to revoke registration. There, personally, I would stop." He emphasized his "strong objection to going any farther in giving the Commissioner ... the power to declare a corporation a monopoly, or to charge it with such character before any court," as provided for in the Foulke plan. He allowed that "if we get the publicity and registration features, theoretically it would not make much difference if we had some other powers," such as those in the Foulke proposal, but in practical political life, he was "afraid the public will insist that I use those other powers to the exclusion of the publicity feature," and that would "inevitably tend toward making this Bureau simply a prosecuting agent." He added, "This is the great objection. I shy away from anything that looks like exercising the powers of prosecution...."[196]

Smith acknowledged, however, that in current political conditions, there was "just one great weakness in my publicity and registration plan, namely, that it does not sound '*strong*,' that it will not appeal to the man in the street as 'having any teeth.'" Smith said he knew the man in the street was wrong, but also "I know ... that I probably cannot convince him that he is wrong." Hence, Smith was prepared to adopt a more flexible posture. As he informed Garfield, "my idea is that in some way or other this proposition of mine must be accompanied by proposed legislation which will make a noise; to put it baldly, which will furnish some 'thunder in the index.'" Such legislation might be

195.   Ibid. and Smith to Garfield, 26 May 1911, JRG, Box 120: SCF.
196.   Ibid.

introduced as "a part (although a separable part) of the publicity and registration proposition," or "separately as another bill." To put the matter even more plainly, "the thunder might be put in such shape," Smith thought, "as to make a lot of noise and practically amount to very little – a political dodge which I am frank to say I would be willing to descend to if necessary."[197]

By the end of May, in the midst of consultations with Newlands, Pinchot, and others, Smith had drafted a bill "for Federal publicity and registration" combined with a little thunder. Its "chief features," as he described it to Garfield, were that in providing for "the usual publicity," it would make registration by corporations voluntary, the inducement for registration being "the exclusive right [of the registered corporation] to use the title 'United States Registered.'" As for the thunder, the bill stated the grounds for revocation of registration "in general terms," thereby including a punitive power but leaving it vague and therefore weak, and it provided for the establishment of a commission. "This, of course," Smith wrote to Garfield, "is the interesting, and probably to you and me the most disputable point." Nevertheless, Smith explained, "The sole duties of the commission are to determine whether a registered corporation shall have its registry revoked, upon complaint of the Commissioner, for the causes named in the act." He had inserted the commission feature, "in the first place, because Senator Newlands and Gifford [Pinchot] were quite vigorous for it, and in the second place because I am fairly well satisfied that it will do no particular harm, if the powers of the commission are no greater than are allowed in this bill." Smith immediately added his fear of having reared a potential Frankenstein monster: "Of course the danger is that in course of passage or by later amendment the powers of this commission might be very materially increased, so as to include positive directory powers over corporate business...." That was the risk, however, necessary to attracting sufficient support for what was otherwise a mild publicity measure. Nevertheless, Smith still worried: "I frankly admit I am rather afraid of this commission feature, because of what it might grow into...."[198]

Toward a trade commission

On 5 July 1911, Senator Newlands introduced in the Senate his bill, S. 2941, "to create an interstate trade commission." It was referred to the

197. Ibid. Smith's emphasis.
198. Smith to Garfield, 1 June 1911, JRG, Box 120: 3CF.

Senate Interstate Commerce Committee, which began hearings on the bill on 4 August 1911.[199] This was a tough license-registration measure, similar in its key provisions to the subsequent draft bills of the Jenks-Clark-Williams NCF subcommittee. The Senator's bill would take the Bureau of Corporations out of the Department of Commerce and Labor and transform it into a five-member independent trade commission. Corporations, except common carriers subject to the ICC (but including pipelines), with gross annual receipts in excess of $5 million would be required to register with the commission and provide full information, as the commission might prescribe. The commission would make public the information so gathered, as well as information collected in the course of its investigations, and it would make annual reports to Congress. Registered corporations would have the right to use the title "United States registered." The commission would have the power, upon complaint or on its own initiative, to revoke or cancel registration for noncompliance with registration regulations, and also for violation of the Sherman Act, for unfair methods of competition, for discriminatory practices, for giving or receiving rebates, or for overcapitalization. Upon revocation or cancellation of a corporation's registration, the commission could order the corporation to cease engaging in interstate or foreign commerce. All decisions of the commission would be final, except that a corporation might appeal in federal court the commission's order to cease from trade, as well as commission decisions or actions "involving the taking of private property without due process of law," and the extent and character of the powers conferred upon the commission.[200]

Smith co-drafted the bill with Newlands, thereby sustaining his influence with the senator in the ensuing committee hearings and redrafting work. Smith reported to Garfield that "In theory, and for publication, I have no connection with this bill," except insofar as Secretary Nagel had authorized him to confer with Newlands on the legislation, but "As a matter of fact, this bill is just about half-and-half the Senator's and mine." This meant that the "registration and publicity features are, of course, mine," including "the cancellation of registration," whereas the "compulsory feature and the power debarring from inter-

199. S. 2941, 62d Cong., 1st Sess., as amended by Newlands in his substitute of the same number, inserted 21 Aug. 1911, at Sen. Rep. 597 (1914), app., pp. 15–19.
200. Ibid. The commission would have had full subpoena powers. Corporations or businesses with less than $5 million annual gross receipts could voluntarily register. Note, there is nothing in this bill exempting registered corporations from prosecution under the Sherman Act, now that the Supreme Court had restored the common-law construction making reasonable restraints legal.

state commerce are the Senator's, against my views." Also, the establishment of the commission and its separation from the Department of Commerce and Labor were "primarily the Senator's." Smith now declared his "views on this point" to be "decidedly mixed." He was still personally in favor of "simply the voluntary registration system under this Bureau," but he had come to "recognize that my prejudices here may be simply conservatism," and he had become "entirely clear that, politically speaking, the Senator is right in saying, first, that my voluntary registration scheme does not have enough 'teeth' in it to appeal to the public, and, second, that it would not be possible to pass a bill giving even the power of revocation of registration to a single officer."[201]

However reluctantly, Smith was preparing himself to acknowledge that the nation's majority political consensus had arrived at a trade commission of some sort, and to shift his own efforts from arguing against a commission as such to influencing the shaping of its composition and powers. "It may be true," he conceded to Garfield, "that the time has come for the establishment of a Trade Commission like the Interstate Commerce Commission. On this point I am not entirely clear." He could see "strong arguments both ways." If there must be a commission, however, "Much would depend upon the personnel," and therefore he "did manage to arrange it so that if the bill passes it will carry with it into the commission both the Commissioner of Corporations and the entire Bureau of Corporations, so that it will preserve the continuity of our own history, and in all probability the traditions and morale of the Bureau will dominate the Commission, at least for the first few years, which will be the most important time." He did not know "what chance the bill has got," he informed Garfield, but Newlands had told him that the Senate committee was "now controlled by the Progressives, and that it will probably report this bill, or something like it, favorably."[202]

Newlands's optimism was premature. The consensus in favor of a trade commission still fell short of agreement, even among progressives, on positive legislation detailing the purposes and powers of a commission, and it was still stalled on the divisions over the labor question. Smith therefore had time to exercise his persuasive powers with Newlands, and in the next several weeks he did so with considerable success. Supplementing his conversations with Newlands, he prepared an extended memorandum in the form of a letter replying to the senator's

201. Smith to Garfield, 8 July 1911, JRG, Box 120: SCF.
202. Ibid.

questions about their draft bill, S. 2941, then before the Senate Interstate Commerce Committee.[203]

Smith observed that the Supreme Court's Rule of Reason decisions in the Standard Oil and American Tobacco cases had prepared the way for an "administrative system of regulation by the Federal Government." The time was "ripe for such action," for on the one hand, "the public is ready and anxious for an advance" to some such system, and on the other, "corporate managers concede more and more the necessity for such regulation and publicity, recognizing both its public necessity and its advantage to fair business." From his own "experience of eight years" in the Bureau, Smith had concluded that the "one imperative change now required in our policy toward the 'corporate problem,' is a change from our present system of ... occasional prosecution, to a system [of] ... continuous administrative action." It was necessary, that is, to "advance from a negative policy to a positive constructive policy; from mere occasional prohibition to permanent regulation and prevention." The policy should be centered in a "Federal administrative system of publicity and registration," which would have both "strength and elasticity," and result in "establishing definite standards of business action, of public economics, and of Government regulation," as well as in stimulating a "closer relationship between large business and public authorities, marked improvement in corporate accounting and in the standing of our industrial securities, and the elimination of unfair practice and business privilege."[204] Thus far, Smith's recommendation accorded with the Roosevelt view, with the general public opinion inclined toward a commission, and with Newlands's pro-commission outlook as embodied in the bill. Beyond this, however, Smith made a concerted argument against the prevalent commission idea and in favor of an agency that would conform more closely with his concept of an expanded Bureau of Corporations.

If the administrative agency's function were to be "simply that of investigation and publicity," its organization under a single chief officer, as was now the case with the bureau, would suffice, but if it were to have "judicial or semijudicial powers," Smith acknowledged, in deference to Newlands's views, the commission form would be preferable, as better adapted to its engaging in judicial deliberation, to its rulings carrying "more weight," and to its securing "stability, continuity of policy, and greater independence of action." Whatever the exact function of a commission, however, "it seems almost necessary that the

203. Smith to Newlands, [Aug. 1911], at Sen. Rep. 597 (1914), app., pp. 28–31.
204. Ibid., pp. 30, 31.

bureau should be merged" into it, as the bureau was "the one unit in the Government service which can immediately supply the experience, trained force, knowledge, and traditions which the commission must have for its work."[205] Thus did Smith, as he planned, turn "bureaucracy" to political account.

As for a commission's functions and powers, Smith marshaled all his major arguments for indirect regulation against direct state control of the market. The regulatory agency should have the functions of "investigation, publicity, and recommendation." For these purposes, it should administer the registration of corporations, "with power of cancellation." The grounds of cancellation should be "broadly stated," leaving the commission with wide discretion in applying the power in specific cases. Registration would afford "a very practical means of control, which at the same time has the great advantage that it does not actually attempt the positive regulation of business." It would bestow government and hence public approval on "proper business conduct," and disapproval on improper conduct, but would assume "no power of direction," and leave the market relatively free of state command, relying on "the public to apply corrective pressure through public opinion and the investment of the public's money." Cancellation of registration should be the only penalty for improper business conduct within the authority of the commission. Especially if voluntary rather than compulsory, therefore, registration would be not a property right subject to due process protections, but simply a privilege "granted through the commission and revocable by it." Limiting the commission's functions and powers in this way would also confine them to the sphere of executive administration and avoid the contention that they represented an unconstitutional delegation of Congress's legislative power to regulate interstate commerce. The commission's registration authority, its information gathering, and its publicity activity would effectively deter business malpractice, stimulate improvements and innovations in business enterprise, and facilitate prosecution of improper business conduct not deterred by publicity alone. In sum, the registration-publicity system should be largely separated from prosecutorial or punitive functions, that is, as far as possible from judicial powers, although the commission might assist the Department of Justice, just as had the bureau, with information "indicating a clear and flagrant violation of the law."[206]

205. Ibid., p. 28.
206. Ibid., pp. 28, 29, 30. Smith gave examples of deterrent, stimulative, and prosecutorial results from the bureau's information-gathering and publicity functions, including changes in the practices of the New Orleans Cotton Exchange, termination of

In accordance with his strong opposition to a commission with intrusive market powers, Smith advised categorically against conferring upon a commission any power to fix prices. He equally strongly advised against a power, which was included in the Newlands bill and was a key feature in all the proposed license plans, to bar from interstate and foreign commerce a corporation whose registration had been canceled or revoked. Smith questioned "both the wisdom and necessity" of barring a corporation from commerce. He argued that it "would require rather elaborate machinery for its enforcement," that it would involve interference with property rights, and that it was therefore "a peculiarly drastic" power. Smith took his argument one step farther, introducing what was for him a rather novel view. "In considering any such treatment of our commercial problem as is attempted in this bill," he said, "it seems to me . . . that the Government should not, at present, commit itself, by way of general policy, either to the theory of 'unlimited competition' or of 'unlimited combination.'" The situation was not "sufficiently advanced to justify us in taking a definite position in favor of either one of these opposing ideas." Hence, whatever the system Congress might now adopt, it "should be so framed as to be alike available for either development."[207]

Such an exaggerated definition of the alternatives (unlimited competition versus unlimited combination), along with a pretense of uncertainty respecting the major tendency of the nation's economic evolution, was uncharacteristic of Smith's thinking. Nor did it correspond with the substance of the prevalent arguments in public discourse; none of the politically organized parties to the debates favored unlimited competition or combination. This theme, however, of whether to recognize competition or combination as the basic principle of policy, would be picked up later by others, including by Luther Conant, Smith's deputy at the bureau and his successor as commissioner, and by Taft, in arguing against the establishment of a commission and in favor of judicial enforcement of the Sherman Act as reconstrued in the Supreme Court's Rule of Reason decisions. It may also have misled scholars seeking to understand the substance of the antitrust debates. It may be surmised that Smith resorted to this argument as a "political dodge," that is, as an effective way of convincing others that it made most sense to establish an executive agency, if one were to be established now, with

rebates by railroads, discontinuation of undesirable conduct in the tobacco industry, and effective utilization of information by the Department of Justice in the successful prosecution of the Standard Oil Company.
207. Ibid., pp. 29, 30. Smith added: "To give the power to fix prices would tend to commit us to a policy of industrial combination."

as few specific powers over the market as possible beyond registration and publicity, or to defer action pending further deliberation. Either way, the bureau as it stood, or something very much like it, would continue to exist as the basis of further policy development. Whatever Smith's motives, his argument on this point in particular, and on his other major points in general, exerted a powerful impact on Newlands, or provided the senator with substantial grounds upon which publicly to change his position.

As late as July, when he introduced the bill, S. 2941, Newlands was a staunch advocate of an administrative commission with quasi-judicial powers over industrial corporations similar to those of the ICC over transportation. In a letter in March 1911, for example, on Democratic legislative strategy, to representative Champ Clark, who was about to become Speaker of the House, Newlands noted that the Interstate Commerce Act and the Sherman Act had been passed at about the same time. The administration of the former "was given to a quasi-judicial board," and that of the latter to the attorney general, so that after "about 23 years of operation, through a gradual process of evolution, the regulation of railroads ... has been practically accomplished," whereas the administration of the Sherman Act "on the contrary, has been lame and halting, changing with the shifting incumbents ... and according to the requirements of political exigencies." The result was that "practically no progress has been made in the control of trusts." From this, Newlands reasoned, "Experience should teach us that with reference to interstate trade a commission or board should be organized similar to the Interstate Commerce Commission, with powers of investigation, of condemnation, and of recommendation." The purpose of such a trade commission, as with the ICC, should be not to restore the old competition but to regulate the new corporate market, "with a view, whilst preserving the good arising from commercial combination, to curing the pernicious practices connected therewith." The commission should have the power, upon complaint or its own initiative, to inquire into interstate corporations and itself bring suit, or recommend prosecution to the attorney general, against those corporations behaving in violation of the law. A trade commission would be necessary, Newlands argued, under any circumstances that assumed the established existence of large-scale corporate enterprise. If such monopolistic combinations as the Standard Oil or American Tobacco corporations were "to be held legal, the regulation of their prices and practices becomes a public necessity"; if they were to be held illegal, "then there should be some law, which, while permitting large capitalization and the ownership of many plants by a single corporation engaged in interstate trade, will protect the public from the abuses ... and the oppression exercised by it." For either purpose, an administrative commission would be necessary.[208]

Newlands stated these same views, consistently, in speeches on the Senate floor from January through June of 1911. On at least three different occasions in the Senate – on 11 January, 16 May, and 22 June – Newlands called for the establishment of a "quasi-judicial" administrative commission "similar to the Interstate Commerce Commission," with powers of "examination, recommendation, and condemnation." The regulation of industry, he held, needed to be embedded in the same kind of continuous executive direction and administrative law as that applying to transportation. If Congress had established a trade commission to enforce the Sherman Act, as it had established the ICC in transportation more than twenty years ago, "we would have had the constant corrective power" applied to industry, "and a great body of administrative law would have been built up and combinations of capital would have been effected without the abuses which have existed during the past 23 years." Newlands noted, with some exaggeration but not without foundation in utterances of some notable corporation executives, that "the trust managers themselves have seen a great light," and in public testimony have agreed that "the time has come for as complete regulation of corporations engaged in interstate trade as of corporations engaged in interstate transportation." It was a matter still to be determined, "Whether that regulation will ever extend so far as the regulation of the price itself." If Congress decided to "maintain the principle of competition, even though it leads to destruction, there will then, of course, be no necessity of regulating prices" – the market would do it, but if Congress recognized "the principle of helpful cooperation instead of destructive competition, then it will be necessary ... in extreme cases to face the question of the regulation of prices just as the prices of any public utility are regulated." Apart from extreme cases, Congress would also have to face, as a matter of routine regulation, the questions of "how great these corporations shall be," the size of their capital, the number of plants they should own, and "the extent of their operations." For the execution of any of these legislative purposes, Congress would need to establish a quasi-judicial administrative commission.[209]

On 4 August 1911, Newlands testified at the opening of the hearings of his own committee on his bill, which, as he had introduced it in the

208. Newlands to Clark, 15 Mar. 1911, at Sen. Rep. 597, app., pp. 19–20.
209. Newlands, in the Senate, 11 Jan., 16 May, 22 June, 1911, at ibid., pp. 36, 37, 38.

Senate in July, provided for a license-registration system presided over by an administrative commission, although it also contained features contributed by Smith. Now, however, Newlands recommended changes in the bill and raised doubts about proceeding directly to the establishment of a strong commission. He drew upon the arguments Smith had made in the commissioner's letter-memorandum to the senator, and placing that letter in the record, Newlands explicitly acknowledged that he relied for many of his revised views on Smith's advice.[210]

Newlands noted the national political consensus in favor of the establishment of a commission, and he reaffirmed his own commitment to it. There could "hardly be any difference of opinion," he observed, "on the point that there should be an administrative tribunal," which should be both "independent of any department of Government" and "quasi judicial" in character. A commission was necessary, because: "We want traditions; we want a fixed policy; we want trained experts; we want precedents; we want a body of administrative law built up." For these reasons, and because "powers of judgment and powers of discretion" were therefore to be exercised, the work could not be done by a bureau under "one executive official," changing with administrations and subject "to higher executive authority," but rather must be done by a "commission of dignity, permanence, and ability, independent of executive authority, except in its selection, and independent in character."[211]

The need for a commission form of regulation arose not only from the nature of its work but also from the current circumstances of corporate enterprise as they stood to be affected by the Supreme Court's Rule of Reason construction of the Sherman Act. Newlands held that left to the courts, the law as now interpreted would result in convicted corporations undergoing reorganization and taking the form of "a large

210. "Hearings Before the Senate Committee on Interstate Commerce," 62d Cong., 2d Sess., 4 Aug. 1911, at ibid., pp. 15–27, 28–31. Newlands informed the committee (Sen. Clapp, chair, presiding) that he had prepared the bill, S. 2941, after consulting with Attorney General Wickersham, Commissioner Smith, members of the ICC, lawyers "engaged in trust prosecutions" – presumably Frank B. Kellogg and James C. McReynolds among others – "men connected with these industrial corporations," and "eminent economists," and, he said, he had "found everywhere a general acquiescence in the view that something in the way of supplemental legislation was required." The senator noted that Smith had "since modified also his views somewhat as to the desirability of a commission, an idea which he at first opposed, and I think that he is now substantially in accord with this bill," that is, as to be amended in accordance with Newlands's testimony. Ibid., pp. 21, 25–26.

211. Ibid., p. 22. Here, Newlands followed Smith's distinction between a bureau with functions of investigation and publicity, for which a single head would suffice, and a quasi-judicial body with "corrective power," which must exercise "judgment and discretion." Ibid.

number of corporations, limited either in the character of the commodity with which they deal or in the area over which they operate." The
stockholders of each of these separate corporations could be expected in
general to feel satisfied with its management and with "the great financial interests and institutions that usually control that management."
"So that we will eventually have," Newlands continued, "in these
industrial corporations, just as we have with railroads, the practical
control of all these subdivided corporations in the hands of a few great
financial institutions or groups in New York," which would "dictate
the membership of the boards and the general policy of all these
corporations." The result would be "an effective unity of policy," not
reachable by the law as a combination in restraint of trade: "A mere
nod, a mere suggestion, will accomplish what is desired." Hence, an
"administrative tribunal" was needed, which "by continuous supervision" would end or prevent "these abuses which the courts are now
called upon sporadically and intermittently to correct by their slow
processes."[212]

Having remained consistent with his past views in favor of an administrative commission, Newlands now proceeded to depart from them in
calling for a commission with relatively weak powers. In this, he
adopted two of Smith's basic points. First, instead of likening the
proposed commission to the ICC, as he had previously, he embraced
Smith's distinction between the regulation of industry, or the economy
in general, and the regulation of common carriers or public utilities.
Accordingly, to the question of whether a commission should have the
power to condemn "an unfair or unreasonable price," as with railroads
subject to the ICC, or the positive power of "fixing a reasonable price,"
as more recently bestowed upon the ICC in the Mann–Elkins Act of
1910, Newlands replied that he was "opposed to any attempt at present
[by a government commission] to fix prices" in industry.[213]

Second, Newlands adopted Smith's opposition to the essence of a
license system: While he persisted in recommending the compulsory
registration of larger corporations, he now argued against barring a
corporation from engaging in interstate commerce upon revocation of
registration as "a rather extreme power" that "had better be left out,"
and he therefore specified that the corresponding section of his bill be
deleted. The commission's punitive powers or quasi-judicial functions
would be limited to the revocation of registration, and to referring to
the attorney general information indicating a corporation's misconduct.

212. Ibid., p. 21.
213. Ibid., p. 25.

As Newlands summarized his position, "we should confine our present exercise of legislation ... to the appointment of an interstate trade commission and the merger in such a commission of the Bureau of Corporations," the commission to have "simply powers of publicity, inquest, and recommendation." Gone were powers of "condemnation."[214]

Newlands further followed Smith in recommending that the law leave general, and not define, such words or phrases as "unfair methods of competition," "overcapitalization," and "financial organization," that is, leaving thereby their interpretation as they applied to registration and its revocation, "to the judgment and discretion of the commissioners without precise legal definition." The courts would not find the law invalid as an unconstitutional delegation to an executive agency of the legislative power to regulate commerce, because, in the absence of a power to bar a corporation from commerce, the commission's actions in these matters could not go beyond "the denial or cancellation of the mere privilege of registration, which affects no substantial property right."[215]

Somewhat incredulously, Senator Cummins, senior Republican member of the committee after Clapp, and an advocate of a strong commission, commented, "You do not propose any rules. The thing would have simply a moral effect if the board or commission did not have the power to determine how the corporation should be organized and how it should carry on its business." Cummins acknowledged that Newlands's plan led in the right direction, toward a commission, but he objected that if there were to be a commission, "we should be able to determine what kind of law it shall administer." Its preventive and punitive powers should be more specifically designated or defined to permit it validly to undertake the regulation of commerce on behalf of the legislative branch. At any rate, he argued, "publicity is of no value unless the facts that are discovered can be compared with some rule of conduct which the law has laid down for the government of corporations ... and if you have no law, publicity is of minor importance."[216]

In reply, Newlands once again relied on Smith, drawing upon Smith's

---

214. Ibid., pp. 23, 25. Newlands followed Smith closely on folding the Bureau of Corporations into the commission: "... it is obviously desirable that we merge the Bureau of Corporations – as this bill does – with all its officials, funds, and powers, in this commission, and that we make, for the first two years, the Commissioner of Corporations one of the new commissioners, and make him, for the first year, the chairman of the commission.... Thus the executive work as at present organized would go on without a break." Ibid., p. 22.
215. Ibid., p. 24.
216. Ibid., pp. 24, 25.

distinction between a policy based on the assumption of competition and one based on the recognition of combination, and holding that with respect "to the great corporate problem," the country was divided into "at least two leading and divergent schools of thought," one seeking "to maintain by government action if need be, the full competitive system and to rely chiefly on competition as the regulator of corporate business," the other inclining "toward freely allowing combinations, both present and future, [and] applying thereto governmental supervision and direction as the prime regulator." Because it was "too early to say which of these opposing tendencies should, or will, ultimately prevail," Congress should adopt legislation along lines he now recommended as "exactly adapted to the undeveloped situation"; it would provide for an agency that would be "available for either tendency" and could "serve either principle," without committing policy to either, while the nation made up its collective mind. It would neither legalize nor forbid combination as such; it would not interfere with the enforcement of the Sherman Act; but in the meantime, pending an ultimate policy commitment, the registration and publicity provisions would "tend strongly to promote fair competition." His bill, therefore, was "eminently fitted by its moderation and ... its own frankly tentative character" to represent "a step upon which all can unite."[217]

In this way, Newlands, following Smith, converted the counterposing of two theoretical principles – competition as market regulator versus corporate combination cum government as regulator – into the two prevalent contending schools of thought in the nation's politics of the trust question, as an argument in favor of a commission without directive powers over the market. Although it tended to settle in as an explanation of the nation's major political division on the issue, among observers then and historians since, Newlands in effect acknowledged that his dichotomy did not really characterize the basic political division on the trust question, first by using the term "competition as the regulator of corporate business," indicating he had no expectation of the nation's seriously considering reverting to the old competitive regime, and second by saying that to put the alternatives as he had was "to state the extremes," not the substantial sides of the debate in the political mainstream.[218] The real division was over whether government regulation of industry should be directive as with public-service cor-

---

217. Ibid., pp. 26–27. Newlands repeated this delineation of the national division on the trust question in subsequent testimony before the committee, on 15 Nov. 1911, Sen. Rep. 1326, 62d, 3d, 26 Feb. 1913, at ibid., pp. 38–39.
218. Ibid., p. 26.

porations (or public utilities), and as Roosevelt was advocating as well as Newlands until recently, or whether government regulation of industry should be indirect by its enforcement of fair business methods and its sustaining thereby the disciplinary impact of intercorporate and "potential competition."

Even with his recommended deletion, Newlands's bill, as drafted, still retained provisions that went beyond a commission limited to registration-publicity functions. In the next several months, with Smith's assistance, Newlands drafted an entirely new bill, S. 5485, and on 26 February 1912, he formally substituted it for the original bill. The new bill would fold the Bureau of Corporations into a small, three-member interstate trade commission. All traces of a registration-license system were deleted. Instead, the commission would be authorized, with injunction and subpoena powers, to gather information from corporations and to make the information public; it would also be required to submit annual reports to Congress, with such legislative recommendations as it saw fit. The commission would also be authorized to assist courts in the framing, implementing, and enforcing dissolution or reorganization decrees in Sherman Act cases. It would, in addition, be authorized to investigate, upon complaint or its own initiative, any corporation to determine if it was in violation of the Sherman Act; it could turn over its findings to the attorney general; it could, alternatively, advise the corporation on changes it should make, and if the corporation did not comply with the advice, the commission would report the noncompliance, along with the information gathered, to the attorney general for possible judicial action.[219]

In essence, this was Smith's bill. As he wrote to Garfield, although he was not publicly endorsing any specific legislation, "this bill comes nearer to meeting my ideas than anything I have seen; in fact, I had a good deal to do with the drafting of it."[220] Smith had succeeded in persuading Newlands to make a complete about-face from advocating an administrative commission with far-reaching registration-license powers to backing a commission without "teeth," reduced largely to information-gathering and publicity functions.

How is this to be explained? Newlands's own testimony may be the best guide. In part, Smith had convinced him that a commission with registration-license powers harbored the dangerous implication of turn-

---

219. S. 5485, at Sen. Rep. 1326, 62d, 3d, at ibid., pp. 36, 39–42. To make the information-gathering function consistent with the Fifth Amendment protection against self-incrimination, natural persons would be granted immunity from prosecution on account of matters related to their testimony.
220. Smith to Garfield, 10 Feb. 1912, JRG, Box 120: SCF.

ing the whole economy into a "public utility" subject to state command. In part, Newlands had come to believe that although a majority
in Congress might agree in general upon the need for a commission, no
such majority could as yet agree on the specific nature, functions, and
powers of a commission. He decided, therefore, to propose, as a possibly viable expedient, the establishment of a commission with minimal
functions and powers, not much more than those already reposed in the
Bureau of Corporations, because such a commission might attract
majority support and might serve as the basis for a gradual evolution
toward a strong regulatory commission, much as had been the case with
the ICC. The important point was to get some kind of commission
established, "in view of the present political status," as Newlands put it,
with "the administration having drifted from one of powerful Republican control, a control entirely in sympathy with the broad exercise of
national powers, to one of divided control."[221]

Newlands was referring to the growing regular-insurgent, Taft–La
Follette–Roosevelt rifts in the Republican party, as well as to the fact
that Congress had come under "divided control," the House by the
Democrats, the Senate by the Republicans. But Newlands also referred
to divisions within his own party, pointing out that with respect to such
proposals for strong national regulation of the market as federal incorporation, he had never been able "to make much headway with my
own party," especially its southern wing, "clinging, as it does, to the
exercise of State functions and guarding against Federal encroach-
ment."[222]

The divisions within the Democratic party extended beyond those
involving states' rights racism or parochialism. To name no others,
Bryanite populists differed with Wilsonite progressives, and labor
Democrats from a good cross section of the others, in attitudes toward
the regulation of the market. As for the Republicans, it was a matter of
division compounded. Among the Taft Republicans, within the administration, Wickersham and Nagel supported proposals for federal incorporation and a strong administrative commission, as did Taft himself
for some time. But especially after the Rule of Reason decisions, and as
the break with Roosevelt deepened, Taft moved away from executive
toward judicial regulation, through prosecutions under the Sherman
Act, a policy that Wickersham implemented with zest, and that dis-
gusted big business Republicans but appealed to smaller manufacturers

221. Newlands's testimony, 4 Aug. 1911, at Sen. Rep. 597 (1914), app., pp. 26–27.
222. Ibid., p. 26.

who wanted the Sherman Act maintained as a weapon against labor. Among anti-Taft Republicans, animosities arose between followers of La Follette and those of Roosevelt; even among Roosevelt loyalists such as Smith and Garfield, as we have seen, there were serious disagreements with Roosevelt over regulatory policy.[223]

With the approach of the 1912 national elections, moreover, the political divisions between and within the parties only deepened. Neither house of Congress could produce legislation for the regulation of industry before the election and inauguration of Woodrow Wilson and what turned out to be the capture of both houses by the Democrats. Senator Cummins's report for the Senate Interstate Commerce Committee, filed 26 February 1913, a week before Wilson's inauguration, was emblematic of the general situation. He declared that the committee was "not yet ready to report any of the bills which are now before it, ... nor is it prepared at this time to report a substitute for them." The committee, however, could report a consensus, but not a unanimous one, on certain general propositions, namely, that the Sherman Act should remain on the books, that a federal incorporation law was "neither necessary nor desirable," that it was "desirable to impose upon corporations ... further conditions or regulations affecting both their organization and conduct," that the Bureau of Corporations should be converted into "an independent commission," that such a commission with administrative and quasi-judicial functions and powers was necessary, and that such a commission should aid corporations and the courts in corporate reorganization or behavioral reform. How all this was to be accomplished the committee left to the future.[224]

223. Smith's and Garfield's disagreement with Roosevelt on regulatory policy did not make them any the less loyal to him as their political leader. They agreed with him on most issues and on what they took to be his general progressive outlook, and they felt they could use their influence to modify his policy positions, especially as he tended to welcome diverse views and dissenting advice among his associates and advisers. When the Taft administration attacked Roosevelt with revelations about Roosevelt's understandings with the International Harvester Corporation, for example, Smith rose to Roosevelt's defense, and as the break between Taft and Roosevelt became irreparable, Smith prepared to leave the bureau and go to work for Roosevelt's presidential renomination and reelection. As he wrote from the bureau to Garfield in late April 1912: "It certainly looks to me as if the Colonel were going to get there, thank Heaven! And if he does, the Republican party will become the Progressive party, the party with a future, and men like you and me will have a political home. Otherwise, we wont. Also, we'll have a chance to elect a Republican President" (punctuation as in original). Smith to Garfield, 24 Apr. 1912, also, on International Harvester, Garfield to Smith, 26 Apr. 1912, and Smith to Garfield, 30 Apr. 1912, all in JRG, Box 120: SCF.
224. Sen. Rep. 1326, 62d, 3d, 26 Feb. 1913, at Sen. Rep. 597 (1911), app., pp. 21-33

The corporate-liberal solution

At the outset of the Wilson administration, the nation's effective political groupings had, since the Civic Federation's initiative of 1907, passed through about six years of intense debate on regulatory policy, which aside from producing legislation strengthening the ICC's powers over common carriers, clarified the alternatives with respect to the regulation of the economy in general and prepared the ground for a consensus capable of legislation. In yielding Democratic party control over both houses of Congress, as well as the White House, the 1912 elections reinforced the conditions favorable to legislation. By the time President Wilson turned to the mechanics of drafting and passing regulatory legislation toward the end of 1913, having made tariff and banking reform his highest priorities in his first year in office, effective political opinion, whatever the diversity of views among the people at large, had defined the main alternatives of regulatory policy along the lines of two kinds of regulation and three modes of implementation, all of which assumed the affirmation of reasonable restraints of trade in the form of large-scale corporate capitalism.

The two kinds of regulation were: (1) statist: government direction of the market, with corporations treated as public utilities and agents of public policy, that is, applying to industry and the economy in general a regime similar to, but ultimately more comprehensive than, that imposed upon transportation under the ICC. (2) nonstatist: indirect government regulation of a corporate-administered market, with industry and the economy in general treated differently from public utilities and, instead, monitored by government to permit reasonable combinations and restraints of trade, but to remedy or prevent unfair business methods and maintain the disciplinary impact of intercorporate (or oligopolistic) and potential competition. Of the two, government direction became a minority view, associated with Roosevelt and some New Nationalists, who wished to combine public control and planning with the advantages of private ownership. Indirect government regulation became the majority view that included a cross section of pro-Taft and insurgent Republicans, Bull Moosers, Wilson progressives, conservative and states'-rights southern Democrats, and populist Democrats. Small-producer anti-corporate partisans, although articulate and influential in party politics, were able to criticize and peripherally modify, but not define, the actionable alternatives, as to both kind and mode. Their major impact, along with that of other small-producer leaders, was to assure that whatever the legal accommodation to corporate capitalism, it should safeguard a wide latitude for the coexistence of small enterprise within the dominant large-corporate order. This was no small accomplishment.

The three modes of implementation were: (1) judicial enforcement of the law against unreasonable restraints of trade, in accordance with the Supreme Court's restoration of the common-law construction of the Sherman Act, in essence a form of indirect government regulation of the market; (2) a federal registration-license system (or its incorporation variation), administered by a trade commission – a form of regulation that in specific proposals tended strongly toward direct government regulation of the market, but that in principle might serve a policy of either direct or indirect regulation, depending upon the provisions respecting license powers and the role of the judiciary; (3) a trade commission, without registration-license powers and closely aligned with judicial process, designed to permit reasonable restraints of trade and remedy or prevent unfair business methods, a form of regulation that would serve the policy of indirect government regulation of the market. Of the three modes of implementation, the first, as a policy excluding a trade commission or restricting its functions to little more than publicity, became viable only after the Supreme Court's Rule of Reason decisions of 1911, when Taft and his allies vigorously took it up, but it quickly became and remained a minority position. The second was associated with Roosevelt and the Civic Federation's subcommittee proposals, as well as, from time to time, with prominent legislators like Newlands, but like the judicial alternative it became, indeed it always was, a minority position, although one with great forensic influence and tenacity. The third, a trade commission in weaker or stronger form, but without license powers, and closely aligned with the first mode, judicial process, became the majority position and the basis of the legislation passed in 1914.

It is in this detailed historical context that President Wilson's message to Congress of 20 January 1914 on antitrust legislation may be best understood, that is, as one deftly supporting the nonstatist kind of indirect regulation, in the trade commission–judicial process mode. In the message, Wilson addressed issues and proposed measures well rooted in the past years' debates and legislative drafting efforts, indicating his proficient familiarity with the established record and the prevalent positions. Accordingly, it was not mere rhetoric or expedient soothing of business sensibilities when, in declaring his intent to seek "constructive legislation," springing not from "recent or hasty opinion" but from "the experience of a whole generation," Wilson stated, "We are now about to give expression to the best business judgment of America." In that sense, also, as he stated, referring more to the torrent of Sherman Act prosecutions under Taft and Wickersham than to circumstances during the several months of his own administration, "The antagonism between business and Government is over."[225]

The market, Wilson noted, needed the certainty of law for its healthy functioning: "Nothing hampers business like uncertainty. Nothing [so] daunts or discourages it," and the remedy lay in the "further and more explicit legislative definition of the policy and meaning of the existing antitrust law." It was possible and appropriate, Wilson explained, to do this "with as few, as slight, as easy and simple business readjustments as possible in the circumstances, nothing essential disturbed, nothing torn up by the roots, no parts rent asunder which can be left in wholesome combination." This meant, implicitly rejecting Roosevelt's position, that "Fortunately, no measures of sweeping or novel change are necessary," and, disowning Taft's prosecutorial hyperactivism, that "our object is *not* to unsettle business or anywhere seriously to break its established courses athwart." The administration sought "a comprehensive but not a radical or unacceptable program." Rather, it was its intent that "the laws we are about to pass" should constitute "the bulwarks and safeguards of industry against the forces that now disturb them." The task ahead was to be carried out "in a new spirit, in quiet moderation, without revolution of any untoward kind."[226]

The proper regulation of the market could be accomplished by eliminating uncertainty of the law by defining explicitly and forbidding "the many hurtful restraints of trade," with which "we are sufficiently familiar" (Wilson here singling out interlocking directorates and the stifling of industrial managements by financier dictation), and by establishing an administrative interstate trade commission, which would not simply enforce the law but also give capitalists "advice, ... definite guidance and information," and thereby function "as an indispensable instrument of information and publicity, as a clearing house for the facts by which both the public mind and the managers of great business undertakings should be guided." The commission would be an instrument, also, of monitoring business against malpractices, "where the processes of the courts or the natural forces of correction outside the courts are inadequate to adjust the remedy to the wrong." The commission would also assist the courts in the dissolution or reorganization of corporations in decisions resulting from Sherman Act cases, in such a way as to avoid "financial consequences likely to overwhelm the security market

225. "Trusts and Monopolies," Special Address to Congress, 20 Jan. 1914, at *PPWW*, 3, pp. 81–88, at p. 82.
226. Ibid., pp. 85, 83. Wilson's emphasis.

and bring upon it breakdown and confusion," because great corporations could "not always be dissected into their component units as readily as railroad companies or similar organizations can." To protect corporations' institutional stability, to insulate corporations from the direct intrusion of government, and to facilitate in business the "processes of self-correction and disturb its legitimate course as little as possible," the law should provide "that penalties and punishments should fall not upon business itself," not upon the corporation, "to its confusion and interruption, but upon the individuals" who misuse the corporation to break the law.[227]

Of particular significance, accurately summarizing the current political consensus against direct government management of the market, and in favor of indirect regulation, Wilson in noting that "The opinion of the country would instantly approve such a commission," emphasized nevertheless that "It would not wish to see it empowered to make terms with monopoly or in any sort to assume control of business, as if Government made itself responsible."[228] The economy in general was to remain a largely autonomous realm of private enterprise; it was not to become a public utility.

Nothing in Wilson's message was unfamiliar to the proposals and draft bills formulated over the previous several years in Civic Federation, Bureau of Corporations, commercial association, and congressional committee circles. Wilson's position tended toward a Smith–Newlands mix, that is, the combining, in an administrative agency, of information-gathering and publicity functions with monitoring and enforcement authority in aid of the Department of Justice and the courts. It corresponded, as well, with his own opposition to direct government intrusion in market transactions in the general economy apart from public utilities, a view he expressed privately, for example, to Charles R. Van Hise, president of the University of Wisconsin, whose regulatory ideas were closely associated with those of Roosevelt. "My own judgment," Wilson told the educator about a month after Van Hise had testified before the House Judiciary Committee, "is that it is not wise to begin, at any rate, by giving the commission the authority you suggest." The commission "ought to be a means of systematic information both for Congress and the country," he explained, and "it ought to be an

227. Ibid., pp. 85–86, 86–87.
228. Ibid., p. 85. Sen. Newlands quoted *en bloc* several of the paragraphs of Wilson's message, from which some of the quotations in the text above are taken, in his report for the Senate Interstate Commerce Committee accompanying an earlier version of what became the final Federal Trade Commission Act. Sen. Rep. 597 (1914), pp. 6–7.

instrument for the Department of Justice and the courts in determining the just and wise things to do with regard to the restoration of normal competition," but the commission's powers ought not to go beyond that, for "to allow it to authorize acts and practices seems to me to be taking a dangerous step." This was essentially the same position as that which Wilson had taken six years before when, in criticizing the Hepburn bill, he stated, "If there must be commissions, let them be, not executive instrumentalities having indefinite powers capable of domineering as well as regulating, but tribunals of easy and uniform process acting under precise terms of power in the enforcement of precise terms of regulation."[229]

The Federal Trade Commission Act, signed by Wilson on 26 September 1914, and passed with his active support, established a five-member commission consisting initially of the Bureau of Corporation's records and employees, and headed by the incumbent bureau chief, Joseph E. Davies, on both counts according with Herbert Knox Smith's design. It declared illegal "unfair methods of competition," without further specifying or defining those methods, leaving the application of the prohibition to the commission and the courts. It empowered the commission, upon notice and hearing, to issue cease and desist orders against unfair methods of competition; these orders, however, were to be fully subject to judicial review. The act authorized the commission, at its discretion, to require annual and special reports from corporations; also, to investigate into business affairs in general and into alleged or

229. Wilson to Van Hise, 10 Mar. 1914, quoted at Link, *Wilson*, 2, pp. 435–436; Wilson, "Law or Personal Power," address delivered to the National Democratic Club, New York, 13 Apr. 1908, *PPWW*, 2, p. 28. Testimony of Van Hise, 13 Feb. 1914, at U.S. House of Representatives, Committee on the Judiciary, *Hearings on Trust Legislation*, 63d Cong., 2d Sess. (Washington: Government Printing Office, 1914), 2 vols. 1, pp. 546–559. Wilson's reference to "normal competition" should not be misread as distinguishing his views from those of people like Van Hise. Among those affirming corporate capitalism, the advocacy of healthy competition was universal. In his testimony, for example, before the House Judiciary Committee, Van Hise declared that "nothing should be done that would prohibit or stand in the way of free and open competition," that private monopoly should be prohibited along with unfair practices, and, at the same time, that although competition was the rule of the nineteenth century, cooperation was the rule of the twentieth, that "this great tendency for cooperation is held by everybody everywhere," that "what we have is this irresistible general tendency to cooperate, this universal tendency, and it exists in every business everywhere in the United States and we all know it," and that although he was "standing for free competiton" and wanted "to prohibit absolutely monopoly and all unfair practices," and did "not stand for private monopoly any more than ... the President of the United States," nevertheless it was necessary to "allow cooperation in contracts and combinations in restraint of trade so far as they are not detrimental to the public welfare." Ibid., pp. 548, 550, 557, 559. Wilson's views on regulatory policy were different from Van Hise's, as they were from Roosevelt's – or Taft's – but on other grounds.

suspected violations of the antitrust laws, to make its findings public, to submit annual and special reports to Congress, with legislative recommendations, and to report alleged violations of the antitrust laws to the attorney general. In aid of its investigatory functions, the commission was to have full subpoena powers, and its orders were to be supported by court injunction. In the capacity of master in chancery or otherwise, the commission was to assist the attorney general and the courts in shaping and implementing Sherman Act decrees respecting corporate dissolutions, reorganizations, or business conduct, and it was to aid in supervising the carrying out of such decrees. All acts, orders, and procedures of the commission were to be subject to judicial review.

This was a commission that corresponded with Herbert Knox Smith's conception supplemented with some of Newlands's "teeth."[230]

230. The Federal Trade Commission Act can be said to have accorded, in Wilson's words, with "the best business judgment of America," that is, with the proposals of the Chicago Association of Commerce, the Illinois Manufacturers' Association, the New York Board of Trade, the Merchants' Association of New York, and the U.S. Chamber of Commerce, as well as with the views of the majority of members of the National Civic Federation. Louis D. Brandeis and George L. Rublee played important roles toward the end of the legislative process that produced the commission, Brandeis in liaison between Wilson and congressional committees, Rublee in drafting work; their contributions, however, were neither novel nor original, but drew upon the large common fund of work and ideas of the previous several years. Brandeis and Rublee were both working in close association with the recently organized (1912) U.S. Chamber of Commerce, Rublee being at the time of the legislation's drafting, a member of the chamber's committee on trade commission legislation, having replaced Brandeis when the latter went off to Washington to advise and work with Wilson and Congress. For details of the last stages in the drafting work, indicating prominent roles played by representatives William C. Adamson (Ga.), James H. Covington (Md.), and Raymond B. Stevens (N.H.), and by senators Newlands and Cummins, and noting Rublee's working with Stevens to insert the section on unfair competition in the act as passed, see Link, *Wilson*, 2, pp. 425–442. See also, M. J. Sklar, "Woodrow Wilson and the Political Economy of Modern United States Liberalism," at Ronald Radosh and Murray N. Rothbard, eds., *A New History of Leviathan* (New York: Dutton, 1972), pp. 7–65, at pp. 21–24; Gerard C. Henderson, *The Federal Trade Commission: A Study in Administrative Law and Procedure* (New Haven: Yale University Press, 1924), pp. 21–22; for Brandeis's views, see his testimony, for example, at House Committee on the Judiciary, *Trust Legislation* (Series No. 2) – *Patent Legislation* (Ser. No. 1), *Hearings on H.R. 11380, H.R. 11381, H.R. 15926, and H.R. 19959*, 26, 27 January and 19 February 1912, 62d Cong., 2d Sess. (Washington: Government Printing Office, 1912), pp. 13–54, and Brandeis, "The Solution of the Trust Problem," *Harper's Weekly* 58, no. 2968 (8 Nov. 1913), pp. 18–19; concerning Rublee, Senate Committee on Interstate Commerce, "Promotion of Export Trade," *Hearings on H.R. 17350*, 64th Cong., 2d Sess., January 1917 (Washington: Government Printing Office, 1917), pp. 10–12, and Rublee, "The Original Plan and Early History of the Federal Trade Commission," *Proceedings of the Academy of Political Science* 11:4 (Jan. 1926), pp. 114–120. Cf. Thomas K. McCraw, "Rethinking the Trust Question," in McCraw, ed., *Regulation in Perspective: Historical Essays* (Cambridge, Mass.: Harvard University Press, 1981), pp. 25–55.

As Smith had strongly advocated, the category "unfair methods" was left general, and not defined with specificity, a position Wilson came to accept as being more practical than seeking to specify all unfair practices in the act itself. The commission was to regulate the market indirectly, with more remedial power than Smith might have desired, but with the ultimate power residing in the courts, as Smith had wanted. The commission's cease and desist power, and the Clayton Act, passed separately a month later, provided what Smith might have called the "thunder in the index." The Clayton Act illegalized three specific unfair business methods subject to FTC enforcement, namely, price discrimination, tying contracts, and some kinds of intercorporate directorships and stockholding, but the prohibitions were so qualified as to leave wide latitude for administrative, and ultimately judicial, judgment as to their meaning and application.[231]

Absent from the regulatory legislation of 1914 were those proposed measures that had been at the heart of the license-registration plans, and that would constitute, or lay the basis for, a government-directed market, namely: (1) registration of all large corporations with the commission; (2) submission of all their contracts, agreements, and combinations to the commission for its approval or disapproval; (3) commission control over prices; (4) commission control over corporations' capitalization, stock issue, or investment policy; (5) commission control over corporations' accounting, bookkeeping, and records; (6) commission condemnation and seizure of monopolistic corporations and their operation by the commission or under the direct command of the commission; finally, and most decisive, as the basis of the foregoing, (7) federal license, or incorporation, as the condition for engaging in commerce, and commission power to issue and revoke license, or corporation charter, and to bar from commerce any corporation without license or charter. Compared with a publicity-information agency, the Federal Trade Commission was "strong"; compared with a license-registration

231. Texts of FTC and Clayton acts at Bureau of Corporations, *Ann. Rep.* (1914), pp. 18–36. For an assessment of the Clayton Act, see Link, *Wilson*, 2, pp. 433–434, 442–444; and for the stinging critique of the Clayton Act by members of Clayton's House Judiciary Committee, see *House Report No. 627*, pt. 3, by John M. Nelson (Wisc.), concurred in by Andrew J. Volstead (Minn.), and pt. 4, by Dick T. Morgan (Okla.), 63d Cong., 2d Sess., "Antitrust Legislation," 13 May 1914, Minority Views to accompany H.R. 15657, at U.S. Senate Committee on the Judiciary, *Amendments to the Sherman Antitrust Law and Related Matters*, pt. 1, 63d Cong., 2d Sess. (Washington: Government Printing Office, 1914), pp. 109–119, 121–125. Cf. Testimony of H. K. Smith in opposition to the Clayton Act, at U.S. House Committee on the Judiciary, *Hearings on Trust Legislation*, 1 (11 Feb. 1914), pp. 423–432.

agency, it was "weak." It is more accurate, however, to understand it not as "strong" or "weak," but as different in kind from either.

The legislation of 1914 marked another defeat for the objectives of organized labor. The American Federation of Labor and the railway brotherhoods made a concerted effort to attain the exemption of trade unions from the antitrust laws, an effort that put a severe strain on the Democratic party and placed the passage of regulatory legislation in serious jeopardy. Wilson and the Democratic congressional leadership, along with key Republicans, overrode labor's demands, resulting in far less for labor than it had been offered in the *pro forma* registration provisions of the Hepburn bill. Labor received, in the Clayton Act, an unactionable declaration, rooted in the socialist and populist traditions, that "the labor of a human being is not a commodity or article of commerce," and it received a restatement of the existing law that trade unions and farm organizations were not, per se, illegal or in violation of the antitrust laws.[232]

The Federal Trade Commission and Clayton acts proved a successful legislative package in embodying, after many years' debate, the national political consensus on the regulation of the market. Together, they represented the accommodation of statute law to corporate capitalism, based upon a putative arrangement for the coexistence of large-corporate and smaller capital. The acts gave organized labor nothing new aside from a platitude, thereby installing a regulatory system without encouraging trade-union organizing or jeopardizing the widespread prevalence of the open shop in industry. The legislation confined the government's authority to an indirect regulation of the market, which included an antitrust law that the Supreme Court, in its 1911 landmark decisions, had construed as legalizing reasonable restraints of trade.[233] The two laws sustained the subordination of executive administration to judicial review, thereby protecting the due process rights of property and insulating contractual relations from direct administrative controls.

In the regulatory legislation of 1914, the nation's prevalent political

232. Link, *Wilson*, 2, pp. 427–431. The provision limiting the issue of court injunctions against strikes and other union actions proved to have no practical effect upon existing union vulnerability to the injunction. It was not until the Norris–La Guardia Act of 1932 that the injunction power against union actions was significantly limited.

233. Symbolic of the modus vivendi between small and large capital, Wilson appointed as charter members of the commission Edward N. Hurley, the prominent Illinois machine tool manufacturer and recent president of the Illinois Manufacturers' Association, and George L. Rublee, the Progressive attorney who had served on the U.S. Chamber of Commerce committee on trade commission legislation (see note 230).

forces found a nonstatist method of market administration that succeeded in "taking the trust question out of politics." Proposals for the statist command of the large-corporate economy as a public utility receded, except in times of total war, before indirect government regulation of the corporate-administered market by "apolitical" experts and judicial process, both of which were removed from the direct impact of electoral politics. The FTC solution, based as it was on the Supreme Court's Rule of Reason decisions, represented an advance in positive government and at the same time a triumph of corporate liberalism, in an early phase of its development, over statist tendencies whether of a libertarian or authoritarian hue.

5

Two progressive presidents

Two presidents

It is customary to think of Roosevelt as the progressive president and Taft as the conservative president in an age of reform. In some respects, the distinction is useful, but more for style than substance, more for the Taft of his postpresidential years, and more for the selective appropriation of the two men's respective views by subsequent political movements, than for the politics with which the two leaders were directly involved in the first decade of the twentieth century. Not for nothing did Roosevelt designate Taft his preferred progressive presidential successor. As political protégé and cabinet member, Taft supported Roosevelt's reform initiatives in general, and he shared, in particular, Roosevelt's views on the need to affirm and regulate large corporate enterprise. The secretary of war and former civil governor of the Philippines was also a leading exponent and practitioner of the internationalism championed by Roosevelt.

If Roosevelt achieved notable reform legislation, so Taft as president established an impressive reform record of his own: parcel post, postal savings, federal tax on net corporate income, the Mann–Elkins Act, establishment of a federal children's bureau, railway and mine safety regulation, employer's liability on government contract work, the eight-hour day for federal employees, the income tax amendment (passed by Congress in 1909 and, with Taft's active support, ratified in 1913).

Although Taft was not successful in substantially reforming the tariff, he did succeed in revising some rates downward; Roosevelt succeeded at neither and, indeed, preferred not to touch the issue. Downward tariff revision may have been progressive, but many progressives, especially from the Midwest and West, opposed it. Taft's ambivalence toward the Cannon–Aldrich leadership in Congress and his decision to work with them to achieve legislation matched

Roosevelt's attitude and practice. If Taft did not achieve new antitrust legislation, neither had Roosevelt, although through much of Taft's term his administration's regulatory proposals bore a large resemblance to Roosevelt's and Taft's antitrust prosecutions far outnumbered Roosevelt's in almost half the time. If Taft warned against the dangers of socialism, so did Roosevelt; if Taft emphasized the importance of the Constitution and of the evenhanded enforcement of the law, so did Roosevelt. Differences there were between the two, but they were differences that divided progressives of the time, not differences that distinguished progressives from conservatives. With respect to the questions under examination here, the issue that ultimately came to divide Roosevelt from Taft, as it did Roosevelt from such of his own progressive loyalists as Smith and Garfield, and Roosevelt from Wilson, was that of the role of the government in regulating the market, and within the government, the role of the executive branch. This was a difference that did not then distinguish progressives from conservatives, but that cut across those lines. It was a difference that divided one progressive president from another, until in the contest for the presidency in 1910–1912, it became intertwined with the question of property rights, and then began to mark the distinctions between American conservatism and liberalism, and between liberalism and left-liberalism, in the twentieth century.

Roosevelt

When Theodore Roosevelt became president, his position on the trust question resided well within the bounds of the antistatist view that the corporations should exercise the primary function of regulating the market, and be subject to a secondary regulation by the government. As to the nature of this regulation, Roosevelt remained cautious and tentative. It was only gradually and by degrees that he came to assume a statist position that assigned the superior regulatory role to the national government and the commanding power within the government to the executive branch.

Roosevelt's position as president rested on three leading elements, two of which remained constant from at least 1901 on and were matters, respectively, of historical perspective and political principle; the third element, policy, underwent change.

Historical perspective

Like his adviser Jenks and such other thinkers and advisers as Perkins, Hadley, and Conant, and in line with the prevalent evolutionary social thought of the time, Roosevelt identified modern progressive civilization with advanced industrial society and large-scale business enterprise. He viewed modern world politics as largely a matter of commercial competition among the civilized industrial powers. Large-scale enterprise constituted the essence of America in its development as a modern civilization and in the assumption of its appropriate role in world politics. The great business combinations were nothing other than the large corporations, and the large corporation was the modern business form of large-scale enterprise. It was also the essential instrument of extending trade and investment abroad, in disposing of surpluses that otherwise would derange the economy and provoke social and political instability. It followed that to prohibit business combination meant to prohibit the large corporation and hence to obstruct America's progressive development as a modern society and a modern world power. The large corporation, in Roosevelt's view, had emerged, therefore, as the inevitable product and vehicle of modern economic development; it was the preeminent instrument of industrial efficiency and progress. The legal order must adapt to this "inevitable development of our modern industrial life," by providing for government regulation of the large corporation, not its prohibition.[1]

1. Roosevelt enunciated these premises in state papers as governor of New York and in his first presidential message to Congress, and he repeated them again and again thereafter. The quotation is from his gubernatorial message in January 1900, composed with Jenks's assistance. Jeremiah W. Jenks, *The Trust Problem* (New York: McClure, Phillips, 1900; 5th ed., New York: Doubleday, Doran, 1929), pp. 6–7, and app., pp. 244–279; Hans B. Thorelli, *The Federal Antitrust Policy: Origination of an American Tradition* (Baltimore: Johns Hopkins University Press, 1955), pp. 414–415. In his first presidential message, of 3 Dec. 1901, Roosevelt rendered a complete statement of what we might call the corporate synthesis, by emphasizing the international dimension in the modern-civilization equation: "An additional reason for caution in dealing with corporations is to be found in the international commercial conditions of to-day. The same business conditions which have produced the great aggregations of corporate and individual wealth have made them very potent factors in international commercial competition. Business concerns which have the largest means at their disposal and are managed by the ablest men are naturally those which take the lead in the strife for commercial supremacy among the nations of the world. America has only just begun to assume that commanding position in the international business world which we believe will more and more be hers. It is of the utmost importance that this position be not jeopardized, especially at a time when the overflowing abundance of our own natural resources and the skill, business energy, and mechanical aptitude of our people make foreign markets essential." *Addresses and Presidential Messages of Theodore Roosevelt, 1902–1904* (New York: Putnam's, 1904), p. 295. The "trust" section of Roosevelt's second annual message was written in collaboration with Hadley, Jenks, Prof. Edwin R. A. Seligman of Columbia University, Secretary Root, and the attorney James B. Dill; William H. Harbaugh, *Power and Responsibility: The Life and Times of Theodore Roosevelt* (New York: Farrar, Straus & Cudahy, 1961), p. 124. Cf. Roosevelt, "The Trusts, the People, and the Square Deal," *Outlook* 99 (18 Nov. 1911), pp. 649–656, at p. 655: "Nothing is gained by depriving the American

Political principle

It was a principle by no means peculiar to Roosevelt, but one that he strongly held, that the law must be both enforceable and enforced without arbitrary imposition or the obstruction of modern economic development. The Supreme Court's construction of the Sherman Act as requiring unrestricted competition and forbidding reasonable restraints of trade, created a legal incongruity that Roosevelt considered intolerable, futile, and dangerous. The law must adapt to the facts of economic evolution lest the market become lawless. Quite apart from the necessity of the certainty of law to the smooth operation of contractual relations, the incongruent legal order laid down by the Court must result either in failure to enforce the law or an enforcement that rendered the society's "leading citizens" – its economic managers and greatest property owners, as well as its labor leaders – criminals and outlaws. In either case, it must breed contempt for the law. Failure consistently to enforce the law was especially dangerous in a republic based in principle upon "the rule of law, not men," and equality before the law, for it must provoke an unusually sharp sense of injustice and class resentment and erode the society's claim to legitimacy in the eyes of its citizens. Hence, Roosevelt insisted upon vindicating the supremacy of the law over the practices of the large corporations: The great capitalists must be made to recognize, respect, and submit to the law and the nation-state as the highest authority in the land. By the same token, however, the law must be made fit for such supremacy.

In 1913, Elihu Root in surveying recent social development, noted the passage of society from individual and personal to highly organized, complex, and impersonal relations in employment, production, and consumption. "In the movement of these mighty forces of organization the individual laborer, the individual stockholder, the individual consumer, is helpless." He noted further that "To-day almost all Americans are dependent upon the action of a great number of other persons mostly unknown." In this situation, the American "inevitably calls

Nation of good weapons wherewith to fight in the great field of international industrial competition." For Roosevelt's historical premises in general, see, e.g., "Message Communicated to the Two Houses of Congress at the beginning of the First Session of the Fifty-Seventh Congress," 3 Dec. 1901, and "Message ...," 2 Dec. 1902, *Adresses and Presidential Messages*, pp. 285–299, 346–351, presidential messages of December 1903–1906, at Oswald W. Knauth, *The Policy of the United States Towards Industrial Monopoly* (Columbia University Studies, 1914), pp. 73–84; the *Outlook* article of 18 Nov. 1911; "My Confession of Faith," address at the Convention of the National Progressive Party, Chicago, Tuesday, 6 Aug. 1912, in George H. Payne, ed., *The Birth of the New Party, or Progressive Democracy* (Naperville, Ill.: Nichols, 1912), pp. 254–263.

upon that great combination of all citizens which we call government to do something more than merely keep the peace – to regulate the machinery of production and distribution and safeguard it from interference so that it shall continue to work." In these circumstances, Root observed, "There are two separate processes going on among the civilized nations at the present time. One is an assault by Socialism against the individualism which underlies the social system of Western civilization. The other is an assault against existing institutions upon the ground that they do not adequately protect and develop the existing social order."[2] Roosevelt found it necessary time and again to disclaim socialism and, indeed, to insist that he was fortifying the ramparts against its assault. But he believed it necessary to modify the legal institutions – and, later, government structure and functions as well – in order to "protect and develop the existing social order," an order, as Roosevelt argued, "of federation and combination, in which great capitalistic corporations and labor unions have become factors of tremendous importance in all industrial centers."[3]

As Roosevelt defined the issue in his message to Congress in December 1905, "This is an age of combination, and any effort to prevent all combination will not only be useless, but in the end vicious, because of the contempt for law which the failure to enforce law inevitably produces." The Sherman Act as construed by the Supreme Court's majority, with its outmoded conception of political-economic conditions and its intent to "prohibit all restraint on competition whether ... reasonable or unreasonable," could only have a negative effect, either useless or harmful. Law that was based upon and that affirmed large corporate enterprise could be beneficial and positive in character and could clothe government with the power to facilitate modern development while it protected the public interest.[4]

2. Elihu Root, "Experiments in Government and the Essentials of the Constitution – I," *N. Am. Rev.* 198 (July 1913), pp. 2–3. Root immediately continued (p. 2): "It is of this latter process in our own country that I wish to speak, and I assume an agreement, that the right of individual liberty and the inseparable right of private property which lie at the foundation of our modern civilization ought to be maintained."
3. Message to Congress, December 1903, at Knauth, *Policy of the United States*, pp. 73–74. For Roosevelt's insistence that he was a bulwark against socialism, "a safety-valve for the popular unrest and indignation," a barrier against "class hatred," against "a tidal wave of violent State action," against "a radical and extreme democracy," and against outright "State ownership" of the large corporations, see, e.g., Roosevelt to Philander C. Knox, 10 Nov. 1904, Roosevelt to Paul Morton (president, Equitable Life Assurance Society), 2 Jan. 1907, Roosevelt to Henry L. Higginson, 11 Feb. 1907, all in TR.
4. Message to Congress, December 1905, at Knauth, *Policy of the United States*, pp. 78, 79.

Roosevelt's historical perspective informed his conception of the principle of legal congruity. If it were true that in the past, small-scale, dispersed enterprise generally distributed only small-scale, dispersed political power among persons or groups, then the public interest could be expected to gain expression in government automatically, as it were, by the interaction of these small and disparate interests within the framework of representative democracy hedged by the separation of powers. The Sherman Act as construed by the Supreme Court from 1897 to 1911 embodied this conception of society. Justice Peckham had stated as much in *obiter dicta*. Concentrated economic power meant the decline of the self-determining citizen in the market and in politics, and it meant the rise of massive political power capable of subordinating the individual to hierarchic organization and the government to special interest; it thus threatened democracy itself. The government, through the Sherman Act and similar legislation, must therefore intervene to redress the balance of power wherever an individual or group amassed so much economic power as to inhibit or negate the interaction of disparate, competing interests.

To Roosevelt, such legal theory and the corresponding legal structure appeared to be atavistic and reactionary. Because large-scale industry and its vehicle, the large corporation, were necessary results of economic evolution, the persistence and enforcement of such legal institutions must mean the strangulation of progress, the artificial preservation of a primitive economy, and the inhibition of the nation's fulfillment as a modern civilization and a great world power. The maintenance of laws without their enforcement, on the other hand, must mean contempt for law and the very subordination of government to concentrated economic power feared by the advocates of the Sherman Act as it stood. Roosevelt therefore argued for a change in the legal structure, which would vindicate government as an instrument of the "interest of the public as a whole," by recognizing and affirming large-scale corporate enterprise along with the reasonable combinations and restraints of trade they implied, and regulating them.[5] The substitute for the dispersed power of the past was to be a vigorous national democracy that subordinated economic power to public policy as determined by the people, codified by their representatives in legislation, and implemented by an executive acting as the steward of the public welfare. The judiciary must not obstruct, but serve, this national democracy.

5. Message to Congress, December 1904, at ibid., pp. 76–77.

Policy

In the formulation of policy respecting the nature and scope of regulation, Roosevelt's views underwent gradual change. Because regulation of the market and of the use of property was so central an issue to Roosevelt and to his times, as his views evolved with respect to regulatory policy, so they did with respect to other issues, and to the government-society relation in general.

It will be recalled that the senators who drafted and sponsored the Sherman Act considered it as essentially a statutory embodiment, at the federal level, of common-law doctrine, and that the federal courts so construed the act from 1890 to 1897. In this period, moreover, as well as during the next fifteen years, the executive branch of the federal government, as represented by the various presidents and attorneys general, who were responsible for enforcing the law, shared this view. Until the Trans-Missouri decision in 1897, this disposition on the part of the executive implied no impropriety and no disharmony between law and policy. The executive branch's outlook, at any rate, was only natural considering the views of the presidents with respect to economic matters and those of their attorneys general, who themselves were corporation lawyers by profession or pro-corporate by association or conviction.[6] After the 1897 decision, however, the conflict between executive policy and the law as judicially construed, combined with Congress's failure to act, yielded an altogether different situation.

The state of the law and policy in the 1890s is well illustrated in the evaluation of the Sherman Act that President Grover Cleveland's attorney general, the Boston Democrat and corporation lawyer Richard Olney, offered in his annual report for 1893. Delivered well before the Supreme Court's decisions of 1897–1899, Olney's opinion can be considered neither disingenuous nor improper. "There has been, and probably still is," Olney observed, "a widespread impression that the aim and effect of this statute are to prohibit and prevent those aggregations of capital which are so common at the present day, and which are sometimes on so large a scale as to control practically all the branches of an extensive industry." Nevertheless, he stated, "It is sufficient to

6. Cf. Thorelli, *Antitrust Policy*, pp. 370–405; William Letwin, *Law and Economic Policy in America: The Evolution of the Sherman Antitrust Act* (New York: Random House, 1965), pp. 100–142. Letwin offers a useful corrective against the view, finding support in Thorelli's treatment, that the attorneys general before 1897 were remiss in neglecting to enforce a duly passed law, if not actually culpable of sabotaging the law; but Letwin is critical of the McKinley administration for failure to bring suits under the law after the Supreme Court's decisions of 1897–1899 gave the law wide applicability.

point out what small basis [there] is for the popular impression referred to." Olney went on to explain that "as all ownership of property is of itself a monopoly, and as every business contract or transaction may be viewed as a combination which more or less restrains some part or kind of trade or commerce, any literal application of the provisions of the statute is out of the question."[7]

Four years later, in 1897, the prominent Pennsylvania Republican and leader of the bar Philander C. Knox, soon to serve as attorney general under McKinley and Roosevelt, revealed in a major address the extent to which his view of the antitrust law was, like Olney's and the Sherman Act's authors', rooted in common-law doctrine. Because monopolies could "only exist by grant from the sovereign," Knox averred, invoking the old common-law definition, and therefore could not be created "by contract between individuals," statutes that "make it a penal offense to make contracts creating monopolies, undertake to punish an impossible act." The principle embedded within this word-play was that not monopoly taken literally, but unreasonable restraint of trade, or "unfair" practices, constituted the proper object of antitrust legislation. Accordingly, Knox considered competition subordinate to freedom of contract, declaring: "Segregated competition in business is not a plank in our platform of rights, but the liberty of contract, included in the right to acquire and possess property is a main one. It is not nearly so important to foster a fanciful system of free trade in a state as to rear a race of free men." A contract "obnoxious to a sound public policy," a common-law concept, he held, properly should be and "is now invalid." But the Supreme Court's Trans-Missouri decision of that year, which pronounced against reasonable as well as unreasonable restraints of trade, violated this principle. It represented an infringement on the common right to acquire and dispose of property. "Combinations, whether of employers or employees, are not essentially bad or essentially good," Knox in part concluded; it was therefore "well-nigh impossible to legislate in reference to them lawfully or wisely."[8]

It remained for President McKinley to confirm the gulf between executive policy and the law, in his annual message to Congress in 1899, delivered on the heels of the Supreme Court's reaffirmation of its

7. Quoted at Thorelli, *Antitrust Policy*, p. 385.
8. Knox, "The Law of Labor and Trade," presidential address before the Pennsylvania Bar Association, at *American Law Register and Review*, n.s., 36. (July 1897), pp. 417–436, at pp. 423–424, 426, 434, 436. One of Pittsburgh's and the nation's eminent corporation lawyers, Knox had assisted, for example, in the formation of the Carnegie Steel Company, that is, in changing the enterprise's organization from a partnership to a corporation.

Trans-Missouri decision in the Joint Traffic and Addyston Pipe cases. Here the president stated that "it is universally conceded that combinations which engross or control the market of any particular kind of merchandise or commodity necessary to the general community, by suppressing natural or ordinary competiton, whereby prices are unduly enhanced to the general consumer, are obnoxious not only to the common law but also to the public welfare."[9] Significantly, in this statement of policy on the trust problem, McKinley chose to define what was obnoxious to the common law and the public welfare rather than what was in violation of the Sherman Act as construed by the Supreme Court in three successive cases.

Roosevelt was the first president to combine the common-law view and the affirmation of large-corporate enterprise with a commitment to legislative reform. In the common-law and pro-corporate outlook, Roosevelt and McKinley were alike. It was the advocacy of legislative reform that distinguished Roosevelt from McKinley and for that matter from Senator Mark Hanna.

Roosevelt inherited a deepening chasm between law and policy. He had no intention of enforcing the Sherman Act as an instrument of restoring the competitive regime. Yet, from political principle, and with the concurrence of such corporate executives as Perkins and Gary, organizations such as the Civic Federation, and pro-corporate eminences such as Knox and Root, he became determined to bring the large corporation and the emerging administered market under the rule of law. Initially, he pursued the cautious call for publicity of corporate affairs, which already enjoyed broad support. Publicity would serve to some extent as a surrogate for the old competitive discipline in imposing fair prices and wages, reasonable profits, and proper capitalization; it would also serve as a basis for intelligent legislation, including, if necessary, remedial taxation.[10]

In the absence of the likelihood that the Supreme Court would reverse or modify its interpretation of the Sherman Act, or that (apart from the regulation of railroads) Congress would take definitive legislative action, Roosevelt phased the publicity idea into the proposal for a bureau of corporations as a presidential agency for information gathering. Information, soberly and objectively analyzed, would provide the grounds for distinguishing between restraints of trade or corporate combinations that were reasonable or in the public interest, and those

---

9. Quoted at Thorelli, *Antitrust Policy*, p. 399.
10. Roosevelt had already covered all this gound in his gubernatorial address of 1900. Ibid., pp. 414–415.

that were unreasonable or detrimental to the public. Once established, the bureau provided an administrative context for proposing federal incorporation or licensing of interstate corporations and their operations. But in addition, it provided a legislative basis for Roosevelt's persistence in enforcing the Sherman Act selectively against unreasonable ("bad") corporations or corporate practices,[11] and thereby reassuring an agitated public that the "trusts" were not above the law, while demonstrating that he would not turn the law against modern industrial evolution.

Roosevelt's selective enforcement of the Sherman Act, in a manner openly renunciatory of the law as the Supreme Court had construed it, represented an executive usurpation of the judicial function, and in effect, therefore, of the legislative function as well. It also violated the president's constitutional obligation "to take care that the laws be faithfully executed" (Article II, section 3). It accorded, however, with his belief in a higher obligation, namely, the readjustment and accommodation of political power and the law to socioeconomic evolution, or, in other words, to the property-production system, or mode of production – not to any property-production system, but to one that was, as he believed corporate capitalism to be, demonstrably modern and progressive. If the law were to be supreme over persons and power, it must first be made fit for its supremacy.

Roosevelt practiced the same temporary subordination of the law to the needs of the evolving property-production system in the sphere of banking, where the national banking law, and hence the banking system, had fallen out of phase with the needs of an emergent corporate capitalism. The latter had increasing need for a central bank and an elastic currency supply (an assets currency, as it was then referred to), neither of which the national banking law provided. Pro-corporate partisans argued that central banking and currency elasticity were needed, among other reasons, to provide countercyclical and counterseasonal protections to the money and capital markets, thereby hedging against panics, and stabilizing investment and employment levels. Central banking was also needed, they believed, to facilitate the financing of a growing corporation-centered international trade and investment. In the absence of a political consensus sufficient to create a congressional majority for banking reform, a consensus not achieved until 1913 with the passage of the Federal Reserve Act, Roosevelt

11. During the approximately seven and a half years of his presidency, Roosevelt brought forty-four actions under the Sherman Act, of which eighteen were bills in equity, twenty-five were criminal indictments, and one, a forfeiture proceeding. Knauth, *Policy of the United States*, p. 86.

permitted Secretary of the Treasury Leslie M. Shaw to dispose of Treasury funds unlawfully, deploying the Treasury as a sort of surrogate central bank, to stabilize the New York money and capital markets.[12] As with large corporations in industry, so here in banking, Roosevelt did not shrink from mobilizing extralegal or illegal executive power in regulating the market, to serve what he considered to be the healthful evolution of the property-production system, where that system was developing within an incongruent legal order. In both cases, however, Congress effectively concurred in Roosevelt's policies by acquiescing in them, thereby in effect affirming the president's view that the law and public policy must serve, and ultimately be accommodated to, progressive evolution.

The Hepburn bill and similar draft bills that Roosevelt backed represented in part a proposal to institutionalize in the legal order, binding upon successor administrations, what had become Roosevelt's policy in practice, that is, the policy of allowing reasonable restraints of trade and of seeking to attain the legitimation of large-scale corporate capitalism. These bills, however, also represented something more: a proposal to expand executive administration at the expense of judicial process – if not entirely replacing it – and to insert the government directly into the work of administering the market as the ultimate arbiter of valid contracts, business practices, and investment strategy.

It was after the defeat of the Hepburn bill, after his departure from office, and in the course of his break with Taft, that Roosevelt arrived at making more fully explicit the statist implications of his heretofore evolving public position. He articulated them most clearly in the campaign for his return to presidential power. Without the inhibitions imposed by the responsibilities of office, Roosevelt spoke out more freely. Reiterating the historical argument for accepting large corporations as inhering in "modern business and modern industrial conditions, . . . [and] all the modern conditions of our civilization," Roosevelt renounced the "sincere rural toryism" of those who would use the

12. Respecting Roosevelt's references to the lack of a consensus, particularly among the big financiers themselves, on currency and banking reform, making legislation impossible, the following letters, e.g., Roosevelt to Conant, 9 July 1900, Roosevelt to N. M. Butler, 29 Aug. 1903, Roosevelt to Lucius B. Swift, 9 Nov. 1907, Roosevelt to Jacob H. Schiff, 9 Nov. 1907, Roosevelt to Frederic A. Delano, 9 Nov. 1907, Roosevelt to Conant, 25 Aug. 1911 (S. 3A), all in TR. On unlawful and interventionist Treasury operations, see, e.g., Abram Piatt Andrew, "The Treasury and the Banks Under Secretary Shaw," *QJE* 21 (Aug. 1907), pp. 519–566; Charles A. Conant, *A History of Modern Banks of Issue* (New York: Putnam, 1927), pp. 436–437; Leslie M. Shaw, *Current Issues* (New York: D. Appleton, 1908), pp. 284–304.

antitrust law "to restore business to the competitive conditions of the middle of the last century," an effort that was "foredoomed to end in failure, and that, if successful, would be mischievous to the last degree." Because it was "absolutely impossible to go back to an outworn social status," Roosevelt reasoned, "we must abandon definitely the *laissez-faire* theory of political economy, and fearlessly champion a system of increased Governmental control, paying no heed to the cries of the worthy people who denounce this as Socialistic."[13]

It followed that "in order to meet the inevitable increase in the power of corporations produced by modern industrial conditions," it was "necessary to increase in like fashion the activity of the sovereign power which alone could control such corporations." Their huge size and power rendered the modern corporations "fraught with potential menace to the community"; this made it "incumbent upon the community to exercise through its administrative (not merely through its judicial) officers a strict supervision" over them. On the one hand, the national government should not be saddled with "a policy of unregulated competition and of the destruction of all big corporations, that is, of all the most efficient business industries in the land." Nor should it, on the other hand, "persevere in the hopeless experiment of trying to regulate these industries by means only of lawsuits, each lasting several years, and of uncertain results." Rather, the large corporation should be subjected primarily to administrative regulation. It should be "so supervised and controlled as to guarantee us, the people, against its doing mischief." In effect drawing upon the constitutional ambiguity residing in the Supreme Court's non-common-law construction of the Sherman Act between 1897 and 1911, Roosevelt combined these premises with the assertion of the national government's paramount authority, as against both the states and private parties, in regulating the national market, a position assuming particular significance from his strongly advocating it after the Supreme Court's Rule of Reason decisions of 1911. In America's system of government, Roosevelt argued, "Congress alone has power under the Constitution effectively and thoroughly and at all points to deal with inter-State commerce, and where Congress, as it should do, provides laws that will give the Nation full jurisdiction over the whole field, then that jurisdiction becomes, of necessity, exclusive...."

Beyond a negative kind of regulation, merely policing the market against improper behavior, the national government's jurisdiction,

13. "The Trusts, the People, and the Square Deal," *Outlook* 99 (18 Nov. 1911), pp. 652–653, 654.

Roosevelt held, should in a positive way "enter upon a course of supervision, control, and regulation of these great corporations – a regulation which we should not fear, if necessary, to bring to the point of control of monopoly prices, just as in exceptional cases railway rates are now regulated." Roosevelt recommended that the authority "to exercise this supervision, this authoritative control," be lodged with a renovated Bureau of Corporations or with "some other governmental body similar to the Inter-State Commerce Commission," which "should be created" for the purpose. Collaterally, the Sherman Act could be invoked against "immoral business practices," as in the cases brought against the Standard Oil and American Tobacco companies, but with provision for positive government powers over convicted corporations, such as those proposed in the Foulke plan. Upon the courts' declaring "a corporation to possess a monopolistic character," it could then be completely dissolved and not reassembled "save on terms and under whatever conditions may be imposed by the governmental body in which is invested the regulatory power."[14]

Ultimately, the overall system of regulatory control, Roosevelt stated, "should undoubtedly indirectly or directly extend to dealing with all questions connected with their [corporations'] treatment of their employees, including the wages, the hours of labor, and the like." As a result, large corporations would be made into well-managed, well-behaved servants of the public interest; "the National Government [would assume] complete power over the organization and capitalization" of all interstate corporations, and it would "control them in such a fashion as amply to safeguard the interests of the whole public, including producers, consumers, and wage-workers." Roosevelt noted that "Against all such increase of Government regulation the argument is raised that it would amount to a form of Socialism." He discounted such objections as familiar echoes of similar opposition to the creation of the Interstate Commerce Commission and to state utilities commissions, stating, "the 'conservatives' will do well to remember that these unfair and iniquitous methods by great masters of corporate capital have done more to cause popular discontent with the propertied classes than all the orations of all the Socialist orators in the country put together."[15]

Nevertheless, Roosevelt's articulation of a comprehensive program of national control of the market, extending to prices, wages, and conditions of labor, combined with his stepped-up public attacks on the

14. Ibid., 652–656.
15. Ibid., 649, 655–656.

courts, in which he endorsed recall of judicial decisions, amounted to a position centered upon a state-directed economy under executive command.[16] In rejecting the Supreme Court's construction of the Sherman Act, before 1911, as dictating unrestricted competition, Roosevelt embraced the other side of the Court's coin and stayed with it after the Court's turnaround of 1911: the nation-state's supreme authority in regulating interstate and foreign commerce. The large corporation would become the agency of the state and its political or social policy. If indulge in shibboleths we must, let it be said that Roosevelt's position was that not of "Trust-Buster" but of "Trust-Muster" – he would muster the trusts into the national service. His repeated disclaimers about socialism went to justify, not to deny, the position.[17]

The Supreme Court's Rule of Reason decisions of 1911 represented a partial vindication of Roosevelt's opposition to the Harlan-led majority of the Court during the previous years. In this instance, Roosevelt all but conceded that the judiciary had exceeded its authority, but he defended it against such charges, thereby implicitly exonerating his own presidential actions that similarly exceeded constitutional or legal authority. "It is contended," Roosevelt noted, "that in these recent decisions the Supreme Court legislated; so it did; and it had to; because Congress had signally failed to do *its* duty by legislating.... The blame in such cases," Roosevelt argued, "lies with the body which has been derelict, and not with the body which reluctantly makes good the dereliction."[18] The higher obligation to use power to facilitate progressive socioeconomic evolution took precedence over formal legality.

16. Cf. John M. Blum, *The Republican Roosevelt* (1954; New York: Atheneum, 1966), p. 96: "Roosevelt envisioned a new kind of federal executive power to control the complex processes of an industrialized state." And ibid., pp. 87–124 passim, for Blum's analysis; and to similar effect, George E. Mowry, *The Era of Theodore Roosevelt and the Birth of Modern America, 1900–1912* (1958; New York: Harper & Row, 1962), pp. 220–225.

17. Cf. e.g., Roosevelt, "... Where We Cannot Work with Socialists," *Outlook* 91 (20 Mar. 1909), pp. 619–623, "... Where We Can Work with Socialists," Ibid. (27 Mar. 1909), pp. 662–664, and speech at Osawatomie, Kansas, 31 Aug. 1910, all at William H. Harbaugh, ed., *The Writings of Theodore Roosevelt* (New York: Bobbs-Merrill, 1967), pp. 303–333, in addition to Roosevelt's *Outlook* article of 18 Nov. 1911, and his "Confession of Faith," both cited in note 1, above.

18. *Outlook* 99 (18 Nov. 1911), p. 653. Roosevelt's emphasis. Perhaps in anticipation of such charges of judicial legislation, made among others by Justice Harlan in his partial dissent, Chief Justice White wrote the Court's opinions in these cases as if they were consistent with, not reversals of, *Trans-Missouri* and the Court's consistently held position thereafter. Given that impossible task, it is no surprise that White's reasoning often appears tortuous and the writing often unintelligible. For a different explanation of White's obscurity in these decisions – the general infelicity of his writing style – an explanation that remains unpersuasive to me in view of White's relative lucidity in his earlier dissenting opinions, see Letwin, *Law and Economic Policy*, pp. 256–265. At the same time, it is only fair to note that *Trans-Missouri* may be equally vulnerable to charges of judicial legislation.

Now that the Supreme Court had accommodated the law to the corporate-administered market, it was no longer relevant to link a license-registration system with dispensations permitting reasonable restraints of trade. The newly construed law, Roosevelt now held, should be "kept on the statute books," but to regard the Sherman Act by itself as adequate was "a sign not of progress, but of toryism and reaction." Instead, the law should be "strengthened" by the establishment of a federal administistative commission with "complete power to regulate and control" the great interstate corporations and to exercise authority similar to that exercised by the ICC over the railroads. In arguing the necessity of giving "the National Government complete power" over the operations and conduct, as well as over "the organization and capitalization of all business concerns engaged in inter-State commerce," Roosevelt recalled that as president, "I urged as strongly as I knew how that the policy followed with relation to railways in connection with the Inter-State Commerce Law should be followed by the National Government as regards all great business concerns," and that accordingly, "there should be created" a commission "with powers somewhat similar to those of the Inter-State Commerce Commission, but covering the whole field of Inter-State business exclusive of transportation."[19] By 1911–1912, what Roosevelt had specifically in mind, as we have seen, was a license-registration system drawn along the more intrusively stringent lines of the Foulke plan. It was a system to be administered by a commission that would, in addition to everything else, secure "conservation of our natural resources, fair wages, good social conditions, and reasonable prices." The commission Roosevelt had in mind, in sum, was not that of the limited powers and scope of the Federal Trade Commission as it was to be established by Congress two years later, but one that would actuate the supremacy of state authority in administering the market and ordering the economy to accord with social policy.

From at least the time of the Hepburn bill through the presidential campaign of 1912, Roosevelt consistently invoked the ICC analogy in

19. "Confession of Faith," 6 Aug. 1912, at Payne, *Birth*, pp. 254, 259–260; *Outlook* 99 (18 Nov. 1911), p. 649. It may be doubted that Roosevelt publicly "urged" these precise policies while president "as strongly as I knew how," but this statement accurately indicates the trend of his policy thinking while he held the executive office, and it of course directly states his position as of late 1911 and thereafter in the campaign of 1912. Although by 1912, Roosevelt's position on regulatory policy was more fully elaborated in its broader implications, Mowry's assessment (*Era of Theodore Roosevelt*, p. 222) that Roosevelt's position on federal regulatory powers was essentially the same in 1910–1912 as in 1908 seems to me accurate. For a similar assessment, see Harbaugh's commentary (*Writings*, p. 315) on Roosevelt's Osawatomie speech of 31 Aug. 1910; cf. Harbaugh, *Power and Responsibility*, pp. 343–348.

indicating the kind of executive-administrative control he thought it necessary to install over the economy as a whole. Rather than distinguish industry, and the economy in general, from public service business like common carriers and public utilities, he argued their similarity and the need to subject them to similar kinds of comprehensive public administration. He was thereby explicitly taking the position that large corporations in the economy as a whole were to be treated as public utilities and the executives of those corporations were to become, in effect, public-service capitalists. Such controls over common carriers and public utilities proper by a large and growing administrative bureaucracy were one thing, and were largely accepted among capitalists, policymakers, and politicians, but the same kind of controls over the economy in general was quite another.[20] It would mean a government-directed economy, one that in Roosevelt's view, as he presented it with greater intensity and eloquence in 1910–1912, would be directed in the service of a national democracy under the stewardship of the federal executive.[21] It was this aspect of Roosevelt's politics that caused concern among such of his own loyalists as Smith and Garfield, and that elicited the widespread opposition of capitalists, large and small, from 1908 onward.

It was therefore not simply farfetched hysteria, but a matter of serious debate over fundamental law and policy, that led political opponents as well as capitalists to criticize and fear Roosevelt for advocating what from their point of view amounted to state socialism or, at any rate, to a basic change in the constitutional framework of the government-society relation.

20. Cf., e.g., Roosevelt's statements: "... the same kind and degree of control and supervision which should be exercised over the public-service corporations should be extended also to combinations which control necessaries of life, ... or which deal in them on an important scale." Speech at Osawatomie, Kan., 31 Aug. 1910, at Harbaugh, *Writings*, pp. 322–323. "We propose to handle the colossal industrial concerns engaged in interstate business as we are handling the great railways engaged in interstate business ..." Address at San Francisco, 14 Sept. 1912, at ibid., p. 289. On the development of ICC powers and functions, and the dramatic growth in the size of its staff in 1906–1908, immediately upon the passage of the Hepburn Act (and even before the Mann–Elkins Act), under Roosevelt's prodding, see Ari Hoogenboom and Olive Hoogenboom, *A History of the ICC: From Panacea to Palliative* (New York: Norton, 1976), pp. 52–53.
21. Blum, *Republican Roosevelt*, pp. 116–124; Henry F. Pringle, *Theodore Roosevelt: A Biography* (New York: Harcourt Brace, 1931), pp. 540–571; Mowry, *Era of Theodore Roosevelt*, pp. 197–225, 290–295; Harbaugh, *Power and Responsibility*, pp. 377–395, 412–426, 437–450; Paolo E. Coletta, *The Presidency of William Howard Taft* (Lawrence: The University Press of Kansas, 1973), pp. 217–247; John M. Cooper, Jr., *The Warrior and the Priest: Woodrow Wilson and Theodore Roosevelt* (Cambridge, Mass.: Harvard University Press, 1983), pp. 187–221.

In response to Roosevelt's speeches and writings in the spring and summer of 1912, where in addition to his regulatory position Roosevelt called for popular restrictions on judicial protections of property, the subordination of wealth to the people's welfare, greater equality of opportunity and of political participation, and redistributive income and inheritance taxation, President Taft, for example, saw the views of his former patron, now his rival, as pointing toward the "undermining of our Constitutional Government," as exemplifying extremism rather than progressivism, and, as he confided to his personal secretary the day after Roosevelt's acceptance address to the National Progressive party, as being "radical to the last degree in state socialism."[22] Even if Taft's view may be in part discounted as that of an adversary in an electoral contest, it was shared by others, not only such others as Root and Lodge but also, to some significant degree of concern, by such Bull Moosers as Smith and Garfield, that is, in both cases, by people who had been longtime political and personal associates of Roosevelt, including some who were fighting at his side during the election.

Representative of opinion in higher circles of corporate capitalism, opinion by no means unfriendly to Roosevelt and reform in the recent past, were the commentaries on political affairs provided by the president of the National City Bank of New York City, Frank A. Vanderlip, to his mentor and the bank's elder statesman and effective chief James Stillman. From 1910 to 1912, Vanderlip, like many other knowledgeable observers, saw "radical politics" as running "rampant" through the American body politic. He analyzed Roosevelt's strategy as that of denouncing "the conservative wing of the Republican party" and seeking to "rally to him the radical wings of both parties." He believed that "Roosevelt at the right moment" would appear "in the guise of the friend of business and will make a play that will bring to him a large part of the business vote along with the radical vote." This, it would seem, had been his previous pattern as president. "That his promises will be worthless goes without saying," Vanderlip thought. "There are some conservative people," he noted, "who believe that Roosevelt, after all, is a bad talker rather than a bad doer, that he would have the courage to meet socialistic tendencies and that by all odds the worst would be in his words rather than his acts." But, on second thought,

22. Coletta, *Presidency*, pp. 228, 229, 233, 239, 242. Latter quotation, Taft to Charles D. Hilles, 7 Aug. 1912, at Donald E. Anderson, *William Howard Taft: A Conservative's Conception of the Presidency* (Ithaca, N.Y: Cornell University Press, 1973), p. 198. Taft continued: "He has not advocated the appropriation of rich men's property to distribute among the poor, but that is only another step and perhaps is one involved in the really successful accomplishment of those steps which he proposes."

Vanderlip added, having in mind the national political temper at the time, "Probably the truth lies in between."[23]

Vanderlip's point was that although it was possible, even supposing it was likely, that Roosevelt did not believe much of what he was saying, or at any rate, that he would not implement his proposals if elected, and although he may have been acting as a safety valve to draw off and render harmless political radicalism in the body politic, as he had in the past and as he himself had claimed to have done, nevertheless, whatever his current motives, the substance of his views represented, or appealed to, a large segment of public opinion. Whether or not he was playing the demagogue, such proposals as he was making in public in the pursuit of votes had better be taken seriously. Accordingly, Vanderlip wrote Stillman in May 1912, "The question of partisan politics ... is serious enough, but the serious thing lies underneath that. It lies in the unreasonable radicalness of the whole social body, quite apart from partisan politics." In view of the election results of the following November, in which presidential candidates publicly perceived as well to the left of center took 75 percent of the popular vote (Roosevelt, Wilson, and Debs), Vanderlip's assessment of the national political tendency was not unreasonable.[24] Hence, he continued, "It seems to me we have reached one of the great crises in our government." Ahead lay "more than a partisan struggle; the questions are not partisan, they are fundamental." That is to say, Vanderlip explained, "It is not the tariff, it is the constitution; it is not the personal success of this man or that, it is the question of the continuance of our form of government; it is not a matter of restrictive legislation, it is the fundamental question of property rights." As a man of affairs who looked upon himself as progressive and open-minded, he concluded, on a note of consoling resignation, "A change in the form of government might even be for the better; I am not sure of that." But, he added, "Whether Roosevelt, should he be elected, would be drunk with power and change our form of government no one can say."[25]

Whatever else Vanderlip's concern may have been, his ruminating over the extent to which Roosevelt was raising fundamental questions

23. Vanderlip to Stillman, 13 May and 2 Sept. 1910, and 17, 24 May 1912, all in FAV.
24. See Coletta's political analysis of the 1912 election results at *Presidency*, pp. 245–247; and the postelection complaint of a socialist that "the new [Progressive] party ... begins its career with the brazen theft of half the working program of the Socialist party," quoted at Harbaugh, *Power and Responsibility*, p. 450.
25. Vanderlip to Stillman, 17 May 1912, FAV. A week later, in a darker mood, Vanderlip wrote, "I believe seed has been sown that will be harvested in great tribulation to this nation." Vanderlip to Stillman, 24 May 1912, FAV.

of "our form of government" and "property rights" was not misplaced. This would be the case whether or not Roosevelt meant what he was saying. In spite of skeptical suspicions, however, the record leaves little reason to doubt that Roosevelt was sincere in the principles and proposals he expounded in 1910–1912 respecting the government-market relation; they bore a large degree of consistency with those he had been both privately and publicly advocating since 1907–1908. The evidence indicates that far from playing the demagogue in this respect, he had every intention of seeking their implementation if reelected.[26]

Although between 1908 and 1912 his regulatory proposals remained rather constant in essentials, his larger political outlook underwent significant movement. It evolved from an evolutionary positivist affirmation of a modern capitalism closely regulated and directed by the state, to a commitment to integrate this affirmation with the American republican political tradition. In that commitment, Roosevelt had set himself in dialogue with socialism, just as such policy-oriented intellectuals as Conant, Hadley, and Seligman had done, but he had not become a socialist, still less a radical or populist. It seems more accurate, and more illuminating of both the substance and thrust of his political thinking, to describe his position by 1910–1912 as that of a left-wing statist who was prepared to play a leadership role in achieving significant changes in the "form of government," the government-society relation, and the nature of property rights. Roosevelt himself put the matter succinctly in his Osawatomie speech in the summer of 1910, when he said that in standing for the "square deal," he meant "not merely that I stand for fair play under the present rules of the game, but that I stand for having those rules changed," and he wanted the rules changed in the direction

---

26. "A broken promise is bad enough in private life. It is worse in the field of politics. No man is worth his salt in public life who makes on the stump a pledge which he does not keep after election; and if he makes such a pledge and does not keep it, hunt him out of public life." Roosevelt, at Osawatomie, Kan., 31 Aug. 1910, Harbaugh, *Writings*, p. 317. For assessments confirming Roosevelt's sincerity of belief and intent, see, Harbaugh, *Power and Responsibility*, pp. 412–426, esp. at pp. 421–424; Blum, *Republican Roosevelt*, pp. 106–124, 142–150; Pringle, *Roosevelt*, pp. 540–571; Cooper, *Warrior and Priest*, pp. 143–163, 206–221; also, Mowry's assessment (*Era*, pp. 222–223, 225) that Roosevelt by 1907–1910 had become "a radical progressive." I agree with these assessments, but for reasons to be indicated, I would not use the term "radical" to describe Roosevelt's position or disposition. See also Herbert Croly's assessment of Roosevelt, as early as 1908–1909, that although the "real meaning of his programme" might have been "more novel and more radical than he himself has publicly proclaimed," his commitment to the program, to "the national and to the democratic ideas is thoroughgoing and absolute." *The Promise of American Life* (1909; New York: Dutton, 1963), pp. 167–175, quotes at pp. 173, 170.

of effecting "a more substantial equality of opportunity and of reward for equally good service."[27]

Roosevelt's statism – he would call it the New Nationalism – may be better understood if two major points are kept in mind. In the first place, it was, in his thinking, the pro-democratic and socially just alternative to the anti-democratic and socially unjust characteristics of a corporate capitalism left less subject to public control; it was, also, the alternative to socialism, that is, to the elimination of private property in large-scale enterprise and its replacement by state ownership. Short of ending capitalism or democracy, the condition of the American people's acceptance of large corporate enterprise was, in his view, not merely its regulation but its close control and direction by the government. In the second place, Roosevelt's statism was a limited one, confined to the management of the economy. In no sense did he believe in extending state power beyond that to the restriction of individual rights, political democracy, or civil liberties. He insisted, indeed, upon a more vibrant political democracy and increasing individual liberty (within current moral bounds), as both the means and the outcome of the achievement of a state-directed economy. His statism was partial and libertarian, not totalistic and authoritarian. Whatever it might become upon establishment, in Roosevelt's conception, incompletely thought out as it may have been, it was a species not of a corporate state but of a liberal-democratic state. That is to say, it was not to be a statism based upon an unlimited control of the individual by the state or by other collectivities so controlled by the state, nor upon an alliance of corporate capital and the state, in which society as manifested factionally in capital and the market rendered the state its servant, and all other groups and individuals along with it. Rather, it was to be one based upon the state's defining, prescribing, limiting, and commanding that part of society represented by corporate-capitalist property and market relations, yet itself limited by law and individual rights. In making the state supreme over society in its corporate-capitalist property and market relations, the state nevertheless remained subject to society in its political relations, that is, so long as the latter were democratic.

Roosevelt held that state power properly followed economic development, specifically, that in the American historical context, the functions and scope of the national government's power had grown, and must grow, in proportion as "the business of the country has become nation-

27. Speech at Osawatomie, 31 Aug. 1910, Harbaugh, *Writings*, p. 321. The Osawatomie speech marked the public crystallization of this integration of positivism and republicanism, and in that sense, I believe, a turning point in Roosevelt's broader political role.

al in character." The extension of government power was necessary both as a check against concentrated corporate power and as a means of thereby protecting and expanding the people's liberties as producers, consumers, individuals, and citizens.[28] The American people were therefore "right in demanding that New Nationalism, without which we cannot hope to deal with new problems." Although "overcentralization" should be avoided, he argued, "a broad and far-reaching nationalism" was needed that put "national need before sectional or personal advantage" and that put an end to "the impotence which springs from the overdivision of governmental powers." Traditional federalism and checks and balances should not be allowed to become a screen for special privilege or a bulwark against democracy. "The National Government belongs to the whole American people, and where the whole American people are interested, that interest can be guarded effectively only by the National Government." Roosevelt tied this proposition about centralized government power to principles of both popular democracy and social justice: "I have scant patience," he declared, "with this talk of the tyranny of the majority. The only tyrannies from which men, women, and children are suffering are the tyrannies of minorities." The American republic "means nothing unless it means the triumph of a real democracy, the triumph of popular government, and, in the long run, of an economic system under which each man shall be guaranteed the opportunity to show the best that there is in him." Hence, for Roosevelt, political democracy and economic democracy, or social justice, were indivisible.[29]

The struggles "for human betterment," Roosevelt noted, had ever been to enlarge "equality of opportunity," and "the essence of any struggle for human liberty" had always been and "must always be, to take from some one man or class of men the right to enjoy power, or wealth, or position, or immunity, which has not been earned by service to his or their fellows." This struggle had been "the central condition of progress"; "this conflict between the men who possess more than they have earned and the men who have earned more than they possess." Here was a class struggle that wise political leadership will not leave to itself or exploit but manage and channel constructively in the direction of progressive democracy, as American political leadership had, at critical junctures, succeeded in doing in the past. In this struggle, the

28. Roosevelt to R. D. Silliman, 25 Feb. 1908, TR; Address at San Francisco, 14 Sept. 1912, Harbaugh, *Writings*, pp. 290–291.
29. Roosevelt at Carnegie Hall, New York City, 20 Mar. 1912, quoted at Harbaugh, *Power and Responsibility*, p. 423; at Osawatomie, Harbaugh, *Writings*, pp. 316, 330.

"New Nationalism regards the executive power as the steward of the public welfare." As for the other two branches of government, the New Nationalism demands of the judiciary that "it shall be interested primarily in human welfare rather than in property"; of the legislature it demands that it "shall represent all the people rather than any one class or section of the people."[30] The nation's leadership, and its governmental institutions, must prepare the way for, and establish, social justice, or class war and revolution from below would prevail, with all their visionary, extreme, and radical consequences. The nation's upper- and middle-class elites and its institutions must embrace, guide, and adapt to, progressive evolution, or be swept aside as reactionary by popular revolution.

In giving notice, in such statements and others like them, that he favored a change in the "form of government," that is, in the composition and balance of its powers, and that this change in form necessarily followed upon the evolution of the production-property system, Roosevelt argued accordingly that the governmental changes he favored meant, as well, a change in the conception of property rights and therefore in the relation of government to the market, and hence to society. "We are face to face," he plainly stated, "with new conceptions of the relation of property to human welfare." It could no longer be accepted that human rights were "secondary" to profit; on the contrary, property rights must now be subordinate to "human welfare." The capitalist "holds his property subject to the general right of the community to regulate its use to whatever degree the public welfare may require it."[31]

It followed that although the profit incentive was still useful and "We

---

30. Roosevelt at Osawatomie, Harbaugh, *Writings*, pp. 319, 320, 330; Roosevelt, "Charter of Democracy," speech at Columbus, Ohio, before Ohio Constitutional Convention, 21 Feb. 1912, quoted and discussed at Harbaugh, *Power and Responsibility*, pp. 419–422.

31. This included "the right to regulate the terms and conditions of labor ... directly in the interest of the common good." Osawatomie speech, Harbaugh, *Writings*, pp. 327–328. Cf. Pringle, *Roosevelt*, pp. 543–544: "The Osawatomie address aroused wide interest for two reasons. The first was that the public mind was better prepared for the reception of such doctrines. The second was that one or two passages were alarmingly close to socialism from which Roosevelt had always shrunk.... Regulate the property of Mr. Morgan or Mr. Harriman in the interest of the people? Do this to 'whatever degree' the public welfare might require? Even Roosevelt became a little alarmed by the storm his Denver and Osawatomie speeches caused.... He confessed to Lodge that it had been 'a blunder of some gravity' to express himself in such a manner that his remarks could be considered apart from their context and misunderstood.... [But soon after] the 1910 campaign, ... [he] then said only that he had nothing to add [to] or subtract from the speeches at Osawatomie and elsewhere ..."

grudge no man a fortune which represents his own power and sagacity," nevertheless his enterprise must be "exercised with entire regard to the welfare of his fellows," and a new standard of legitimate profit-making would have to be instilled in the nation's capitalists: "It is not even enough," Roosevelt explained, "that it [wealth] should have been gained without doing damage to the community. We should permit it to be gained only so long as the gaining represents benefit to the community." That was a matter not simply of restrictive but of positive standards that would have to be determined by the people through their government. Roosevelt did not fail to draw the logical conclusion: "This, I know, implies a policy of a far more active government interference with social and economic conditions in this country than we have yet had, but I think we have got to face the fact that such an increase in governmental control is now necessary." Property must be made "the servant and not the master of the commonwealth"; Americans as citizens of the republic "must effectively control the mighty commercial forces which they have themselves called into being." In short, "The object of government is the welfare of the people." The market, which so decisively determined the people's welfare, was to be subordinated to public policy, that is, to politics and the state.[32]

The broad political principles enunciated by Roosevelt in 1910–1912, taken together with the specific regulatory and distributive reforms he called for, articulated a new role of government and a redefinition of property rights that, if effected, would constitute a legal-administrative framework of a state-directed capitalism.[33] As formulated by Roosevelt, this New Nationalism was designed to make capitalist property serve the public welfare; it was intended to assure both distributive justice, or, as he put it, "the fair distribution of prosperity," and economic efficiency, by providing for equal opportunity while acknowledging and allowing the inequality of service and reward. It would, in other words, seek to combine the advantages of

32. Osawatomie speech, Harbaugh, *Writings*, pp. 324, 321, 332. Also, at Columbus, Ohio, 21 Feb. 1912: "The only prosperity worth having is that which affects the mass of the people. We are bound to strive for the fair distribution of prosperity.... our fundamental purpose must be to secure genuine equality of opportunity." And, at Carnegie Hall, 20 Mar. 1912: "If on this new continent we merely build another country of great but unjustly divided material prosperity, we shall have done nothing ..." Quoted and discussed at Harbaugh, *Power and Responsibility*, pp. 420, 423.
33. In addition to the regulatory measures, other reforms Roosevelt advocated included: conservation, graduated income and inheritance tax, workmen's compensation, workplace safety, regulation of child and woman's labor, improvements in general and vocational public education, farm cooperatives, day-care centers, better wages and hours, limitation of injunctions against strikes.

private ownership with a public-service economy under state direction. As Roosevelt expressed it at one point in the campaign of 1912, he did "not care a rap" about the extent or concentration of the corporations' ownership of industry: "What I am interested in is getting the hand of government on all of them – this is what I want." Combination and competition alike must be made to serve the achievement of efficiency, fair prices, good wages and working conditions, equality of opportunity, and social mobility.[34]

The incentive of reward for service, the incitement to initiative from contention in the market, would remain but would be limited both by state administrative authority and by redistributive taxation. In providing for the general economic welfare, the state at the same time would prevent a concentration of wealth that could corrupt or destroy political democracy, while permitting and facilitating a concentration of productive forces suited to modern enterprise as the basis of national progress and world power. The state would safeguard a relatively equalitarian republic, where differences in wealth that were just and economically serviceable would nevertheless be consistent with a political democracy in which wealth gave no person or group significantly more power, or access to power, than others, where, in sum, "human rights are supreme," and wealth was made "the servant, not the master, of the people," where, by state direction, the use and ownership of property were made to serve both social justice and progressive economic efficiency.

It was essential, in Roosevelt's view, that state policy modulate the mix of competition and combination to yield equality of opportunity, fair and efficient prices, and improving conditions of work, in order to guarantee that the political economy operated to distribute to the majority, to the farmers, and especially to the workers as the new rising class in modern society, the wealth commensurate with their weight in the body politic: a good Whig principle inverted for adaptation to a rising propertyless class. As he had once told his attorney general, Philander C. Knox, and as he continued to believe, "More and more the labor movement in this country will become a factor of vital importance, not merely in our social but in our political development." Development must be managed by responsible leaders to prevent the division of political parties along class lines, and the consequent inundation of national politics by class hatred and class warfare with their

---

34. On inequality of service and reward, see Roosevelt's essays on working with socialists, at Harbaugh, *Writings*, pp. 303–315. Quotation, Roosevelt in Chicago, 12 Oct. 1912, at Cooper, *Warrior and Priest*, p. 200.

impulses toward revolution from below. "It would be a dreadful calamity," Roosevelt warned, "if we saw this country divided into two parties, one containing the bulk of the property owners and conservative people, the other the bulk of the wage workers and the less prosperous people generally...."[35]

A state-directed economy, then, was the alternative to class war, proletarian revolution, an "extreme and radical democracy," and socialism. It would convert the old-style capitalism into a public-service economy and the old-style capitalists into public-service capitalists. It was, in Roosevelt's mind, the progressive response to modern industrial conditions that, by implementing reforms that populists and socialists may have initiated or advocated, sustained continuing material progress within a framework of a market society, private property, and the American democratic tradition. If the American democratic tradition warranted a political economy that acquired socialist characteristics alongside, and intermeshed with, capitalist characteristics, so be it.

In his public discourse, Roosevelt increasingly identified his position with Lincoln and the republican tradition, tracing back through Lincoln to the Declaration of Independence, with its emphasis on equality and equal liberty as the fundamental basis of democracy. He invoked Lincoln as having "forecast our present struggle," as having "showed the proper sense of proportion in his relative estimates of capital and labor, of human rights and property rights." Lincoln had pointed out that capital had its rights, that as "the fruit of labor," it was "desirable," and "a positive good in the world." Capital's rights should therefore be respected, but only its rights, not privileges or exploitative impulses. Those rights, Roosevelt held, were to be understood within the framework of Lincoln's other major proposition, that "Labor is prior to, and independent of, capital.... Labor is the superior of capital, and deserves much the higher consideration." Hence, capital's rights existed on the basis of its subordination to human rights.[36]

It was in this context that Roosevelt declared, "We Progressives believe that ... human rights are supreme ... that wealth should be

35. Roosevelt to Knox, 10 Nov. 1904, also, Roosevelt to Paul Cravath, 31 Oct. 1906, Roosevelt to David Scull, 16 Aug. 1907, Roosevelt to T. M. Patterson, 8 Apr. 1907, all in TR; also, to similar effect, Roosevelt's essays on working with socialists, and his speech at Milwaukee, 14 Oct. 1912, at Harbaugh, *Writings*, pp. 303–315, 336–337, and his speech at Columbus, Ohio, 21 Feb. 1912, at Harbaugh, *Power and Responsibility*, pp. 420, 423.
36. Roosevelt, and Roosevelt quoting Lincoln, at Osawatomie speech, 31 Aug. 1910, Harbaugh, *Writings*, pp. 318–319, 316–317. Roosevelt also stated: "If that remark was original with me, I should be even more strongly denounced as a Communist agitator than I shall be anyhow. It is Lincoln's. I am only quoting it." Ibid., p. 319.

the servant, not the master, of the people." It was, also, in this context that he stated that the American republic "means nothing unless it means the triumph of real democracy, the triumph of popular government." The nation and its natural resources "belong to the people." The republic therefore required a government that had for its fundamental purpose the vindication of human rights over property rights. With respect to the structure of power within the nation, that would mean more specifically that "Our purpose is to increase the power of the people themselves," in order "to make the people in reality," not merely in name, "the governing class." This was what popular government meant under modern conditions of an industrial society. The people must be empowered as the governing class to use their government for its "fundamental purpose," namely, "to secure genuine equality of opportunity" by requiring the proper use of property and the equitable distribution of its fruits. "If the American people are not fit for popular government," so that they might use their power for these ends, "then Lincoln's work was wasted," Roosevelt argued, "and the whole system of government upon which this great democratic Republic rests is a failure."[37]

Roosevelt believed, he said, "in shaping the ends of government to protect property as well as human welfare," and he assumed that "normally, and in the long run, the ends are the same," but, he warned, "whenever the alternative must be faced, I am for men and not for property." Here he drew the analogy between the current times and circumstances and those of the Civil War, and, not insignificantly, between slave property and capitalist property. "In our day," he stated, the struggle for progress, the essence of which was the struggle for the enlargement of equality of opportunity, "appears as the struggle of freemen to gain and hold the right of self government as against special interests." At the time of the Civil War, it was "the special interests of cotton and slavery"; now it was "the great special business interests." Just as the slave interest had threatened the equality of the people and the integrity of the republic in the past, so the great capitalist interests, unless they acquiesced in their subordination to human rights, democracy, and the public welfare, posed a similar threat, and as the slave

37. "Charter of Democracy," Columbus, Ohio, 21 Feb. 1912, at Harbaugh, *Power and Responsibility*, pp. 419–421; Carnegie Hall speech, 20 Mar. 1912: "I stand on the Columbus speech." Ibid., p. 423. "Limitation of Governmental Power," speech at San Francisco, 14 Sept. 1912, Harbaugh, *Writings*, p. 289; Osawatomie speech, 31 Aug. 1910, ibid., p. 316. Note that Roosevelt did not subscribe to the oft-repeated contention that in the American political tradition a distinction was to be made between popular democracy and republican institutions.

interest was dealt with, so must be the corporate interests. "The true friend of property," Roosevelt insisted, "the true conservative, is he who insists that property shall be the servant and not the master of the commonwealth; ... that the creature of man's making shall be the servant and not the master of the man who made it."[38] With friends like that, property needs no enemy; with conservatives like that, the people need no revolutionary.

By 1910–1912, Roosevelt tied his historical perspective and his political principle of legal congruity into the political ethic of the American republican tradition. He oriented his policy thinking toward reconciling the former two with the latter. In articulating the outlook of a public-service capitalism and seeking a legal-administrative framework that would combine the advantages of private ownership with service to the public welfare, Roosevelt eventually came to advocate the subordination of property to the dictates of the state, but a state understood as subject to, and expressing, a political democracy and a popular will to progress toward an increasingly equalitarian republic. The new dispensation was to embody majority rule with protection for minority, property rights, but only on the condition of the minority interest and rights serving the people's welfare: in sum, a public-service capitalism under state direction and with increasing public-sector provision for distributive justice. If capital were to balk or resist, it would be dealt with accordingly by the republic, but capitalists such as George W. Perkins represented a model of the public-service disposition that capitalists might be expected to emulate.

Roosevelt's outlook, in seeking, in effect, the reconciliation of commutative and distributive justice in the modern industrial society, embodied what might be called the quest of the American Dream of reconciling liberty and equality and, in so doing, of reconciling republican institutions with technological progress. That is to say, it represented the search for the fulfillment of republicanism within the framework of Progress, or the fulfillment of republicanism through its adaptation to the modern industrial age – what Herbert Croly called "The Promise of American Life." The adaptation had come to mean, in Roosevelt's view, the application of the principle of self-government to a state-directed economy that would make property socially responsible to equalitarian goals.

38. Osawatomie speech, ibid., pp. 330–331, 330–321. "... the essence of the struggle is to equalize opportunity, destroy privilege, and give to the life and citizenship of every individual the highest possible value both to himself and to the commonwealth." Ibid., p. 321.

In assessing Roosevelt's political position as it was evolving in the years 1908–1912, it is of some significance to note that not only in public but also in his private political discourse he identified himself with Lincoln and compared his own times with that of the American Civil War, "a period of revolution."[39] He rejected both the tepid reformism of mugwumpery and the ineffective fanaticism of populistic or doctrinaire radicalism. He saw himself, rather, as the moderate who, like Lincoln, united the majority, extending from left to right of center, in the struggle for fundamental changes in political alignments, the form of government, property rights, and the government-society relation. It might be said that he saw himself as a revolutionary – or reconstructionist – in the Anglo-American, rather than in the French, tradition. He had for some time been interested in the question of leadership in revolutionary times, that is, of how wise leadership might balance and intermesh the claims of change and order, historical perspective and immediate practicalities, theory and practice, without which revolutionary or great social movements degenerate into chaos or peter out in rebellious protest without accomplishing any lasting transformations, at least not those desired. While governor of New York, he had written his book *Oliver Cromwell*, inquiring into these matters, and his attraction to Lincoln reflected a similar interest and disposition.[40]

Roosevelt expressed his thinking along these lines with respect to his own times and politics, in a letter, for example, to the progressive Republican senator of Oregon, Jonathan Bourne, Jr., in early 1911, a letter that he began by requesting that Bourne show it to Senator La Follette.[41]

The immediate subject of the letter was whether progressives should insist on such measures as the direct primary, referendum, initiative, and recall, which Roosevelt ultimately came to support. He now raised the question as to their real efficacy in achieving "popular government," which he believed, in agreement with Bourne, to be "fundamental to all

39. Osawatomie speech, ibid., pp. 316–318, quotation at p. 317.
40. Roosevelt's strong aversion to mugwumpery is expressed, e.g., at Roosevelt to Foulke, 4 Jan. 1907, Roosevelt to Lodge, 8 Aug. 1908, TR. On Roosevelt's book on Cromwell, cf. Cooper, *Warrior and Priest*, p. 43: "... it was perhaps Roosevelt's best single work. It contained a probing inquiry into leadership in a time of upheaval and a careful consideration of the competing requirements of order and change. Roosevelt was once more using historical interpretation to shed light on his own time. He also reflected on the balance between intellect and action in statesmen. 'Cromwell, like many a so-called "practical" man,' he wrote, 'would have done better work had he followed a more clearly defined theory, for though the practical man is better than the mere theorist, he cannot do the highest work unless he is a theorist also.'"
41. Roosevelt to Bourne, 2 Jan. 1911, S. 3A, TR.

other questions," and as to the tactical wisdom of placing them at the top of the progressive list of demands and unnecessarily risking the estrangement of leaders and voters from support for other substantive changes in government-market relations.[42]

In dealing with these immediate matters, however, Roosevelt moved to broader political and historical ground. He was "particularly anxious," he wrote, lest "the progressive movement" end "where so many other movements have landed when they have allowed enthusiasm to conquer reason." Most recently, in American history, although the "Populists and the Bryanites both advocated many admirable reforms," they freighted them "with so much of the fantastic and the irrational and with so much downright demagogy and indifference to public faith, that they richly earned their own overthrow." In the less recent past, but in times of crisis like those at present, "Abraham Lincoln showed as much wisdom in his contemptuous refusal to ally himself with the Free Soil Party as he did in immediately joining the Republican Party." Lincoln had understood the necessity, in accomplishing great change in the nation, to wed interest and principle and, in thereby avoiding doctrinaire radicalism, carry an effective political majority. The Free Soil party, which Lincoln disdained, Roosevelt observed, "was in the hands of fantastic extremists, who, however good" – and note that Roosevelt acknowledged their objectives as good – "can accomplish nothing practical," whereas the Republican "movement was guided by practical men who also possessed high ideals."[43]

In general, these examples indicated that it was "not wise" to proceed with a progressive movement "in such fashion as to make it look as if a

---

42. Ibid. Roosevelt wrote, in this respect: "Don't forget that the direct primary, the referendum, the direct nomination of Senators, are all merely means to ends. On the other hand, such legislation as railroad legislation, the physical valuation of railroads, the great bulk of what has been done in the State of Wisconsin, the workmen's compensation act in New York, much that has been done in New Jersey under [Republican] Governor [John F.] Fort [Woodrow Wilson's immediate predecessor] etc etc: all represent not merely means but ends." In addition to Fort, who had "accomplished an extraordinary amount of progressive work" in New Jersey, Roosevelt cited Governor Robert P. Bass of New Hampshire and Henry L. Stimson of New York, then serving as Taft's secretary of war, as well as insurgent Republican Senator Cummins, as leaders who, although progressive on many or all other important matters, had grave reservations about or opposed the referendum, initiative, and recall. Cummins had recently told Roosevelt "that he personally, and he believed the State of Iowa, were opposed to the initiative and referendum, and so far as the initiative is concerned were very strongly opposed to it. Now I certainly think we ought to find out how Cummins feels, and not only that, but as a matter of expediency we should find out what the attitude in Iowa is before we split up the progressive forces." Ibid. Roosevelt's punctuation.
43. Ibid.

small knot of men were trying to dictate popular policies instead of rallying the people to their support." The end result would be a despotic negation of popular democracy, not its fulfillment. "One of the worst vices of the Jacobins who brought on the Red Terror," Roosevelt noted, "was their tendency, after deifying the will of the people in the abstract, unhesitatingly to override the will of the people if they thought it did not agree with their beliefs as to what was good for the people." Unlike Lincoln and the Republican party, the Jacobins devoured themselves and lost democracy to an imperial despotism. "The progressives can only win," Roosevelt held, "if they carry moderates with them." He no longer cared "to bring over the reactionary leaders," as he thought that "however useful these men have been in the past, their usefulness is at an end, and that they can do nothing more of good to the people." But, he continued, "I very emphatically desire to bring over the great bulk of their followers." Nothing was to be gained "by making the progressives a small knot of people with advanced ideas which they cannot persuade the bulk of their fellow citizens to adopt." "In other words," Roosevelt concluded, in effect drawing the distinction between moralistic radicalism and reconstructionist, if not revolutionary, politics, "I wish to follow in the path of Abraham Lincoln rather than in the path of John Brown and Wendell Phillips."[44]

The John Browns and Wendell Phillipses, the populists and the Bryanites, the radicals and the fantastic visionaries, have their role to play in preparing the events and the public opinion for the elevation of the Lincolns, and the Roosevelts, to leadership of potentially transformative movements. The great secret divulged by American history is not that America is a conservative country, for all peoples are conservative, according to their prevailing beliefs and customs, most of the time; rather, it is that those revolutions that expand human rights against property rights or other traditional usage, need not, and probably cannot, be simply or mainly radical events. Such revolutions are, in effect, if not in intent, synthesizers of radical, liberal, and conservative trends, heretofore seemingly at loggerheads. They are great synthesizers of change and order, tradition and innovation, resulting in a transformative reordering, a transcendance, or revolution. If revolutions are this reordering of principles and traditions, and the establishment and fulfillment of this reordering in institutions, then they are made by a coalition embodying the interplay of radical, liberal, and conservative principles and values, and the true revolutionaries are those most suited to synthetic thought. All great revolutions await their appropriate

44. Ibid.

"moderate" leaders who are neither wholly radical, nor liberal, nor conservative, but who are synthetic in their thought and appeal. Revolutions need radicals, no less than the other persuasions, but are seldom if ever made by radicals. That is why, at the right time and place, revolution may become the true calling of the prescient moderate, who may relish the self-image of, and even be perceived as, being conservative.

Roosevelt's problem was that he was a prescient moderate in an age of great change – the transition from the competitive to the corporate stage of capitalism – but not yet of revolution, and that he articulated – some might say flirted with – proposed changes unrealizable without a revolution that the American body politic was neither ready nor willing to transact. On the one hand, he was preparing himself to be drafted as revolutionary leader if necessary and practical; on the other hand, he presented himself and his program as the alternative to revolution. He aroused thereby both strong allegiance and deep distrust. Richard Hofstadter memorably and perhaps indelibly painted Roosevelt "the Conservative as Progressive,"[45] but it may be more revealing to see in Roosevelt also, or instead, the upper-class progressive appearing as Conservative. As president he did not scruple to bend or disregard the law for purposes of forwarding what he regarded as progressive social change, but in general he remained within the mainstream American political tradition of pursuing substantial change through, rather than against or around, the established political and governmental institutions. Similarly, he disclaimed belief in socialism, but he placed himself in constructive dialogue with socialists, and he came to advocate programs and principles that were consistent with many of those originating or associated with socialists, and that, if implemented, looked toward basic changes in the government-society relation and the use and rights of property. His outlook, moreover, mixed traditional American republican beliefs in liberty and equality and self-government with an untraditional statism that would make government supreme over the society in its property relations, rather than serving, facilitating, and regulating those relations as they more or less freely evolved.

Roosevelt thereby represented, or personified, the emergence in twentieth-century American political life of the left-statist tendency of modern corporate liberalism, as against the nonstatist regulatory corporate liberalism on the left of center, represented by Wilson, and as

---

45. Richard Hofstadter, *The American Political Tradition* (1948; New York: Random House, Vintage Books, n.d.), chap. 9: "Theodore Roosevelt: the Conservative as Progressive," pp. 206–237.

against the property-rights liberalism, become a neoconservatism, personified by Taft, on the right of center. The nation was ready for a John Quincy Adams in defeat, not yet a Lincoln in victory.

Taft

At the outset of his presidential term, William Howard Taft's views on the trust question bore a large similarity to those of Roosevelt. Like Roosevelt, he defined the trust problem historically in terms of the emergence of the large corporation, and he affirmed the latter as the form of business organization necessitated by modern economic evolution and as most suited to America's role as a world power. Like Roosevelt, he identified restraint of trade and monopoly not with bigness or restriction of competition as such, but with unfair practices and the transgression of the public interest. Like Roosevelt, and particularly as a former judge with a distinct legalistic bent of mind, he believed strongly in the principle of legal congruity and especially in the absolute necessity of enforcing the law.[46] Like Roosevelt, finally, Taft had for some time advocated a federal policy that would sanction corporate consolidation and reasonable restraints of trade, while providing for a federal administrative supervision of corporate affairs directed against unfair practices, supplemented by legislative prohibition of specific unfair practices, such as exclusive tying contracts, underselling competitors at a loss to suppress them, and overcapitalization.[47]

Taft differed, however, from Roosevelt on three points of government, law, and ideology that did not assume their full political significance until Roosevelt turned against Taft's presidential leadership and embarked upon the campaign to displace him after mid-1910. It was

46. Cf. Anderson, *Taft: Conservative's Conception*, p. 59: "Taft's previous judicial and administrative careers had imbued him with a strong respect for the rule of law and a firm belief in a juridical administrative style...." Also, ibid., p. 60, and chap. 1, pp. 4–27, passim. Cf. also Vanderlip's assessment of Taft after an extended White House conference with the president on 5 Feb. 1910: "In gauging the President's actions, it is necessary, I think, always to have in mind the background of his personality and training. He was trained as a lawyer and spent much of his life as a Judge, and it is as a Judge, executing existing law, that one will usually find him." Vanderlip to Stillman, 11 Feb. 1910, and to similar effect, Vanderlip to Stillman, 27 Oct. 1911, both in FAV. See also Stanley I. Kutler, "Chief Justice Taft and the Delusion of Judicial Exactness – A Study in Jurisprudence," *Virginia Law Review* 48 (1962), pp. 1407–1426.

47. Cf. Knauth, *Policy of the United States*, pp. 86–92; *Address of Henry L. Stimson, Secretary of War, at the Republican Club, New York City on December 15, 1911* (released for morning papers of Saturday, 16 Dec. 1911), pamphlet in State Historical Society of Wisconsin, Madison, a statement of the Taft administration's trust policy.

not that Taft had first moved to the right; he had stood essentially the same ground that had earlier earned him Roosevelt's confidence and support.[48] The Ballinger–Pinchot dispute, although irritating and latent with issues pertinent to the subsequent division, had not led Roosevelt to attack Taft or break with him. It was, rather, that in standing ground he had previously shared with Roosevelt, Taft gradually moved to the right in defense of property rights as Roosevelt moved to the left in defense of equalitarian human rights. The two progressive Republicans thereby opened an ample area between them for Wilson, the progressive Democrat, to occupy. The twentieth-century American political landscape may be said to have formed, in its dominating features, around this three-way progressive split: Roosevelt's statist-tending leftism, Wilson's nonstatist left-tending liberalism, Taft's property rights–oriented liberal conservatism – a landscape with a long-term glacial tilt to the left.

The three points of difference between Taft and Roosevelt may be described as follows.

First, although he strongly affirmed the need for positive government, to regulate market relations and, as he reiterated in the campaign of 1912, "to further equality of opportunity," Taft did not favor a statist version of the administered market, nor such a degree of regulation as seriously to modify or restrict private property rights.[49] He conceived of federal incorporation and such other proposals as methods of vigorous government regulation, not direction, of the market. To Taft, property rights constituted a basic human right and were not to be viewed as in conflict with, and hence subordinate to, human rights.

Second, as one trained in the law and as above all, in his own mind, a jurist to whom the law was fundamental to a well-ordered and progressive modern society, Taft believed it essential to uphold the rule of law as against a government of persons. He could not bring himself to affirm, although to an extent he uneasily continued to practice, the selective implementation or disregard of the law that Roosevelt as president had as a matter of policy engaged in. The law, in Taft's view, must be accommodated to the progressive evolution of society's social and economic relations, but this was to be accomplished not by picking and choosing the laws to be enforced, nor by executive fiat or stratagem, but by consistent enforcement, so that those laws seen to be obstructive of progress or the public interest might be properly changed, in accordance with the Constitution, by the legislative branch. An

48. At the outset of his administration, Taft himself defined his task, in Anderson's words, as that of translating "the ideals of Roosevelt into permanent social institutions and policies." Anderson, *Taft: Conservative's Conception*, p. 60.
49. Ibid., p. 195, respecting Taft's affirmation of positive government.

independent judiciary was essential to the rule of law, and particularly to the rule of law as embodied in the American constitutional system of checks and balances.[50] An independent judiciary was also, therefore, indispensable to the protection of individual and property rights. As Roosevelt moved from seeking to replace judicial process by administrative powers in regulating the market, to attacking the judiciary as obstructive of the popular will, and to advocating the recall of judicial decisions, Taft came to believe that his difference with Roosevelt had become not simply personal or a matter or specific policy, but one of fundamental principle.

Taft viewed Roosevelt as having gone beyond the positions he had taken as president, to one that implied a basic "revision of the Constitution," even "revolution."[51] Taft's determination to resist Roosevelt's return to the presidency now combined personal political interest with principle. As he told his brother, Horace, after Roosevelt's Osawatomie speech, "the thing of all others that I am not going to do is to step out of the way of Mr. Roosevelt when he is advocating such wild ideas...."[52] Judicial recall, Taft believed, would mean the evisceration of the constitution and the abandonment of limited government: "It lays the axe at the foot of the tree of well ordered freedom," Taft declared at Toledo, Ohio, early in 1912, for it "subjects the guarantees of life, liberty and property without remedy to the fitful impulses of a temporary majority of the electorate."[53]

Third, Taft considered it necessary, in principle, to reject socialism

---

50. "We have a government of limited power under the Constitution, and we have got to work out our problems on the basis of law. Now, if that is reactionary, then I am a reactionary." Taft to William Kent, 29 June 1909, quoted at ibid., p. 59. Also, Vanderlip to Stillman, 27 Oct. 1911, FAV: "Taft's mind is purely a legal mind and takes no collateral factors into account, except his own political ambitions. There is burned into his brain the idea that we have a law on the statute books that was designed to correct economic evils; the law has been judicially interpreted by the highest courts; he is the executive and his duty is to enforce the law, and any argument designed to change his course seems to him like an argument designed to swerve him from his duty...."
51. Taft, quoted at Harbaugh, *Power and Responsibility*, p. 393.
52. Taft, quoted at Coletta, *Presidency*, p. 111. Also, Vanderlip to Stillman, 27 Oct. 1911, FAV: "[Taft] is in a state of mind where his conception of his political future and also of official duty correspond and, while he undoubtedly believes that he is doing the right thing, he honestly believes that he is doing the thing which will best forward his political chances and the political element, I believe, is very potent in shaping every action that he takes at the present time."
53. Taft, reported by *New York Tribune*, 9 Mar. 1912, quoted at Norman M. Wilensky, *Conservatives in the Progressive Era: The Taft Republicans of 1912* (Gainesville: University of Florida Press, 1965), pp. 49–50. Roosevelt sought to parry this criticism and substantiate his support for an independent judiciary, by distinguishing between recall of judges, which he opposed, and recall of judicial decisions.

outright, and not enter into dialogue with it. As he confided to his military aide and friend, Archie Butt, in mid-August 1910, he saw growing in the United States at the time a movement for "absolute socialism," and although Roosevelt sought "to guide it," Taft believed that "the way to meet it was by direct challenge and by fighting it out at the ballot box."[54] From about mid–1910 onward, Taft viewed Roosevelt not only as entering dialogue with socialism but as increasingly aligning himself with it. "The ultimate issue," Taft stated, as it presented itself in the United States in its current stage of development, "is socialism," and along with it, "an unlimited control of the majority of the electorate on the one hand," as against "our present [form of] government on the other."[55] In this way, Taft in effect drew the line between what would become left and right in modern American politics: on the left, those who would enter dialogue with socialism and align with it in some degree; on the right, those who would confront socialism and reject it outright. It was a line, it might be noted, that cut across the older liberal-conservative divide.

From these convictions, and from the necessities of political maneuvering imposed upon him by Roosevelt's challenge to his party leadership and to his renomination for a second term, Taft extended his general break with Roosevelt to specific policy respecting regulation of the market. He receded from support of administrative methods of regulation, such as those embodied in license-registration, federal incorporation, and trade commission proposals, and ultimately reverted to judicial supremacy in the regulation of corporations, with the corollary insistence upon the primacy of the corporations, or the private sector, in administering the market, subject to a secondary policing by the government. It was not, however, until after the Supreme Court's Rule of Reason decisions in May 1911, that Taft made this break overt and clear-cut.

As circuit court judge in the late 1890s, Taft, like a number of other federal judges, had disagreed with the Supreme Court's decisions in *Trans-Missouri* and *Joint Traffic* insofar as they had refused to apply common-law doctrine to the construction of the Sherman Act. His authoritative decision in *Addyston Pipe*, which the Supreme Court later upheld unanimously, had reaffirmed the application to Sherman Act cases of the common-law distinction between ancillary and direct restraints. Otherwise, however, he had been obliged to submit to the Supreme Court's ruling against the common-law distinction between

54. As related by Butt in Butt to Clara Butt, 15 Aug. 1910, quoted at Cooper, *Warrior and Priest*, p. 151.
55. Taft, quoted at Wilensky, *Conservatives*, p. 40.

reasonable and unreasonable restraints in construing the meaning of the Sherman Act.[56]

After leaving the bench, both in his capacity as secretary of war and as president, Taft, not unlike Roosevelt, made frequent public criticisms of the Sherman Act as then construed by the Supreme Court. He advocated federal incorporation of interstate corporations, administered by a federal agency loosely analogous to the Interstate Commerce Commission, but with functions more like the supervisory oversight role of the comptroller of the currency in the field of national banks. Taft, in other words, did not see federal incorporation as a device for the government direction of the economy. Rather, in his view, a federal agency, administering an incorporation system, would police the market against unfair methods of competition and certain specified business malpractices, and would advise, not dictate to, corporate executives as to what combinations or contracts they might undertake as reasonable and what they should avoid as unreasonable. The agency would provide publicity of corporate affairs, and it would generally aid Congress in drafting legislation regulating business practices, and in particular, legislation that might define and prohibit specific unreasonable or unfair business practices. Among the duties of the federal agency, Taft, like Roosevelt, recommended the supervision of security issues and the prevention of intercorporate stockholding without the agency's permission.[57]

Although, therefore, to a large extent similar to Roosevelt's, Taft's views on policy concerning the trust question were far from identical to Roosevelt's. Taft, furthermore, was adamant on the obligation to enforce the Sherman Act to demonstrate the supremacy and impartiality of the law, as well as to force the issue with Congress and thereby build up pressure for expediting legislative action. Unlike Roosevelt, he be-

---

56. In *Addyston Pipe*, Taft had found the restraint of trade complained of to be an unreasonable one, thereby making possible a unanimous Supreme Court decision. See discussion of the case in Chapter 3, above.

57. See, e.g., Taft's special message to Congress, 7 Jan. 1910 (*H.R. Doc. No. 484*, 61st, 2d), at Knauth, *Policy of the United States*, pp. 86–87. Like Roosevelt, Taft had come to believe it unnecessary and unwise to amend the Sherman Act itself, preferring the alteration of antitrust law in the form of collateral and supplementary legislation. Cf. Vanderlip to Stillman, 11 Feb. 1910, FAV (reporting on his talk with Taft at the White House on 5 Feb. 1910): "[Taft] does not desire to have the Sherman Act repealed or altered. He thinks it might have been better drawn, but in view of the fact that there have already been twelve important Supreme Court decisions elucidating it and two more are soon to come [the Standard Oil and American Tobacco cases], he believes it much better to permit the law to stand as it is than it would be to alter it and again have to wait for the Supreme Court to decide exactly what the new law means."

lieved the law should be enforced, pending its revision, even if it disrupted progressive development. Taft believed, however, that prosecutions under the Sherman Act could go much farther than they had under Roosevelt against improper corporate practices and unwarranted combinations without restoring the old competitive regime or endangering the new corporate order. Taft thought, also, that in any event, prosecutions of large corporations were necessary, where malpractices were plainly palpable, as an antidote to popular socialistic sentiment.[58] Finally, and most significant of all his differences with Roosevelt over government regulation of the market, Taft believed it more consistent with the nation's traditions, with the principles of liberty and property rights, and with standards of economic vitality and efficiency, to maintain the primacy of individuals and corporations in administering the market, while reserving to the state a secondary regulatory role.

For all these reasons, and as a person with a judicial background, Taft favored keeping administrative regulatory powers strictly limited by and subordinate to judicial review and sustaining judicial process as the preeminent regulatory instrument of government. Taft and his attorney general George W. Wickersham, accordingly, downgraded the role

---

58. Cf., e.g., Vanderlip to Stillman 11 Feb. 1910, FAV: "[Taft] believes that the great corporations have been engaged in methods which he groups under the head of pernicious practices. These he defines as the underselling of competitors in certain markets while higher prices are charged elsewhere, using the size of the corporation, rather than its economic advantages, to crush rivals and obtain a monopoly, the making of combinations and agreements that tend to create a monopoly, – any practice, in fact, that does not depend on good business management and economic saving but does depend on the size of the corporation, can be stopped under the Sherman Anti-Trust Law, and ought to be stopped for the welfare of the country and to save us in the end from socialistic tendencies.... His federal incorporation act, he says very frankly, is not designed to permit corporations to avoid in any degree the responsibilities of the Sherman Act, and if anybody is looking for that law as a means of escape from the penalties that law imposes or a method that is designed to continue the practices that law is meant to prevent, he will not find it in the federal incorporation act." Also, Vanderlip to Stillman, 3 June 1910, FAV (discussing the injunction brought by Attorney General Wickersham against the Western Freight Association's attempted rate increase): "Mr. [William C.] Brown [vice-president of the New York Central Railroad] quoted Taft as saying that not only the railroads but a great many other corporations were in contravention of the law as it stands, and he did not propose to take the personal responsibility of permitting such a condition of affairs to continue, that he had pointed out the situation to Congress and that if Congress did not act he should act, and that for one thing the [Steel?] Company was doing business outside of the law and he should take steps to dissolve it... [Brown also reported] that the President clearly sees the impossible position in which the roads are in reference to the Sherman Anti-Trust law, ... that he has said repeatedly that if the law were not changed so as to put the roads in a legal position – so far as their working together in ... the Western Freight Association – he then proposed to enforce the law to the letter, and by making it obnoxious secure its reasonable change."

of the Bureau of Corporations and reinvigorated the prosecutory processes of the Department of Justice against some of the largest corporations, including the American Sugar Refining Company (of *E. C. Knight* fame), General Electric, the meat-packers, and against the great transcontinental railways in the Western Freight Association in 1910 when they moved in concert to raise rates.

In the face of the continued failure of Congress to act, except for the passage in 1910 of the Mann–Elkins Act regulating common carriers, Taft's policy came increasingly to center upon enforcement of the Sherman Act in the courts, with a declining commitment to eventual enactment of a federal incorporation law.[59] With the lower federal court rulings, in 1908 and 1909, against the Standard Oil and American Tobacco companies, which reaffirmed the non-common-law construction of the Sherman Act, judicial regulation appeared all the more menacing to corporate leaders. As there was every reason to expect that these rulings would be upheld by the Supreme Court in the pending appeals, Taft's policy jeopardized the entire corporate structure of industry as it currently stood. By early 1910, a powerful segment of corporation leaders, including many who were cool or hostile to Roosevelt, had become deeply disaffected with Taft's policies, viewing

59. Corporation executives looked upon federal incorporation with mixed emotion and divided views. E.g., Vanderlip to Stillman, 3 Feb. 1910, FAV: "I do not find anyone of importance who is satisfied with the federal incorporation scheme, which Taft has proposed. In at Morgan's, Kuhn, Loeb's and elsewhere, the view seems to be that the federal incorporation really cures none of the disabilities that corporations are under in respect to the Sherman Anti-Trust law, and, on the other hand, does add a new master in the shape of the federal Bureau of Corporations, if the act should be availed of. There is a quite general opinion that the act would be unconstitutional." At the same time, there was some opinion that federal incorporation would offer "a settled position" for "certain classes of corporations," particularly the packers; while in other quarters it was felt (Vanderlip to Stillman, 21 Jan. 1910, FAV) that should the Supreme Court uphold the lower courts in the Standard Oil and American Tobacco cases, a federal incorporation act might be "the only door that offers any escape." In that case, however, another difficulty would arise: Aside from Taft's warning that he would not permit federal incorporation to become a way around the Sherman Act, Congress might well refuse to act against what would be a very popular Supreme Court decision. As Vanderlip explained to Stillman (ibid.), "Of course, ever since the old Standard Oil decision [in the lower court], everybody has been more or less concerned as to what would happen should the Supreme Court affirm that decision, but it seems to have dawned on people pretty generally after Mr. Morgan's recent conference with the President and some talks that various people here had with Senator Aldrich that, if the Supreme Court should affirm the veiw taken by the lower court, there is little possibility of any corrective legislation being obtained from the present Congress, and the result might, therefore, be extremely embarrassing.... [Senator Elihu Root is] much impressed with this view and presented it to the President in the strongest sort of light a few days ago, telling him that he believed it was quite possible that his Administration would go down in a greater political wreck than any Administration of our times had seen."

them as at best inappropriate and potentially disastrous. "There is great disgust expressed in all circles here with the present attitude of Wickersham," Vanderlip reported from Wall Street to Stillman sojourning in Europe, in February. "Wickersham, it appears, has developed political ambitions, and that seems to be accountable for the new views he is taking of affairs." A few months later, the news of the former Wall Street lawyer's actions as attorney general was no better. "Wickersham," Vanderlip observed, "has out-radicaled the radicals. Bonaparte was a suckling dove compared to him." Apparently, Washington had worked "an absolute mental change" on Wickersham, and he had become "really the most feared member of the Administration."[60]

Confronted with growing opposition within his own party from corporate executives, from insurgents like La Follette, and from other progressives led by Roosevelt, Taft moved away from administrative regulation and toward stepped-up prosecutions under the Sherman Act.[61] He thereby served his own sense of principle and at the same time bolstered his political standing among smaller manufacturers and others who since the fight over the Hepburn bill, whether from antipathy to labor unions or to "big business," had been opposed to amending the Sherman Act and were calling for its judicial enforcement.[62]

In this situation, the Standard Oil and American Tobacco cases

60. Vanderlip to Stillman, 3 Feb. and 3 June 1910, FAV.
61. Cf., e.g., Vanderlip's impressions of Taft's disposition after his White House conference with the president on 5 Feb. 1910: "The President is extremely frank and impresses me as being absolutely sincere in what he is trying to accomplish. To find just where his mind is on any particular subject seems to be a very simple matter, – one has nothing to do but ask him.... He is absolutely without political sense, and of course, with little or no business training, so that he has neither the point of view of the politician nor of the business man; and I do not believe that the arguments either of the politician or of the business man are going to influence his actions very much. If to enforce the law as he sees it means a cataclysm in industrial affairs (and I use the word 'cataclysm' as his own and not as mine), or if it means the wreck of his political fortunes and the end of his political career with his first term of office, I believe neither fact will greatly influence his determination." "After Judge [Robert S.] Lovett [of the Union Pacific and other Harriman properties] saw the President, he characterized his attitude to me as that of 'trembling between two great fears, – the fear of the return of Roosevelt and the fear of a panic.' That may be a good characterization, but I should strike out the word 'trembling.' I think the President is fearful for his political future and sees strong probability of Roosevelt's return to power. I think he looks with great apprehension on the possibilities of industrial [dis]organization for a time, but he strikes me as a man with a certain bovine sort of courage, who would march straight ahead to an execution of the laws as he finds them, even though he knew his action would result in both these calamities." Vanderlip to Stillman, 11 Feb. 1910, FAV. See also Robert L. Raymond, "The Federal Anti Trust Act," *Harvard Law Review* 23 (Mar 1910), pp. 353–379, esp. pp. 375–378.
62. Cf., e.g., Vanderlip to Stillman, 27 Oct. 1911, FAV, at note 52, above.

assumed a crucial political importance. With the Supreme Court in a pivotal position in the deepening political-legal crisis, Taft in late 1910 took the unprecedented step of appointing as chief justice, after Melville W. Fuller's death, a sitting associate justice, Edward D. White, the longtime leader of the Court's minority that since 1897 had been arguing for a common-law construction of the Sherman Act.[63]

Already in early 1910, there were reports that the Supreme Court justices were preparing to give the cases special attention. As president of the National City Bank of New York, with its close ties to the Rockefellers, Vanderlip had a particular interest in the Standard Oil and American Tobacco cases, and was in a good position to be well informed on the legal proceedings. Persons "in close touch with the Court," he informed Stillman in January 1910, told him that "they are awake to the full significance of the matter" and believed "that the Court will weave out some sort of a decision which will, perhaps, in general terms affirm the decision of the lower court, but which will be so modified that it will lose a good deal of its serious character so far as business interests are concerned." A month later, Vanderlip could report that "some effective work has been done to get into the Court's mind the effect upon business that an adverse decision will have," and that there was "reason for the hope which exists in some quarters that the Court will go beyond merely a cold-blooded decision of the case of law and will try to formulate a decision in such a way that some road will be pointed out for business to proceed along, without an absolutely chaotic interruption, even though the Court should in general terms affirm the lower decision." A year later, with White now the sitting chief justice, Vanderlip reported to Stillman that he had received "some exceedingly interesting and highly confidential information in regard to the attitude of the Supreme Court in the Standard Oil case." According to his information, Vanderlip said, "I know that some of the members of the Court are greatly impressed with radical sentiment throughout the country," which led them to "believe that if a decision were rendered favorable to the Company it would be followed by such radical political developments as would be dangerous to the whole national life." Hence, Vanderlip had been given to understand, "the case is going

---

63. Fuller died on 4 July 1910. Taft announced his nomination of White on 12 Dec. 1910, passing over Charles Evans Hughes, whom he nominated as associate justice earlier in the year (confirmed on 2 May 1910), with an intimation that he might elevate Hughes to chief justice upon Fuller's retirement or death. White became "the first sitting jurist to be promoted to that post in the history of the Court." Henry J. Abraham, *Justices and Presidents: A Political History of Appointments to the Supreme Court* (New York: Penguin, 1975), pp. 156–159, quotation at p. 159.

to be decided from the point of view of statesmanship rather than law." The puzzle was, how to assuage the widespread radical public opinion without destabilizing the nation's business system. "There is undoubtedly every disposition," Vanderlip explained, "to protect property rights, and the Court will be chiefly concerned in trying to find some middle ground with which this radical sentiment with which they are so impressed will be appeased, but the business of the country not seriously upset." Vanderlip noted that the "difficulty of evolving a clear-cut formula which will do that and can be applied generally to other corporations that are in the same position as the Standard Oil [Company] is extremely great," and as yet – more than four months before the Rule of Reason decisions would be handed down – he was "pretty certain that no important progress has been made in the minds of the Court toward evolving such a formula."[64]

By whatever political or jurisprudential process behind the scenes – and Vanderlip's intelligence sources appear to have been rather well informed – Chief Justice White's Rule of Reason decisions of May 1911 went far toward resolving the crisis. The Court sustained the lower court rulings in directing the dissolution of the two corporations; it thereby satisfied popular anti-corporate sentiment, at least to some extent, and demonstrated the effectiveness of the law against the high and mighty. At the same time, the Court restored the common-law construction of the Sherman Act and with it the legalization of reasonable restraints of trade. As the other side of the same coin, the decisions also opened the way to extensive prosecutions of large corporations under the Sherman Act by Taft's Department of Justice under Wickersham's direction, which, however appealing to "radical" opinion and galling to corporate executives, did not "seriously upset" the nation's corporate structure.[65]

As late as December 1911, Taft and his administration spokesman, Henry L. Stimson, were still formally recommending a federal incorporation measure supervised by a federal commission, as well as sup-

64. Vanderlip to Stillman, 21 Jan. and 3 Feb. 1910, and 6 Jan. 1911, FAV.
65. Cf., e.g., Vanderlip to Stillman, 17 Oct. 1911, FAV (about five months after the Standard Oil decision): "The public is beginning to get somewhat used to dissolutions under the Sherman law. They have seen the Standard Oil dissolution go through without a ripple and, apparently, without making any change whatever in the situation. We are just in the midst of the Tobacco settlement, which is much more knotty, but its general effects have been to advance its securities.... We have, within a week, had court orders on the electrical combine, the 'Bath Tub Trust' and two or three other things, without apparently any disastrous effect upon the business situation, and a good many people are beginning to wonder if such dissolutions are really such a serious menace as has been popularly supposed."

plementary legislation against specific unfair practices.[66] But after May 1911, with the restoration of the common-law construction of the Sherman Act, Taft placed increasingly greater emphasis upon judicial enforcement of the law.

The Rule of Reason decisions came as a personal victory for Taft, who, as federal judge in 1898, had discreetly suggested the need for common-law guidance in the interpretation of the Sherman Act. Less than a month after the American Tobacco case decision, Taft publicly praised the Rule of Reason decisions as beneficial to "all the business of the country," and as prescribing a standard of business practices "not difficult for honest and intelligent business men to follow."[67] Later, in his annual message to Congress, 5 December 1911, Taft referred to the two decisions as epoch-making and definitive, which indeed they proved to be. He pointed out that the rule of legality "thus finally established" corresponded with the rule of reasonableness as well understood at common law. The Supreme Court, he explained, had finally clarified and pronounced the true meaning of the Sherman Act. It was not intended to condemn "combinations of capital or mere bigness of plant organized to secure economy in production and reduction of cost." Taft still recommended in this message the measures for federal incorporation and prohibition of specific unfair practices, although now in the context, not of altering the general thrust of the antitrust law, but of advising the business community so that it might more readily conform with the newly construed law.[68] Because the courts no longer construed the Sherman Act as destructive of all combinations and restrictions of competition, but only those that were unreasonable in the common-law sense (as involving unfair or unlawful methods or as in contravention of the public interest), it was once again, in Taft's view, effective. The law could be enforced with renewed vigor without threatening the existence of large corporations or reasonable agreements among them; it could strike at practices that were unfair or against the public interest, and from time to time even dissolve or reorganize a specific corporate combination as the merits of the individual case might warrant.[69]

This was precisely the policy Taft and Attorney General Wickersham

---

66. Knauth, *Policy of the United States*, pp. 90–91; *Address of Henry L. Stimson* (15 Dec. 1911), pp. 5–8.
67. Taft, speech delivered 21 June 1911, quoted at Knauth, *Policy of the United States*, p. 89.
68. Ibid., pp. 89–91.
69. Cf. Vanderlip to Stillman, 29 Sept. 1911, FAV: "Taft believes that something might be worked out with a national incorporation plan," but he "does not think it possible to discriminate between good and bad trusts by any statute definition and does apparently intend to go on with further prosecutions."

adopted after the Rule of Reason decisions. The president soon abandoned the program of administrative supervision of corporations and
legislative prohibition of specified unfair practices, leaving their definition to the courts, and he became increasingly critical of such proposed
measures. At the same time, he seized upon the wholesale enforcement
of the Sherman Act as the only safe and effective solution of the trust
problem. By the autumn of 1911, Wickersham had brought suit against
United States Steel and was proceeding against International Harvester,
two of the great corporations that under Roosevelt had cooperated
closely with the Bureau of Corporations in disclosing their affairs and in
return had received assurances of immunity from prosecution under the
Sherman Act. If any president deserves the reputation as "the Trust
Buster," surely it is Taft. The record of no administration before or
since Taft's stands comparison with the number of antitrust suits
against major corporations brought in the space of one term, most of
them in less than two years. As George E. Mowry observed, Taft and
Wickersham pursued "possibly the most active antimonopoly campaign
that the nation has ever witnessed."[70] Taft's policy horrified corporate
executives, both those aligned with the National Civic Federation and
those not. With the 1912 elections not far off, many corporate executives prepared to throw their support to another candidate, although
many of them found none of the three major choices in 1912
desirable.[71]

---

70. Mowry, *Era of Roosevelt*, p. 286. Or as Robert H. Wiebe put it, Taft's administration "mined the Sherman Act for all it was worth." "The House of Morgan and the
    Executive, 1905–1913," *AHR* 65:1 (Oct. 1959), p. 58.
71. Cf. Vanderlip to Stillman, 27 Oct. 1911, FAV: "We opened a new chapter in the
    administration of the Sherman Law this morning with the complaint of the Government for the dissolution of the Steel Trust. Of course it is not unexpected; as I wrote
    you two or three months ago, Wickersham told [Steve] Palmer [of Farmers Loan &
    Trust Co.] that the complaint would be filed. The Steel people, however, have been
    hopeful up to the last that this would not happen and have tried to do everything
    possible to avoid it and to bring themselves in line with official opinions. It is idle for
    me to speculate on what the effect is going to be.... The only thing that is of
    interest is a mental speculation as to where this is all leading to [¶] Mr. [J. P.]
    Morgan [Sr.], Senator Aldrich, Senator [Winthrop M.] Crane [Mass.], Mr. [George
    F.] Baker and [Henry P.] Davison all spent Saturday and Sunday [21 and 22 Oct.
    1911] with Mr. [Theodore N.] Vail [of AT&T] in Vermont. The time was put in
    pretty generally discussing the trust outlook. The opinions of these men I think may
    interest you. Mr. Morgan was extremely pessimistic, in that he saw no road or alley
    to get out of the present situation. He said he had never been in a situation before
    where there was darkness from every aspect and where he had no intuition even of a
    way out. Senator Aldrich was as pessimistic about the political outlook as was Mr.
    Morgan about the business side of the question. He felt that all old moorings were
    cut loose politically and that the outlook was only that a bad situation might get still
    worse in that respect. On the other hand, Mr. Vail was the optimist of the party. He

In its four years, the Taft administration instituted twice as many Sherman Act prosecutions as did the Roosevelt administration in more than seven years. If from the outset of his administration, Taft moved to a move vigorous enforcement of the act by judicial proceeding than had Roosevelt, before May 1911, the difference was still more a matter of degree than of kind. Of the eighty-nine cases brought under the Sherman Act during the Taft administration, about two-thirds were instituted after the Rule of Reason decisions. To put it differently, by the end of Taft's first twenty-six months as president (that is, up to the Rule of Reason decisions), well past the halfway point of his presidential term, petitions had been first filed or indictments returned in only twenty-six cases; but in his last twenty-two months as president (after the Rule of Reason decisions), petitions were first filed or indictments returned in sixty-three cases. The list of large corporations prosecuted in the latter period was not only longer, but in signifying a break with Roosevelt's policies, more impressive; it included the United States Steel Corporation, the National Cash Register Company, the United Shoe Machinery Company, the Keystone Watch Company, the International Harvester Corporation, the Aluminum Company of America, the Corn Products Refining Company, the American Thread Company, the Burroughs Adding Machine Company, and the American Coal Products Company.[72]

There were other manifestations of Taft's policy change. For example, Attorney General Wickersham, in his annual report to Congress in December 1911, now emphasized the excellence of the Sherman Act

declared the whole thing was a political phase and would pass, as political phases always have. Mr. Baker was conservatively on the side of Mr. Vail and Mr. Davison, of course, was also on that side. [¶] The result of the discussion was to favor one positive action. It was decided that ——— and ——— [Senators Aldrich and Crane?] should see Mr. Taft immediately on his return [from his western tour] and try to present to him in the most forceful way possible the industrial chaos that is ahead if the administration's policy is followed to a logical conclusion and to endeavor to get him to put into his message something that will be reassuring. [¶] That plan is interesting, but, in my opinion, will get nowhere at all." Cf. also, the denunciation of Taft for his change of policy, in George W. Perkins, "The Sherman Law, Where It Has Failed, Why It Has Failed, and a Constructive Suggestion," an address before the Economic Club of Philadelphia, Pa., 22 May 1915 (reprinted from *The Market World*, New York, pamphlet in the State Historical Society of Wisconsin, Madison), p. 6.

72. *The Federal Antitrust Law with Amendments, List of Cases Instituted by the United States, and Citations of Cases Decided thereunder or Relating thereto*, 1 Jan. 1914, in U.S. Senate, Committee on the Judiciary, *Hearings ... together with Briefs and Memoranda ... Compiled for Use in Consideration of H.R. 15657* (Washington, D.C.: Government Printing Office, 1914), pp. 164–183. The Standard Oil and American Tobacco cases were among the forty-four cases instituted during Roosevelt's tenure as president. Ibid., pp. 154–164.

and strongly opposed legislation to specify and prohibit unfair practices.[73] On 18 July 1912, Herbert Knox Smith resigned as commissioner of corporations to join the campaign for the Republican presidential nomination of Roosevelt. On 7 August 1912, Taft replaced Smith with his deputy commissioner, Luther Conant, Jr., the Boston statistician, former editor of *Industrial Securities* and the *Journal of Commerce*, author of an authoritative study of corporate combinations, and an outspoken opponent of the current trade commission proposals.[74]

Commissioner Conant forcefully argued the Taft administration's policy, in a way that Smith, as a Roosevelt loyalist, could not, in spite of the fact, as we have seen, that Smith's position on regulatory policy was closer to Taft's than to Roosevelt's. Conant attacked the establishment of a federal trade commission as representing "the substitution of a marked degree of paternalism for ... freedom of individual action." The trade commission idea, Conant noted, was based upon the premise that where free competition no longer existed or was impossible, the government, in the absence of competition as the automatic regulator, must intervene and regulate on behalf of the public interest, as in the case of the Interstate Commerce Commission with respect to common carriers and state or municipal public ownership or strong commission control with respect to other public-service corporations. Establishment of trade commission regulation over industrial corporations was therefore tantamount to official government acknowledgment that competition no longer existed in industry and had been replaced by monopolistic conditions. Such an admission would not only justify, but require, government regulation of, and interference with, the everyday affairs of private industry, ranging from contractual relations to prices (as indeed, Gary, Perkins, Carnegie, and Roosevelt proposed).[75]

Although the subordination of enterprise to such government regulation appeared harmless and mandatory in the special cases of natural monopolies possessing public franchises or businesses affected with a vital public interest, such as common carriers and public utilities, the general application of such a principle to industrial corporations and, in effect, to the economy at large, would constitute, Conant argued, much like Smith, "a radical departure" from the nation's practice and tradi-

---

73. Knauth, *Policy of the United States*, pp. 91–92.
74. U.S. Bureau of Corporations, *Ann. Rep.* (1913), p. 3. Luther Conant, Jr., may have been related to Charles A. Conant. Charles had also been with the *Journal of Commerce* (Chap. 2, above). The two men, however, did not necessarily share the same views on the issues of the day.
75. *Ann. Rep.* (1912), pp. 3–5.

tion. At best, it would mean "regulated monopoly," but this in turn must constitute a standing invitation to unlimited government intervention in market enterprise, which would in effect validate and implement Roosevelt's state-directed economy, and could well proceed to a state socialism upon which Roosevelt's proposals, combined with his call for equalitarian human rights, seemed very much to verge. Better that the government refuse to concede the passing of competition from the industrial scene, and instead judicially enforce the Sherman Act, which by the "recent decisions ... [had become] effective to reach those consolidations which so cross the border line of monopolistic control as to be detrimental to the public interest...."[76]

By this formula, reasonable combination would remain legal, and along with it corporate administration of the market, while by presuming to the preservation of the principle of competition, the door would remain closed to government intervention on a comprehensive scale, that is, closed to governmental "paternalism" in economic affairs and, ultimately, to socialism. As Taft put it succinctly in early October, 1911, "We must get back to competition. If it is impossible then let us go to socialism, for there is no way between."[77] This should not be misinterpreted, however, to mean that Taft favored a reversion to the old competitive regime, and still less to laissez-faire. He was stating the alternatives, as he saw it, in principle, and as they appeared to be emerging in political life in the context of the position staked out by Roosevelt and gaining growing public support, and against which he found himself battling for political survival. He is better understood, perhaps, from his longer formulation along these lines: "If the abuses of monopoly and discrimination can not be restrained; if the concentration of power made possible by such abuses continues and increases, and it is made manifest that under the system of individualism and private property the tyranny and oppression of [the] wealthy can not be avoided," Taft warned, "then socialism will triumph and the institution of private property will perish."[78]

It was on the basis of this conception of the issues and the principle involved that Taft developed his administration's policy on the regulation of the market, moving away from administrative supervision

76. Ibid.
77. Taft, 6 Oct. 1911, quoted at Mowry, *Era of Roosevelt*, p. 286.
78. Taft, quoted at Wilensky, *Conservatives*, p. 44. In Senate debate on the Federal Trade Commission bill, Senator William E. Borah of Idaho argued along similar lines: "So far as I am concerned, rather than undertake merely to regulate monopoly through commissions, which is about the same thing as undertaking to regulate a cancer in the human system, I would prefer to try State Socialism." Quoted at Thomas C. Blaisdell, Jr., *The Federal Trade Commission* (New York: Columbia University Press, 1932), p. 10.

toward judicial process.[79] Taft's Secretary of War Henry L. Stimson explained the principle clearly and directly in public discourse. He told the Republican Club of New York City in December 1911, for example, that the disadvantage in acquiescing in the principle of monopoly was this: "The moment business claims the right to control prices through monopoly, that moment will the arm of the State claim the right to fix prices. We cannot legalize monopoly without bringing on State regulation of prices. Are we ready in our ordinary business to face that alternative?" Stimson reminded his fellow Republicans that public-service corporations such as railways and gas and electric companies, which necessarily enjoyed a monopoly, were already regulated by the state as to prices. The same condition, he suggested, was approaching for industries based on the right to appropriate limited resources, such as water power, phosphate lands, and perhaps eventually coal. "If we grasp at monopoly," he continued, "we must face the condition exacted of monopoly. We need not deceive ourselves with the idle dream that our virile American democracy will permit the prices of the things it buys to be controlled by a monopoly which is beyond the reach of the hand of its Government. If therefore," Stimson concluded, "we are unwilling to accept State regulation of prices, we must accept the only other regulation which is possible – that of competition, actual or potential." As Stimson's reference to "potential" competition implied, and as he made explicit in this same address, he did not favor the restoration of the old competitive market, but rather the assurance of fair prices and earnings to be attained by government regulation to prevent unfair trade methods, which would thereby keep "the field free for new competing capital to come in whenever the prices in the field are sufficient to tempt it."[80]

This concept of competition accorded essentially with Jenks's idea of monopolistic price, and what subsequently became known as oligopolistic price. Hence the emphatic, indeed impassioned, advocacy of publicity of corporate affairs by Roosevelt, Taft, and Wilson alike, to guard against stock-watering and secretive accounting, which might conceal

---

79. In early 1910, although publicly he still supported programs originating with the Roosevelt administration, including federal incorporation administered by a federal commission, Taft told Frank A. Vanderlip in a private White House talk that (in Vanderlip's words) "some of the great corporations have become so monopolistic in character that they are practically as much a quasi-public corporation as is a railroad company, because the people have no choice, but to patronize them, and that this gives the warrant for federal supervision in the form that he proposes." Vanderlip to Stillman, 11 Feb. 1910, FAV. It was this type of federal supervision that Taft came to view as dangerous and that he moved away from toward the end of his term.

80. Stimson, *Address* (15 Dec. 1911), pp. 3–4, 5.

improper prices and excessive returns. Publicity was essential to the concept of oligopolistic price, defined as that price which yielded a fair return on real investment and assets, and which spurred or did not obstruct innovation and rising efficiency; that price and rate of return above which competition, either direct or indirect by substitution, would be induced. In keeping the field open to the threat of new investment, if not new investment itself, publicity was the corollary of regulation against unfair practices. Together, publicity and policing business practices constituted the regulatory equivalent of competition.

By a legal fiction, namely, the preservation of competition in principle, the administered market could be validated under the primary control of the corporations, or the private sector, subject secondarily to government regulation, without embracing the statist command of the economy implied in such proposals as the Hepburn bill and Roosevelt's later trade commission proposals.

Although restrained during the campaign of 1912 by the Republican party's platform commitment to a federal trade commission and to legislation defining and prohibiting specific unfair practices, after the election, Taft emerged as the leading advocate of the judicial enforcement of the Sherman Act, construed in common-law terms, as in itself a sufficient solution of the trust problem.

The former president elaborated his views in his book *The Anti-Trust Act and the Supreme Court*, published in 1914. Agreeing with Chief Justice White's decision in the Standard Oil and American Tobacco cases, Taft argued that by determining that the Sherman Act denounced unreasonable restraints of trade at common law, the Rule of Reason decisions contained principles both logical and precisely applicable to modern conditions, affording a firm guide to judges responsible for administering the law. This made supplementary legislation unnecessary and harmful. The attempt to enumerate and define by legislation unfair practices would only duplicate the "well measured and definite yard stick" already developed by the courts at common law and result in confusion. A trade commission act that gave an administrative commission the power to define and prevent unfair practices would be similarly redundant, or it would be unconstitutional. If it went beyond those practices already "included in unreasonable restraints of trade at common law now denounced by the anti-trust law," the act would confer upon the commission legislative powers in violation of the constitution. If it did not, the commission would merely duplicate the work of the Justice Department and the courts.[81]

81. Taft, *The Anti-Trust Act and the Supreme Court* (New York: Harper Bros., 1914), pp. 115–117, and passim. *Cf.* Gerard C. Henderson, *The Federal Trade Commission: A Study in Administrative Law and Procedure* (New Haven: Yale University

Taft therefore argued that enforcement of the Sherman Act, now that the Supreme Court had restored its proper common-law meaning, offered the safest and most effective method of handling the trust problem. Without permitting government administrative agencies to interfere directly with the affairs of private enterprise, as various trade commission plans proposed, the judicial enforcement of the Sherman Act would best achieve the objectives of legitimizing the corporate order, preventing unfair practices and unreasonable restraints of trade, preserving the principle of competition as against a socialist-tending statist intervention, and protecting the public interest.[82]

By the end of the Taft administration and the opening months of the Wilson administration, three major positions on the trust question had formed from the previous years' debates, namely: (1) that associated with Roosevelt, of moving toward a government-directed public-service economy enforced by executive commission with minimal judicial review; (2) that associated with Taft, of regulating business methods through judicial enforcement of an antitrust law restored to common-law construction; and (3) that associated with Wilson, of regulating business methods through a mix of commission and judicial enforcement of a common-law-based antitrust law, with ultimate judicial supremacy in the process as a whole. It would take some time for Wilson's position, representing the majority view, to assume an adequate legislative embodiment. Once it had, however, it effectively "settled" the trust question. In combination with the Rule of Reason decisions of 1911, the Federal Trade Commission and the Clayton Acts of 1914 became the sustained basis for all subsequent national antitrust policy. Never again, moreover, would the trust question as such lie at the center of major party politics. At last, in short, the trust question was "taken out of politics." The legal order and the economic order were, in this respect, brought into phase, the one with the other, a signal achievement of Wilsonian progressivism, and a culminating landmark of the ascendancy of corporate liberalism.

In the course of extended conflicts among large-corporate and smaller capitalists, among capitalists and labor organizations, among those with proprietary and those with corporate outlooks, among competing wings of the major parties, the legal order moved, unevenly, into correspon-

---

Press, 1925), pp. 5–11. Letwin, *Law and Economic Policy*, pp. 279–282, presents a cogent argument in criticism of regulatory commissions more or less repeating, or at any rate agreeing with, that of Taft.

82. Taft, *Anti-Trust Act*, pp. 115–117; also, e.g., Taft's lengthy address at the banquet of the National Association of Manufacturers, 26 May 1915, Waldorf-Astoria Hotel, New York City, "Justice and Freedom for Industry," NAM, Twentieth Annual Convention, *Proceedings*, 25, 26 May 1915, pp. 279–280.

dence with the corporate reorganization of industry and the rise of the administered market. The legal order changed under the pressure of a great social movement among capitalists, political leaders, and intellectuals, aligned with movements among farm, labor, and civic associations, for the reorganization of the market. It was an accommodation that settled upon the rejection of a statist solution: It gave to corporations and other private parties in the market the primary responsibility, and the power, for regulating the market, and it assigned to government the secondary role of regulating the corporations. In the accommodation, Taft played a decisive role. In his unyielding legalism, he built a major bridge from Roosevelt's incipient statist corporate liberalism to Wilson's antistatist, regulatory corporate liberalism. The interplay of the three tendencies would recur again and again in the nation's politics in the ensuing years of the twentieth century – and Wilson himself would embrace an extensive statism during World War I – with Republican as well as Democratic presidents claiming Wilson's legacy as their own. That legacy, however, owed much to Taft. Indeed, the symbolism holds: Corporate liberalism has ever been a blend, in shifting proportions, of Wilsonian Democracy and Taft Republicanism, holding the line against, while drawing piecemeal upon, Rooseveltian statism whether square-dealing or new-dealing on the equalitarian left.

6

Woodrow Wilson and the corporate-liberal ascendancy

Introduction

On 23 May 1912, before a group of banqueting capitalists and civic notables, Woodrow Wilson, governor of New Jersey and presidential aspirant, anticipating misconceptions among members of his audience about his position on economic matters and the government-society relation, introduced his address on the relation of government to business with the complaint, "Most persons are so thoroughly uninformed as to my opinions that I have concluded that the only things they have not read are my speeches."[1]

Wilson's chagrin may well have been justified. Not only were some of the less informed capitalists and conservatives belaboring under frightening notions of Wilson as a near-populist, an unreliable vote-chaser, or an irresponsible trust-buster, but probably even greater numbers within, or leading, the ranks of Bryan-type Democrats and insurgent Republican progressives pictured the presidential candidate in terms of their own wishful interpolations rather than facts. For many of these, it would lead inevitably to disillusionment with, and bitter hostility toward, Wilson the president – a hostility not altogether fair because directed against a Wilson of their hopes and dreams, not a Wilson of reality; yet, in afterthought, not altogether unfair, because as is characteristic of politics in the United States, as perhaps elsewhere, Wilson the candidate, while refusing responsibility for such hopes and dreams,

---

1. "Government in Relation to Business," address at the Annual Banquet of the Economic Club, Hotel Astor, New York City, 23 May 1912, *PPWW*, 2, p. 130.

found therein powerful propulsion for his rise to the presidency and did not undertake decisively and publicly to disavow them.[2] From historical perspective, it may be said that in a time of conflict between an ascending corporate capitalism and a receding competitive capitalism, Wilson, although a political leader in transacting the ascendancy of the one, appealed to partisans of both. He thereby personified the transition from the competitive stage to the corporate stage of capitalism through the workings of normal, electoral politics, albeit under somewhat abnormal circumstances of party politics, in which in neither of his two elections to the presidency was he able to attract a majority of the popular vote.

"A history of developments"

As was the case with many United States intellectuals, capitalists, and political leaders of the time, the long depression of the 1890s, and the related social-political eruptions, exerted a strong impact upon Wilson's thinking. Previously, although a firm believer in private enterprise and market relations as essential components of democracy, he had focused his major attention on the evolution of political institutions.[3] This was perhaps to be expected: A belief in the free market may nourish an assumption that economic conditions, being basic to social life, are natural and will take care of themselves quite apart from deliberate, rational determination, and that political institutions offer the legitimate arena of human deliberation and intervention where people sustain their values, ideals, and principles in adapting them to natural evolutionary change. The depression of the 1890s, however, indicated that economic conditions no longer were taking care of themselves, if they ever did, without generating social dislocation and political upheaval. Even before the 1890s, Wilson had placed strong emphasis on economic causes of political events; for example, he interpreted the causes of the American Civil War as lying in the social and economic differences between the North and the South.[4] The trauma of the

---

2. Reference may be made, for example, to Col. Edward M. House's conference, with Wilson's approval, with leaders of Wall Street on 26 February 1913, including Henry C. Frick, Henry P. Davison, Otto Kahn, and others, where he assured them that the president-elect had no intention of making an attack on business, that Wilson's idealistic utterances were for the moral education of the people and "not for the purpose of writing such sentiment into law ..." House Diary, 26 Feb. 1913, cited at Link, *Wilson*, 2, p. 27.
3. E.g., his books *Congressional Government* (1885), and *The State* (1889). Cf. Link, *Wilson*, 1, p. 25.
4. See John M. Mulder, *Woodrow Wilson: The Years of Preparation* (Princeton: Princeton University Press, 1978), p. 93.

depression reinforced and perhaps solidified in Wilson's thinking the conviction, which remained prominent in his thought throughout the rest of his life, not simply that economic relations were basic to social relations, but that politics in the modern industrial era must above all be concerned with understanding, and making the necessary institutional adjustments to, changing economic conditions.

A conviction of this type may be understood logically and epistemologically as fitting nicely into Wilson's evolutionary-positivist conception of society and its historical development.[5] Nevertheless, the manner in which Wilson applied this conviction in both his scholarly writings and his policy-oriented thinking about political issues can be more fully understood in the context of his personal and intellectual association with Frederick Jackson Turner.

Wilson as professor and Turner as student became friends, lodging at the same residence, in 1888–1889, while Wilson lectured at Johns Hopkins University. Each had a lasting intellectual impact on the other. It was during this period that the young Turner was developing his frontier thesis, which was to reach a culmination in his Columbian Exposition address in Chicago in 1893, before the American Historical Association, "The Significance of the Frontier in American History." Arguing in 1891 that each age tends to write history "anew with reference to the conditions uppermost in its own time," Turner noted that inquiry into "the economic basis of society in general" had begun to assume the central place in United States historiography, because "Today the questions that are uppermost, and that will become increasingly important, are not so much political as economic questions. The age of machinery, of the factory system, is also the age of socialistic inquiry."[6]

Beyond this, Turner himself believed that the "careful student of history ... must seek the explanation of the forms and changes of

5. Martin J. Sklar, "Woodrow Wilson and the Political Economy of Modern United States Liberalism," in Radosh and Rothbard, eds., *A New History of Leviathan* (New York: Dutton 1972), pp. 10–12. See also, Karl Mannheim, *Ideology and Utopia* (New York: Harvest Books, n.d.), pp. 120–121. Mannheim refers to this outlook as "conservative-historicist."
6. Frederick Jackson Turner, "The Significance of History," *Wisconsin Journal of Education* 21 (Oct. 1891), in Ray A. Billington, ed., *Frontier and Section: Selected Essays of Frederick Jackson Turner* (Englewood Cliffs, N.J.: Prentice-Hall, 1961), p. 17. On the reciprocal intellectual relation between Wilson and Turner at Johns Hopkins during the last years of the 1880s, see Mulder, *Preparation*, p. 121; Henry W. Bragdon, *Woodrow Wilson: The Academic Years* (Cambridge, Mass.: Harvard University Press, 1967), pp. 193–194, 236, 241–242; and William Diamond, *The Economic Thought of Woodrow Wilson* (Baltimore: Johns Hopkins University Press, 1943), pp. 35–37.

political institutions in the social and economic forces that determine them. . . . These are the vital forces that work beneath the surface and dominate the external form." It was, then, "to changes in the economic and social life of a people that we must look for the forces that ultimately create and modify organs of political action." Responding to the great impact of the social turmoil and changes of the 1890s, Turner characterized his era as one of "profound economic and social transformation," which had witnessed within one decade, 1890–1900, four "marked changes" that "taken together . . . constitute a revolution." These he listed as: (1) ". . . the exhaustion of the supply of free land and the closing of the movement of Western advance as an effective factor in American development"; (2) a contemporaneous "concentration of capital in the control of fundamental industries . . . [signifying] a new epoch in the economic development of the United States," and "side by side with this concentration of capital . . . the combination of labor in the same vast industries," resulting in "the lines of cleavage which begin to appear . . . between capital and labor . . . accentuated by distinctions of nationality"; (3) ". . . connected with the two just mentioned . . . the expansion of the United States politically and commercially into lands beyond the seas," so that having "completed the conquest of the wilderness, and having consolidated our interests, we are beginning to consider the relations of democracy and empire"; and (4) the fact that "the political parties of the United States now tend to divide on issues that involve the question of socialism."[7]

It was largely in terms of the development of modern industrial capitalism in both its domestic and its international dimensions, the capitalism-socialism dialogue, and the specifically American situation portrayed by Turner's frontier thesis, that Wilson comprehended and wrote about the intensification of class conflict and economic dislocation in the United States, the emergence of economic questions as the preeminent issues of the day, and the consequent trend toward changing government-society relations.

As to the affinity of their thinking, Wilson wrote to Turner in 1889 of "our agreement that the role of the west in this development [of United States nationality] has a very great, a leading, role, though much neglected by our historians."[8] According to Wilson, "Turner and I were close friends. He talked with me a great deal about his idea. All I ever

7. Turner, "Contributions of the West to American Democracy," *Atlantic Monthly* 91 (Jan. 1903), in Billington, ed., *Frontier and Section*, pp. 78–80.
8. Wilson to Turner, 23 Aug. 1889, in Ray S. Baker, *Wilson, Life and Letters*, 8 vols. (New York: Doubleday, Page, various dates), 2, p. 125. Cf. William A. Williams, "The Frontier Thesis and American Foreign Policy," *Pacific Historical Review* 24:4 (Nov. 1955), pp. 379–395.

wrote on the subject came from him."[9] In fact, before delivering his address of 1893, Turner read it aloud to Wilson, upon whom it "made a deep impression."[10]

The impact of Turner's thesis on United States historiography had scarcely had time to make itself felt, when Wilson, in December 1893, appeared in print as a firm advocate of the frontier interpretation of the nation's history. In a critical review of Goldwin Smith's book on United States political history, Wilson rejected and assailed the "expansion of New England" interpretation of United States history, insisting instead upon the importance of the middle colonies, and particularly of the nation's westward-moving development as the peculiar and determining characteristic of United States civilization.[11]

As a scholar, no less than as a public figure, Wilson turned again and again to this theme, defining the nation's development and the American character in terms of westward expansion and the frontier.[12] Addressing the New Jersey Historical Society in 1895, Wilson applied Turner's thesis to conclude that the frontier "is, so far, the central and determining fact of our national history." The westerner, he argued, had been "the type and master of our American life."[13] "The typical Americans," Wilson had already asserted two years earlier in 1893, "have all been western men, with the exception of Washington," but even Washington "got his experience and his notions of what ought to be done for the country from ... actual life on the western frontier." Hamilton, Madison, John Adams, John Quincy Adams, were "not Americans in the sense in which Clay and Jackson and Lincoln were Americans." No mention of Jefferson here at all.[14] In his widely read essay published in the *Atlantic Monthly* in 1897, Wilson articulated Turner's thesis at length in defining the nation's evolution and its newly

9. Wilson to Professor William E. Dodd, n.d., in Baker, *Wilson*, 2, p. 125.
10. Ibid. Further evidence of Wilson's high esteem for Turner appears in his private appraisal in 1902 of Turner as a historian: "... it is a little difficult for me to answer the question, who is the coming man in American history? But on the general question no man who knows the field need hesitate a moment for the answer. He is Professor Frederick J. Turner, of the University of Wisconsin. Both in knowledge and in the gift of expression he is already in the first class. He has not yet published a book. When he does various other writers to the country will be willingly accorded a back seat." Wilson to J. B. Gilder, 30 Jan. 1902, *Woodrow Wilson Letters, Miscellaneous*, State Historical Society of Wisconsin, Madison.
11. Wilson, "Mr. Goldwin Smith's 'Views' on Our Political History," *Forum* 16 (Dec. 1893), pp. 489–499; see also "The Puritan," speech before the New England Society of New York City, 22 Dec. 1900, *PPWW*, 1, pp. 362–364; cf. Baker, *Wilson*, 2, p. 108.
12. Cf. Link, *Wilson*, 1, pp. 30–31.
13. Quoted at ibid., p. 31.
14. Wilson, "Mr. Goldwin Smith's 'Views'," pp. 497–498; see also Baker, *Wilson*, 2, p. 104.

attained stage of development: The "'West'," Wilson noted was not "a region," but, "in Professor Turner's admirable phrase, a stage of development." It was now, however, "a stage of development with a difference, as Professor Turner has shown, which makes it practically a new thing in our history." Wilson continued:

> The "West" was once a series of States and settlements beyond which lay free lands not yet occupied, into which the restless and all who could not thrive by mere steady industry, all who had come too late and all who had stayed too long, could pass on, and, it might be, better their fortunes. Now it lies without outlet. The free lands are gone. Now communities must make their life sufficient without this easy escape.... It is as if they were caught in a fixed order of life and forced into a new competition.[15]

Again in 1901, Wilson wrote, "Until 1890 the United States had always a frontier; looked always to a region beyond, unoccupied, unappropriated, an outlet for its energy.... For nearly three hundred years their growth had followed a single law, – the law of expansion into new territory."[16] Indeed, thought Wilson, the nation's history since independence, its determining events, were to be seen as a function of the westward-moving frontier, and hence as the function of stages of development over expanding territory: "The history of the United States," Wilson noted, "is very far from being a history of origins. It is just the opposite: it is a history of developments."[17]

Westward expansion, according to Wilson, "set the pace of our life; forced the slavery question to a final issue; gave us the civil war with its stupendous upheaval and its resettlement of the very foundations of the government; spread our strength from sea to sea; created us a free and mighty people, whose destinies daunt the imagination of the Old World looking on. That increase, that endless accretion, that rolling, resistless tide, incalculable in its strength, infinite in its variety, has made us what we are; ... has provoked us to invention and given us mighty captains of industry. This great pressure of a people moving always to new frontiers, in search of new lands, new power, the full freedom of a virgin world, has ruled our course and formed our policies like a Fate."[18] Understood as incessant development, westward expansion

15. "The Making of the Nation," *Atlantic Monthly* 80 (July 1897), *PPWW*, 1, pp. 313–314.
16. "Democracy and Efficiency," *Atlantic Monthly* 87 (Mar. 1901), *PPWW*, 1, p. 403. See also, Wilson, "The Ideals of America," *Atlantic Monthly*, 90 (Dec. 1902), address delivered 26 Dec. 1901, *PPWW*, 1, p. 426.
17. Wilson, "Mr. Goldwin Smith's 'Views'," p. 495.
18. "Ideals of America," *PPWW*, 1, p. 425.

was, to Wilson the political scientist, the natural law of the nation's history, the dominant mode of organic evolution as it operated in the United States, the creative force propelling and shaping the American people; because his was no blaspheming mind, to Wilson the ethical Christian it was also the providential End All and Be All: If this was God's country, developmental expansion was the Spirit itself, no mere pagan Fate at the head of a barbarian wave, but *der heilige Geist*, marching through history in the New World as the daunted Old World looked on. The history of the United States, in short, was "a history of developments."

The central position of developmental expansion in Wilson's thinking about the nation's past and its prospects makes itself evident alike in his scholarly and in his political works. In one of his major scholarly works, *Constitutional Government* (published in 1908), for example, he applied the frontier thesis to an analysis of the nation's constitutional history. It was the dynamics of westward expansion and the frontier, Wilson here argued, that provided the constitution with a steadily growing national, as against a strictly federal, character. He wrote: "It is familiar matter of history that it is this westward expansion, this constant projection of new communities into the West, this never ceasing spread and adaptation of our institutions and our modes of life, that has been the chief instrumentality in giving us national feeling, that has kept our eyes lifted to tasks which had manifest destiny in them, and could be encompassed by no merely local agencies."[19]

Wilson viewed the passing of the frontier and the industrial revolution as interrelated phenomena, as inevitable and irresistible developments, which in turn determined the course of United States history from the Civil War to the turn of the century. The fact that the two processes had reached a climax in the crisis of the 1890s reinforced Wilson's conception of economic processes as basic to an understanding of the nation's history; it also largely determined the terms in which Wilson comprehended these economic processes. Whether one examines Wilson's writings of the 1890s, of his Princeton period, 1900–1909, or of his political officeholding period, 1910 and after, the emphasis upon the post–Civil War industrial revolution as having effected a fundamental

19. Wilson, *Constitutional Government in the United States* (New York: Columbia University Press, 1908), pp. 47, 48 (eight lectures delivered at Columbia University in 1907). For further such statements both before and after 1907, see Wilson's "Democracy and Efficiency" (1901) and "The Ideals of America" (1901), *PPWW*, 1, pp. 403–404, 425, and "Richmond Address" (1912), *PPWW*, 2, pp. 372–373.

transformation of the United States, is to be found.[20] But repeatedly Wilson discussed the broad consequences of the industrial revolution in relation to the passing of the frontier. Taken together, as essentially economic processes, the two impelled Wilson, like Turner, to see an inseparable connection between the nation's domestic and international relations, and to assume an economic interpretation of United States history, at least in large part, and at times an economic determinism in his analysis of political institutions and human behavior.[21]

"The life of America," Wilson declared in 1911, "is not the life it was twenty years ago. It is not the life it was ten years ago. We have changed our economic conditions from top to bottom, and with our economic conditions has changed also the organization of our life."[22] Note that here Wilson did not limit the impact of economic conditions to political life or to some relatively narrow sphere of institutional arrangements, but ascribed that impact as exerting itself universally: "the organization of our life." Indeed, he was not reluctant to insist, at least on some occasions, upon the primacy of economics in subjective consciousness, not alone in objective institutions. "For whatever we say of other motives," Wilson observed in 1898 in a talk at Johns Hopkins, "we must never forget that in the main the ordinary conduct of men is determined by economic motives."[23]

Like Turner, then, Wilson defined the foremost political questions of his times as, in essence, economic questions. In 1897, for example, observing that "an industrial revolution separates us" from the Civil War, he declared, "It is not now fundamental matters of [governmental] structure and franchise upon which we have to centre our choice," but

20. See, e.g., "Leaderless Government," address before Virginia State Bar Association, 4 Aug. 1897, *PPWW*, 1, pp. 353, 354; *Constitutional Government*, pp. 46–47; "Issues of Freedom," address at banquet of Knife and Fork Club of Kansas City, Mo., 5 May 1911, *PPWW*, 2, pp. 285, Wilson, *The New Freedom* (New York: Doubleday, Page, 1914), chap. 1, "The Old Order Changeth," pp. 3–32, comprising selections from Wilson's 1912 campaign speeches.

21. This is not to say that Wilson embraced economic determinism as a systematic way of thinking in the totality of his writings, but that it constituted a basic, if not always consistent, component of his thinking about social and political evolution, and political questions, from the 1890s onward, if not before; at the same time, it should be noted, it was generally consonant with his evolutionary-positivist view of society. Wilson noted the noneconomic motives from which people acted, but he regarded economic motives and thinking as in essence rational in contrast to other kinds, and he regarded economic laws to be rational, indefeasible, and hence impervious to legislation or government policy that ignored or violated them. See Diamond, *Economic Thought*, pp. 51–55; Sklar, "Woodrow Wilson," pp. 9–12.

22. "Issues of Freedom" (1911), *PPWW*, 2, p. 285. This statement appears again in slightly altered form in *The New Freedom*, p. 3.

23. Quoted at Diamond, *Economic Thought*, p. 52 n. 45.

upon "questions of economic policy chiefly." Among those matters he regarded as "questions of economic policy chiefly," Wilson cited not only those that are transparently economic in character such as "customs tariffs, coinage, currency, ... the regulation of railway traffic and of the great industries," but also "immigration, the law of corporations and trusts," and "foreign policy, our duty to our neighbors."[24]

That the main questions of the day were economic in character was related, in Wilson's mind, to the circumstance that the United States had reached a new stage of development requiring institutional reform. Conceiving the new stage of development as itself the result of economic changes, he proceeded accordingly to a broader generalization that defined economic relations as basic to the overall character of modern society. Hence in 1910, before the American Bar Association convened in Chattanooga, Tennessee, Wilson stated, "The life of the nation running upon normal lines, has grown infinitely varied. It does not centre now upon questions of governmental structure or of the distribution of governmental powers. It centres," he stressed, "upon economic questions," and these were "questions of the very structure and operation of society itself, of which government is only the instrument."[25] It would be hard to find a more emphatic statement of a belief in the economic basis of modern society. Five months later, in his inaugural address as governor-elect of New Jersey, Wilson declared, "The whole world has changed within the lifetime of men not yet in their thirties; the world of business, and therefore the world of society and the world of politics.... A new economic society has sprung up, and we must effect a new set of adjustments."[26]

It may be noted, in assessing the significance of the economic interpretation of society in Wilson's thought, that sixteen years before Charles A. Beard published his book on the question, Wilson had already offered an economic interpretation of the United States Constitution and the founding of the new government under it. The Founders had "first met to make a commercial arrangement and upon that commercial arrangement built the institutions of the Nation." The new government "had been fostered in the making by the commercial classes."[27] In similar fashion, Wilson interpreted sectional conflict between the East and the West and South as rooted in differential econom-

---

24. "Leaderless Government" (1897), *PPWW*, 1, p. 354.
25. "The Lawyer and the Community," 31 Aug. 1910, *PPWW*, 2, pp. 250–251; this statement appears again in altered form in *The New Freedom*, p. 4.
26. Inaugural Address, 17 Jan. 1911, *PPWW*, 2, pp. 270–271, 273.
27. "The Making of the Nation" (1897), *PPWW*, 1, p. 322; "The Tariff and the Trusts," 24 Feb. 1912, *PPWW*, 2, pp. 406–407.

ic development and as resolvable with further economic evolution.[28]

It was therefore as a genuine component of his intellectual framework, and not merely as a rhetorical response to political issues, that Wilson explained the need for government regulation of business on the ground that business "is the foundation of every other relationship, particularly of the political relationship," and that, therefore, "no study of the history of the Government can candidly be made which will not lead to this conclusion – that the very thing that Government cannot let alone is business, for business underlies every part of our life; the foundation of our lives, of our spiritual lives included, is economic." It is of particular interest that Wilson posited the effective, if not complete, identity of economy and society in the modern industrial capitalist epoch where society was so largely coterminous with market relations. The government-business relation, in this view, will therefore essentially determine, if not actually constitute, the government-society relation. Upon that determination must rest the future of the liberal principle, strongly affirmed by Wilson, that the state serve society, not society the state, and it was precisely on this issue that Wilson would eventually shape a position distinguished from both that of Taft and that of Roosevelt.[29]

"A *modus vivendi* in America for happiness"

An economic interpretation of history, society, and more particularly of politics, was not unusual in the Anglo-American political tradition, and around the turn of the century it was common to thinkers of the most diverse opinions in other respects – liberals, conservatives, populists, social Darwinists, social gospelers, pragmatists, social reformers, and socialists. It would therefore be a mistake to think that Wilson accepted a populist or radical economic diagnosis of the social conflicts of the late nineteenth and early twentieth centuries while simply rejecting proposed populist or radical remedies. For this erroneously implies not only that an economic diagnosis was peculiar to populists or radicals, but also that Wilson's and their diagnoses were necessarily the same.[30]

28. "The Making of the Nation" (1897), *PPWW*, 1, pp. 324–325, 327–328; *Constitutional Government*, pp. 48, 49.
29. "Government in Relation to Business" (1912), *PPWW*, 2, pp. 431, 432. On the liberal principle of the state-society relation in the modern world, Wilson, *The State: Elements of Historical and Practical Politics* (Boston: D.C. Heath, 1906), chaps. 15, 16, pp. 612–639 (on the functions and objects of government).
30. For Wilson's hostility to the populists and Bryan Democrats in the opening years of the new century, carrying over from the 1890s, see, e.g., Diamond, *Economic Thought*, pp. 52–59; Link, *Wilson*, 1, pp. 96–97; Link, *Papers*, 15, pp. 545–551.

Wilson did not have to depend upon populists or radicals for an economic interpretation of society. Aside from classical political economy and Walter Bagehot, he had plenty of good Gold Democrats to commune with, such as Conant, Reinsch, and Walter Hines Page. Like theirs and like that of Turner and such solid Republicans as McKinley, Hay, Root, Jenks, and Theodore Roosevelt, his diagnosis found a large common ground with that of socialists and, precisely therein, was as different from that of populists as were his remedies. Populists viewed United States society as having become unnaturally unjust and exploitative, with the large industrial corporations, the railroads, and the great banking and finance houses disrupting the natural laws of competition and commerce by their monopolistic and parasitic practices, which injured or destroyed the real producers – farmers, workers, and smaller entrepreneurs – and corrupted and defeated republican institutions. If socialists viewed these phenomena as the natural and inevitable outcome of capitalist development, so intensifying exploitation and injustice as to set the stage for an equally inevitable revolution, Wilson viewed United States society as moving toward larger and more concentrated units of enterprise according to natural laws of evolution and commerce, but as essentially just, beneficent, and progressive, precisely in its obedience to the dictates of economic evolution along modern lines.

Imbalances of economic and political power, class conflicts, political upheaval, social turmoil and discontent, all these were understandable, in Wilson's view, as the results of uneven sectional development and the lag of legal, institutional, and cultural change in the face of a profound economic transformation wrought by the industrial revolution and aggravated by the concomitant passing of the continental frontier. When adjusted to the new economic conditions, the laws and new customs and attitudes would prevent irresponsible individuals from turning novel conditions to their selfish advantage, and would foster social harmony by establishing, on a new basis of modern industrialization, the national welfare and the public interest as the transcendent principles of statecraft. Populists sought to throttle, dismantle, or publicly expropriate the large corporations and big banks. Wilson and like-minded progressives sought to harness and regulate them by adjusting law and government policy to the new economic order they represented. Whereas populist diagnosis implied a significant restorationist restructuring of the market and society, Wilson's was essentially positivistic and viewed the trends of social dislocation and political turbulence as the understandable, and not entirely avoidable, pains of a generally progressive and inevitable, although uncommonly accelerated, process of national development and reconstruction that required urgent, but careful, adjustments in both domestic and foreign policy.

Wilson's recurrent and deeply troubled concern over the intensification of "sharp class contrasts and divisions"[31] was accordingly accompanied by his insistence upon the urgency of composing the conflicts of interest within a new social harmony, defined by the national interest and the general welfare, before such conflicts could erupt in irreparable social disintegration and revolution. At the same time, his concern was accompanied by a confidence that by wise adjustments to the economic and social forces that lay beneath the conflict, a new accommodation and harmony of interests could be achieved on the basis of those same forces.

Again and again, Wilson sought to analyze the intensification of social conflict and to define the problem that had to be solved, in terms of the passing of the frontier and rapid industrialization. In the midst of the crisis of the 1890s, for example, Wilson spoke of "commercial heats and political distempers in our body politic which warn of an early necessity for carefully prescribed physic." In spite of the organic metaphor, Wilson's "prescribed physic" fell in with classic liberal instrumentalism: "Under such circumstances some measure of legislative reform is clearly indispensable."[32] In 1897, before the Virginia State Bar Association, Wilson warned, "This is not a day of revolution; but it is a day of change, and of such change as may breed revolution should we fail to guide and moderate it."[33] "If ever a nation was transformed," he noted, "this nation has been, under the eyes of a single generation – and processes that run so fast are perilous." The industrial revolution of the previous decades "has left us more various and more unequal ... than ever before. ... there is an unprecedented diversification of interests ... [which] for the time ... mark also differences of region and development. And these differences of condition and of economic

31. "The Banker and the Nation," address delivered at annual convention of American Bankers' Association, Denver, Colo., 30 Sept. 1908, *PPWW*, 2, p. 55.
32. "Government Under the Constitution" (1896), quoted at Diamond, *Economic Thought*, p. 58. Although Wilson liked to characterize his own view of society as organic, patterned after Bagehot, Burke, and Maine, as against a mechanistic view, one must be careful about accepting that self-appraisal from him and, for that matter, from any significant American political figure. Upon analysis, "organic" to Wilson really meant an instrumentalist evolutionary-positivism, that is, in the American political universe, a progressive liberalism. To my knowledge, there is no genuine organicist or "corporativist" strain in twentieth-century mainstream American political thought, although associational thought, or theory centered upon sociality, is sometimes mistaken for it.
33. "Leaderless Government" (1897), *PPWW*, 1, p. 337.

growth as between region and region, though temporary, are more sharply marked than they ever were before."[34]

The differences were the result of "the two forces which were to dominate" the United States from the early national period "till the present," and which determined "the present issues of our politics: an open 'West' into which a frontier population was to be thrust from generation to generation, and a protective tariff which should build up special interests the while in the 'East,' and make the contrast ever sharper between section and section." The West, he continued, now simply noted more keenly and distastefully than before "this striking contrast between her own development and that of the 'East.'" While the sectional conflict deepened, moreover, the conflict among interests in the more settled parts of the nation had quickened. There was "no longer any outlet for those who are not the beneficiaries of the protective system, and nothing but the contrasts it has created remains to mark its triumphs." In short, Wilson declared, "The old sort of growth is at an end, – the growth by mere expansion." It had become necessary "now to look more closely to internal conditions, and study the means by which a various people is to be bound together in a single interest."[35]

Wilson's concern with deepening conflicts of interests in American society occupied a central place in his thinking throughout the first decade of the new century and in the years afterward at Trenton and Washington. The United States, he said in 1908, had "come upon a time of crisis when it is made to appear, and is in part true, that interest is arrayed against interest," and it was the duty of the nation's leaders "to turn the war into peace."[36] Arguing the necessity, under the circumstances, for strong executive leadership of the caliber of Lincoln's at another time of protracted and bitter strife, Wilson declared, "The country is going to have crisis after crisis. God send they may not be bloody crises, but they will be intense and acute." Underlying the conditions "that perplex us at this moment," he warned, "are the things which mark, I will not say a warfare, but a division among classes," which had rendered the nation "divided into rival and contestant interests by the score," and had yielded a "much more dangerous" situation than that at the time of the Civil War because, Wilson held, at least in that previous contest the nation had divided "into only two perfectly

34. Ibid., pp. 337, 353.
35. "The Making of the Nation" (1897), *PPWW*, 1, pp. 324–325, 327.
36. "The Banker and the Nation" (1908), *PPWW*, 2, p. 61. See also "Democracy and Efficiency" (1901), *PPWW*, 1, pp. 399–400; and "The Ideals of America" (1901), *PPWW*, 1, p. 126.

distinguishable interests, which you ... [could] discriminate and deal with."[37]

If the crisis resided merely in the "contest ... between capital and labor," it might perhaps have been less dangerous and more easily manageable. But, in Wilson's view, that was "too narrow and too special a conception of it." For the crisis lay in a multiplicity of antagonistic interests engaged in hostile, mutually suspicious conflict that threatened wholesale social disintegration if not stemmed, and that involved a widespread loss of confidence, on the part not only of labor but also of many business and middle-class elements, in the ability of the existing society to dispense welfare and justice. Defining the national crisis, in effect, as centering in the passage from the proprietary-competitive stage to the corporate stage of capitalism, Wilson held that the contest was "rather between capital in all its larger accumulations and all other less concentrated, more dispersed, smaller, and more individual economic forces." It had resulted in the "anatomizing of our social structure, this pulling it to pieces," as if each part "had an independent existence and interest and could live not only separately but in contrast and contest with its other parts, as if it had no organic union with them or dependence upon them, ... a very dangerous and unwholesome thing at best." This "process of segregation and contrast," Wilson warned, "is always a symptom of deep discontent.... It has given occasion to that extensive and radical programme of reform which we call socialism and with which so many hopeful minds are now in love." At certain times in history, however, like this one, such a crisis was inevitable, because it grew out of profound economic transformation, to which political and legal institutions had yet to adjust. It was necessary, therefore, Wilson counseled, to "make the best of it, if only to hasten the process of reintegration."[38]

Among the most eloquent statements of Wilson's analysis of the social crisis as the product of the passing of the frontier in the midst of

37. "Abraham Lincoln: A Man of the People," address on the occasion of the celebration of the hundredth anniversary of the birth of Abraham Lincoln, Chicago, 12 Feb. 1909, *PPWW*, 2, pp. 93, 99.
38. "The Banker and the Nation" (1908), *PPWW*, 2, pp. 55–56. For later examples of Wilson's description of the United States during the early years of the twentieth century as characterized by social crisis punctuated by conflicts of classes and interests, see his Acceptance Address, Seagirt, N.J., 7 Aug. 1912, *Official Report of the Proceedings of the Democratic National Convention* (Baltimore, 25 June to 2 July 1912), p. 403; *The New Freedom*, p. 36; "The Uneasiness of Business," address to Virginia Editorial Association, Washington, D.C., 25 June 1914, *PPWW*, 3, pp. 135, 177; public letter to Secretary of the Treasury McAdoo, 17 Nov. 1914 (printed in *New York Times*, 18 Nov. 1914), quoted at Arthur S. Link, *Wilson and the Progressive Era, 1910–1917* (New York: Harper Bros., 1954), p. 79.

rapid industrialization, is that to be found in his Richmond address, which he delivered in early 1912 as a prominent candidate for the Democratic party's presidential nomination. On that occasion, he observed, "only in our day has the crowding gotten so close and hot that there is no free outlet for men. Don't you remember that until the year 1890, every ten years when we took the census, we were able to draw a frontier in this country? . . . But when we reached the year 1890 there was no frontier discoverable in America." That meant, he stated, "that men who found conditions intolerable in crowded America no longer had a place free where they could take up land of their own and start a new hope." Indeed, it was "true that we needed a frontier so much that after the Spanish war we annexed a new frontier some seven thousand miles off in the Pacific." But still America's "seething millions" turned upon themselves "and the cauldron grows hotter and hotter." The problem to be defined, he continued, was the nation's "great duty . . . to see that her men remain free and happy under the conditions that have now sprung up." For, Wilson explained, "now we realize that Americans are not free to release themselves. We have got to live together and be happy in the family. . . . We have got to put up with one another, and . . . so regulate and assuage one another that we will not be intolerable to each other. We have got to get a *modus vivendi* in America for happiness, and that is our new problem. And I call you to witness it *is* a new problem. America never had to finish anything before."[39]

The modus vivendi for happiness, Wilson thought, would result in large part naturally from the onward evolution of extant economic forces, as the latter exerted their influence in domestic and foreign affairs. "Many differences will pass away of themselves," he predicted in 1897. "'East' and 'West' will come together by a slow approach, as capital accumulates where now it is only borrowed, as industrial development makes its way westward in a new variety, . . . until all the scattered parts of the nation are drawn into real community of interest."[40] "The processes which knit close and unite all fibres into one cloth," he asserted ten years later, "are now everywhere visible to any one who will look beneath the surface. . . . influences that operate silent and unobserved in the economic and social changes that are working a great synthesis upon us, are carrying the nationalizing process steadily and irresistibly forward to the same great consummation."[41]

39.   "Richmond Address" (1 Feb. 1912), *PPWW*, 2, pp. 372–373. Wilson's emphasis.
40.   "The Making of the Nation" (1897), *PPWW*, 1, pp. 327, 328.
41.   *Constitutional Government*, pp. 48, 49.

The appropriate acquiescence in, and adjustment to, evolutionary and integrative socioeconomic development required strong and intelligent national leadership capable of discovering and implementing the legal and ideological framework best suited to facilitating developmental forces, lest popular unrest, discontent, and conflicts of interest and class evoked by them preempt their harmonizing, nationalizing "consummation." In this sense, Wilson, too, was a New Nationalist. Not everything could "be left to drift and slow accommodation," he admonished. Years before Walter Lippmann would define the alternatives as drift or mastery, Wilson urged, "It will require leadership of a much higher order to teach us the triumphs of cooperation, the self-possession and calm choices of maturity."[42]

Because the central policy questions of the day were economic in nature, their determination "must turn upon economics – that is to say, upon business questions," and therefore the "question of statesmanship" was the "question of taking all the economic interests of every part of the country into the reckoning," to achieve "an all-around accommodation and adjustment." But economic questions could not be settled "except upon grounds of interest"; what was needed, therefore, was "some guiding and adjusting force," in the person of the president of the United States functioning as a "single organ of intelligent communication between the whole Nation and the Government which determines the policy of the Nation," that is, the federal government, and able "to reconcile our interests and extract what is national and liberal out of what is sectional and selfish."[43]

Wilson's emphasis upon the necessary to submit and adjust to the facts of social life, that is, to naturally evolving socioeconomic development, was, in essence, the logical expression of his evolutionary-positivist view of society. It was therefore central to, and it permeated, his thought on political and social questions in general, and on the trust question in particular. The evolutionary determinism in Wilson's thought is quite understandable in an outlook rooted in the predestination of Calvinism, the natural laws of commerce and liberty of Smith, Cobden, and Bright, and the evolutionary historicism of Burke and Bagehot. In passage from the Old World to the New, evolutionary determinism translated into the future-looking evolutionary positivism of Wilsonian Democracy, or of modern American Liberalism.[44]

42. "The Making of the Nation" (1897), *PPWW*, 1, p. 328.
43. "Leaderless Government" (1897), *PPWW*, 1, p. 354; "Government in Relation to Business" (1912), *PPWW*, 2, pp. 436, 437. Also, respecting the new presidential role, *Constitutional Government*, pp. 73, 220–221.
44. For this translation, it should be noted, Wilson already had warrant in the evolu-

The function of a "national and liberal" statecraft, as Wilson saw it, therefore, was to comprehend the facts and effect the corresponding adjustments of the people's thinking, habits, laws, and institutions. As he put it in his paper delivered before the history division of the International Congress of Arts and Science, at the St. Louis World's Fair in 1904, "Law and government" in the modern age had become "regulative rather than generative." Statecraft, therefore, could not negate or re-create the "laws of trade" or basically alter the facts of social and economic evolution by mere legislation or executive fiat; these were the natural, inevitable, and irresistible products of evolution; what statecraft could do was to shape law and administration in submission to and correspondence with the facts, and from time to time thereby also "mould" the facts. Otherwise law and administration must stand as retrogressive or visionary, and in either case invite or exacerbate social discontent, class conflict, political upheaval, and the danger of revolution. In a time of transition such as his, when the facts were not yet sufficiently understood by the people, or accepted by them as legitimate, the need for leadership capable of comprehending social reality, reconciling the people to it, and translating that accommodation into corresponding law and institutions, was particularly acute. As Wilson had written in 1897, "It is not simply the existence of facts that governs us, but the consciousness and comprehension of the facts." For this reason, he believed, "The whole process of statesmanship consists in bringing facts to light, and shaping law to suit, or, if need be, mould them."[45]

Wilson's view of the relation of the law to facts rested on his evolutionary conception of society. "All history," he noted, "has society as its subject matter," and society existed as an "organic order." Yet, not all themes of history "lie equally close to the organic processes of

tionary liberalism of Bagehot and the social progressivism of the German historical school that he had encountered and absorbed as a younger scholar. The translation, then, is not strictly American-exceptional. Wilson's evolutionary positivism also found reinforcement in his adaptation of Darwin's theory of natural evolution to social evolution, although not in the sense of the "social Darwinism" associated with Spencer, Sumner, or Fiske. See *Constitutional Government*, pp. 56–57, 199–200, and *The New Freedom*, pp. 46, 47–48, where Wilson describes government and social life as "organic," Darwinian, as against what he denotes as the mechanistic, Newtonian conceptions of Montesquieu, the Enlightenment thinkers, and Jefferson. See also notes 65 and 66 and accompanying text, below, Cf. Wilson, "The Variety and Unity of History," delivered at the St. Louis World's Fair, 20 Sept. 1904, at Link, *Papers*, 15, pp. 472–491; Link, *Wilson*, 1, pp. 21–22; Diamond, *Economic Thought*, pp. 39, 47.

45 "The Variety and Unity of History," Link, *Papers*, 15, p. 475; "The Making of the Nation" (1897), *PPWW*, 1, p. 328.

society," which were "most prominent in political and economic history." Historically, "the organic order is: politics, economics, religion, law, literature, art, language." Wilson was not sure whether throughout all of history, religion or law should be considered as taking precedence over the other, for "most history is not modern," but "in modern society, certainly law." In modern society, so largely devoted to economic development, "Law occupies a place singular and apart. Its character is without parallel in our list." The law in modern society, Wilson held, "consists of that part of the social thought and habit which has definitely formed itself, which has gained universal acquiescence and recognition, and which has been given the sanction and backing of the state itself, a final formulation in command." In its origins, the law "comes, not independently and of itself, but . . . is itself a product of the state. But not of politics, unless we speak of public law, the smaller part, not of private, the greater." Viewed "from the historian's point of view," Wilson explained, "The forces which created it [the law] are chiefly economic, or else social," that is, "bred amidst ideas of class and privilege." As such, "It springs from a thousand fountains."[46] Private law facilitated, and gave expression to, the evolutionary development of the market, the economy, under the protection of the state, without state direction or command; public law adjusted to, and regulated, that development.

During both his academic and political years, Wilson maintained his views on the intimate relation of law and fact, but he became, if anything, more emphatic on the need to acknowledge the subordination of law to fact. The laws of the United States, he declared in 1912, "have not kept up with the change of economic circumstances," and they had "not kept up with the change of political circumstances." "We have not kept our practices adjusted to the facts of the case," he argued, "and until we do, and unless we do, the facts of the case will always have the better of the argument; because if you do not adjust your laws to the facts, so much the worse for the laws, not for the facts, because law trails after the facts. . . . I do not say we may or may not [adjust the laws to the facts]; I say we must; there is no choice." Leaving little unsaid, Wilson explained further, "If your laws do not fit your facts, the facts are not injured, the law is damaged; because the law, unless I have studied amiss, is the expression of the facts in legal relationships. Laws have never altered the facts; laws have always necessarily expressed the facts; adjusted interests as they have arisen and have changed toward one another."[47] Hence, in assuming a position on the law similar to

46. "The Variety and Unity of History," Link, *Papers*, 15, pp. 478, 479.
47. *The New Freedom*, pp. 33, 34, 35; also, "Richmond Address" (1 Feb. 1912), *PPWW*, 2, p. 376, for an almost identical statement.

that of Roosevelt and Taft, Wilson placed it in his own broader philosophical framework, in accordance with which, it might be said, the New Freedom presupposed the knowledge and recognition of (evolutionary) necessity.[48] It was the "necessity," the "facts," which Wilson recognized, that determined his position on the trust question, that is to say, on the place of the large corporation in American life, or on the "question" of corporate capitalism and the government-society relation.

A "middle ground" between socialism and capitalism

More than a decade before Theodore Roosevelt denounced agrarian and small-enterprise trust-busters as "rural tories" and reactionaries, whose passion for the preservation of the republic of small producers would turn back the clock of progress, Wilson, in December 1900, had directed the same criticism at the populists and Bryan Democrats. "Most of our reformers," he disparaged them, "are retro-reformers. They want to hale us back to an old chrysalis which we have broken; they want us to resume a shape which we have outgrown."[49] Their program was not only retrogressive but, because it was that and therefore did not correspond with the facts of the modern industrial order, it was impossible of achievement; its enactment would result in contempt for law, lawlessness, and social chaos.

In this most basic respect, Wilson was no more a "Jeffersonian" than were Roosevelt, Taft, Chief Justice Edward D. White, Justice Oliver Wendell Holmes, George W. Perkins, or Herbert Croly. If "Jeffersonian" is meant to connote a return to an agrarian-yeoman or small-producer republic, or to the regime of unrestricted competition among individual entrepreneurs or small-business units, or to a governmental policy of laissez-faire, that is, nonintervention in economic affairs, then as much as it obscures more than clarifies our understanding of any major twentieth-century political figure in the United States, including Bryan and La Follette, it certainly fails, even allegorically, to characterize, or provide insight into, Wilson's thought or policy positions.

It is doubtful that by the early 1900s Wilson thought of himself in terms either of "Jeffersonianism" or "Hamiltonianism." In 1889 he had described himself as a Federalist, and in the 1890s he felt more favorably disposed toward Hamilton than Jefferson, with respect to the role of the federal government and its national character.[50] On occasion, he

---

48. See also *Constitutional Government*, pp. 5–6, and *The New Freedom*, pp. 281–282.
49. "The Puritan" (22 Dec. 1900), *PPWW*, 1, p. 365.
50. Link, *Wilson*, 1, p. 22; Baker, *Wilson*, 2, p. 103.

referred to the steady growth of the national government's authority at the expense of the state governments as a natural development and as more in line with Hamilton's than with Jefferson's political conceptions. But in his later scholarly works, particularly in his *Constitutional Government*, he associated both Jefferson and the *Federalist Papers*, written largely by Madison and Hamilton, with what he called the Newtonian, mechanistic view of government and society, as against the organic, Darwinian view that he espoused – although in this work, inconsistently, he elsewhere identified Hamilton, but not Jefferson, with the organic view.[51]

It has been suggested, not without cogency and worthy authority, that the course of Wilson's political thought may be divided into three periods, that of "an academic sort of conservatism," from 1879 to 1902, that of "a belligerent political and economic conservatism," from 1902 to 1908, and that of "a gradual transition from conservatism to militant progressivism," from 1908 to 1912.[52] This periodic distinction, however, may be somewhat presentist in judgment; it posits a dramatic change, moreover, that in taking only four years resembles less a "gradual transition" than a short-order flip-flop inconsistent with the long-term integrity of Wilson's basic premises and principles. Wilson's thinking belongs, rather, to the broad trend of thought that embraced evolutionary change within a framework that affirmed development on the basis of liberal capitalism, or what later came to be known as modernization western style.

Granting for the moment, however, the periodic distinctions, it may nevertheless be said that in Wilson's two "conservative" periods, as a Gold Democrat who identified himself with the Cleveland–Olney wing of the party, he all but dissociated himself from Jefferson, Virginia native though Wilson was, while in his later "progressive" period, as a gubernatorial and presidential candidate in need of the votes of Bryan Democrats, although he perhaps more often praised and invoked Jefferson,[53] he clearly differentiated himself and modern conditions from Jefferson and the conditions of Jefferson's times. To the extent that Wilson during his New Freedom period invoked Jefferson and his ideas, it was largely to emphasize the two general principles that the people and their interests must be the source of all laws, and that individual liberty must be the object of law – principles not peculiar to Jefferson, but Wilson did not invoke Jefferson to define or illuminate his

51. Wilson, *Constitutional Government*, pp. 56–57, 199–200; Baker, *Wilson*, 2, p. 104.
52. Link, *Wilson*, 1, pp. 31–32.
53. Baker, *Wilson*, 2, p. 103.

own position on either the trust question or the role of government in economic affairs and social welfare.

For all practical purposes, Wilson ruled out Jefferson's ideas as a guide to the great economic issues of the modern industrial world. During his "militant progressive"–New Freedom period, 1908–1912, when he has been perceived by some scholars to have been at his most Jeffersonian disposition, where Wilson did invoke the Sage of Monticello, he invariably took pains to translate Jefferson's thought for modern times, to show that only certain of Jefferson's broad principles were still relevant, and then in altered form. His invocation of Jefferson was more politically ritualistic than substantive.

As if to emphasize his difference from Jefferson, Wilson on 13 April 1912 took the occasion of the Democratic party's annual Jefferson Day banquet – when Democratic politicians ambitious for higher office usually accentuate the universal goodness and perennial relevance of Jefferson's thought – to disparage the idea that Jefferson could lend useful assistance in dealing with the specific issues of the day. "The circumstances of our day," said Wilson, "are so utterly different from those of Jefferson's day that it may seem nothing less than an act of temerity to attempt to say what Jefferson would do if he were now alive and guiding us with his vision and command." To make his point plainly and clearly, Wilson then went into a rather full bill of particulars: "The world we live in is no longer divided into neighborhoods and communities; the lines of the telegraph thread it like nerves uniting a single organism. . . . America has swung out of her one-time isolation and has joined the family of nations. . . . She is not the simple, homogeneous, rural nation that she was in Jefferson's time . . .; she is great and strong; above all . . . infinitely varied; her affairs are shot through with emotion and the passion that comes with strength and growth and self-confidence." In short, Wilson stated flatly, "We live in a new and strange age and reckon with new affairs alike in economics and politics of which Jefferson knew nothing."[54]

In his New Freedom campaign speeches of the late summer and early autumn of 1912, Wilson maintained and reemphasized this theme as central to achieving a proper approach to modern industrial conditions. "We used to think," he declared, "in the old-fashioned days when life was very simple that all that government had to do was to put on a

---

54. "What Jefferson Would Do," *PPWW*, 2, p. 424. Wilson went on to say, in the most general of terms, that Jefferson would have opposed monopoly, special privilege, and a special-interest tariff, and favored an elastic currency system, and government responsible to and run by the people rather than by special interests. Ibid., pp. 424–429.

policeman's uniform, and say, 'Now don't anybody hurt anybody else.'
We used to say that the ideal of government was for every man to be
left alone and not interfered with, except when he interfered with
somebody else; and that the best government was the government that
did as little governing as possible. That was the idea that obtained in
Jefferson's time." But, Wilson contended, "we are coming now to
realize that life is so complicated that we are not dealing with the old
conditions, and that the law has to step in and create new conditions
under which we may live, the conditions which will make it tolerable
for us to live." He went on to point out that business in the main was
no longer conducted by independent entrepreneurs or single employers
operating with individualized private property and capital, but by huge
corporations employing scores, hundreds, thousands of workers. The
new organization of business differed from the old, just as the teeming
tenement houses differed from the family-owned and -inhabited dwell-
ing. "A corporation is very much like a large tenement house; it isn't
the premises of a single commercial family; it is just as much a public
affair as a tenement house is a network of public highways," in need of
government inspection and regulation to maintain health and safety
standards. Corporate securities were offered on the public market,
which therefore justified and required public inspection. "Similarly,"
said Wilson, "the treatment of labor by the great corporations is not
what it was in Jefferson's time. Whenever bodies of men employ bodies
of men, it ceases to be a private relationship.... Similarly, it was no
business of the law in the time of Jefferson to come into my house and
see how I kept house." But, insisted Wilson, under the new corporate
organization of modern industrial enterprise, private property had
assumed a public character, and government must intervene in the
national interest to assure social welfare. The central problem, as he
saw it, was not that a way must be found to apply Jeffersonian maxims
to modern conditions, but on the contrary, that the modern "centralized and complex society" constituted "a new world, struggling under
old laws," laws rooted precisely in the bygone regime of competitive-
individual enterprise and the corresponding laissez-faire conceptions of
government commonly associated with Jefferson.[55] It was the task of
statecraft to balance public with private law to fashion a state suited to,
and regulative of, the modern economy.

Wilson's affirmation of "positive government" did not have to wait
upon the advent of "square dealers," New Nationalists, or Rule of

55. *The New Freedom*, pp. 19–24.

Reason regulators; it dated back at least to 1889 with the publication of his book *The State*, if not earlier. In that book, as well as in its revised edition of 1906, spanning his two "conservative" periods, Wilson attributed to government two major types of functions: *constituent*, or essential, functions, and *ministrant*, or optional, functions; each type varied historically in character and scope, although not necessarily in principle.[56]

The constituent functions of government included the guarantee of life and liberty, the regulation of the family, the definition of crime, the administration of justice, the determination of political rights and obligations, and the provision for defense and foreign relations; but as these functions implied, they centered upon the protection and regulation of property relations. Whether in ancient or modern times, Wilson observed, "every government must regulate property in one way or another and may regulate it as much as it pleases." This was because by definition it was "of the nature of the state to regulate property rights," while it was "of the policy of the state to regulate them *more* or *less*." It followed that "Administrators must regard this as one of the Constituent functions of political society."[57]

The ministrant, or optional, functions of government, according to Wilson, were in principle limitless. "Government," Wilson held, "does not stop with the protection of life, liberty, and property, as some have supposed; it goes on to serve every convenience of society. Its sphere is limited only by its own wisdom, alike where republican and where absolutist principles prevail."[58] Among the ministrant functions, Wilson included the regulation of trade, industry, and labor, the maintenance and regulation of postal, transportation, and communications systems, the provision for all manner of internal improvements, the provision for public utilities, for education, for conservation, for public sanitation and health and safety, including in trades and work, for relief of the poor and infirm, and for many other matters of public concern.

In the basic area of the regulation of property and labor, Wilson held, much like Roosevelt, "The birth and development of the modern industrial system has changed every aspect of the matter." The modern situation "reveals the true character of the part which the state plays": It yielded the "rule ... that in proportion as the world's industries grow must the state advance its efforts," both in the regulation of labor relations and in "the regulation of corporations," which together made

56. Wilson, *The State*, pp. 613–615.
57. *State*, pp. 613–614, 623–624. Wilson's emphasis.
58. Ibid., p. 621.

up the two major sides of "the modern regulation of the industrial system."[59]

In general, and again like Roosevelt, Wilson held that modern conditions required the expansion of government functions along a "middle ground" between socialism, which he regarded as having "the right end in view," of reconciling the individual with the general interest, and modern self-interested individualism, which, he judged, "has much about it that is hateful, too hateful to last." The middle ground cut a wide swath: In the modern industrial society, the state in both its constituent and ministrant functions "has been relieved of very little duty by alterations of political theory." As compared with the ancient state, in ministrant functions "one would expect the state to be less active." But, Wilson held, "there is in fact no such difference: *government does now whatever experience permits or the times demand.*"[60] Or, as Wilson put it in his *History of the American People* in 1902, by the turn of the century in the United States, "Statesmen knew that it was to be their task to release the energies of the country for the great day of trade and manufacture which was to change the face of the world," and this meant that it was their job "to ease the processes of labor, govern capital . . ., and make law the instrument, not of justice merely, but also of social progress."[61] If this be conservatism, it is nevertheless indistinguishable in spirit or principle from liberalism in twentieth-century American political history.

Wilson articulated the principle of positive government in the ensuing years to mean that the modern government's role in an industrial capitalist society like the United States included distributive, among its regulative, functions. As he moved from Princeton, through New Jersey state politics, to national presidential politics, Wilson's view of those functions grew more and more comprehensive, not unlike Roosevelt's experience in these years. In this sense, it is undoubtedly true that Wilson became more liberal, that is, that he moved more to the left, from 1908 to his first years as president.

"No one now advocates the old *laissez faire*," he noted in 1908; "no one questions the necessity for a firm and comprehensive regulation of business operations"; whatever the differences over methods, Demo-

59. Ibid., pp. 614–615, 626.
60. Ibid., pp. 632–633, 624–625. Wilson's emphasis.
61. *A History of the American People*, vol. 5: *Reunion and Nationalization* (New York: Harper Bros., 1907), p. 300. See Diamond's astute discussion at *Economic Thought*, pp. 32–34, 37, 45–47, 52, 157. For cordial personal and intellectual relations between Wilson and Roosevelt, before 1910, see, e.g., Link, *Papers*, 15, p. 547; Henry F. Pringle, *Roosevelt, A Biography* (New York: Harcourt Brace, 1931), pp. 545–546.

crats and Republicans alike "are all advocates of a firm and effective regulation."[62] Regulation included not merely policing business practices, but the extension of aid to individuals and groups for the improvement of their living conditions, such aid as workers' compensation, the guarantee of proper working conditions and hours, and the protection of the right of workers to organize into unions. In the modern capitalist society, "the individual is caught in a great confused nexus of all sorts of complicated circumstances and . . . to let him alone is to leave him helpless"; "therefore, law in our day must come to the assistance of the individual," for without "the watchful interference, the resolute interference, of the government, there can be no fair play between individuals." Hence, Wilson the presidential candidate declared, "The Democratic party does not stand for the limitation of powers of government, either in the field of state or in the field of the federal government. There is not a Democrat that I know who is afraid to have the powers of the government exercised to the utmost." For Democrats had come to understand that "Freedom today is something more than being let alone. The program of a government of freedom must in these days be positive, not negative merely." Or, as Wilson had stated in 1911 while governor of New Jersey, "the service rendered the people by the *national government must be of a more extended sort and of a kind* not only to protect it against monopoly, but also to facilitate its life."[63]

Wilson's evolving commitment to positive government of both the regulative and distributive kind found practical expression during his New Jersey political career. In his campaign for governor in 1910, and in his inaugural address in January 1911, Wilson advocated supervision and regulation of corporations and public utilities by the state government, including powers to prevent such corporate malpractices as overcapitalization, to regulate and restrict security issues, to regulate and fix transportation, communication, and utility rates by a state administrative commission, and to regulate public utilities' financial operations, service, and equipment. As governor, he worked for and achieved these measures, and in addition he urged and achieved the passage of laws for

---

62. "Law or Personal Power," address delivered before the National Democratic Club, New York, 13 Apr. 1908, *PPWW*, 2, pp. 30–31.
63. *The New Freedom*, pp. 292, 283–284; "The Vision of the Democratic Party," address at New Haven, Conn., 25 Sept. 1912, in John Wells Davidson, ed., *A Crossroads of Freedom: The 1912 Campaign Speeches of Woodrow Wilson* (New Haven: Yale University Press, 1956), p. 264; also, Wilson's Labor Day Speech, Buffalo, N.Y., 2 Sept, 1912, ibid., p. 80; "Democracy's Opportunity," address at rally of Democratic Clubs, Harrisburg, Pa., 15 June 1911, *PPWW*, 2, p. 306. Wilson's emphasis.

workers' compensation, factory inspection, and the regulation of hours and conditions of labor of women and children. In his second annual message to the state legislature in January 1912, he outlined a broad program to provide, as Arthur S. Link has summarized it, for "a greatly expanded system of state intervention and regulation in order to insure the health, happiness, and general welfare of the people of the state," including a more comprehensive public health program and supplemental labor legislation.[64]

The views Wilson expressed in *The State*, his other writings, and his public addresses, lacked context neither in American politics nor in American scholarship and intellectual life in the three decades before World War I. Strong political forces in the electoral arena pushed municipal and state governments toward greater regulatory, and even direct, involvement in the market, just as they also exerted a powerful impact on the role of the federal government. The Interstate Commerce and Sherman acts, the activity of the ICC, and the cases brought under the two acts by 1900, if nothing else, established in principle a legislative, judicial, and administrative framework of a national regulatory system, which provided the basis for further development in judicial process, in the establishment and work of the Bureau of Corporations and the Federal Trade Commission, and in other complementary regulatory legislation. What remained to be determined at the opening of the twentieth century, and what became the central issue of national politics in the Progressive Era, was the nature, scope, and purposes of the government's regulatory system, in both its constituent and ministrant functions, to use Wilson's terms.

The world of scholarship and intellect, too, provided fertile soil for the cultivation of the theories, principles, and views that Wilson expounded in *The State* and afterward. By the time of his residence at Johns Hopkins University in the years 1883–1885, the German historical-institutional and the British anthropo-evolutionary schools were already exerting their strong and lasting impact on American graduate studies in political science and political economy. Wilson attended Herbert Baxter Adams's seminar along with Richard T. Ely, J. Franklin Jameson, Albert Shaw, and Davis Rich Dewey, and although he did not seem to care for Adams's style, he nevertheless rubbed shoulders and ideas with colleagues who were absorbing, and who became leading practitioners of, the new learning. His friendship later

64. Link, *Wilson*, 1, pp. 179, 242, 246, 263–267, 297 (quotation); Wilson, Inaugural Address as Governor of New Jersey, 17 Jan. 1911, *PPWW*, 2, pp. 270–282.

with Turner at Hopkins had a like significance. John Bates Clark's *Philosophy of Wealth*, published in 1885 but composed of articles printed in previous years, exerted a similar influence. Wilson, like his young colleagues, was strongly impressed with Clark's critique of classical political economy, which tended to reinforce that which Wilson had also found in Bagehot, and with Clark's argument that the competitive market was receding before monopolistic powers of large-scale enterprise, that the cooperative principle was largely to be preferred to the competitive principle on both moral and economic grounds, and that market relations should be subject to modifications suited to attaining distributive and social justice.[65]

These influences during his graduate studies and his early teaching years at Bryn Mawr were reinforced by Wilson's strong attraction to Edmund Burke's and Walter Bagehot's emphasis upon society as a naturally evolving organism, and to Bagehot's critique of classical political economy and of laissez-faire. Hence, Wilson's departure from the strict Manchestrian economics of Smith, Cobden, and Bright went hand in hand with a growing belief in "positive government." Indeed, far from embracing Jeffersonian or any other peculiarly American homiletics on government, Wilson insisted upon the inadequacy of trying to understand United States political institutions as unique, and upon the need instead, as the historical-evolutionary schools suggested, to grasp those institutions on the basis of comparative study applicable in principle to all societies. Turner's frontier thesis satisfied this requirement, because it interpreted United States history, including its peculiar characteristics, in terms of such universal determinants as land-people ratios, stages of development, corresponding class formation and class relations, and economic realities.

"Certainly it does not now have to be argued," wrote Wilson in his Preface to *The State*, "that the only thorough method of study in politics is the comparative and historical." From this standpoint, Wilson held, "the wide correspondences of organization and method in government" would become evident and would reveal "a unity in structure and procedure much greater than the uninitiated student of institutions is at all prepared to find." It was a unity that would no

---

65. Diamond, *Economic Thought*, pp. 32–34, 37, 47, 57; Link, *Wilson*, 1, pp. 11–23; Mulder, *Preparation*, pp. 83, 117–120; Bragdon, *Academic Years*, pp. 101–123; Lee Benson, *Turner and Beard* (New York: Free Press, 1960), pp. 1–91; Sidney Fine, *Laissez Faire and the General-Welfare State* (Ann Arbor: University of Michigan Press, 1967), pp. 247–248. Clark later shifted to an affirmation of the competitive principle, but not without acknowledging the realities of large-corporate anti-competitive tendencies and the need for government regulation. See Chapter 4, under "Between Roosevelt and Wilson."

doubt contribute "to the upsetting of many pet theories as to the special excellencies of some one system of government." That meant that "our own institutions can be understood and appreciated only by those who know other systems of government as well, and the main facts of general institutional history."[66]

Applying the comparative-historical method to the United States, Wilson viewed it as a matter of natural evolution that with economic development, power and authority should pass from the states to the national government. Wilson argued that under the Constitution, the general commercial, financial, transportation, and industrial interests of the nation, as they reached the stage of development that made them interstate and international in their operations, "were meant to be brought under the regulation of the federal government," on behalf of the general welfare. All in all, the ever-expanding frontier together with the natural transformation of the nation's economic life, made the growth of the powers of Congress both as against the states and as to their quality and reach, inevitable, and to an extent not conceived by earlier Americans. Put another way, in industrializing America, conservative change, which to Wilson meant providing for justice and orderly social progress, by adjusting laws and institutions to facts, or to evolutionary reality, involved the transfer of functions from the states and localities to the federal government.[67]

The acquisition of empire and a more active role in world affairs, moreover, requiring the "administration of distant dependencies" and the "plunge into international politics" that accompanied industrialization and the passing of the continental frontier, constituted another fundamental condition, in Wilson's view, contributing to the transfer of power from the states to the national government, and the propulsion of the president within the national government to the preeminent position as the nation's leader, representative in world politics, and initiator of foreign and domestic policy. Here, again, Wilson's view of

---

66. *The State*, pp. xxxiv, xxxv. Wilson made four acknowledgments in his preface: Herbert B. Adams and J. M. Vincent of Johns Hopkins; J. Franklin Jameson, then at Brown; and Munroe Smith of Columbia. He stated that the work "upon which I have chiefly relied in describing modern government is the great *Handbuch des oeffentlichen Rechts der Gegenwart*, edited by the late Professor Heinrich Marquardsen of the University of Erlangen." Among those authors he listed in end-of-chapter bibliographies, he included Bagehot, Darwin, T. H. Huxley, Spencer (*Principles of Sociology*), Lecky, Lubbock, Maine, von Maurer, Lewis H. Morgan, Tylor, Westermarck, Austin, Bluntschli, G. Jellinek, Pollock, Savigny, and Thibaut. Ibid., pp. xxxv, 24–25, 610–611.
67. *Constitutional Government*, pp. 173–174, 185–187, 194; see also "The States and the Federal Government," *N. Am. Rev.* 187 (May 1908), *PPWW*, 2, p. 50.

the presidency was much like that of Roosevelt. "The President of the United States," he noted in 1900, with war in the Philippines and McKinley running for reelection against Bryan, "is now, as of course, at the front of affairs, as no president, except Lincoln, has been since the first quarter of the nineteenth century, when the foreign relations of the new nation had first to be adjusted.... Upon his choice, his character, his experience hang some of the most weighty issues of the future." As compared with the old federal system delicately balanced between mutually jealous state and national sovereignties, the new system generated a continuing centralization of power: "It is evident," Wilson noted in a nutshell, "that empire is an affair of strong government."[68] Indeed, Wilson believed, once more, much like Roosevelt, "we have come within sight of the end of the merely nationalizing process," to the point where "we must think less of checks and balances and more of coordinated power, less of separation of powers and more of the synthesis of action." In this juncture of historical development, the president had become "undoubtedly the only spokesman of the whole people."[69]

The transfer of power from the states to the national government does not necessarily imply positive government; for example, in the late nineteenth century, national power at times operated to void or vitiate state or local government regulation of railroads and industry. In Wilson's mind, however, the superiority of national jurisdiction and positive government increasingly converged under modern conditions. Wilson warned against the nonneutral use of positive government, and it was in this respect that he invoked Jefferson, although he might no less have aptly invoked countless prominent Americans of the most diverse persuasions. It is important, however, not to confuse Wilson's concern for the neutrality of government intervention in social and economic affairs, with a disposition on Wilson's part against intervention in principle or with anything like a prejudice for laissez-faire dogma. To Wilson, the primary objective was the general welfare, or the national interest, which meant perfecting justice and promoting social progress, which by definition was neutral, and which could not be achieved under modern conditions without a positive government operating to achieve the accommodation of all those interests that themselves were consistent with the general welfare. The general welfare, in turn, in modern

68. "Preface to Fifteenth Printing," 15 Aug. 1900, *Congressional Government* (New York: Meridian Books, 1956), pp. 22–23; "The Reconstruction of the Southern States," *Atlantic Monthly* 87 (Jan. 1901), *PPWW*, 1, p. 394; cf. *Constitutional Government*, pp. 59, 73–74, 77–79, 194; Diamond, *Economic Thought*, pp. 48, 49; Link, *Wilson*, 1, pp. 27, 108; 2, pp. 145–149.
69. *Constitutional Government*, pp. 73, 220–221.

times, presumed a society founded upon large-scale corporate capital-ism in an advanced stage of industrialization.

However circular the reasoning, to Wilson it was sufficiently compell-ing, because it accorded with natural social evolution, with the facts. Wilson believed that every legitimate economic interest, small and large – farm, labor, mercantile, industrial, financial – was consistent with the general welfare, but it was a general welfare defined implicitly in terms of the indefeasibility of the leading role of large corporations in the economy as a whole. Those interests not so cohering with the general welfare could be considered to have relinquished legitimacy, that is, as having been disestablished, displaced, superseded, or bypassed, by evolution. Interests requiring tariff protection, for example, might be so considered. Progressive development, after all, implied evolutionary change and therefore the decline and passing away, as well as the rise, of interests. The fact that numerous legitimate interests, not to mention those falling into obsolescence, came frequently into conflict with, and were injured by, progressive change, whether in the form of the admin-istered market, new technology, regulatory measures, or the power of large corporations, accounts in part for the failure of many of Wilson's domestic and foreign policies to achieve their avowed conciliatory intent. The evolutionary creed implied a large ethical loophole: The neutralism of positive government consisted not in satisfying every interest but, as Wilson had put it, in distilling national and long-term from narrow, sectional, particular, or transient interests. The distillation must accord with the dictates of evolution. For those interests, and people, bypassed by evolution, conciliation often lies on the other side of paradise – or the grave.

"A world-wide economic tendency"

Wilson altered his views respecting government regulation of business practices as he moved from a general affirmation, in his academic years, of comprehensive governmental powers, to the concrete legislative proposals of his political and officeholding years. Although changing in detail in this way, and hence in political coloration, his views remained anchored in his evolutionary outlook. To Wilson, the disposal of the trust question as a matter or practical statecraft, began with recognizing that the law and government action must correspond with the facts of economic life. That is, the law must accommodate the people, their habits and institutions to, and at the same time facilitate, evolving economic development, and in the process strive to serve the public interest and hence the general welfare. As the general welfare was to be defined not in terms of abstract reason or visionary dreams, but historically in terms of evolving economic relations and organization, the facts, for Wilson, were that the corporation and large-scale industrial enterprise had displaced the individual entrepreneur and small-business unit as the dominant feature of modern capitalism. Smaller enterprise would remain, even multiply and prosper, and government must protect it, but as complementary and auxiliary to the large-enterprise economy. It was therefore this new industrial order to which the law must be adjusted, which government must both facilitate and regulate, and in terms of which the general welfare must be shaped.

Wilson's pronouncement as governor-elect of New Jersey that a "new economic society has sprung up, and we must effect a new set of adjustments," succinctly stated his general evolutionary view of social questions and served as his central principle with respect to the trust question.[70] The trust question, in turn, in Wilson's mind, because it involved the basic structure and operation of market relations, encompassed essential components of society as a whole. As he had already stated in 1907, "It is manifest that we must adjust our legal and political principles to a new set of conditions which involve the whole moral and economic makeup of our national life." Indeed, he held, one could "state the matter in a way that makes it sound very subtle, very philosophical," but it was "a plain question for practical men after all." There were "many things to define," it seemed; "yet there is only one thing." The "problem for statesmen," the one thing, "is the problem of the control of corporations." The corporation, Wilson held, "stands in the foreground of all modern economic questions, so far as the United States are concerned." As modern business had changed, so must law and morals. Wilson put it quite plainly: "Our thinkers, whether in the field of morals or in the field of economics, have before them nothing less than the task of translating law and morals into terms of modern business."[71] Note the trinitarian intimacy of economy, law, and morals, in Wilson's mind, and note that modern business was not to be prescribed by law and morals, but that the latter were to be reformulated and work their way in the world to suit the naturally, perhaps preternaturally, evolving requirements and capacities of modern business: father (economy), son (law), holy spirit (morals).

The problem to be defined, more precisely, according to Wilson, was that "Our laws are still meant for business done by *individuals*; they

70. Inaugural Address, 17 Jan. 1911, *PPWW*, 2, p. 273.
71. "Politics (1857–1907)," *Atlantic Monthly* 100 (Nov. 1907), *PPWW*, 2, pp. 18–20; "The Lawyer and the Community" (1910), *ibid.*, pp. 255–256.

have not been satisfactorily adjusted to business done by great *combinations*, and we have got to adjust them. ... there is no choice." The "greater part of the business of the country has come into the hands of great corporations and trusts." The country was therefore "a very different America from the old." It was "no longer a scene of individual enterprise, ... individual opportunity and individual achievement." Instead, "Comparatively small groups of men in control of great corporations wield a power and control over the wealth and the business operations of the country," so that they "seem rivals of the government itself," and they have "put at the head of every great industry a dominating corporation, or group of corporations." It was these new circumstances that made "unquestionably" necessary "adjustments and reformulations of the law." "Law must be strengthened and adapted to keep them [the great corporations] in curb and to make them subservient to the general welfare."[72]

The adjustment and reformulation of the law was not to be an attempt to restore the proprietary-competitive regime of bygone days, but was to affirm and facilitate the development of business in its large-scale corporate stage of development, while providing for its regulation and for its serving the general welfare in a reconstituted society. The law could only express and regulate the facts, and in so doing perhaps "mould" or modify them; it could not negate them. Government, in Wilson's view, must regulate the economic institutions that formed the basis of society, but by the very nature of the case, it must also facilitate their function and development. The general welfare required both. "It is perfectly legitimate, of course," as Wilson stated in the 1912 campaign, "that the business interests of the country should not only enjoy the protection of the law, but that they should be in every way furthered and strengthened and facilitated by legislation."[73]

It was, accordingly, central to Wilson's thinking about regulatory policy that he distinguished between the large corporation and the "trust." A corollary of his evolutionary positivism, it was at the same

72. "Richmond Address" (1912), *PPWW*, 2, p. 376; *The New Freedom*, p. 35. Wilson's emphasis. "Law or Personal Power" (1908), *PPWW*, 2, pp. 24–25; "The Tariff Make-Believe," *N. Am. Rev.* 190 (Oct. 1909), *PPWW*, 2, pp. 134–135. See also "Bankers and Statesmanship," address before New Jersey Bankers' Association, Atlantic City, 6 May 1910, *PPWW*, 2, p. 228: "What is our problem? We conceive it to be the absence of that sort of free competition which used to make monopoly almost impossible. The competitors were once many; they are now few, and those who compete are gigantic combinations rather than individuals. Where the competitors are few and powerful the danger is much greater than when they are numerous and individually weak."

73. *The New Freedom*, pp. 177–118.

time a distinction in every essential respect the same as that drawn by
Roosevelt, Herbert Knox Smith, Garfield, Taft, Chief Justice White, and
all such other like-minded authorities, between reasonable and unreasonable restraints of trade, or between "good" and "bad" trusts.
The large corporations, as the inevitable product of economic evolution,
having replaced individuals "engaged in business on their own capital
and separate responsibility," were, as Wilson noted, "indispensable to
modern business enterprise"; they had become the employers of a
growing sector of the industrial work force, "marshalled in great numbers for the performance of a multitude of particular tasks under a
common discipline." Large corporations were "society's present means
of effective life in the field of industry," its "new way of massing its
resources and its power of enterprise"; they were "organizations of a
perfectly intelligible sort which the law has licensed for the convenience
of extensive business." Large corporations, in short, were "the combinations necessarily effected for the transaction of modern business."[74]

Trusts were those large corporations perverted, by those who organized or operated them, with unfair methods in pursuit of unlawful
monopolistic ends; they were unreasonable restraints of trade. Their
rise was therefore inseparable from the legitimate rise of large-scale
corporate capitalism and from the "new economic society" of modern
America. The corporation "grew just as naturally as an oak grows," the
trust "just as naturally as a weed grows." Hence, Wilson observed,
"The trusts do not belong to the period of infant industry.... They
belong to a very recent and very sophisticated age." Their rise was
"another chapter in the natural history of power and of governing
classes." The distinction, then, to be made between the large corporation and the trust was that although "the elaboration of business upon
a great co-operative scale is characteristic of our time and has come
about by the natural operation of modern civilization," and although
"Big business is no doubt to a large extent necessary and natural," and
its development "upon a great scale, upon a great scale of cooperation,
is inevitable," that was "a very different matter from the development
of trusts, because the trusts have not grown" in the same natural and
beneficial way as large corporations as such had grown. "They have

---

74. "The Lawyer and the Community," 31 Aug. 1910, *PPWW*, 2, pp. 254–257, 262;
Inaugural Address, 17 Jan. 1911, ibid., pp. 271–272; *The New Freedom*, pp. 5, 7,
8, 11; "Bankers and Statesmanship," 6 May 1910, *PPWW*, 2, p. 229; *The New
Freedom*, p. 5: "In most parts of our country men work, not for themselves, ... but
generally as employees, – in a higher or lower grade – of great corporations. There
was a time when corporations played a very minor part in our business affairs, but
now they play the chief part, and most men are servants of corporations."

been artificially created; they have been put together not by natural processes, but by the will, the deliberate planning will, of men who ... wished to make their power secure against competition." The trust was an unnatural, illegitimate canker in the naturally evolving large-corporation economy; conversely, and by the same token, "any large corporation built up by the legitimate processes of business, by economy, by efficiency, is natural; I am not afraid of it, no matter how big it grows."[75]

The remedy for the trust problem was not to be found in seeking to thwart legitimate power or governing classes that had naturally evolved. The remedy, in other words, Wilson held, was "not to disintegrate what we have been at such pains to piece together in the organization of modern industrial enterprise." The dissolution of large corporations, or "trust-busting," as a general policy, would, at the level of the firm, "disorganize some important business altogether," and "throw great undertakings out of gear," while at the level of the economy as a whole, it would retrogressively derange and dismantle modern productive and distributive systems.[76]

The large modern corporation, Wilson noted, was indeed "an economic society, a little economic state, – and not always little, even as compared with states." Many of them "wield revenues and command resources which no ancient state possessed, and which some modern bodies politic show no approach to in their budgets." This was a description, however, of legitimate modern enterprise, not an indictment, and not a call to "trust-busting." "The economic power of society itself," Wilson emphasized, "is concentrated in them [modern corporations] for the conduct of this, that, or the other sort of business.... Society, in short, has discovered a new way of massing its resources and its power of enterprise...." Hence, as Wilson explained, "I would not have you think that I am speaking with a feeling of hostility towards the men who have in our day given the nation its extraordinary material power and prosperity by an exercise of genius such as in days gone by was used, in each great age, to build empires and alter the boundaries of states. I am drawing no indictment; no indictment that I could draw would be just." In fact, he stated, "No indictment that has been drawn has been just, but only exaggerated and disquieting." He was "simply trying to analyze the existing constitution

75. Richmond Address (1912), *PPWW*, 2, pp. 376–377; *The New Freedom*, pp. 163–165, 166; Acceptance Address, Seagirt, N.J., 7 Aug. 1912, *Official Report of the Democratic National Convention*, p. 407.
76. "The Lawyer and the Community" (1910), *PPWW*, 2, p. 254; cf. Jackson Day Dinner Address, 8 Jan. 1912, ibid., p. 348.

of business in blunt words of truth, without animus or passion of any kind." For, as he put it in 1912, in arguing that "the things that have happened by operation of irresistible forces" could not be considered "immoral things": "I am not one of those ... who speak of the interests in big letters as if they were enemies of mankind.... I am not here, in other words, to suggest that the things that have happened to us must be reversed, and the scroll of time rolled back on itself. To attempt that would be futile and ridiculous."[77]

As both a politician compelled to take a stand on the issues, and an intellectual adhering to the evolutionary-positivist mode of thought, Wilson consistently acknowledged and affirmed the historical development of large-scale corporate enterprise and its liquidation of the old proprietary-competitive regime. What history, or evolution, had wrought it was "futile and ridiculous" to oppose. "Modern business," he held, "is no doubt best conducted upon a great scale, for which the resources of the single individual are manifestly insufficient." Capital and labor "must be massed in order to do the things that must be done for the support and facilitation of modern life." Whether, therefore, judgment was to be based upon the standard of "energy or economy," it was "plain enough that we cannot go back to the old competitive system under which individuals were the competitors." In the course of progressive evolution, in Wilson's view, "Wide organization and cooperation have made the modern world possible and must maintain it." Indeed, great enterprises and "the opportunities they have afforded exceptional men" had "developed genius as well as wealth," as a result of which, "The nations are richer in capacity and in gifts comparable to the higher gifts of statesmanship."[78] The large corporation was no mere necessary evil; it was a positive good – society's instrument for its own progressive development.

In sum, as Wilson put it in his inaugural address as New Jersey's governor-elect in 1911, "Corporations are no longer hobgoblins which have sprung up at us out of some mysterious ambush, nor yet unholy inventions of rascally rich men...." On the contrary, Wilson stated, in one of his major addresses as a prominent progressive presidential hopeful early in 1912, "Nobody can fail to see, no matter how clearly you perceive the evils that have come upon the country by the use of them, – nobody can fail to see that modern business is going to be done by corporations. *The old time of individual competition is probably*

---

77. "The Lawyer and the Community" (1910), *PPWW*, 2, pp. 255–257, 262; Richmond Address (1912), ibid., pp. 376–377.
78. "The Lawyer and the Community" (1910), *PPWW*, 2, p. 258.

gone by." If it were ever to return, "it will not come back within our time, I dare say." There was no alternative to recognizing and affirming evolutionary necessity: "We will do business henceforth when we do it on a great and successful scale, by means of corporations."[79]

The remedy for the trust problem, then, began with the affirmation of large corporate enterprise as the vehicle of economic progress, as the characteristic form of modern business organization, and as the basic component of a progressive modern society. Beginning there, the remedy proceeded by distinguishing the large corporation from the "trust" – that is, from its unreasonable, inefficient, and deleterious uses or forms. The proper policy was so to regulate business practices as to prevent the misuse of corporations and market power by individuals and, as Herbert Knox Smith similarly held, so also Wilson, to make guilt and punishment for unfair methods and unreasonable restraints of trade individual rather than corporate. "If you want to cure men of joy riding," as Wilson explained in 1912, "you won't break up their automobiles, but catch the men that do the joy riding and see that these very useful and pleasant vehicles of our modern life are left for legitimate uses." In the same way, "If you want to stop joy riding in corporations ... you will not break up the corporations; we may need them; but you will break up the game, namely, that use of corporations." Upon the commission of a wrongdoing, "we will ... find the officer who ... ordered that thing done, and we will indict him *not as an officer of the corporation but as an individual who used that corporation for something that was illegal.*" For, Wilson asked, "Do you see any other way to avoid interrupting the natural and normal processes of American business?"[80]

It was therefore significant, and consistent with his previously stated views spanning a decade and more, that in his address of 7 August 1912, accepting the Democratic party's presidential nomination, Wilson in effect repudiated that section of the party's platform that denounced the Supreme Court's Rule of Reason decisions of 1911 and that represented the position of the party's Bryan–Clark, and perhaps majoritarian, wings. Clearly dissociating himself from that plank, Wilson candidly lay down his own, and in so doing stressed one of the central themes that he shared with the Roosevelt Progressives and Taft Republicans: "I am not one of those who think that competition can be established by law against the drift of a world-wide economic tendency," he told his

79. Inaugural Address as Governor of New Jersey, 17 Jan. 1911, *PPWW*, 2, p. 271; "The Tariff and the Trusts," 24 Feb. 1912, ibid., pp. 410–411. Wilson's emphasis.
80. "The Tariff and the Trusts," ibid., pp. 412–413, 414. Wilson's emphasis.

party's and the nation's populists; "neither am I one of those who believe that business done upon a great scale by a single organization – call it corporation, or what you will – is necessarily dangerous to the liberties, even the economic liberties, of a great people like our own, full of intelligence and indomitable energy." Reiterating his evolutionary outlook as it applied specifically to the trust question, so that he could now convincingly expect not to be misunderstood, Wilson told his party and the American public, "I am not afraid of anything that is normal. I dare say we shall never return to the old order of individual competition," Wilson declared about as categorically as one can get, "and that the organization of business upon a great scale of co-operation is, up to a certain point, itself normal and inevitable."[81]

"The modern idea ..."

In remedies offered for the trust question, Taft and Wilson during the period from 1911 to 1914 passed each other, traveling in opposite directions: Wilson moved from serious reservations about commission regulation with a preference for judicial enforcement of the law to prevent unfair business methods, to support for the Federal Trade Commission Act that Congress ultimately passed. Taft moved from initial support for commission regulation to judicial enforcement of the Sherman Act as sufficient for regulatory purposes. Their similar objectives, however, placed them on the same antistatist road. They both sought to prevent unreasonable restraints of trade as understood at common law, and to permit reasonable combination and intercorporate arrangements. Accordingly, Wilson's attitude toward, and the remedies he proposed for, the trust question, should be considered within the broad context of the debate between the Supreme Court's majority and its critics from 1897 to 1911, and of the position of political leaders like Roosevelt and Taft, groups like the Civic Federation, and government agencies like the Bureau of Corporations. In that context, it is evident that Wilson stood among those who defined the trust question as the corporation question, who affirmed that large corporation as a natural and progressive development of economic evolution, who opposed the

81. The "certain point" was, as with Roosevelt, that beyond which unfair methods or inefficiency set in. Acceptance Address, Seagirt, N.J., 7 Aug. 1912, *Official Report of the Democratic National Convention*, p. 407. For a similar statement by Wilson that competition could not be established by statute law, see his Jackson Day Dinner Address, Washington, D.C., 8 Jan. 1912, *PPWW*, 2, p. 348. Cf. Link, *Wilson*, 1, pp. 472–473 n. 28: In his acceptance address, Wilson "did not cater to the popular demand for destruction of the trusts." But Link's view of Wilson's position on the trust question, as presented in the work just cited, is different from that offered here.

Harlan construction of the Sherman Act, and who sought the restoration of common-law doctrine in the antitrust law of the nation. The alterations in Wilson's position on the issue of government regulation of business during his gubernatorial campaign and term of office, during the 1912 presidential campaign and his first two years in the White House, marked a change not in basic objectives but rather in preferred methods of achieving them. Wilson's position on methods as of 1912–1914 may be regarded as a synthesis of Roosevelt's and Taft's: the establishment of a federal administrative commission charged with policing the market against unfair business methods, but limited in its powers by statute and judicial review; judicial enforcement of the Sherman Act, but in a spirit of consultation with corporate officers, where appropriate, that might as often as not result in their entering consent decrees. These methods were expected to achieve the legalization of contracts and combinations in reasonable restraint of trade – that is, of the corporate reorganization of the market – while inducing and, where necessary, enforcing intercorporate competition. In sum, the objective embraced by Wilson's position, and embodied in the Federal Trade Commission and Clayton acts of 1914, was a market administered directly by corporate and other parties endogenous to the private sector, subject to a system of indirect government policing and regulation in which judicial process remained supreme.[82] More politic than Taft, Wilson understood that the political consensus in favor of a regulatory commission could not be resisted, but it could be readily adapted to policy sound in substance.

There was more than a Tweedledee-Tweedledum difference between Roosevelt's New Nationalism and Wilson's New Freedom, but it did not reside in significant disagreement over "regulated monopoly" versus "regulated competition," or over affirming the corporate reorganization of the market in general and the demise of the old competitive regime, or over laissez-faire as against positive government. It resided, rather, in defining the role of the state, or its positive action, in legalizing and legitimizing the corporate order and guaranteeing that it serve the public interest. With respect to objectives, in short, Wilson stood with Taft as an antistatist against Roosevelt. He did not want the state to command society. Yet, he stood with Roosevelt against Taft, in wanting

82. Cf. Link, *Wilson*, 2, p. 441; Thomas C. Blaisdell, Jr. *The Federal Trade Commission* (New York: Columbia University Press, 1932), p. 289; Gerard C. Henderson, *The Federal Trade Commission: A Study in Administrative Law and Procedure*, (New Haven: Yale University Press, 1924, 1925), pp. 48, 336; Susan Wagner, *The Federal Trade Commission* (New York: Praeger, 1971), pp. 15, 17; Sklar, "Woodrow Wilson," at Radosh and Rothbard, eds., *New History*, pp. 41–44, 51–59.

the state actively to serve society, and in entering dialogue with socialism, particularly with respect to government measures on behalf of distributive justice and equalitarian expectations.

The arguments of such antistatists as Taft and Luther Conant, and no less of such Roosevelt loyalists as Herbert Knox Smith and Garfield, played an influential role in the debates on the trust question in the several years ending with the passage of the Federal Trade Commission Act in 1914. They received their full force, however, from Taft's policy, and Wickersham's, of relentless judicial enforcement of the Sherman Act against one great corporation after another. In so doing, Taft demonstrated the effectiveness of judicial process in policing and altering corporate practices without abolishing the corporate order, and without direct government involvement in administering the market. He thereby at the same time satisfied small-business sentiment that opposed amending the Sherman Act and called for its enforcement, especially as a curb against trade unions.

Taft's policy also cleared space and bought time for the majority antistatist opinion in corporate circles to mobilize and assert itself in a positive manner. The incessant prosecutions of large corporations demonstrated to harassed corporation executives, stockholders, and their lawyers the urgent need for some federal executive agency not directly involved in administering the market but mediating between corporations and the market, on the one side, and the Department of Justice and the courts, on the other. As Stimson had put it, "Nobody thinks that modern business can be run permanently by a series of explosions. Nobody believes that the American people intend to regulate permanently the delicate operations of their modern trade from the office of the District Attorney."[83] Organizations like the Merchants' Association of New York, the New York Board of Trade, the Chicago Association of Commerce, and the newly formed (1912) United States Chamber of Commerce, now came forward, overshadowing the Civic Federation, and took the lead in aiding the Wilson administration and Congress in the shaping of legislation. The Federal Trade Commission Act, in abandoning the license-registration scheme and, instead, in au-

83. Stimson, *Address of Henry L. Stimson, Secretary of War, at the Republican Club, New York City, on December 15, 1911*, pamphlet, State Historical Society of Wisconsin, Madison. pp. 10, 11. Stimson differed from Taft in that he favored the establishment of a trade commission. As for the Sherman Act, he pointed out that there was "no use railing at the Sherman Law" or "demanding its repeal," for "No state or national legislature has existed during the past twenty years which would dream of repealing it; and any party which made repeal a part of its programme would commit suicide." The American people would "not have it repealed." Ibid., pp. 5–7.

thorizing the commission to enforce the antitrust laws and prevent unfair methods of competition, represented the legislative embodiment, and the administrative complement, of the Supreme Court's common-law restoration of the Sherman Act. It also represented, at last, the harmonizing of policy among the three branches of the federal government, concerning regulatory policy, for the first time since 1897. Although the act granted the commission investigatory, subpoena, and cease and desist powers, nevertheless by subjecting all its actions, orders, and procedures to judicial review, it maintained judicial supremacy over executive administration, and with it the supremacy of society in its market relations over the state, in accordance with time-honored liberal principles. Under its first chair, Joseph E. Davies, President Wilson's commissioner of corporations before the Bureau of Corporations was merged into the FTC, the commission as its first order of business and as a guide to its enforcement of antitrust law, proceeded to catalogue unfair methods of competition as defined at common law by the courts over the years.[84]

If corporate liberalism may be understood as the prevalent political, ideological, and programmatic outlook of the movements transacting the corporate reconstruction of American capitalism, then the national reform legislation of 1913–1916 represented the culmination of corporate liberalism in its emergent phase of ascendancy.

The legislation of Wilson's first presidential term embodied three fundamental premises of corporate liberalism, namely, (1) the indivisibility of the corporate reorganization of the economy at home and its expansion abroad, or the internationalization of the investment-trade system as the condition of national prosperity; (2) the accommodation of large-corporate capitalism to the continued existence and general viability of a broadly based small-enterprise capitalism; and (3) the supremacy of society over the state as the basis of the government-society relation, and especially as the basis of a government-society relation involving an ever-growing and more comprehensive regulatory and distributive government role.

In changing two of the major components of the legislative framework of industrialization since the Civil War, namely, tariff protection and the decentralized national banking system, the tariff, tax, and banking reforms of 1913 signified the triumph of the emergent

---

84. Joseph E. Davies, *Trust Laws and Unfair Competition* (Bureau of Corporations, 1916), pp. 10, 24, and passim; "Memorandum on Unfair Competition at the Common Law" (printed for office use only by the FTC, 1915), cited and discussed at Blaisdell, *Federal Trade Commission*, pp. 21–23.

corporate-capitalist order. The Underwood tariff act's downward revision of rates reflected the international orientation of large corporate industry, as well as the principle of international competition as a vital spur to efficiency and innovation in an administered market. The income tax, implementing the new constitutional amendment, at the same time provided the revenue source for the federal government's continuing growth in size and function.

The Federal Reserve Act marked a victory, after protracted efforts going back to the 1890s, of a movement that had intermeshed leaders in the corporate reorganization of industry with those in currency and banking reform. The Federal Reserve system sought to answer the need for a banking and monetary system that could contribute to the stabilization of capital markets against seasonal and cyclical fluctuations, that could regulate credit and money supply to head off tendencies toward panic or redundant investment, that could thereby facilitate corporate organization of enterprise, that could at the same time accommodate smaller enterprise with short-term credit, and that could significantly aid in channeling surplus capital into international trade and investment. The Federal Reserve system served these domestic and international purposes, theoretically, if not altogether effectively in practice, by providing for supplementing the bond-based bank note currency with an assets currency, massing reserves and altering discount rates in accord with business fluctuations, discounting short-term commercial and agricultural paper, inaugurating a market for commercial acceptances in export trade, and permitting national banks for the first time to establish branches abroad. Segmented into twelve district reserve banks owned by their member banks, and provided with a management, which although it included government appointees, consisted predominantly of private bankers and other capitalists, the new central banking system remained insulated from national party politics and executive fiat. In providing a banking system more suited to the needs of a developing corporate capitalism, the Federal Reserve Act, at the same time, accommodated small enterprise with new credit facilities. In general, the new central banking system represented the principle of the administered market given legislative sanction, under government regulation but without state command. The banking and tariff measures together represented the idea of providing a legal framework within which in the first instance, the market, or society in its market relations, not the state, not social goals or political objectives, would shape, manage, and direct banking and currency policy as well as international trade and investment. Primary authority in administering the market would remain with private parties, subject to a secondary government oversight. In effect, the corporate-administered market was to be, in this respect, less "political" than the old competitive market with its government-ridden currency system and tariff protection.[85]

The antitrust legislation of 1914, as we have seen, embodied the same accommodationist and antistatist premises. It also addressed the international dimension of corporate capitalism. The Federal Trade Commission Act, for example, provided in section 6(h), inserted at the urging of the United States Chamber of Commerce and other business associations, for commission authority to investigate conditions of international trade and recommend legislation. In its first year, the FTC undertook four investigations, and three of these dealt with foreign trade, one of which resulted in the two-volume *Report on Cooperation in American Export Trade* (1916) and its recommendation of what became, with Wilson's strong support, the Export Trade (Webb–Pomerene) Act of 1918, permitting American companies to combine for purposes of promoting their export trade. The Clayton Act, for its part, exempted the export trade from its prohibitions against discriminatory prices and exclusive agencies or tying contracts.[86]

Legislation during the rest of Wilson's first term similarly extended positive government in regulatory and distributive functions, affecting both domestic and international relations, without embracing methods of statist command: the Adamson Act establishing the eight-hour day for railroad workers; the child labor act (later struck down by the Supreme Court); the La Follette (Furuseth) Seaman's Act, regulating working conditions on merchant ships operating under United States registry; the rural credits act, establishing federal farm land banks, paralleling the twelve district federal reserve banks, to provide farmers with long-term credit; new taxes on upper incomes, corporations, and estates; the Tariff Commission and the Shipping Board acts; federal aid to agricultural and vocational education; the cotton futures and grain standards acts; the agricultural warehouse licensing and credit act; the federal roads act. Statist tendencies there were, especially in the regulation of common carriers and, perhaps ironically, in aiding agriculture,

---

85. See, e.g., Wilson, "Efficiency" (27 Jan. 1912), *PPWW*, 2, pp. 357–360, 372–375, 380; "The Tariff and the Trusts" (1912), ibid., pp. 407–409; and Speech of Acceptance (1912), ibid., pp. 471–472. Also, Sklar, "Woodrow Wilson," pp. 26–27, 45–50. Cf. Link, *Wilson*, 2, chaps. 6, 7, pp. 177–240. For a new study of the relation of the Federal Reserve system to the corporate stage of capitalism, see James Livingston, *Origins of the Federal Reserve System: Money, Class, and Corporate Capitalism, 1890–1913* (Ithaca: Cornell University Press, 1986).
86. For a more detailed discussion of the international dimensions of the legislation of 1913–1914, see Sklar, "Woodrow Wilson," pp. 41–50.

but they remained confined to a minor key in the corporate-liberal score.

As expressed in the legislative accomplishments of his first presidential term, Wilson gave leadership to, and presided over, a movement beginning to lay the institutional foundations, in law, jurisprudence, and executive administration, of corporate capitalism at home and of its expansion abroad. Just as the Open Door policy may be said to have ended the debate between imperialists and anti-imperialists,[87] so the Wilson legislation ended the debate over the legitimacy of the large corporation – if nothing else, it took the trust question and the central bank question "out of politics" – by beginning the setting down in law, on a comprehensive scale that had not yet been possible under Roosevelt and Taft, of rudimentary adjustments to, and regulation of, the domestic and international requirements of corporate capitalism.

With Wilson's presidency, Congress joined the executive in becoming responsible for legitimizing, regulating, and facilitating corporate capitalism in its domestic and international dimensions. Whereas previously, under Roosevelt and Taft, primarily the executive branch, now both the executive and the legislative branches, and increasingly the judiciary as well, assumed coordinated, or at least complementary, responsibility for the new order. Executive and judicial regulation of the market became executive, judicial, and legislative regulation for the first time in a comprehensive manner, just as executive promotion of Open Door expansion abroad now found its counterpart in legislation. The corporate-capitalist order was thereby becoming increasingly legally institutionalized, in the name of the public interest, as the joint property of both policy-making branches of government, and thus of the judicial branch as well.[88]

---

87. William A. Williams, *The Tragedy of American Diplomacy* (Cleveland: World, 1959), chap. 1: "Imperial Anticolonialism."
88. In the United States Steel case, for example, initiated by Wickersham under Taft, the circuit court in its 1915 decision, later affirmed by the Supreme Court, found "that the Steel Corporation was largely formed, that its large financial resources were designed, and the varied lines of its constituent manufacturing units were bought to enable it to successfully enter foreign trade," and that "the Federal Steel Company was driven to further expansion and integration in order to enter foreign trade." The court concluded: ". . . the foreign trade of the Steel Corporation, its mode of building it up, and its retention when built up are not contrary to the Sherman Law. To hold otherwise would be, practically and commercially, to enjoin the steel trade of the United States from using the business methods which are necessary in order to build up and maintain a dependable business abroad, and if the Sherman Law were so construed, it would itself be a restraint of trade and unduly prejudice the public by restraining foreign trade." *United States* v. *United States Steel Corporation et al.*, 223 Fed, 105, 109, 111. Upholding the circuit court's decision, the Supreme Court

Wilson's achievement was to preside over the extension of responsibility for the adjustment of the law and government to the corporate-capitalist "facts," as he would put it, from the executive to all branches of government, thereby providing the nonstatist regulatory and distributive framework of corporate capitalism with a legislative and growing judicial sanction it had theretofore lacked, and elevating corporate capitalism in both its property-market relations and its governmental dimensions to the realm of public policy and national interest. As Wilsonian democracy, corporate liberalism, it might be said, represented a first phase in the Americanization of corporate capitalism.

It was the part of wise statecraft, as Wilson held, to make the law the expression of the necessities and facts of the time; to institutionalize the ground rules of the corporate economy at home and the mechanisms of its expansion abroad, so that day-to-day business, the laws of commerce, and the government's role with respect to them, might flow smoothly along settled paths, rather than by the fits and starts of fire brigade policy, ad hoc administrative decisions subject to change with elections and administrators, or executive fiat. As Wilson had put it in 1907, "an institution is merely an established practice, an habitual method of dealing with the circumstances of life or the business of government."[89] It was this, with respect to the institutionalization of the modern corporate-capitalist order, that the legislation of 1913–1916 promised, as a beginning, to do.

Each standing in the national political tradition, Wilson was more the "economic determinist," Roosevelt more the republican. That is to say, Wilson more than Roosevelt thought systematically in terms of the

in 1920 concluded that the "public interest" would not be served by dissolving the Steel Corporation. It held, "we do see in a contrary conclusion a risk of injury to the public interest, including a material disturbance of, and, it may be a serious detriment to, the foreign trade. And in submission to the policy of the law and its fortifying prohibitions the public interest is of paramount regard." Idem, 251 U.S. 457. Although the Wilson administration continued the case to its conclusion, the Court's decision was not, in essence, inconsistent with Wilson's principles in general, and it was entirely consistent with its own Rule of Reason, common-law construction of the Sherman Act. There is an analogy here with the Northern Securities case. There, Roosevelt approved on political grounds the Court's dissolution of the holding company, although he disagreed with the Court's basic construction of the law, and he volubly expressed irritation with Justice Holmes for dissenting in the case on the side of the company, although Holmes's construction of the law agreed with Roosevelt's view of what the law should be. In the U.S. Steel case, Wilson may have preferred a different specific outcome, but his view of the proper construction of the law agreed with that of the Court's. In any case, Wilson did not express the sharp irritation with the Court's decision in the U.S. Steel case that Roosevelt expressed with respect to Holmes's dissent in the Northern Securities case.

89. *Constitutional Government*, p. 14.

centrality of the market in modern society and its implications for the government-society relation and, therefore, for policy-making. At least as he expressed himself in 1910–1912, Roosevelt was more inclined to believe that the economy could be considered, and be kept, distinct from political society; for him, as well, "the people" was a more important, and more real, category than "society" – so that, the people in their political relations could use the state to run the economy in their interests, without giving the state despotic power over society. The people would remain supreme over the state, while they made their state supreme over the economy. In this way, they might control their own wealth-creating forces and remain freely self-determining in all their other social relations as well as in their politics. It was precisely this species of thinking in traditional American thought that Wilson renounced as mechanistic.

Wilson saw economic relations as nearly coterminous, or as intimately intertwined, with the essential social relations of modern society. In this important, but limited, sense, it might be said that Wilson's outlook was "organic"; that is, not only did he see economic relations as basic to political, legal, and social relations, and to politically prevalent modes of thought, but he saw economic relations in modern society as inextricable from all the others, that is, as "organically" bound up with them or, in his words, as involving "the very structure and operation of society itself." So that were the state to direct the market, it must necessarily direct, and stand supreme over, society as a whole, and therefore over individuals as members of society. This would mark a retrogression to premodern conditions. Just because business, or the economy, was so critical a constituent of society and hence "the very thing Government cannot let alone," as he had put it, how government dealt with, or related to, business was a matter of the utmost importance in determining the state-society relation. For Wilson, the real categories were individuals and society, not "the people"; if government in a modern society were made the master of the economy, it would also be made the master of individuals and the society.

"The modern idea," Wilson had held in *The State*, "is this: the state no longer absorbs the individual; it only serves him." Projected onto the plane of society, this meant that "Government should serve Society, by no means rule or dominate it.... The State exists for the sake of Society, not Society for the sake of the State." Or as he put it to Congress on 20 January 1914 in his special message on trust legislation, a regulatory commission such as he recommended should not be "empowered ... in any sort to assume control of business, as if Government made itself responsible." The fundamental consideration, in Wilson's view, was to avoid statist command of any sort, whether in the form of a state functioning as a right-wing instrument of capital, as a left-wing instrument of labor, or perhaps worst of all as a leviathan – an "autonomous" – state, standing "above," and dictating to, society and all its components alike. Society was the organism, the state its "executive organ," through which society's "will becomes operative"; society "is vastly bigger and more important than its instrument, Government."[90]

In the modern world, society was the originative, the generative, organism, Wilson held, invoking Hegelian terms, "the Whole" that had become "self-conscious" and "self-directive"; the state was the regulative organ, subordinate to, and serving, the ends of the organism. In serving society, the aim of the state was to "aid the individual to the fullest and best possible realization of his individuality, instead of merely to the full realization of his *sociality*," and "the way to do this is by no means itself to undertake the administration of the individual by the old-time futile methods of guardianship." In contrast to the ancient state of Greece and Rome, "the state is ours, not we the state's." This did not mean embracing Taft's tendency toward a minimalist state. Modern industrial society required a growing government role in service of "social convenience and advancement."[91] This made it all the more imperative, however, to draw the line between positive government, an urgent necessity in modern times, and the placing with government of a power of statist command over society. Positive government based on the sovereignty of society and its supremacy over the state represented the enduring, "organic," national political tradition.

Wilson's outlook articulated an awareness of the need to bring the system of authority and power lodged in capitalist property ownership, as it changed from the competitive stage to the corporate stage, into phase with the system of authority and power lodged in the law, party politics, and government. For this purpose, as Wilson expressed it, it was in general the law, party politics, and government that would have to accommodate to the changing system of property, or the changing property-production system, not the other way around. In specifics, the property system would also have to adjust to the particular political culture of the United States. There would have to be reciprocity in the adjustment, but an asymmetrical one.

90. *The State*, pp. 576, 619, 636; "Trusts and Monopolies," Special Address to Congress, 20 Jan. 1914, *PPWW*, 3, p. 85.
91. *The State*, pp. 586, 620. Wilson's emphasis.

In historical perspective, Wilson's outlook may be summarized, in part, as follows: Law, politics, and government did not in some passive or reflective sense accommodate to the property system and its pattern of authority. Rather, law, politics, and government constituted the ways in which those favoring or representing the evolving property system translated its system of authority into society's system of power, and brought the two into alignment. To leave the two in protracted non-alignment would be to court the disorder of stagnation or social up-heaval. Reform represented alignment on the basis of the extant property system as it was evolving, that is, as it was being reshaped by the movement for corporate capitalism in the Progressive Era. Revolution would have represented alignment on the basis of ending or seriously interdicting the evolving property system to make way for another.

The characteristic quality of Wilson's thought was not an idiosyn-cratic distinctiveness in content but, on the contrary, its conformity to an emerging mode of consciousness and the large extent to which in substance it thereby stood as representative and typical of what became the prevalent corporate-liberal outlook, an outlook that sought to rec-oncile a highly centralized corporate capitalism with social and econom-ic diversification and a form of political democracy, and that also sought to reconcile an ever-developing positive government with the supremacy of society over the state. The distinctive quality of Wilson's thought, which made it remarkable and uniquely his contribution, re-sided rather in its style and impact. Wilson articulated the prevailing corporate-liberal outlook with a scholarly acumen, a conceptual rigor, and an exalted form of public discourse, which at the same time rendered it accessible to popularization and suffused it with the civic rectitude and political axioms of the national political tradition.

Wilson's style of discourse clothed the emerging corporate-capitalist order in the vestments of the national tradition by presenting change as continuity to those who treasured the old, and continuity as change to those who demanded or savored the new. This was the mark of its adequacy, in a transitional period, to the transacting of the corporate-capitalist reconstruction of American society. Wilson's was a synthetic outlook – more suited to nonrevolutionary times than Theodore Roosevelt's – which was at once reformist and liberal and strongly attractive, however grudgingly, to conservatives and radicals alike. If it may be said that Roosevelt's style of public discourse tended to accentu-ate the sense of change at the expense of that of continuity, and Taft's the sense of continuity at the expense of that of change, Wilson's struck the right balance – or interconvertibility – in the form of high and familiar principle fortified with strong moral tone, which gave a classic political expression, in its characteristic liberal embodiment, to the corporate reconstruction of American capitalism.

7

Conclusion: Fathers and prophets

Practically the whole of our industrial and economic mechanism has been reconstructed within the past few years.

— Henry Clews, 1905

They were making the first tentative combinations of the ideas and materials they found ready at their hands — ideas destined to become, in future years, first articulate, then startling and finally commonplace. At the moment ... they were sitting with disarming quiet upon the still unhatched eggs of the mid-twentieth century.

— F. Scott Fitzgerald,
"The Scandal Detectives," *Taps at Reveille*

The transformation of capitalist market and property relations, along with the rise of new thinking about those relations and their implications for public policy, gave to the period of 1890–1916 its distinctive character in American history. The property-production system, or the mode of production, passed from the proprietary-competitive stage to the incipient phase of the corporate-administered stage of capitalism.

The transformation of the market and of the form of capitalist property included changes in the organization and management of labor, production processes, finance, distribution, and administration. These changes generated new professional, technical, and managerial functions with their corresponding social strata and, in turn, their values, attitudes, and ideological dispositions. Along with these strata came provision for their training and for the propagation of forms of consciousness appropriate to their functions, provision especially lodged in newly established or reoriented university professional and graduate schools and professional associations. The new market and property relations also generated movements for the alteration of government roles in social and economic affairs, that is, new governmental functions and administrative structures.

These developments in both the private and public sectors corresponded with what historians take social science theory to designate as systemic tendencies toward bureaucratic organization, professionalization, and the continuing modernization of a mature or highly developed industrial society. Hence, as such leading figures of the time as Roosevelt and Wilson believed, the changes in the market, in property relations, in class relations – in the mode of production – that transpired in the late nineteenth and early twentieth centuries, may be understood as having constituted the substance, the causal or motive force, of "modernization," as well as of the reforms and political thought that affirmed both the corporate reorganization of the political economy and government regulation on behalf of the general welfare. These were the reforms and political thought that became associated with progressivism and with modern liberalism, or corporate liberalism, in the United States.

The transformation of capitalist market and property relations exerted an immediate and formative impact on the nation's foreign policy, its legal order, its party politics, and its prevalent forms of political-economic and historical thought. In modes of thought, business-cycle and crisis theory displaced or amended the older equilibrium theory, evolutionary positivism refashioned older principles of natural liberty, and republican principles shifted from their old roots in the self-employed producer to new roots in principles of citizenship, individuality, opportunity, and the general welfare. Not only socialists reinterpreted American history as fundamentally shaped by evolutionary economic development; so did such historians and social scientists as Turner, Veblen, Commons, and Beard, and such pro-corporate-capitalist policy-making intellectuals and political leaders as Conant, Jenks, Reinsch, Root, Hay, Roosevelt, Taft, and Wilson. A broad capitalist-socialist, reformer-revolutionary, intellectual consensus emerged in this respect, forming the common soil of modern liberalism. The transformation of American capitalism, therefore, was not simply a matter of techno-economic structural change that occurred behind people's backs and over their heads. It proceeded as a dialogue of consensus and conflict among social movements and their trends of thought, in which people not only transformed their relations of production and exchange, their inter-class and intra-class relations, but they also, as might be expected in a society in which market relations constitute the dominant social relations, transformed the law of the market, the structure and role of government, party politics, foreign relations, and basic forms of thought.

The antitrust debates are trivialized if their importance is thought to have resided essentially in the conflict between partisans of regulated monopoly and partisans of competition, and they are misunderstood if dismissed as jousts between Tweedledee and Tweedledum. The antitrust debates gave expression to the conflict among the representatives of two stages of American capitalism – the proprietary-competitive and the corporate – in which those on both sides sought to regulate competition and the market, but in different ways and for different purposes. The debates gave expression at the same time to differences, which cut across the other lines, over how to regulate the market, whatever the purpose, that is, over the respective roles of federal and state government, of the executive and the judiciary, and the extent to which government or private parties should regulate the market to the exclusion of the other. Fundamentally, the debates revolved around the relation of the state to society in resolving the general questions of whether the law should permit or prevent the corporate reorganization of the political economy, and in either case whether it should do so along statist or nonstatist lines.

A statist resolution might have ensued had the American capitalist class been less developed and more dependent on the state for its wealth and power; had the republican ideology of equal liberty and the supremacy of society over the state (the sovereignty of the people) been weaker; had the working class been less imbued with the republican ideology, less developed, and hence more inclined to (Lassallean) state-socialist rather than (Marxian) associative-socialist ideas; had the corporate sector of the capitalist class sought and made an alliance with a statist-oriented sector of the working class or a statist-oriented petty bourgeoisie, especially in the farm and rural population; had the corporate sector of the capitalist class sought and made an alliance with civilian or military professionals, technicians, administrators, and managers – or a "managerial class" – looking to the state as a base of power. None of these circumstances were strongly rooted in the American historical soil at the turn of the century, and none found translation, with the rise of corporate-capitalism, into politically prevalent tendencies, however much they may have found significant literary expression.

Instead of a statist route, a broad pro-regulatory consensus defined the common ground of the great debate over the reorganization of the market. Upon this ground, disagreement proceeded over the role of the state, the status of labor, and not least of all the prospects of small enterprisers in the emergent corporate order. Small-producer thinking, as expressed in the policy positions of many organizations, favored government regulation to protect the small enterprisers from concentrated power, whether corporate or trade-union, as well as from com

petition among themselves, and they favored government intervention
to aid them in a positive way to control or interdict competitive forces
by subsidies, credit, or laws protecting their own restraints of trade.

Small-enterpriser opinion divided between those, increasingly the
minority, who from interest or principle opposed the corporate reorganization of the market altogether, and those, increasingly the majority,
who sought survival or growth within it and adaptation to it. Large-
corporate sentiment, for its part, opposed the old competitive market;
in its prevalent tendency it favored federal regulation not only to
preempt state or local authority but, more positively, to facilitate,
legitimize, police, and complement corporate regulation of the market.
Pro-corporate opinion then divided on questions of regulatory ways and
means, and on statist as against nonstatist proposals.

The origin of what is designated here as corporate liberalism centered
in, although it was not coterminous with, a continuing adjustment of
interest and outlook, hence a shifting but continuing alliance, between
sectors of corporate capitalists and ever-widening sectors of the smaller
bourgeoisie, including farmers, among which pro-statist proclivities suc-
cumbed to the much stronger antistatist tradition in the American
political culture. The birth and early rise of the corporate-liberal dispensation turned upon including a numerous and politically potent
small bourgeoisie, or sufficient segments of it, in the new administered
marketplace on favorable terms that largely excluded labor from participation in the administering function, that reconciled regulation with
wide latitude for private initiative on a small scale as well as large, and
that guaranteed the continuing supremacy of society over the state.
These terms found institutional embodiment in the Rule of Reason
decisions of 1911, the Federal Reserve and the tax and tariff laws of
1909 and 1913, in the Federal Trade Commission and Clayton acts of
1914, and in the reform legislation of the remainder of Wilson's first
term.

The corporate reconstruction of the American political economy
emerged from reciprocal accommodations of corporate and smaller or
proprietary capitalists, one to the other, based upon the affirmation of
the corporate reorganization of industry, and the receding of the competitive before the administered market. As such, it was not a unilinear
but a zigzagging process, as with the law of restraint of trade, and as,
for example, with the reversion to tariff protection in the 1920s and
1930s, and the prolonged retardation of trade-union organization and
collective bargaining in industry. With respect to the latter, it was not
until a later phase (the 1930s–1950s) in this process of mutual accommodation of large and small capital that organized labor (outside of

railroads and some local or limited markets, particularly in the building trades) assumed a substantial, although subordinate, role in administering the market. It was not until this later time that distributive functions, although beginning to emerge in the Progressive Era, significantly complemented regulatory functions in the government's secondary role in administering the market, and that direct statist-tending functions in peacetime, not simply as wartime measures, appeared. Nevertheless, the corporate reconstruction also involved from the outset some adjustments in the capital-labor relation, which, on the one hand, maintained the open shop generally in industry, and, on the other hand, embarked government at the local, state, and national levels on the first, if halting, phases of protective and distributive measures that responded to, and drew upon, programs and demands of the trade-union, women's, and socialist movements. The American working-class movements, including those inclined toward, or significantly influenced by, socialism, were predominantly constitutional-republican, as against statist, in outlook.[1] They were therefore strongly attracted to corporate liberalism, an attraction that facilitated the accommodation between smaller and corporate capital, and hence the ascendancy of corporate liberalism in the transition from the competitive stage to the corporate stage of capitalism.

The emergence of corporate capitalism in the years 1890–1916 coincided with the rise of an associative and cooperative outlook on society, politics, and economic organization in leading intellectual, political, and business circles. The prevalent American associative-cooperative current differed from contemporary and subsequent trends in European corporative thought. The prevalent American current was corporate-*liberal*: It assigned to the corporation, including investment banking and central banking, and to a lesser degree to other private entities, the

---

1. For the distinction between the constitutional-republican and the statist trends in American working-class politics, see Richard Schneirov, "The Knights of Labor in the Chicago Labor Movement and in Municipal Politics, 1877–1887" (Ph.D. diss. Northern Illinois University, 1984; Champaign: University of Illinois Press, forthcoming); also, John B. Jentz and Richard Schneirov, "Social Republicanism and Socialism: A Multi-Ethnic History of Labor Reform in Chicago, 1848–1877," paper presented at the Social Science Historians Convention, Chicago, November 1985. The whole topic of the relation of republicanism and American working-class politics, as well as the reconceptualization of the relation between socialism and the American working class, has its origins in the essays of Herbert G. Gutman, dating back to the 1950s, later published in the collection, Gutman, *Work, Culture, and Society in Industrializing America: Essays in American Working Class and Social History* (New York: Knopf, 1976). See also, for important interpretive formulations by Gutman, "Interview with Herbert Gutman," conducted by Michael Merrill, *Radical History Review* 27 (1983), pp. 203–222. Gutman's critique there of "corporate liberalism" as conceived and applied by some writers is one with which I agree.

primary task of managing the market, and to the state the secondary task of regulating the corporations and the lesser entities in the private sector. In renouncing laissez-faire and implementing programs of positive government on an ever-growing scale, it nevertheless affirmed the supremacy of the society over the state and the subordination of state policy to the dominant forces in society that composed the corporate-capitalist property-production system. It "transcended" the old small-producer republican ideal of the sovereignty of the self-governing people by incorporating it in the new political-economic order, specifically, for example, through adaptation of small-business and professional opportunities to the corporate economy, through civic and professional associations and their political influence, through the attractions, absorptions, or distractions of consumer sovereignties, and through both legal extension of the suffrage (to women, amidst its withdrawal from southern blacks) and expansion of popular electoral functions (direct election of United States senators, the initiative, recall, and referendum, the primary, working-class participation in big-city politics, rural and city people's participation in "third party" or "nonpartisan" movements). Although giving first priority in its early phase to intra-capitalist adjustments, corporate liberalism nevertheless prepared the ground for the reconstruction of capital-labor relations by giving what was at first limited sanction to trade-union organization, and by adapting socialist programmatic ideas and some socialist values to positive government measures suited to regulating the corporate-capitalist order.

In the prevalent political-intellectual trend, there was no "corporate ideal" in any meaningful sense of the words beyond the view, with its corollaries and implications, that the corporate mode of capitalist enterprise, and the corporation as a form of capitalist property, were progressive and beneficent and taking the place of individual enterprise as the dominant form of property relations in the economy. Neither corporate capitalism nor corporate liberalism in the United States should be confused with European or Latin American versions of "corporative" social relations or modes of thought. The prevalent forms of extrafamilial social relations in the United States remained contractual, associative, and bureaucratic rather than corporative in any organicist sense or in any coercively collectivistic sense. The prevalent mode of thought among American partisans of the corporate reorganization of capitalism was not organicist, but instrumental and associational, and its prevalent mode of implementation was through voluntary and contractual relations in the private sector and through electoral political and legislative processes in the public sector, with both sectors subject to the oversight of an independent judiciary. It was, in other words, not a traditionalist, or a peasant, or an artisan or early-working-class (guild or communitarian), or a fascist, but a liberal, mode of thought and politics adapted to the corporate stage of industrial capitalism.

Corporate-liberal thought did acknowledge and affirm the displacement of the individual by the group (or association) as the basic functional unit of a modern capitalist economy, but it was a group that the individual might freely join or quit, according to opportunity and circumstance, and was not bound to involuntarily as a matter of kinship, custom, law, or binding obligation other than contractual. In this sense, natural-liberty principles became part of the evolutionary-positivist outlook. Hence, although corporate-liberal thought designated the organized group (corporation, trade union, cooperative) as the basic unit of the economy, it still made room and affirmed support for individual enterprise (including the family farm), and it still defined the individual as the basic unit of the body politic and society. In principle and at law, rights and obligations remained fundamentally individual, not corporative; the basic categorical concepts remained the individual, society, and government, not "the people," or "the class," and the state.

As the American corporate-liberal outlook was not "organicist" in the conservative, or in the "traditionalist," sense, so neither was it simply or statically oriented to "organizational" order or social stability. It highly valued innovation, the reordering of economic and social relations, as well as the physical landscape, and the instabilities of growth, both at home and in America's role in the world. The perennial search for order was the handmaiden of the perennial impulse of American corporate capitalism to disruption and change. The quest for countercyclical stabilizing mechanisms in the economy, for example, proceeded as a function of the corporate reorganization and transformation, that is, the disruption, of the older small-producer political economy.

Although evolutionary-positivist in certifying the legitimacy of corporate capitalism, the corporate-liberal outlook went with the older American grain in being economic-determinist, acquisitive, materialist, instrumentalist, pragmatic, and simultaneously idealist, altruist, and moralist – almost, one might say, latter-day Emersonian and Whitmanesque in spirit. As with similar reform or social-liberal movements in England and continental Europe, but with deep roots in the American experience tracing back through Lincoln to Jackson, Jefferson, and the Founders, corporate liberalism combined an outlook favoring reform at home with that favoring imperialist expansion. It was, in sum, committed to, while it refashioned, the democratic political tradition as it had developed in the United States.

Corporate liberalism expressed the accommodation of corporate capitalism to representative government based on population, geographical district, and the American federalist tradition – it rejected syndicalism in this respect – while it afforded strong support to the shifting of the balance of decision-making initiative away from the electoral arena, party politics, and the legislative branch, to the executive and judicial branches of government and to extra-electoral bodies of experts and administrators insulated from the fluctuations of electoral politics. It gave expression to the dominant power of the capitalist class in society and in the state by validating a revised definition of property at law and by affirming a change in the rules of the market, while it embraced the political tradition of defining society as superior to the state in accordance with the doctrine of limited government under law – constitutional government. In particular, while oriented to the expansion of executive power as against the legislative branch, the prevalent corporate-liberal outlook never challenged in principle, and often strongly asserted, the paramount authority of the legislative branch in making public policy, and it affirmed the limitation of executive power by constitutional and statute law, and in the last analysis by the authority of an independent judiciary.[2] To say the same things differently, the ascendancy of corporate liberalism represented an alternative to, and rejection of, the corporate state associated with European "organicist" thought and politics of either the left or the right. It corresponded with the prevalent antistatism of all major classes and strata of a highly developed capitalist society – a strong and diversified capitalist class, an advanced, largely literate, functionally and ethnically heterogeneous, and politically sophisticated working class,[3] growing, differentiated strata of professionals and technicians, and a largely business-oriented, diversified farm population. At every step of the way, the corporate-liberal movement had to fight, and also accommodate to, in order to defeat or contain, the small-producer

---

2. Hence, the Supreme Court's decision against provisions of the National Industrial Recovery Act in 1935, on the grounds that they authorized an unconstitutional delegation of legislative power to the executive, endowing the executive with "unfettered" discretionary powers over the market, and through, the executive, to private collectivities with, in effect, coercive powers of the state over individuals; also, the almost instinctive revulsion of liberals as well as conservatives against Franklin D. Roosevelt's attempted court-packing. *Panama Refining Co.* v. *Ryan*, 293 *U.S.* 388, and *Schecter Poultry Corp.* v. *United States*, 295 *U.S.* 495.
3. This characterization implies disagreement with conventional views of the American working class as being antisocialist or nonsocialist, or as being politically "backward" or "undeveloped," insofar as it rejected the leadership or the ideological doctrines of professed socialist parties or movements.

tradition, and, less in earlier phases but more in later phases, an organized labor movement and socialism.

There was in the period 1890–1916 a widespread and highly charged sense of the emergence of a new era in American history among capitalists, politicians, and intellectuals – a sense of an evolutionary outcome that marked a distinct break with the past, comparable to that of the Revolutionary and Civil War eras. It was a sense of a new departure in both domestic and foreign affairs. It was particularly strongly felt and explicitly expressed in connection with the transformation of the political economy. Those in opposition to the rise of corporate capitalism, and even many who favored or acquiesced in it, feared the passing of the old republic of small producers and its attendant set of values. Those who affirmed the rise of corporate capitalism often sought to ease that fear by portraying it as another chapter in the evolutionary, and providential, progress of the American people, by adapting the ethic of self-reliance to associative modes of social intercourse (voluntarism), and by transporting the concept of freedom from its old moorings in the self-employed producer to the new environs of the self-reliant worker accorded equality of opportunity, the self-determining investor protected from unfair competition, and the sovereign consumer safeguarded against fraud, all interacting and cooperatively competing as Americans in an administered marketplace and a political democracy that combined fairness and opportunity with progress and ever-growing abundance.[4] The affirmers of corporate capitalism tended to see themselves as founders of a new progressive dispensation, like the generation of Washington and that of Lincoln. They conceived themselves as the heirs of the American republican tradition and the founders of a new age of progress fulfilling the national destiny of assuming the leadership of a grateful world. Hence, many of their eminent figures did not shrink from seeing their founding in universal-imperial terms.

John Hay, who some two score years before as President Lincoln's private secretary was present at one creation, the national republic that arose from the Civil War, now at the outset of the new century declared

---

4. Cf. Warren I. Susman, *Culture as History: The Transformation of American Society in the Twentieth Century* (New York: Pantheon, 1984), esp. pts. 2 and 3, pp. 53–97, 101–229; William A. Williams, *The Contours of American History* (New York: World, 1961), esp. pp. 390–450; Martin J. Sklar, "On the Proletarian Revolution and the End of Political-Economic Society," *Radical America* 3:3 (May–June 1969), pp. 1–41; and Martin J. Sklar, "The Corporate Ascendancy and the Socialist Acquiescence: An Inquiry into Strange Times," *The Maryland Historian* 12:2 (Fall 1981), pp. 49–59.

himself and his colleagues present at, and indeed the authors of, another creation. Before a joint session of Congress and in the presence of Washington's international diplomatic corps, the secretary of state in his eulogy of the assassinated President McKinley, proclaimed the birth of the corporate-imperial order, which promised the redemption of the American Edenic dream of a nation at last wrenching itself free of the past – not alone of the Old World's past, but of the New World's as well – to assume its destined role. By history was the nation freed of history. "The 'debtor nation,'" Hay stated, "has become the chief creditor nation. The financial center of the world, which required thousands of years to journey from the Euphrates to the Thames and the Seine, seems passing to the Hudson between daybreak and dark." A new epoch in world history had begun – at last the *novus ordo seclorum* – in which, Hay judged, "the past is past, and experience vain."

> Every young and growing people [said Hay] has to meet, at moments, the problem of its destiny.... The fathers are dead; the prophets are silent; the questions are new, and have no answer but in time.... The past gives no clue to the future. The fathers, where are they? and the prophets, do they live forever? We are ourselves the fathers! We are ourselves the prophets![5]

America had fulfilled, by surpassing, the Founders and the Lincolns. An astonishing statement, indeed, at least for the secretary of state to make in public, on an official occasion, not alone before Congress but also to the world. Once again Ahab, the self-made American, hell-bent on sailing through an open door to new frontiers, new worlds, new beginnings, a new epoch – and age-old tragedies.

> Ay, Democracy
> Lops, lops; and where's her planted bed?
> The Future, what is that to her

5. *Congressional Record*, vol. 35, pts. 3–5, 57th Cong., 1st Sess. (27 Feb. 1902), pp. 2201, 2202. Here, also, Hay cited the 1890s as one of "the three great crises of our history," ranking with the Revolutionary and Civil War eras, each of which, Hay said, produced a great national leader – Washington and Lincoln in the two earlier crises, respectively, and McKinley in that of the 1890s. Theodore Roosevelt made a similar comparison; see "At the Banquet at Canton, Ohio, January 27, 1903, in Honor of the Birthday of the Late President McKinley," *Addresses and Presidential Messages of Theodore Roosevelt, 1902–1904* (New York: Putnam, 1904), pp. 100–101. Wilson, as we have seen, similarly saw his times as representing a new era in the nation's history. Hay's eulogy ranks as a Periclean oration on the American imperial republic, except that it came at the dawn instead of at the twilight of the "new empire." In any case, it deserves as much notoriety as Bryan's "Cross of Gold" speech of 1896 as a piece of oratory and as, much more than Bryan's, an evocation of the "American Spirit" as it entered the twentieth century.

Who vaunts she's no inheritor?
'Tis in her mouth, not in her heart.[6]

The movement for corporate capitalism reconstructed American society during the years 1890–1916. In effecting a reorganization of property ownership and the market, and in attaining a revision of the law and of government-market relations, this movement established the fundamental conditions of what many historians regard as the mass-culture society and also as the organizational or bureaucratic society with its concomitant rise of a professional, managerial, and technical middle class. Corporate capitalism, and the reconstruction of American society that it represented, constituted the essence of that movement, corporate liberalism, which in renouncing statism, or a corporate state, pacified agrarian populism, transcended proprietary capitalism, and, in the inclusive as well as the exclusive sense, contained socialism. It was the movement that gave America "the fathers and the prophets" of its national development and international relations well beyond the mid–twentieth century.

6. Herman Melville, *Clarel* (1876).

Bibliography

Unpublished collections

Nelson W. Aldrich Papers. Library of Congress, Washington, D.C.

James R. Garfield Papers. Library of Congress, Washington, D.C.

Seth Low Papers. Rare Book and Manuscript Library, Butler Library, Columbia University, New York City.

McCormick Collection. State Historical Society of Wisconsin, Madison.

National Civic Federation Papers. New York Public Library, New York City.

George W. Perkins Papers. Rare Book and Manuscript Library, Butler Library, Columbia University, New York City.

Paul S. Reinsch Papers. State Historical Society of Wisconsin, Madison.

Theodore Roosevelt Papers. Library of Congress, Washington, D.C.

Elihu Root Papers. Library of Congress, Washington, D.C.

Robert Stewart Taylor Papers. Indianapolis State Library, Indianapolis, Indiana.

U.S. Bureau of Corporations. Record Group 122. National Archives, Washington, D.C.

U.S. Department of War. Record Group 350. National Archives, Washington, D.C.

Frank A. Vanderlip Papers. Rare Book and Manuscript Library, Butler Library, Columbia University, New York City.

Woodrow Wilson Letters, Miscellaneous. State Historical Society of Wisconsin, Madison.

Published government sources

U.S. Attorney General. *Federal Anti-Trust Decisions*. III: *1890–1912; IV: 1890–1917*; VI: *1890–1917*; VIII: *1917–1923*. Washington, D.C.: Government Printing Office, 1912, 1917, 1918, 1924, respectively.

U.S. Attorney General. *Report of the Attorney-General's National Committee to Study the Antitrust Laws*, Stanley N. Barnes and S. Chesterfield Oppenheim, co-chairmen. Washington, D.C.: Government Printing Office, 1955.

U.S. Bureau of Corporations. *Annual Report of the Commissioner of Corporations*, Department of Commerce. Washington, D.C.: Government Printing Office, various years.

U.S. Bureau of Corporations. *Trust Laws and Unfair Competition*, by Joseph E. Davies, Commissioner of Corporations, Department of Commerce, 15 March 1915. Washington, D.C.: Government Printing Office, 1916.

U.S. Commission on International Exchange. *Report on the Introduction of the Gold Standard into China, the Philippine Islands, Panama and Other Silver Using Countries.* Washington, D.C.: Government Printing Office, 1904.

U.S. Commission on International Exchange. *Stability of International Exchange: Report on the Introduction of the Gold Exchange Standard into China and Other Silver Using Countries.* Washington, D.C.: Government Printing Office, 1903.

U.S. *Congressional Record.* Washington, D.C.: Government Printing Office, various volumes and dates.

U.S. Department of War. *Report on Certain Economic Questions in the English and Dutch Colonies in the Orient,* by Jeremiah W. Jenks, Special Commissioner, Bureau of Insular Affairs. War Department Doc. No. 168, September 1902. Washington, D.C.: Government Printing Office, 1902.

U.S. Department of War. *A Special Report on Coinage and Banking in the Philippine Islands, Made to the Secretary of War by Charles A. Conant of Boston,* 25 November 1901. Appendix G in *Annual Report of the Secretary of War,* 1901. Washington, D.C.: Government Printing Office, 1901.

U.S. Federal Trade Commission. *Report on Cooperation in American Export Trade.* 2 vols. Washington, D.C.: Government Printing Office, 1916.

U.S. House of Representatives, Committee on Banking and Currency. *Hearings and Arguments,* "Currency Responsive to the Needs of Business." H.R. 13303, 56th Cong., 2d Sess. Washington D.C.: Government Printing Office, 1901.

U.S. House of Representatives, Committee on Insular Affairs. *Hearings,* "Coinage System in the Philippine Islands." 57th Cong., 1st and 2d Sess., 1901–1903. Washington D.C.: Government Printing Office, 1903.

U.S. House of Representatives, Committee on the Judiciary. *Hearings on House Bill 19745, An Act to Regulate Commerce, etc.* Subcommittee No. 3, 60th Cong., 1st Sess. Washington, D.C.: Government Printing Office, 1908.

U.S. House of Representatives, Committee on the Judiciary. *Hearings on Trust Legislation.* 2 vols. 63d Cong., 2d Sess. Washington, D.C.: Government Printing Office, 1914.

U.S. Industrial Commission, XIX: *Final Report of the Industrial Commission.* Washington, D.C.: Government Printing Office, 1902.

U.S. Industrial Commission, I: *Preliminary Report on Trusts and Industrial Combinations.* H.R. Doc. No. 476, pt. 1, 56th Cong., 1st Sess., 1 March 1900. Washington, D.C.: Government Printing Office, 1900.

U.S. Industrial Commission, XIII: *Report of the Industrial Commission on Trusts and Industrial Combinations.* H.R. Doc. No. 182, 57th Cong., 1st Sess., 4 December 1901. Washington, D.C.: Government Printing Office, 1901.

U.S. Industrial Commission, II: *Trusts and Industrial Combinations: Statutes and Decisions of Federal, State, and Territorial Law, Together with a Digest of Corporation Laws Applicable to Large Industrial Corporations,* in two parts. H.R. Doc. No. 476, pt. 2, 56th Cong., 1st Sess. Washington, D.C.: Government Printing Office, 1900.

U.S. Senate, Committee on Interstate Commerce. "Federal Trade Commission." *Senate Report No. 597*, 63d Cong., 2d Sess., Calendar No. 518, 13 June 1914. Washington, D.C.: Government Printing Office, 1914.

U.S. Senate, Committee on Interstate Commerce. *Trusts in Foreign Countries: Laws and References concerning Industrial Combinations in Australia, Canada, New Zealand, and Continental Europe*, compiled by Fred A. Johnson. Washington, D.C.: Government Printing Office, 1912.

U.S. Senate, Committee on the Judiciary. *Adverse Report*, "Amending Antitrust Act." *Senate Report No. 848*, 60th Cong., 2d Sess., 26 January 1909. Washington, D.C.: Government Printing Office, 1909.

U.S. Senate, Committee on the Judiciary. *Amendments to the Sherman Antitrust Law and Related Matters*, pt. 1, 63d Cong. 2d Sess. Washington, D.C.: Government Printing Office, 1914.

U.S. Senate, Committee on the Judiciary. *Hearings Before Subcommittee of the Committee on the Judiciary, U.S. Senate, During 60th, 61st, 62nd Congresses, Compiled for Consideration of H.R. 15657*, 63rd Cong., 2d Sess., 1914. Washington, D.C.: Government Printing Office, 1914.

U.S. Senate, Committee on the Philippines. *Hearings.* "Affairs in the Philippine Islands," Sen. Doc. No. 331, pt. 1, 57th Cong., 1st Sess. Washington, D.C.: Government Printing Office, 1902.

Articles, books, and other published sources (selected)

Allen, Arthur M. "Criminal Conspiracies in Restraint of Trade at Common Law." *Harvard Law Review* 23:7 (May 1910), pp. 531–548.

American Academy of Political and Social Science. *Corporations and the Public Welfare.* New York: McClure, Phillips, 1900.

Anderson, Donald F. *William Howard Taft: A Conservative's Conception of the Presidency.* Ithaca N.Y.: Cornell University Press, 1973.

Andrew, Abram Piatt. "The Treasury and the Banks Under Secretary Shaw." *Quarterly Journal of Economics* 21 (August 1907), pp. 519–566.

Apter, David E. *The Politics of Modernization.* Chicago: University of Chicago Press, 1965.

Arac, Jonathan. "The Politics of *The Scarlet Letter*." In Sacvan Bercovitch and Myra Jehlen, eds., *Ideology and Classic American Literature.* Cambridge University Press, 1986, pp. 247–266.

Avineri, Shlomo, ed. *Karl Marx on Colonialism and Modernization.* New York: Doubleday, Anchor Books, 1969.

Bain, Joe S. *Barriers to New Competition.* Cambridge, Mass.: Harvard University Press, 1956.

Bain, Joe S. "Industrial Concentration and Anti-Trust Policy." In Harold F. Williamson, ed., *The Growth of the American Economy.* 2d ed. New York: Prentice-Hall, 1951.

Baker, Ray S. *Wilson, Life and Letters.* 8 vols. New York: Doubleday, Page, various dates.

Baltzell, E. Digby. *An American Business Aristocracy.* New York: Collier Books, 1962.

Baltzell, E. Digby. *Puritan Boston and Quaker Philadelphia: Two Protestant Ethics and the Spirit of Class Authority and Leadership.* New York: Free Press, 1979.

Baritz, Loren. *The Servants of Power: A History of the Use of Social Sciences in American Industry.* New York: Wiley, 1960.

Benson, Lee. *Turner and Beard.* New York: Free Press, 1960.

Berle, Adolph A., Jr., and Means, Gardiner C. *The Modern Corporation and Private Property.* New York: Macmillan, 1933.

Berman, Harold J. *Law and Revolution: The Foundation of the Western Legal Tradition.* Cambridge, Mass: Harvard University Press, 1983.

Billington, Ray Allen, ed. *Frontier and Section: Selected Essays of Frederick Jackson Turner.* Englewood Cliffs, N.J.: Prentice-Hall 1961.

Black, Cyril E. *The Dynamics of Modernization: A Study in Comparative History.* New York: Harper & Row, 1966.

Black, R. D. C., Coats, A. W., and Goodwin, C. D. W., eds. *The Marginal Revolution in Economics: Interpretation and Evaluation.* Durham, N.C.: Duke University Press, 1973.

Blaisdell, Thomas C., Jr. *The Federal Trade Commission.* New York: Columbia University Press, 1932.

Blum, John M. *The Republican Roosevelt.* 1954; New York: Atheneum, 1966.

Bork, Robert H. "Legislative Intent and the Policy of the Sherman Act." *Journal of Law & Economics* 9 (October 1966), pp. 7–48.

Bragdon, Henry W. *Woodrow Wilson: The Academic Years.* Cambridge, Mass.: Harvard University Press, 1967.

Braibanti, Ralph, and Spengler, Joseph J., eds. *Tradition, Values, and Socio-Economic Development.* Cambridge University Press, 1961.

Brown, E. H. Phelps, with Handfield-Jones, S. J. "The Climacteric of the 1890s: A Study in the Expanding Economy." *Oxford Economic Papers*, New Series, 4:3 (October 1952), pp. 266–307.

Brown, Richard D. *Modernization: The Transformation of American Life 1600–1865.* New York: Hill & Wang, 1976.

Bushman, Richard L. *From Puritan to Yankee: Character and Social Order in Connecticut, 1690–1765.* Cambridge, Mass.: Harvard University Press, 1967.

Carnegie, Andrew. "The Bugaboo of the Trusts." *North American Review* 148 (February 1889), pp. 141–150.

Carosso, Vincent P. *Investment Banking in America: A History.* Cambridge, Mass.: Harvard University Press, 1970.

Cary, William. "Federalism and Corporate Law: Reflections upon Delaware." *Yale Law Review* 83 (March 1974), pp. 663–705.

Chamberlin, Edward H. *The Theory of Monopolistic Competition.* Cambridge, Mass.: Harvard University Press, 1933.

Chandler, Alfred D., Jr. "The Beginnings of 'Big Business' in American Industry." *Business History Review* 33:1 (Spring 1959), pp. 1–31.

Chandler, Alfred D., Jr. "The Large Industrial Corporation and the Making of the Modern American Economy." In Stephen E. Ambrose, ed., *Institutions in Modern America: Innovation in Structure and Progress*. Baltimore: Johns Hopkins University Press, 1967.

Chandler, Alfred D., Jr. *The Visible Hand: The Managerial Revolution in American Business*. Cambridge, Mass.: Harvard University Press, 1977.

Chessman, G. Wallace. *Theodore Roosevelt and the Politics of Power*. Boston: Little, Brown, 1969.

Civic Federation of Chicago. *Chicago Conference on Trusts: Speeches, Debates, Resolutions, List of Delegates, Committees, Etc.*, 13, 14, 15, 16 September 1899. Chicago: The Civic Federation of Chicago, 1900.

Clark, John Bates. "Education and the Socialistic Movement." *Atlantic Monthly*, October 1908, pp. 433–441.

Clark, John Bates. "Introduction" to Karl Rodbertus, *Overproduction and Crises*. Ed. J. B. Clark. New York: Burt Franklin, 1898.

Clark, John Bates. (Review of) Charles A. Conant, *The United States in the Orient* and other books. *Political Science Quarterly* 16 (March 1901), pp. 142–144.

Cochran, Thomas C. *The American Business System, 1900–1955*. 1957; New York: Harper & Row, 1962.

Cochran, Thomas C., and Miller, William. *The Age of Enterprise: A Social History of Industrial America*. Rev. ed. New York: Harper & Row, 1961.

Coletta, Paolo E. *The Presidency of William Howard Taft*. Lawrence: The University Press of Kansas, 1973.

Commons, John R. *Legal Foundations of Capitalism*. 1924; Madison: University of Wisconsin Press, 1957.

Compton, William R. "Early History of Stock Ownership by Corporations." *George Washington Law Review* 9 (1940).

Conant, Charles A. "Crises and Their Management." *Yale Review* 9 (February 1901), pp. 374–398.

Conant, Charles A. "The Development of Credit." *Journal of Political Economy* 7:2 (March 1899), pp. 161–181.

Conant, Charles A. "The Economic Basis of 'Imperialism.'" *North American Review* 167 (September 1898), pp. 326–340.

Conant, Charles A. "The Functions of Centralized Banking." *The Bankers Magazine* (N.Y.), 89 (October 1914), pp. 388–398.

Conant, Charles A. "The Future of Political Parties." *Atlantic Monthly* 86 (September 1901), pp. 365–373.

Conant, Charles A. *A History of Modern Banks of Issue: with an Account of the Economic Crises of the Present Century*. New York and London: Putnam, 1896; 6th ed., New York: Putnam, 1927.

Conant, Charles A. "The Struggle for Commercial Empire." *Forum* 27 (July 1899), pp. 427–440.

Conant, Charles A. "The United States as a World Power, I. The Nature of the Economic and Political Problem," and "The United States as a World Power. II. Her Advantages in the Competition for Commercial Empire." *Forum* 29 (July 1900), pp. 608–622, *Forum* 29 (August 1900), pp. 673–687.

Conant, Charles A. *The United States in the Orient: The Nature of the Economic Problem.* 1901; Port Washington, N.Y.: Kennikat Press, 1971.

Conant, Charles A. *Wall Street and the Country: A Study of Recent Financial Tendencies.* 1904; Westport, Conn.: Greenwood, 1968.

Conant, Luther, Jr. "Industrial Consolidations in the United States." *Quarterly Publications of the American Statistical Association,* New Series, 7:53 (March 1901), pp. 1–20.

Cooper, John Milton, Jr. *The Warrior and the Priest: Woodrow Wilson and Theodore Roosevelt.* Cambridge, Mass: Harvard University Press, 1983.

Coyajee, Sir J. C. *The Indian Currency System, 1835–1926.* Madras: Thompson & Co., 1930.

Davidson, John Wells, ed. *A Crossroads of Freedom: The 1912 Campaign Speeches of Woodrow Wilson.* New Haven: Yale University Press, 1956.

Davis, Lance E. "The Capital Markets and Industrial Concentration: The U.S. and U.K., A Comparative Study." *Economic History Review,* Second Series, 19:2 (August 1966), pp. 255–272.

Davis, Lance E. "The Investment Market, 1870–1914: The Evolution of a National Market." *Journal of Economic History* 25:3 (September 1965), pp. 355–399.

Dawes, Charles G. "Trusts and Trade Combinations." Delivered at Annual Meeting of Merchants' Club of Boston, 17 October 1899. Washington, D.C.: Judd & Detwiler, 1899.

Dewey, Donald. "The Common-Law Background of Antitrust Policy." *Virginia Law Review* 41:6 (October 1955), pp. 759–786.

Dewey, Donald. *Monopoly in Economics and Law.* Chicago: Rand McNally, 1959.

Diamond, William. *The Economic Thought of Woodrow Wilson.* Baltimore: Johns Hopkins University Press, 1943.

Dobb, Maurice. "The Falling Rate of Profit." *Science & Society* 23:2 (Spring 1959), pp. 97–103.

Dobb, Maurice. *Theories of Value and Distribution Since Adam Smith: Ideology and Economic Theory.* Cambridge University Press, 1973.

Dorfman, Joseph. *The Economic Mind in American Civilization.* Vol. 3: 1865–1918. 1949; New York: Viking, 1959.

Eakins, David W. "Policy-planning for the Establishment." In Ronald Radosh and Marray N. Rothbard, eds., *A New History of Leviathan.* New York: Dutton, 1972, pp. 188–205.

Eakins, David W., and Weinstein, James, eds. *For a New America.* New York: Random House, Vintage Books, 1970.

Eichner, Alfred S. *The Emergence of Oligopoly: Sugar Refining as a Case Study.* Baltimore: Johns Hopkins University Press, 1969.

Etherington, Norman. "The Capitalist Theory of Capitalist Imperialism." *History of Political Economy* 15:1 (Spring 1983), pp. 38–62.

Etherington, Norman. "Reconsidering Theories of Imperialism." *History and Theory* 21:1 (1982), pp. 1–36.

Fabricant, Solomon. *Employment in Manufacturing, 1899–1939: An Analysis of Its Relation to the Volume of Production.* New York: National Bureau of Economic Research, 1942.

Fabricant, Solomon. *The Ouput of Manufacturing Industries, 1899–1937.* New York: National Bureau of Economic Research, 1940.

Feavearyear, Albert E. *The Pound Sterling: A History of English Money.* 2d ed. Oxford: Clarendon Press, 1963.

Fellner, William. *Emergence and Content of Modern Economic Analysis.* New York: McGraw-Hill, 1960.

Fieldhouse, D. K. "'Imperialism': An Historiographical Revision." *Economic History Review*, Second Series, 14:2 (1961), pp. 187–209.

Fine, Sidney. *Laissez Faire and the General-Welfare State.* Ann Arbor: University of Michigan Press, 1967.

Foraker, Joseph B. *Notes of a Busy Life.* 2 vols. Cincinnati: Stewart & Kidd, 1916.

Freyer, Tony A. "The Federal Courts, Localism and the National Economy, 1865–1900." *Business History Review* 53:3 (Autumn 1979), pp. 343–363.

Freyer, Tony A. *Forums of Order: The Federal Courts and Business in American History.* Greenwich, Conn: JAI Press, 1979.

Friedman, Lawrence M. *A History of American Law.* New York: Simon & Schuster, 1973.

Friedman, Milton, and Schwartz, Anna Jacobson. *A Monetary History of the United States, 1867–1960.* Princeton: Princeton University Press, 1963.

Furner, Mary O. *Advocacy and Objectivity: A Crisis in the Professionalization of American Social Science, 1865–1905.* Lexington: University Press of Kentucky, 1975.

Galambos, Louis. "The AFL's Concept of Big Business: A Quantitative Study of Attitudes Toward the Large Corporations, 1894–1931." *Journal of American History* 57 (March 1971).

Galambos, Louis. "The Agrarian Image of the Large Corporation, 1879–1920: A Study in Social Accommodation." *Journal of Economic History* 28 (September 1968), pp. 341–362.

Galambos, Louis. "The Emerging Organizational Synthesis in Modern American History." *Business History Review* 44:3 (Autumn 1970), pp. 279–290.

Gallman, Robert E. "Gross National Product in the United States, 1834–1909." In *Output, Employment and Productivity in the United States After 1800, Studies in Income and Wealth by the Conference on Research in Income and Wealth,* vol. 30. New York: National Bureau of Economic Research, 1966.

Genovese, Eugene D. *Roll, Jordan, Roll: The World the Slaves Made.* 1974; New York: Random House, Vintage Books, 1976.

Goldin, Claudia D. "The Economics of Emancipation." *Journal of Economic History* 33:1 (March 1973), pp. 66–85.

Goldsmith, Raymond W. *A Study of Saving in the United States*, vol. 1. Princeton: Princeton University Press, 1955.

Green, Marguerite. *The National Civic Federation and the American Labor Movement, 1900–1925*. Washington, D.C: Catholic University of America Press, 1956.

Gunderson, Gerald. "The Origin of the American Civil War." *Journal of Economic History* 34:4 (December 1974), pp. 915–950.

Gutman, Herbert G. *Work, Culture, and Society in Industrializing America: Essays in American Working Class and Social History*. New York: Knopf, 1976.

Hadley, Arthur Twining. *Economics: An Account of the Relations Between Private Property and Public Welfare*. New York: Putnam, 1896, 1899.

Hadley, Arthur Twining. "The Good and the Evil of Industrial Combinations." *Atlantic Monthly* 79:473 (March 1897), pp. 377–385.

Hadley, Arthur Twining. *Railroad Transportation: Its History and Its Laws*. New York: Putnam, 1885.

Hammond, John Hays. *The Autobiography of John Hays Hammond*. 2 vols. New York: Farrar & Rinehart, 1935.

Harbaugh, William Henry. *Power and Responsibility: The Life and Times of Theodore Roosevelt*. New York: Farrar, Straus & Cudahy, 1961.

Harbaugh, William Henry, ed. *The Writings of Theodore Roosevelt*. New York: Bobbs-Merrill, 1967.

Hartz, Louis. *The Liberal Tradition in America: An Interpretation of American Political Thought Since the Revolution*. New York: Harcourt Brace & World, 1955.

Harvey, Richard S., and Notz, William F. *American Foreign Trade as Promoted by the Webb–Pomerene and Edge Acts*. Indianapolis: Bobbs-Merrill, 1921.

Hawley, Ellis. "The Discovery and Study of a 'Corporate Liberalism.'" *Business History Review* 52:3 Autumn (1978), pp. 309–320.

Hawley, Ellis W. "Herbert Hoover, the Commerce Secretariat and the Vision of an 'Associative State,' 1921–1928." *Journal of American History* 62 (June 1974), pp. 116–140.

Hays, Samuel P. "The New Organizational Society." In Jerry Israel, ed., *Building the Organizational Society: Essays on Associational Activities in Modern America*. New York: Free Press, 1972.

Hays, Samuel P. *The Response to Industrialism: 1885–1914*. Chicago: University of Chicago Press, 1957; reprint, 1973.

Healy, David. *United States Expansionism: The Imperialist Urge in the 1890s*. Madison: University of Wisconsin Press, 1970.

Hechler, Kenneth W. *Insurgency: Personalities and Politics of the Taft Era*. New York: Columbia University Press, 1940.

Henderson, Gerard C. *The Federal Trade Commission: A Study in Administrative Law and Procedure*. New Haven: Yale University Press, 1924; 2d printing, 1925.

Hepburn, A. Barton. *History of Coinage and Currency in the United States and the Perennial Contest for Sound Money*. New York: Macmillan, 1903.

Hilton, George W. "The Consistency of the Interstate Commerce Act." *Journal of Law & Economics* 9 (October 1966), pp. 87–113.

Hobson, John A. "The Economic Taproot of Imperialism." *The Contemporary Review* 82 (August, 1902), pp. 219–232.

Hobson, John A. *The Evolution of Modern Capitalism: A Study of Machine Production*. London: W. Scott, 1894; New York: Scribner, 1894.

Hobson, John A. *Imperialism* (1902). Ed. Philip Siegelman. Ann Arbor: University of Michigan Press, 1965.

Hobson, John A., and Mummery, A. F. *The Physiology of Industry*. 1889; New York: Kelley & Millman, 1956.

Hoffmann, Charles. *The Depression of the Nineties: An Economic History*. Westport, Conn.: Greenwood, 1970.

Hofstadter, Richard. *The Age of Reform*. New York: Random House, Vintage Books 1955.

Hofstadter, Richard. *America at 1750: A Social Portrait*. New York: Random House, Vintage Books, 1973.

Hofstadter, Richard. *The American Political Tradition*. New York: Knopf, 1948; Random House, Vintage Books, n.d.

Hofstadfer, Richard. *Social Darwinism in American Thought*. Rev. ed. Boston: Beacon, 1955.

Holaind, R. I. "The Chicago Trust Conference." *Annals* 15 (January 1900), pp. 69–80.

Hollander, Samuel. *The Economics of David Ricardo*. Toronto: University of Toronto Press, 1979.

Holt, James. *Congressional Insurgents and the Party System, 1909–1916*. Cambridge, Mass.: Harvard University Press, 1967.

Hoogenboom, Ari, and Hoogenboom, Olive. *A History of the ICC: From Panacea to Palliative*. New York: Norton, 1976.

Horwitz, Morton J. "The Emergence of an Instrumental Conception of American Law, 1780–1820." *Perspectives in American History* 5 (1971), pp. 285–326.

Horwitz, Morton J. "*Santa Clara* Revisited: The Development of Corporate Theory." *West Virginia Law Review* 88 (1985), pp. 173–224.

Horwitz, Morton J. *The Transformation of American Law, 1780–1860*. Cambridge, Mass.: Harvard University Press, 1977.

Hubbard, Evelyn. "American 'Trusts' and English Combinations," *Economic Journal* (London), 12 (June 1902), pp. 159–176.

Hurst, J. Willard. *Law and the Conditions of Freedom in the Nineteenth-Century United States*. Madison: University of Wisconsin Press, 1956.

Hurst, J. Willard. *Law and Economic Growth: The Legal History of Lumber Industry in Wisconsin, 1836–1915*. Cambridge, Mass.: Harvard University Press, 1977.

Hurst, J. Willard. *Law and Markets in United States History: Different*

Modes of Bargaining Among Interests. Madison: University of Wisconsin Press, 1982.

Hurst, J. Willard. "Legal Elements in United States History." *Perspectives in American History* 5 (1971), pp. 3–92.

Hurst, J. Willard. *The Legitimacy of the Business Corporation in the Law of the United States, 1780–1970*. Charlottesville: University Press of Virginia, 1970.

Iriye, Akira. *Pacific Estrangement: Japanese and American Expansion, 1897–1911*. Cambridge, Mass.: Harvard University Press, 1972.

Israel, Jerry. *Progressivism and the Open Door: America and China, 1905–1921*. Pittsburgh: University of Pittsburgh Press, 1971.

James, John A. *Money and Capital Markets in Postbellum America*. Princeton: Princeton University Press, 1978.

James, John A. "Structural Change in American Manufacturing, 1850–1890." *Journal of Economic History* 43:2 (June 1983), pp. 433–549.

Jastram, Roy W. *The Golden Constant: The English and American Experience, 1560–1976*. New York: Wiley, 1977.

Jenks, Jeremiah W. *The Trust Problem*. New York: McClure, Philips, 1900; 5th ed., New York: Doubleday, Doran, 1929.

Johnson, Arthur M. "Antitrust Policy in Transition, 1908: Ideal and Reality." *Mississippi Valley Historical Review* 48:3 (December 1961), pp. 415–434.

Johnson, Arthur M. "Theodore Roosevelt and the Bureau of Corporations." *Mississippi Valley Historical Review* 45:4 (March 1959).

Jones, Eliot. *The Trust Problem in the United States*. New York: Macmillan, 1926.

Kahn, Otto H. *Our Economic and Other Problems: A Financier's Point of View*. New York: George H. Doran, 1920.

Kemp, Tom. *Theories of Imperialism*. London: Dennis Dobson, 1967.

Keynes, John M. *The Collected Writings of John Maynard Keynes*, vol. 15. ed. Elizabeth Johnson. London: Macmillan, 1971.

King, Willard Leroy. *Melville Weston Fuller: Chief Justice of the United States, 1889–1910*. New York: Macmillan, 1950.

Knauth, Oswald W. *The Policy of the United States Towards Industrial Monopoly*. Columbia University Studies in History, Economics, and Public Law (56:2, whole no. 138), 1914.

Knox, Philander C. "The Law of Labor and Trade." Presidential address before the Pennsylvania Bar Association. *American Law Register and Review*, New Series, 36:7 (July 1897), pp. 417–436.

Koebner, Richard, and Schmidt, Helmut Dan. *Imperialism: The Story and Significance of a Political Word, 1840–1960*. Cambridge University Press, 1964.

Kohlsaat, Herman H. *From McKinley to Harding*. New York: Scribner 1923.

Kolko, Gabriel. *Railroads and Regulation, 1877–1916*. Princeton: Princeton University press, 1965.

Kolko, Gabriel. *The Triumph of Conservatism*. New York: Free Press, 1963.

Kramer, Helen. "Harvesters and High Finance: Formation of the International Harvester Company." *Business History Review* 38:3 (Autumn 1964), pp. 283–301.

Kutler, Stanley, I. "Chief Justice Taft and the Delusion of Judicial Exactness – A Study in Jurisprudence." *Virginia Law Review* 48 (1962), pp. 1407–1426.

Kutler, Stanley, I. *Privilege and Creative Destruction: The Charles River Bridge Case*. Philadelphia: Lippincott, 1971.

Lamoreaux, Naomi R. *The Great Merger Movement in American Business, 1895–1904*. Cambridge University Press, 1985.

Lande, Robert H. "Wealth Transfers as the Original and Primary Concern of Antitrust: The Efficiency Interpretation Challenged." *Hastings Law Journal* 34 (September 1982), pp. 67–151.

Landes, David S. *The Unbound Prometheus: Technological Change and Industrial Development in Western Europe from 1750 to the Present*. Cambridge University Press, 1969.

Langer, William L. "A Critique of Imperialism." *Foreign Affairs* 14 (1935–1936), pp. 102–119.

Langer, William L. *The Diplomacy of Imperialism, 1890–1902*. 2 vols. New York: Macmillan, 1935.

Laughlin, J. Laurence. "Our Monetary Programme." *Forum* 20 (February 1896), pp. 652–666.

Lenin, Vladimir I. *Collected Works*, vol. 39. Moscow: Progress Publishers, 1968.

Lenin, Vladimir I. *Imperialism: The Highest Stage of Capitalism* (1917). New York: International Publishers, 1939.

Lerner, Ralph. "Commerce and Character: The Anglo-American as New-Model Man." *William & Mary Quarterly*, Third Series, 36:1 (January 1979), pp. 3–26.

Letwin, William. *Law and Economic Policy in America: The Evolution of the Sherman Antitrust Act*. New York: Random House, 1965.

Leupp, Francis E. "The Father of the Anti-Trust Law." *Outlook* 99 (30 September 1911), pp. 271–276.

Lindblom, Charles E. *Politics and Markets: The World's Political-Economic Systems*. New York: Basic, 1977.

Link, Arthur S. *Wilson: The New Freedom*. Princeton: Princeton University Press, 1956).

Link, Arthur S. *Wilson: The Road to the White House*. Princeton: Princeton University Press, 1947.

Link, Arthur, S. *Woodrow Wilson and the Progressive Era, 1910–1917*. New York: Harper Bros., 1954.

Link, Arthur S. ed. *The Papers of Woodrow Wilson*. vol. 15: 1903–1905. Princeton: Princeton University Press, 1973.

Livingston, James. *Origins of the Federal Reserve System: Money, Class, and*

Corporate Capitalism, 1890–1913. Ithaca, N.Y.: Cornell University Press, 1986.

Lustig, R. Jeffrey. *Corporate Liberalism: The Origins of Modern American Political Theory, 1890–1920.* Berkeley: University of California Press, 1982.

Macrosty, H. W. "Business Aspects of British Trusts." *Economic Journal* (London), 12 (September 1902), pp. 347–366.

Macrosty, H. W. (Review of) *American Industrial Conditions and Competition. Reports of British Iron Trade Commission.* London: British Iron Trade Association, 1902; *Economic Journal* (London), 12 (September 1902), pp. 367–370.

Martin, Albro. *Enterprise Denied: Origins of the Decline of American Railroads, 1897–1917.* New York: Columbia University Press, 1971.

Marx, Karl. *Capital*, vol. 1. Moscow: Foreign Languages Publishing House, n.d.

Marx, Karl. *A Contribution to the Critique of Political Economy.* Trans. N. I. Stone. Chicago: Charles H. Kerr, 1904.

McCraw, Thomas K., ed. *Regulation in Perspective: Historical Essays.* Cambridge, Mass.: Harvard University Press, 1981.

McCurdy, Charles W. "American Law and the Marketing Structure of the Large Corporation, 1875–1890." *Journal of Economic History* 38:3 (September 1978), pp. 631–649.

McCurdy, Charles W. "The *Knight* Sugar Decision of 1895 and the Modernization of American Corporation Law, 1869–1903." *Business History Review* 53:3 (Autumn 1979), pp. 304–342.

Meade, Edward Sherwood. "Financial Aspects of the Trust Problem." *Annals* 16 (November 1900), pp. 1–59.

Meade, Edward Sherwood. *Trust Finance.* New York: D. Appleton, 1903; 2d ed., 1906.

Means, Gardiner C. *The Corporate Revolution in America: Economic Reality vs. Economic Theory.* New York: Collier Books, 1964.

Meek, Ronald L. *Smith, Marx, and After: Ten Essays in the Development of Economic Thought.* London: Chapman & Hall, 1977.

Merchants' Association of New York. "Concerning the Amendments to the Sherman Anti-Trust Law of 1890." *Bulletin of the Merchants' Association of New York, No. 47, April 13, 1908.*

Mommsen, Wolfgang J. *Theories of Imperialism* (1977). Trans. P. S. Falla. New York: Random House, 1980.

Moody, John. *The Truth about the Trusts: A Description and Analysis of the American Trust Movement.* 1904; Westport, Conn.: Greenwood, 1968.

Morgan, Donald G. *Congress and the Constitution: A Study of Responsibility.* Cambridge, Mass.: Harvard University Press, 1966.

Morgan, H. Wayne. *From Hayes to McKinley: National Party Politics, 1877–1896.* Syracuse, N.Y.: Syracuse University Press, 1969.

Morison, Elting E., ed. *The Letters of Theodore Roosevelt*, vol. 6. Cambridge, Mass.: Harvard University Press, 1952.

Mowry, George E. *The Era of Theodore Roosevelt and the Birth of Modern America: 1900–1912.* 1958; New York: Harper & Row, 1962.

Mulder, John M. *Woodrow Wilson: The Years of Preparation.* Princeton: Princeton University Press, 1978.

National Civic Federation. *Proceedings of the National Conference on Trusts and Combinations,* under the auspices of the National Civic Federation, Chicago, 22–25 October 1907. New York: National Civic Federation, 1908.

National Civic Federation. *The Trust Problem: Replies of 16,000 Representative Americans to a Questionnaire Sent Out by Department on Regulation of Industrial Corporations of the National Civic Federation.* Compiled and edited by Henry Mann. New York: National Civic Federation, 1912.

National Foreign Trade Council. *Official Report of the Third National Foreign Trade Convention.* New Orleans, 27–29 January 1916. New York: NFTC, 1916.

National Industrial Conference Board. *Mergers in Industry: A Study of Certain Ecomonic Aspects of Industrial Consolidation.* Prepared by Myron W. Watkins. New York: NICB, 1929.

Navin, Thomas R., and Sears, Marian V. "The Rise of a Market for Industrial Securities, 1887–1902." *Business History Review* 29:2 (June 1955), pp. 105–138.

Nelson, Ralph L. *Concentration in the Manufacturing Industries in the United States: A Midcentury Report.* New Haven: Yale University Press, 1963.

Nelson, Ralph L. *Merger Movements in American Industry, 1895–1956.* Princeton: Princeton University Press, 1959.

Nelson, William E. *Americanization of the Common Law: The Impact of Legal Change on Massachusetts Society, 1760–1830.* Cambridge Mass: Harvard University Press, 1975.

Noble, David F. *America by Design: Science, Technology, and the Rise of Corporate Capitalism.* New York: Knopf, 1977.

North, Simon Newcomb Dexter. "The Federal Census of Manufactures, 1900." Paper read before the National Association of Manufacturers, Boston, 25 April 1900. Pamphlet. State Historical Society of Wisconsin, Madison.

North, Simon Newcomb Dexter. "The Industrial Commission." *North American Review* 168 (June 1899), pp. 708–719.

Nutter, G. Warren, and Einhorn, Henry A. *Enterprise Monopoly in the United States, 1899–1958.* New York: Columbia University Press, 1969.

Official Report of the Proceedings of the Democratic National Convention. Baltimore, 1912.

Oppenheim, Saul Chesterfield. *Cases on Federal Anti-Trust Laws, Including Restraints of Trade at Common Law: Trade Regulation.* St. Paul, Minn.: West Publishing, American Casebook Series, 1948.

Parrini, Carl P. *Heir to Empire: United States Economic Diplomacy, 1916–1923.* Pittsburgh: University of Pittsburgh Press, 1969.

Parrini, Carl P., and Sklar, Martin J. "New Thinking About the Market, 1896–1904: Some American Economists on Investment and the Theory of Surplus Capital." *Journal of Economic History*, 43:3 (September 1983), pp. 559–578.

Parsons, Talcott. "The Distribution of Power in American Society." *World Politics* 10:1 (October 1957), pp. 123–143.

Patterson, George Stuart. "The Case of the Trans-Missouri Freight Association." *The American Law Register and Review*, New Series, 36:5, (May 1897), pp. 307–321.

Payne, George H., ed. *The Birth of the New Party, or Progressive Democracy. A Complete Official Account of the Formation and Organization of the Progressive Party*. Naperville, Ill: Nichols, 1912.

Payne, P. L. "The Emergence of the Large-Scale Company in Great Britain, 1870–1914." *Economic History Review*, Second Series, 20:3 (December 1967), pp. 519–542.

Perkins, George W. "Some Things to Think About." Address at the Graduate School of Business Administration, Harvard University, 15 April 1910. *Commercial Pamphlets*, vol. 1. Madison: University of Wisconsin Library.

Porter, Glenn. *The Rise of Big Business, 1860–1910*. New York: Crowell, 1973.

Potter, David M. *The Impending Crisis, 1848–1861*. New York: Harper & Row, 1976.

Presser, Stephen B. "'Legal History' or the History of Law: A Primer Bringing the Law's Past into the Present." *Vanderbilt Law Review* 35:4 (May 1982), pp. 849–890.

Pringle, Henry F. *The Life and Times of William Howard Taft: A Biography*. 2 vols. New York: Farrar & Rinehart, 1939.

Pringle, Henry F. *Theodore Roosevelt, A Biography*. New York: Harcourt Brace, 1931.

Radosh, Ronald. "The Corporate Ideology of American Labor Leaders from Gompers to Hillman." *Studies on the Left* 6:6 November-December 1966, pp. 66–87.

Radosh, Ronald, and Rothbard, Murray N., eds. *A New History of Leviathan: Essays on the Rise of the American Corporate State*. New York: Dutton, 1972.

Raymond, Robert L. "The Federal Anti-Trust Act." *Harvard Law Review* 23:5 (March 1910), pp. 353–379.

Reinsch, Paul S. *Colonial Administration*. New York: Macmillan, 1905.

Reinsch, Paul S. *Colonial Government: An Introduction to the Study of Colonial Institutions*. 1902; Freeport, N.Y.: Books for Libraries Press, 1970.

Reinsch, Paul S. "The New Conquest of the World." *World's Work* 1:4 (February 1901), pp. 425–431.

Reinsch, Paul S. *World Politics at the End of the Nineteenth Century, As Influenced by the Oriental Situation*. New York: Macmillan, 1900.

Robinson, Joan. *The Economics of Imperfect Competition*. London: Macmillan, 1933.

Rohlfing, Charles C. et al. *Business and Government*. 5th ed. Chicago: Foundation Press, 1949.

Roosevelt, Theodore. *Addresses and Presidential Messages of Theodore Roosevelt, 1902–1904*, with an Introduction by Henry Cabot Lodge. New York: Putnam, 1904.

Roosevelt, Theodore. "The Trusts, the People, and the Square Deal." *Outlook* 99 (18 November 1911), pp. 649–656.

Root, Elihu. "Experiments in Government and the Essentials of the Constitution – I." *North American Review* 198 (July 1913), pp. 1–17.

Ross, Howard N. "Economic Gowth and Change in the United States Under *Laissez-Faire*: 1870–1929." In Frederic C. Jaher, ed., *The Age of Industrialism in America: Essays in Social Structure and Cultural Values*. New York: Free Press, 1968, pp. 6–48.

Rothman, David J. *Politics and Power: The United States Senate, 1869–1901*. New York: Atheneum, 1969.

Rozwenc, Edwin C., ed. *Roosevelt, Wilson and the Trusts*. Boston: D.C. Heath, 1950.

Rubin, Paul H. *Business Firms and the Common Law: The Evolution of Efficient Rules*. New York: Praeger, 1983.

Rublee, George L. "The Original Plan and Early History of the Federal Trade Commission." *Proceedings of the Academy of Political Science* 11:4 (January 1926), pp. 114–120.

Saul, S. Berrick. "The American Impact on British Industry, 1895–1914." *Business History* 3:1 (December 1960), pp. 19–38.

Scheiber, Harry N. "Federalism and the American Economic Order, 1789–1910." *Law & Society Review* 10:1 (Fall 1975), pp. 57–118.

Scheiber, Harry N. "The Road to *Munn*: Eminent Domain and the Concept of Public Purpose in the State Courts." In Donald Fleming and Bernard Bailyn, eds., *Perspectives in American History 5: Law in American History*. Cambridge, Mass.: Harvard University Press, 1971, pp. 329–402.

Scheinberg, Stephen J., "Theodore Roosevelt and the A.F. of L.'s Entry into Politics, 1906–1908." *Labor History*, 3:2 (Spring 1962), pp. 131–148.

Schneirov, Richard. "The Knights of Labor in the Chicago Labor Movement and in Municipal Politics, 1877–1887." Ph.D. Diss., Northern Illinois University, 1984; Champaign: University of Illinois Press, forthcoming.

Schwab, Charles M. "What May Be Expected in the Steel and Iron Industry." *North American Review*, no. 534 (May 1901), pp. 655–664.

Schwartz, Bernard. *The Law in America: A History*. New York: McGraw-Hill, 1974.

Scranton, Philip. *Proprietary Capitalism: The Textile Manufacture at Philadelphia, 1800–1885*. Cambridge University Press, 1983.

Seager, Henry R., and Gulick, Charles A., Jr. *Trust and Corporation Problems*. New York: Harper Bros., 1929.

Seligman, Edwin R. A., ed. *The Currency Problem and the Present Financial Situation*. New York: Columbia University Press, 1908.

Seltzer, Alan L. "Woodrow Wilson as 'Corporate-Liberal': Toward a Reconsideration of Left Revisionist Historiography." *Western Political Quarterly* 30:2 (June 1977), pp. 183–212.

Semmel, Bernard. *The Rise of Free Trade Imperialism: Classical Political Economy, the Empire of Free Trade, and Imperialism, 1750–1850*. Cambridge University Press, 1970.

Shaw, Leslie Mortier. *Current Issues*. New York: D. Appleton, 1908.

Shepherd, William G. "Bain's Influence on Research into Industrial Organization." In Robert T. Masson and P. David Qualls, eds., *Essays on Industrial Organization in Honor of Joe S. Bain*. Cambridge, Mass.: Ballinger, 1976.

Sherwood, Sidney. "The Function of the Undertaker." *Yale Review*, Old Series, 6 (November 1897), pp. 233–250.

Sherwood, Sidney. "Influence of the Trust in the Development of Undertaking Genius." *Yale Review* 8 (February 1900), pp. 362–372.

Sklar, Martin J. "The Corporate Ascendancy and the Socialist Acquiescence: An Inquiry into Strange Times." *The Maryland Historian* 12:2 (Fall 1981), pp. 49–59.

Sklar, Martin J. "On the Proletarian Revolution and the End of Political-Economic Society." *Radical America* 3:3 (May-June 1969), pp. 1–41.

Sklar, Martin J. "Woodrow Wilson and the Political Economy of Modern United States Liberalism." *Studies on the Left* 1:3 (Fall 1960), pp. 17–47. In Ronald Radosh and Murray N. Rothbard, eds., *A New History of Leviathan*. New York: Dutton, 1972, pp. 7–65.

Sklar, Richard L. "On the Concept of Power in Political Economy." In Dalmas H. Nelson and R. L. Sklar, eds., *Toward a Humanistic Science of Politics: Essays in Honor of Francis Dunham Wormuth*. Washington, D.C.: University Press of America, 1982.

Smart, William. *An Introduction to the Theory of Value, on the Lines of Menger, Wieser, and Böhm-Bawerk*. 1891; 3d ed., London: Macmillan, 1914.

Smart, William. *Studies in Economics*. London: Macmillan, 1895.

Solomon, Rayman L. "The Politics of Appointment and the Federal Courts' Role in Regulating America: U.S. Courts of Appeals Judgeships from T.R. to F.D.R." *American Bar Foundation Research Journal*, No. 2 (Spring 1984), pp. 285–343.

Sowell, Thomas. *Say's Law: An Historical Analysis*. Princeton: Princeton University Press, 1972.

Stimson, Henry L. *Address of Henry Lewis Stimson, Secretary of War, at the Republican Club, New York City, on December 15, 1911*. Pamphlet. State Historical Society of Wisconsin, Madison.

Stokes, Eric. "Late Nineteenth-Century Colonial Expansion and the Attack on the Theory of Economic Imperialism: A Case of Mistaken Identity?" *The Historical Journal* 12:2 (1969), pp. 285–301.

Susman, Warren I. *Culture as History: The Transformation of American Society in the Twentieth Century.* New York: Pantheon, 1984.

Sylla, Richard. *The American Capital Markets, 1846–1914.* New York: Arno Press, 1975.

Sylla, Richard. "Federal Policy, Banking Structure, and Capital Mobilization in the United States, 1863–1913." *Journal of Economic History* 29:4 (December 1969), pp. 657–686.

Taft, William Howard. *The Anti-Trust Act and the Supreme Court.* New York: Harper Bros., 1914.

Taft, William Howard. "Justice and Freedom for Industry." *Proceedings of the Twentieth Annual Convention of the National Association of Manufacturers of the United States of America,* 25, 26 May 1913, New York City, pp. 276–288.

Thompson, James H. "Mill's Fourth Fundamental Proposition: A Paradox Revisited." *History of Political Economy* 7:2 (Summer 1975), pp. 174–192.

Thorelli, Hans B. *The Federal Antitrust Policy: Origination of an American Tradition.* Baltimore: Johns Hopkins University Press, 1955.

Thorp, Willard L. *The Integration of Industrial Operation.* Census Monograph no. 3. Department of Commerce, Bureau of the Census. Washington, D.C.: Government Printing Office, 1924.

Timberlake, Richard Henry, Jr. *The Origins of Central Banking in the United States.* Cambridge, Mass.: Harvard University Press, 1978.

Tipps, Dean C. "Modernization Theory and the Comparative Study of Societies: A Critical Perspective." *Comparative Studies in Society and History* 16 (1973), pp. 199–226.

Tocqueville, Alexis de. *Democracy in America.* 2 vols. 1840; New York: Knopf, 1945.

Trubek, David M. "Max Weber on Law and the Rise of Capitalism." *Wisconsin Law Review* no. 3 (1972), pp. 720–753.

Vatter, Harold G. *The Drive to Industrial Maturity: The U.S. Economy, 1860–1914.* Westport, Conn.: Greenwood, 1975.

Veblen, Thorstein. "The Preconceptions of Economic Science. II." *Quarterly Journal of Economics* 13 (July 1899), pp. 396–426.

Veblen, Thorstein. *The Theory of Business Enterprise.* 1904; New York: Mentor, 1958.

Vietor, Richard H. K. "Businessmen and the Political Economy: The Railroad Rate Controversy of 1905." *Journal of American History* 64:1 (June 1977), pp. 47–66.

Wagner, Susan. *The Federal Trade Commission.* New York: Praeger, 1971.

Walker, Albert Henry. "Who Wrote the Sherman Law?" *Central Law Journal* 73:15 (13 October 1911), pp. 257–259.

Walker, Francis. "The Law Concerning Monopolistic Combinations in Continental Europe." *Political Science Quarterly* 20:1 (March 1905), pp. 13–41.

Wall, Joseph F. *Andrew Carnegie.* New York: Oxford University Press, 1970.

Watkins, Myron W. *Industrial Combinations and Public Policy: A Study of Combination and the Common Welfare.* Boston: Houghton Mifflin, 1927.

Weber, Max. *Economy and Society: An Outline of Interpretive Sociology.* 3 vols. Ed. Guenther Ross and Claus Wittich. New York: Bedminster, 1968.

Weber, Max. *Max Weber on Law in Economy and Society.* ed. Max Rheinstein. Cambridge, Mass: Harvard University Press, 1954.

Weber, Max. *Theory of Social and Economic Organization.* Trans. A. M. Henderson and Talcott Parsons; ed. Talcott Parsons. New York: Free Press, 1964.

Weinberg, Albert K. *Mainfest Destiny: A Study of Nationalist Expansionism in American History.* Baltimore: Johns Hopkins University Press, 1935; Chicago: Quadrangle Books, 1963.

Weinstein, James. *The Corporate Ideal in the Liberal State, 1900–1918.* Boston: Beacon, 1968.

Wells, David Ames. *Recent Economic Changes, and Their Effect on the Production and Distribution of Wealth and the Well-Being of Society.* New York: Appleton, 1889.

White, G. Edward. *The American Judicial Tradition: Profiles of Leading American Judges.* New York: Oxford University Press, 1976.

Wiebe, Robert H. "Business Disunity and the Progressive Movement, 1901–1914." *Mississippi Valley Historical Review* 44:4 (March 1958), pp. 664–685.

Wiebe, Robert H. *Businessmen and Reform: A Study of the Progressive Movement.* Cambridge, Mass.: Harvard University Press, 1962; Chicago: Quadrangle Books, 1968.

Wiebe, Robert H. "The House of Morgan and the Executive, 1905–1913." *American Historical Review* 65:1 (October 1959), pp. 49–60.

Wiebe, Robert H. *The Search for Order, 1877–1920.* New York: Hill & Wang, 1967.

Wieser, Friedrich von. *Natural Value.* Trans. Mrs. Mallock; ed. with a Preface and Analysis by William Smart. 1893; New York: Augustus M. Kelley, 1971.

Wilensky, Norman M. *Conservatives in the Progressive Era: The Taft Republicans of 1912.* Gainesville: University of Florida Press, 1965.

Williams, William A. *The Contours of American History.* Cleveland: World, 1961.

Williams, William A. "The Frontier Thesis and American Foreign Policy." *Pacific Historical Review* 24:4 (November 1955), pp. 379–395.

Williams, William A. *The Tragedy of American Diplomacy.* Cleveland: World, 1959.

Williams, William A., ed. *The Shaping of American Diplomacy.* Chicago: Rand McNally, 1964.

Willoughby, William F. "The Concentration of Industry in the United States." *Yale Review* 7 (May 1898), pp. 72–94.

Willoughby, William F. "The Integration of Industry in the United States."
    Quarterly Journal of Economics 16 (November 1901), pp. 94–115.
Wilson, Woodrow. *Congressional Government* (New York: Meridian Books,
    1956.
Wilson, Woodrow. *Constitutional Government in the United States.* New York:
    Columbia University Press, 1908.
Wilson, Woodrow. *A History of the American People.* Vol. 5: *Reunion and
    Nationalization.* New York: Harper Bros., 1907.
Wilson, Woodrow. *The New Freedom.* New York: Doubleday, Page, 1914.
Wilson, Woodrow. *The Public Papers of Woodrow Wilson.* Ed. Ray S. Baker
    and William E. Dodd. 4 vols. New York: Harper Bros., 1925, 1926.
Wilson, Woodrow. *The State: Elements of Historical and Practical Politics.*
    Boston: D.C. Heath, 1906.
Wright, Carroll D. *Industrial Depressions.* First Annual Report of the Commis-
    sioner of Labor, March 1886. Washington, D.C.: Government Printing
    Office, 1886; New York: Augustus M. Kelley, 1968.
Wright, Carroll D. "The Relation of Production to Productive Capacity. I."
    Forum 24 (November 1897), pp. 290–302.
Wright, Carroll D. "The Relation of Production to Productive Capacity. II."
    Forum 24 (February 1898), pp. 660–675.
Young, Marilyn B. *The Rhetoric of Empire: American China Policy, 1895–
    1901.* Cambridge, Mass.: Harvard University Press, 1968.

Index

461